MOON HANDBOOKS®

OAXACA

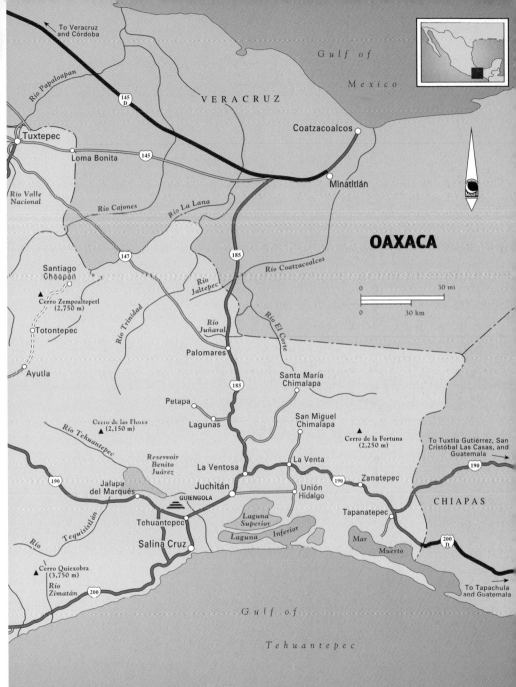

To Veracruz
and Córdoba

Gulf of

Mexico

Río Papaloapan

145
D

VERACRUZ

Coatzacoalcos

Tuxtepec

145

Loma Bonita

Minatitlán

Río Valle
Nacional

Río Cajones

Río La Lana

OAXACA

147

Río Coatzacoalcos

185

Santiago
Choapan

Río
Jaltepec

30 mi

Cerro Zempoaltepetl
(2,750 m)

0   30 km

Totontepec

Río
Juñaral

Río El Corte

Río Trinidad

Ayutla

Palomares

185

Santa María
Chimalapa

Cerro de las Flores
(2,150 m)

Petapa

San Miguel
Chimalapa

Río Tehuantepec

Lagunas

Cerro de la Fortuna
(2,250 m)

To Tuxtla Gutiérrez, San
Cristóbal Las Casas, and
Guatemala

Reservoir
Benito
Juárez

La Ventosa

La Venta

190

190

Jalapa
del Marqués

190

Zanatepec

Juchitán

CHIAPAS

GUIENGOLA

Unión
Hidalgo

Tequisistlán

Tehuantepec

Laguna
Superior

Tapanatepec

200
D

Río

Salina Cruz

Laguna   Inferior

Mar

Muerto

Cerro Quiexobra
(3,750 m)

Río
Zimatán

200

To Tapachula
and Guatemala

Gulf of

Tehuantepec

MOON HANDBOOKS®
OAXACA

THIRD EDITION

BRUCE WHIPPERMAN

AVALON
TRAVEL

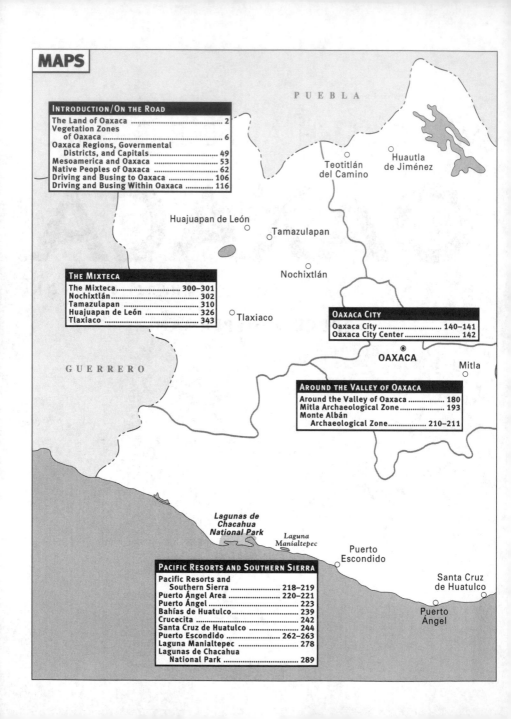

MAPS

INTRODUCTION/ON THE ROAD

The Land of Oaxaca 2
Vegetation Zones
    of Oaxaca 6
Oaxaca Regions, Governmental
    Districts, and Capitals 49
Mesoamerica and Oaxaca 53
Native Peoples of Oaxaca 62
Driving and Busing to Oaxaca 106
Driving and Busing Within Oaxaca 116

PUEBLA

Teotitlán
del Camino

Huautla
de Jiménez

Huajuapan de León

Tamazulapan

Nochixtlán

THE MIXTECA

The Mixteca.............................. 300–301
Nochixtlán................................ 302
Tamazulapan 310
Huajuapan de León 326
Tlaxiaco 343

Tlaxiaco

OAXACA CITY

Oaxaca City.............................. 140–141
Oaxaca City Center.................... 142

OAXACA

Mitla

GUERRERO

AROUND THE VALLEY OF OAXACA

Around the Valley of Oaxaca 180
Mitla Archaeological Zone...................... 193
Monte Albán
    Archaeological Zone................. 210–211

Lagunas de
Chacahua
National Park

Laguna
Manialtepec

Puerto
Escondido

Santa Cruz
de Huatulco

PACIFIC RESORTS AND SOUTHERN SIERRA

Pacific Resorts and
    Southern Sierra 218–219
Puerto Ángel Area 220–221
Puerto Ángel 223
Bahías de Huatulco............................... 239
Crucecita 242
Santa Cruz de Huatulco 244
Puerto Escondido 262–263
Laguna Manialtepec 278
Lagunas de Chacahua
    National Park 289

Puerto
Ángel

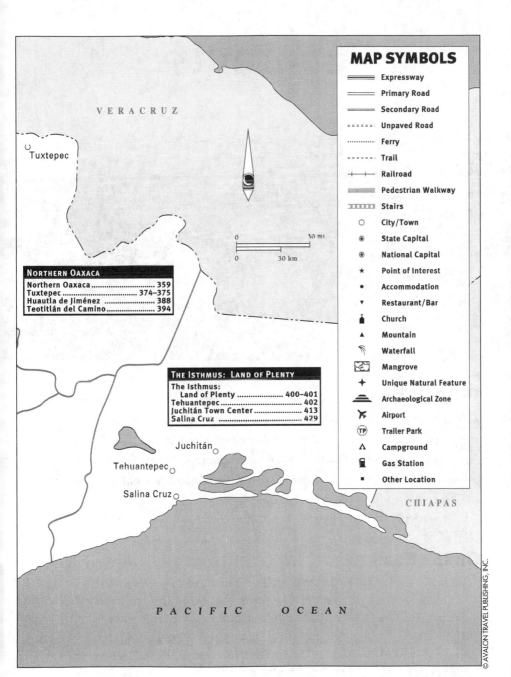

MAP SYMBOLS

- ═══ Expressway
- ─── Primary Road
- ─── Secondary Road
- ╌╌╌ Unpaved Road
- ⋯⋯ Ferry
- ‒ ‒ ‒ Trail
- ┼─┼─ Railroad
- ▓▓▓ Pedestrian Walkway
- ▥▥▥ Stairs
- ○ City/Town
- ◉ State Capital
- ✪ National Capital
- ★ Point of Interest
- • Accommodation
- ▼ Restaurant/Bar
- ⛪ Church
- ▲ Mountain
- ⬙ Waterfall
- Mangrove
- ✦ Unique Natural Feature
- Archaeological Zone
- ✈ Airport
- (TP) Trailer Park
- ▲ Campground
- ⛽ Gas Station
- ■ Other Location

VERACRUZ

Tuxtepec

NORTHERN OAXACA
Northern Oaxaca 359
Tuxtepec 374–375
Huautla de Jiménez 388
Teotitlán del Camino 394

0   30 mi
0   30 km

THE ISTHMUS: LAND OF PLENTY
The Isthmus:
  Land of Plenty 400–401
Tehuantepec 402
Juchitán Town Center 413
Salina Cruz 429

Juchitán ○

Tehuantepec ○

Salina Cruz ○

CHIAPAS

PACIFIC   OCEAN

Contents

Introduction 1

Like its renowned mole *sauces, Oaxaca is a rich mixture of influences—indigenous and colonial, traditional and modern. This is a land with 16 native languages, in hundreds of dialects, where even today Spanish is often a foreign tongue. With countless fiestas, crafts villages, colorful markets—and of course, the incomparable cuisine—you'll find much to savor.*

Land and Sea **2**; Flora and Fauna **5**; History **18**; Economy and Government **44**; People **52**

On the Road 74

What's your vision of paradise? Whether it's snorkeling in hidden coves, figuring out where to string your hammock, or dining on fresh-caught fish under a shady palapa, *you'll find all the practical information you need right here.*

Sports and Recreation **74**; Festivals and Events **80**; Arts and Crafts **84**; Accommodations **90**; Food and Drink **95**; Shopping **99**; Getting There **102**; Getting Around **115**; Information and Services **119**; Health and Safety **127**; What to Take **133**

Oaxaca City 135

Stroll the cobbled streets of Oaxaca's capital city, soaking in the colonial charm of its stone buildings. Sit at a zócalo sidewalk café and watch the world glide by. Discover handicraft-shopping heaven browsing through traditional markets and private galleries. Or let the whirling colors and dazzling spectacle of July's Guelaguetza folk dance festival draw you in.

Around the Valley of Oaxaca 179

Welcome to the Zapotec heartland, where villages famed for woodcarving and weaving thrive alongside stunning ruins such as Monte Albán, where long ago a majestic city endured for over 1,000 years.

EAST SIDE: THE TEXTILE ROUTE 184
Santa María del Tule; Tlacochahuaya; Dainzu and Lambityeco Archaeological Sites; Teotitlán del Valle; Santa Ana del Valle; Tlacolula; Yagul Archaeological Zone; San Bartolomé Quialana and San Marcos Tlapazola; Mitla; Hierve el Agua Mineral Springs

SOUTH SIDE: THE CRAFTS ROUTE 197
San Bartolo Coyotepec; San Antonino Castillo Velasco; San Martín Tilcajete; Santo Tomás Jalieza; Ocotlán; Ejutla; Zimatlán; San Sebastián de las Grutas; Sola de Vega; Zaachila; Cuilapan de Guerrero and Arrazola

WEST SIDE: THE ARCHAEOLOGICAL ROUTE 208
Monte Albán; Santa María Atzompa; San José El Mogote; Etla; Suchilquitongo and Cerro de la Campana Archaeological Zone

Pacific Resorts and Southern Sierra 217

Adventure awaits along the Pacific Coast, from kayaking lagoons teeming with birds to riding the pipeline at Playa Zicatela, Mexico's best surfing beach. Heading upland into the Sierra Madre, you'll find spectacular waterfalls and jungle coffee farms to explore.

PUERTO ÁNGEL AND VICINITY 219
Playa Zipolite; Playas San Agustinillo and Mazunte; San Pedro Pochutla; Chacalapa; San José del Pacífico

BAHÍAS DE HUATULCO AND VICINITY 238
  Crucecita; Santa Cruz de Huatulco; Chahue; Tangolunda; Santa María Huatulco;
  Santa María Xadani; Santiago Astata; San Pedro Huamelula
PUERTO ESCONDIDO AND VICINITY 260
  Playa Zicatela; Laguna Manialtepec; Atotonilco Hot Springs
UPLAND EXCURSION INTO CHATINO COUNTRY 281
  Santos Reyes Nopala; Santa Magdalena Tiltepec; Santa Catarina Juquila
WEST TO THE MIXTEC COAST 287
  Lagunas de Chacahua National Park; Río Grande; Roca Blanca; San Pedro
  Tututepec; Charquito Atotonilco Warm Springs; Santiago Jamiltepec; San Andres
  Huaxpaltepec; Santa María Huazolotitlán; Pinotepa Nacional; Pinotepa Don Luis;
  San Juan Colorado; Cacahuatepec; San Pedro Amusgos; Playa Corralero

The Mixteca 299

Stretching from the jungle-draped Pacific coastline across the cool, cloud-shadowed highlands to the warmth of a sunny desert plateau, the Mixteca is both vast and diverse. Its human legacy is just as impressive, with grand Dominican churches dotting the countryside and ancient Mixtec kingdoms that stir the imagination.

NORTHWEST FROM OAXACA CITY 300
  Nochixtlán; Yucuita; Tilantongo and Monte Negro Archaeological Zones; The
  Vale of Apoala
DOMINICAN ROUTE SOUTH 309
  Tamazulapan; Teposcolula; Yucunama; Yanhuitlán
DOMINICAN ROUTE NORTH 317
  Coixtlahuaca; San Miguel Tequixtepec; Tepelmeme de Morelos
THE MIXTECA BAJA: LAND OF THE SUN 325
  Huajuapan de León; Cerro de las Minas Archaeological Zone; Santiago
  Huajolotitlán; Río Mixteco Valley and Asunción Cuyotepeji; San Pedro y San Pablo
  Tequixtepec; Santiago Chazumba; Yosocuta Reservoir; Tonalá Canyon; Santo
  Domingo Tonalá; Santiago Juxtlahuaca; Laguna Encantada
THE MIXTECA ALTA: ROOF OF OAXACA 342
  Tlaxiaco; Chalcatongo; Yosundua and Cascada Esmeralda; San Miguel Achiutla;
  San Martín Huamelulpan; Santa María Cuquila; San Miguel Progreso;
  Putla de Guerrero

Northern Oaxaca 357

The north offers something for every outdoor enthusiast: high mountains for hiking, climbing, and camping; tropical rivers and glassy lakes for fishing, swimming, and boating; and crystalline springs for refreshing dips and relaxing afternoon picnics.

NORTHERN SIERRA 358
Benito Juárez and Cuajimoloyas; Santa Catarina Ixtepeji; Ixtlán de Juárez; Calpulalpan; Guelatao

INTO THE PAPALOAPAN 368
Valle Nacional; Santa María Jacatepec; San José Chiltepec; Tuxtepec; Temascal and Miguel Alemán Dam and Reservoir; San Pedro Ixcatlán and the Islands; Isla Soyaltepec; San Lucas Ojitlán

THE MAZATECA 385
Jalapa de Díaz; Cerro Rabón; Huautla de Jiménez; Las Regaderas; Nindo-Da-Gé; Sotano de San Agustín

THE CAÑADA: CANYON COUNTRY 393
Teotitlán del Camino; Cuicatlán

The Isthmus: Land of Plenty 397

This is a land worth celebrating, with vivid marketplaces and near-continuous velas—as fiestas are known to ist-meños. The grandest vela of them all is late December's Vela Tehuantepec, when an entire town dances to the strains of Sandunga music all night long.

TEHUANTEPEC AND VICINITY 398
Guiengola; Jalapa del Marqués; Tequisistlán

JUCHITÁN AND VICINITY 412

NORTH OF JUCHITÁN 420
Magdalena Tlacotepec; Santiago Laollaga; Lagunas; Santo Domingo Petapa

EAST OF JUCHITÁN 423
La Venta; The Chimalapa; Unión de Hidalgo; Playa Copalito and San Dionisio del Mar; Santo Domingo Zanatepec; San Pedro Tapanatepec; Rincón Juárez and the Calm Sea

SALINA CRUZ AND VICINITY 428
Playa La Ventosa; San Mateo del Mar; Santa María del Mar

Resources

Resources 439
TRAILER PARKS AND CAMPING 440
GLOSSARY 444
SPANISH PHRASEBOOK 447
SUGGESTED READING 454
INTERNET RESOURCES 462
INDEX 464

ABOUT THE AUTHOR
Bruce Whipperman

In the early 1980s, the lure of travel drew Bruce Whipperman away from a 20-year career of teaching physics. The occasion was a trip to Kenya, which included a total solar eclipse and a safari. He hasn't stopped traveling since.

With his family grown, he has been free to let the world's wild, beautiful corners draw him on: to the ice-clawed Karakoram, the Gobi Desert's trellised oases, the pink palaces of Rajasthan, Japan's green wine country, Bali's emerald terraces, and now, Oaxaca's traditional markets, spectacular ruins, picture perfect vistas, and parklike green pastures.

Bruce has always pursued his travel career for the fun of it. He started with slide shows and photo gifts for friends. Others wanted his photos, so he began selling them. Once, stranded in Ethiopia, he began to write. A dozen years later, after scores of magazine and newspaper feature stories, *Moon Handbooks Pacific Mexico* became his first book. For him, travel writing heightens his awareness and focuses his own travel experiences. He always remembers what a Nepali Sherpa once said: "Many people come, looking, looking; few people come, see."

Travel, after all, is for returning home, and that coziest of journeys always brings a tired but happy Bruce back to his friends, son, daughter, and wife Linda in Oakland, California.

Bruce invites the readers of *Moon Handbooks Oaxaca* to likewise "come see"—and discover and enjoy—Oaxaca's delights with a fresh eye and renewed compassion.

*To those valiant Oaxacan people who,
inspired by Benito Juárez's immortal words—
"Respect for the Right of All Is Peace"—
give their all in the struggle for justice.*

Introduction

The once-neglected state of Oaxaca is now fulfilling its promise. Its capital has become one of Mexico's most enjoyable colonial cities. By day, people relax at plaza-front sidewalk cafés beneath shady arches and take in a seemingly slow-motion scene, reflecting the best of old Mexico. By night, the same plaza comes alive with entertainment, from mimes and crafts and dessert stalls to folkloric dance shows and band concerts.

Within a few blocks of the plaza, good restaurants and hotels, traditional markets, and a host of handicrafts shops and galleries offer a feast of food, comforts, and shopping opportunities.

The list goes on. Visitors who venture into the surrounding Valley of Oaxaca can sample much more—regal ruined cities, crafts villages, colorful native markets, beloved old churches, small community museums, and comfortable tourist Yu'u accommodations.

Farther afield, the delights of Oaxaca's regions beckon. Head south and explore the tufted strands of the Pacific coastal resorts of Huatulco, Puerto Ángel, and Puerto Escondido. Here visitors opt for a trove of outdoor adventures, from fishing and river rafting to paddling wildlife-rich coastal mangrove lagoons and hiking butterfly- and flower-bedecked tropical forest trails.

Travel northwest from Oaxaca city to the Mixteca to explore its magnificent old Dominican churches, ancient Mixtec kingdoms, waterfalls, limestone caves, great cypress groves, crystal springs, and colorful country markets. Or head to northern Oaxaca and the pine-tufted, wildlife-rich Sierra heights and beyond, to the fertile, tropical river country of the Papaloapan basin and Tuxtepec, Oaxaca's second largest city.

As a finale, head southeast to the Isthmus, the rich land of vivid, bustling markets and near-continuous festivals. Here virtually everyone

© BRUCE WHIPPERMAN

enjoys an abundance of food and dancing—to the lovely, lilting strains of the beloved *Sandunga,* melody of the Isthmus.

Whatever options you choose, Oaxaca offers excitement, lots of friendly folks, relatively low prices, and a host of traditional Mexican delights. Regardless of the route you prefer, whether by back-road adventure or via the lap of luxury or a little bit of both, Oaxaca offers it. This book will show the way.

Land and Sea

On the map of North America, Mexico's state of Oaxaca (wah-HAH-kah) makes up the southern bulge of Mexico, the region where the Mexican coastline thrusts into the Pacific like the belly of a frolicking Pacific dolphin. Oaxaca is a sizable place—with about 36,800 square miles (95,400 square km)—and Mexico's fifth largest state, as big as a midsize U.S. state, such as Indiana, or an entire small European country, such as Portugal.

As in Mexico as a whole, mountains rule Oaxaca's landscape. From the U.S. border, Mexico's grand pair of mother ranges, the Sierra Madre Oriental in the east and Sierra Madre Occidental in the west, sweep southward a thousand miles until they reach Oaxaca, where they bend eastward and practically merge. In Oaxaca, the ranges, respectively called the Sierra Madre de Oaxaca and the Sierra Madre del Sur, form a broad, rumpled, pine-tufted landscape, dotted with 20 peaks in excess of 10,000 feet (3,000 meters). Only the mostly narrow southern coastal plain, one large valley, and a few scattered lesser vales provide enough level cropland to support large towns. From those few valleys, a handful of streams, blocked and forced by the mountains to twist through deep canyons, make their way to the sea.

A Closer Look

Imagine navigating a high-altitude airship, borne

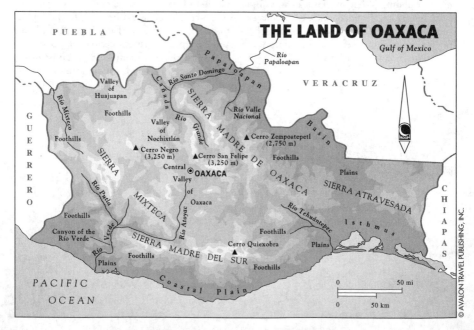

by the tropical breezes, over Oaxaca's vivid shoreline, mountain, and valley panorama. Start your adventure in the southwest, at Oaxaca's coastal border with its neighboring state of Guerrero. Here, as you drift eastward above the green coastal plain directly below, the broad estuary of the **Río Verde** empties into the sea. The mightiest river system entirely within the state, the Río Verde's tributaries drain a major fraction of western Oaxaca, including the central valley, where it is known as the Río Atoyac.

As you continue easterly, the forest-swathed peaks of the Sierra Madre del Sur stretch ahead, cresting at cloud-capped 12,300-foot (3,750-meter) **Cerro Quiexobra,** Oaxaca's tallest mountain. To your right far below, Pacific waves wash a coastline indented with small bays and lined with wildlife-rich mangrove wetlands and pearly, palm-tufted strands. In succession, you pass over the small resorts of **Puerto Escondido, Puerto Ángel,** and the **Bahías de Huatulco,** where visitors flock year-round to enjoy the delights of South Seas Mexico.

To the Isthmus and North

As you continue, the coastal plain gradually broadens as the Sierra shrinks to mere foothills at the **Isthmus of Tehuantepec,** the neck of land where Mexico (and indeed the entire American continent) shrivels to a scant 125 miles (200 km) in width. East beyond the Isthmus, in the remote region Oaxacans call the **Chimalapas,** you spot a new range of mountains, the **Sierra Atravesada,** rising and stretching east into the neighboring state of Chiapas. The Atravesadas' isolated, rugged, summits, sylvan forests, and deep gorges shelter one of Mexico's last remaining troves of endangered plants, birds, mammals, and reptiles.

From the Isthmus, other Oaxaca regions beckon. Turning around to the left and heading your airship northwest, you follow the valley of the **Río Tehuantepec,** passing over the bustling, tradition-rich small cities of Juchitán and Tehuantepec and their luxuriant hinterlands of fruit, corn, and cotton. Soon, on your right toward the north, rises the grand **Sierra Madre de Oaxaca.** You see a succession of peaks stretching west a hundred miles, from the rugged homeland of the

indigenous **Mixe** (MEE-shay) people in Oaxaca's northeast to the equally mountainous domain of their neighbors, the Sierra **Zapotec** at the northern center of the state.

Drawn by what you might find beyond the mountain crest, you navigate your airship due north, over the Mixe country, above the gigantic spreading massif of **Zempoaltepetl** (only 9,000 feet, 2,700 meters, but composed nevertheless of a dozen separate peaks), the Mixes' holy mountain. Beyond that, the mountains gradually drop to foothills, where you see a great river-laced plain of tropical forest checkered with pasture, farms, and small towns, stretching north past Oaxaca's northern lowland border with the state of Veracruz all the way to the Gulf of Mexico. The Oaxaca portion, known as the **Papaloapan** (pah-pah-loh-AH-pahn) for the great river system that drains it, encompasses the **Chinantla** and the **Mazateca,** homelands of the indigenous Chinantec and Mazatec peoples.

The Central Valley of Oaxaca and the Mixteca

Continue your breeze-blown journey, now turning southwest, over the Sierra Zapoteca (Zapotec Highland) country to the **Valley of Oaxaca,** the heartland of the Zapotec people and Oaxacan civilization for more than 3,000 years. Below you spreads Oaxaca's great highland central valley complex: farms, pastures, towns,

OAXACA SUMMARY

Land area: 36,860 square miles, or 95,470 square kilometers (fifth largest among 31 Mexican states and the federal district)
Tallest mountain: Cerro Quiexobra, 12,300 feet (3,750 meters)
Population (2000): 3,440,000 (tenth largest among Mexican states)
Indigenous population: 39 percent of the total
Population density: 93 per square mile, 36 per square kilometer
Average daily income per active worker: $4.80
Average school grade attained per person: 5.8
Illiteracy: 20 percent

and villages, radiating in three 50-mile fingers (east, northwest, and south) from the capital city, Oaxaca.

Drawn on by the mystery of the mist-shrouded western mountains, you continue a hundred miles northwest, following the valley of the upper **Río Atoyac,** where the Sierra de Oaxaca rises again. There, you gaze down on a broad mountain and high plateau landscape, much of it tragically eroded. Oaxacans call this the **Mixteca,** the domain of the Mixtec people, proud transmitters of a major share of Oaxaca's ancient tradition. From your high vista, you see a landscape as creased as an old chopping board, dotted with tiny settlements scattered atop rugged mesas and tucked into deep gorges.

A closer look reveals natural divisions in the land. In the center you see the **Mixteca Alta**—high, cool, and cloud-shadowed. To the northwest, bordering the states of Guerrero and Puebla, lies the **Mixteca Baja,** a lower, desert-like plateau-land of cactus, maguey, and dwarf palm. To the south, toward the Pacific, at the place where your imaginary journey began, the mountains drop to the verdant, jungle-draped foothills, lush river canyons, and coastal farms of the **Mixteca de la Costa** (Mixtec coastal region).

CLIMATE

Despite its deep southern latitude, Oaxaca's elevation, cooling sea breezes, and summer rain showers moderate the heat of its plentiful sunshine. Most of the state, excepting the remote mountain summits, basks in the tropics, never feeling the bite of frost.

The seashore and coastal plain, including all of the Isthmus, is truly a land of endless summer. Winter days are typically warm and rainless, peaking at 82–88°F (28–31°C) and dropping to 65–75°F (18–24°C) by midnight.

Summers on the Oaxaca beaches are warmer and wetter. Mornings are usually bright and balmy, warming to around 90°F (32°C). Early afternoons, clouds often gather and bring short, sometimes heavy, cooling showers. Later, the sun reappears, drying the beaches and warming the breeze just in time to enjoy a dazzling Oaxaca *puesta del sol* (sunset).

Visitors to Oaxaca city experience similar but more temperate seasons. Midwinter days are mild, typically peaking between 70 and 75°F (21–24°C). Expect cool but frost-free winter nights between 45 and 60°F (9–16°C). Oaxaca city summers are delightful, with afternoons typically in the mid- to upper 80s (28–32°C) and pleasant evenings in the mid-70s (24–26°C), perfect for strolling. May, before the rains, is usually the warmest, with June, July, and August highs being moderated by afternoon showers.

Visitors should take note that Oaxaca's rainfall, like all of Mexico's, is strongly seasonal. Most years, nearly all the rainfall accumulates during the summer and early fall. Rains taper off in October and November and don't usually return until June. May, before the rains, is typically Mexico's warmest month. Relief comes with the cooling summer showers.

Many trees, especially along the coast, respond to the winter–spring drought by losing their leaves by February. This might make a typical late winter–early spring Oaxaca landscape

Many dozens of butterfly species thrive in Oaxaca's woodlands.

appear barren to the visitor in March even though the same area will be blooming with greenery by July or August. If you prefer lush, jungle verdure to be part of your Mexico experience, you'll enjoy plenty if you visit during the seven months from July through January.

Flora and Fauna

Luxuriant tropical foliage is one of the reasons that visitors are pleasantly surprised when they visit Oaxaca during the rainy summer-fall season. Then, excursions through Oaxaca's forest hinterlands offer an exotic experience. Leafy trees are swathed with mats of vines; giant-leafed **philodendrons** climb toward the canopy, while tropical hangers-on, such as spiny, pineapple-like red bromeliads and big, white-flowered **orchids** perch atop available branches.

Forests are not the only places that bloom. Wildflowers sprout everywhere, especially on upland plateaus. There, summer rains bring carpets of roadside blossoms—petite purple daisies, blue and yellow lupine, morning glories, tiny magenta sweet peas, and dozens more.

The dry winter–spring season also brings its surprising rewards. Many trees, especially along the coast, having lost their leaves, flower in February. Hundreds of varieties of the **pea family** bloom in riotous red, pink, yellow, and white. Now and then visitors stop, attracted by something remarkable, such as a host of white flowers blooming from the apparently dead branches of the appropriately named *palo de muerto* (tree of the dead). Other times, strikingly beautiful tree blossoms, such as the yellow, roselike *rosa amarilla,* tempt one's poetic imagination.

In dry country, cactus-like plants rule. Dotted all over the state, fields of **maguey** in ranks and files like obedient botanical battalions wait to be harvested for *mescal.* In other places, you will often see farmyards fenced with bulging nopal (prickly pear) cacti, their thick leaves studded with red **tunas** (cactus apples). And, on the road some drowsy afternoon, when you least expect it, a big **candelabra cactus** might appear around a bend, bristling with a house-size row of dozens of upright fluted green columns.

VEGETATION ZONES

Plants must adapt to the soil, sun, and rain, and Oaxaca's astonishingly diverse plant population reflects the state's varied landscape. Of Mexico's 14 major vegetation zones, ranging from high desert to tropical rainforest, at least eight occur in Oaxaca.

Directly along Oaxaca's paved national highways you can visit six of these zones: Near the seacoast lie extensive swaths of **savanna, deciduous tropical forest,** and **pine-oak forest.** Inland you can add the **tropical evergreen forest, tropical rainforest,** and **arid tropical scrub** to your botanical itinerary. Oaxaca's remaining major two vegetation zones, the **cloud forest** and **high coniferous forest,** are accessible only on high, often roadless, mountain slopes and summits.

Savanna

In their natural state, Oaxaca's savanna lands appear as flat, palm-dotted grasslands, watery during the summer and dry and brown during the winter and spring. Although much savanna has been converted to pasture or farmland, some pristine stretches lie along the coast, notably along Highway 200 near the Lagunas de Chacahua and along the Isthmus shoreline south of Highway 190, east of Juchitán.

Although grass rules the savanna, palms give it character. One of the most familiar in Oaxaca is the **Mexican fan palm,** or *palma real (Sabal Mexicana),* seasonally festooned with black fruit with leaves spread flat like a señorita's fan. The *palma real,* sometimes called the Oaxaca palm, resembles its cousin, the palmetto of the American southeast. The *palma real,* moreover, doesn't limit itself to the savanna. It appears in many other Oaxaca landscapes, notably in picturesque dwarf form in the cactus forest alongside Highway 190,

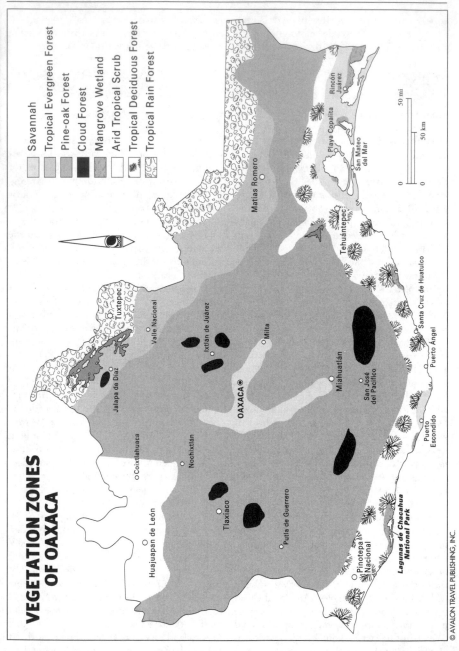

VEGETATION ZONES OF OAXACA

Savannah
Tropical Evergreen Forest
Pine-oak Forest
Cloud Forest
Mangrove Wetland
Arid Tropical Scrub
Tropical Deciduous Forest
Tropical Rain Forest

Rincón Juárez
Playa Copalita
San Mateo del Mar
Matías Romero
Tehuántepec
Santa Cruz de Huatulco
Puerto Ángel
Tuxtepec
Valle Nacional
Ixtlán de Juárez
Mitla
Miahuatlán
San José del Pacífico
Jalapa de Díaz
OAXACA
Puerto Escondido
Coixtlahuaca
Nochixtlán
Putla de Guerrero
Huajuapan de León
Tlaxiaco
Pinotepa Nacional
Lagunas de Chacahua National Park

50 mi
50 km
0

© AVALON TRAVEL PUBLISHING, INC.

just north of Huajuapan de León, in desertic northwest Oaxaca.

Visitors to Oaxaca's coastal resorts usually enjoy the sight of plenty of **coconut palms** *(Cocos nucifera),* by many measures the world's most useful tree. Local folks, who call it the *cocotero,* use nearly all of its parts: fronds for thatch, mats, and baskets; lumber for construction; and nuts for cooling drinks, fruit, candy, and oil. Nothing seems to symbolize the tropics more than a coconut palm drooping lazily over the beach or its fronds rustling gently in the tropical breeze. The coconut is completely benign with one exception: Falling coconuts are no joke. Watch out for them, especially during a breeze.

Another interesting savanna resident is the **sea grape** *(Coccolobis uvifera),* a genuine, although unusual, grape, often found growing on or behind seashore sand dunes. Like many true grapes, its vines sprout large round leaves and edible reddish-purple berries, which are probably too sour and astringent for wine.

If you see what look like several grapefruits sprouting from a tree trunk, you are probably looking at a **gourd tree,** or *calabaza (Crescentia alata).* The mature gourds, brown and hard, were handsomely carved and fitted with gold handles for Aztec emperors to drink chocolate out of. Oaxacans, who still call them by the ancient name *jícaras,* use them as bowls (notably women, on the west Oaxaca coast, who carry them all day at market on their heads, like a hat).

Its petite, pumpkin-shaped gourds both identify and name the **sandbox tree,** or *jabillo,* because they once served as desktop boxes full of sand for drying ink. The Aztecs, however, named it the exploding tree, because its ripe fruits burst their seeds forth with a bang like a firecracker. Beware of its poisonous seeds and its irritating sap.

A **mangrove wetland** *(manglar),* a vegetation sub-zone, often borders a savanna's watery seaward edge. Healthy mangrove wetlands are primary nurseries for uncounted forms of aquatic plants and animals. While a number of prime spots exist, Laguna Manialtepec, a half-hour drive west of Puerto Escondido, is one of Oaxaca's richest and most accessible mangrove wetlands.

The plant both synonymous with and essential to the mangrove wetland is the **red mangrove,** or *mangle colorado,* a tree that seems to stand in the water on stilts. Its new roots grow downward from above; a time-lapse photo would show it marching, as if on stilts, into the lagoon.

Tropical Deciduous Forest

Great swaths of this "friendly" or "short-tree" forest coat Oaxaca's coastline, especially along coastal Highway 200 around Puerto Ángel and the Bahías de Huatulco. As the label "deciduous" implies, this is the forest where the trees, in response to the dry winter weather, go dormant and lose their leaves. For visitors, the upside to all the winter barrenness is that many trees' leaves show bright fall colors; then, at the height of winter bleakness, they sprout profusions of bright red, yellow, pink, and white winter blossoms from apparently lifeless branches.

One of the most strikingly beautiful of these is the *rosa amarilla,* or yellowsilk shellseed *(Cochlospermum vitifolium).* Although not a rose, it looks every bit like a wild yellow rose when its big flowers sprout from bare branches in the early spring. After the flowers fall, leaves bud and apple-shaped green fruit grows, turning into brown pods, which pop open and release silky fluff.

The **silk cotton tree** *(Ceiba pentandra),* another of the tropical deciduous forest's major actors, yields a form of lightweight, cottony kapok fiber. Local folks, who call it the *cuajilote,* prize it for its spectacular large white (or red in cultivated varieties) blossoms with big, brushy pink stamens. In dense forest the silk cotton tree stays relatively short, but isolated it can grow to a wide-crowned giant with bulging buttresses on the lower trunk.

Lovers of Hawaii will be pleasantly surprised to find that a number of their favorite island plants are Mexican natives. The **frangipani** or **plumeria,** prized by native Mexicans for its heavenly orange blossom–like fragrance, was first classified and named as *Plumeria acutifolia* by French botanist Plumier. Pick some of its white, pink, or yellow whorl-lobed five-petaled flowers and put one behind your ear to get yourself into the mañana mood.

cottony puffs of the silk cotton tree, or *cuajilote*, in the coastal tropical deciduous forest

In Oaxaca as in Hawaii, you always know Christmas is coming because of another famous Mexico native, the **poinsettia** or *catarina (Euphorbia pulcherrima)*, first classified in 1828 by Joel R. Poinsett, an early ambassador to Mexico. Interestingly, the poinsettia's red blooms, in great abundance at Oaxaca city's Christmas fiestas, are not actually flower petals, but green leaves turned red, known technically as bracts.

Not nearly so benign is the *mala mujer* (bad woman), southern Mexico's poison ivy bush *(Cnidoscolus urens)*. Before venturing out through the Oaxaca coastal forest, ask someone to point out its drooping, oak-like, five-lobed leaves and tiny flowers. Otherwise, you might risk a stinging rash from the nettle-like hairs on the leaf surfaces and the long stalks.

If you go out on your hike but forget your makeup kit, you can improvise with the **lipstick tree** or *achiote (Bicha orellana)*. It appears as an ordinary shrub, but marked with brownish-green soft burrs above long, heart-shaped leaves. The surprise comes when you crush the burrs and discover their bright red-orange pulp, source of annatto dye, which warriors used to make

themselves look fierce and which manufacturers now use to color cheese, silk, and lipstick.

One of the showiest of roadside inhabitants is *mata ratón* (mouse killer, *Gliricidia sepium*). Despite its fragrant spring swirls of pink and white pea-like blossoms, this plant lives up to its name. Oaxacans grind its bark and leaves with cooked corn for a very effective rat and mouse poison (which, beware, is also poisonous to dogs). It can be further identified by its four- to six-inch-long seedpods.

Pine-Oak Forest

About an hour's drive inland, at elevations of about 5,000 feet (1,500 meters), the tropics give way to the cooling heights of the pine-oak forest, Oaxaca's most extensive vegetation zone.

Although pine-oak forest once covered half of Oaxaca's landscape, people, beginning thousands of years ago with Oaxaca's original farmers, cleared much of it for fields, especially in the central valley and surrounding mountainsides. Nevertheless, extensive upland tracts of pine-oak forest still remain, doing their beneficent work, storing moisture, anchoring soil against erosion, and providing food and shelter for hosts of animals.

As you enter the pine-oak forest from lower elevations, you usually see the oaks first, occurring in two broad families. Mexicans identify them as either the *encino* (evergreen, small-leafed) or the *roble* (deciduous, large-leafed), both resembling oaks that dot the hills and valleys of California and the U.S. Southwest. Clustered in their branches and scattered in the shade are the *bellota* (acorns), which unmistakably mark them as oaks.

At higher elevations the oaks gradually give way to pines, which, in Oaxaca, often grow in pure stands above six or seven thousand feet (1,800–2,100 meters). Pines are easy to identify, because of their long needle-like leaves, which grow in bundles, in contrast to the shorter needles of other conifers, such as spruce and fir, which commonly grow feather-shaped leaves made of rows of needles individually attached to the leaf stem.

Although pines are easily distinguished from other tree families, individual pine species are often hard to differentiate from each other. Nevertheless, examining the cones (which often conceal edible, tasty nuts) and the needles may yield identifying clues to at least a few members of this populous and very useful Mexican tree family.

Among the varieties you may encounter is the **Mexican white pine** *(Pinus ayachuite)*, similar to the white pine of the western United States. Local folks, who call it the *pinabete* or *ayacahuite,* know it by its very large (more than eight inches or 20 centimeters) cones and long, four- to six-inch needles, which hang in clusters of five.

Others you might see are the **Montezuma pine,** locally called the *ocote macho* (dark three- to nine-inch dark cones, long, drooping needles, five to a bundle) or the **Aztec pine** or *pino real* (shiny, small brown one- to two-inch cones and long, bright green needles in bundles of three—very useful for turpentine, tar, soap, and medicines).

Often associated in the same territory as pines and oaks is Mexico's renowned national tree, the *ahuehuete* (ah-way-WAY-tay) or *sabino.* Nearly every visitor to Oaxaca city sees the country's most famous specimen, at the village of Santa María del Tule, half an hour east of the city, where droves of visitors arrive, some on bended knee, to wonder at what is known locally as El Tule. Probably the most massive tree in Latin America, it's as big around at the trunk as it is high: approximately 150 feet (46 meters).

Other more modest but still impressive *ahuehuete* specimens occur in outlying areas, often in majestic groves near water, which accounts for its name, which translates as "old one of the water." When traveling through the inland countryside, especially along stream bottoms in the Mixteca (northwest Oaxaca), you may be able to spot an old *ahuehuete* by its general appearance, unusual for Mexico: a thick, deep green crown and reddish-brown, vertically grooved bark, not unlike a California redwood. Up close you will identify it by its round, reticulated two-inch cones and its feathery green spruce-like leaves (which led botanists to classify it as a type of cypress, namely the Montezuma bald cypress, *Taxodium mucronatum).*

Tropical Evergreen Forest

In rainy foothill and low mountain areas, especially along the north Gulf slope, the lush, dense undergrowth and tall, leaf-crowned trees of the tropical evergreen forest decorate the hillsides. Here, most extensively in the north along Highway 175 around Valle Nacional, and, to a lesser extent, in the southern Sierra foothills along highways north from the Pacific Coast, huge trees and vine-strewn thickets often overhang the highway. As the road curls through a dark, isolated, liana-draped canyon, momentarily you might feel as if you're traversing a forgotten corner of some prehistoric lost world, where a last remnant dinosaur might rear up at any moment.

But the bright visions of the tropical evergreen forest invariably dissipate such Jurassic Park images and jolt you back to its vivid jungle realities: A green iguana, looking every bit as primitive as a dinosaur, slithers across the road; a screeching swarm of bright green parrots swoops overhead; or a big, bird-size butterfly flutters in a roadside patch of sunlight. Overhead, huge-leafed climbing plants, such as the **ceriman** *(Monstera deliciosa),* hang by thick ropy vines on the trunks of accommodating trees. Local people, who know the ceriman as the *piñanona,* enjoy its sweet, juicy, corn cob–shaped fruit and find relief from aches and pains by drinking a tea brewed from its leaves.

No Oaxaca jungle trip would be complete without experiencing the **strangler fig,** known by the hideously accurate local label *matapalo* (killer tree). A strangler fig seed, once it sprouts in the crotch of a victim tree, will grow, finally entwining its host in a suffocating embrace. By then the strangler fig will have planted hairy "air roots" for ground support and will most likely go on living long after its victim has died. In a peculiarly national quirk of character, many Mexicans prize such dead victim-tree trunks. Workers scour the forests, cutting, gathering, and polishing these death embraces, to decorate living room corners or support elaborate outdoor *palapa* roofs, especially in fancy open-air restaurants.

In numerous stretches of Oaxaca's tropical evergreen forest, local folks cultivate **coffee** beneath the shady canopy. Even if coffee *(Coffea arabica),* known to its Mexican growers as *cafeto,* weren't commercially important, people could still enjoy it as an attractive ornamental, with its shiny, ribbed green leaves and red holly-like berries. Even though coffee shrubs are quite common in Oaxaca's jungly foothills, you have to look carefully for them, because they grow best in the deep shade beneath taller trees. If you don't spot the ripe red berries, look instead for the white flowers, which are as fragrant as those of coffee's cousin, the gardenia.

Another popular import to Oaxaca's tropical forestland is the **African tulip tree** *(Spathodea campanulata)*. Often seen right at roadside, a host of spectacular big red blooms caps a lush leafy crown like a host of heavenly scarlet bells.

Nearly as spectacular in its own exotic way is that cousin of the banana, the **heliconia** *(Heliconia latispatha)*. Because of the resemblance, Mexicans call it the *platanillo,* or "little banana." In contrast to the fruit of the banana, the heliconia's golden-orange flower-like leaves (bracts), reminiscent of bird-of-paradise blossoms, are the main attraction. To happen upon one for the first time in a garden or in the wild—hanging amongst the greenery in descending golden-orange segments like a ladder for leprechauns—is an experience rarely forgotten.

Tropical Rainforest

This is the "forest primeval" of legend, where heavy rains nourish grand evergreen hardwoods whose great leafy crowns tower up to 200 feet (60 meters) over layers of lesser trees. Here and there, rays of sunlight shine through and nurture a luxuriant undergrowth of palms, bamboo, orchids, and bromeliads.

The rainforest gives rise to many unique, sometimes bizarre, adaptations. The big trees fortify themselves against their top-heavy bulk by developing ponderous buttresses, reaching up to a dozen feet from the ground and spreading six or eight feet from the trunk. On the other hand, shorter, lower-canopy trees commonly drop fibrous filaments, which eventually root and grow into strange, stilt-like side-trunks as far as 50 feet (15 meters) from the original trunk.

Oaxaca's rainforests, which once spread in a continuous green swath along its northern border with the state of Veracruz, are steadily being logged and replaced by farms and ranches. Nevertheless, sizable tracts still remain, much in roadless areas

on both sides of Highway 175 around Valle Nacional, Isthmus Highway 185, and its offshoot, Highway 147, which runs northwest, through lowland Mixe territory, paralleling the Veracruz border.

The acknowledged king of the Mexican rainforest community is the **mahogany,** which local people, who call it the *caoba,* often point to with pride. The label refers to a number of similar trees of the genus *Swietenia,* which grow throughout the Mexican and Central American rainforests. Although the original mahogany *(Swietenia mahogani)* does not grow in Mexico, some of its cousins, such as *Swietenia macrophylla,* do. Oaxacans prize it for its handsome reddish wood, much valued for furniture. You can identify it by its half-foot-long slender leaves and four-inch woody fruits, curved like a vulture's head, thus the tongue-twisting indigenous label *zopilo zontecomacuahuitl* (buzzard-head tree).

If, along the roadside, you spot a tall tree with diagonal slashes on its bark (for gathering sap), it's most likely either a rubber tree or the chewing-gum tree, the **chicle,** locally known as the *chicozapote.* Chewing gum, made from the chicle's sap (notice the Chiclets in every store), spread all over the world during the early 20th century and continues to gum up sidewalks and schoolroom desks from San Francisco to Samarkand. Additionally, chicle trees, known to botanists as *Acrasuzapote,* yield hard, very durable wood and, from small pinkish-white flowers, luscious round, cream-colored fruits.

Of both commercial and decorative importance is the **rubber tree** *(Castilla elastica),* the source of so-called Panama rubber, once made (before synthetics) for raincoats, tennis balls, and tires. Indigenous Mexicans, who still call it the *hule* (OO-lay), have used it for millennia for making the ball for the ceremonial game of *tlatchtli.* Besides the diagonal grooves (which guide the milky sap into cups) on the trunk, you can identify the rubber tree by its foot-long, elliptical, leathery dark-green leaves, shiny on the top side and hairy underneath.

Among Oaxaca's most useful rainforest natives is the **chocolate tree** *(Theobromo cacao),* the "food of the gods" of the pre-conquest kings of Mexico. Before the conquest, *cacao* seeds served as currency. Although these days most people don't like to think of such things, historical records indicate that a healthy slave usually traded for about 100 beans; a small animal, for perhaps about five. Most likely you'll identify the *cacao*, growing as a smallish tree beneath the forest canopy, by spotting its 10-inch (25-centimeter) pods, which sprout right from the trunk. Workers break open the ripe, leathery yellow pods to harvest the trove of beans inside.

Arid Tropical Scrub

Although it looks a lot like a desert, Oaxaca's arid tropical scrub vegetation zone, along its northwest border with the states of Guerrero and Puebla, averages as much rainfall as San Francisco, California. In Oaxaca, however, the rain comes within a few summer months, often in cloudburst deluges that quickly drain away, leaving the people, animals, and plants to cope with six months of winter–spring drought.

The arid tropical scrub zone's most successful plants, succulents, such as the **cactuses** and their cousins the **agaves,** cope by storing moisture in fleshy leaves, trunks, and stems. None is more successful or important than the **prickly pear** *(Opuntia tuna),* which, from its role in Aztec legend and consequent presence on the Mexican flag, is an important national symbol. Moreover, it is especially useful as a fence plant, for cattle food, and, most of all, for its delicious red tunas, "cactus apple" fruit, which festoon its fleshy leaves.

The prickly pear is but one member of a broad look-alike family, known in Mexico generally as the *nopal.* Another, especially benign relative, known by botanists as *Platyopuntia,* is cultivated both for its tasty, spine-free leaves and, in Oaxaca, for red **cochineal** dye. Once commercially very important but now largely supplanted by synthetics, cochineal is still produced in a few Valley of Oaxaca communities. It turns out that a certain scale insect, *Dactylopius coccus,* loves to munch on the *Platyopuntia* cactus leaves. When the insects have eaten their fill, the people gather, dry, and crush their bodies, which yield a brilliant scarlet dye prized by weavers.

Another useful domesticated member of the arid tropical scrub community is the **maguey** (mah-GAY), or century plant, so-called because it's said to bloom once, then die, after 100 years of growth, although its lifetime is usually closer to 50 years. The maguey, moreover, has a number of well-known relatives. These include the very useful *mescal,* renowned for distilled liquor; *lechuguilla,* for *ixtle* fiber; and sisal, also useful for fiber. All of these, of the genus *Agave,* mature as a rose-like cluster of leathery, long, pointed gray-green leaves, from which a single flower stalk eventually blooms.

Wondrous gardens of wild cacti proliferate in the arid tropical scrub zone of northwest Oaxaca. Hard to miss is the **bravo** *(Neobuxbaumia mexcalaensis),* which often appears right at roadside, rising as pencil-shaped fluted columns. Bravos frequently grow in spectacular grand forests stretching to far rocky horizons.

Often growing in the same habitat is the *candelabro,* or **candelabra cactus** (Stenoceris weberi), which, most likely, you will see in a community of stunning many-columned giants, like house-size menorahs, dotting the landscape for miles.

Cloud Forest and High Coniferous Forest

Oaxaca's two rarest plant and wildlife communities lie on the slopes and summits of high, remote mountains. Oaxaca's most accessible cloud forests coat the northern mountains around Ixtlán de Juárez and the crest of the Mazatec's holy mountain, Cerro Rabón, near Jalapa de Díaz. The easiest, safest route is to hire a local guide who can take you to these dewy mountaintops where, beginning around 6,000 feet (1,800 meters), you will first meet the plant and wildlife community of the cloud forest. Most botanists believe the cloud forest plants to be Ice Age remnants of a time when Mexico's climate was much cooler than today. The proof is in the unusual specimens, many of which appear to have been transported directly across the Gulf of Mexico from the mountain forests of Georgia or North Carolina. In Oaxacan cloud forests, you may see the brilliant reds and oranges of **liquidambar,** the lovely white flowers of **dogwood,** or the white bark and tan falling leaves of **beech.**

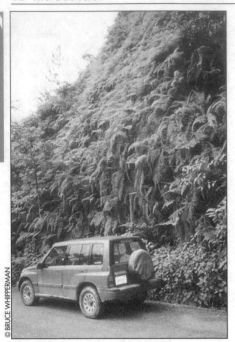

© BRUCE WHIPPERMAN

Tree ferns flourish in Oaxaca's cloud forest zones.

Besides those, you might observe some of the cloud forest's even more ancient vestiges, dating from the age of the dinosaurs. They include the giant Mexican **tree ferns** *(Cyathea mexicana)* with their long feathery fronds, dotted underside with ranks of brown spores. New fronds, which are born curling out of the treetops, account for the tree fern's local name, *rabo de mico* (monkey's tail).

Other such relics are the bromeliads and orchids, which as epiphytes merely enjoy physical support in their hosts' branches (unlike parasites, which feed on their hosts). **Bromeliads,** members of the pineapple family, love the drippy cloud forest environment, collecting water in their cup-like leaf folds. Of the dozens of Mexican species, one of the best known is the showy *piñuela (Guzmannia lingulata),* whose roseate central leaf cluster matures from green to red, finally appearing as an exotic scarlet flower.

Among the **orchids,** you will most likely first see the very widespread *bayoneta* or *pata de paloma* (dove's foot), which thrives in every humid Oaxaca environment from mangrove lagoons to cloud forests. You can recognize the *bayoneta* by its clusters of fleshy, drooping green leaves, topped by showy white flowers that age to a mellow golden hue.

Follow your guide even higher and you will reach the zone of **high coniferous forest,** which in Oaxaca probably exists only as a few scattered roadless, cloud-swathed green alpine islands, with vegetation resembling upper Rocky Mountain slopes in the United States and Canada. In Oaxaca, as you climb above about 9,000 feet (2,700 meters), you will likely pass through a zone of mixed pines, alders, and firs, reigned over by the regal **Montezuma pine** *Pinus montezumae,* distinguished by its long, pendulous cones and rough, ruddy bark, reminiscent of the sugar pine of the western United States.

Ascending still higher, you may pass through pure stands of **sacred fir** (Abies religiosa), which your guide will probably know as *oyamel* or *abeto.* You can identify them by lovely violet-blue cones and typical fir-like needles, which grow in rows along the branches. Even higher, the firs will eventually thin out, giving way to bunchgrass and bushy **Mexican juniper** *(monticola),* with its edible, waxy blue berries.

For more details of Oaxaca's marvelous plants, consult M. Walter Pesman's delightfully readable *Meet Flora Mexicana* (which, unfortunately, is out of print, but major libraries often have a copy). Also informative is the popular paperback *Handbook of Mexican Roadside Flora,* by Charles T. Mason Jr. and Patricia B. Mason. (See Suggested Reading.)

MAMMALS

Although thousands of years of human hunting and habitat encroachment have generally reduced their numbers, many of Oaxaca's native animal species still thrive in the wild. While some animals sensitive to human presence, such as **jaguars, howler monkeys,** and **tapirs,** are now rarely seen in Oaxaca, others, such as **foxes,**

coyotes, coatimundis, and wild pig-like jaba-
lines, seem unaffected by, and sometimes even
appear to benefit from, human presence.

The excitement of seeing animals in the wild is
the reward of visitors who take time to visit them
in their own wilderness home grounds. Sylvan
stretches, such as the pine-oak woodlands coating mountainsides northeast of Oaxaca city, the
thick forests of the Huatulco preserve, or the rich
mangrove wetland of Manialtepec near Puerto
Escondido, are ripe with wildlife-viewing opportunities for those willing to get off the beaten track
and quietly watch and wait.

Armadillos, Coatimundis, Peccaries, and Bats

The benefits of quiet isolation once came to me
when, lazing on a tropical beach, I spotted my
first armadillo (Dasypus novemcinctus). Although
it behaved much like the familiar opossum, I was
struck by its reptilian-like shell. The armadillo
was going about its business, nosing through the
forest-edge leaf cover nearby. Not seeming to possess particularly good eyesight, the preoccupied armadillo didn't notice when I crept in for a closer
look. He waddled right up and sniffed my shoe,
which evidently gave him such a scare that he
scuttled back into the woods in a flash.

One of the Mexicans' favorite animals is the
raccoon-like coatimundi (Nasua narica), known
in Mexico as coati, or tejón, the Spanish name
for badger. While many urban Mexicans,
charmed by the coatimundi's acrobatic antics
and inquisitive nature, keep them as pets, hungry
country folks enjoy them for culinary reasons.
You can identify one by its long nose and straight,
usually vertically held tail. Watch for them at
country markets.

The pig-like collared peccary (Tayassu ta-
jacu) is definitely not one of Oaxaca's endangered
species. Known locally as the jabalí, the Spanish
name for the much larger European wild boar, it
eats most anything and thrives in nearly all envi-
ronments—often not far from towns and villages. The gray-to-brown, short-haired jabalís,
although normally shy when encountered alone,
sometimes congregate in large groups and become aggressive. People have occasionally

reported being chased and, in one case, forced up
a tree, by collared peccaries.

Bats (murciélagos) are widespread in Oaxaca,
home to around two or three times as many bat
species as the entire United States. In Oaxaca,
bats were once widely worshipped, and even
today, as everywhere, they are both feared and
misunderstood. Shortly before sundown, bats
emerge from their cave and forest roosts and
silently flit through the air in search of insects.
Most people, sitting outside enjoying the early
evening, will mistake their darting silhouettes
for those of birds, who, except for owls, don't
generally fly at night.

The nonvampire Oaxacan bats carry their
vampire cousins' odious reputation with forbear-
ance. They go about their good works, pollinat-
ing flowers, clearing the air of pesky gnats and
mosquitoes, ridding cornfields of mice, and dropping seeds, thereby restoring forests.

Monkeys

Oaxaca's remote mountains and jungles, notably in
the Chimalapas region in the eastern Isthmus of
Tehuantepec, still shelter a number of rare and
endangered species. Accompanied by a competent tracker and suitably equipped with a jeep and
a week's worth of supplies, you may be lucky
enough to catch glimpses of Mexico's two seldom-
seen primates, the spider and howler monkeys.
The black spider monkey, whom your tracker will
probably know as the chango or mono de araña,
congregates in groups and uses its spindly arms
and legs (thus the "spider" label) and its prehensile
tail to reach its favorite wild fruits. Although its entertaining antics and endearingly mischievous
ways have earned the chango a place as a pet in
many Mexican homes, its present rarity is due in
large part to its contribution to the diet of many
poor indigenous families.

The even rarer howler monkey, called locally
saraguato or aullador, is, by contrast, extremely shy
and retiring. Seldom seen even in captivity,
howler monkeys (Alouatta palliata) withdraw far
into the forest as mankind encroaches. Consider
yourself lucky if somewhere in Oaxaca's eastern
jungle wilderness you can draw close enough to
hear a big male howler's far-off booming call.

Consider yourself doubly fortunate if, on such an excursion, you also hear the chesty cry of a jaguar, the fabled *tigre.*

El Tigre

The jaguar's cunning, stealth, and strength are the stuff of Mexican legend. In ancient times, the jaguar was the supreme source from whom kings, princes, and warriors drew their power. And when Mexicans recall the old proverb etched in their memories that "Each hill has its own *tigre,*" they remember that untamable presence out there beyond the campfire, the gate, the town limits, lurking somewhere in the darkness.

The legend is well deserved; at 250 pounds and six feet (110 kilograms, two meters) in length, the jaguar *(Felis onca)* is America's largest, most powerful cat. With dark reticulated spots over a tan coat, the jaguar resembles a beefy, short-legged leopard. Although hunting and human encroachment have driven jaguars into Oaxaca's deepest forest reaches, a few still live on, mostly in the southern coast and Sierra and the northeastern isthmus, where they hunt along thickly forested stream bottoms and foothills. Unlike its more common cousin, the mountain lion, or *león,* the jaguar will eat any game. They have even been known to wait patiently for fish in rivers and stalk beaches for turtle and egg dinners. If they have a favorite food, it is probably the pig-like collared peccary.

Although government rules strictly prohibit jaguar hunting, the temptation for a poor campesino to earn a year's wages by shooting a jaguar and clandestinely selling its pelt is too great for the jaguar to survive for many more years in the wild in Oaxaca.

Despite their fearsome reputation and the demonstrated fact that they will fight back when cornered, little or no evidence indicates that jaguars are deliberate man-eaters.

Ocelots, Margays, and Jaguarundis

Although jaguars are extremely endangered, other Mexican cats are less so. Besides the bobcat and mountain lion, both familiar north of the border, three other wild cat species make their home in Oaxaca. In descending order of size, first comes

the **ocelot** *(Felis pardalis).* Its appearance, like a miniature jaguar, with a spotted yellowish-tan coat and stout legs, reflects its Mexican name, *tigrillo.* Full-grown male ocelots measure about 25 pounds (10 kilograms) and three feet (one meter) in length. Its soft, fine fur, highly valued as a pelt, has unfortunately led to the ocelot's near-disappearance from Oaxaca's forests.

Approaching large house-cat size is the **jaguarundi** or *leoncillo,* which, full-grown, weighs in at around 13 pounds (six kilograms). Although its species label *(Felisjaguarundi)* clearly puts the jaguarundi in the cat family, its elongated head gives it a somewhat otterlike appearance.

With its spots and diminutive size, a full-grown **margay** appears at first glance to be a baby jaguar. A closer look, however, reveals spots more aligned in rows than the jaguar's. Moreover, a domesticated margay, in contrast to the untamable jaguar, can be as endearing as your own family cat.

Like their larger cousins, the jaguarundi and margay are gradually disappearing from Oaxaca's forest wildlands. They hunt mostly along stream banks in deep remote valleys and roadless mountainsides. They feast on small game, birds, and fish, and, as a matter of self-preservation, make it their business to see you before you see them.

BIRDS

Oaxaca's coastal wetlands and upland forests straddle the southern zone of the great Pacific Flyway, the major western pathway for hosts of birds migrating south from the United States and Canada. These familiar winter visitors, such as Canada geese and ducks, including the Muscovy, black-bellied whistler, gadwall, baldpate, and shoveler, arrive and join an already-rich resident population of ibis, parrots, jacanas, egrets, herons, and anhingas, swelling the numbers into the millions.

Some of the most commonly seen residents are also the most spectacular and entertaining. The cootlike, blackish **northern jacana** *(Jacana spinosa)* amuses bird-watchers by appearing to walk on water. Actually, its clownishly large feet

Oaxaca seagulls, as everywhere, are on the watch for a meal.

allow it to scoot across gardens of water-borne lily pads as if they were solid land, earning it the label "lily walker."

Always impressive is the graceful swoop of a **great blue heron** *(Ardea herodius)* gliding to rest in a Oaxacan wetland. Unmistakable because of its regal six-foot (two-meter) wingspread and blue-gray coloring, the male great blue heron also sports a proud blue head plume. In the same marshland, you will also probably spot its smaller (about two feet, or half a meter, long), more numerous cousin, the **snowy egret** *(Egretta thula),* pure white except for its black beak. Although differing sharply in appearance, both species single-mindedly stalk through a pond ever so slowly, freezing rock still when prey is spotted. After several seconds, pop! Down goes the bill, snaring a hapless crab, fish, or frog.

Try not to confuse the snowy egret with the smaller (18-inch) yellow-billed **cattle egret** *(Bubulcus ibis),* an African native that began appearing in Mexico around 1900. True to their name, cattle egrets usually flock around cow pastures, where they feed on the hordes of bugs that follow livestock. Local Mexican people generally identify all herons and egrets collectively as *garzas.*

Seabirds

Oaxaca's prime beach-bird actors, in addition to the swarms of gulls, terns, sandpipers, and boobies, are **brown pelicans** and big, black-and-white **frigate birds.** Their collective feeding rituals, although quite distinct, are equally entertaining. That of the brown *pelícano* (pay-LEE-cah-noh) is the most deliberate. After spotting a school of their preferred prey, the pelicans, singly or in pairs, circle once or twice, then dive headlong into the billows, usually coming up with fish in their gullet. They rest, bobbing over the waves for a spell, seemingly waiting for their comrades to take their turns.

Frigate birds *(fragatas),* by contrast, prefer either being fed or stealing food to hunting for themselves. They often reap bonuses from the efforts of villagers who haul in nets of fish right on the beach. Once the salable part of the catch is gone, kids have great fun throwing the residue overhead to a gaggle of wheeling frigate birds. In contrast to the pelicans' mannerly behavior, it's every frigate bird for itself. Frigates who miss a tossed morsel often try to snatch their fellow's prize.

Parrots

Flocks of small parrots screech, shriek, swoop, chatter, and swarm above Oaxaca's coastal mangrove lagoons and tropical foothills. The best places to spot them are in fields or pastures adjacent to thick forests, far from town. Half a dozen species—mostly green, with a patch of color on their throat or forehead—are common. If you don't get far enough into the country to see them, ask where *péricos* (PAY-ree-kohs) are for sale in big markets, such as Oaxaca city, Tlacolula, Etla, Tehuantepec, Tuxtepec, Pinotepa Nacional, and Valle Nacional.

Although you might be tempted to buy such a market parrot, don't. Like all wild animals, parrots outside of their forest homelands present manifold difficulties. For starters, they quickly chew their way out of bamboo cages. Later, your airline will probably require that you buy a special "parrot ticket" for the flight back home. Moreover, after you arrive, parrots are all but impossible to get through customs. On the other hand, if you must have a pet parrot, best buy a pair of (never a single) certified healthy birds from a pet shop back home.

Among the parrots you're most likely to encounter in Oaxaca is the foot-long **green parakeet** *(Aratinga holochlora).* A long tail and a red throat further mark the species, whose members prefer to flock in the drier woodlands above 3,000 feet (1,000 meters). Another, commonly seen in tropical lowlands, is the **Aztec parakeet** *(Aratinga astec),* at nine inches (23 centimeters), all green with an olive-brown throat. For colored drawings and details, consult *Field Guide to Mexican Birds* by Roger Tory Peterson and Edward L. Chalif. (See Suggested Reading.)

REPTILES AND AMPHIBIANS
Snakes
Of Oaxaca's many dozens of snake species, the great majority couldn't harm you even if they tried. Furthermore, most snakes are shy and will clear out if you give them plenty of warning. In Oaxaca, poisonous snakes have been largely driven out of city and tourist areas. In the bush or jungle, however, carry a stick and beat the shrubbery in front of you while watching where you put your feet. When hiking or rock-climbing in the country, don't put your hands in niches you can't see into.

While such precautions minimize potential hazards, outback travelers should be prepared to encounter members of Oaxaca's most notorious snake families, the **rattlesnakes** and the **fer-de-lances.** Each occurs in a number of species, all potently venomous and generally aggressive. Mexican rattlesnakes or *cascabeles* (kahs-kah-BAY-lays), with the same warning rattle and the diamondback markings as their north-of-the-border U.S. relatives, need little introduction. Their tropical viper-cousins, the fer-de-lances *(Bothrops atrox),* are known locally by various names, such as *nauyaca, cuatro narices, palanca,* and *barba amarilla.* Although about the same size (to six feet, or two meters) and general appearance as rattlesnakes, fer-de-lances *lack warning rattles* and are consequently even more dangerous. On treks into the jungle, where the fer-de-lance commonly

lives, *guard* against them by wearing high-topped leather boots and watching carefully where you put your feet.

Snakes in the tropics are not confined to land. Although very unlikely, it is possible that you may encounter a **sea snake** *(culebra marina)* while swimming offshore at an isolated Oaxaca beach. If small, yellow, and black, it will be certainly the *Pelamis platurus,* which, although shy, lives in groups and has been reported to inflict a serious, venomous bite. Some **eels,** which resemble snakes but have gills like fish and inhabit rocky crevices, can inflict nonpoisonous bites and should also be avoided.

The Oaxacan land counterpart of the poisonous sea snake is the **coral snake** *(coralillo),* which occurs in several species, all with bright multicolored bands that always include red. Although relatively rare, small, and shy, coral snakes occasionally bite, sometimes fatally.

Gila Monsters, Iguanas, and Geckos
The Gila monster (confined in Mexico to northern Sonora) and its southern tropical relative, the black-with-yellow-spots *escorpión,* are the world's only poisonous lizards. Despite its beaded skin and menacing, fleshy appearance, the *escorpión (Heloderma horridum)* bites only when severely provoked; even then, its venom is rarely, if ever, fatal.

The rest of Oaxaca's many lizard species are much more benign; some are even endearing. Of them, the **iguana,** locally called the *garrobo,* is most popular, mainly because of its tasty flesh. Although usually masked in the bush by its spotted green camouflage, you may glimpse an iguana scurrying, in a flash of green, across the road in front of your car or bus. Despite their fierce dinosaurian aspect, iguanas are peaceful vegetarians, often munching flowers in a favorite treetop.

One of Oaxaca's most endearing reptilian residents is the **gecko,** known as *guerita* (blondie) in the coastal towns and villages where they are common. Visitors usually encounter them in their hotel rooms. If you hear their homey clicking sound (for which residents affectionately call them *besucona,* the "kissing one"), don't be alarmed. Quite the contrary, for each room cannot be without its resident gecko to properly cleanse it of gnats and mosquitoes. If your room doesn't have one, ask the management to find a *guerita* for you.

Crocodiles

The crocodile, *cocodrilo* or *caiman,* once prized for its meat and hide, came close to vanishing from Oaxaca's coastal lagoons until the government stepped in to ensure its survival. Now officially protected, a few isolated breeding populations live in the wild, while government and private hatcheries are breeding more for the eventual repopulation of lagoons where they once were common. A hatchery open for touring is located in Lagunas de Chacagua.

Two crocodile species are native to Oaxaca. The true **crocodile** *(Crocodilus acutus)* has a narrower snout than its local cousin *(Caiman crocodilus fuscus),* a type of **alligator** *(lagarto).* Although past individuals have been recorded up to 15 feet (five meters) long, wild native crocodiles are usually young and a few feet or less in length.

Sea Turtles

The story of Mexican sea turtles is similar. They once swarmed ashore on Mexican beaches to lay their eggs. Prized for their meat, eggs, hide, and shell, the turtles were severely devastated. Now officially protected, growing numbers of sea turtles are hatching and returning to the sea from Oaxaca's beaches, thanks to the increasing ranks of eco-volunteers who guard against poachers. Very accessible Oaxaca turtle sanctuaries include the entire Bahías de Huatulco, a pair of home-grown sanctuaries near Puerto Escondido, and especially Playa Mazunte, near Puerto Ángel. There, a government **turtle aquarium and hatchery** occupies the site of a former turtle processing factory.

Of the four locally occurring species, the **olive ridley** *(tortuga golfina)* and the **green turtle** *(tortuga verde)* are the most common. From tour boats, green turtles can often be seen grazing on sea grass offshore from Puerto Escondido and the Bahías de Huatulco.

For more details of Mexico's mammals and birds in general, check out Starker Leopold's very readable (but unfortunately out-of-print)

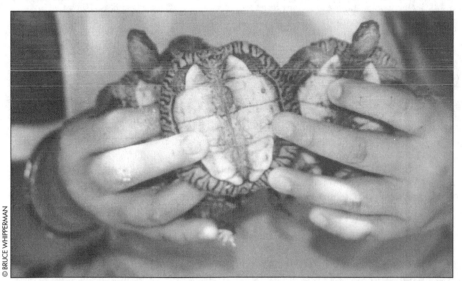

© BRUCE WHIPPERMAN

Once fished nearly to extinction, sea turtles are now making a comeback on the Oaxaca Pacific Coast.

classic, *Wildlife of Mexico: The Game Birds and Mammals,* and other works in the Suggested Reading section.

FISH

Shoals of fish abound in Oaxacan waters. Four billfish species are found in deep-sea grounds several miles offshore: **swordfish, sailfish,** and **blue and black marlin.** All are spirited fighters, though the sailfish and marlin are generally the toughest to bring in. The blue marlin is the biggest of the four. Although 10-foot, 1,000-pound (three-meter, 450-kilogram) fish used to be brought in occasionally, four-foot, 200-pound marlin (one-meter, 90-kilogram) and 100-pound (45-kilogram) sailfish are more typical of late. Recognizing the need for conservation, forward-looking captains now encourage victorious anglers to return these magnificent "tigers of the sea" (especially the sinewy, poor-eating sailfish and blue marlin) to the deep after they've won the battle.

Billfish are not the only prizes of the sea. Serious fish lovers also seek varieties of tunalike **jack,** such as **yellowtail, Pacific amberjack, pompano, jack crevalle,** and the tenacious **roosterfish,** named for the "comb" atop its head. These and the **yellowfin tuna, mackerel,** and *dorado,* which Hawaiians call mahimahi, are among the delicacies sought in Oaxacan waters.

Accessible from small boats offshore and by casting from shoreline rocks are varieties of **snapper** *(huachinango, pargo)* and **sea bass** *(cabrilla).* Closer to shore, **croaker, mullet,** and **Goliath fish** often can be found foraging along sandy bottoms and in rocky crevices.

Sharks and **rays** inhabit nearly all depths, with smaller fry venturing into beach shallows and lagoons. Sometimes, huge **Pacific manta rays** appear to be frolicking, their great wings flapping like birds, not far off Oaxacan shores. Just beyond the waves, local fisherfolk bring in **hammerhead, thresher,** and **leopard sharks.**

Also common is the **stingray,** which can inflict a painful wound with its barbed tail. Experienced swimmers and waders avoid injury by both shuffling (rather than stepping) and watching their feet in shallow, sandy bottoms.

Captains from marinas at Santa Cruz de Huatulco, Puerto Ángel, and Salina Cruz routinely pilot big boats equipped for four or five anglers to try for the big marlin, sailfish, and swordfish. Launches and tackle, suitable for smaller but still exciting catches, can be hired at those same marinas, in addition to Puerto Escondido and a number of other beach villages along the Oaxacan coast.

For more fish details, including a chart of species encountered in Oaxacan waters, turn to the Sports and Recreation section in the On the Road chapter.

History

An age ago—perhaps as long as 20,000 years—small bands of hardy people, ancestors of the adventurers who had crossed the Arctic land bridge from Siberia thousands of years earlier, were hunting and foraging in what is now the Valley of Oaxaca. The forests and meadows abounded with edible plants and game—from squirrels and rabbits to great Ice Age herds of camels, horses, and mammoths. Supplied with abundant food, the people multiplied.

But by around 7000 B.C. the climate had warmed several degrees, and the great game animals were extinct. Perhaps in response, the people began to sow seeds of their favorite edible wild

grains, legumes, vegetables, and fruits. As their descendants still do today, those ancient Oaxacans picked out the biggest and healthiest seeds to plant for the succeeding year's crop. After many generations, their fields were blooming with domesticated beans, squash, corn, and avocados nearly as robust as those enjoyed today.

EARLY CIVILIZATION
The Village Era
Millennia later, around 2000 B.C., those early Oaxacans, supplied with the bounty of their fields, no longer had to wander in search of food

and were settling into permanent villages. Although initially small—typically only a dozen houses—the villages prospered and grew. Discovered remains reveal that many aspects of Oaxacan village life have remained fundamentally unchanged. Then, as now, planting, harvesting, and preparation of food occupied most of the day. Men used flint ax-heads hafted to wooden handles to clear brush, which they would burn in preparation for seeding. Women ground corn with the familiar *mano* and *metate*, combination roller-crusher. They patted tortillas and baked them on the flat clay *comal* griddle and stewed meats, beans, and chili sauces in round clay pots.

Excavated ceramic figurines reveal the villagers' dress: for women, woven cloth or frond skirts, fiber or leather sandals, and long, often attractively braided hair, earrings, and necklaces; for men, ordinarily a simple loincloth and sandals.

Village people buried their dead family members, laid out flat, in graves near their houses. A few offerings for the afterlife accompanied the deceased: a bowl with food, drinks, favored personal objects, and jewelry, including a semiprecious stone placed in the mouth.

Gradually, population increased. By 500 B.C. some villages, such as at **San José Mogote** about 10 miles (16 km) northwest of Oaxaca city, had grown into small towns, with as many as 500 residents. At San José Mogote investigators have uncovered early evidence of social classes—large, regally elevated houses—and specialization, in the form of a factory where workers polished iron-rich magnetite into small mirrors, which were traded hundreds of miles away.

Gradually during the few thousand years when villages were growing into towns, abundant food and burgeoning commercial wealth lifted a small but significant fraction of Oaxacans to a privileged leisure status. They became the artists, architects, warriors, and ruler-priests—with time to think and create. Over time, they devised symbols, writing, and a calendar that tied the constant wheel of the firmament to life on earth, defining the days to plant, to harvest, to feast, to travel, and to trade. Eventually, a grand city arose.

Monte Albán

Around 500 B.C., ancestors of Oaxaca's present-day Zapotec peoples founded what many experts believe to have been the Americas' earliest metropolis. On the central valley summit known today as Monte Albán, they raised monumental platforms, pyramids, palaces, and ceremonial ball courts. These they decorated with inscriptions, in a language yet to be deciphered, recording the exploits of their god-kings. The ordinary family homes of adobe bricks, arranged around central patios, occupied the hillside just below the ceremonial summit.

For centuries, Monte Albán flourished, overflowing halfway down its hillsides. Although starting from a population of only 2,000 at its founding, Monte Albán flourished to a city of as many as 40,000 at its height a thousand years

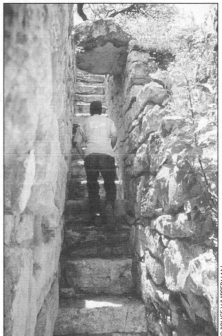

© BRUCE WHIPPERMAN

Archaeologists have gradually uncovered the remains of a sizable early urban-stage town (circa 500 B.C.) at San José Mogote, 20 minutes' drive north of Oaxaca city.

later. By A.D. 500 Monte Albán encompassed three square miles (seven square km), interlaced with vegetable and flower gardens and spreading to several monumental neighborhood subcenters downhill.

Although Monte Albán ruled, upwards of two dozen subsidiary cities administered local areas throughout Oaxaca. Their ruins litter the present-day state: sites such as **Yucuita** and Yucuñudahui in the Mixteca Alta, **Cerro de las Minas** in the Mixteca Baja, and **Dainzu** and **Lambityeco** in the central valley. War appears to have been a scourge of Oaxaca's early cities. Like Monte Albán, and in contrast to most village-era sites, most cities lay atop defensible hilltops.

Monte Albán's days were nevertheless numbered. After dominating Oaxaca and beyond for more than a thousand years, its power was fading fast by around A.D. 750. Although experts argue over what combination of drought, disease, war, or overpopulation ended Monte Albán's glory days, they agree that it was virtually abandoned by A.D. 1000 and eclipsed by a crowd of tussling city-states. A similar mysterious fate befell other southern and central Mexican cities, most notably Teotihuacán, Monte Albán's great rival metropolis in the north.

Teotihuacán

Although founded half a millennium later than Monte Albán, Teotihuacán grew rapidly, attaining population and wealth on a par with the ancient world's great cities by A.D. 300. Its epic pyramids still stand, not far north of Mexico City, along a grand avenue of fearsome, rubyeyed stone effigies of Quetzalcoatl, the feathered serpent king of gods.

After Teotihuacán was abandoned around A.D. 700, a host of its former vassal cities rose to power, among them Xochicalco, in the highlands in the present state of Morelos, an hour's drive south of Mexico City.

The Living Quetzalcoatl

Xochicalco became renowned as a center of learning, where noble families sent their sons to study the healing arts, astronomy, architecture, and agriculture. A prominent student among them

was **Topiltzín** (literally, Our Prince), who left Xochicalco in A.D. 968 to found his own city-state, Tula, north of old Teotihuacán.

After an enlightened 20-year rule, Topiltzín became so revered that his people began to know him as the living incarnation of Quetzalcoatl, the plumed god of gods. He was not universally loved, however. Jealous priests, who hated Quetzalcoatl-Topiltzín's persuasive opposition to their bloody rites of human sacrifice, drugged him with alcohol. He awoke, bleary-eyed, in bed with his sister. Devastated by shame, Quetzalcoatl-Topiltzín banished himself from Tula with a band of retainers. In A.D. 987, they headed east, toward Yucatán. Although he sent word he would reclaim his kingdom during the 52-year cyclical calendar year of his birth, Ce Acatl, Quetzalcoatl-Topiltzín never returned. Legends say that he sailed east and rose to heaven as the morning star.

The Rise of Oaxacan City-States

By A.D. 1000, the power vacuum left by the demise of Monte Albán had been filled by its dozens of former tributary cities, whose rulers carved out their own little kingdoms, mostly in the central valley and the Mixteca. Each had a dominant town, typically with a population of 5,000–10,000, which ruled a dispersed walking-distance village hinterland of about 100 square miles (250 square km) and 10,000 or 20,000 people. Some of these, notably **Zaachila** and **Mitla** near present-day Oaxaca city, remain thriving towns, still dominating their districts, while others, such as **Yagul**, near Mitla; **Huijazoo**, in the Etla Valley northwest of Oaxaca city; and **Guiengola**, in the Isthmus west of Tehuantepec, are uninhabited ruins.

8-Deer and the Mixtec Invasion

In A.D. 1011, not long after the great Quetzalcoatl-Topiltzín had trekked east, another renowned noble, known to historians as 8-Deer, the calendar name-date of his birth, was born in Oaxaca. Scholars have learned details of his life through pre-conquest hieroglyphic documents, collectively called **codices** (or singularly, codex). Although most were destroyed by Spanish priests all over Mexico early in the conquest, eight Oaxaca codices, folded deerskin hieroglyphic books whitened with lime, survived, all from the Mixtec region of Oaxaca, respectively called Becker I, Becker II, Bodley, Colombino, Nuttall, Sánchez Solis, Selden, and Vienna. Six of these eight Mixtec codices commemorate 8-Deer's adventures. Among the most enlightening, Codex Nuttall records 8 Deer's given name as "Tiger Claw," portending his ruthless exploits.

As Monte Albán's power faded, the Mixtec city-states, west and northwest of the central valley, thrived. But overpopulation, and perhaps pressure from Xochicalco and the Toltecs (People of Tula), forced ambitious Mixtec nobles to look southward at the fertile lands of the Oaxaca central valley.

The stage for Mixtec expansion was set when 8-Deer Tiger Claw came of age. He moved quickly, forming alliances and setting his rivals against one another. Codex Nuttall depicts one of 8-Deer Tiger Claw's expeditions. It shows him, along with two allies, 4-Tiger and 9-Water, spears and shields in hand, crossing a lake by canoe toward an island, the Hill of Mixtlatl. The document records the expedition's three consecutive dates: 10-Serpent, 11-Death, and 12-Deer, of A.D. 1046, when 8-Deer was in his 35-year-old fighting prime.

After bringing the entire Mixteca, from the Tehuacán Valley in the north to the coastal stronghold at Tututepec, under his control, 8-Deer led Mixtec armies southeast from his capital at **Tilantongo** and defeated a number of Zapotec central valley city-states. Although 8-Deer met his end as a sacrifice victim in Cuilapan, not far south of present-day Oaxaca city, in 1061, Mixtec nobles ruled on as an elite minority in Zaachila, Mitla, and other valley city-states. They preserved their dominance by the tactic of political marriage, taking daughters of the Zapotec nobility as near-hostage wives who raised Mixtec-speaking heirs.

Although virtually no Mixtec speakers remain living today in the central valley, the old Mixtec influence lives on in the Zapotec-Mixtec stylistic fusion of the architecture, pottery, jewelry, and other remains found at Zaachila, Mitla, Monte Albán, and other sites. Admire the elaborately

fine **greca** mosaic frets decorating the Mitla ruins and you're enjoying the Mixtec influence; likewise, at the Santo Domingo Cultural Center museum in Oaxaca city, Mixtec craftsmanship and sophistication gleam from the **golden mask of death** and the trove of gold and turquoise jewelry taken from **tomb 7** at Monte Albán.

The Aztecs Invade Oaxaca

At the time the Mixtecs were consolidating their rule of the Valley of Oaxaca, the Aztecs (People of Aztlán), a collection of seven aggressive immigrant subtribes, had eclipsed the Toltec civilization that Quetzalcoatl-Topiltzín had founded north of present day Mexico City. After migrating from a mysterious **western land of Aztlán** (Land of the Herons) into the lake-filled valley that Mexico City now occupies, around 1250, the Aztecs' fiercest tribe, whose members called themselves the **México** (MAY-shee-kah), clawed its way to dominion over the Valley of Mexico. In 1325, the México founded their capital, Tenochtitlán, on an island in the middle of the valley-lake. During the next century, Tenochtitlán grew into a magnificent city, from which Aztec armies, like Roman legions, marched out and subdued kingdoms for hundreds of miles in all directions.

In 1434, the Aztecs, under Emperor Itzcóatl, conquered the northern Mixtec domains in the Tehuacán Valley; several years later his successor, Moctezuma Ilhuicamina, attacked southward, defeating Atonaltzin, the Mixtec lord of Coixtlahuaca. Besides yielding booty and a small army of captives, the victory opened the path to the entire Mixteca and the Valley of Oaxaca.

By 1456, the Aztecs were firmly fixed in the valley, having established a garrison at **Huaxyacac,** the site of present-day Oaxaca city. From that point, however, the Aztecs found their access to the remainder of the central valley and the coveted southern lands of Tehuantepec blocked by the strong Zapotec city-state of Zaachila. After 30 frustrating years, the Aztecs, then under Emperor Ahuizotl, bargained with **Cosijoeza** (koh-see-hoh-EY-zah), the king of Zaachila, for peaceful access toward Tehuantepec in the southeast. Cosijoeza soon regretted the concession. In 1494, the Aztecs broke the agreement and seized and subjugated

Mitla, at the eastern end of the valley. Enraged, Cosijoeza rushed his forces southeast and fortified their Isthmus hilltop bastion at Guiengola, which blocked the Aztecs' progress to their southern capital at Tehuantepec and Chiapas beyond.

After a seven-month siege of Guiengola, the frustrated Aztecs again resorted to diplomacy. They proposed a new alliance, in the form of a marriage between King Cosijoeza and **Coyollicatzin** (koh-yoh-yee-KAH-tseen), the daughter of the new Aztec Emperor Moctezuma I. The Aztecs' hidden agenda: They expected Coyollicatzin to spy upon Cosijoeza; true love, however, won out as Coyollicatzin refused to play the pawn and remained loyal to her husband Cosijoeza. The Aztecs eventually made peace in return for tribute. Cosijoeza turned his Tehuantepec domain to his son **Cosijopí** and returned home to reign over his Zapotec people at Zaachila in the central valley.

Despite a king's ransom in yearly tribute—mounds of quetzal feathers, dozens of sacks of cochineal, hundreds of pounds of gold, thousands of bolts of cloth—the Aztec's millions of Oaxacan subjects always seemed to be rebelling someplace until the Spanish conquistadores arrived and toppled the Aztecs from power in 1521.

THE CONQUEST

Although Christopher Columbus and the generation of explorers who followed him had discovered a new world in America, their dreams of riches had eluded them. In Spain's new Caribbean island colonies both gold and native workers, who had mostly died from European diseases, were scarce. A new wave of adventurers, among them **Hernán Cortés,** a minor nobleman from the poor Spanish province of Extremadura, turned their vision toward new fabled empires—perhaps even the elusive Cathay—beyond the setting sun. In Cuba, Cortés patched together a motley force of 550 men, an assortment of small ships, a few horses, and a cannon and sailed west in early 1519. By the time they landed on Mexico's Gulf Coast on April 22, 1519, Cortés's men, torn by dissension and realizing the impossible odds against them, were near mutiny.

Cortés, however, cut his losses and exploited his opportunities with extraordinary aplomb. He won over the doubters, isolated the dissenters, and ended any thoughts of retreat to Cuba by burning his ships. Next he capitalized on the lucky coincidence that he had landed on the Mexican coastline in the Aztec year of Ce Acatl, exactly the same 52-year cyclical anniversary year in which Quetzalcoatl-Topiltzín had vowed to return from the east to reclaim his kingdom.

As he led his band of adventurers westward over the mountains toward the Aztec capital of Tenochtitlán, Cortés played Quetzalcoatl to the hilt, awing local leaders. Coaxed by **Doña Marina,** his wily native translator-mistress-confidante, local chiefs began to add their armies to Cortés's march against their Aztec oppressors.

Tenochtitlán, Capital of the Empire

A few months later, inside the gates of Tenochtitlán, the Venice-like island-metropolis, it was the Spaniards' turn to be awed: by gardens full of animals, gold and palaces, and a great pyramid-enclosed square where tens of thousands of people bartered goods gathered from all over the empire. Tenochtitlán, with perhaps a quarter of a million people, was the great capital of an empire as large and rich as any in Europe.

Moctezuma II, the lord of that empire, fearing that Cortés was in fact the god Quetzalcoatl incarnate, had followed Cortés's progress toward Tenochtitlán with trepidation. Wishing not to offend, Moctezuma II had sent Cortés sumptuous gifts of gold, coupled with warnings to stay away. Encouraged by the gold, Cortés demanded an early audience with the emperor, who pathetically surrendered himself to Cortés's custody and "donated" his entire empire to the Spanish crown.

Spaniards Enter Oaxaca

With his position temporarily secure, Cortés dispatched emissaries west, east, and south. To Oaxaca he sent Hernando Pizarro and Diego de Ordaz, each with small detachments, to reconnoiter for riches. Pizarro searched for gold in the Papaloapaon basin around Tuxtepec and later the Chinantla, while Ordaz passed through the

Mixtec kingdoms of Yanhuitlán and Sosola on his way to the Gulf Coast.

The Aztecs Force a Spanish Retreat

Meanwhile, however, the people of Tenochtitlán were rioting against Spanish brutality. On July 1, 1520, with Moctezuma II mortally wounded by his own countrymen, Cortés and his men, forced by the sheer numbers of rebellious Mexicans, retreated, hacking a bloody path through thousands of screaming Aztec warriors to safety on the lakeshore.

Hearing the news of Cortés's defeat, Mexican garrisons in Oaxaca dealt a similar blow against the local Spanish expeditions, attacking and killing dozens of Spaniards and their indigenous allies.

Although Cortés was down, he wasn't out. In succeeding months, as his forces regathered strength in the Valley of Mexico, he pushed the conquest of the south. Alonso de Avila arrived in Oaxaca in late 1520 and accepted the ambassadors of Zapotec kings Cosijoeza and Cosijopí, who were more than willing to ally themselves against their Aztec overlords. Concurrently, other Spanish expeditions thrust into Oaxaca: Gonzalo de Sandoval successfully counterattacked against the Aztec garrisons, while Juan Cedeño obtained the submission of the Chinantecs and the northern Zapotecs.

Tenochtitlán Falls and Oaxaca Is Conquered

In late 1521, reinforced by fresh soldiers, horses, a small fleet of armed sailboats, and 100,000 indigenous allies, Cortés retook Tenochtitlán. The stubborn defenders, led by Cuauhtémoc, Moctezuma's nephew, fell by the tens of thousands beneath a smoking hail of Spanish grapeshot. The Aztecs, although weakened by smallpox, refused to surrender. Cortés found, to his dismay, that he had to destroy the city in order to take it.

Soon after Cortés's triumph, the Zapotec kings Cosijoeza and Cosijopí sent ambassadors declaring their submission to him and his king, Charles V. This alarmed the Mixtecs, who, with the backing of the Chinantec king of Tuxtepec, declared war on the Zapotecs. At the request of his new

Zapotec allies, Cortés dispatched Francisco de Orozco in December 1521 and Pedro de Alvarado a month later with a few hundred infantry and a handful of cavalry to pacify Oaxaca. After a few skirmishes, Orozco took possession of Huaxyacac, the site of present-day Oaxaca city, which the Aztec garrisons had occupied since 1456. A few hours later, on the same day, December 25, 1521, padre Juan Díaz celebrated the first Catholic mass in Oaxaca territory. A month later at the same spot, Alvarado, with the help of padre Bartolomé de Olmedo, helped negotiate a peace agreement between the Mixtecs and Zapotecs.

With the valley and northern Oaxaca pacified, Cortés sent Alvarado to conquer the Oaxacan Pacific Coast. On March 4, 1522, Alvarado defeated Casandoo, the Mixtec king of Tututepec, and with colonists displaced from the Valley of Oaxaca by Cortés orders, he founded the Villa Segura de la Frontera (Secure Village of the Frontier). He went on to pacify the whole coast, including Tonameca, Pochutla, Huatulco, and Astata, all the way east to Tehuantepec.

NEW SPAIN

With much of the former Aztec empire firmly in his grip and his lieutenants continuing to lead their forces in triumph in all directions, Cortés anticipated the grand domain that would eventually expand to more than a dozenfold the size of old Spain. He wrote his king, Charles V, ". . . the most suitable name for it would be New Spain of the Ocean Sea, and thus in the name of your Majesty I have christened it."

Even as he was building the new Mexico City atop the ruins of old Tenochtitlán, Cortés dreamed of a kingdom of his own. His first information of the fertile, spring-like Valley of Oaxaca came from his own scouts and from the ambassadors the Oaxacan kings had sent. Cortés moved quickly to carve out his Oaxaca domain, sending orders with Pedro de Alvarado to remove all Spanish settlers from the valley.

When Cortés personally arrived in Oaxaca in 1523 he found to his chagrin that settlers that he had previously ordered out of the valley had returned and were squatting on the land he wanted for himself. He sent the instigators to Mexico City in chains and dispersed the settlers again. He granted his friends and relatives, including his son Martín and his two illegitimate daughters, *encomiendas* (rights to land and native labor) at strategic points all over Oaxaca, then, in October 1524, marched off on an exhausting two-year expedition to Honduras.

By the time Cortés returned in 1526, the settlers had again returned and reestablished their village at Huaxyacac. Moreover, they had petitioned the king of Spain, Carlos I, for a charter for their settlement, which they had christened **Antequera,** in honor of the ancient Granada town of the same name. To Cortés's great displeasure, the petition was granted, by royal decree, on September 14, 1526.

Undeterred, Cortés took charge and began building his Valley of Oaxaca domain. He staked out the best bottomland, built haciendas, and set his native laborers to planting wheat and sugarcane. Cortés then traveled to Huatulco and Tehuantepec, where he built a port and ships to explore the Pacific. Concurrently, Cortés strengthened his alliance with King Cosijopí, who reciprocated by converting (along with thousands of his Tehuantepec subjects) to Christianity, taking the name Juan Cortés Cosijopí.

Hernán Cortés, Marquis of the Valley of Oaxaca

Cortés realized that his de facto kingdom needed both a queen and royal recognition, so he traveled to Spain in 1528 to get both. A year later he returned with his young noble bride, Juana de Zúñiga, and the grand title of Marqués del Valle de Oaxaca, which included a singularly generous grant of land, subjects, and privileges. For many years thereafter, he and his heirs received upward of 80,000 gold pesos a year from tens of thousands of indigenous subjects on three million acres of domain scattered from the Valley of Mexico through the present states of Morelos, Mexico, Guerrero, and Veracruz to Oaxaca.

Cortés's Valley of Oaxaca holdings, the crown jewel of his domain, encompassed most of the best valley land. In a wide, 350,000-acre swath, it stretched 25 miles, including 34 villages and towns, from Etla in the north to Coyotepec in the south. Excluded, however, was the one-league square (two square miles) of the town of Antequera, which grew into the present-day Oaxaca city.

The Missionaries

While the conquistadores scoured the countryside for gold and subjugated the local people, missionaries began arriving to heal, teach, and baptize them. The Dominicans were the first and most numerous in Oaxaca. Padre Minaya built the first Oaxaca convent, dedicated to Saint Paul, in Antequera around 1530. Other Dominicans settled in Tlaxiaco, Etla, and Tehuantepec, where King Cosijopí financed a church for them in 1538. Other orders—Franciscans, Augustinians, Bethlehemites, and more—soon joined them. Missionary authorities customarily enjoyed a sympathetic ear from Charles V and his successors, who earnestly pursued Spain's Christian mission, especially when it coincided with their political and economic goals.

Besides saving souls, the missionaries introduced new plants, flowers, and vegetables, and useful European crafts, such as ironwork, glassmaking, wool processing, and pottery glazing. They learned native tongues and wrote catechisms in Zapotec, Mixtec, and other local dialects. Within a few dozen years, the fields, orchards, and vineyards dotted with dozens of churches around the Valley of Oaxaca and beyond testified to the dedication of both the missionaries and their native converts.

Unfortunately, in order to speed the process of conversion, which the missionaries viewed as a sort of divine manifest destiny, native temples, idols, and paintings were destroyed. Historical records were irretrievably lost. The Spaniards also banned native song and dance, fearing that they kept alive old beliefs.

Although the missionaries on the whole provided a kinder, gentler counterbalance to the often brutal and exploitative conquistadores and colonists, they were not entirely blameless. In their zeal to build churches, convents, and monasteries, they also demanded the backbreaking labor of the newly converted. Moreover, those resistant to conversion were dealt with harshly, sometimes beaten, tortured, or killed.

In Oaxaca, however, which was primarily a Dominican stronghold, *indígenas* were spared the worst excesses of the more zealous Franciscans. **Bartolomé de las Casas,** a Dominican friar, devoted his life to fighting for the rights of the native people. This champion of social justice earned the sobriquet "Apostle of the Indians."

The King Takes Control

By 1530, the crown, through the Council of the Indies, had begun to wrest power away from Cortés and his conquistador lieutenants. Cortés had granted many of them rights of *encomienda:* taxes and labor of an indigenous district. In exchange, the *encomendero,* who often enjoyed the status of feudal lord, pledged to look after the welfare and souls of his native charges.

From the king's point of view, though, tribute pesos collected by *encomenderos* translated into losses to the crown. Moreover, many *encomenderos* callously exploited their indigenous wards for quick profit, sometimes selling them as slave labor in mines and on plantations. Such abuses, coupled with European-introduced diseases, began to reduce the native population at an alarming rate.

By 1540, strongly influenced by Dominican padre Bartolomé de las Casas, the outspoken "Apostle of the Indians," the king and his councillors realized that the native Mexicans were in peril, and without their labor New Spain would vanish.

They acted decisively. New laws would shift power toward the crown and limit abuses to the king's native subjects. Decreed in 1542 and enforced by a powerful *visitador* (inspector general), the **New Laws of the Indies** abolished perpetual rights of *encomienda,* outlawed slavery of native Mexicans, and limited their labor and tribute payments.

Although Oaxacan colonists protested vehemently, some native groups benefited. With the support of the new bishop of Antequera, Juan López de Zárate, and the missionary padres, Zapotecs around the Valley of Oaxaca mounted a legal fight against excessive *encomienda* payments.

COLONIAL OAXACA

Congregación

Despite the Oaxaca Valley Marquesate, Spanish garrisons, a score of Spanish-run haciendas, a few mines, and the capital town Antequera, Oaxaca had a sparse population of no more than a thousand Spaniards around 1550. On the other hand, the native population, while reduced, still numbered several hundred thousand, widely dispersed over the entire territory, and largely controlled by the hereditary native nobility. The Spanish authorities, in order to break the hold of the old chiefs on the natives, began moving indigenous populations into *congregaciones:* new townships in potentially productive areas—valleys, mines, and along royal roads. Each township had its *cabecera* (head town) and *sujeto* (subject) villages. Indigenous governing councils, supervised by Spanish

POPULATION CHANGES IN NEW SPAIN

	Early Colonial (1570)	Late Colonial (1810)
peninsulares	6,600	15,000
criollos	11,000	1,100,000
mestizos	2,400	704,000
indígenas	3,340,000	3,700,000
negros	22,000	630,000

agents, were responsible for local order and collection of tribute.

The missionary clergy initially went along with *congregación* because it led to more converts, but after a generation of seeing the cruel reality of people displaced from their land and traditions, opposed it. In 1604, although the policy was officially abandoned and some of the people returned to their original way of life, many did not. Their descendants remain living in the original *caberceras*, which comprise a significant portion of present-day Oaxaca's 570 *municipios* or governmental townships.

The natives, in being shifted toward traditional Spanish occupations, in which they worked mines, harvested sugarcane and wheat, and tended sheep and cattle, were forced to abandon the way of life that had sustained them for millennia. In a few generations, even the memory of their extensive irrigation works—diversion dams and canals that fed terraced fields—was lost.

The severe consequences of this forgotten water-conservation tradition have become acute in modern Oaxaca. An increasing population has led to lack of bottomland, forcing families to poor uplands that without irrigation cannot sustain them. Slash-and-burn dry farming, noncontour plowing, overgrazing, and overcutting of forest have turned large tracts of Oaxaca into eroded wasteland.

Population Collapse

In a real sense, European disease, rather than the conquistadores, subdued Mexico. Despite the missionary fathers' most benign efforts and the most beneficial effects of the king's New Laws, typhus, measles, smallpox, and other European plagues wiped out about 90 percent of the Mexican indigenous population within a few generations after the conquest. Although estimates vary, most experts agree that pre-conquest Mexico's 15–25 million native population had shrunk to a mere 1.3 million by 1650.

Oaxaca's figures reflect a similar tragedy. Of a population that archaeologists estimate at around two million in 1500, only 150,000 remained in 1650. In some cases, such as the mines of Santa Catalina Martir, in 1580, a combination of overwork and disease killed thousands; those remaining simply fled into the hills. In the southern Oaxaca Valley towns, plagues reduced thriving towns such as Teitipac, Ocotlán, and Miahuatlán from populations of thousands to a few dozen inhabitants nearly overnight.

Today's Mexicans can, ironically, look forward to the year 2019, the 500th anniversary of Cortés's landing, when Mexico's native-speaking population will have recovered to its pre-conquest level of approximately 25 million.

The Changing Role of the Church

During the colonial era, civil and church authorities increasingly came into conflict with missionary orders, whose independent status derived directly from Papal authority, in contrast to locally administered ("secular") clergy, who answered to local bishops. Disputes usually revolved around treatment of the natives, whose welfare missionaries often outspokenly championed. The kettle, always bubbling, sometimes boiled over. In 1647, Bishop Cerda Benevente of Antequera tried to kick all Dominican fathers out of their churches; in 1749 Bishop Maldonado tried to replace 27 Dominicans with clergy under his control. The issue of power was finally settled in 1767 when the King of Spain *expelled all Jesuit missionaries* from his New World colonies. This chilled the liberal activist tendencies of clergy everywhere in Mexico and led to an increasingly conservative church establishment.

During Spain's Mexican colonial twilight, the church, increasingly profiting from the status quo, became fat and largely complacent. The biblical tithe—one-tenth of everything, from crops and livestock to rents and mining profits—filled church coffers. *By 1800, the church owned half of Mexico.* Moreover, all clergy (including the lay church officers) and the military were doubly privileged. They enjoyed right of *fuero* (exemption from civil law) and could be prosecuted by ecclesiastical or military courts only.

The Colonial Economy

In trade and commerce, New Spain existed for the benefit of the mother country. Spaniards enjoyed absolute monopolies by virtue of the complete prohibition of foreign traders and goods.

Colonists, as a result, paid dearly for often shoddy Spanish manufactures. The Casa de Contratación, the royal trade regulators, always ensured the colony's yearly balance of payments would result in deficit, which would be made up by bullion shipments from New Spain mines (from which the crown raked 10 percent off the top).

If New Spain was a tradition-bound feudal domain, Oaxaca was even more so. The crown regulated nearly everything. Any kind of enterprise required a royal license, issued through a bureaucracy that required bribes as part of the cost of doing business. Wealth flowed directly from the labor of the native people. Although Oaxaca people produced lots of corn, wheat, cattle, sheep, wool, and some silk, **cochineal** was by far Oaxaca's most valuable export.

Whatever native people produced, they all had to pay taxes, whether directly to the local collector or as tribute to the *encomendero* owner of the estate where they lived. For many poor native families, the problem of getting enough to eat year-round was doubly acute because of the seasonal nature of their produce. They began to rely upon *alcaldes mayores,* local royal officials, for cash advances on crops, especially cochineal. Through their official posts, *alcaldes mayores* enjoyed a monopoly, which forced local folks to sell to them for a pittance. This hated monopoly payment system, known as *repartmiento,* although officially forbidden, was rampant during the mid-1600s, when a swarm of Oaxaca uprisings led to the killing of Tehuantepec's greedy *alcalde mayor* and a number of his henchmen by an angry crowd of native cochineal producers.

Reform didn't come until the 18th century, when Spanish authorities saw the light and banned the *repartmiento* system, replacing the *alcaldes mayores* with less corruptible salaried agents known as *intendentes.*

The bustling cochineal trade led to boom times in colonial Oaxaca. The region, previously a backwater, neglected by Mexico City authorities, benefited from a monopoly on cochineal production after 1745. The population tripled during the 1700s, reaching 20,000 and making the city of Oaxaca (whose name was officially changed from Antequera in 1786) New Spain's third largest city by 1800.

The benefits of the new prosperity did not extend equally to all Oaxacans, however. As the administrative center for the entire region, most wealth flowed to Oaxaca city, where a rich elite, of mostly Spanish-born government and church officials and owners of large estates, raked in the lion's share of the profits. Below them, a modicum of treasure and respectability trickled down to the small locally born white and mixed-blood

COCHINEAL—NATURE'S RICHEST RED DYE

Cochineal *(cochinilla)* is a prized rich scarlet dye, long cultivated in Mexico before the conquest. The Spanish, immediately seeing its export value, expanded production, especially in Oaxaca, where its production became a major source of cash for native Oaxacans faced with increasing tribute demands. The rise of the textile industry in England, the Low Countries, France, and Spain further propelled demand for Oaxacan cochineal, renowned as the most brilliant, richest red dye in the world. The word spread, and, by its peak during the 17th and 18th centuries, Spain's cochineal trade extended as far as China. Although largely replaced by cheaper synthetic dyes by 1900, cochineal is still locally cultivated in the Valley of Oaxaca.

The actual source of the dye is the female of a type of scale insect, *Dactylopius coccus,* which feeds off a variety of nopal (prickly pear) cactus. Typically, families or village cooperatives own patches of nopal, from which they brush the female beetles during the fall harvest. The beetles are then dried, ground, and boiled in water. The resulting dye suspension is filtered and evaporated, leaving pure crimson cochineal crystals, still preferred by many Oaxaca Valley weavers.

A **demonstration farm,** dedicated to the revival of cochineal, welcomes visitors to see its experimental cactus garden and small museum at Santa María Coyotepec, on the highway about four miles (6 km) south of the Oaxaca airport.

professional and merchant class. Finally, the great majority of mixed and pure native descent who did the hard work—the spinners, weavers, masons, shoemakers, bakers, farmers, and laborers—plugged along as best they could at the city's least desirable margins.

Despite its faults, New Spain lasted three times longer than the Aztec empire. By most contemporary measures, both Oaxaca in particular and New Spain as a whole were prospering in 1800. The native and mixed-blood labor force was completely subjugated and increasing, and the galleon fleets were carrying home increasing tonnages of silver, gold, and cochineal worth many millions of gold pesos. Spanish authorities, however, failed to recognize that Mexico had changed in 300 years.

Criollos, the New Mexicans

Nearly three centuries of colonial rule gave rise to a burgeoning population of more than a million criollos—Mexican-born descendants of Spanish colonists, many rich and educated—to whom top status was denied.

High government, church, and military office had always been the preserve of a tiny but powerful minority of *peninsulares*—European-born Spaniards. Criollos (kree-OH-yohs) could only watch in disgust as unlettered, unskilled *peninsulares* (derisively called *gachupines*—wearers of spurs) were boosted to authority over them.

Although the criollos stood high above the mestizo (mixed native-Spanish), *indígena*, and black (African-Mexican) underclasses, that seemed little compensation for the false smiles, the deep bows, and the costly bribes that *gachupines* demanded.

Mestizos, Indígenas, and African Mexicans

Upper-class luxury existed by virtue of the sweat of Mexico's mestizo, *indígena,* and black laborers and servants. African slaves were imported in large numbers during the 17th century after typhus, smallpox, and measles epidemics had wiped out most of the indigenous population. In Oaxaca, a small African-born black population of around 2,000 in 1650 rose gradually to approximately 10,000, both pure and mixed, by 1800.

Although the African Mexicans contributed significantly (crafts, healing arts, dance, music, drums, and marimba), they had arrived last and experienced discrimination from everyone.

INDEPENDENCE

The chance for change came during the aftermath of the French invasion of Spain in 1808, when Napoléon Bonaparte replaced King Ferdinand VII with his brother Joseph on the Spanish throne. Most *peninsulares* backed the king; most criollos, however, inspired by the example of the recent American and French revolutions, talked and dreamed of independence. One such group, urged on by a firebrand parish priest, acted.

El Grito de Dolores

"¡Viva México! Death to the Gachupines!" Father **Miguel Hidalgo**'s impassioned *grito* from the church balcony in the Guanajuato town of Dolores on September 16, 1810, ignited passions. A mostly *indígena,* machete-wielding army of 20,000 coalesced around Hidalgo and his compatriots, **Ignacio Allende and Juan Aldama.** Their ragtag mob raged out of control through the Bajío, killing hated *gachupines* and pillaging their homes.

Hidalgo advanced on Mexico City but, unnerved by stiff royalist resistance, retreated and regrouped around Guadalajara. His rebels, whose numbers had swollen to 80,000, were no match for a disciplined, 6,000-strong royalist force. Hidalgo (now "Generalisimo") fled north but was soon apprehended, defrocked, and executed. His head and those of his comrades—Aldama, Allende, and Mariano Jiménez—were hung from the walls of the Guanajuato granary (site of the slaughter of 138 *gachupines* by Hidalgo's army) for 10 years as grim reminders of the consequences of rebellion.

The 10-Year Struggle

Others carried on, however. A former student of Hidalgo, mestizo **José María Morelos,** carried the Independence struggle to Oaxaca in earnest by defeating the Oaxaca capital's royalist defenders on November 25, 1812. He set up a revolutionary government and fanned the flames with his liberationist newspaper *El Correo Americano del Sur (The American Post of the South)* until seriously defeated in Michoacán a year later. The victorious royalists retook Oaxaca city on January 29, 1814, sending defending *insurgente* commander Ramón Rayón fleeing north to Tehuacán, Puebla.

Although the royalists seriously damaged the rebel cause by capturing and executing Morelos in December 1815, Morelos's compatriot **Vicente Guerrero** continued the fight, joining forces with criollo royalist Brigadier **Agustín de Iturbide**. Their **Plan de Iguala** promised "**Three Guarantees**"—the renowned Trigarantes: Independence, Catholicism, and Equality—which their army (commanded by Iturbide, of course) would enforce. On September 21, 1821, Iturbide rode triumphantly into Mexico City at the head of his army of Trigarantes. Mexico was independent at last.

But the cost of the struggle had been great, especially in Oaxaca. Ten years of war had decimated the cochineal industry and sent Oaxaca's rich Spaniards and their capital fleeing to Mexico City and Europe. The criollo professional and business class now found themselves at the top of the social ladder, but with little money for rebuilding. Everyone tightened their belts as Oaxaca industry reverted to traditional products: soap, *aguardiente* (white lightning) distillation, *pulque* (native beer), wool, leather, and pottery.

Moreover, in Mexico as a whole, Independence had resolved few grievances except to expel the *peninsulares*. With an illiterate populace and no experience in self-government, Mexicans began a tragic 40-year love affair with a fantasy: the general on the white horse, the gold-braided hero who could save them from themselves.

The Rise and Fall of Agustín I

Iturbide—crowned Emperor Agustín I by the bishop of Guadalajara on July 21, 1822—soon lost his charisma. Attempting to assert his authority, Iturbide dissolved the national Congress on October 31, igniting a roar of protests. Among the loudest protesters was Iturbide's military governor of Oaxaca, Colonel Antonio de León. In a pattern that became sadly predictable

for succeeding generations of topsy-turvy Mexican politics, ambitious commanders issued *pronunciamientos,* declarations against the government. Supporting *pronunciamientos* followed, and old revolutionary heroes Guerrero, Guadalupe Victoria, and Nicolás Bravo endorsed a "plan"—the Plan of Casa Mata (not unlike Iturbide's previous Plan de Iguala)—dethroning Iturbide in favor of a republic. Iturbide, his braid tattered and brass tarnished, abdicated in mid-February 1823.

On June 1, 1823, carried away by liberationist zeal, León set up a local provisional government that declared Oaxaca to be a "free and independent" state and wrote a state constitution. Simultaneously, delegates in Mexico City were doing the same, creating the republic of the Estados Unidos Mexicanos ("United Mexican States"), which Oaxaca soon joined.

The country overflowed with republican zeal. Oaxacans rewrote their state constitution to conform with the federal document, creating a governor, bicameral legislature, local governments, and state departments, including public instruction and the **Institute of Sciences and Arts** (now the Benito Juárez Autonomous University). Graduates of the institute, notably Mexico's famous pair of presidents, Benito Juárez and Porfirio Díaz, both of indigenous descent, gradually began to fill the leadership vacuum left by the departed Spanish elite.

The Disastrous Era of Santa Anna

Antonio López de Santa Anna, the eager 28-year-old military commander of Veracruz, whose *pronunciamiento* had pushed Iturbide from his white horse, maneuvered to gradually replace him. Throughout the latter 1820s the government teetered between liberal and conservative hands six times in three years. Finally, unhappy with the 1828 presidential election result, Santa Anna "pronounced" in favor of the losing candidate, old independence *insurgente* Vicente Guerrero. This put Santa Anna at odds with government commanders all over the country—especially in Oaxaca city, which he attacked—but he soon found himself seriously besieged in the fortress-like convent of Santo Domingo.

But Lady Luck, as usual, intervened in favor of Santa Anna. At the height of the siege, on November 20, 1829, government agents discovered that a Spanish force was being assembled in Cuba to re-invade Mexico. Faced with the external threat, former bitter enemies soon joined hands. On January 5, 1829, Santa Anna rushed from Oaxaca city with a combined force that, a few months later, defeated an abortive Spanish invasion attempt on the Gulf at Tampico. People called Santa Anna "The Victor of Tampico."

In 1831, a rebellious, still-powerful Vicente Guerrero was kidnapped in Acapulco and handed over to agents of conservative President Anastasio Bustamante in Huatulco. He was taken to Oaxaca city and executed at the old convent in Cuilapan on February 14, 1831. Later, upon the initiative of young Oaxaca legislative deputy **Benito Juárez,** Guerrero's remains were placed in an elaborate silver urn and reinterred during six days of solemn ceremonies at Santo Domingo convent in the city.

In late 1832, the national government was bankrupt; mobs demanded the ouster of President Bustamante in retaliation for Guerrero's execution. Santa Anna issued a *pronunciamiento* against Bustamante, which Congress soon obliged, elevating Santa Anna to "Liberator of the Republic" and "Conqueror of the Spaniards" and naming him president in March 1833. More interested in the hunt than the prize, Santa Anna quickly resigned his office to Vice President Gómez Farías.

Santa Anna would pop in and out of the presidency like a jack-in-the-box 10 more times before 1855. First, he foolishly lost Texas to rebellious Anglo settlers in 1836. He later lost his leg (which was buried with full military honors) fighting the emperor of France.

Santa Anna's greatest debacle, however, was to declare war on the United States with just 1,839 pesos in the treasury. With his forces poised to defend Mexico City against a relatively small 10,000-man American invasion force, Santa Anna inexplicably withdrew. U.S. Marines surged into the "Halls of Montezuma," Chapultepec Castle, where Mexico's six beloved Niños Héroes cadets fell in the losing cause on September 13, 1847. In the subsequent Treaty of Guadalupe

Hidalgo, Mexico lost two-fifths of its territory—the present states of New Mexico, Arizona, California, Nevada, Utah, and Colorado—to the United States. Mexicans have never forgotten; they have looked upon gringos with a combination of admiration and disgust ever since.

Despite the national debacle, Oaxaca prospered under the 1848–1852 governorship of Benito Juárez. Among his first acts was to deny Santa Anna, who was fleeing from U.S. invaders, transit across Oaxaca territory. Besides keeping the peace, Juárez opened hundreds of elementary schools, a swarm of teacher's academies, and nearly wiped out the state debt. Improved roads and new bridges attracted Italian investment in mines; new coffee production began to replace Oaxaca's lost cochineal output. English entrepreneurs built a textile and hat factory, and artisans in Atzompa, near Oaxaca city, resumed producing their renowned pottery again in earnest. Oaxaca city's population swelled by more than 25 percent, to 24,000, between 1844 and 1854.

But for Santa Anna, however, enough was not enough. Called back as president for the last and 11th time in 1853, Santa Anna, now "His Most Serene Highness," financed his war against the liberals by selling off a part of southern New Mexico and Arizona, known as the Gadsden Purchase, for $10 million.

REFORM, CIVIL WAR, AND INVASION

The Reforms

Mexican leaders finally saw the light and exiled Santa Anna forever. While conservatives fumbled, searching for a king to replace Santa Anna, liberal leaders (whom Santa Anna had exiled or kept in jail) stirred up their own successful revolution. Juárez, having triumphantly returned to the Oaxaca governorship, and others plunged ahead with three controversial reform laws: the Ley Juárez, Ley Lerdo, and Ley Iglesias. These *reformas,* integrated into a new liberal Constitution of 1857, directly attacked the privilege and power of Mexico's corporate landlords, clergy, and generals: Ley Juárez abolished *fueros,* the separate military and church courts; Ley Lerdo forbade excess corporate (read: church) landholdings, and Ley Iglesias reduced or transferred most church power to the state.

Despite their liberal authors' good intentions, some of the reform provisions resulted in negative consequences. Although Ley Lerdo (the "Law of the Divestiture of the Property of the Dead Hand") succeeded in wiping out bloated church landholdings, it also forced thousands of native communities to sell their traditional land. Such sales invariably benefited the few rich individuals who could afford to buy, at the expense of the great mass of native Mexicans who became landless as a result. The consequence was equally negative. It created a new class of superlandowners: *latifundistas,* who soon ruled small kingdoms with impunity all over Mexico.

Oaxaca, fortunately, ran counter to the national trend. Lack of local capital and isolation from Mexico City led to little investment in Oaxaca land, so most communal holdings remained in indigenous hands. Moreover, of the several hundred church parcels sold in Oaxaca, one-third were, surprisingly, bought by native Mexicans.

Alarmed by the reforms, conservative generals, priests, and businessmen and their mestizo and *indígena* followers revolted. The resulting **War of the Reforms** (not unlike the U.S. Civil War) ravaged the countryside for three long years until the victorious liberal army paraded triumphantly in Mexico City on New Year's Day 1861. In a thumping congratulations from the electors, Juárez outdistanced all rival candidates and became president in March 1861.

Juárez and Maximilian

Benito Juárez, the leading *reformista,* had won the day. His similarity to his contemporary, Abraham Lincoln, is legend: Juárez had risen from humble Zapotec native origins to become a lawyer, a champion of justice, and the president who held his country together during a terrible civil war. Like Lincoln, Juárez's triumph didn't last long.

Imperial France invaded Mexico in January 1862. Despite a formidable French force, which eventually ballooned to 60,000, Mexican regulars and guerrillas achieved a number of victories, several under the leadership of Oaxacan colonel (later general) **Porfirio Díaz.** Díaz rocketed to fame as the "Victor of Puebla" whose troops routed the French on May 5 (Cinco de Mayo), 1862. The French nevertheless managed to occupy Mexico City and several state capitals, including Oaxaca city, by summer 1864.

After two costly years pushing Juárez's liberal army into the hills, the French installed the king Mexican conservatives thought the country needed. Austrian Archduke Maximilian and his wife Carlota, the very models of modern Catholic monarchs, were crowned emperor and empress of Mexico in June 1864.

The naive **Emperor Maximilian I** was surprised that some of his subjects resented his presence. Meanwhile, Juárez refused to yield, stubbornly performing his constitutional duties in a somber black carriage one jump ahead of the French occupying army. After Díaz's signal victories at Carbonera and Miahuatlán in Oaxaca in late 1866, the climax came in May 1867, when liberal forces besieged and defeated Maximilian at Querétaro. Juárez, giving no quarter, sternly ordered Maximilian's execution by firing squad on June 19.

Juárez Reelected; Díaz Rebels

Benito Juárez's tumultuous popular approval and reelection to the presidency in October 1867 was not without its costs. His critics, notably Sebastián Lerdo de Tejada and Porfirio Díaz (who retired from active military duty to seek the presidency himself) accused Juárez of heavy-handed constitutional violations. Under Díaz's influence, a number of military commanders stirred up local uprisings. Undeterred, Juárez worked day and night at the double task of reconstruction and reform. Single-mindedly, he pushed to amend the Constitution of 1857, a course that triggered a major armed revolt, the Rebellion of La Noria, by Díaz in 1871 to "restore the purity" of the constitution against Juárez's alleged transgressions. Although his political momentum was weakened, Juárez was reelected president over both Tejada and Díaz in October 1871, but he died of a heart attack on July 18, 1872. In his honor,

PORFIRIO DÍAZ: HERO OR VILLAIN?

Porfirio Díaz, Mexico's most controversial and longest-serving president, was born in the city of Oaxaca on September 15, 1830. His parents, José de la Cruz Díaz and Petrona Mori, were of poor Mixtec-mestizo origin. Porfirio's father died when he was three, and he spent his childhood working at odd jobs to support his mother while attending public and parochial schools. He entered seminary in Oaxaca in 1843, dropped out after three years, and resumed studies in law at the Institute of Arts and Sciences, where he briefly taught in 1854.

A seminal event occurred for young Porfirio in 1854, when it was publicly announced that the entire faculty of the institute unanimously supported the notorious conservative dictator Antonio López de Santa Anna. Díaz asked that his abstention be recorded, and when publicly accused of siding with the liberal cause, he declared his support for General Juan Álvarez, leader of the liberal rebellion in Guerrero. The die was thus cast: For the next 50 years, Díaz never wavered from the image of a resolute, determined liberal, who possessed the courage of his convictions.

Forced to flee, Porfirio joined a rebel guerrilla band in the northern Sierra and, later, in 1856, the Oaxaca National Guard, where he found purpose fighting for Benito Juárez's liberal side during

the civil War of the Reforms. His valor and ability elevated him to the rank of brigadier general at the time of the liberal triumph in 1861.

During the imperialist French intervention, his military reputation skyrocketed when his forces defeated the French army at Puebla on May 5, 1862, the still celebrated Cinco de Mayo national holiday. After 25 battles and the liberation of Oaxaca, Puebla, and Mexico City, Díaz retired from the military in 1867 at the age of 37.

It turned out that Díaz's insatiable ambition was driving him toward the presidency. He opposed Juárez and Lerdo de Tejada in the 1871 election, which, with no clear winner, was thrown into Congress, where Juárez was re-elected. Díaz revolted unsuccessfully; Juárez died and Lerdo de Tejada became president. Díaz rebelled again, in 1876, promulgating the doctrine of *"No Reelección"* in his Plan of Tuxtepec. Lerdo de Tejada fled, and Porfirio Díaz finally assumed the presidency legally on May 5, 1877.

Mexico, however, remained a hotbed of revolt. Díaz found that he had to put some of his democratic principles aside to remain in office and keep the country together. He reasoned in essence that, after all, if you don't have a government, you can't have democracy. His treatment of captured local

Oaxaca city fathers renamed their city, officially, **Oaxaca de Juárez.**

The passing of Benito Juárez, the stoic partisan of reform, signaled hope to Mexico's conservatives. They soon got their wish: General Don Porfirio Díaz, the "Coming Man," was elected president in 1876.

ORDER AND PROGRESS
Pax Porfiriana

Don Porfirio is often remembered wistfully, as old Italians remember Mussolini: "He was a bit rough, but, dammit, at least he made the trains run on time."

Although Porfirio Díaz's humble Oaxaca mestizo origins were not unlike Juárez's, Díaz was not a democrat: When he was a general, his officers

often took no captives; when he was president, his country police, the *rurales,* shot prisoners in the act of "trying to escape."

Order and progress, in that sequence, ruled Mexico for 34 years. Foreign investment flowed into the country; new railroads brought the products of shiny factories, mines, and farms to modernized Gulf and Pacific ports. Mexico balanced its budget, repaid foreign debt, and became a respected member of the family of nations.

Oaxaca also gained material benefits from the Porfiriato, the label Mexican historians attach to Díaz's long rule. The Mexico City rail link, which arrived in 1892, was the high point of three decades of public works improvement: bridges, roads, ports, electricity, sewage, an elegant theater, an Isthmus rail line, a state museum, and an enlarged Institute of Arts and Sciences. Rich rebels—*Matalos en caliente* ("Kill them on the spot")—was typically brutal.

Díaz retained enough of his liberal idealism to follow his own *No Reelección* prescription and stepped down from the presidency in 1880 to become governor of Oaxaca, but after that he was re-elected consecutively and held office for 28 more years, until 1911.

The 34-year period (1876–1910) known as the Porfiriato was marked by stability and modernization. Díaz managed stability by conciliation, negotiation, cajolery, and, if all these failed, repression. He accomplished what no other president had been able to do—control the army. Under Díaz, the army quieted down, stayed in its barracks, and left politics to the politician.

A stable Mexico attracted foreign investment. Mostly American and British entrepreneurs and engineers expanded railroads from a mere 400 miles in 1876 to 15,000 miles by 1910. New factories, mills, and mines blossomed along the railroads, which brought raw materials and took away manufactured goods to cities and modernized ports.

Díaz's industrialization plans were directed by a clique of advisers who professed to apply scientific principles to government and became known as the Científicos. Their policies, however, were decidedly elitist and ended up concentrating land, wealth, and power in foreign and upper-class hands, pushing Mexico's already poor indigenous population into even deeper poverty.

In 1908, Díaz hinted in an interview that he would retire in 1910 at the age of 80. This encouraged his growing political opposition, and when Díaz changed his mind and stood for another term in 1910, he was opposed by northern factory owner Francisco I. Madero, who campaigned on Díaz's original *"No Reelección"* slogan. Díaz had Madero jailed and won election to his eighth presidential term.

But this time, Díaz was too tired to keep the lid on; his long rule collapsed partly because of its own success. Díaz had transformed the country. In many ways it reflected his original liberal vision of a stronger, richer, and better-educated Mexico, with a democratic balance of power and a procedure for orderly succession. But Díaz's failures, driven by cynicism, complacency, and a thirst for dominance, produced a regime that, like a dinosaur, fell under its own weight on May 31, 1911.

Porfirio Díaz, in exile in Paris, complaining of French food and yearning for some home-cooked Oaxacan fare, died on July 2, 1915.

---

foreign and Mexican investors dug dozens of new mines and built several factories, producing shoes, soap, hats, matches, glassware, cigarettes, and beer. In the southern mountains, coffee farms proliferated after the government offered a rebate for planting 2,000 coffee trees or more. Oaxaca city's population doubled, to nearly 40,000, during Díaz's rule.

The human price, nevertheless, was high. The rich, who included hundreds of resident foreigners, soaked up most of the profits while Oaxaca's poor, who lacked the money to benefit directly from the new civic improvements, struggled along as best they could. And although in Oaxaca most natives were able to hold on to their land, nationally Díaz's government did not intervene to prevent more than a hundred million acres—one-fifth of Mexico's land area

(including most of the arable land)—being turned over to rich Mexicans and foreigners. Poor Mexicans suffered the most. By 1910, 90 percent of Mexico's *indígenas* had lost their traditional communal land. In the spring of 1910, a smug, now-cultured, and elderly Don Porfirio anticipated with relish the centennial of Hidalgo's Grito de Dolores.

REVOLUTION AND STABILIZATION
¡No Reelección!

Porfirio Díaz himself had first campaigned on the slogan. It expressed the idea that the president should step down after one term. Although Díaz had stepped down once in 1880, for an interregnum as Oaxaca's governor, in 1884 he got himself elected president again and remained in office for 26 consecutive years. In 1910, **Francisco I. Madero,** a short, squeaky-voiced son of rich landowners, opposed Díaz under the same banner.

Although Díaz had jailed him before the election, Madero refused to quit campaigning. From a safe platform in the United States, he called for a revolution to begin on November 20. The response in Oaxaca was typical: In the countryside, a few leaders rallied around Madero's banner, but Díaz had them rounded up and then got his nephew, Félix, installed as governor.

After all, *¡No Reelección!* is not much of a platform. But millions of poor Mexicans were going to bed hungry, and Díaz hadn't listened to them for years.

Villa and Zapata

In May 1910, those millions of poor Mexicans began to stir. In Oaxaca, a swarm of small rebellions broke out, then coalesced into a general revolution, which toppled Félix Díaz from the governorship. Simultaneously, up north in Chihuahua, followers of **Francisco (Pancho) Villa,** an erstwhile ranch hand, miner, peddler, and cattle rustler, began attacking the *rurales,* dynamiting railroads, and raiding towns. Meanwhile, in Morelos state, just north of Oaxaca, horse trader, farmer, and minor official **Emiliano Zapata** and his *indígena* guerrillas were terrorizing rich *hacendados* and forcibly recovering stolen ancestral village lands. Zapata's movement gained steam and by mid-May had taken the Morelos state capital, Cuernavaca. Meanwhile, Madero crossed the Río Grande and joined with Villa's forces, who took Ciudad Juárez. Soon the *federales,* government army troops, began deserting in droves, and on May 25, 1911, Díaz submitted his resignation.

As Madero's deputy, General Victoriano Huerta, put Díaz on his ship of exile in Veracruz, Díaz confided: "Madero has unleashed a tiger. Now let's see if he can control it."

Madero's star, nevertheless, was still rising. As he paraded triumphantly into Mexico City, revolutionary state governments were blossoming all over the country. Benito Juárez's son, Benito Juárez Maza, served briefly as Oaxaca's *maderista*

governor in 1911–1912 until he was killed in a local skirmish.

The Fighting Continues

Emiliano Zapata turned out to be that very tiger whom Madero had unleashed. Meeting with Madero in Mexico City, Zapata fumed over Madero's go-slow approach to the "agrarian problem," as Madero termed it. By November 1912, Zapata had denounced Madero. *"¡Tierra y Libertad!"* ("Land and Liberty!") the Zapatistas cried, as Madero's support faded. The army in Mexico City rebelled; Huerta forced Madero to resign on February 18, 1913, then murdered him four days later.

The rum-swilling Huerta ruled like a Chicago mobster; general rebellion, led by the **"Big Four"**—Villa, Alvaro Obregón, and Venustiano Carranza in the north, and Zapata in the south—soon broke out. Pressed by the rebels and refused United States recognition, Huerta fled into exile in July 1914.

Meanwhile in Oaxaca, fighting between liberals and conservatives, much like the wars for Independence and the Reforms, laid waste to the countryside, killing commerce and sending foreign investors fleeing. But unlike the rest of the country, Oaxaca had no majority class of landless campesinos and consequently no great radical cause or leader to champion it.

Disgusted with the barbaric war of attrition ravaging the rest of the country, many Oaxaca leaders publicly repudiated the "Big Four" and declared **Oaxaca a "sovereign" republic** and tried to deny access to revolutionary outsiders.

Oaxacan conservatives, however, made a serious error in betraying and murdering Jésus Carranza, brother of El Primer Jefe (First Chief) Venustiano Carranza. Soon *Carranzista* battalions invaded Oaxaca and quickly defeated local forces, sending Oaxacan leaders scurrying to Mexico City or to the mountains, where they fought on for years as guerrillas.

The national struggle ground on for three more years as authority see-sawed between revolutionary factions. Finally Carranza, who controlled most of the country by 1917, got a convention together in Querétaro to formulate political and social goals. The resulting Constitution of 1917, while restating most ideas of the Reformistas' 1857 constitution, additionally prescribed a single four-year presidential term, labor reform, and subordinated private ownership to public interest. Every village had a right to communal *ejido* land, and subsoil wealth could never be sold away to the highest bidder.

The Constitution of 1917 was a revolutionary expression of national aspirations and, in retrospect, represented a social and political agenda for the entire 20th century. In modified form, it has lasted to the present day.

Obregón Stabilizes Mexico

On December 1, 1920, General Alvaro Obregón legally assumed the presidency of a Mexico still bleeding from 10 years of civil war. Although a seasoned revolutionary, Obregón was also a negotiator who recognized that peace was necessary to implement the goals of the revolution. In four years, his government pacified local uprisings, disarmed a swarm of warlords, executed hundreds of *bandidos*, obtained U.S. diplomatic recognition, assuaged the worst fears of the clergy and landowners, and began land reform.

With Obregón as an example, Oaxaca's new governor **García Vigil** went to work. Despite the irritant of remnant revolutionary guerrilla bands in the countryside, Vigil pushed a successful land reform and wrote a new constitution, which is essentially in effect today. His tax reform plans, however, ran into trouble with Oaxaca's rich landowners and came to nothing when he was assassinated in 1924.

At the national level, Obregón's success set the stage for Plutarco Elías Calles, Obregón's Secretaría de Gobernación and handpicked successor, who won the 1924 national election. Aided by peace, Mexico returned to a semblance of prosperity. Calles brought the army under civilian control, balanced the budget, and shifted Mexico's revolution into high gear. New clinics vaccinated millions against smallpox, new dams irrigated thousands of previously dry acres, and campesinos received millions of acres of redistributed land.

Simultaneously, Calles threatened foreign oil companies, demanding they exchange their titles

for 50-year leases. A moderate Mexican supreme court decision over the oil issue and the skillful arbitration of U.S. Ambassador Dwight Morrow smoothed over both the oil and church troubles by the end of Calles's term.

Calles, who started out brimming with revolutionary fervor and populist zeal, became increasingly conservative and dictatorial. Although he bowed out peaceably in favor of Obregón (the constitution had been amended to allow one six-year nonsuccessive term), Obregón was assassinated two weeks after his election in 1928. Calles continued to rule for six more years through three puppet-presidents: Emilio Portes Gil (1928–1930), Pascual Ortiz Rubio (1930–1932), and Abelardo Rodríguez (1932–1934).

Calles Forms the PRI

In 1929, President Calles united three of Mexico's major constituencies: the country poor (represented by the Confederación Nacional de Campesinos, CNC), the workers (Confederación de Trabajadore Méjicanos, CTM), and the middle classes (Confederación Nacional de Organizaciones Populares, CNOP). Calles christened his new super political party the **Partido Revolucionario Institucional** (Institutional Revolutionary Party), or **PRI**, or, pronounced simply, the "pree."

The PRI dominated Mexican, and especially Oaxacan, politics during the 60 years after its founding. PRI presidents handpicked their PRI successors, who always got elected. Federal government contracts and salary money flowed from PRI headquarters in Mexico City to state and municipal officials, who were nearly always loyal local members of the PRI.

Oaxaca, isolated from the national economy and with no influential revolutionary ex-general to demand its fair share of national patronage, was consistently underfunded and mostly ignored by the central government. Nevertheless, despite a severe earthquake in 1931 and general economic depression, Oaxacans managed some modest public works improvements during the 1930s and early 1940s. A paved road to Monte Albán led to important archaeological discoveries; other new highways branched out from the valley to the Mixteca, the Isthmus, and to Puerto Ángel. Oaxaca city residents benefited from a few improvements, such as a new water works and restoration of the opera house. But revolution and hard times had taken their toll: In 1940, Oaxaca city's population, about 40,000, was still the same as in 1910.

Lázaro Cárdenas, President of the People

Although he had received Calles's blessing for the 1934 presidential election, ex-general Lázaro Cárdenas, the 40-year-old former governor of Michoacán, immediately set his own agenda. Cárdenas worked tirelessly to fulfill the social prescriptions of the revolution. As morning-coated diplomats and cabinet ministers fretted in his outer office, Cárdenas ushered in delegations of campesinos and factory workers and sympathetically listened to their problems.

In his six years of rule, Cárdenas moved public education and health forward on a broad front, supported strong labor unions, and redistributed 49 million acres of farmland, more than any president before or since.

Cárdenas's resolute enforcement of the constitution's Artículo 123 brought him the most renown. Under this pro-labor law, the government turned over a host of private companies to employee ownership and, on March 18, 1938, expropriated all foreign oil corporations.

In retrospect the oil corporations, most of which were British, were not blameless. They had sorely neglected the wages, health, and welfare of their workers while ruthlessly taking the law into their own hands with private police forces. Although Standard Oil cried foul, the U.S. government did not intervene. Through negotiation and due process, U.S. companies eventually were compensated with $24 million plus 3 percent interest. In the wake of the expropriation, President Cárdenas created Petróleos Mexicanos (Pemex), the national oil corporation that continues to run all Mexican oil and gas operations to the present day.

Manuel Avila Camacho

Manuel Avila Camacho, elected in 1940, was the last general to be president of Mexico. His administration ushered in a gradual shift of Mexican politics, government, and foreign policy as Mexico allied itself with the U.S. cause during World War II. Foreign tourism, initially promoted by the Cárdenas administration, ballooned. Good feelings surged as Franklin Roosevelt became the first U.S. president to officially cross the Río Grande, when he met with Camacho in Monterrey in April 1943.

As World War II moved toward its 1945 conclusion, both the United States and Mexico were enjoying the benefits of four years of governmental and military cooperation and mutual trade in the form of a mountain of strategic minerals, which had moved north in exchange for a similar mountain of U.S. manufactures that moved south.

CONTEMPORARY MEXICO AND OAXACA
The Mature Revolution

During the decades after World War II, beginning with moderate President **Miguel Alemán** (1946–1952), Mexican politicians gradually honed their skills of consensus and compromise as their middle-aged revolution bubbled along under liberal presidents and sputtered haltingly under conservatives. Doctrine required of all politicians, regardless of stripe, that they be "revolutionary" enough to be included beneath the banner of the PRI, Mexico's dominant political party.

Mexico's revolution hasn't been very revolutionary about **women's rights,** however. The PRI didn't get around to giving Mexican women, millions of whom fought and died alongside men during the revolution, the right to vote until 1953.

Alemán's government in 1947 began construction of a huge power and irrigation dam in the Río Papaloapan watershed of northern Oaxaca. The resulting **Miguel Alemán Dam,** completed a few years later, created a mammoth 2.3-million-acre reservoir. Although providing a large chunk of the region's growing electricity demand and an assured irrigation supply for thousands of new fruit, dairy, and vegetable farms, the project required the painful relocation of many thousands of poor Mazatec, Chinantec, and Mixe *indígena* families.

Political Trouble in Oaxaca

Meanwhile, in Oaxaca city, trouble was breaking out, triggered by the unpopular actions of Governor Edmund Sánchez Cano. Merchants, who objected to his new taxes, and students, who resented the governor's interference in university affairs, got together and occupied the state government palace. Before the dust settled, federal troops were occupying the city and Mexico's second in command, the Secretaría de Gobernación, had forced Governor Sánchez's resignation and taken over the state government.

Trouble erupted again in 1951. This time, the dispute had roots among coffee farmers in Oaxaca's southern Sierra. Growers, far removed from Oaxaca city, had been shipping their coffee directly from Pacific ports or by remote roads directly to Mexico City, where they had developed strong commercial and political connections. Although responsible for Oaxaca's major export, coffee growers enjoyed little influence among state officials in Oaxaca city. One of these growers, Mayoral Heredia, had become a close family friend of President Miguel Alemán, who endorsed Heredia's successful PRI candidacy for governor of Oaxaca in 1950.

Upon taking office in December 1950, Heredia replaced the local politicos with his own Mexico City cadre, then proceeded with plans to modernize Oaxaca's agriculture, with subsidies paid by new state taxes. The ensuing dispute revolved fundamentally around the question of power: Who should control Oaxaca—the city leaders as usual, or Mexico City–oriented appointees?

Soon, most townspeople—notably among them, local businesspeople and university professors and students—lined up angrily against the governor. The governor's sole supporters were the state police, who, in the heat of action, shot two protesting university students. After a one-day national student strike and weeks of daily protests, the merchant-student-professor coalition mounted a **citywide general strike.** Finally, President

Alemán had to send in a federal regiment to restore order. Discredited, Governor Heredia was forced to replace his cabinet with city leaders. They reversed his modernization plans: They judged the present dirt roads adequate and found no need for tractors or irrigation. Oaxaca agriculture would sputter along as it had for the past hundred years. Rebuffed, Governor Heredia soon resigned in July 1952.

Political Activism of the 1960s and 1970s

Women, voting for the first time in a national election, kept the PRI in power by electing liberal **Adolfo López Mateos** in 1958. Resembling Lázaro Cárdenas in social policy, López Mateos redistributed 40 million acres of farmland, forced automakers to use 60 percent domestic components, built thousands of new schools, and distributed hundreds of millions of new textbooks. *"La electricidad es nuestra"* ("Electricity is ours"), Mateos declared as he nationalized foreign power companies in 1962.

Despite his left-leaning social agenda, unions were restive under López Mateos. Protesting inflation, workers struck; the government retaliated, arresting Demetrios Vallejo, the railway union head, and renowned muralist David Siqueiros, former Communist party secretary.

Despite the troubles, López Mateos climaxed his presidency gracefully in 1964 as he opened the celebrated National Museum of Anthropology, appropriately located in Chapultepec Park, where the Aztecs had first settled 20 generations earlier.

In 1964, as several times before, the outgoing president's Secretaría de Gobernación succeeded his former chief. Dour, conservative **Gustavo Díaz Ordaz** immediately clashed with liberals, labor, and students. The pot boiled over just before the 1968 Mexico City Olympics. Reacting to a student rebellion, the army occupied the National University; shortly afterward, on October 2, government forces opened fire with machine guns on a peaceful downtown rally crowd, killing hundreds and wounding thousands.

The Mexico City troubles reignited political activism in Oaxaca. Local university students, organized as the **Federación Estudiantil de**

Oaxaca (FEO), mounted a successful campaign in support of bus drivers in 1970. In 1972, the students joined with workers and poor farmers, forming the **Coalición de Obreros, Campesinos, y Estudiantes de Oaxaca (COCEO).** They led off with a fight on behalf of sidewalk vendors to prevent the Saturday market being moved to the city's southern outskirts. After that, a disgruntled student splinter faction set off three small bombs: in the PRI-dominated union office, at an English-language library, and in the (empty) folk-dance amphitheater on the hill above the city. Fortunately, no one was injured. Later, in the mid-1970s, the COCEO supported and helped organize rural land invasions by villagers, organized and supported city workers' unions, and backed hillside squatters on the city's northern edge.

The actions in the capital inspired activists in other parts of Oaxaca. In Juchitán, on the Isthmus, students united with workers and poor farmers to form the **Coalición Obero, Campesino, y Estudiantil del Istmo (COCEI).** Unlike its Oaxaca city counterpart, the COCEI had a strong indigenous Zapotec cultural orientation, with women exerting important, although behind-the-scenes leadership roles. Moreover, their cultural unity produced unusual militancy and political skill. Through a series of actions—strikes, boycotts, marches, and demonstrations—they opposed city hall cliques and local *caciques* (bosses) at the painful cost of 20 of their number killed or kidnapped by police, soldiers, and hired thugs. Their payment in blood, however, led to significant improvements in working and living conditions for poor people in Juchitán and other Isthmus communities. Moreover, they forced the local establishment politicos to recognize their legitimacy by winning the 1980 local elections and making Juchitán one of the few towns in Mexico without a PRI-dominated city government.

Meanwhile, back in Oaxaca city, student influence peaked, then faded in 1977 over a dispute that started with election of the university (Universidad Autonoma de Benito Juárez de Oaxaca, UABJO) rector, equivalent to a university president in the United States. Actions escalated until snipers were killing people in university buildings. As police stepped in to restore order, students protested and organized strikes. Fed up with the turmoil, merchants, property owners, and the local PRI organized their own anti-student shutdown, triggering a student-worker march upon the central plaza. State police opened fire, killing one and wounding dozens. That night, the federal government clamped down. Troops took control, and Zárate Aquino, the third Oaxaca governor to be forced from office within a generation, left permanently. Soldiers patrolled the city for nine months, demonstrations were banned, and the anti-establishment COCEO coalition collapsed.

Having had to deal with a generation of Oaxacan political turmoil, the federal government began to direct more resources to Oaxaca. Federal expenditures and employment in Oaxaca city doubled during the 1970s. Improved roads linked villages to the city; electric lines extended into formerly isolated mountain villages; a host of schools and health centers proliferated; and many villages and towns got clean water systems for the first time. With the money and power flowing from Mexico City, Oaxaca's local merchant and professional old guard gradually lost their influence over state government.

New Mexican Industrialization

Despite its serious internal troubles, Mexico's relations with the United States were cordial. President Lyndon Johnson visited and unveiled a statue of Abraham Lincoln in Mexico City. Later, President Díaz Ordaz met with President Richard Nixon in Puerto Vallarta.

Meanwhile, bilateral negotiations produced the **Border Industrialization Program.** Within a 12-mile strip south of the U.S.-Mexico border, foreign companies could assemble duty-free parts into finished goods and export them without any duties on either side. Within a dozen years, a swarm of such plants, called **maquiladoras,** were humming as hundreds of thousands of Mexican workers assembled and exported billions of dollars worth of shiny consumer goods—electronics, clothes, furniture, pharmaceuticals, and toys—worldwide.

Concurrently, in Mexico's interior, Díaz Ordaz pushed Mexico's industrialization ahead full steam. Foreign money financed hundreds of new plants and factories. Primary among these was the giant Las Truchas steel plant at the new industrial port and town of Lázaro Cárdenas at the Pacific mouth of the Río Balsas.

Very little of Mexico's new industrial development reached Oaxaca, however. Oaxaca's sparse industry, with few exceptions, remained simple, producing raw materials or goods for local consumption only.

Oil Boom, Economic Bust

Discovery in 1974 of gigantic new oil and gas reserves along Mexico's Gulf Coast added fuel to Mexico's already rapid industrial expansion. During the late 1970s and early 1980s, billions in foreign investment, lured by Mexico's oil earnings, financed other major developments—factories, hotels, power plants, roads, airports—all over the country.

A modest share of Mexico's new oil wealth trickled to Oaxaca, in increased government jobs, infrastructure construction, and the new cross-Isthmus pipelines and Salina Cruz oil refinery, completed in 1977. Soon 3,000 Oaxacan workers were processing 800,000 barrels of Gulf crude a year into gasoline, diesel and jet fuel, and liquid propane and butane, which tank trucks, railway cars, and ocean tankers distributed all over Mexico and the Pacific Rim.

The negative side to these expensive projects was the huge dollar debt required to finance them. President **Luis Echeverría Alvarez** (1970–1976), diverted by his interest in international affairs, passed Mexico's burgeoning balance of payments deficit to his successor, **José López Portillo.** As feared by some experts, a world petroleum glut during the early 1980s burst Mexico's ballooning oil bubble and plunged the country into financial crisis. When the 1982 interest came due on its foreign debt, Mexico's largest holding company couldn't pay the $2.3 billion owed. The peso plummeted more than fivefold, to 150 per U.S. dollar. At the same time, prices doubled every year.

In the mid-1980s President **Miguel de la Madrid** (1982–1988) was straining to get Mexico's economic house in order. He sliced government and raised taxes, asking rich and poor

alike to tighten their belts. Despite getting foreign bankers to reschedule Mexico's debt, de la Madrid couldn't stop inflation. Prices skyrocketed as the peso deflated to 2,500 per U.S. dollar, becoming one of the world's most devalued currencies by 1988.

Such economic belt-tightening invariably hits the poor hardest, and Oaxacans are among Mexico's poorest. Oaxaca's families average only about $2,000 income per year—about one-third of the Mexican average, and less than a tenth of the U.S. average. The problem is much worse for Oaxaca's dirt-poor, who, in Oaxaca city, make up about one-third of the population. Their yearly average family income hovers somewhere around $1,000, less than $100 per month. With basic food prices not much different from those in the United States, hunger, if not outright starvation, has been an everyday fact for many Oaxacans for as long as they can remember.

Salinas de Gortari, Solidaridad, and NAFTA

Public disgust led to significant opposition during the 1988 presidential election. The conservative National Action Party candidate Michael Clothier and liberal National Democratic Front candidate Cuauhtémoc Cárdenas ran against the PRI's Harvard-educated technocrat Carlos Salinas de Gortari. Although Salinas de Gortari eventually won the election, his showing, barely half of the vote, was the worst ever for an Institutional Revolutionary Party president.

Salinas de Gortari, nevertheless, lost no time getting started. His biggest domestic success was the popular "Solidarity" (Programa Nacional de Solidaridad, PRONASOL) program, which aided poor communities in locally run self-help, cultural, sanitation, health, agricultural, and other projects. Especially targeted were small, mostly indigenous Oaxaca coffee producers who, through local Solidaridad committees, received hundreds of interest-free loans.

Salinas de Gortari's major international achievement, despite significant national opposition, was the North American Free Trade Agreement (NAFTA), which the Canadian, U.S., and Mexican legislatures ratified in 1993.

The Zapatista Revolt

However, on the very day in January 1994 that NAFTA took effect, rebellion broke out in Oaxaca's neighboring state of Chiapas. A small but well-disciplined campesino force, calling itself Ejército Zapatista Liberación Nacional (**Zapatista National Liberation Army, EZLN**) or "Zapatistas," captured a number of provincial towns and held the former governor of Chiapas hostage.

The Zapatista revolt rattled Oaxaca. In a social trend that had been growing at least since the Isthmus Zapotec community became politicized and formed the COCEI during the 1970s, indigenous communities all over the state began pushing for their rights under the Mexican constitution. Prime actors in this movement have been liberationist Catholic priests and nuns, especially in remote country parishes.

Although successful clergy-led projects have sprung up all around Oaxaca, the Isthmus provides the most successful examples. Under the leadership of clergy, in dozens of communities around Tehuantepec, thousands of indigenous people—Mixe, Chontal, Huave, Zapotec, and others—have organized self-help, cultural, political, and communal work programs. Their moneymaking activities range from raising coffee, sheep, and chickens to milling corn and producing pottery, which they sell in the Tehuantepec, Salina Cruz, and Juchitán markets.

One of the most successful organizations in all this ferment has been the **Unión de Comunidades de la Region del Istmo (UCIRI)**, headquartered in Lachaviza, north of Tehuantepec. Fed up with corrupt middlemen and discouraged by the lack of governmental help, small coffee growers banded together and now represent 3,000 growers in 50 communities. Besides working together in production, transportation, and sales, they organize cooperative self-education (especially in organic farming) and run a savings bank, a clinic, and cooperative grocery, hardware, and drug stores.

The Zapatista revolt has struck the common chord—of autonomy—among virtually all of Oaxaca's indigenous social-political groups. Echoing the Zapatistas in Chiapas, their political goals usually include the right of self-rule by their own traditional means.

A National Tragedy

In mid-1994, Mexico's already tense political drama veered toward tragedy. While Salinas de Gortari was trying to settle the Zapatista revolt, Luis Donaldo Colosio, Salinas's handpicked presidential candidate, was gunned down just months before the August balloting. However, instead of disintegrating, the nation united in grief; opposition candidates eulogized their fallen former opponent and later earnestly engaged his replacement, stolid technocrat **Ernesto Zedillo**, in Mexico's first presidential election debate.

In a closely watched election relatively unmarred by irregularities, Zedillo piled up a solid plurality against his PAN (National Action Party) and PRD (Revolutionary Democratic Party) opponents. By perpetuating the PRI's 65-year hold on the presidency, the electorate had again opted for the PRI's familiar, although imperfect middle-aged revolution.

A New Economic Crisis

Zedillo, however, had little time to savor his victory. The peso, long propped up by his predecessor's fiscal policies, lost one-third of its value in the few days before Christmas 1994. The peso kept falling, and to stave off a worldwide financial panic, **U.S. President Bill Clinton** in February 1995 secured an unprecedented multibillion-dollar international loan package for Mexico.

Although economic disaster was temporarily averted, the cure for the country's ills required another painful round of belt-tightening for poor Mexicans. During 1995, national inflation soared. More and more families became unable to purchase staple foods and basic medicines. Malnutrition increased sixfold, and third world diseases, such as cholera and dengue fever, resurged in the countryside.

The Political Cauldron Bubbles On

At the same time, Mexico's equally serious political ills seemed to defy cure. Raul Salinas de Gortari, an important PRI party official and the former president's brother, was arrested for money laundering and political assassination. As popular sentiment began to implicate Carlos Salinas de Gortari himself, the former president fled Mexico to an undisclosed location.

Meanwhile, as negotiations with the rebel Zapatistas sputtered on and off in Chiapas, popular discontent erupted in Oaxaca's western neighbor-state, Guerrero, leading to the massacre of 17 unarmed campesinos at Aguas Blancas, in the hills west of Acapulco, by state police in June 1995. One year later, at a demonstration protesting the massacre, a new, well-armed revolutionary group, **Ejército Popular Revolucionario** (People's Revolutionary Army, EPR) made its appearance. Scarcely two months later, on August 28, EPR guerrillas killed more than two dozen police and soldiers at several southwest Mexico locations, including four sailors at the naval garrison in Huatulco, Oaxaca. Soon, platoons of soldiers and police were scouring rural Guerrero, Oaxaca, Michoacán, and other states, searching homes and arresting suspected dissidents.

Mexican democracy got a much-needed boost, when notorious Guerrero governor Ruben Figueroa, who had tried to cover up the Aguas Blancas massacre with a bogus videotape, was forced from office. At the same time, although the official negotiations with the Zapatista rebels were stalled over the issue of indigenous rights, the Zedillo government gained momentum in addressing other local grievances in Chiapas by building new rural electrification networks and refurbishing health clinics. Similar federal action seemed to be forthcoming in Oaxaca also, when, in early 1996, President Zedillo recognized that "success or failure of [his] social policy" depended on Oaxaca and announced an unprecedented $1 billion in federal expenditures in Oaxaca for the upcoming fiscal year.

Nevertheless, continued federal military presence, especially in Guerrero, Oaxaca, and Chiapas, seemed to trigger violent incidents. Worst was the massacre of 45 indigenous campesinos, including women and children, at Acteal, Chiapas, in late December 1997 by paramilitary gunmen. Federal investigators later linked the perpetrators to local PRI officials. In mid-1998, the EPR appeared in Ayutla, Guerrero, leafleting villagers

and giving impromptu speeches. Government soldiers responded with repression, violent searches, and torture. Finally, federal troops cornered and killed 11 suspected EPR members in a schoolhouse 50 miles (80 km) east of Acapulco.

The rough federal army and police searches, arrests, and jailings have energized a flurry of political action. Oaxacan human rights groups, already protesting against unpunished violence, have upped the pressure for reforms at the state and national level. The official **Oaxaca State Human Rights Commission** (Comisión Estatal de Derechos Humanos, CNDH) hears complaints and issues "nonbinding and autonomous recommendations" to relevant authorities.

Fortunately, **foreign visitors** in Oaxaca have been unaffected by such disputes. In Oaxaca city especially, and along well-traveled highways, in resorts, towns, and sites of touristic interest, foreign visitors are generally much safer than in their home cities in the United States, Canada, or Europe.

Economic Recovery and Political Reforms

The best news for which the Zedillo government could justly claim credit was the dramatically improving national economy. By mid-1998, annual inflation had dropped below 15 percent, investment dollars were flowing back into Mexico, the peso had stabilized at about eight to the U.S. dollar, and Mexico had paid back every penny of its borrowed U.S. bailout money.

Moreover, in the political arena, although the justice system in Oaxaca and other states left much to be desired, a pair of unprecedented events signaled an increasingly open political system. In the 1997 congressional elections, voters elected a host of opposition candidates, depriving the PRI of an absolute congressional majority for the first time since 1929. A year later, in early 1998, Mexicans were participating in their country's first **primary elections**—in which voters, instead of political bosses, chose party candidates.

Although Ernesto Zedillo's presidential ride had been rough, he entered the twilight of his 1994–2000 term able to take credit for an improved economy, some genuine political reforms, and relative peace in the countryside. The election of 2000 revealed, however, that the Mexican people were not satisfied.

End of an Era: Vicente Fox Unseats the PRI

During 1998 and 1999 the focal point of opposition to the PRI's three-generation rule had been shifting to relative newcomer Vicente Fox, former President of Coca Cola Mexico and clean former PAN governor of Guanajuato.

Fox, who had announced his candidacy for President two years before the election, seemed an unlikely challenger. After all, the minority PAN had always been the party of wealthy businessmen and the conservative Catholic right. But blunt-talking, six-foot-five Fox, who sometimes campaigned in *vaquero* boots and a 10-gallon cowboy hat preached populist themes of coalition building and "inclusion." He backed up his talk by carrying his campaign to hardscrabble city *barrios,* dirt-poor country villages, and traditional outsider groups, such as Jews.

In a relatively orderly and fair July 2, 2000 election, Fox decisively defeated his PRI opponent Labastida, 42 percent to 38 percent, while

A protest crowd assembles in the Huautla plaza—the victory of Vicente Fox has ignited renewed interest in politics.

PRD candidate Cárdenas polled a feeble 17 percent. Fox's win also swept a PAN plurality (223/209/57) into the 500-seat Chamber of Deputies lower house (although the Senate remained PRI-dominated).

Nevertheless, in pushing the PRI from the all-powerful presidency after 71 consecutive years of domination, Fox had ushered Mexico into a new, more democratic era.

Despite stinging criticism from his own ranks, **President Zedillo,** whom historians were already praising as the real hero behind Mexico's new democracy, made an unprecedentedly early appeal for all Mexicans to unite behind Fox.

On the eve of his December 1, 2000, inauguration, Mexicans awaited Fox's speech with hopeful anticipation. He did not disappoint them. Although acknowledging that he couldn't completely reverse 71 years of PRI entrenchment in his one six-year term, he vowed to ride the crest of reform, by revamping the tax system and reducing poverty by 30 percent, by creating a million new jobs a year through new private investment in electricity and oil production, and by forming a new common market with Latin America, the United States, and Canada.

He promised, moreover, to secure justice for all by a much-needed reform of police, the federal attorney general, and the army. Potentially most difficult of all, Fox called for the formation of an unprecedented congressional "Transparency Commission" to investigate a generation of past grievances, including the 1968 massacre of student demonstrators and assassinations of, among others, a Roman Catholic cardinal in 1993 and a popular presidential candidate in 1994.

Vicente Fox, President of Mexico

Wasting little time getting started, President Fox first headed to Chiapas to confer with indigenous community leaders. Along the way, he shut down Chiapas military bases and removed dozens of military roadblocks. Back in Mexico City, he sent the long-delayed **peace plan,** including the **indigenous bill of rights,** to Congress. Zapatista rebels responded by journeying en masse from Chiapas to Mexico City, where, in their black masks, they addressed Congress, arguing for

© BRUCE WHIPPERMAN

indigenous rights. Although by mid-2001, Congress had passed a modified version of the negotiated settlement, and the majority of states had ratified the required constitutional amendment, indigenous leaders condemned the legislation plan as watered down and unacceptable, while proponents claimed it was the best possible compromise between the Zapatistas demands and the existing Mexican constitution.

On the positive side, by mid-2002, Vicente Fox could claim credit for cracking down on corruption and putting drug lords in jail, negotiating a key immigration agreement with the United States, keeping the peso stable, clamping down on inflation, and attracting a record pile of foreign investment dollars.

Furthermore, Fox continued to pry open the door to democracy in Mexico. In May 2002, he signed Mexico's first **freedom of information act,** entitling citizens to timely copies of all public documents from federal agencies. Moreover, Fox's long-promised **"Transparency Commission"** was taking shape. In July 2002, federal attorneys were taking extraordinary action. They were questioning a list of 74 former government officials, including ex-President Luí Echeverrí, about their roles in government transgressions, notably political murders and the University of Mexico massacres during the 1960s and 1970s.

But, Mexico's economy, reflecting the U.S. economic slowdown, began to sour in 2001, losing half a million jobs and cutting annual growth to 2.5 percent, down from the 4.5 percent that the government had predicted. Furthermore, a so-called "Towelgate" furor (in which aides had purchased dozens of $400 towels for the presidential mansion) weakened Fox's squeaky-clean image.

During 2002 and 2003, the Mexican economy continued its lackluster performance, increasing public dissatisfaction. In the July 7, 2003, congressional elections, voters took their frustrations out on the PAN and gave its plurality in the Chamber of Deputies to the PRI. When the dust settled, the PRI total had risen to 225 seats, while the PAN had slipped to 153. The biggest winner, however, was the PRD, which gained more than 40 seats, to a total of about 100.

At the end of 2003, with his term half finished, critics were increasingly claiming that Fox was "running out of time" to accomplish what he promised. Although Fox had won concessions from U.S. President George W. Bush on immigration policy, Mexican men and women in the street were seeing little improvement in their lives and were increasingly impatient with Fox's efforts to remake the economy and political system. Nevertheless, most still believed that unseating the PRI was good for Mexico, and that even Fox couldn't completely undo in six years what 71 years of PRI dominance created.

And regardless of how history will judge Vicente Fox, it's important to remember the prime fact of July 2, 2000: that, in pushing out the PRI after 71 years and cleanly electing an opposition president, Mexicans have taken a crucial, irreversible step in their long journey toward democracy and justice for all.

Economy and Government

THE ECONOMY

Postrevolutionary National Gains

By many measures, Mexico's 20th-century revolution appears to have succeeded. Since 1910, illiteracy has plunged from 80 percent to 10 percent; life expectancy has risen from 30 years to nearly 70; infant mortality has dropped from a whopping 40 percent to about two percent; and, in terms of caloric intake, most Mexicans are eating about twice as much as their turn-of-the-century forebears.

Decades of near-continuous economic growth account for rising Mexican living standards. The Mexican economy rebounded from its 1982 and 1995 recessions and is presently recovering from its 2001–2002 recession, due to plentiful natural resources, notably oil and metals; diversified manufacturing, such as cars, steel, and petrochemicals; steadily increasing tourism; exports of fruits, vegetables, and cattle; and its large, willing, low-wage workforce.

Recent Mexican governments, moreover, have skillfully exploited Mexico's economic strengths. The **Border Industrialization Program** has led to millions of jobs in thousands of border maquiladora factories, from Tijuana to the mouth of the Río Grande. Foreign trade, a strong source for new Mexican jobs, has burgeoned since the 1980s, due to liberalized tariffs as Mexico joined the General Agreement on Tariffs and Trade (GATT) in 1986 and NAFTA in 1994. As a result, Mexico has become a net exporter of goods and services to the United States, its largest trading partner. Although Mexico suffered a peso collapse of about 50 percent (in relation to the U.S. dollar) in 1995, the Zedillo administration acted quickly. Belt-tightening measures brought foreign investment flowing back to Mexico by 1997 and annual inflation, which had initially surged, cooled down to around six or seven percent during 2003. Although some factory and business closures led to increased unemployment in 1995 and 2001, benefits from the devalued peso, such as increased

tourism and burgeoning exports, despite the 2001–2002 slowdown, spell an increasingly prosperous future for Mexico during 21st century.

The Oaxacan Economy

Despite huge gains, Mexico's Revolution of 1910 is nevertheless incomplete. In Oaxaca, it remains especially so. Oaxaca lags behind the rest of Mexico by many measures of economic success. Median income, for example, hovers at about half the national average. The year 2000 national census figures indicate that median daily earnings per active worker stood at about $3 for Oaxacans and about $6 for Mexicans in general. Such numbers demonstrate the difficult reality confronting the poorest Oaxacan families. When asked by 2000 census takers to categorize their incomes, a whopping 28 percent of Oaxacan active wage earners said they received no income. The next two higher categories, totaling about 20 percent (one in five) reported incomes of between zero and $2 and between $2 and $4 per day, respectively.

A look at more government figures provides clues as to who most of Oaxaca's poor are. According to recent figures, **agriculture**—overwhelmingly corn farming, but also cattle, fruit, and fish—occupies about half of Oaxaca's active workers, but accounts for only one-fifth of the value of Oaxaca's yearly economic output. The remaining four-fifths is generated by the other half of Oaxaca's workers who are, consequently, responsible for approximately four times as much production value as the farmers.

At the human level, the typical Oaxacan lives on a farm and is poor, even by Mexican standards. The typically six-member family, dad José, 36, mom María, 31, three kids, 2, 6, and 11, and grandma, 56, earn next to no cash income and must subsist on what they can produce and gather. This generally is limited to corn, squash, beans, eggs, garden vegetables, an occasional chicken or turkey, and maybe a little wild game. Staples that they don't produce must be bought or bartered for at the village market. So once a week María bundles up some tomatoes, carrots, and potatoes from her garden and maybe one of her half dozen young roosters. With her middle child in tow, she walks the six miles uphill to the village. With luck, María will return by early evening, having sold or traded everything for perhaps a liter of cooking oil, a kilo of sugar, a spool of thread, and a yard or two of bright ribbon.

While María is at the market, José pulls weeds for a few hours in his *milpa* (cornfield). Although his acreage is small, perhaps no more than two or three acres, he usually manages two harvests of corn a year. In a good season, this might amount to two tons, as long as he keeps the mice and rats away from it. Every year he stores about a ton of corn for home consumption and sells the other ton for about $100 to Conasupo, the government commodity agency. If all goes well, he reckons, in three years he'll save enough to replace his family's present stick-and-adobe, dirt-floor house with a new, sturdy two-room concrete house with an interior water tap and a toilet.

Solving the Problems

Like José, many thousands of Oaxacan farmers must struggle to better their lot. The government is generally sympathetic to their efforts and recog-

Pre-primary schooling stands high among modern Mexico's fiscal priorities.

nizes that Oaxaca, with its plentiful sun and adequate (but sharply seasonal) rainfall, is a potential trove of grain, fruit, fiber, meat, and fish for the rest of the country and maybe even for export. But the problems are manifold. Although Oaxaca has expanses of rich land, especially in the Isthmus,

SOCIOECONOMIC STATISTICS: OAXACA VS. MEXICO VS. THE UNITED STATES

	Oaxaca	Mexico	U.S.
Approximate average daily income per active worker	$5	$11	$81
Corn productivity	.5 ton/acre	.5 ton/acre	1.6 ton/acre
Tractor use by farmers	20%	38%	100%
Infant mortality	1.6%	1.6%	.7%
Inhabitants per doctor	1,370	935	400
Average grade attained in school	5.8	7.6	13
Illiteracy	20%	9%	3%
Population (year 2000)	3,440,000	97,500,000	281,000,000
Yearly population growth	.60%	.67%	1.4%

Sources: Mexican government census, U.S. Census Statistical Abstract, World Bank, and the *World Almanac and Book of Facts*

ECONOMIC ACTIVITY—REGIONAL VS. NATIONAL

The following figures represent categories by percent of population engaged in the activity and percent of value of total output.

	Agriculture	Industry	Construction	Commerce	Transportation	Private Services	Gov't Services
MEXICO							
Population	23%	21%	7%	13%	4%	16%	13%
Value of Output (% of total)	7%	23%	5%	22%	9%	14%	20%
OAXACA							
Population	53%	12%	5%	8%	3%	8%	10%
Value of Output (% of total)	18%	13%	5%	20%	9%	15%	20%

Note: Population percentages, from census figures, do not add to 100% because some respondents declined to categorize their occupations.

INCOME DISTRIBUTION—REGIONAL VS. NATIONAL

Approximate percent of active workforce that earns the equivalent US$ per day:

	$0	$0–2	$2–4	$4–8	$8–12	$12–20	$20–40	more than $40
Mexico	8%	4%	9%	32%	18%	15%	8%	4%
Oaxaca	27%	6%	11%	23%	8%	9%	3%	12%

Note: Estimated from the 2000 Mexican national census. Percentages do not add to 100% because some respondents declined to categorize their earnings.

the Papaloapan, and the central valley, about a fifth of Oaxaca's land, especially in the Mixteca, is useless because of severe erosion. Another third is partly so. Before the conquest, much of Oaxaca's farmland was **terraced and irrigated,** not unlike the millet terraces of Nepal and the rice terraces of Bali. Although Oaxacans largely lost that precious knowledge, it could be relearned, and the old water channels and hillside terraces (which are still visible at many locations) could be restored.

Meanwhile, on the present land, productivity could be greatly increased. To raise corn production from the current half ton per acre to the U.S. level of two tons per acre would require mechanization, fertilizer, an irrigation water supply, and the know-how to make everything come together. At present, however, only about one-fifth of Oaxaca's farmers have access to a tractor (compared to 38 percent nationwide); very few have the money for fertilizer; only about 15 percent have access to irrigation water; and most have completed five years or less of schooling. Nevertheless, a focused, long-term government-to-people partnership, not unlike the Tennessee Valley Authority in the United States, could restore prosperity in the Oaxacan countryside.

One route to a better life for many Oaxacans has been to get out. Census figures indicate that about 40 percent of people born in Oaxaca are living and working in other parts of Mexico, the United States, or Canada. While Oaxacan people don't want to leave home, lack of local jobs forces them to. Unlike northern Mexican states close to U.S. cities filled with people who want to buy Mexican-made shoes, telephones, mops, lamp fixtures, and bicycles, Oaxaca, in the far south, is surrounded by other equally disadvantaged Mexican states. Oaxaca, with few nearby markets, attracts only a dribble of new factories and consequently generates scant new jobs. If Oaxaca had oil or gold, the story would be much different.

Although emigration has slowed Oaxaca's population growth in general, Oaxaca city is an exception. Country people seeking a better life started arriving in Oaxaca city in the 1940s when the population was about 40,000, and they're still coming. Most estimates put Oaxaca city's rising population at around 350,000.

All the new neighbors make life more crowded for the average Oaxaca city family—parents with two or three children—who typically must manage on about $10 per day. The survival mode for many such city families has been enterprise: Mom takes in laundry or starts a neighborhood store on the front porch; Dad works one or two jobs; and both Mom and Dad sell *taquitos* out front on Saturday and Sunday nights. Oaxacans, like everyone, do what they must to get by.

Tourism

Partly because of their isolation and difficult economic circumstances, Oaxaca folks are in many ways like people of yesteryear. Unlike richer people in some parts of Mexico and much of the United States, Canada, and Europe, most Oaxacans have yet to join the headlong race into the future. And therein lies Oaxaca's charm. The native women's bright traditional costumes, the venerable, monumental buildings, the stick-and-adobe

Concrete block–making earns about $5 a day in Oaxaca.

© BRUCE WHIPPERMAN

Street vending supplements many Oaxaca family incomes.

© BRUCE WHIPPERMAN

thatched houses, the *vaqueros* on horseback, the oxcarts, all of which symbolize backwardness and poverty in some eyes, are a sentimentally picturesque sight to increasing numbers of visitors, both domestic and foreign.

But as a visitor, *please remember the reality behind Oaxaca's charm*. Please be tolerant, generous in your gratuities, and bargain gently. If you do, Oaxacans will welcome your presence and try even harder to make your visit worthwhile.

State and federal government planners years ago recognized Oaxaca tourism's potential benefits. Their strategy, formulated in the late 1980s, is yielding results. While tourist visitations have burgeoned, Oaxaca city's proud old monuments have been restored, the central plaza blooms with old Mexico charm, village-run tourist accommodations have sprouted in the countryside, and the coastal Bahías de Huatulco resort continues to grow gradually while retaining its precious tropical forest hinterland.

This is all good news if Oaxaca's increasing tide of visitors doesn't ruin the charm that they came to enjoy in the first place. Instead, let's hope that Oaxaca's culture and natural assets will be enriched *because* of their tourist value. If so, campesinos

will preserve, rather than wipe out, the local wildlife because they realize that visitors come *because* of the wildlife. For the same reason, artisans will fashion more enticing handicrafts; people will continue to dress up and dance in their bright costumes; towns will build museums and conserve their old monuments; and archaeologists will restore crumbled cities to their original glory.

GOVERNMENT AND POLITICS

The Constitution of 1917

Mexico's governmental system is rooted in the Constitution of 1917, which incorporated many of the features of its reformist predecessor of 1857. State constitutions, including Oaxaca's, must conform to the federal Constitution, which, with some amendments, remains identical to the 1917 document. Although drafted at the behest of conservative revolutionary Venustiano Carranza by his handpicked Querétaro "Constitucionalista" congress, the 1917 Constitution was greatly influenced by Alvaro Obregón and generally ignored by Carranza during his subsequent three-year presidential term.

Whereas many articles resemble those of its U.S. model, the Constitution of 1917 contains provisions developed directly from Mexican experience. **Article 27** addresses the question of land. Private property rights are qualified by societal need; subsoil rights are public property; and foreigners and corporations are severely restricted in land ownership. Although the 1917 constitution declared *ejido* (jointly held) land inviolate, recent 1994 amendments allow, under certain circumstances, the sale or use of communal land as loan security.

Article 23 severely restricts church powers. In declaring that "places of worship are the property of the nation," it stripped churches of all title to real estate, without compensation. **Article 5 and Article 130** banned religious orders, expelled foreign clergy, and denied priests and ministers all political rights, including voting, holding office, and even criticizing the government.

Article 123 establishes the rights of labor: to organize, bargain collectively, strike, work a

OAXACA REGIONS, GOVERNMENTAL DISTRICTS, AND CAPITALS

Governmental Districts
Caxaca Regions

maximum eight-hour day, and receive a minimum wage. **Women** are to receive equal pay for equal work and be given a month's paid leave for childbearing. Article 123 also establishes social security plans for sickness, unemployment, pensions, and death.

On paper, Mexico's constitutional government structures appear much like their U.S. prototypes: a federal presidency, a two-house (Senate and Chamber of Deputies) congress, and a supreme court, with their counterparts in each of the 31 states and the Mexico City *Distrito Federal.* Political parties field candidates, and all citizens vote by secret ballot.

In Oaxaca, local federal elections determine Oaxaca's national legislative delegation: **11 deputies** *(diputados)* of the approximately 500-seat lower house and **four senators** *(senadores)* of the 120-odd upper house seats. **PRI dominance** of Oaxaca elections, although not as complete as in the past, still continues, with a plurality of Oaxaca's deputies and senators usually being PRI members.

Although ideally providing for **separation of powers,** the Constitution of 1917 subordinates both the legislative and judicial branches, with the courts being the weakest of all. The supreme court, for example, can only, through repeated deliberations, decide upon the constitutionality of legislation. Five separate individuals must file successful petitions for writs *amparo* (protection) on a single point of law in order to effect constitutional precedent.

The President, the PRI, and the PAN

Despite Mexico's increasingly active legislative bodies, Mexican presidents still enjoy greater powers than their U.S. counterparts. They can suspend constitutional rights under a state of siege, can officially initiate legislation, veto all or parts of bills, refuse to execute laws, and replace state officers. The federal government, moreover, retains nearly all taxing authority, relegating the states to a role of merely administering federal programs.

Mexican presidents successively built upon their potent constitutional mandate during the last three generations of the 20th century. The

Institutional Revolutionary Party (PRI), whose handpicked candidates held the presidency continuously from 1929 to 2000, became an extralegal parallel government, as powerful as or more so than the formal constitutional government. The PRI is organized hierarchically, in three separate labor, farmer, and "popular" (this last mostly government, business, and professional workers) columns, which send delegates from local committees to state and, ultimately, national conventions.

Past Mexican presidents, as heads of the PRI, traditionally reigned at the top of the party apparatus, sending orders through the national PRI delegates, who in turn looked after their respective state delegations. The delegates reported on the performance of the state and local PRI committees to get out the vote and carry out party mandates. If the local committee's performance was satisfactory, then federal subsidies, public works projects, election funds, and federal jobs flowed from government coffers to the state and local level through PRI organizations. In your hometown, if you were not in the PRI or didn't know someone who was, you might have found it difficult to get a small business loan, crop subsidy, government apartment, teaching job, road-repair contract, or government scholarship.

The successful election of PAN opposition presidential candidate **Vicente Fox** in 2000, although erasing PRI executive dominance, still left the Senate (and later, in 2003, also the Chamber of Deputies) under PRI control. Consequently, President Fox has found himself in much the position of a U.S. president, having to negotiate, sometimes unsuccessfully, with legislators from the opposition party (and sometimes even his own party).

State and Local Government

Oaxaca, like all 31 Mexican states, has an elected governor and state legislature. The Oaxaca voters elect 42 representatives to the state legislature, which holds its sessions in the Palacio de Gobierno, adjacent to Oaxaca city's central plaza. With minimal tax powers, the state government is mostly relegated to oversight of federal public works, social welfare, health, and education programs in 30 regional administrative *distritos* (districts).

Distritos vary widely in extent, from the largest, Juchitán, in the Isthmus, to tiny Zaachila, the smallest, in the central valley, not far south of Oaxaca city. Although second smallest in area, Oaxaca's most populous and economically most important district is the Centro district, which contains the capital, Oaxaca city.

Oaxaca's 30 *distritos* are in turn divided, often along ethnic lines, into a host of 570 *municipios* (townships), each with its *cabercera* (head town) and subsidiary *agencias,* usually country villages, each of which oversees a scattering of surrounding *rancherias* (hamlets). Oaxaca's crazy quilt of 570 *municipios,* by far the most of any Mexican state, reflects Oaxaca's ethnic richness. Many of the *municipios* encompass a single ethnic group whose members are united by common kinship, language, and costume.

Its *municipios* are where much of Oaxaca's civic action is. If you get a traffic ticket, you'll probably be told to go to the *municipio's presidencia municipal* (like a city hall) to pay your fine and recover your driver's license. From the *presidencia municipal* reigns the *municipio's* publicly elected *presidente* (like a mayor), *alcaldes* (judges), and *regidores* (administrators) of various ranks, who oversee the *municipio's policía municipal* and organize public works.

Parallel to and interlocking with this formal Spanish-derived hierarchy is the less formal indigenous *consejo de ancianos* (council of elders), members of which attain their status by a cumulative lifetime of civic service. Operating mostly by discussion and consensus, the council of elders (which sometimes includes the *presidente* and other elected officials) gets its way through discussion, persuasion, and final approval or veto of civic proposals.

Oaxaca's former progressive governor and legislature, in 1995, recognized indigenous demands for local election by traditional *Usos y Costumbres* (Use and Custom) procedures. Now, a majority of (but by no means all; notably not Oaxaca city) *municipios* elect their mayor and city council members in town hall meetings.

Although *municipios* collect minimal monetary taxes, they often require community members to perform *tequio* (public service) in lieu of taxes. For men, such work might be repairing a local bridge or police or fire duty; women, on the other hand, might perform child care or sweep the city streets or the municipal market.

Political Reform

Reforms in Mexico's stable but top-heavy "Institutional Revolution" has come only gradually. Characteristically, street protests were brutally put down at first, with officials only later working to address grievances. Dominance by the PRI led to widespread cynicism and citizen apathy. Regardless of who got elected, the typical person on the street used to tell you that office-holders were bound to retire with their pockets full.

Nevertheless, during the last dozen years of the 20th century, Mexico took significant strides toward pluralism. Minority parties increasingly were electing candidates to state and federal office. Although none captured a majority of any state legislature, the strongest non-PRI parties, such as the conservative pro-Catholic **Partido Acción Nacional,** or National Action Party (PAN), and the liberal-left **Partido Revolucionario Democratico (PRD),** elected governors. As early as 1986, minority parties were given federal legislative seats, up to a maximum of 20, for winning a minimum of 2.5 percent of the national presidential vote. In the 1994 election, minority parties received public campaign financing, depending upon their fraction of the vote.

Following his 1994 inaugural address, in which he called loudly and clearly for more reforms, President **Ernesto Zedillo** quickly began to produce results. He immediately appointed a respected member of the PAN opposition party as attorney general—the first non-PRI cabinet appointment in Mexican history. Other Zedillo firsts were federal Senate confirmation of both supreme court nominees and the attorney general, multiparty participation in the Chiapas peace negotiations, and congressional approval of the 1995 financial assistance package received from the United States. Zedillo, moreover, organized a series of precedent-setting meetings with opposition leaders, which led to a written pact for political reform and the establishment of permanent working groups to discuss political and economic questions.

Of major symbolic importance was Zedillo's campaign and inaugural vow to separate both his government and himself from PRI decision-making. He kept his promise, becoming the first Mexican president in as long as anyone could remember who did not choose his successor.

A New Mexican Revolution

Finally, on July 2, 2000, like a Mexican Gorbachev, Ernesto Zedillo, the man most responsible for Mexico's recent democratic reforms, watched as PAN opposition reformer Vicente Fox swept Zedillo's PRI from the presidency after a 71-year rule. Moreover, despite severe criticism from his own party, Zedillo quickly called for the country to close ranks behind Fox. Millions of Mexicans, still dazed but buoyed by Zedillo's statesmanship and Fox's epoch-making victory, eagerly awaited Fox's inauguration address on December 1, 2000.

He promised nothing less than a new revolution for Mexico, and backed it up with concrete proposals. Reduce poverty by 30 percent with a million new jobs a year from revital-

ized new electricity and oil production, a Mexican Silicon Valley, and free trade between Mexico, all of Latin America, the United States, and Canada. Fox promised justice for all, through a reformed police, army, and the judiciary. He promised conciliation and an agreement with the Zapatista rebel movement in the south, including a bill of rights for Mexico's native peoples.

Although recession in 2001–2002 and the realities of PRI legislative majorities slowed his reform agenda, President Fox, by late 2003, had pushed through a number of his democratic reform promises. The pace, however, was slow, and the Mexican in the street has come to realize that it will take longer than Vicente Fox's earnest six-year tenure to reverse generations of ingrained public habits and heavy-handed government.

Nevertheless, hope for a prosperous, democratic Mexico still burns bright, based on the same urgent vision that Vicente Fox expressed in his inaugural address: "If I had to summarize my message today in one sentence, I would say: Today Mexico has a future, but we have lost much time and wasted many resources. Mexico has a future, and we must build that future starting today."

People

Let a broad wooden chopping block represent the high plain, the *altiplano* of Mexico; imagine hacking at one half of it with a sharp cleaver until it is grooved and pocked. That fractured surface resembles Mexico's central highlands, where most Mexicans have lived for millennia. The most severely shattered southern end of the Mexican landscape encompasses Oaxaca, whose rugged topography has isolated its original inhabitants behind high ridges and yawning barrancas for untold generations. In their seclusion, they developed separate tongues and hierarchical societies that viewed outsiders with suspicion and hostility, as odd-speaking, barely human barbarians from across the canyon or behind the mountains. When the Spanish conquerors arrived in Oaxaca, they

found a region divided among hundreds of separate subtribes, speaking 16 main languages broken down into scores of mutually unintelligible dialects. The Oaxacans' own divisions, as much as Spanish horses and steel, led to their quick downfall. The Spanish merely added their own layers atop the existing divisions—of territory, language, caste, class, and wealth—that continue to shape both Mexico and Oaxaca to the present day.

Mesoamerica

Although Oaxacan native peoples are divided by their diverse languages and rugged topography, they nevertheless share many folk customs, not only with each other but with tens of millions of other native peoples in a broad belt, beginning around Mexico's Tropic of Cancer and stretching south and east to Honduras and El Salvador. Anthropologists call the entire region Mesoamerica, a single label reflecting its broad cultural unity. Anthropologists believe that this universal symphony of belief and practice flows from tenaciously held traditions handed down from Mexico's great pre conquest civilizations. And nowhere are these folk practices more persistent than in Oaxaca, Mesoamerica's heartland. If you're curious about how most Americans lived before Columbus and Cortés, you needn't look any farther than the Oaxaca countryside.

POPULATION

The Spanish colonial government and the Roman Catholic religion provided the glue that over 400 years has welded Mexico's fragmented population into a nation. In recent years, increased emigration, mostly to the United States, has slowed the growth of the population of both Mexico at large and Oaxaca. At about 98 million in 2000, Mexico's population is growing at less than one percent per year, less than half the pace of previous decades. The same is true for Oaxaca's population, which stood at about 3.4 million in the year 2000.

A growing population was not always the case in Mexico. Historians estimate that European diseases, largely measles and smallpox, probably wiped out as many as 20 million—perhaps 95 percent—of Mexico's *indígena* population within a few generations after Cortés stepped ashore in 1519. Oaxaca's population dropped correspondingly from a pre-conquest level of about two million to a mere 150,000 by 1650. Oaxaca's native peoples, ironically, can look forward to the year 2019, five centuries after Cortés, when their population will have recovered approximately to its pre-conquest level.

By 1600, Mexico's indigenous population had dropped so low that the Spanish began to import sizable numbers of **African slaves,** whose numbers swelled to several tens of thousands by 1650. Although much of the African lineage has been absorbed into Mexico's general population, several thousand African-Mexicans still maintain separate small communities in the Costa Chica, the coastal region

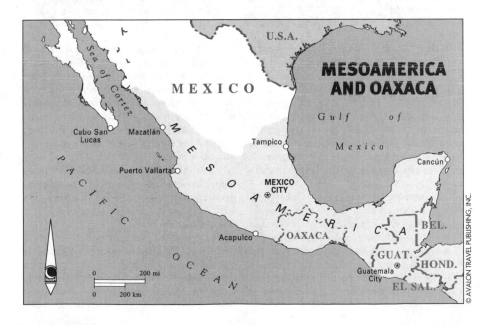

MESOAMERICAN CALENDAR

The Mixtec and Zapotec ancestors of present-day Oaxacans ordered their lives with the same calendric system as many Mesoamerican linguistic groups, including the Maya, the Aztecs (Nahuatl), the Tarascans (Purépecha), and many others. Their system combined two major calendric cycles. First, they used the agricultural calendar, tied to the seasons and derived from the approximately 365-day (actually 365.2422) cycle of the sun through the background of stars and constellations.

The Mesoamerican counting system was basic to the calendar's operation. The Mesoamericans didn't count by decimals, but rather used a vigesimal (20-count) system. They logically divided their agricultural year into 18 "months" of 20 days each, with a five-day short month at the year-end. A given day, for example, might be called, instead of June 11 or June 12, 5-Deer or 6-Deer and so forth.

They tracked ceremonial dates, such as birthdays, with a separate ritual or divinatory calendar of 260 days that combined 20 separate named days with numbers one through 13. Succeeding days were identified as, for example, 2-Water, 3-Monkey, 4-Dog, and so on.

A given date was a unique coincidence of both calendars, which you can imagine as a pair of meshed cogwheels, turning in lockstep. As you picture the calendric cogwheels turning, at a given moment a certain cog (marked as 5-Deer, for example) in the solar calendar will always be meshing with some slot (marked as 3-Monkey, for example) in the ritual calendar, producing a unique combination of two numbers and two names (since the solar and the ritual calendars have different—365 vs. 260—respective totals of cogs and slots). For example, June 11, 1999, might be represented by the unique coincidence of cog 5-Deer and slot 3-Monkey; June 12, 1999, by 6-Deer and 4-Dog, and June 13 by 7-Deer, 5-Water, and so on. (Note that the solar calendar progresses through named "months," such as "Deer" in the example, while the ritual calendar does not.)

In this system dates are unique, but only for a determined time period, because the entire calendric cycle repeats itself after all dual-number–dual-name combinations have occurred. This happens every 52 solar years (or, in days, 52 times 365 or 18,980 days). During this time the intermeshed ritual calendar must pass through exactly the same

spreading both east and west from the Oaxaca-Guerrero border.

ETHNIC GROUPS

Although by 1950 Mexico's population had recovered to 25 million, it was completely transformed. The **mestizo,** a Spanish-speaking person of mixed blood, had replaced the pure native Mexican, the *indígena* (een-DEE-hay-nah), as the typical Mexican.

This trend is not as strong in Oaxaca. Although perhaps three of four Mexicans would identify themselves as mestizo, only about half of Oaxacans probably would. Among many native Oaxacans, the label "mestizo" borders on the derogatory, despite the long colonial tradition that, by virtue of their part-European blood, mestizos were elevated to the level of *gente de razón*—people of "reason" or "right."

The typical mestizo family enjoys many of the benefits of the modern world. They typically own a modest concrete house in town. Their furnishings, simple by developed-world standards, will often include an electric refrigerator, washing machine, propane stove, television, and a car or truck. The children go to school every day, and the eldest son sometimes even looks forward to college.

Above the mestizos, a tiny **criollo** (Mexican-born, European blood) minority, a few percent of the total population, inherits the privileges—wealth, education, and political power—of their colonial Spanish ancestors.

The typical *indígena* family lives in a small adobe house in a remote valley, subsisting on corn, beans, and vegetables from their small, unirrigated *milpa* (cornfield). They usually raise chickens, a few pigs, and sometimes a cow, and have electricity, but no sewage connection. Their few number of days. Dividing 18,980 by its number of 260 cogs, you come up with the exactly 73 revolutions that the ritual calendar must undergo in the same 52 solar years.

Besides the Mixtecs and Zapotecs, all other Mesoamerican groups probably feared that cataclysmic events might occur at the end of each 52-year period, measured from some mythical beginning. High priests and presumably the populations at large observed solemn ceremonies, performed sacrifices, and watched the sky for auspicious portents, such as a bright overhead star, a conjunction of planets, or a comet, on the eve of their 52-year cyclical "millennium."

Knowledge of the Zapotec and Mixtec calendars is gradually being accumulated. Scholars believe that they have been used since at least the early urban stage, around 500 B.C., approximately the founding of Monte Albán. Alfonso Caso, the discoverer of Monte Albán's earliest stages, associated a common but undeciphered Monte Albán glyph, of a headdress in profile, with the solar year. For Caso, this indicated that certain personages wearing such headdresses either interpreted, read, or manipulated the calendar. The ritual calendar,

called *piye* in Zapotec, was also certainly used at Monte Albán.

As in other parts of Mesoamerica, persons were named by their birth date, such as 8-Deer, 3-Dog, or 7-Monkey, in the ritual calendar. Such name-dates occur as glyphs associated with personages recorded in stone or on the surviving hieroglyphic paper books, called codices, such as the Codex Nuttall.

The Mesoamericans, as the Europeans, had to apply corrections to keep the solar calendar in correspondence with the seasons. This will happen only if the year averages, over the millennia, 365.2422 days. The presently used Gregorian calendar (which was instituted by Pope Gregory VIII in 1582) corrects the solar year approximately to 365.2425 days (compared to the actual 365.2422) by omitting the leap year every three out of four centuries. Therefore, although the years 1700, 1800, and 1900 were not leap years (that is, they were permitted only 365 days, instead of 366), the year 2000 was permitted 366 days. The Mayas, scholars believe, did a little better than this; they corrected the solar calendar to 365.2420 days.

hundred dollars a year cash income isn't enough to buy even a small tractor or refrigerator, much less a truck. The *indígenas* (or, mistakenly but commonly, Indians), by the usual measurements of income, health, or education, squat at the bottom of the social ladder. (See also Indigenous Groups.)

Sizable **African Mexican** communities, or *negros,* descendants of 17th- and 18th-century African slaves, live in the Gulf states and along the Guerrero-Oaxaca coastline. Last to arrive, they experience discrimination at the hands of everyone else and are integrating very slowly into the mestizo mainstream.

SHARED OAXACAN CUSTOMS

Settlement Patterns

Oaxaca's present 570 *municipios* (townships), each with its main town and market, reflect

community boundaries often dating back more than a thousand years. Although the Spanish imposed their civic pattern of church, *presidencia* (city hall), and major stores and prominent residences all clustered around a central plaza, the native people still hold to their tradition of concentrating their homes in a number of *barrios* (neighborhoods) on the outskirts. Native peoples have sometimes stretched the Spanish pattern, reverting to their ancient **"empty town"** custom. Here, only the mestizo and criollo elite permanently live in town, while natives maintain empty in-town houses, which they occupy only during market and ceremonial occasions. Most of their days they spend by their country *milpas.*

Birth, Life, and Death

Christian baptism is everyone's first major life event; it's so important that a number of communities believe that a baby is not fully human until

Oaxaca's people, who are gradually moving from the country to the cities and towns, are requiring new housing, such as this new tract of minihomes near Huajuapan de León in northwest Oaxaca.

© BRUCE WHIPPERMAN

baptized. If an unbaptized baby dies, the parents must make haste to bury the body immediately, with little ceremony. If not, the spirit of the unbaptized baby might escape and become a *nagual* (nah-WAHL), a malevolent animal that will harm people who cross its path.

Baptism is also the time when the web of *compadrazgo* relationships starts to influence a person's life. This begins when parents designate their *compadres* (best friends) as *padrinos* (godparents) to their newly born. As children mature, with parental consent they designate their own *compadres*. Formal ceremonies often solemnize *padrino* and *compadrazgo* bonds, which might continue through generations of loyal *padrino* and *compadre* relationships.

With babies, nursing often lasts two or three years, or at least until the next child comes along. Preschool children experience little imposed discipline except the responsibility of watching after younger siblings. Loud or disruptive children might get spanked or shunned, however. Formal schooling is usually considered so important that families often sacrifice so that children,

especially boys, may attend at least six grades of school. Although children of poorer parents experience few, if any, puberty rites, richer parents often honor their children, especially girls, with a number of Catholic ceremonies, such as first communion, confirmation, blessing of their pet animals, and *quinceana* (coming out) at age 15. Among poorer folks, a girl becomes an adult with marriage, often by age 14 or 15. A boy enters manhood through either marriage or entering *servicio* (community service). He's expected to pay community assessments and perform *tequio* (communal work) service. As a young man matures, he is expected to fulfill the duties of a series of increasingly important *cargos* (offices). If successful, at middle age he is rewarded with the rank of *principal* (elder) and admitted to the village council of elders.

Death is usually marked by 24 hours of mourning while the body lies in state at home, usually with candles, incense, and flowers. Wrapped in a *petate* (reed mat) or a coffin, the body is buried, along with the deceased's favored trinkets, and perhaps favorite food. Rituals continue periodically thereafter, especially at nine days as well as one year after burial.

Marriage, Family, and Inheritance

Traditional marriage is an alliance between families, initiated by the groom's parents, often through a go-between. Girls marry as early as 14, boys at 16 or 17. The more well-to-do marry later. Often prospective grooms and brides perform services for the other's family, sometimes even taking up temporary residence (but not sleeping with their intended) while everyone gets acquainted. The contents of the couple's dreams often carry weight in the decision to marry. Polyandry, marriage of a woman to two brothers, although sanctioned in some communities, is not common. On the other hand, well-to-do husbands, while remaining married, sometimes support additional women in separate households.

Although extended families generally encompass two, three, or four generations, couples often establish their own households after the birth of their first child. Even though both the wife's and the husband's relatives enjoy equal kinship status, couples are more likely to live near the husband's relatives. Other practices are male-weighted. Boys usually inherit more land than their sisters, and family names, nearly always Spanish, are inherited from the father. Among some Mixtecs and Mazatecs, the father's first name, interestingly, becomes his children's surname. (This is not unlike the practice among some northern Europeans—"Johnson," "Svensen," and "Mendelsohn," for example.)

Household Life

The basic house has a single room, a dirt floor, stick-and-adobe walls, and a thatched roof. Better houses have more rooms, adobe or concrete walls, a concrete floor, and perhaps a flush toilet. Household goods hang on pegs and nails all around the walls. Overhead, rafters support grain and other heavy storage. Beds are either on floor mats or hammocks. A small altar with saint and candle occupies one corner, with the kitchen in the other. Cooking is either over open fire or on an adobe stove. Tortillas are heated on a flat adobe *comal* (griddle); beans, chilies, and stews are cooked in pottery jars *(ollas)* or metal pots over the open fire. Women grind corn by rolling with their stone *mano* on

Indigenous campesinos, especially in remote areas, still wear traditional cottons.

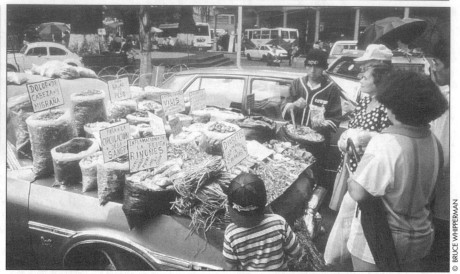

© BRUCE WHIPPERMAN

Traditional healers *(curanderos)* frequently use time-tested natural plants for curing sickness.

the *metate* basin. They grind chilies in their *molcajete* (mortar).

Men do the heavier outside work: clearing, burning, farming, building, repairing, plus fishing, hunting, and tending cattle and horses. If fields are far from the homestead, men sometimes take up temporary residence there during planting and harvest. Women cook, sew, wash clothes, gather fruit, flowers, and wild herbs, and tend household animals, such as pigs, goats, chickens, and turkeys. Women do most, if not all, of the marketing. Both men and women carry heavy loads.

Dress

Verbal descriptions pale in comparison to the color and excitement of a Oaxaca town fiesta or big market day. Country people, especially in remote areas, still wear the traditional cottons that blend the Spanish and native styles. Men usually wear the Spanish-origin fiber **sombrero** (literally, shade-maker) on their heads, loose white cotton shirt and pants, and leather huaraches on their feet. Women's dress is often more colorful. It can include a *huipil* (long, sleeveless dress), often embroidered in bright floral and animal motifs, or a

handwoven *enredo* (wraparound skirt that identifies the wearer with a particular locality). A very common addition is the Spanish-tradition all-purpose woven shawl *(rebozo),* which can carry a baby, a bag of corn, or maybe even a chicken or two, as well as protect from the rain or sun. A *faja* (waist sash) and, in the winter, a *quechquémitl* (shoulder cape) complete the costume.

Making a Living

The great majority of Oaxacan indigenous people cultivate native corn, along with a number of other secondary crops, such as beans, squash, pumpkins, potatoes, chili peppers, and tomatoes. Depending upon soil and climate, they may also harvest potatoes, maguey (for alcoholic drinks), and fruits, such as mangos, papaya, cherimoya, *zapote,* and avocado. Other native crops might be cotton or maguey, for *ixtle* fiber, and perhaps cocoa beans, *hule* (rubber), and chicle (chewing gum) for cash. Locally cultivated introduced cash crops include wheat, bananas, coffee, sugarcane, sesame seeds, and peanuts.

Many families or sometimes entire villages specialize in **crafts,** such as pottery, cloth weaving, or basketry. Although the appearance of cheap, machine-made cloth has weakened the tradition, many Oaxacan women still weave family garments with the ancestral backstrap loom. Treadle looms, introduced by the Spanish and operated by either men or women, are common around Oaxaca city. Potters, both women and men, practice their craft all over Oaxaca. Methods vary; they might confine themselves to the native hand-coiling or the Spanish-introduced potter's wheel, or use a combination of both. (See the Arts and Crafts section in the On the Road chapter.)

Governmental and Religious Institutions

Although women exercise considerable behind-the-scenes influence, men customarily occupy the formal community leadership positions. Minor *presidencia* (city hall) positions are usually appointive; senior positions, such as *regidor* (administrator), *alcalde* (judge), and *presidente* (mayor) are often elective. In-town native homes cluster in one or more *barrios* on the outskirts. A town *regidor* acts as a representative agent for one or more *barrios*.

Paralleling such formal civil institutions are the religious, which center on the *mayordomía*, the office responsible for the oft-elaborate ceremonial trappings and yearly fiesta of the barrio's patron saint. The barrio's *regidor* or one of its *cofradias* (religious fraternities) designates the *mayordomo* for a one-year *mayordomía* responsibility. If donations for the patronal fiesta are inadequate, the *mayordomo,* often a wealthy individual, is expected to add a generous contribution of his or her own. Although this may spell temporary poverty for the *mayordomo,* the reward is great community prestige. A lifetime of such service will often assure election to the status of elder *(principal* or *anciano)* and exalted (so exalted that elders are rarely prosecuted for wrongdoing) membership in the council of elders, upon whose resources and sage advice the community relies.

RELIGION

Although the vast majority of Oaxacan *indígenas* consider themselves Catholics, their religion blends the catechism of the missionary fathers with ancient native beliefs. Deities in

© BRUCE WHIPPERMAN

Banners are carried by *cofradia* (religious fraternity) members in saint's day processions.

THE VIRGIN OF GUADALUPE

Conversion of the *indígenas* to Catholicism was sparked by the vision of Juan Diego, a poor farmer. On the hill of Tepeyac north of Mexico City in 1531, Juan Diego saw a brown-skinned Virgin Mary enclosed in a dazzling aura of light. She told him to build a shrine in her memory on that spot, where the Aztecs had long worshipped their "earth mother," Tonantzín. Juan Diego's brown Virgin told him to go to the cathedral and relay her instruction to Archbishop Zumárraga.

The archbishop, as expected, turned his nose up at Juan Diego's story. The vision returned, however, and this time Juan Diego's brown Virgin realized that a miracle was necessary. She ordered him to pick some roses at the spot where she had first appeared to him (a true miracle, since roses had been previously unknown in the vicinity) and take them to the archbishop. Juan Diego wrapped the roses in his rude fiber cape, returned to the cathedral, and placed the wrapped roses at the archbishop's feet. When he opened the offering, Zumárraga gasped: Imprinted on the cape was an image of the Virgin herself—proof positive of a genuine miracle.

In the centuries since Juan Diego, the brown Virgin—La Virgen Morena, or Nuestra Señora La Virgen de Guadalupe—has blended native and Catholic elements into something uniquely Mexican. In doing so, she has become the virtual patroness of Mexico, the beloved symbol of Mexico for *indígenas*, mestizos, African Mexicans, and criollos alike.

offerings, candles, food, and sacrificial turkeys and chickens.

Other old beliefs persist. Many folks, especially in remote areas, believe that *ánimas* (spirits) of the dead, besides the Catholic God and the saints, influence the living. Appeasement of *ánimas* peaks on November 1 and 2, respectively, the Day of All Saints and Day of the Dead, when many families gather all night at graves of their departed, with candles, flowers, incense, and the deceased's favorite foods. People also appease saints for favors; however, if prayers are not answered, a person may also punish a saint by abusing its figurine. Sometimes evil dwarfs, the devil, or malevolent female spirits lure men to ruin. At birth, people acquire *tonos*, powerful guardian spirits, often in the guise of mountain lions, jaguars, and eagles who, if treated with respect, might protect them throughout life. Sickness, commonly thought to be afflicted by an evil spell, loss of soul by fright, or "bad air," *mal aire*, is treated by the incantations of a traditional village healer *curandero* or *curandera*.

Healers employ other remedies, such as consumption or avoidance of certain foods, sucking (to remove the mysterious object causing the illness), herbs and poultices, and also modern medicine. Especially common is a steam bath in the traditional *temascal*, a permanent wood or stone structure or temporary mat-covered brush hut, which many Oaxacan households maintain individually (rather than communally).

Catholicism, spreading its doctrine of equality of all persons before God and incorporating native gods into the church rituals, eventually brought the native Mexicans into the fold. Within a hundred years of the Conquest, nearly all natives had accepted the new religion, which raised the universal God of all humankind over local tribal deities.

Every Mexican city, town, and village celebrates the cherished memory of their **Virgin of Guadalupe** on December 12. This celebration, however joyful, is but one of the many fiestas that Mexicans, especially the *indígenas*, rejoice in. Each village holds its local fiesta in honor of its patron saint, who is often a thinly

their age-old Mesoamerican pantheon assume thinly disguised identities among the host of Catholic saints. Besides paying obeisance at the village church altar, Oaxacan country folks also appease mountain, water, and underworld spirits with offerings and sacrifices at sacred summits, springs, and caves. Before killing a deer, for example, a hunter often asks permission of the *señor del monte* (lord, or spirit, of the mountain). Sometimes *hechiceros* (wizards) or *ancianos* lead entire communities in cornfield ceremonies for a successful harvest, with flower veiled sit-in for some local pre-Cortesian deity. Themes appear Spanish—Christians vs. Moors, devils vs. priests—but the native element is strong, sometimes dominant. During Semana Santa (Holy Week) at Pinotepa Nacional in coastal Oaxaca, for example, Mixtec people, costumed as Jews, shoot arrows skyward, simultaneously reciting traditional Mixtec prayers.

LANGUAGE

Oaxacan Indigenous Languages

Linguists recognize 16 separate languages spoken in Oaxaca today. Experts identify each of them with one of five language families. North American language family names are conventionally derived by combining the names of the northernmost and southernmost languages of the group. Thus, Otomanguean, Oaxaca's most widespread language family, derives its label from Otomi, spoken northwest of Mexico City, and Mangue, spoken in southeast Mexico. All of Oaxaca's native language speakers occupy pretty much the same territories that they did at the time of the conquest. The Otomanguean, by location, moving generally west to east, are: **Amusgo, Chatino, Trique, Mixtec, Chocho, Ixcatec, Popoluca, Cuicatec, Mazatec, Chinantec, and Zapotec.** A language pair of eastern Oaxaca, **Mixe** (MEE-shay) and **Zoque** (SOH-kay), probably distantly related to Mayan dialects, are often lumped into a second family, the Mixe-Zoque family. Three other languages are the only representatives of their respective families.

INDIGENOUS LANGUAGES

The 2000 national census figures list populations of those over five years old who speak an indigenous Oaxacan language:

Language	Population	% of Total Oaxacans	Important Centers in Oaxaca
Zapotec	377,000	13.5%	Tlacolula, Juchitán, Pochutla
Mixtec	245,000	8.8%	Tlaxiaco, Huajuapan de León, Jamiltepec
Mazatec	174,000	6.5%	Huatla de Jiménez, Jalapa de Díaz
Chinantec	108,000	3.9%	Valle Nacional, Ojatitlán
Mixe	105,000	3.8%	Ayutla, Zacatepec
Chatino	40,000	1.4%	Nopala, Juquila
Trique	15,200	.55%	Tilapa
Huave	13,700	.49%	San Mateo del Mar, San Dionisio del Mar
Cuicatec	12,000	.43%	Cuicatlán
Nahua	11,000	.39%	Salina Cruz, Tuxtepec
Zoque	5,300	.19%	San Miguel Chimalapa, Santa María Chimalapa
Amusgo	4,800	.17%	San Pedro Amusgos
Chontal	4,600	.16%	Santiago Astata
Chocho	500	.018%	Coixtlahuaca
Popoluca	500	.018%	Santiago Chazumba
Ixcatec	200	.0072%	Ixcatlán
Totals	1,076,000	38.7%	

Nahuatl (the language of the Aztecs) of the Uto-Aztecan family; **Chontal,** of the Hokan-Coahuiltecan family; and **Huave,** of its own family, Huave.

Understanding in Oaxaca is further complicated by a proliferation of **dialects.** Mixtec speakers from Jamiltepec, on the Pacific Coast, for example, do not generally comprehend the Mixtec dialect of a town, such as Tlaxiaco, across half a dozen ridges 100 miles away. The same is true for Oaxaca's other major languages—Zapotec, Mazatec, Chinantec, and Mixe—and to a lesser degree, for the minor languages.

Few nonindigenous people, whether foreigners or Mexican, have made the intense effort required to speak and understand a Oaxacan native language. All of the Otomanguean languages, like the Chinese dialects, are **tonal.** This means that a given word takes on different meanings depending upon the pitch—low, high, rising, or falling—with which it is enunciated. Consequently, in big market towns, Spanish is often the lingua franca of buying and selling. Nevertheless, at many country markets, aware visitors

notice many people, usually older folks, who speak no Spanish at all.

Please take note that the Spanish names for the Zapotec, Mixtec, Mazatec, and Chinantec languages are *Zapoteco, Mixteco, Mazateco,* and *Chinanteco,* while the respective home territories of each group are the Zapoteca, Mixteca, Mazateca, and Chinantla.

INDIGENOUS GROUPS

Although anthropologists and census takers classify them according to language groups (such as Mixtec, Zapotec, or Nahua), *indígenas* typically identify themselves as residents of a particular locality rather than by language or ethnic grouping. And although as a group they are referred to as *indígenas* (native, or aboriginal), individuals are generally made uncomfortable (or may even feel insulted) by being labeled as such.

While the mestizos are the emergent self-conscious majority class, the *indígenas* remain mostly invisible, keeping to their country hamlets, except during town market days and

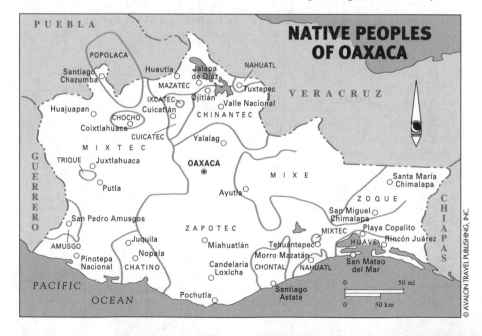

NATIVE PEOPLES OF OAXACA

PUEBLA

POPOLACA

Santiago Chazumba

Huautla Jalapa de Díaz

MAZATEC

NAHUATL

Tuxtepec

VERACRUZ

IXCATEC Ojitlán

Huajuapan Cuicatlán Valle Nacional

CHOCHO

CHINANTEC

Coixtlahuaca

CUICATEC Yalalag

MIXTEC

TRIQUE Juxtlahuaca

OAXACA

GUERRERO

Putla

MIXE

Santa María Chimalapa

Ayutla

ZOQUE

San Miguel Chimalapa

San Pedro Amusgos

ZAPOTEC

MIXTEC Playa Copalito

Rincón Juárez

CHIAPAS

AMUSGO Juquila

Miahuatlán

Tehuantepec

HUAVE

Nopala

Morro Mazatán

San Mateo del Mar

Pinotepa Nacional CHATINO

Candelaria Loxicha

CHONTAL NAHUATL

PACIFIC OCEAN

Pochutla

Santiago Astata

0   50 mi

0   50 km

fiestas. Typically, they are politically conservative, socially traditional, and tied to the land. On market day, the typical *indígena* family might make the trip into town. They bag up some tomatoes, squash, or peppers, and tie up a few chickens or a pig. The rickety country bus will often be full, and the mestizo driver may wave them away, giving preference to his friends, leaving the *indígenas* to trudge stoically along the road.

Their lot, nevertheless, has been slowly improving. *Indígena* families now often have access to a local school and a clinic. Improved health has led to a large increase in their population. Official census counts, however, probably run low. *Indígenas* are traditionally suspicious of government people, and census takers, however conscientious, seldom speak the local dialect.

Recent figures nevertheless indicate that about 40 percent of Oaxacans are *indígenas*—that is, they speak one of Oaxaca's 16 native languages. Of these, about a fifth speak no Spanish at all. These fractions, moreover, are changing only gradually. Many *indígenas* prefer the old ways.

Once a year, in mid-July, thousands of indigenous people, from hundreds of ethnically distinct Oaxaca communities, converge on Oaxaca city for the **Guelaguetza** (gay-lah-GHET-sah) folk dance festival. Dazzled by the whirling color and spectacle, visitors begin to grasp the richness and sheer magnitude of Oaxacan folk tradition. Although their diversity is staggering, the simple fact is that the majority—about three of every five—of indigenous Oaxacans speak some dialect of one of two languages, Zapotec or Mixtec. Of these, the most numerous and visible are the Zapotecs, the people whom visitors encounter first in excursions from Oaxaca city.

Zapotecs

The Spanish label "Zapoteco" comes from Aztec, rather than Zapotec tradition. The Zapotecs call themselves **Ben Zaa,** or "People of the Clouds." The Aztecs heard this as *Tsapotécatl,* or Zapote People, a less-than-flattering "fruit eater" label.

Zapotec speakers, who number upward of 400,000, make up about one-third of Oaxaca's native people. The Zapotecs, moreover, are the

Many Indigenous folks sell their handmade pottery at weekly markets.

most visible for more reasons than their numbers. In contrast to the Mixtecs, the Zapotecs, led by their kings Cosijoeza and Cosijopí, allied themselves with the Spanish right from the beginning. Nearly unique among Mexican indigenous groups, Zapotecs have figured prominently in national politics. Mexico's most beloved president, Benito Juárez, was of pure Zapotec origin. Lately, Zapotecs, including many women, have strongly influenced politics and government in the **Isthmus,** through the Coalición Obero, Campesino, y Estudiantil de Istmo, or **COCEI (Confederation of Workers, Farmers, and Students of the Isthmus).**

Zapotec influence goes much further. Although frequented by nearly all of Oaxaca's indigenous groups, a number of Oaxaca's largest native markets, such as Oaxaca city, Tlacolula, Tehuantepec, and Juchitán, are run by Zapotecs. Backcountry centers, where Zapotecs own and manage most stalls and stores, are hostile to penetration by mestizo merchants.

Individual Zapotec-speaking persons usually identify themselves more strongly with region

TAKING PEOPLE PICTURES

Like most folks everywhere, typical Oaxacan people on the street rarely appreciate strangers taking their pictures. The easiest route to overcoming this is a local friend, guide, or even a willing interpreter-bystander who can provide an introduction. Lacking that, you'll need to be at least semi-fluent in Spanish in order to introduce yourself or say something funny to break the ice.

A sometimes useful way to go is to offer to send them a copy of their picture. If they accept, make sure that you follow through. If somehow the picture doesn't come out, at least send them a picture of you, explaining why.

Although it's becoming less common, some people still believe that they might lose their souls if they let you take their picture. In such a case, humor again might help (or perhaps offering to let them take a picture of you first).

Markets are wonderful picture-taking places but pose challenges. Vendors are often resistant, to the point of hostility, if you try to take their picture behind their sumptuous pile of tomatoes or stack of baskets. The reasons aren't hard to understand. They're grumpy partly because sales are probably disappointing, and, since they have to stay put, they probably feel used. Buying something from them might go a long way toward soothing their feelings.

As for church picture-taking, remember churches are places of worship and not museums. Don't be

Markets are great places for taking pictures—but they pose challenges.

rude by trying to take pictures of people at the altar. Moreover, churches are usually dark inside, and, unless you have a flash-suppress option or unusually high-speed film, your flash will disturb worshippers.

or locale than language. (You might expect this, since the several Zapotec regional dialects are virtually separate languages, differing as much as French, Spanish, Italian, and Portuguese.) Living and work patterns, likewise, depend much more on locale—tropical coast, cool mountain, or highland valley—than ethnicity. Oaxaca's four Zapotec regions (and their important market centers), moving clockwise from Oaxaca's center, are the central valley (Oaxaca, Tlacolula, Ocotlán), northern Sierra (Ixtlán, Yalalag, Villa Alta), Isthmus (Tehuantepec, Juchitán), and southern Sierra (Miahuatlán, Pochutla).

Zapotec communities, moreover, are generally skillful at resolving disputes. If informal

means—neighborly discussion, arbitration, or the council of elders—fail, then the argument will nearly always be resolved in the local court. Blood feuds, common in some Oaxacan indigenous communities, are rare among the Zapotecs.

Although Zapotec speakers are gradually adopting new ways, many still remember the old gods, especially the god of rain, fertility, and lightning, known as **Cocijo,** in the central valley. On masks you may see him as a lizard. He controls the clouds and may even release *granizo* hail onto a wrongdoer's crops. Some southern Zapotecs visualize the world as an island in a vast sea, watched down upon by Cocijo and his retinue-hierarchy of heavenly hosts.

Other old beliefs persist. Influential animals, such as the *correcamino* (roadrunner), who brings good luck, the *tecolote* (small owl), who brings bad, and the *mariposa* (butterfly), who signifies death, are important actors in Zapotec fables. Besides mysterious incantations, Zapotec traditional healers, both men and women, use a wealth of herbal cures: wild garlic for high blood pressure, cloves for toothaches, *rosa de fandango* (a type of mint) for conception, *epazote morada* (a type of basil) for worms.

Although midwives traditionally preside over **birthing,** fathers are expected to be present to ensure a healthy baby. Pregnant women are often exhorted not to eat honey or mamey fruit. If possible, mothers are treated royally after giving birth. They traditionally remain in bed for three weeks, get plenty of massages, take *temascal* steam baths, and eat lots of chicken, chilies, and salt.

Mixtecs

It's probably not an accident that the Mixtecs' self-label, Nyu-u Sabi, "People of the Rain" (or "Clouds") has the same meaning as the Zapotecs' name for themselves. Linguists estimate that around 3,000 years ago, they were, in fact, the same people. They're not the same today, however. Their languages, although related, are mutually unintelligible, and their homelands are on opposite sides of Oaxaca.

The Mixtecs, who number around 350,000, comprise about a quarter of all Oaxacan native speakers. Nearly all live in three geographic zones in western Oaxaca: the Mixteca Baja, Mixteca Alta, and Mixteca de la Costa. The **Mixteca Baja** is the dry plateau-land basin of the Río Mixteco, which runs adjacent to the Puebla-Guerrero border, about 100 miles (160 km) west by northwest of Oaxaca city. Major centers are Santiago Juxtlahuaca in the southwest and Huajuapan de León in the north. Bordering the Mixteca Baja to the southwest is the **Mixteca Alta,** a highland of pine-tufted peaks cut by lush deep canyons. Its major market centers, moving from north to south, are Tamazulapan, Teposcolula, and Tlaxiaco. Bordering the Mixteca Alta on the south is the **Mixteca de la Costa,** a roughly 50- by 50-mile (160-sq-km)

Oxen yokes are still an important item in Oaxaca, where only about a third of the farmers have access to a tractor.

© BRUCE WHIPPERMAN

region of hills and valleys abutting the Guerrero border on the west and spreading southward from the foothills to the mangrove-fringed coastline. Its major centers are Pinotepa Nacional in the center and Santiago Jamiltepec to the east.

A few thousand Mixtec speakers also occupy a pair of intriguingly isolated enclaves: Cuyamecalco (near the market town of San Juan Chiquihuitlán) in the northern Sierra, and around Mixtequilla, the "Little Mixteca" just north of Tehuantepec, in the Isthmus.

Although Mixtec-speaking people have passed down a rich heritage, as a group they are now among Oaxaca's poorest. Of the Mixteca's three regional groupings, the people in the Costa are generally the best off. Santiago Jamiltepec, for example, where Mixtec-speakers compose 70 percent of the population, has many Mixtec shop owners, in contrast to upland Mixtec centers where mestizos often dominate commerce.

Coastal Mixtec folks congregate from miles around to trade at the spring San Andres Huaxpaltepec fair.

Exceptions notwithstanding, most Mixtecs are subsistence farmers. Agriculture is typically based on age-old **slash-and-burn,** methods. Fields lie fallow for five years, then brush is burned, cleared, and the ground planted with corn, usually employing a *coa* (digging stick). Oxen, when they are used for plowing or hauling, are often rented. Irrigation, except near valley-bottom creeks, is not common. On the coast, the warmer climate allows more options for cash crops, such as bananas, mangos, *panela* (brown sugar from cane), cotton, and peanuts, although distribution is limited and local.

Another cash possibility that Mixtecs have not generally developed is **coffee,** which mestizo, Trique, and European immigrant growers harvest successfully on the Mixteca Alta's semitropical forested mountainsides, using Mixtec day labor.

Moreover, despite their proximity to rich ocean resources, very few coastal Mixtecs fish. Instead, they buy dried fish from the many African Mexicans, descendants of African slaves, whose modest houses and fields dot the coastline.

Nevertheless, the Mixtecs seem to have cornered the **palm-frond weaving** market. In the dry Mixteca Baja, homeland to wild forests of short palms, people gather and dry the fronds, and whenever two hands are free, everyone—father, mother, children, grandmother, grandfather—weaves them into everything, from mats and hats to toys and baskets.

Lack of good roads hinders market access all over the Mixteca. A large proportion of Mixtec homesteads lie at the end of foot trails, along which produce must be hauled by hand or burro. Even if a farmer could harvest a ton of mangos (potentially worth maybe $500) from his four trees, how could he, his wife, a baby, and two children, and three neighbors haul them five miles by trail, then 20 miles by dirt road, to some market where people have the money to buy his mangos? He tells himself that maybe he and his neighbors will get together, widen the trail and buy a used truck. Yes . . . someday.

Faced with such odds, instead of saving for that someday truck, many Mixtec farmers opt to accumulate prestige by fulfilling *compadrazgo* (contributing to friends) or *mayordomía* (religious festival) obligations. Although such charitable action often leads to poverty, generosity, in the Mixtec (and Mexican) mind is, after all, much preferable to parsimony.

Coastal Mixtec women enjoy an unusual degree of autonomy. Besides often handling family purse strings and doing all the marketing, they typically keep their own family names and own property independently of their husbands. For some Mixteca Alta and Mixteca Baja men, traveling to the coast is believed to be dangerous, partly for fear that some Costa Mixteca woman, through witchcraft, might steal (or disable) their penis. So, men, watch out for the women, especially around the Pinotepa Nacional market, where they often wear their best finery, which customarily includes an heirloom *pozahuanco* wraparound skirt of brilliant natural-dyed red cochineal and deep purple horizontal stripes. From afar, you'll easily recognize them, carrying themselves proudly, with their hat-like *jícara* gourd bowl tipped whimsically on their heads. Some women sell handloomed *pozahuancos* in the market. The authentic ones, by which coastal Mixtec women judge each other, sell for $150 or more.

Mazatecs

In contrast to the Zapotecs and Mixtecs, the Mazatec territory, the **Mazateca,** is relatively concentrated into a roughly 35- by 50-mile (56- by 80-km) corner at Oaxaca's very northern tip. Mazatec villages and farms spread across two very fertile climatic zones: lush semitropical forested uplands and tropical rainforest river bottomland of the Papaloapan River basin. Major market centers are **Jalapa de Díaz and Huautla de Jiménez,** both in the western highlands. Important subsidiary centers, many in the highlands around Huautla, are Cosolapa, Santa María Chilchotla, Huehuetlán, Eloxotitlán, San José Tenango, Mazatlán, Chiquihuitlán, and Ayautla. The eastern lowland has no dominant Mazatec center, partly because of the displacement of thousands of families during construction of the Miguel Alemán Dam. Although the Mazatecs' homeland spills over into neighboring Puebla and Veracruz states, around 170,000, or about 90 percent, live in Oaxaca.

The Mazatecs' own name for their homeland, **Ampaad,** which translates as the "Place Where the People Are Born," reflects their own creation myth. Legends say that the great tropical trees of Ampaad gave birth to three types of people: giants; ordinary-size humans, who became the present Mazatecs; and smaller people, who became the monkeys. The label "Mazatec" derives from the Aztec Nahuatl language and translates as "People of the Deer."

Left largely to themselves, the Mazatecs have retained many of their own traditions. Many of these they hold in common with their Chocho-, Popoloca-, and Ixcatec-speaking neighbors, whose tongues linguists sometimes lump into a Mazatec-language subfamily. Their isolation has left Mazatec speakers among the least hispanicized of Oaxacans; as a group, as many as 40 percent speak little or no Spanish.

In 1944, government planners initiated the **Papaloapan Project,** which called for a huge hydroelectric works in the Mazatec heartland. The project's centerpiece, christened as the Miguel Alemán Dam and Reservoir in 1955, created a mammoth lake in the Mazatec lowland, drowning hundreds of thousands of acres of fertile Papaloapan basin forest and farmland. Although water and electric power were the projected benefits, the human cost turned out to be enormous. Mazatec society was torn by the forced removal of 22,000 poor Mazatec people to unfamiliar, often undesirable territory. Fortunately, the rest of the Mazatec population, largely in the western highlands around Huautla de Jiménez, remained undisrupted. Mexican authorities have since generally avoided such socially disruptive mega-projects.

Although most Mazatec families are subsistence corn, bean, and squash farmers, many cultivate fruits (mango, mamey, *zapote,* papaya, banana, and avocado) and coffee as cash crops on their fertile acreage. Although some farmer cooperatives have found national and international markets for their fruit and coffee, many individuals seem content to sell their produce for low local prices at Huatla de Jiménez and other Mazateca markets.

Mazatec women are renowned for their costumes and adornments. At markets and festivals especially, watch for them in their famously bright *huipiles,* horizontally striped in the middle, vertically on the sides. Beneath the *huipil* they often wear a loom-woven blue and white horizontally striped skirt. Their hair is also part of their decoration. They keep it soft and dark with a preparation called *pistle,* made from the core of the mamey fruit, and typically braid it with bright ribbons. Many women take pride in their home embroidery and hand-woven cotton, silk, and wool, which they sometimes sell at markets.

As in the past, scarcity of priests weakens Catholic influence in the Mazateca. Priestly visits are so rare that many Mazatec campesino couples have two or three children by the time they enjoy a Catholic church wedding ceremony. When a priest does arrive, rustic churches are customarily thronged with husbands and wives bringing children for baptism. For the ceremony, they buy a small lead cross, which they hang with a bright ribbon around their child's neck. In addition to Catholic baptism, Mazatec parents sometimes ask a diviner to read the ancient *tonalpohualli* 260-day ritual calendar to discover their newborn's *tona* or *tono* guardian spirit.

Mazatec people often gather for non-Catholic religious rites in fields and at sacred springs, caves, or mountains. Mazatec people especially venerate El Rabón peak, which towers over Jalapa de Díaz, and whose .6-mile-high (one-km) vertical rock wall is said never to have been scaled. There on that lofty summit live the *dueñes* (earth spirits), who must be appeased with prayers and *copal* incense for the return of lost souls. In the Mazateca lowland, *brujos* (witch doctors) carry out similar ceremonies at Cabeza de Tilpan cave near San José Tenango.

Traditional *curandero* or *curandera* healers are very busy in the Mazateca. Among their weapons against illness, many include natural forest-gathered hallucinogens. Common are *hongos alucinantes* (hallucinogenic mushrooms), *semillas de la Virgen* (seeds of the Virgin) or *ololiuhqui,* and *hojas*

de la pastora (leaves of the shepherdess). These, used by either the patient or the healer, will induce enlightening visions that may lead to a cure.

Chinantecs

Although Oaxaca's approximately 100,000 Chinantec-speaking people live on some of Mexico's best-watered land, the majority are poor. Inaccessibility, tropical forests that were not easily tillable, and lack of gold or silver relegated the Chinantecs to the margin during colonial times. The Chinantecs' homeland, the **Chinantla,** is a 70- by 40-mile (112- by 64-km) region around the important market town of **Valle Nacional,** in northeast Oaxaca. The Chinantla's natural division into eastern lowland (Chinantla Grande) and western upland (Chinantla Pichinche) was apparent to the first Spanish arrivals in the 1520s. For the Spanish conquistadores, the Chinantecs weren't pushovers. After years of seesaw skirmishes, the Spanish mounted their final push at Yetzelalag. Chinantec legend recounts that at the battle's height the Chinantec warriors invoked their gods, who opened the mountain, allowing them to escape. Nevertheless, the Chinantecs submitted to three centuries of labor on Spanish tobacco and sugarcane plantations and cattle ranches.

Although the Spanish colonial policy of *congregación* led to the abandonment of many original town sites, the upland Chinantla retained a number of important market centers. Among the most important and colorful are Sochiapan, Tlacozintepec, Usila, Quiotepec, and San Pedro Yolox in the western uplands; Valle Nacional and San Lucas Ojitlán in the center; and Petlalpa, Lalana, and Jocotepec in the southwest lowlands.

During the 19th century, new colonists introduced coffee, pineapple, and rice agriculture, which, with the Papaloapan Project, continues in modern form today. Although the project forced painful relocations on thousands of lowland Mazatec and Chinantec peoples, it ended their isolation. Government jobs, schools, clinics, electricity, and sanitary and water systems changed life forever in the Chinantec lowlands. At the height of the disorder, swarms of protests erupted. Oaxacan bishops denounced government relocation efforts: "The *indígenas* continue to be the ones always exploited, those who must pay the price of any progress."

For good or bad, the Papaloapan Project lifted the native residents' health, literacy, and general standard of living at the expense of erasing many of their age-old ways of life. In contrast to the Chinantla highlands, few traditional markets function in the lower Chinantla. On the other hand, the government-planned communal and corporate plantations have greatly increased productivity. The Chinantla regularly produces the lion's share of Oaxaca's tobacco, rice, sugarcane, chilies, and pineapples. The workers, however, receive only a minimum of the benefits. Most profits flow to the government agencies, which control everything—seeds, planting, credit, harvesting, and marketing.

Nevertheless, tradition still rules in much of the upper Chinantla. In the minds of many Chinantec-speakers, the old fertility gods **"Father and Mother Maize"** still command the rain even though their prayers are Catholic. The cosmos is still a battleground between day, ruled by the young and vigorous sun, and night, ruled by the twinkling old stars. Some still believe that Creation's original people, who refused to bow down before the god-sun, were changed to monkeys and banished to the forest forever for their error. In some villages, *rayos*, powerful members of lightning cults, can still hurl lightning bolts against neighboring villages and know how to defend the home village against reverse attacks.

Mixes and Zoques

Their cultural and common Mayan linguistic linkages have led most experts to believe that the original Mixe and Zoque (MEE-shay and SOH-kay) people, together with the Popoluca of present Veracruz state, occupied a single territory. Invasions, first by the Zapotecs and Aztecs and then the Spanish forced the present territorial divisions. The Mixes (population around 100,000) occupy the mountainous belt that stretches about 100 miles (160 km) from the central valley's eastern edge to the most easterly Mixe center, San Juan Guichicovi, several miles short of the cross-Isthmus highway-rail line. Thirty-five miles (55

km) farther east, Zoque territory (population around 5,000), divided between two sprawling *ejido* grants, begins. From the Santa María Chimalapa–San Miguel Chimalapa line it spreads east, across the wild Chimalapas mountainous jungle to the Chiapas border. The few remaining Popoluca-speakers are limited to a few isolated villages in eastern Veracruz state.

Despite several costly campaigns, the Spanish force of arms never really conquered the Mixes. If they were conquered at all, it was by 16th-century Dominican missionaries who accomplished with kindness what Spanish guns and steel could not. By the end of the colonial era, they had established nine vicarages, among them Juquila Mixes, San Miguel Quetzaltepec, Asunción Puxmecatan, Ayutla, and San Juan Guichicovi, which all remain important Mixe market towns. Ayutla, closest to the central valley, is dominant.

Anthropologists generally describe Mixe traditions as "less developed" than other Oaxacan groups. They describe a "culture unsuited to the environment," as if the Mixe ways of life first flowered in fairer, more fertile lands and never completely adjusted to the cold, marginal, mountainous regions where the Mixes fled in the face of foreign invasions. Such a speculation also explains the Mixes' well-known wariness and avoidance of outside contact. The Zoque, by contrast, adapted relatively easily to Spanish ways and share little of the Mixes' shyness.

Spanish attempts to congregate the Mixes into towns were only minimally successful. Mixe people largely moved back into the countryside, leaving little-used empty houses in town. Today most live in country hamlets clinging to mountainsides, with individual houses built on level stilt platforms.

Turbulence has marred the Mixes' recent history. In 1938, President Lázaro Cárdenas wanted to reward the Mixe people for their support of the Republic against the infamous 1865 French Intervention. He persuaded the Oaxaca legislature to award them semi-autonomous status in an all-Mixe district. However, a dispute broke out over the location of the district capital. The towns of Ayutla, Cacalotepec, and Zacatepec had their leading supporters, but **Luis Rodríguez** of Zacatepec was the most ruthless. While the others protested weakly, he led a four-year reign of terror—kidnapping, cattle rustling, torture, murder, and pillage—with the implicit support of Governor Vicente González. In 1943, Rodríguez cut off the feet and tongue of one prominent opponent and had another assassinated on the steps of the Government Palace in Oaxaca city. Enough was enough for Governor Sánchez Canom, who left Oaxaca city to intervene. But while he was gone, Rodríguez got him replaced. After that, Rodríguez was in complete control, murdering opponents with impunity, collecting tribute from towns and even 10 percent from religious fiestas and holding 500 prisoners in forced labor. Even after his death in 1952, his heirs tried to extend their reign until the 1970s. Despite Luis Rodríguez's notorious legacy, **Zacatepec** remains the Mixe district capital to the present day.

In 1972, partly in response to the trouble, Mixe people organized themselves into the grassroots social-political Federación Mixe. They soon coalesced with the already-existing local Worker's Federation of Chinantecs, Zapotecs, and Mixes and the national General Union of Workers and Farmers of Mexico (UGOCM).

Mixe and Zoque social traditions closely follow Mesoamerican patterns. Mixe religion has striking parallels to those described in the Maya sacred book, the *Popol Vuh.* Their legends say that the Mixe god **Kondoy** was hatched from an egg, grew rapidly, and traveled, battling Aztec armies. He returned and arranged the world in the Mixe image, then retired to the Mixe sacred mountain, **Zempoaltepetl,** where he still lives.

Belief in the *nagual* persists among the Mixes. If an unbaptized baby dies, the parents must make haste to bury the body immediately, with little ceremony. If not, the spirit of the unbaptized baby might escape and become a *nagual,* a malevolent animal that will harm people who cross its path. Sometimes the *nagual* takes human form as a witch that can transform itself into an animal or other scary form and cause general mischief and illness by infusing some type of object into the victim's body. Traditional

healers combine a number of remedies, such as *temascal* steam bathing, rubbing with herbs, prayers, sucking, and vision-inducing plants, to remove such infusions.

Chatinos

The southern Sierra country of the nearly 40,000 strong Chatinos is a 1,200-square-mile (3,072-sq-km) enclave surrounded by Mixtecs on the west, Zapotecs on the north and east, and mestizos and African-Mexicans on the south coast. Their language, part of the Zapotec subfamily, resembles Sierra Zapotec. Chatino market centers, besides the central and dominant **Santa Catarina Juquila,** are Panixtlahuaca, San Juan Quiahije, San Pedro Juchatengo, Nopala, and Zacatepec. Besides its commercial and political influence, Santa Catarina Juquila is a major pilgrimage center, especially for the hundreds of thousands of faithful who arrive on December 8 to honor their beloved Virgin of Juquila.

Most Chatino families are subsistence farmers; Zapotec and mestizo traders dominate commerce in the market centers. In addition to the customary corn, beans, and squash, farmers also cultivate coffee, either as day laborers or on their own land, in which case they sell the surplus for cash at the market.

Amusgos

The approximately 30- by 30-mile (48- by 48-km) Amusgo territory straddles the Oaxaca-Guerrero border. Only about 5,000 of 40,000 Amusgo speakers live in Oaxaca, around the small centers of Cacahuatepec and San Pedro Amusgos, while the remainder live on the Guerrero side, near the centers of Ometepec, Xochistlahuaca, and Tlacoachistlahuaca.

Linguists reckon that the Amusgo language, a member of the Mixtec language subfamily, separated from Mixtec between 2000 and 1000 B.C. Around A.D. 1000 the Amusgos came under the domination of the strong coastal Mixtec kingdom of Tututepec. In 1457 they were conquered by the Aztecs and not long after, by the Spanish in the 1520s. Decimation of the Amusgo population by disease during the 16th century led to the importation of African slave labor, whose descendants, known locally as *negros* or *costeños* live along the Guerrero-Oaxaca coastline.

Although the Amusgo population eventually recovered, many of the old colonial-era haciendas remained intact until modern times. The Amusgos, isolated from the mainstream of modern Mexican life, retain their age-old corn-bean-squash farming tradition. Moreover, they have received little attention from anthropologists or archaeologists, although several likely archaeological mounds exist near Amusgo villages.

Amusgo women are nevertheless famous for their hand-embroidered *huipiles,* whose colorful floral and animal designs fetch willing customers in Oaxaca tourist centers. Even better, Amusgo women often wear their *huipiles,* appearing as heavenly visions of spring on dusty small-town side streets.

Triques

About 50 miles (80 km) farther north from the Amusgo territory, about 15,000 Trique (TREE-kay) people live in their 20- by 15-mile (32- by 24-km) highland pocket of the Mixteca Alta. You'll see plenty of them in the **Juxtlahuaca** town market—especially Trique women—selling their brilliant red-striped wool *huipiles* in the middle of the town square. Long ago, the Trique fled into the mountain vastness, from first Mixtec, then Aztec, and finally Spanish invaders. Some of their main centers are San Isidro Chicahuaxtla, San Juan Copala, and Tilapa, all south of Juxtlahuaca and north of Putla de Guerrero.

The Trique have only grudgingly accepted outside authority. Rebellions broke out often during the colonial era and later. In 1843 Trique forces rebelled against state and federal authorities, who needed five years to jail and execute the responsible leaders. Subsequently, during the later 19th and 20th centuries, coffee became a major Trique product and coffee beans became their money, which traders turned into alcohol and guns. Rebellion, which again required federal forces to suppress, broke out in Copala in 1956. The federal garrison remains in Copala to the present day.

Only at Chicahuaxtla, in the high Mixteca

country (just off of Highway 125, about 25 miles, 40 km west of Tlaxiaco), did Christianity have much effect. This was due to the compassionate persuasion of Father Gonzales Lucero hundreds of years ago. Consequently, much of the Trique's folklore survives to the present day. An oft-told creation myth describes the sun and the moon, gods who once lived in a *calabaza* (calabash), but who broke out and rode a rabbit and a cat into the heavens to light the world. Around March 25, traditional *curanderos* lead services to appease the old gods at a sacred cave near Copala, about 13 miles (20 km) down the highway south of Juxtlahuaca. They sacrifice a lamb and a goat while the gathered crowd offers incense and flowers.

Chochos, Ixcatecs, and Popolucas

Emigration and Spanish literacy are fast reducing the number of speakers of Chocho, Ixcatec, and Popoluca, three related tongues of the dry canyon-lands of the northwest Oaxaca. Of the three, the Chocho people are dominant in their extensive homeland around Coixtlahuaca and subsidiary centers of Tequixtepec and Tepelmeme. If you're going to hear any of the Chocho language, it will probably be in the market at **Tepelmeme de Morelos,** just off the Oaxaca-Puebla expressway about 15 miles (24 km) north of Coixtlahuaca.

Defeated by the Mixtecs in the 1300s and the Aztecs a hundred years later, the Chochos were again subdued by Spanish conquistadores Orozco and Alvarado in 1522 and later converted by Dominican Father Fermín Abrego. Coixtlahuaca was a thriving Chocho and Ixcatec market until around 1900, but loss of topsoil to erosion has forced many families to emigrate.

If you're going to hear any Ixcatec at all, it will be in **Ixcatlán,** the sole Ixcatec *municipio,* accessible by dirt road about 20 miles (32 km) northeast from Coixtlahuaca. The same is approximately true of Popoluco, whose few remaining speakers in Oaxaca live in the sliver of territory by the Puebla border, around Santiago Chazumba on Highway 125.

Cuicatecs

The Cuicatec language, by contrast, is holding its own, due to the isolation and richness of the homeland of the Cuicatecos ("People of Song"). About 15,000 Cuicatec people inhabit their present territory, mainly the *municipios* of Concepción Pápalo, San Juan Tepeuxila, San Pedro Teutila, and Santiago Nacaltepec in the mountains east of district capital **Cuicatlán** and south of the Santo Domingo River canyon.

Archaeological digs around Pápalo and other sites reveal Toltec influences, hinting that the Cuicatec lands may have been a haven for some of the refugees from the fall of Tula, the Toltec capital in the north, around A.D. 1060.

Historians believe that Cuicatec speakers numbered about 60,000 before the conquest. They were defeated by both the Aztecs, around 1456, and Spanish soldiers, commanded by conquistador Martín Mezquita in 1526. Nevertheless, during the colonial era the Cuicatecs resisted both Catholic conversion and forced plantation labor by fleeing into the mountains, where they remain today. Although the Dominicans established a church in Pápalo in 1630 and tried to convert them, Catholic influence remains weak. The old gods, notably já iko, the lord of their sacred mountain, **Cerro Cheve**, still live on in the hearts and minds of many Cuicatec people.

Today you might hear some Cuicatec spoken at the busy market at Cuicatlán, where Cuicatec women come down from the mountains to sell their highland handicrafts: wool serapes and jackets, flower- and animal-motif embroidered *huipiles*, and palm-leaf sombreros, *petates*, and *cestas* (hats, mats, and baskets, respectively).

Cuicatec people also earn cash collectively from the concession in which they allow the paper mill in Tuxtepec to harvest some of their forest trees. The money goes to finance community projects.

Huaves

The Isthmus territory of the Huave people encompasses the shoreline of the big tidal **Lagunas Superior, Inferior,** and the **Mar Muerto.** About 15,000 Huave-speaking people live there, notably around the villages of **San Mateo del Mar, Santa María del Mar, San Dionisio del Mar,** and San Francisco del Mar.

The Huave language, not clearly identified with any other language family, is generally classified in a family of its own. This is supported by studies by colonial historians, indicating that the Huave may have migrated from the Nicaraguan Pacific Coast and settled around present-day Jalapa del Marqués on the Isthmus. The more numerous Zapotecs, invading around 1375, forced them to the edges of the lagoons, where they now live.

Generally ignored and neglected by everyone, the Huaves hold on to many pre-conquest beliefs. In the absence of Catholic priests, native *curanderos* practice thinly veiled pagan rites in some village churches.

Although they subsist mainly on corn, beans, chilies, vegetables, and occasional meat, Huave-speaking people earn cash from their fish catches. Men sell fresh fish to wholesalers who arrive afternoons at the shoreline villages, while women sell the surplus as dried fish at Salina Cruz, Tehuantepec, and Juchitán markets.

Nahuas

Along the coast, in a 20-mile (32-km) strip west of Salina Cruz and with the small town of Morro de Mazatán at its center, lies an enclave of Nahua (Nahuatl- or Aztec-speaking people). Besides this small region, several thousand more Nahuatl speakers live in two other small Oaxaca enclaves in the north, one around Tuxtepec and the other next to the Puebla border, wedged between Mazatec, Ixcatec, Chocho, and Popoluca territories. Such Nahuatl enclaves are probably remnants of early colonies established by the Aztec emperors after their armed expansion into Oaxaca in the 1400s.

Chontals

Finally, a few miles farther west lies the Chontal (sometimes known as "Tequistlatec") territory. The Chontals are most visible on the coast, at **Santiago Astata** and **San Pedro Huamelula.** Today, about 25,000 speakers of Chontal, a language of the Hokan language family (widespread, from the north Gulf Coast to Central America) live in their approximately 1,000-square-mile (2,560-sq-km) domain.

The Chontals are among the least modernized of Oaxaca indigenous groups. They have always tenaciously resisted invasion (although many in the zone due west of Tequisistlán have adopted the Zapotec language). Although many live near the coast, they do little fishing. They live mostly by corn-based subsistence farming, emigrating to the Isthmus or elsewhere for cash employment.

Relatively unaffected by Catholicism, their traditions remain strong. A popular fable is of their folk-hero **King Fane Kansini,** whom, legend says, an elderly couple hatched as an infant from an egg that they had found. The old couple soon discovered that the infant had supernatural powers. As he matured, Fane Kansini acquired the burning desire to save his people from the Zapotecs. He invented body armor and a wondrous new kind of arrow, which he used to defeat the Zapotec king in battle and thus save the Chontal people from annihilation. The Chontal-Zapotec mutual enmity continues to the present time.

On the Road

ON THE BEACH

It's easy to understand why many Oaxaca vacationers stay right at the beach. And not just at the popular crystalline stretches around the Bahías de Huatulco, Puerto Ángel, and Puerto Escondido. Some adventurers flee the resorts to find even more pristine strands hidden in far corners along the entire Oaxaca coast. There they discover solitude and wildlife-rich shorelines varying from mangrove-edged lagoons and algae-decorated tidepools to shoals of pebbles and sand of a dozen colors and consistencies.

Sand makes the beach, and Oaxaca has plenty, from warm, black mica dust to cool, velvety, white coral. Some beaches drop steeply to tur-bulent, close-in surf fine for fishing. Others are level, with gentle, rolling breakers made for surfing and swimming.

Oaxaca's beaches yield fascinating troves of shells and treasures of flotsam and jetsam. **Beachcombing** is more rewarding during the summer storm season when big waves deposit acres of fresh shells—among them clams, combs of Venus, conch, cowries, limpets, olives, sand dollars, scallops, starfish, and whelks.

During the summer–fall rainy season, beaches near river mouths are often fantastic outdoor galleries of wind- and water-sculpted snags and giant logs deposited by the downstream flood.

Viewing Wildlife

Wildlife watchers should keep quiet and always be on the alert. Animal survival depends on them seeing you first. Occasional spectacular offshore sights, such as whales, dolphins, and manta rays, or an onshore giant constrictor, beached squid or octopus, crocodile, or even a jaguar looking for turtle eggs may reward those prepared to wait and watch for them. Don't forget your binoculars and Steve Howell and Sophie Webb's *A Guide to the Birds of Mexico and Northern America.* (See Suggested Reading.)

WATER SPORTS

Swimming, surfing, windsurfing, snorkeling, scuba diving, and kayaking are Oaxaca's water sports of choice. For details on local conditions, favorite spots, equipment, and rental shops, see the travel chapters.

Safety First

As viewed from Oaxaca beaches, the Pacific Ocean usually lives up to its name. Many protected inlets, safe for child's play, dot the coastline. **Unsheltered shorelines,** on the other hand, can be deceiving. Smooth water in the calm forenoon often changes to choppy in the afternoon; calm ripples lapping the shore in March can grow to hurricane-driven walls of water in November. Such storms can wash away sand, changing a wide, gently sloping beach into a steep, rocky one plagued by turbulent waves and treacherous currents.

Undertow, whirlpools, crosscurrents, and occasional oversized waves can make ocean swimming a fast-lane adventure. Getting unexpectedly swept out to sea or hammered onto the beach bottom by a surprise breaker are potential hazards.

Never attempt serious swimming when tipsy or full of food; *never* swim alone where someone can't see you. *Always* swim beyond the breakers (which come in sets of several, climaxed by a big one, which breaks highest and farthest from the beach). If you happen to get caught in the path of such a breaker, avoid it by *diving under* and letting it roll harmlessly over you. If you do get caught by a serious breaker, try to roll and tumble with it (as football players tumble) to avoid injury.

Poisonous sea snakes, although rare and shy, do inhabit Oaxaca waters. Much more common,

SPRINGS, CAVES, AND WATERFALLS

A trove of crystalline springs, limestone caves, and gushing waterfalls fills the state of Oaxaca. Refer to the specific destination chapters for details (* means especially recommended):

Around the Valley of Oaxaca: *Hierve El Agua, *San Sebastián las Grutas

Pacific Resorts and Southern Sierra: Chacalapa, Balneario El Paraiso, Santa María Xadani, Atotonilco Hot Springs, Charco Atotonilco Hot Springs

The Mixteca: *Apoala, *Tamazulapan, *Juxtlahuaca (Laguna Encantada), Yosundua (Cascada Esmeralda)

Northern Oaxaca: Ixtlán de Juárez (Arco de Yagela), Valle Nacional (*Balnearios Monte Flor and El Zuzul), San José Chiltepec, Jalapa de Díaz (*Río Uluapa), Huautla de Jiménez (Las Regaderas, Nindo-Ga-Gé, and Sotano de San Agustín)

The Isthmus: Jalapa de Marqués, *Magdalena Tlacotepec, *Santiago Laollaga

especially around submerged rocks, is the **moray eel.** Don't stick your fingers or toes in any concealed cracks.

Now and then, swimmers get a nettle-like **jellyfish sting.** Be careful around coral reefs and beds of sea urchins; corals can sting (like jellyfish), and you can get infections from coral cuts and sea-urchin spines. Shuffle along sandy bottoms to scare away stingrays before stepping on one. If you're unlucky, its venomous tail spines may inflict a painful wound.

First Aid: If you suffer a coral scratch or jellyfish sting, experts advise you to wash the afflicted area with ocean (not fresh) water and pour alcohol (rubbing alcohol or a liquor, such as *mescal,* tequila, or *aguardiente*), if available, over the wound, then apply hydrocortisone cream from your first-aid kit or the *farmacia.*

© BRUCE WHIPPERMAN

Sand makes the beach, and Oaxaca has plenty.

Injuries from sea urchin spines and sting-ray barbs are both painful and sometimes serious. Physicians recommend similar first aid for both: First remove the spines or barbs by hand or with tweezers, then soak the injury in hot-as-possible fresh water to weaken the toxins and provide relief. Another method is to rinse the area with an antibacterial solution—rubbing alcohol, vinegar, wine, or ammonia diluted with water. If none is available, the same effect may be achieved by rinsing with urine, either your own or someone else's in your party. Get medical help immediately.

Snorkeling and Scuba Diving

Many exciting clear-water sites, such as the Bahías de Huatulco and Playa Estacahuite at Puerto Ángel and Playa Angelito in Puerto Escondido, await both beginner and expert snorkelers and divers. Veteran divers usually arrive during the dry winter and early spring when river outflows are mere trickles, leaving offshore waters clear. In Huatulco and Puerto Escondido, professional dive shops rent equipment, provide lessons and guides, and transport divers to choice sites.

While convenient, rented equipment is often less than satisfactory. To be sure, serious divers

bring their own gear. This might include wetsuits in the winter, when some swimmers begin to feel cold after an unprotected half hour in the water.

Surfing, Sailing, Windsurfing, and Kayaking

Oaxaca has the Mexican Pacific's acknowledged best surfing beach, the renowned **Playa Zicatela** "pipeline" at Puerto Escondido. The surf everywhere is highest and most exciting during the July–November hurricane season, when big swells from storms far out at sea attract platoons of surfers to favored beaches.

Sailboarders, sailboaters, and kayakers—who, by contrast, require more tranquil waters—do best in the Oaxaca winter or early spring. Then they gather to enjoy the near-ideal conditions at many coves and inlets near the resorts.

While beginners can have fun with the equipment available from rental shops, serious surfers, sailboarders, sailboaters, and kayakers should pack their own gear.

POWER SPORTS

Power sports, such as waterskiing, parasailing, and personal watercraft riding, are not widespread

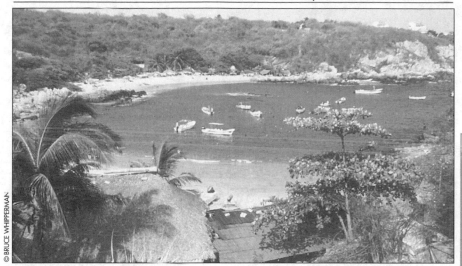

© BRUCE WHIPPERMAN

Bahía Puerto Angelito in Puerto Escondido is a favorite for sunbathers, snorkelers, and picnickers.

on Oaxaca beaches. In parasailing, a motorboat pulls while a parachute lifts you, like a soaring gull, high over the ocean. After 10 minutes, they deposit you (usually gently) back on the sand. Personal watercraft are like snowmobiles except they operate on water, where, with a little practice, even beginners can quickly learn to whiz over the waves.

Although the luxury hotels at Huatulco provide experienced crews and equipment for such activities, practice while sober and with caution. Moreover, you, as the paying patron, have a right to expect that your providers and crew are themselves both cautious and sober besides being well-equipped.

Beach Buggies and ATVs

Some visitors enjoy racing along the beach and rolling over dunes with beach buggies and ATVs (all-terrain vehicles—*motos* in Mexico), balloon-tired, three- or four-wheeled motor scooters, and mini-jeeps. While certain resort rental agencies cater to the growing use of such vehicles, limits are in order. Of all the proliferating high-horsepower beach pastimes, these are the most intrusive. Noise, exhaust and gasoline pollution, injuries to operators and bystanders, scattering of

wildlife and destruction of their habitats have led (and I hope will continue to lead) to the restriction of beach buggies and ATVs on beaches and in forest habitats.

TENNIS AND GOLF

Most Oaxacans are working too hard to be playing much tennis and golf. Consequently, tennis and golf courses are nearly completely restricted to Oaxaca city and the Bahías de Huatulco. If you are planning on a lot of golf and tennis, check into one of the several Oaxaca city or Huatulco hotels with easy access to these facilities. Use of hotel tennis courts is sometimes included in your hotel tariff. If not, fees will run about $10 per hour. Golf greens fees, which begin at about $50 for 18 holes, are usually extra.

FISHING

Experts agree that the Oaxaca coast is a world-class deep-sea and surf fishing ground. Sportfishing enthusiasts routinely bring in dozens of species from among the several hundred that have been identified in Oaxaca waters.

ON THE ROAD

© BRUCE WHIPPERMAN

Although Playa Zicatela in Puerto Escondido is the mecca, surfing is fine at many other Oaxaca beaches, such as at Playa Chacahua, shown.

Surf Fishing

Most good fishing beaches away from the immediate resort areas will typically have only a few locals (mostly with nets) and fewer visitors. Oaxacans do little sportfishing. Most either make their living from fishing or do none at all. Some local folks catch fish for supper with nets. Consequently, few Oaxaca shops sell fishing equipment. Plan to bring your own, including hooks, lures, line, and weights.

In any case, the cleaner the water, the more interesting your catch. On a good day, your reward might be *sierras, cabrillas,* porgies, or pompanos pulled from the Oaxaca surf.

You can't have everything, however. Foreigners cannot legally take Mexican abalone, clams, coral, lobster, rock bass, sea fans, seashells, shrimp, or turtles. Neither are they supposed to buy them directly from fishermen.

Deep-Sea Fishing

Santa Cruz de Huatulco, and to a lesser extent, Salina Cruz and Puerto Ángel, are well-known jumping-off-spots for the big prize marlin and sailfish.

A deep-sea boat charter generally includes the boat and crew for a full or half day, plus equipment and bait for 2–6 persons, not including food or drinks. The full-day price depends upon the season. Around Christmas and New Year and before Easter (when reservations will be mandatory), a boat can run $400 at Huatulco, less during low seasons and at the other spots.

Renting an entire big boat is not the only choice. *Pangas,* outboard launches seating up to six passengers, are available for as little as $40, depending on the season. Once, six of my friends hired a *panga* for $50, had a great time, and came back with a boatload of big tuna, jack, and mackerel. A restaurant cooked them up as a banquet for a dozen of us in exchange for the extra fish, and I discovered for the first time how heavenly fresh *sierra veracruzana* can taste.

Bringing Your Own Boat

If you're going to be doing lots of fishing, your own boat may be your most flexible and economical option. One big advantage is you can go to the many excellent fishing grounds the charter boats do not frequent. Keep your

FISH

A bounty of fish dart, swarm, jump, and wriggle in Oaxaca's surf, reefs, lagoons, and offshore depths. While many make delicious dinners (albacore, red snapper, pompano), others are tough (sailfish), bony (bonefish), and even poisonous (puffers). Some grow to half-ton giants (marlin, Goliath fish), while others are diminutive reefgrazers (parrot fish, damselfish, angelfish) whose bright colors delight snorkelers and divers. Here's a sampling of what you might find underwater or on your dinner plate.

albacore *(albacora, atún):* 2–4 feet in size; blue; found in deep waters; excellent taste

angelfish *(ángel):* one foot; yellow, orange, blue; reef fish*

barracuda *(barracuda, picuda):* two feet; brown; deep waters; good taste

black marlin *(marlin negro):* six feet; blue-black; deep waters; good taste

blue marlin *(marlin azul):* eight feet; blue; deep waters; poor taste

bobo *(barbudo):* one foot; blue, yellow; found in surf; fair taste

bonefish *(macabi):* one foot; blue or silver; found inshore; poor taste

bonito *(bonito):* two feet; black; deep waters; good taste

butterfly fish *(muñeca):* six inches; black, yellow; reef fish*

chub *(chopa):* one foot; gray; reef fish; good taste

croaker *(corvina):* two feet; brownish; found along inshore bottoms; rare and protected

damselfish *(castañeta):* four inches; brown, blue, orange; reef fish*

dolphinfish, mahimahi *(dorado):* three feet; green, gold; deep waters; good taste

grouper *(garropa):* three feet; brown, rust; found offshore and in reefs; good taste

grunt *(burro):* eight inches; black, gray; found in rocks, reefs*

jack *(toro):* 1–2 feet; bluish-gray; offshore; good taste

mackerel *(sierra):* two feet; gray with gold spots; offshore; good taste

mullet *(lisa):* two feet; gray; found in sandy bays; good taste

needlefish *(agujón):* three feet; blue-black; deep waters; good taste

Pacific porgy *(pez de pluma):* 1–2 feet; tan; found along sandy shores; good taste

parrot fish *(perico, pez loro):* one foot; green, pink, blue, orange; reef fish

pompano *(pómpano):* one foot; gray; inshore bottoms; excellent taste

puffer *(botete):* eight inches; brown; inshore; poisonous

red snapper *(huachinango, pargo):* 1–2 feet; reddish pink; deep waters; excellent taste

roosterfish *(pez gallo):* three feet; black, blue; deep waters; excellent taste

sailfish *(pez vela):* five feet; blue-black; deep waters; poor taste

sardine *(sardina):* eight inches; blue-black; offshore; good taste

sea bass *(cabrilla):* 1–2 feet; brown, ruddy; reef and rock crevices; good taste

shark *(tiburón):* 2–10 feet; black to blue; in- and offshore; good taste

snook *(robalo):* 2–3 feet; black-brown; found in brackish lagoons; excellent taste

spadefish *(chambo):* one foot; black-silver; found along sandy bottoms; reef fish*

swordfish *(pez espada):* five feet; black to blue; deep waters; good taste

triggerfish *(pez puerco):* 1–2 feet; blue, rust, brown, black; reef fish; excellent taste

wahoo *(peto, guahu):* 2–5 feet; green to blue; deep waters; excellent taste

yellowfin tuna *(atún amarilla):* 2–5 feet; blue, yellow; deep waters; excellent taste

yellowtail *(jurel):* 2–4 feet; blue, yellow; offshore; excellent taste

*fish that are generally too small to be considered edible

equipment simple, scout around, and keep your eyes peeled and ears open for local regulations and customs, plus tide, wind, and fish-edibility information.

Fishing Licenses and Boat Permits

Anyone 16 or older who is either fishing or riding in a fishing boat in Mexico is required to have a fishing license. Although Mexican fishing licenses are obtainable from certain travel and insurance agents or at government fishing offices everywhere along the coast, save yourself time and trouble by getting both your fishing licenses and boat permits by mail ahead of time from the Mexican Department of Fisheries. Call at least a month before departure, tel. 619/233-6956, fax 619/233-0344, and ask for applications and the fees (which are reasonable, but depend upon the period of validity and the fluctuating exchange rate). On the application, fill in the names (exactly as they appear on passports) of the persons requesting licenses. Include a cashier's check or a money order for the exact amount, along with a stamped, self-addressed envelope. Address the application to the Mexican Department of Fisheries, 2550 5th Ave., Suite 101, San Diego, CA 92103-6622.

Freshwater Fishing

Oaxaca has four large reservoirs: Yosocuta, in the Mixteca near Huajuapan de León; Cerro de Oro and Miguel Alemán, in the north near Tuxtepec; and Benito Juárez Reservoir, in the Isthmus not far from Tehuantepec. Their shorelines are scenic and easily accessible, and their waters are home to several varieties, mostly *mojarra* (bass), plentiful enough for local folks to a make living cooking fish dinners.

Festivals and Events

Mexicans love a party. Urban families watch the calendar for midweek national holidays that create a *puente* or bridge to the weekend and allow them to squeeze in a three- to five-day mini-vacation. Visitors should likewise watch the calendar. Such holidays (especially Christmas and Semana Santa, pre-Easter week) mean packed buses, roads, and hotels, especially around Oaxaca's beach resorts.

Country people, on the other hand, await their local saint's day or holy day. The name of the locality often provides the clue. For example, in Santa Cruz Papalutla, just east of Oaxaca city, expect a celebration on May 3, El Día de la Santa Cruz (Day of the Holy Cross). People dress up in their traditional best, sell their wares and produce in a street fair, join a procession, get tipsy, and dance in the plaza.

Bullfighting

Oaxaca, unique among Mexican states, has no bullfights. Benito Juárez, as governor during the 1850s, was instrumental in outlawing bullfights in Oaxaca. In his honor, they remain banned.

FIESTAS

The following calendar lists national and notable Oaxacan holidays and festivals. For many more details, see the destinations cited. Call ahead to confirm dates. If you happen to be where one of these is going on, get out of your car or bus and join in!

January

January 1: ¡**Feliz Año Nuevo!** (New Year's Day; national holiday), especially in Santiago Jamiltepec and Teotitlán del Valle.

January 6: **Día de los Reyes** (Day of the Kings), especially in Santos Reyes Nopala—traditional gift exchange; townsfolk perform favorite traditional dances.

January 13–17: **Fiesta del Dulce Nombre de Jesús** (Festival of the Sweet Name of Jesus), in Santa Ana del Valle, Tlacolula and Zimatlán—troupes perform many traditional dances, including the Dance of the Feathers.

January 17: **Día de San Antonio Abad**—decorating and blessing animals.

January 20–21: **Fiesta de San Sebastián,**

Mojigangos, giant dancing effigies, are popular in Oaxaca festivals, such as Oaxaca city's Guelaguetza festival.

especially in San Pedro and San Pablo Tequixtepec, Pinotepa Don Luis, and Jalapa de Díaz.
January 25: **Fiesta del Apóstol de San Pablo** (Festival of Apostle St. Paul), in Mitla—masses, processions, feast, fireworks, *jaripeo* (bull-roping and riding), and dancing.

February
February 2: **Día de Candelaria,** especially in Tututepec—plants, seeds, and candles blessed; procession and bullfights.
February 5: **Constitution Day** (national holiday)—commemorates the constitutions of 1857 and 1917.
February 24: **Flag Day** (national holiday).
February: During the four days before Ash Wednesday, usually in late February, many towns, especially San Juan Colorado, Putla, Pinotepa Don Luis, and Juxtlahuaca, celebrate **Carnaval**—Mardi Gras-style extravaganzas.

February–March: Celebrations continue during **Cuaresma** (Lent), especially in Santiago Jamiltepec and Pinotepa Nacional, for several weeks.

March
Second Friday of Lent (nine days after Ash Wednesday): **Fiesta del Señor del Perdón** (Festival of the Lord of Forgiveness), in San Pedro and San Pablo Tequixtepec—big pilgrimage festival.
Second Friday of Lent: **Fiesta del Señor de Piedad,** in Santiago Astata.
Fourth Friday of Lent (23 days after Ash Wednesday): **Fiesta del Señor de Misericordias,** in Santa María Huatulco.
Fourth Friday before Easter Sunday: **Fiesta of Jesus the Nazarene,** in Huaxpaltepec.
Week before Palm Sunday: **Week of Ramos,** especially in Jamiltepec.
Friday before Good Friday (11 days before Easter Sunday): **Feria Comercial** (Commercial Fair), in Huatla de Jiménez—many traditional folk dances.
March 18–19: **Fiesta de San José,** in Valle Nacional; on the weekend closest to March 10 in San José Mogote.
March 21: **Birthday of Benito Juárez,** the "Hero of the Americas" (national holiday), especially in Benito Juárez's birthplace, Guelatao—a whirl of traditional dances.
March 21–31: **Juegos Florales** (Flower Games), in Oaxaca city.

April
April: **Semana Santa** (pre-Easter Holy Week, culminating in Domingo Santa, Easter, national holiday), in many locales, especially San Juan Colorado, Pinotepa Don Luis, and Pinotepa Nacional.
Good Friday, two days before Easter Sunday: **Fiesta de la Santa Cruz de Huatulco** (Festival of the Holy Cross of Huatulco).
Saturday before Easter Sunday: **Sábado de Gloria** in San Miguel Tequixtepec—people, called *mecos,* don masks and do a kind of adult trick or treat for the occasion.
First week in April: **Feria del Mango** (Mango Fair), in Tapanatepec.

April 26–29: **Fiesta de San Pedro Mártir de Verona,** in San Pedro Yucunama.

May

May 1: **Labor Day** (national holiday).

May 3: **Fiesta de la Santa Cruz** (Festival of the Holy Cross), in many places, especially Salina Cruz, Tehuantepec, and Unión Hidalgo.

May 5: **Cinco de Mayo** (national holiday)—celebration of the defeat of the French at Puebla in 1862.

May 10: **Mothers' Day** (national holiday).

May 10–12: **Fiesta of the Coronation of the Virgin of the Rosary.**

May 11–16: **Fiesta de San Isidro Labrador** (Festival of Saint Isador the Farmer), in Ixcatlán.

May 15–30: **Velas de San Vicente Ferrer,** in Juchitán (also many more—see the sidebar "Velas: Fiestas of the Isthmus" in The Isthmus chapter).

Late May–early June: **Feria Tuxtepec,** in Tuxtepec—big expo and folkloric dance festival.

June

June 2–3: **Fiesta de San Antonio de Padua,** in Jalapa de Díaz.

June 23–24: **Fiesta de San Juan Bautista** (Festival of St. John the Baptist), especially in Tuxtepec, Valle Nacional, Cuicatlán, and Coixtlahuaca.

June 25: **Fiesta de San Pedro,** in Santa María Huamelula; June 27–30 in San Pedro Tapanatepec; June 29 in San Pedro Amusgos; June 26–30 in Unión Hidalgo.

June 26–30: **Fiesta de Santa María Santísima** in Unión Hidalgo.

June 26–30: **San Isidro el Labrador** (Saint Isador the Farmer) in Unión Hidalgo.

June 29: **Fiesta de San Pablo y San Pedro** (Festival of St. Paul and St. Peter); June 21–28 in San Pedro Pochutla.

July

July 1–15: **Fiesta of the Precious Blood of Christ,** in Teotitlán del Valle—featuring the Danza de la Pluma (Dance of the Feather).

Two Mondays following July 16: **Lunes de Cerro** or **Guelaguetza** in Oaxaca city—all-Oaxaca dance extravaganza.

July 20–24: **Fiesta de Santa María Magdalena** (Festival of St. Mary Magdalen), in Tequisistlán.

July 20–30: **Fiesta de Santiago Apóstol** (Festival of St. James the Apostle), in Santiago Laollaga; July 22–27 in Suchilquitongo; July 23–26 in Jamiltepec and in Pinotepa Nacional; and July 25 in Juxtlahuaca.

August

August 1–5: **Fiesta de Santo Domingo de Guzmán,** in Unión Hidalgo.

August 13–18: **Fiesta del Barrio de Santa María Relatoca,** in Tehuantepec.

August 14: **Fiesta de la Virgen de la Asunción** (Festival of the Virgin of the Assumption), in Tlaxiaco; August 15 in Nochixtlán; August 13–16 in Huazolotitlán.

August 25–29: **Fiesta de San Bartolomé,** in San Bartolomé de Quiliana; August 23–24 in San Bartolo Tuxtepec; August 24–27 in San Bartolo Coyotepec.

August 26–September 2: **Fiesta de Santa Rosa de Lima,** in Salina Cruz; August 28 in Ojitlán.

August 31–September 11: **Fiesta Laborio,** in Tehuantepec.

September

September 7–8: **Fiesta de la Vírgen de La Navidad,** in Huatla de Jiménez.

September 7–9: **Fiesta del Señor de La Natividad** (Festival of the Lord of the Nativity), in Teotitlán del Valle.

September 11: **Fiesta de la Virgen de los Remedios,** in Jamiltepec.

September 14: **Charro Day** (Cowboy Day), all over Mexico—rodeos.

September 16: **Independence Day** (national holiday)—mayors everywhere reenact Father Hidalgo's 1810 Grito de Dolores from city hall balconies on the night of September 15.

September 21: **Fiesta of San Mateo,** in Calpulalpan.

September 23–30: **Fiesta de la Preciosa Sangre de Cristo** (Festival of the Precious Blood of Christ), in Tlacochahuaya—eight days of processions, dances, fireworks, and food.

September 27–29: **Fiesta de San Miguel,** in San Miguel Tequixtepec and Teotitlán del Camino—highlights include traditional dances, such as the Cristianos y Moros (Christians and Moors).

October

October 1–2: **Fiesta de San Miguel Arcangel,** in Puerto Ángel.

First Sunday in October: **Fiesta de la Virgen del Rosario** (Festival of the Virgin of the Rosary), in San Pedro Amusgos.

October 3–5: **Fiesta de San Francisco Asis,** in Salina Cruz.

October 6–8: **Fiesta de San Dionisio,** in San Dionisio del Mar—pilgrimage.

Second Sunday in October: **Fiesta del Santa Cristo de Tlacolula** (Festival of the Holy Christ of Tlacolula), in Tlacolula.

Second Monday in October: **Fiesta de los Lunes del Tule,** in Santa María del Tule—locals in costume celebrate with rites, folk dances, and feats of horsemanship beneath the boughs of their beloved great cypress tree.

Third Sunday in October: **Fiesta de Octubre,** in Tlaxiaco—includes fireworks, basketball and *pelota mixteca* (traditional ball game) tournaments, and popular dances.

October 12: **Día de la Raza** (Columbus Day)—national holiday that commemorates the union of the races.

November

November: **Fiestas de Noviembre,** in Puerto Escondido—features the big folk dance festival **Fiesta Costéño.**

November 1: **Día de Todos Santos** (All Saints Day)—in honor of the souls of children; the departed descend from heaven to eat sugar skeletons, skulls, and treats on family altars.

November 2: **Día de los Muertos** (Day of the Dead), especially in Tuxtepec and Cacahuatepec—in honor of ancestors; families visit cemeteries and decorate graves with flowers and favorite foods of the deceased.

November 11–16: **Fiesta de San Diego,** in Salina Cruz.

November 13: **Fiesta de San Marcos,** in San Marcos Tlapazola (tourist Yu'u town in the Valley of Oaxaca).

November 20: **Revolution Day** (national holiday)—anniversary of the revolution of 1910–1917.

November 22: **Fiesta de Santa Cecilia,** in Unión Hidalgo.

November 25: **Fiesta de Santa Catarina,** in Santa Catarina Ixtepeji.

November 29: **Fiesta de San Andrés,** in San Juan Colorado.

December

December 1: **Inauguration Day**—national government changes hands every six years: 2000, 2006, 2012 . . .

December 8: **Día de la Purísima Concepción** (Day of the Immaculate Conception).

December 8: **Fiesta de la Vírgen of Soledad,** in Oaxaca and Juxtlahuaca.

Late November–December 8: **Fiesta de la Virgen de Juquila,** in Santa Catarina Juquila—Oaxaca's biggest fiesta.

December 8–11: **Fiesta de Nuestra Señora de la Concepción,** in Santa María Huatulco.

December 12: **Día de Nuestra Señora de Guadalupe** (Festival of the Virgin of Guadalupe), nationwide—processions, music, and dancing honoring the patroness of Mexico.

December 16–18: **Fiesta de la Virgen de Soledad,** in Oaxaca city.

December 16–24: **Christmas Week**—week of *posadas* and piñatas, with midnight mass on Christmas Eve.

December 19–22: **Fiesta de Santo Tomás Apóstol,** in Ixtlán de Juárez.

December 23: **Fiesta de los Rábanos** (Festival of the Radishes), in Oaxaca city.

December 24: **Nochebuena** (Christmas Eve), in Oaxaca city and Yucunama.

December 25: **¡Feliz Navidad!** (Christmas Day; national holiday)—Christmas trees and gift exchange.

December 26: **Vela Tehuantepec,** in Tehuantepec—everyone in town dances to the lovely melody of the *Sandunga.*

December 31: **New Year's Eve.**

Arts and Crafts

Oaxaca abounds with attractive, reasonably priced handicrafts. A sizable fraction of Oaxacan families still depend upon homespun items—clothing, utensils, furniture, native herbal remedies, religious offerings, adornments, toys, musical instruments. Many such traditions reach back thousands of years, to the beginnings of Mesoamerican civilization. The accumulated knowledge of manifold generations of artisans has in many instances resulted in finery so prized that whole villages devote themselves to the manufacture of a certain class of goods.

Handicrafts (*artesanías,* ar-tay-sah-NEE-ahs) shoppers who venture away from the Oaxaca city center and the coastal tourist enclaves to the source villages and towns will most likely benefit from lower prices, wider choices, and, most importantly, the privilege of meeting the artisans themselves. There, perhaps in a patio shop on a dusty Teotitlán del Valle side street or an Arrazola family patio, you might encounter the people and perhaps view the painstaking processes by

which they fashion humble materials—clay, wool, cotton, wood, metal, straw, leaves, bark, paper, leather—into irresistible works of art.

BASKETRY AND WOVEN CRAFTS

Weaving straw, leaves, and reeds is among the oldest of Oaxacan crafts traditions. Mat- and basket-weaving methods and designs go back as far as 5,000 years and are still used today.

The drier regions of Oaxaca are sources of fronds from the dwarf palms that populate the hillsides. In the Mixteca, in places such as Huajuapan de León and Coixtlahuaca and the east side of the Valley of Oaxaca around Tlacolula, you might see people sitting on a doorstep or at a bus stop or even walking down the street while weaving a *petate* (mat) or *tenate* (tumpline basket) of creamy white palm leaf, prized for its soft, pliable texture. All over Oaxaca, nearly everyone uses *petates,* from vacationers, for stretching out

© BRUCE WHIPPERMAN

Basket weavers, although greatly diminished in numbers, still continue their craft in Oaxaca, in places such as Suchilquitongo, in the Oaxaca Valley, northwest of Oaxaca city.

on the beach, to local folks, for keeping tortillas warm and shielding babies from the sun. *Tenates* have been raised to nearly a fine art in a number of Oaxaca localities, such as San Luis Amatlán, near Ejutla in the southern Valley of Oaxaca. There, craftspeople interweave dyed fibers with the natural palm, creating attractive, sensitively executed geometric designs.

Carrizo, a bamboo-like reed that grows on stream banks all over Oaxaca state, is the source of stronger, more rigid baskets, usually called *canastas* when they have handles, *tenates* when they don't. Well-known Oaxaca Valley sources are San Juan Guelavía and Magdalena Teitipac, on the east side, and Santa Ana Zegache near Ocotlán in the south. Familiar variations include the prized *tenate para tortillas,* round at the top and tapering to square at the base, and *cajas para pájaros* (birdcages), sometimes fashioned in two, three, or four levels.

A third important weaving fiber in Oaxaca is *ixtle,* the dried strands from the leaves of maguey and related agave-family plants. Artisans all over Oaxaca craft *ixtle* into useful items, such as ropes for pulling, string bags for carrying, and hammocks for relaxing.

CLOTHING AND EMBROIDERY

Although *traje* (ancestral tribal dress) has become uncommon in Oaxaca city, significant numbers of Oaxacan native women make and wear *traje,* especially in the Mazateca, Chinantla, and Zapotec Sierra in the north, the Isthmus in the southeast, the coastal Mixteca in the southwest, and the Trique in the Mixteca Alta in the west.

The most common *traje* garment is the *huipil,* a full, square-shouldered, short- to mid-sleeved dress, often hand-embroidered with animal and floral designs and embellished with ribbons. Probably the most popular Oaxaca *huipiles* are the captivating designs from San Pedro de Amusgos (Amusgo tribe; white cotton embroidered with abstract colored animal and floral motifs). Others nearly as prized include the Trique styles from around San Andrés Chicahuaxtla (white cotton, richly embroidered red stripes, interwoven with green, blue, and yellow, and hung with colored ribbons); Mazatec, from Huatla de Jiménez (white cotton with bright flowers embroidered in multiple panels, crossed by horizontal and vertical purple and magenta silk ribbons); and Isthmus Zapotec, from Tehuantepec (brightly colored cotton densely embroidered with either geometric designs or a field of flamboyant, multicolored flowers).

Oaxaca shops and stalls also sell other, less common types of *traje.* These include the *quechquémitl* (shoulder cape), often made of wool and worn as an overgarment in winter, and the *enredo,* a full-length skirt that wraps around the waist and legs like a Hawaiian sarong.

Mixtec women in Oaxaca's warm southwest coastal region around Pinotepa Nacional commonly wear the *enredo,* known locally as the *pozahuanco* (poh-sah-WAHN-koh) below the waist and, when at home, go bare-breasted. When wearing their *pozahuancos* in public, they usually tie a *mandil,* a wide apron, around their front side.

Women weave the most prized *pozahuancos* using cotton thread dyed a light purple with secretions of tidepool-harvested snails, *Purpura patula pansa,* and silk dyed deep red with **cochineal,** an extract from the dried bodies of a locally cultivated scale insect, *Dactylopius coccus.* On a typical day, two or three women will be selling handmade *pozahuancos* at the Pinotepa Nacional market.

Ropa Típica

Colonial-era Spanish styles have blended with native *traje,* producing a wider class of dress, known generally as *ropa típica.* Lovely embroidered *blusas* (blouses), *rebozos* (shawls), and *vestidos* (dresses) fill shop racks and market stalls all over Oaxaca. Among the most popular is the so-called **Oaxaca wedding dress,** made of cotton with a crochet-trimmed riot of diminutive flowers hand-stitched about the neck and yoke. Some of the finest examples are made in **San Antonino Castillo Velasco,** just north of Ocotlán on the Valley of Oaxaca's south side.

In contrast to women, only a small fraction of Oaxacan men—members of remote groups, such as mountain Mazatec and Chinantecs in the north, the Mixes in the east, and rural Chatinos and Amusgos in the southwest—wear *traje*. Nevertheless, shops offer some fine men's *ropa típica*, such as wool jackets and serapes for highland or winter wear and *guayaberas,* hip-length, pleated tropical dress shirts.

Fine *bordado* (embroidery) embellishes much traditional Oaxacan clothing, *manteles* (tablecloths), and *servilletas* (napkins). As everywhere, women define the art of embroidery. Although some work is still handmade at home, cheaper machine-made factory lace and needlework is more commonly available in shops.

Among the most renowned handmade example is the embroidery of **Santo Tomás Jalieza,** the "town of belts" *(cinturones),* in the Oaxaca central valley south of Coyotepec. Although best known for their attractive embroidered cloth and leather belts, the townsfolk have adapted their colorful designs to clothing, purses, bags, and much more.

LEATHER

Some Oaxaca shops offer selections of locally produced *huaraches* from around Miahuatlán in the south valley and Yalalag, north in the Sierra Juárez. Shops import most other leather goods from other Mexican centers, such as Guadalajara and León. For unique and custom-designed articles you'll probably have to confine your shopping to the expensive tourist resort shops. For the more usual though still attractive leather items, such as purses, wallets, belts, coats, and boots, veteran shoppers go to **Mercado Juárez** or **Mercado de Artesanías** in Oaxaca city.

GLASS AND STONEWORK

Glass manufacture, unknown in pre-Columbian times, was introduced by the Spanish. Today factories scattered all over Mexico turn out mountains of *burbuja* (boor-BOO-hah) bubbled-glass tumblers, goblets, plates, and pitchers, usually in blue, yellow, green, or red.

Artisans work stone, mostly near sources of supply. Puebla and **Tequisistlán** (in the Oaxaca isthmus) are Mexico's main sources of decorative **onyx** (*onix,* OH-neeks). Factory shops turn out the galaxy of mostly roughhewn, cream-col-

ored items, from animal charms and chess pieces to beads and desk sets, which you'll see on some Oaxaca city curio shop shelves.

Cantera, a volcanic tufa stone, occurs in pastel shades from pink to green and is quarried in several locations in the Valley of Oaxaca. Most preferred is the light jade-green *cantera* from Magdalena Etla, northwest of Oaxaca city. It has replaced the original but exhausted *cantera* source that supplied stone for most of Oaxaca city's original buildings.

For a keepsake from a truly ancient Oaxacan tradition, don't forget the hollowed-out stone *metate* (may-TAH-tay), or corn-grinding basin, and the three-legged *molcajete* (mohl-kah-HAY-tay), a mortar for grinding chilies. Most examples you'll see in Oaxaca are from Teitipac, in the west valley near **Tlacolula.**

JEWELRY

Gold and silver were once the basis for Mexico's wealth. Her Spanish conquerors plundered a mountain of gold—ritual offerings, necklaces, pendants, rings, plates—masterfully crafted by a legion of indigenous jewelers. Unfortunately, much of that native tradition was lost as the colonial Spanish denied Mexicans access to precious metals and introduced Spanish methods. Nevertheless, a small native gold-working tradition survived the dislocations of the 1810–1821 War of Independence and the 1910–1917 Revolution. Meanwhile, silver crafting, moribund during the 1800s, was revived in **Taxco, Guerrero,** during the 1920s, principally through the joint efforts of architect-artist William Spratling and the local community.

Today, spurred by the tourist boom, jewelry-making is thriving in Mexico. Taxco, where guilds, families, and cooperatives produce sparkling silver and gold adornments, is the acknowledged center. Several Oaxaca shops offer Taxco-made jewelry—shimmering ornamental butterflies, birds, jaguars, serpents, turtles, and fish from the pre-conquest tradition. Pieces, mostly in silver, vary from humble but attractive trinkets to glittering necklaces, silver candelabras, and place settings for a dozen, sometimes embellished with precious stones.

Oaxaca also has a healthy local jewelry-making tradition. Acknowledged leader in Oaxaca city is the family firm of **Oro de Monte Albán.** Their several city and coastal resort shops offer replicas of the ancient Mixtec designs, notably of many pieces found at Monte Albán's tomb 7.

Tehuantepec women *(tehuanas)* have created a demand for elaborate **gold filigree jewelry,** made from fine wires and often decorated with pearls and precious stones. The finest, ranging from 10 to 18 karat (42–75 percent pure) gold, is more often kept in safe deposit boxes and used only on ceremonial occasions. Much more common is *chupa de oro,* gold look-alike filigree that contains no gold at all. Women sell this jewelry in Oaxaca city, at the north-central entrance of the 20 de Noviembre market and in the Isthmus, at the Juchitán and Tehuantepec markets.

© BRUCE WHIPPERMAN

For-tourist masks, widely available in Oaxaca city markets and handicrafts stores, are a continuation of both indigenous and Spanish religious festival tradition.

WOOD CARVING AND MUSICAL INSTRUMENTS

Masks

Spanish and Native Oaxacan traditions have blended to produce a multitude of masks—some strange, some lovely, some scary, some endearing, all interesting. The tradition flourishes in Oaxaca and the strongly indigenous neighboring states of Michoacán, Guerrero, and Chiapas. Here campesinos gear up all year for the village festivals—especially Semana Santa (Easter week), early December (Virgin of Guadalupe), and of the local patron, whether it be San José, San Pablo, San Pedro, Santa Barbara, Santa María, or one of a host of others. Every local fair has its favored dances, such as the **Dance of the Conquest, the Christians and Moors, the Old Men,** or the **Tiger,** in which masked villagers act out age-old allegories of fidelity, sacrifice, faith, struggle, sin, and redemption.

Although artisans craft Oaxaca masks of many materials—from stone and ebony to coconut husks and paper—**wood,** where available, is the medium of choice. For the entire year, workers carve, sand, and paint to ensure that each participant will be properly disguised for the festival. Although Oaxaca's larger municipalities usually have their cadres of mask makers, towns in the

coastal Mixteca region, notably Santa María Huazolotitlán, are among Oaxaca's busiest authentic mask sources.

The popularity of masks has resulted in an entire made-for-tourist mask industry, which has led to mass-produced duplicates, many cleverly antiqued. Examine the goods carefully; if the price is high, don't buy unless you're convinced it's a real antique.

Alebrijes

Tourist demand has made zany wooden animals called *alebrijes* (ah-lay-BREE-hays) a Oaxaca growth industry. Virtually every family in certain Valley of Oaxaca villages—notably **Arrazola and San Martín Tilcajete**—runs a factory studio. There, piles of *copal* wood, which men carve and women finish and intricately paint, become whimsical giraffes, dogs, cats, iguanas, gargoyles, and dragons, including most of the possible permutations in between. The farther from the source you get, the higher the *alebrije* price becomes; what costs $5 in Arrazola will probably run about $10 in Oaxaca city and $30 in the United States, Canada, or Europe.

Musical Instruments

Virtually all of Mexico's guitars are made in **Paracho, Michoacán** (southeast of Lake Chapala), north of Uruapan. There, scores of cottage factories turn out guitars, violins, mandolins, ukuleles, and a dozen more variations every day. Products vary widely in quality, so look carefully before you buy. Make sure that the wood is well cured and dry; damp, unripe wood instruments are more susceptible to warping and cracking.

METALWORK

A score of Oaxaca city family factories turn out fine cutlery, forged ironwork, and a swarm of bright tinware mirror frames, masks, and glittering Christmas decorations.

Cutlery tradition—knives, machetes, scissors, swords, and more—arrived in Oaxaca with the Spanish. Today, several family shops offer their wares in town shops and market stalls, notably at the Benito Juárez market in Oaxaca city.

Traditional **ironwork,** admittedly heavy to carry home in your luggage, is made to order,

boxed, and shipped at a number of specialty shops in Oaxaca city. Some of the more commonly requested items, such as medieval-style lanterns and garden benches, are available on display.

Tinware *(hojalata)* (oh-hah-LAH-tah), especially the colorfully lacquered Christmas decorations—winsome angels, saints, Santas, butterflies, and fruits—constitute Oaxaca city's most sought-after metal craft. Running closely behind are the hosts of old-fashioned lead figures—soldiers, ballerinas, antique automobiles, angels—and fancy silvery mirror frames, metal boxes, birds, flowers, and much more. Many downtown handicrafts shops, in addition to stalls at the 20 de Noviembre market and the Mercado de Artesanías (Handicrafts Market), sell metal work.

Moreover, be sure to ask at the same shops and stalls for *milagros,* one of Mexico's most charming forms of metal work. Usually of brass, they are of homely shapes—a horse, dog, or baby, or an arm, head, heart, or foot. The faithful pin them, along with a prayer, to the garments of their favorite saint, whom they hope will

© BRUCE WHIPPERMAN

Papier-mâché bakery goods, although made of glued and lacquered layers of newsprint, appear as inviting as the real thing.

© BRUCE WHIPPERMAN

One of dozens of innovative pottery designs of Atzompa, in the Oaxaca Valley not far northwest of the city.

intercede to cure the ailment or fulfill the wish designated by the *milagro.*

PAPER AND PAPIER-MÂCHÉ

Papier-mâché has risen to nearly a fine art in **Tonalá, Jalisco.** Many Oaxaca handicrafts stores stock small flocks of Tonalá-made birds, cats, frogs, giraffes, and other animal figurines, meticulously crafted by building up repeated layers of glued paper. The results—sanded, brilliantly varnished, and polished—resemble fine sculptures rather than the humble newspaper from which they were fashioned.

Other paper goods you shouldn't overlook include **piñatas** (durable, inexpensive, and as Mexican as you can get), available in every town market; colorful, decorative **cutout banners** (string overhead at your home fiesta) from San Salvador Huixcolotla, Puebla; and *amate,* wild fig tree bark paintings in animal and flower motifs, from Xalitla and Ameyaltepec, Guerrero.

POTTERY AND CERAMICS

The Valley of Oaxaca is the focus of a vibrant pottery tradition. Many of the most celebrated examples come from the village of **Atzompa,** a few miles northwest of the city. Traditionally popular for their green-glazed clay pots, dishes, casseroles, and bowls, Atzompa potters have evolved a host of fresh styles, from graceful vases and plates blooming with painted lilies to red clay pots and bowls inscribed with artfully flowing blossoms.

San Bartolo Coyotepec village, south of the city, has acquired equal renown for its **black pottery** *(barro negro),* sold all over the world. **Doña Rosa,** now deceased, pioneered the crafting of big round pots without using a potter's wheel. Now made in many more shapes by Doña Rosa's descendants, the pottery's celebrated black hue is produced by the reduction (reduced air) method of firing, which removes oxygen from the clay's red (ferric) iron oxide, converting it to black (ferrous) iron oxide. Workers burnish the result to produce an exquisite, pearly sheen.

Although most latter-day Oaxacan potters are aware of the health dangers of **lead** pigments, some for-sale pottery may still contain lead. The hazard comes from low-fired pottery in which the lead has not been firmly melted into the glaze. **Acids** in foods, such as lemons, vinegar, and tomatoes, dissolve the lead pigments, which, when ingested over a period of time, can result in lead poisoning. In general, the shiniest pottery, stoneware that has been twice fired, is the safest for dinnerware.

Although Mexican pottery tradition is as diverse as the country itself, some varieties stand out. Among the most prized is the so-called **Talavera** (or Majolica), the best of which is made by a few family-run shops in Puebla. The names Talavera and Majolica derive from Talavera, the Spanish town from which the tradition migrated to Mexico; prior to that, it originated on the Spanish Mediterranean island of Majorca, from a combination of still older Arabic, Chinese, and African ceramic styles. Shapes include plates, bowls, jugs, and pitchers, hand-painted and hard-fired in intricate bright yellow, orange, blue, and green floral designs. So few shops make true Talavera these

ON THE ROAD

days that other, cheaper look-alike grades, made around Guanajuato, are more common, selling for a small fraction of the price of the genuine article.

WOOLEN WOVEN GOODS

Mexico's finest wool weavings come from **Teotitlán del Valle** and the neighboring town of **Santa Ana del Valle,** less than an hour's drive east of Oaxaca city. Although they learned to work wool from the Spanish, the weaving tradition, continued by Zapotec-speaking families, dates back at least a thousand years before the conquest. Most families still carry on the arduous process, making everything from scratch. They gather the dyes from wild plants and the bodies of insects and sea snails. They hand-wash, card, spin, and dye the wool and even travel to remote mountain springs to gather water. The result, they say, is *vale la pena* (worth the pain): intensely colored, tightly woven carpets, rugs, and wall hangings that retain their brilliance for generations.

Although many handicrafts shops and a host of stalls in all the Oaxaca city markets sell the Teotitlán and Santa Ana weavings, a trip to Teotitlán (where Santa Ana weavers send most of their products for sale) is a must for Oaxaca Valley first-time visitors.

Accommodations

Oaxaca has lodgings to suit every style and pocketbook: world-class resorts, small beachside hotels, bed-and-breakfasts, homey *casas de huéspedes* (guesthouses), friendly trailer parks, community-maintained tourist lodgings (see Tourist Yu'u and Community Cabana Accommodations), and many miles of breezy beaches, ripe for camping.

In Oaxaca city, the busy **high seasons,** when hotel reservations are generally necessary, are July, Day of the Dead (late October through early November), and December. On the coast, high seasons are mid-December through January 2, February 1 through Easter, and the months of July and August. Excellent, quiet **low-season** times to visit anywhere in Oaxaca are November after the Day of the Dead and the month of January after New Year, when prices are low and the weather is consistently temperate and dry.

The dozens of accommodations described in this book are positive recommendations—checked out in detail—good choices from which you can pick according to your taste and purse.

Hotel Rates

The rates listed in this book are U.S. dollar equivalents of peso prices, taxes included, as quoted by the hotel management at the time of writing. Low- and high-season rates are quoted whenever possible. They are intended as a general guide only, and probably will only approximate the asking rate when you arrive. Some readers unfortunately try to bargain by telling desk clerks that, for example, the rate should be $30 because they read it in this book. This is unwise, because it makes hotel managers and clerks reluctant to quote rates for fear readers might hold their hotel responsible for such quotes. As private businesses, hotels are free to raise their rates; conversely, if the price is too high, you the customer are entitled to take your business elsewhere.

In Oaxaca, hotel rates depend strongly upon inflation and season. To cancel the effect of relatively steep Mexican inflation, rates are reported in U.S. dollars. However, when settling your hotel bill, you should always insist on paying in pesos.

Websites listed in the Internet Resources section might be a useful supplement to the accommodations described in the destination chapters.

Saving Money

The hotel prices quoted here are **rack rates:** the maximum tariff, exclusive of packages and promotions, that you would pay if you walked in off the street and rented an unreserved room for one day. Savvy travelers seldom pay the maximum. Always inquire if there are any **discounts or packages** (*descuentos o paquetes,* pronounced "dees-koo-AYN-tohs OH pah-KAY-tays"). At any time other than the high seasons, you can generally bargain for a discount. Don't be shy; if the hotel asking price is $60, offer $30 or $40. At best, you'll get what you want; at worst, you can always walk away. Often discounts come as one or two free days for a one-week stay. Promotional packages available during slack seasons sometimes include free extras, such as breakfast, a car rental, a boat tour, or a sports rental. A travel agent or Internet travel site can be of great help in shopping around for such bargains.

You will virtually always save money if you deal in pesos only. Insist on both booking your lodging for an agreed price in pesos and paying the resulting hotel bill in pesos, rather than dollars. The reason is that dollar rates quoted by big resorts are often based on the hotel desk exchange rate, which is customarily about 10 percent less favorable than bank rates. For example, if the clerk tells you your hotel bill is $1,000, instead of handing over the dollars, or having him mark $1,000 on your credit card slip, ask him how much it is in pesos. Using the desk conversion rate, he might say something like 10,000 pesos (considerably less than the 11,000 pesos that the bank might give for your $1,000). Pay the 10,000 pesos or have the clerk mark 10,000 pesos on your credit card slip, and save yourself $90.

GUESTHOUSES, BED-AND-BREAKFASTS, AND HOMESTAYS

A growing fraction of Oaxaca city lodgings fall into these categories. On city residential side streets, often several blocks removed from the tourist zone, are many of the *casas de huéspedes* (guesthouses), bed-and-breakfasts, and homes where increasing numbers of families are renting rooms to visitors.

Such lodgings vary from scruffy to spic-and-span, humble to luxurious. At minimum, you can expect a plain room, a shared toilet and hot-water shower, and plenty of atmosphere for your money. In Oaxaca city and the Bahías de Huatulco, rates are highest, ranging between $20 and about $100 for two. Discounts are often available for long-term stays.

In addition to the guesthouse, bed-and-breakfast, and homestay-style lodgings listed in the destination chapters of this book, you should

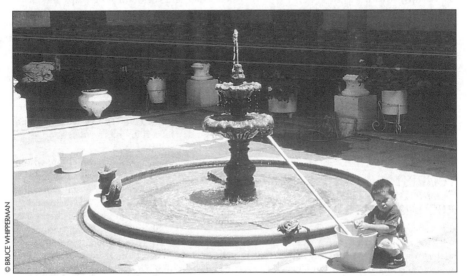

Casas de huéspedes (guesthouses) and small local hotels are often converted colonial-era family houses that surround a quiet inner patio.

© BRUCE WHIPPERMAN

ON THE ROAD

also consult the many classified advertisements of the local tourist newspapers, especially in Oaxaca city and Puerto Escondido, and travel websites in the destination chapters and the glossary.

APARTMENTS AND HOUSE RENTALS

For longer stays in Oaxaca city, many visitors prefer the convenience and economy of an apartment or house rental. Choices vary, from spartan studios to deluxe homes big enough for entire extended families. Prices depend strongly upon season and amenities, from $250 per month for the cheapest to around $1,000 for the most luxurious.

At the low end, you can expect a clean, furnished apartment with kitchen and bathroom and once- or twice-a-week housecleaning service. Higher up the scale, houses vary from moderately luxurious homes to sky's-the-limit mansions, blooming with built-in designer luxuries, such as a swimming pool or tennis court, and including at least a gardener, cook, and maid.

Shopping Around

The Oaxaca City chapter of this book recommends several solid guesthouse, bed-and-breakfast, and apartment rentals. You can find many more through on-the-spot local contacts, such as the tourist newspapers' want ad sections, websites, neighborhood For Rent or *Renta* signs, and local listing agents. If you prefer making rental arrangements prior to arrival, you can usually email, fax, telephone, or write managers—many of whom speak English—directly, using the numbers given in the destination chapters of this book.

TOURIST YU'U AND COMMUNITY CABANA ACCOMMODATIONS

A number of rural communities, mostly on the east side of the central Valley of Oaxaca, encourage visitors to come and stay in their tourist lodges, called Yu'u (say "You") in Zapotec. Other communities call them simply cabanas. These are government-built, spartan but comfortable,

modern-standard accommodations, managed and maintained by a community-appointed *gerente* (manager). Most Yu'u and some cabanas have two separate one-room units that sleep up to six persons each and share a single toilet and shower bath between them. Units rent for about $8 per night per person, or $30 per family group, with towels, blankets, kitchenette, and hot water.

The tourist Yu'u and cabanas offer a unique opportunity for visitors weary of the city tourist rush and who hanker for more people-to-people contact. Moreover, a number of the participating communities produce uniquely fine handicrafts and/or enjoy scenic locations.

Obtain tourist Yu'u and cabana reservations through the government alternative tourism office in Oaxaca city. Contact them downtown, at Murguia 206 (up the driveway, in the back), tel. 951/516-4828, sedetur5@oaxaca.gob.mx. (If somehow you are not able to make contact with alternative tourism, try Oaxaca government tourism, at 607 Independencia, corner G. Vigil, tel./fax 951/516-0123, info@oaxaca.gob.mx.)

For Yu'u and cabana location details, see the sidebar "Where to Find Tourist Yu'u and Cabañas" and the destination maps and chapters, beginning with the Around the Valley of Oaxaca chapter.

LOCAL HOTELS

Locally owned and operated hotels make up most of the recommendations of this book. Many veteran travelers find it hard to understand why people come to Oaxaca and spend $200 a day for a hotel room when good alternatives run as little as $25.

In Oaxaca city, many such hotels are within two or three blocks of the town center, with its lovely plaza, old monuments, restaurants, and shops. In the Puerto Escondido and Puerto Ángel resorts, most of them are right on the beach. Local hotels, which depend at least as much on Mexican tourists as foreigners, generally have clean, large rooms, often with private view balconies, ceiling fans, and toilet and hot-water bath or shower. What they often lack are the plush extras—air-conditioning, cable TV, phones,

WHERE TO FIND TOURIST YU'U AND CABAÑAS

The Oaxaca Federal-State Department of Tourism (SEDETUR) built several tourist Yu'u lodgings in communities on the east side of the Valley of Oaxaca during the 1990s. Although five of the original nine are not now being used, 10 more (now called Cabañas) have been built, so a total of 14 are now operating.

Reservations for the active Yu'u and Cabañas listed below can be made at the Oaxaca alternative tourism office, at Murguia 206, Oaxaca, Oaxaca 68000, tel. 951/514-1778, sedetur5@oaxaca.gob.mx. For access details, see specific destinations.

Location	Highlights
IN THE VALLEY OF OAXACA:	
San Sebastián Abasolo	16th-century church, January 20 San Sebastián fiesta, ruins
Santa Ana del Valle	Master weavers' shops, museum, lake, scenic views, hikes
Hierve El Agua	Hikes, scenic vistas, mineral springs, frozen stone cascades
San Miguel del Valle	Foothill hikes, visits to weaver family homes, camping
San Sebastián de las Grutas	Historic town, forested river, limestone cave
IN THE MIXTECA:	
Apoala	Idyllic village, wild canyon, cave, cascade, springs, camping
Huamelulpan	Ruined city, museum, hikes to other archaeological sites
San Miguel Tequixtepec	Museum, hike to hieroglyphic rock paintings, palm weaving, restored 17th-century church, wayside lodge
Tepelmeme de Morelos	Museum, canyon hike to Puente Colosal natural bridge and rare Nuiñe glyph
IN NORTHERN OAXACA:	
Benito Juárez	Cool, pine-scented air, camping, panoramic views
Cuajimoloyas	Mountain-top village, hiking, rock climbing
Llano Grande	Woodland hikes, wildflowers
Ixtlán de Juárez	Cloud forest, wildlife viewing, Benito Juarez's birthplace and museum, limestone cave

tennis courts, exercise gyms, spas, and saunas—of the luxury resorts.

Booking local hotels is straightforward. Many of them can be emailed and all of them can be dialed or faxed directly (from the United States, dial 011-52, followed by the telephone or fax number given in this book) for information and reservations. If your Spanish is rusty, ask for someone who speaks English. Alternatively, repeat, in Spanish: "*¿Por favor, hay alguien que habla Inglés?*" (por fah-VOR, AY ahhl-ghee-AYN KAY AB-lah een-GLAYS?) Always ask about money-saving packages and promotions when reserving.

INTERNATIONAL-CLASS RESORTS

Oaxaca has several beautiful, well-managed international-class resort hotels in Oaxaca city and the Bahías de Huatulco. Their super-deluxe amenities, moreover, need not be overly expensive. While high-season room tariffs ordinarily run $100–300, low-season packages and promotions sometimes cut these prices by half or even more. Shop around for savings through travel agents, and by calling the hotels directly through their toll-free 800 numbers (see the chart "Resort Toll-Free Numbers and Websites").

ON THE ROAD

ON THE ROAD

RESORT TOLL-FREE NUMBERS AND WEBSITES

The following resort hotels and chains have branches (** = outstanding, * = recommended) at Bahías de Huatulco (HU), Oaxaca city (OA), and Puerto Escondido (PE).

Barceló (formerly Sheraton), tel. 800/346-5454, www.barcelo.com, www.mexicotravelnet.com, HU*

Best Western, tel. 800/528-1234, www.best-western.com, OA*, HU*, PE

Camino Real, tel. 800/7-CAMINO (800/722-6466), www.caminoreal.com, HU**, OA**

Fiesta Americana, tel. 800/FIESTA-1 (800/343-7821), www.fiestaamericana.com, OA

Las Brisas, tel. 866/226-3161 or 888/559-4329, www.lasbrisas.com.mx, HU*

Mexico Boutique Hotels, U.S. tel. 877/278-8018, Can. tel. 866/818-8342, www.mexicoboutiquehotels.com, HU**, OA**

Misión de los Angeles, www.hotel-mision-oaxaca.com, OA**

Victoria, www.hotelvictoria.com.mx, OA**

CAMPING, PALAPAS, AND TRAILER PARKS

Although Oaxaca has only a sprinkling of formally maintained places for camping, many inviting beach and inland country spots are customarily used informally. For camping locations, see the maps at the beginning of each destination chapter. For descriptions and details, see Trailer Parks and Camping in the Resources section and specific destinations.

Beach Camping

Camping at beaches is popular among middle-class Mexican families, especially during the Christmas–New Year week and during Semana Santa, the week before Easter. Other times, tent and RV campers usually find prospective camping spots uncrowded. The best beach spots typically have a shady palm grove for camping and a *palapa* (palm-thatched) restaurant that serves drinks and fresh seafood. (Heads up for falling coconuts, especially in the wind.) Cost for parking and tenting is often minimal, typically only the price of food at the restaurant.

Beach days are often perfect for swimming, strolling, and fishing; nights are usually balmy—too warm for a sleeping bag, but fine for a hammock (which allows more air circulation than a tent). Good tents, however, keep out mosquitoes and other pests, which may be further discouraged with good bug repellent. Tents are generally warm inside, requiring only a sheet or light blanket for cover.

As for camping on isolated beaches, opinions vary, from dire warnings of *bandidos* to bland assurances that all is peaceful along the coast. The truth is probably somewhere in between. Trouble is most likely to occur in the vicinity of resort towns, notoriously, on the outskirts of Puerto Escondido, where a few local thugs have harassed isolated campers.

Checking out a beach site: When scouting out a place to camp, a good general rule is to arrive early enough in the day to get a feel for the place. Buy a soda at the *palapa* or nearby store and take a stroll around. Say *"Buenos días"* to the people along the way; ask if the fishing is good: *"¿Pesca buena?"* Use your common sense. If the people seem friendly, ask if it's *seguro* (safe). If so, ask permission: *"¿Es bueno acampar acá?"* ("Is it OK to camp around here?"). You'll rarely be refused.

Beach Palapas

Visitors can still rent beachfront *palapas* (thatched houses) in Puerto Escondido and Zipolite, near Puerto Ángel, and adjoining Mazunte and Ventanilla. Amenities typically include beds or hammocks, a shady thatched porch, cold running water, a kerosene stove, and shared toilets and showers, for $5–15 per day per person.

The bad news is that security has been a problem in some *palapas*, notably at Puerto Escondido. The good news is that Zipolite has some of the better *palapas*, such as Lo Cosmico and Shambhala. The best news of all is that *palapas* are usually right on the beach, so you can walk right out your front door onto the sand, where surf, shells, and seabirds will be there to entertain you.

Mountain and Backcountry Camping

Oaxaca's mountain and rural backcountry offer additional camping opportunities. Private owners and communities maintain picnic areas and informal campgrounds at choice sites, such as springs, waterfalls, caves, *sabineras* (cypress groves), and on rivers and reservoir shorelines.

Invariably, such inland sites are on private (*particular*—par-tee-koo-LAHR) or communal land. As a courtesy, you should obtain permission to set up camp either from the site manager, the closest neighboring restaurant or house, or at the nearest *presidencia municipal* or *agencia*. Such permission, sometimes for a small fee, is usually granted almost automatically. Please reciprocate by keeping your campfire, if permitted,

modest and under control, respecting local etiquette (don't swim or sunbathe in the nude), cleaning up thoroughly, and carrying away all your trash.

For an informative and entertaining discussion of camping in Mexico, check out *The People's Guide to Mexico*. (See Suggested Reading.)

Trailer Parks

Campers who prefer company to isolation usually stay in trailer parks. Oaxaca has four recommendable but modest trailer parks, two in Oaxaca city, one in Zipolite by the beach, near Puerto Ángel, and one in Puerto Escondido, on the beach. For more details, see the destinations chapters.

Food and Drink

Some travel to Mexico for the food. True Mexican food is old-fashioned, homestyle fare requiring many hours of loving preparation. Such food is short on meat and long on corn, beans, rice, tomatoes, chilies, spices, onions, eggs, and cheese.

Mexican food is the unique end-product of thousands of years of native tradition. It is based on corn—*teocentli,* the Aztec "food of the gods"—called *maíz* (mah-EES) by present-day Mexicans. In the past, the typical Mexican woman spent much of her time grinding and preparing corn: soaking the grain in limewater (which swells the kernels and removes the tough seed-coat) and grinding the bloated seeds into meal on a stone *metate.* Finally, she would pat the meal into tortillas and cook them on a hot, baked mud griddle.

Sages (men, no doubt) have wistfully imagined the gentle pat-pat-pat of women all over Mexico to be the heartbeat of Mexico, which they feared would someday cease. Fewer women these days make tortillas by hand. The gentle pat-pat-pat has been replaced by the whir and rattle of automatic tortilla-making machines in myriad *tortillerías,* where women and girls line up for their family's daily kilostack of tortillas.

Tortillas are to the Mexicans as rice is to the Chinese and bread to the French. A Mexican family meal, more often than not, is some mixture of sauce, meat, beans, cheese, and vegetables

© BRUCE WHIPPERMAN

Special Oaxacan-style rice is a savored, essential part of every *comida corrida* (midday set lunch) in Oaxaca.

wrapped in a tortilla, which becomes the culinary be-all: the food, the dish, and the utensil all wrapped into one.

This most Mexican style of meal usually includes one or two of a number of specialties known by Mexicans as *antojitos* and known to everyone else as "Mexican food." These are the familiar burritos, *chiles rellenos,* enchiladas, guacamole, nachos, quesadillas, refried beans, tacos, tamales, and other combinations of beans, cheese, corn, eggs, meat, sauces, and spices that make up the menus of Mexican restaurants in the United States and Canada.

Hot or Not?

Much food served in Mexico is not "Mexican." Eating habits, as most other Mexican customs, depend upon social class. Upwardly mobile Mexicans typically shun the corn-based native food in favor of the European-style food of the Spanish colonial elite: chops, clams, cutlets, fish, omelettes, pasta, potatoes, rice, soups, and steaks.

Such fare is often as bland as Des Moines on a summer Sunday afternoon. *"No picante"*—not spicy—is how the Mexicans describe bland food. *Caliente,* the Spanish adjective for "hot" weather or water, does not, in contrast to English usage, also imply spicy, or *picante.*

Vegetarian Food

Strictly vegetarian cooking is the exception in Mexico, although a few macrobiotic-vegetarian restaurants and health-food stores have opened in Oaxaca city, Puerto Escondido, Puerto Ángel, and Huatulco. Meat is such a delicacy for most Oaxacans that they can't understand why people would give it up voluntarily. If vegetable-lovers can manage with beans, cheese, corn, eggs, fruit, and *legumbres* (vegetables) and not be bothered by a bit of *manteca de cerdo* (pork fat), Mexican (and Oaxacan) cooking will suit them fine.

If you require strictly vegetable fare, all is not lost. Even a humble Mexican *comedor* or *fonda* will almost always be able to fill some hot corn tortillas with fresh diced tomatoes, avocados, and onions, add some piquant fresh

© BRUCE WHIPPERMAN

Traditional food starts with humble dried corn, beans, and chiles, served up as steaming, delicious *moles,* tamales, soups, enchiladas, tacos, and much more.

salsa, and serve it all up as several tasty and nutritious hot tacos.

Seafood

Early chroniclers wrote that Aztec Emperor Moctezuma employed a platoon of runners to bring fresh fish 300 miles (480 km) every day to his court from the sea. On the Oaxaca Pacific Coast, fresh seafood is fortunately much more available from scores of shoreline establishments, ranging from thatched beach *palapas* to five-star hotel restaurants.

Oaxaca seafood is literally there for the taking. When strolling on the beach, I have seen well-fed, middle-class local vacationers breaking and eating oysters and mussels right off the rocks. Villagers up and down the coast use small nets (or bare hands) to retrieve a few fish for supper, while communal teams haul in big nets full of silvery, wriggling fish for sale right on the beach.

Despite the plenty, Oaxaca seafood prices reflect high worldwide demand, even at the humblest seaside *palapa.* The freshness and variety, however, make even the typical dishes seem bargains at any price.

CATCH OF THE DAY

Ceviche (say-VEE-chay): a chopped raw fish appetizer as popular on Mexican Pacific beaches as sushi is on Tokyo side streets. Although it can contain anything from conch to octopus, the best ceviche consists of diced young *tiburón* (shark) or *sierra* (mackerel) fillet and plenty of fresh tomatoes, onions, garlic, and chilies, all doused with lime juice.

Filete de pescado: fish fillet sautéed *al mojo* (ahl-MOH-hoh) with butter and garlic.

Pescado frito (pays-KAH-doh FREE-toh): fish, pan-fried whole; if you don't specify that it be cooked *a medio* (lightly), the fish may arrive well done, like a big, crunchy french fry.

Pescado veracruzana: a favorite everywhere. Best with *huachinango* (red snapper) smothered in a savory tomato, onion, chili, and garlic sauce. *Pargo* (snapper), *mero* (grouper), and *cabrilla* (sea bass) are also popularly used in this and other specialties.

Shellfish: *ostiones* (oysters) and *almejas* (clams) by the dozen, *langosta* (lobster) and *langostina* (crayfish) *asado* (broiled), *al vapor* (steamed), or *frito* (fried). Pots of fresh-boiled *camarones* (shrimp) are sold on the street by the kilo; cafés will make them into *cóctel* (cocktail) or prepare them *en gabardinas* (breaded) at your request.

Fruits and Juices

Squeezed vegetable and fruit juices (*jugos,* HOO-gohs) are among the widely available delights of Oaxaca. Among the many establishments—restaurants, cafés, and *loncherías*—willing to supply you with your favorite *jugo,* the *jugerías* (juice bars) are often the most fun. Colorful fruit piles usually mark *jugerías.* If you don't immediately spot your favorite fruit, ask anyway; it might be hidden in the refrigerator.

Besides your choice of pure juice, a *jugería* will often serve **licuados.** Into the juice, they whip powdered milk, your favorite fruit, and sugar to taste for a creamy afternoon pick-me-up or evening dessert. One big favorite is a cool banana chocolate *licuado,* which comes out tasting like a milk shake, but minus the calories.

Alcoholic Drinks

The Aztecs usually sacrificed anyone caught drinking alcohol without permission. The later, more lenient, Spanish attitude toward getting *borracho* (soused) has led to a thriving Mexican renaissance of native alcoholic beverages: *aguardiente,* Kahlua, *mescal, pulque,* and tequila. **Mescal,** distilled from the fermented juice of the maguey (century) plant, originated in Oaxaca, where the best *mescales* are still made. Quality **tequila** and *mescal* come 76 proof (38 percent alcohol) and up. A small white worm, endemic

to the maguey plant, is often added to each bottle of factory *mescal* for authenticity.

Pulque, although also made from the sap of the maguey, is locally brewed to a small alcohol content, between beer and wine. The brewing houses are sacrosanct preserves, circumscribed by traditions that exclude both women and outsiders. The brew, said to be full of nutrients, is

Oven-fresh bread and *panes dulces* (sweet rolls) are usually available fresh on the street near markets in most Oaxacan towns.

A TROVE OF FRUITS AND NUTS

Besides carrying the usual temperate fruits, *jugerías* and especially markets are seasonal sources of a number of exotic varieties (followed by an *):

avocado *(aguacate*—ah-wah-KAH-tay): Aztec aphrodisiac

banana *(platano):* many kinds—big and small, red and yellow

chirimoya* *(chirimoya):* green scales, white pulp; sometimes called an *anona*

coconut *(coco):* coconut "milk" is called *agua coco*

grapes *(uvas):* Aug.–Nov. season

guanabana* looks, but doesn't taste, like a green mango

guava *(guava):* delicious juice, widely available canned

lemon *(limón*—lee-MOHN): uncommon and expensive; use lime instead

lime *(lima*—LEE-mah): douse salads with it

mamey* *(mamey*—mah-MAY): yellow, juicy fruit; excellent for jellies and preserves

mango *(mango):* king of fruit, in a hundred varieties June–Nov.

orange *(naranja*—nah-RAHN-ha): greenish skin but sweet and juicy

papaya *(papaya):* said to aid digestion and healing

peach *(durazno,* pronounced doo-RAHS-noh): delicious and widely available as canned juice

Fresh fruit and juices are one of the delights of a Oaxaca visit.

peanut *(cacahuate*—kah-kah-WAH-tay): home roasted and cheap

pear *(pera):* fall season

pecan *(nuez):* for a treat, try freshly ground pecan butter

piña anona* looks like an ear of corn without the husk; tastes like pineapple

pineapple *(piña):* huge, luscious, and cheap

strawberry *(fresa*—FRAY-sah): local favorite

tangerine *(mandarina):* common around Christmas

watermelon *(sandía*—sahn-DEE-ah): perfect on a hot day

*zapote** (sah-POH-tay): yellow, fleshy fruit; said to induce sleep

*zapote colorado** brown skin, red, puckery fruit, like persimmon; incorrectly called *mamey*

---

sold to local *pulquerías* and drunk immediately. If you are ever invited into a *pulquería,* it will be an honor you cannot refuse.

Aguardiente, by contrast, is the notorious fiery Mexican "white lightning," a locally cane-fermented and distilled, dirt-cheap ticket to oblivion for poor Mexican men.

While *pulque* comes from an age-old indigenous tradition, **beer *(cerveza)*** is the beverage of modern mestizo Mexico. Full-bodied and tastier than "light" U.S. counterparts, Mexican beer enjoys an enviable reputation.

Those visitors who indulge usually know their favorite among the many brands, from light to dark: Superior, Corona, Pacífico, Tecate (served with lime), Carta Blanca, Modelo, Dos Equis, Bohemia, Tres Equis, and Negra Modelo. Nochebuena, a flavorful dark brew, becomes available only around Christmas.

Mexicans have yet to develop much of a taste for *vino* (wine), although some domestic wines, such as the Baja California labels Monte Xanic, Domecq, and Cetto are often quite good and sometimes excellent.

Bread and Pastries

Excellent locally baked bread is a delightful surprise to many first-time visitors to Oaxaca. Small bakeries everywhere put out trays of hot, crispy-crusted *bolillos* (rolls) and sweet *panes dulces* (pastries). They range from simple cakes, muffins, cookies, and doughnuts to fancy fruit-filled turnovers and puffs. Half the fun occurs before the eating: Grab a tray and tongs, peruse the goodies, and pick out the most scrumptious. With your favorite dozen finally selected, you take your tray to the cashier, who deftly bags everything up and collects a few pesos (two or three dollars) for your whole mouthwatering selection.

Shopping

What to Buy

Although bargains abound in Mexico, savvy shoppers are selective. Steep import and luxury taxes drive up the prices of foreign-made goods, such as cameras, computers, English-language books, and sports equipment. Instead, concentrate your shopping on locally-made items: cotton resort wear, jewelry, leather, Mexican-made designer clothes, and the galaxy of handicrafts for which Mexico is renowned.

Handicrafts

Shops and markets in Oaxaca city and the Oaxaca Valley towns of Teotitlán del Valle, Santa Ana del Valle, Tlacolula, Mitla, San Bártolo Coyotepec, San Martín Tilcajete, Santo Tomás Jalieza, Ocotlán, Arrazola, and Atzompa are Oaxaca's most renowned sources of handicrafts. And, although most crafts are not made in the coastal resorts of Huatulco and Puerto Escondido, each has several good private handicrafts stores and a number of crafts markets where local folks maintain stalls stuffed with their homemade goods. Moreover, the rich cornucopia of crafts from other Mexican centers, such as the neighboring state of Guerrero, the Lake Pátzcuaro region of Michoacán, and around Guadalajara, spills over to Oaxaca. For a multitude of specifics, see the destination chapters and the Handicrafts section in this chapter.

Bargaining

Bargaining will stretch your money even further. It comes with the territory in Mexico and needn't be a hassle. On the contrary, if done with humor and moderation, bargaining can be an enjoyable path to encountering Mexican people and gaining their respect, and even friendship.

The local crafts market is where bargaining is most intense. For starters, try offering half the asking price. From there on, it's all psychology: You have to content yourself with not having to have the item. Otherwise, you're sunk; the vendor will probably sense your need and stand fast. After a few minutes of good-humored bantering, ask for *el último precio* (the final price), in which, if it's close, you may have a bargain.

Buying Silver and Gold Jewelry

Silver and gold jewelry, the finest of which is crafted in Taxco, Mexico City, Guanajuato, and Oaxaca, is sold in a number of shops in Oaxaca, Huatulco, and Puerto Escondido.

© BRUCE WHIPPERMAN

An automobile hood on a town backstreet serves as a jewelry counter.

TIANGUIS: NATIVE MARKETS

Most important Oaxaca towns have a public outdoor market every day but a *tianguis* (tee-AHN-gees) only once a week. The word *tianguis* is an ancient native expression, synonymous with "awning," the colorful tarpaulins that shade the mini-mountains of fruits, vegetables, crafts, and merchandise, which native people flock to buy and sell everywhere in Oaxaca.

Although trade appears to be the prime mover, people really come to *tianguis* for human contact, not only in the buying and selling itself, but for gossip, entertainment, flirtation—all of the other diversions that make life worth living.

People gather regularly for many Oaxaca *tianguis:*

The awning *(tianguis)* provides both the shelter and the name for the traditional indigenous market.

OAXACA CITY

Abastos	Saturday

VALLEY OF OAXACA

Tlacolula	Sunday
Miahuatlán	Monday
Etla	Wednesday
Zimatlán	Thursday
Zaachila	Thursday
Ejutla	Thursday
Ocotlán	Friday

PACIFIC RESORTS AND SOUTHERN SIERRA

Nopala	Saturday and Sunday
Juquila	Saturday and Sunday
Santa María Huatulco	Saturday and Sunday
Cacahuatepec	Sunday
Sola de Vega	Sunday
Pochutla	Monday
Astata	Tuesday
Huamelula	Thursday
Jamiltepec	Thursday

MIXTECA

Nochixtlán	Sunday
Putla	Sunday
Huajuapan	Wednesday
Juxtlahuaca	Thursday, Friday biggest
Chalcatongo	Thursday
Tonalá	Friday
Tlaxiaco	Saturday

NORTHERN OAXACA

Yalalag	Sunday
Huatla	Sunday
Valle Nacional	Sunday
Tuxtepec	Sunday
Teotitlán del Camino	Wednesday and Sunday
Jalapa de Díaz	Thursday and Sunday
Ojitlán	Wednesday

ISTHMUS

Juchitán	every day
Tehuantepec	Wednesday and Sunday

Although bargaining is traditional for most purchases in Oaxaca, most folks don't haggle much over fruits and vegetables.

One hundred percent pure silver is rarely sold because it's too soft. Silver (most of which is sent from processing mills in the north of Mexico to be worked in Taxco shops) is nearly always alloyed with 7.5 percent copper to increase its durability. Such pieces, identical in composition to sterling silver, should have ".925," together with the initials of the manufacturing jeweler, stamped on their back sides. Other, less common grades, such as "800 fine" (80 percent silver), should also be stamped.

If silver is not stamped with the degree of purity, it probably contains no silver at all and is an alloy of copper, zinc, and nickel, known by the generic label "alpaca," or "German" silver. Once, after haggling over the purity and prices of his offerings, a street vendor handed me a shiny handful and said, "Go to a jeweler and have them tested. If they're not real, keep them." Calling his bluff, I took them to a jeweler, who applied a dab of hydrochloric acid to each piece.

Tiny, tell-tale bubbles of hydrogen revealed the cheapness of the merchandise, which I returned the next day to the vendor.

Some shops price sterling silver jewelry simply by weighing, which typically translates to about $1 per gram. If you want to find out if the price is fair, ask the shopkeeper to weigh it for you.

Oaxaca city itself is a **gold jewelry** center, mainly due to the skill and enterprise of the family-owned *Oro de Monte Albán* business. They maintain a number of shops in Oaxaca city, Puerto Escondido, and Huatulco.

People universally prize pure gold, partly because, unlike silver, it does not tarnish. Gold, nevertheless, is rarely sold pure (24 karat); for durability, it is alloyed with copper. Typical purity levels, such as 18 karat (75 percent) or 14 karat (58 percent), should be stamped on the pieces. If not, chances are they contain no gold at all.

Getting There

BY AIR

From the United States and Canada

The majority of foreign visitors reach Oaxaca by air, and a large fraction of those through Mexico City. There, travelers transfer to flights bound for either Oaxaca city, Puerto Escondido, or Bahías de Huatulco–Puerto Ángel. Two possible exceptions are Mexicana Airlines and American Airlines flights that have connected directly (but at this writing do not) with Huatulco from Los Angeles and Dallas, respectively.

Most air travelers begin their Oaxaca vacations through the Mexico City gateways of **Atlanta, Chicago, Dallas, Denver, Houston, Los Angeles, Miami, New York, Orlando, Phoenix, San Antonio,** or **San Francisco.**

Although very few if any scheduled flights go directly to Mexico City or Oaxaca from the northern United States and Canada, **charters** do, especially during the winter. In locales near Boston, Buffalo, Calgary-Edmonton, Cleveland, Detroit, Minneapolis, Montreal, Ottawa, Seattle, Toronto, Vancouver, and Winnipeg, consult a travel agent or website for charter flight options. Be aware that charter reservations, which often require fixed departure and return dates and provide minimal cancellation refunds, decrease your flexibility.

Air travelers can save money by shopping around, through independent ticket agents and the airlines, both by telephone and the Internet. Don't be bashful about trying for the best price. Make it clear to the airline or agent that you're interested in a bargain. Ask the right questions. Are there special incentive, advance-payment, night, midweek, tour-package, or charter fares? Peruse the ads in your Sunday newspaper travel section for bargain-oriented travel agencies. An agent usually costs you no money, although some don't like discounted tickets because their fee often depends on a percentage of ticket price. Nevertheless, many agents will work to get you a bargain.

You may be able to also save money by booking an air/hotel package. Mexicana (tel. 800/531-9321) and Aeromexico (tel. 800/245-8585) agencies routinely offer Oaxaca air/hotel packages.

From Europe, Latin America, and Australasia

A few airlines fly across the Atlantic directly to Mexico City. These include **Lufthansa,** which connects directly from Frankfurt; and **Aeroméxico,** which connects directly from Paris and Madrid. In Mexico City, several connections with the Acapulco Region are available, mostly via Mexicana and Aeroméxico airlines.

From Latin America, **Aeroméxico** connects directly with Mexico City, from Sao Paulo, Brazil; Santiago, Chile; and Lima, Peru. A number of other Latin American flag carriers also fly directly to Mexico City. From there, easy Oaxaca connections are available via Mexicana Airlines and Aeroméxico Airlines and their respective affiliate airlines, Aerocaribe and Aeromar.

Very few flights cross the Pacific directly to Mexico, except for **Japan Airlines,** which connects Tokyo to Mexico City, via Vancouver. More commonly, travelers from Australasia routinely transfer at Los Angeles, Phoenix, San Francisco, or Seattle for connections to Mexico City.

Baggage, Insurance, "Bumping," and In-Flight Meals

Tropical and temperate Oaxaca makes it easy to pack light. (See the "Packing Checklist" sidebar.) Veteran tropical travelers often condense their luggage to carry-ons only. Airlines routinely allow a carry-on (not exceeding 45 inches in combined length, width, and girth) and a small book bag and purse. Thus relieved of heavy burdens, your trip will become much simpler. You'll avoid possible luggage loss and long baggage check-in lines by being able to check in directly at the boarding gate.

Even if you can't avoid having to check luggage, loss of it needn't ruin your vacation. Always carry your irreplaceable items in the cabin with you. These should include all cameras, checks, credit cards, eyeglasses, money, passport, prescription drugs, tickets, and traveler's keys.

At the X-ray security check, insist that your film and cameras be hand-inspected. Regardless of what attendants claim, repeated X-ray scanning will fog any film, especially the sensitive ASA 400 and 1,000 high-speed varieties. (You can assure both protection and hand inspection for your film by packing it in the special lead-lined film bags available in any good camera store.)

Travelers packing lots of expensive baggage, or who (because of illness, for example) may have to cancel a nonrefundable flight or tour might consider buying **travel insurance.** Travel agents routinely sell packages that include baggage, trip cancellation, and default insurance. Baggage insurance covers you beyond the customary $1,250 domestic, $400 international baggage liability limits, but check with your carrier. **Trip cancellation insurance** pays if you must cancel your prepaid trip, while default insurance protects you if your carrier or tour agent does not perform as agreed. Travel insurance, however, can be expensive. Traveler's Insurance Company, for example, offers about $1,000 of baggage insurance per person for two weeks for about $50. Carefully weigh both your options and the cost against benefits before putting your money down.

It's wise to reconfirm both departure and return flight reservations, especially during the busy Christmas and Easter seasons. This is a useful strategy—as is prompt arrival at check-in—against getting "bumped" (losing your seat) because of the tendency of airlines to overbook the rush of high-season vacationers. For further protection, if possible get your seat assignment and boarding pass included with your ticket.

Airlines generally try hard to accommodate travelers with dietary or other special needs. When booking your flight, inform your travel agent or carrier of the necessity of a low-sodium, low-cholesterol, vegetarian, lactose-reduced meal or other requirements. (Seniors, persons with disabilities, and parents traveling with children, see also the Specialty Travel section under Information and Services.)

BY BUS

As air travel rules in the United States, bus travel rules in Mexico. Hundreds of sleek luxury- and first-class bus lines with names such as Elite, Estrella de Oro (Star of Gold), and Estrella Blanca (White Star) roar out daily from the border, headed south.

Since U.S. bus lines ordinarily terminate just north of the Mexican border, you must usually disembark, collect your things, and after having filled out the necessary but very simple paperwork at the immigration booth, proceed on foot across the border to Mexico, where you can bargain with a local taxi driver to drive you the few miles to the *camionera central* (central bus station). Inside the station door, handy words to have in mind are *taquilla* (ticket booth), *guardaequipajes* (baggage checkroom), *llegada* (arrival), *salida* (departure), and *sanitario* or *baño* (toilet or bathroom).

First- and luxury-class bus service in Mexico is generally cheaper and at least as good as in the United States. Tickets for comparable trips in Mexico cost less than half (as little as $60 for a 1,000-mile, 1,600-km trip), compared to perhaps $150 in the United States.

In Mexico, as on U.S. buses, you often have to take it as you find it. *Asientos reservados* (reserved seats), *boletos* (tickets), and information must generally be obtained in person at the bus station, and credit cards and traveler's checks are sometimes not accepted. Reserved bus tickets are typically nonrefundable, so don't miss the bus. On the other hand, plenty of buses roll south almost continuously. Two basic routes are available, either through Mexico City or down the Pacific Coast all the way.

Pacific Coast Route

The route to Oaxaca along the Pacific shore, although the longest, requiring one or two transfers and at least three full 24-hour days, is the most scenic. Try to go luxury class all the way; the small additional cost is well worth it. Cross the border at **Tijuana, Mexicali,** or **Nogales,** where you can choose from at least three bus lines along the Pacific Coast route,

AIRLINES SERVING OAXACA (VIA MEXICO CITY)

The following scheduled airlines connect with Mexico City (MX), where connecting flights continue on to the Oaxaca destinations of Oaxaca city, Huatulco–Puerto Ángel (HU), and Puerto Escondido. American Airlines and Mexicana Airlines sometimes seasonally connect Huatulco–Puerto Ángel (HU) directly from Dallas and Los Angeles, respectively.

Airline	Origin	Destinations
Aeroméxico	Los Angeles	.MX
tel. 800/237-6639	Tijuana	.MX
www.aeromexico.com	New York	.MX
	Miami	.MX
	Houston	.MX
	San Diego	.MX
	Atlanta	.MX
	Phoenix	.MX
	Dallas	.MX
Mexicana	Los Angeles	.MX, HU
tel. 800/531-7921	San Francisco	.MX
www.mexicana.com.mx	Tijuana	.MX
	Denver	.MX
	Chicago	.MX
	Toronto	.MX
	Montreal	.MX
	Miami	.MX
	San Antonio	.MX
	San José	.MX
Delta	Los Angeles	.MX
tel. 800/221-1212	Dallas	.MX
www.delta.com	Atlanta	.MX
	Orlando	.MX
	New York	.MX
	Miami	.MX

Airline	Origin	Destinations
American tel. 800/433-7300 www.aa.com	Dallas ....HU, MX Chicago ....MX Miami ....MX	
Aerocalifornia tel. 800/237-6225	Los Angeles ....MX Tijuana ....MX	
Continental tel. 800/231-0856 www.continental.com	Houston ....MX	
America West tel. 800/363-2597 www.americawest.com	Phoenix ....MX	
Allegro tel. 877/443-7585	Oakland ....MX Las Vegas ....MX	
Azteca tel. 888/754-0066	Laredo ....MX El Paso ....MX	
Air Canada tel. 888/247-2262 www.aircanada.com	Toronto ....MX	
Aviacsa tel. 800/758-2188	Los Angeles ....MX	

ON THE ROAD

DRIVING AND BUSING TO OAXACA

UNITED STATES

MEXICO

Gulf of Mexico

GUATEMALA

San Diego
Tijuana
Calexico
Mexicali
159/193
3:15

Sonoyta
165/266
2:45

Tucson
Nogales

El Paso
Juárez
233/375
5:00

282/452
6:30

Hermosillo
173/279
3:15

Chihuahua

Ciudad Obregón
181/290
3:05

45D
284/457
6:30

Culiacán
288/431
5:00

Torreón
220/354
5:30

Durango
197/253
3:30

Zacatecas
290/370

45
196/318
6:00

39/224
2:30

Mazatlán

104/167
3:00

Laredo
Nuevo Laredo

Monterrey
174/280
3:45

40D

McAllen
Reynosa
1:00

85D
143/230
2:30

Saltillo
53/85
3:15

54

155/250
3:15

Matehuala
112/180
2:30

57

San Luis Potosí
129/208
2:50

Ciudad Victoria
4:15

197/317
4:30

Tampico
7:30

180/290

227/366

Querétaro
134/215
2:30

40/84
1:00

154/246
4:30

Morelia
74/119
2:15

Toluca
76/122
2:30

MEXICO CITY

150D

Tehuacán
350/564
8:00

259/417
5:15

Taxco
150/242
4:00

95D

Guadalajara

Tepic
141/227
3:00

198/318
5:45

90D

200

Playa Azul
Ixtapa-Zihuatanejo

Acapulco
291/469

6:16

OAXACA

131

148/238
6:15

Puerto Ángel

182/293
4:00

Puerto Vallarta
172/276
4:30

Manzanillo
191/1/311

54D

190/314
6:30

PACIFIC OCEAN

Sea of Cortez

Baja California

La Paz
Cabo San Lucas

Gulf of California

150 mi
150 km
0

NOTE: DISTANCES ARE SHOWN AS MILES/KILOMETERS.
APPROXIMATE DRIVING TIMES ARE SHOWN AS HOURS/MINUTES.

© AVALON TRAVEL PUBLISHING, INC.

via combined National Highways 15 and 200, via Mazatlán, Puerto Vallarta, Zihuatanejo, Acapulco, and finally, Puerto Escondido, in Oaxaca. At the border, get a bus as far south as you can, maybe even **Elite** all the way to Acapulco; or if not, at least to Tepic or Puerto Vallarta, where you change to a bus headed south for, most likely, Lázaro Cárdenas, Zihuatanejo, or Acapulco, at the end of your second day. There, you catch a third bus, which will take you at least to Acapulco, and at most to Puerto Escondido by the end of your third day. On the other hand, make it easy on yourself and stretch the trip to five days by resting overnight in Puerto Vallarta and Zihuatanejo along the way. (In Puerto Vallarta, stay at Hotel Rosita, $45, tel./fax 322/223-2000, tel. 322/223-2177, on the beach; in Zihuatanejo, stay at Hotel Irma, $60–80 d, tel./fax 755/554-3738, on the beach, or Posada Citlali, $35 d, tel./fax 755/554-2043, a block from the beach.)

Mexico City Route

This is the quickest bus route to Oaxaca, typically about 36 hours from the south Texas border, a day longer from California or Nogales, Arizona, via Guadalajara. From the western United States, cross the border at either Tijuana, Mexicali, or Nogales. From the United States Midwest, Southeast and East, cross the border at Laredo to Nuevo Laredo or McAllen to Reynosa. For the most speed and comfort, at only a small extra cost, go by luxury-class bus to Mexico City.

MEXICO CITY DRIVING RESTRICTIONS

To reduce smog and traffic gridlock, authorities have limited which cars can drive on which days in Mexico City, depending upon the last digit of their license plates. If you violate these rules, you risk getting an expensive ticket. On Monday, no vehicle may be driven with final digits 5 or 6; Tuesday, 7 or 8; Wednesday, 3 or 4; Thursday, 1 or 2; Friday, 9 or 0. Weekends, all vehicles may be driven.

Mexico City has four bus terminals—north, east, south, and west (respectively, Terminal Norte, Terminal Tapo, Terminal Sur, and Terminal Poniente). You will most likely arrive in the Terminal Norte, although a few buses from the west via Guadalajara might arrive at Terminal Poniente. (For an overnight rest break, Guadalajara is especially handy, at semi-deluxe but moderately priced Hotel La Serena, $35 d,tel.333/600-091 0, fax333/600-1974, with pool, conveniently adjacent to the bus station.)

In any case, at Mexico City, if you're heading to Oaxaca city, from Terminal Norte, board an **Autobuses del Oriente (ADO)** or **Cristóbal Colón** bus, via the Puebla expressway (*autopista* or *corta*) to Oaxaca city. If you're heading for the Oaxaca Pacific Coast, best board an **Estrella Blanca** affiliate (such as **Turistar** or **Futura**) or an **Estrella de Oro** bus bound for Acapulco, where you can transfer to a Puerto Escondido–bound bus.

If somehow the above connections are not available at Terminal Norte (or Terminal Poniente), share a taxi (don't try it by public transit) to Terminal Sur (or Terminal Tapo for Oaxaca city via ADO) and catch an Estrella Blanca subsidiary (such as Elite, Turistar, Futura, Flecha Roja, or Transportes Cuauhtémoc) all the way to Puerto Escondido via Acapulco. If you miss the direct Puerto Escondido connection, settle for an express connection to Acapulco, where plenty of local departures head out southeast for Puerto Escondido.

Get across town to your continuing bus terminal via **private taxi** (*taxi especial*) or **collective taxi** (*colectivo*). Although such a trip is possible by public transportation, don't try it. If you do, you're either a Mexico City veteran traveling light and know what you're getting into or are willing to bear a load of frustration, pain, and the dirty looks from fellow passengers as you unwittingly poke them with your bulging backpacks and luggage in a crowded subway or local bus.

BY CAR OR RV

If you're adventurous and enjoy going to out-of-the-way places, but still want to have all the comforts of home, you may prefer to drive your

ROAD SAFETY

Hundreds of thousands of visitors enjoy safe Mexican auto vacations every year. Their success is due in large part to their frame of mind: Drive defensively, anticipate and adjust to danger before it happens, and watch everything—side roads, shoulders, the car in front, and cars far down the road. The following tips will help ensure a safe and enjoyable trip:

- **Don't drive at night.** Range animals, unmarked sand piles, pedestrians, one-lane bridges, cars without lights, and drunk drivers are doubly hazardous at night.
- Although **speed limits** are rarely enforced, *don't break them.* Mexican roads are often narrow and shoulderless. Poor markings and macho drivers who pass on curves are best faced at a speed of 40 mph (64 kph) rather than 75 mph (120 kph).
- **Drive on sand only sparingly.** Even with four-wheel-drive, you'll eventually get stuck if you drive either often or casually on beaches. When the tide comes in, who'll pull your car out?
- **Slow down** at the *topes* (speed bumps) at the edges of towns and for *vados* (dips), which can be dangerously bumpy and full of water.
- Extending the **courtesy of the road** goes hand-in-hand with safe driving. Both courtesy and machismo are more infectious in Mexico; on the highway, it's much safer to spread the former than the latter.

RV or car to Oaxaca. On the other hand, consideration of cost, risk, wear on both you and your vehicle, and the congestion hassles in towns may change your mind.

Mexican Car Insurance

Mexico does not recognize foreign insurance. When you drive into Mexico, Mexican auto insurance is at least as important as your passport. At the busier crossings, you can get it at insurance "drive-ins" just north of the border. The many Mexican auto insurance companies are government-regulated; their numbers keep prices and services competitive.

Sanborn's Mexico insurance, one of the best-known agencies, certainly seems to be trying hardest. It offers a number of books and services. These include a guide to RV campgrounds, road map, *Travel with Health* book, "smile-by-mile" *Travelog* guide to "every highway in Mexico," hotel discounts, and more. All of the above are available to members of Sanborn's "Sombrero" Club. You can buy insurance, sign up for membership, or order books through its toll-free number, tel. 800/222-0158. For other queries, call tel. 956/682-7433 or write Sanborn's Mexico, P.O. Box 310, McAllen, TX 78502, or log on to www.sanbornsinsurance.com.

Alternatively, look into **Vagabundos del Mar,** an RV-oriented Mexico fishing and travel club that offers memberships that include a newsletter, caravanning opportunities, discounts, insurance, and much more. Call tel. 800/474-2252 for a free information packet or look at their website, www.vagabundos.com.

Mexican car insurance runs from a barebones rate of about $5 a day to a more typical $10–15 a day for more complete coverage ($50,000/$40,000/$80,000 public liability/property damage/medical payments), including collision and theft on a vehicle worth around $15,000. On the same scale, insurance for a $50,000 RV and equipment runs about $30 a day. These daily rates decrease sharply for six-month or one-year policies, which run from about $200 for the minimum to $350–1,600 for complete coverage.

If you get broken glass, personal effects, and legal expenses coverage with these rates, you're lucky. Mexican policies don't usually cover them.

You should get something for your money, however. The deductibles should be no more than $300–500; the public liability/medical payments should be about double the legal minimum (which is $50,000 total public liability, including property damage and medical payments); and you should be able to get your car fixed in the United States and receive payment in U.S. dollars for losses. If not, shop around.

Crossing the Border

Squeezing through the border traffic bottlenecks during peak holidays and rush hours can be time-consuming. Avoid crossing 7–9 A.M. and 4:30–6:30 P.M.

The Green Angels

The Green Angels have answered many motoring tourists' prayers in Mexico. (They've rescued so many stalled drivers that on my next trip I think I'll carry some gifts to give whenever I see them on the road.) Bilingual teams of two, trained in auto repair and first aid, help distressed tourists along main highways. They patrol fixed stretches of road twice daily by green truck. To make sure they stop to help, pull completely off the highway and raise your hood. You may want to hail a passing trucker to call them for you (toll-free Mex. tel. 800/903-9200 for the tourism hot line, which might alert the Green Angels for you).

If, for some reason, you have to leave your vehicle on the roadside, *don't leave it unattended.* Hire a local teenager or adult to watch it for you. Unattended vehicles on Mexican highways are quickly stricken by a mysterious disease, the symptoms of which are rapid loss of vital parts.

A Sinaloa Note of Caution

Although *bandidos* no longer menace Mexican highways (but loose burros, horses, and cattle still do), be cautious in the infamous marijuana- and opium-growing region of Sinaloa state north of Mazatlán. Best not stray from Highway 15 between Culiacán and Mazatlán or from Highway 40 between Mazatlán and Durango. Curious tourists have been assaulted in the hinterlands adjacent to these roads.

Mexican Gasoline

Pemex, short for Petróleos Mexicanos, the government oil monopoly, markets diesel fuel and two grades of gasoline: 92-octane premium and 89-octane Magna. Magna (MAHG-nah) is good gas, yielding performance similar to that of U.S.-style regular or super-unleaded gasoline. (My car, whose manufacturer recommended 91 octane, ran well on Magna.) It currently costs about $.55 per liter (or about $2.07 per gallon).

On federal highways, Pemex makes sure that major stations (spaced typically about 30 miles or 48 km apart) stock Magna.

Gas Station Thievery

Although the problem has abated considerably in recent years, boys who hang around gas stations to wash windows are notoriously light-fingered. When stopping at the *gasolinera,* make sure that your cameras, purses, and other movable items are out of reach. Also, make sure that your car has a lockable gas cap. If not, insist on pumping the gas yourself, or be super-watchful as you pull up to the gas pump. Make certain that the pump reads zero before the attendant pumps the gas.

A Healthy Car

Preventative measures spell good health for both you and your car. Get that tune-up (or long-delayed overhaul) *before,* rather than after, you leave.

Carry a stock of spare parts, which will probably be both more difficult to get and more expensive in

roadside gasoline service

© BRUCE WHIPPERMAN

ON THE ROAD

DETOUR INTO A CORNFIELD

Driving hazards—poorly marked roads, potholes, pedestrians, roadside horses, cattle, and burros, rattletrap cars and trucks with no lights—make rural nighttime driving in Oaxaca an iffy proposition. Add speed to the mix and you have a recipe for close calls at least and disaster at worst.

I was only doing about 30 or 35 miles per hour (about 50 or 55 kph), and although the road was paved (something that probably lulled me into complacency), it was dark, wet, gravelly, and completely lacking either a white center line or edge markings.

I blundered into a sharp left curve and in a split second found that I had to either roll my car or leave the road. I chose the latter and hurtled into someone's tall-corn *milpa*. As green stalks slapped the windshield and I bounced up and down like a Ping-Pong ball, I wondered if I was going to go over a cliff (this was hilly country), something that probably would have postponed publication of the *Oaxaca Handbook* indefinitely.

This time I was lucky. After a very long second or two, my little truck lurched to a stop, tilted at a crazy sideways angle against a big round boulder. Somehow something managed to seriously crack the front windshield and cave in both passenger-side doors, but the car didn't roll, and miraculously the motor would still run.

What does a writer on a short deadline do on such an occasion? Go get help and get rolling again if possible. The only problem: I was way out in the country, 100 miles (160 km) from the crane (Tow truck? No way!) that seemed necessary to pull my truck from where it was lodged over the boulders and up the long embankment.

It turned out that I couldn't have been in a better place to get help. I climbed out of the cornfield to a nearby village, where, at 9 P.M. on Saturday night, everybody was out and about. I asked a man, named German ("Herman"), who, it seems, knew Agustín, who had a tractor. Agustín, German said, was at his girlfriend's house, where we went next.

Agustín came outside for a conference. Given his tractor, it was not a question of if the job could be done, but when.

"Can't we wait until tomorrow?" Agustín asked. "It's dark now. Best to try in the morning."

My deadline pushed me on.

"You may be right, but if possible I'd like to try now. I've got 1,500 pesos ($150) cash. It's yours if you pull my *camioneta* out of the *milpa*."

By this time a small crowd had gathered around. Several of us piled into German's truck and headed to Agustín's place, where Agustín maneuvered a huge green John Deere tractor with seven-foot (two-meter) wheels out of his barn. Agustín's brother went to get a long cable and met us at the site.

With about five guys helping me, we wrapped the cable around the axle. I got behind the steering wheel, and miracle of miracles, Agustín and his tractor, like the strong right hand of God, pulled my *camioneta* straight up the rocky incline and onto the road.

Overjoyed, I immediately wanted to fulfill my promise to Agustín. I started counting out the $10 bills, one by one. When I got to eight or nine, Agustín protested.

"Stop. That's enough."

I distributed the rest of the bills to the other men and was about to leave when someone spied that the crash had flattened the right front tire. Quickly, one of the men replaced it with my spare, and I was ready to go. I thanked everyone all round again and headed out through the Oaxaca night, shaken but unhurt and grateful to my kind rescuers.

Mexico than at home. Carry an extra tire or two, a few cans of motor oil and octane enhancer, oil and gas filters, fan belts, spark plugs, tune-up kit, points, and fuses. Carry basic tools and supplies, such as screwdrivers, pliers (including Vise-Grip), lug wrench and jack, adjustable wrenches, tire pump and patches, pressure gauge, steel wire, and electrical tape. For breakdowns and emergencies, carry a folding shovel, a husky rope or chain, a gasoline can, and flares.

Car Repairs in Mexico

The American big three—General Motors, Ford, and Chrysler—and Nissan and Volkswagen are well represented by extensive dealer networks in Mexico. Latecomers Toyota and Honda are only sparsely represented by comparison. Getting your car or truck serviced at such agencies is usually straightforward. While parts will probably be higher, shop rates run about a third of U.S. prices, so repairs will generally come out cheaper than back home.

The same is not true for repairing other makes. Mexico has few, if any other Japanese or European car or truck dealers; other than Volkswagen and Mercedes-Benz, which has some Mexican truck agencies, officially certified mechanics for British and European makes are generally difficult to find.

Many clever Mexican independent mechanics, however, can fix virtually any car that happens to come their way. Their humble *talleres mecánicos* (tah-YER-ays may-KAH-nee-kohs), or repair shops, dot the town and village roadsides everywhere.

Although most mechanics are honest, beware of unscrupulous operators who try to collect double or triple their original estimate. If you don't speak Spanish, find someone who can assist you in negotiations. *Always* get a cost estimate, including needed parts and labor, in writing, even if you have to write it yourself. Make sure the mechanic understands, then ask him to sign it before he starts work. Although this may be a hassle, it might save you a much nastier hassle later. Shop labor at small, independent repair shops should typically runs between $15 and $25 per hour. For much more information, and entertaining

anecdotes of car and RV travel in Mexico, consult Carl Franz's *The People's Guide to Mexico*. (See Suggested Reading.)

Highway Routes from the United States

If you've decided to drive to Oaxaca, you have your choice of four general routes. At safe highway speeds, from the Mexican border these routes require as much as five days or as little as two days, depending on your route.

The longest but most scenic route is the **Pacific route,** which starts out as Mexican National Highway 15 from the border at Nogales, Sonora, an hour's drive south of Tucson, Arizona. Soon you join Highway 15 D *cuota* (toll) expressway—or continue along old *libre* (free) Highway 15—proceeding southward smoothly, over cactus-studded plains mountains that give way to irrigated farms and groves and palmy tropical coastal plain by the time you arrive in Mazatlán. Follow the *periféricos* (peripheral bypasses) that conduct traffic past the congested downtowns of Hermosillo, Guaymas, Culiacán, and Mazatlán. Between these centers, you can speed along via the *cuota* Highway 15 D expressway virtually the entire way. If you prefer not to pay the high tolls (around $60 total for a passenger car, much more for multiple-wheeled RVs) you should stick to the old *libre* Highway 15. Hazards, bumps, and slow going might force you to reconsider, however.

At **Tepic,** the Pacific route leaves Highway 15-15 D and continues south via Highway 200, winding past tobacco farms and mango orchards, through lush forest, climbing vine-hung canyons, crossing a score of rivers, past a host of palm-tufted beaches, and passing the renowned vacation lands of **Puerto Vallarta, Manzanillo, Ixtapa-Zihuatanejo,** and **Acapulco.** Finally, several days after you crossed the border, you arrive at the heart of the tropical Oaxaca coast at Puerto Escondido or Puerto Ángel.

A speedier variation on the Pacific route is the **Pacific–Mexico City route,** which starts out as the Pacific route but departs from the Pacific Coast, eastward, at Tepic, continuing along

ON THE ROAD

HIGHWAY ROUTES FROM THE U.S. BORDER TO OAXACA

Route	Via	Miles/Km	Hours at the Wheel	Travel Days
Pacific	Nogales–Mazatlán			
	Puerto Vallarta			
	Acapulco–Puerto Ángel	1,911/3,075	46	5
Pacific–Mexico City	Nogales–Mazatlán			
	Guadalajara–Mexico City			
	Puebla–Oaxaca city	1,749/2,814	34	3
Central	Ciudad Juárez–Chihuahua			
	Torreón–Zacatecas			
	Querétaro–Mexico City			
	Puebla–Oaxaca city	1,370/2,204	29	3
Eastern	Reynosa–Ciudad Victoria			
	Tampico–Pachuca–Mexico City			
	Puebla–Oaxaca city	967/1,556	22	2

Highway 15 or 15 D past Guadalajara, via Toluca to Mexico City.

Across town, at the Los Reyes southeast-side suburb, pick up the Puebla-Veracruz expressway Highway 150 D, where you continue about an hour past Puebla to a fork. Follow the south fork expressway, via Tehuacán and Nochixtlán, to Oaxaca city. This nearly all-expressway route minimizes the road time from the western U.S. border to three very long, or, to be safe, four days to Oaxaca. *Note:* Be sure to arrive in Mexico City on a day of the week when driving restrictions (determined by the last digit of your license plate; see the sidebar "Mexico City Driving Restrictions") do not apply to your car.

If, however, you're driving to Oaxaca from the central United States, go via the **central route**, crossing the border at El Paso to Ciudad Juárez, Chihuahua. There, National Highway 45, preferably via the *cuota* multilane expressway (or, if not, the old *libre* two-lane highway), leads you

southward past high, dry plains and the cities of Chihuahua and Jiménez (use *perifécos*—peripheral highways—to bypass downtowns). Continue via Highway 49 southwest, through Gómez Palacio and the silver colonial cities of Zacatecas to San Luis Potosí, where you connect with Highway 57 expressway, via Querétaro, to the northern outskirts of Mexico City.

At that point, best use the east-bound *periférico* expressway via Carpio and Tezcoco instead of trying to fight your way through downtown Mexico City. At Los Reyes on the southeast side of town, pick up Highway 150 D, the expressway east to Puebla, where you continue southeast via the toll expressway to Oaxaca (as described two paragraphs above). To be safe, allow three daytime-only driving days for this route.

Folks heading to Oaxaca from the eastern and southeastern United States probably save the most time by crossing the border from McAllen, Texas, to Reynosa and taking the **eastern route** to

Oaxaca. Continue south, via Highway 97 then Highway 101, to Ciudad Victoria, bypassing the downtown by the *periférico*. Then connect with Highway 80 to Tampico. There, again bypass the downtown and pick up Highway 105 south headed for Tempoal de Sánchez. After a long, winding, mountain climb via Huejutla de Reyes, you reach Pachuca and continue southward via expressway Highway 85 to Mexico City. At Carpio in the northern suburb, take the east bypass expressway, via Tepexpan and Tezcoco, continuing to east-bound expressway 150 D for Puebla. There, you continue southeast to Oaxaca city (as described three paragraphs above). If you start off at dawn each morning, you could probably get to Oaxaca safely in two driving days, under optimal conditions. Best do it in three leisurely days, including two overnights.

Bribes (Mordidas)

The usual meeting ground between visitors and Mexican police is in their car on the highway or a downtown street. To tourists, such cases sometimes appear as mild harassment, accompanied by vague threats of having to go to the police station or having their car impounded for such-and-such a violation. The tourists often go on to say, "It was all right, though. We paid him $10 and he went away. Mexican cops sure are crooked, aren't they?"

And I suppose, if people want to go bribing their way through Mexico, that's their business. But calling the Mexican cops crooked isn't exactly fair. Police, like most everyone else in Mexico, have to scratch for a living, and they have found that many tourists are willing to slip them a $10 bill for nothing. Rather than crooked, I would call them hungry and opportunistic.

BY TOUR

For travelers on a tight time budget, a prearranged tour package can provide a hassle-free route for sampling Oaxaca's attractions. For tour information, read on about the Special Tours and Study Options, call a travel agent, or visit a travel website (see Internet Resources).

If, however, you prefer a self-paced vacation, or desire thrift over convenience, you should probably defer tour arrangements until after arrival. Many Oaxaca tour agencies as close as your hotel telephone or lobby-front tour desk can customize a tour for you. For recommendations, see the Oaxaca city destination chapter.

Special Tours and Study Options

Oaxaca's rich archaeological and cultural heritage provides a focus for some noteworthy tour-study programs. Some of the agencies that offer such options include Adventures into Art, Elderhostel, Field Guides, Journey Mexico, Manos de Oaxaca, Mexi-Maya Tours, Siemer and Hand, and Zapotec Tours.

A pair of **Elderhostel** tours lead participants on Oaxaca explorations: "Oaxaca: Spanish Language and Hispanic Culture" emphasizes practice in conversational Spanish, while "Exotic Mexican Birds and Their Habitat" centers on natural history in the countryside. Both programs include visits to the archaeological sites of Monte Albán and Mitla and appreciation of indigenous tradition through visits to pottery, weaving, and woodcraft villages and evening excursions to enjoy Oaxacan food and folkloric music and dance. Accommodations include both hotel rooms and homestays with Mexican families. For details, write or phone for the international catalog: Elderhostel, 75 Federal St., Boston, MA 02110-1941, tel. 877/426-8056, www.elderhostel.org.

Chicago-based **Zapotec Tours,** tel. 800/44-OAXAC (800/446-2922), leads three Oaxaca tours: a "Food of the Gods" (beginning of October) gastronomical tour, a crafts and shopping tour (mid-November), and a cultural tour, focused on the famous November 1–2 Day of the Dead festival. For many details, log on to www.oaxacainfo.com/zt/htm. You may also contact Zapotec Tours by mail or fax in the United States, 4955 N. Claremont Ave., Suite B, Chicago, IL 60625, tel. 773/506-2444, fax 773/506-2445.

Journey Mexico organizes outdoor, people-to-people-oriented tours that include off-the-beaten-track villages in the Oaxaca northern mountains and southern tropical coast. Tours start in Mexico City and move on to Oaxaca city and Valley archaeological sites and crafts villages.

The itinerary continues with hiking around the Sierra Norte villages of Benito Juarez and Cuajimoloyas. Tours usually climax with explorations, including sea turtle conservation and wildlife viewing in the tropical coastal villages around Puerto Ángel.

The **Mexi-Maya** tours feature broad cultural experiences, customarily including visits to museums, historical and archaeological sites, crafts villages, and markets. Programs often include extensions to Oaxaca's palmy coastal resorts. For more information, contact Mexi-Maya at 12S675 Knoebel Dr., Lemont, IL 60439, tel./fax 630/972-9393.

Birding tour operator **Field Guides** leads Oaxaca tours centering on the wildlife-rich foothill forests and lagoons of the tropical coast. Along the way, trips often include archaeological and historical sites and colorful native markets. For more information, contact Field Guides at tel. 800/728-4953, fax 512/263-0117, fieldguides@fieldguides.com, www.fieldguides.com.

Siemer and Hand Travel, a broad-based high-end tour agency, specializes in both individual and group educational tours. Their Oaxaca group tours have included "Tropical Birding," in cooperation with the National Audubon Society, and "The Valley of Oaxaca: Archaeology, Arts, and Traditions," for both Bryn Mawr College and the Harvard Alumni Association. For more information, contact Siemer and Hand at 750 Battery St., Suite 300, San Francisco, CA 94111, tel. 415/788-4000 or 800/451-4321, fax 415/788-4133, www.siemerhand.com.

Oaxaca arts and crafts tours are the specialty of **Travel Adventures into Art,** often in cooperation with art institutes and museums. Tours frequently include festivals, such as Easter, Day of the Dead (November 1 and 2) and Christmas–New Year. Other tours have focused on a special interest, such as contemporary art, textiles, or women artists. Hands-on tours emphasize

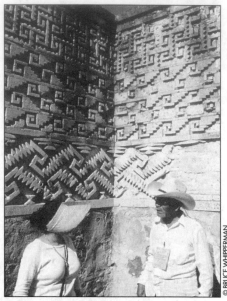

© BRUCE WHIPPERMAN

A tour guide can provide unique insights into Oaxaca's fascinating cultural heritage.

actually doing art, such as painting, pottery, or photography, in a Oaxaca setting. For more information, contact President Joan LeVine Mellion, 3030 Bridgeway, Sausalito, CA 94965, tel./fax 415/331-6238, taia1@mindspring.com, www.arttraveladventures.com.

Adventurous travelers might check out **Manos de Oaxaca,** of artisan-guide–Oaxaca lover Eric Mindling. His bliss is leading like-minded folks in explorations of traditional clay and fiber arts by country artisans in communities in Oaxaca Valley, the Mixteca, and the Coast. The approach is people to people, the accommodations sometimes rustic, the prices very reasonable, but the rewards potentially great. Eric customarily leads about four or five 7-to-10-day tours per year. For info, log on to www.manos-de-oaxaca.com.

Getting Around

BY AIR

Travelers on tight time budgets find it useful to save a day flying, instead of driving or busing, over the Sierra between Oaxaca city and the Pacific resorts of Puerto Ángel, Bahías de Huatulco, and Puerto Escondido.

Mexicana Airlines affiliate **Aerocaribe** connects Oaxaca city with Huatulco and Puerto Escondido daily (in addition to Cancún, Mérida, Villahermosa, and Tuxtla Gutiérrez). For reservations call tel. 951/516-6088 or 951/516-0229. For flight information, call tel. 951/511-5247.

Alternatively, charter airline **Aerotucán** regularly connects Oaxaca city with both Puerto Escondido and Huatulco. In Oaxaca city, contact Aerotucán at Alcalá 201, upper floor, suite 204, tel. 951/501-0530 or 951/501-0532; in Huatulco, call tel. 958/587-2427, and in Puerto Escondido tel. 954/582-3461 or 954/582-1725. For more details, visit www.aerotucan.com, or contact a travel agent.

Moreover, **Aerovega,** the experienced local air-taxi service, routinely connects Oaxaca city with Puerto Escondido and other Oaxaca destinations. For information and reservations in Oaxaca city, call tel. 951/515-4982. In Puerto Escondido, call tel. 954/582-0151.

Local Flying Tips

Mexican airlines have operating peculiarities that result from their tight budgets. For example, don't miss a flight—you might lose half the ticket price. Adjusting your flight date may cost 25 percent of the ticket price. Get to the airport at least an hour ahead of time. Last-minute passengers are often "bumped" in favor of early-bird standbys. Conversely, go to the airport and get in line if you must catch a flight that the airlines have claimed to be full. You might get on anyway. Keep your luggage small so you can carry it on. Lost luggage victims receive scant compensation in Mexico.

BY BUS

The bus is the king of the Oaxaca road. A host of lines connect virtually every town and most villages in Oaxaca. Three distinct levels of service—luxury or super-first class, first class, and second class—are generally available. **Luxury-class** (usually called something like Primera Plus or Ejecutivo, depending upon the line), super-deluxe express coaches speed between major towns, seldom stopping en route. In exchange for somewhat higher fares (about $50 Oaxaca city–Puerto Escondido, for example, compared with $40 for first class), luxury-class passengers enjoy rapid passage and airline-style amenities: plush reclining seats, air-conditioning, on-board toilet, video, and aisle attendant.

Although much less luxurious, **first-class** service costs less, is frequent, and always includes reserved seating. Additionally, passengers usually enjoy soft reclining seats and air-conditioning (if it is working). Besides making regular stops at or near most towns and villages en route, first-class bus drivers, if requested, will usually stop and let you off anywhere along the road.

Second-class bus seating is unreserved. In outlying parts of Oaxaca, there is a class of buses even beneath second class, but given the condition of many second-class buses, it usually seems as if third-class buses wouldn't run at all. Such buses are the stuff of travelers' legends: the recycled old GMC, Ford, and Dodge school buses that stop everywhere and carry everyone and everything to the smallest villages tucked away in the far mountains. As long as there is any kind of a road to it, such a bus will most likely go there.

Now and then, you'll read a newspaper story of a country bus that went over a cliff somewhere in Mexico, killing the driver and a dozen unfortunate souls. The same newspapers never bother to mention the half-million safe passenger trips the same bus provided during its 15 years of service prior to the accident.

Second-class buses are not for travelers with weak knees or stomachs. You will often initially have to stand, cramped in the aisle, among a crowd of campesinos. They are warm-hearted

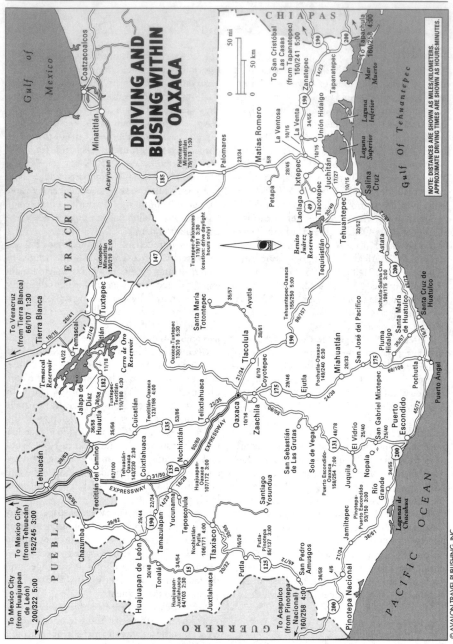

DRIVING AND
BUSING WITHIN
OAXACA

© AVALON TRAVEL PUBLISHING, INC.

people, but poor, so don't tempt them with open, dangling purses or wallets bulging in back pockets. Stow your money safely away. After a while, you will probably be able to sit down. Such privilege, however, comes with obligation, such as holding an old lady's bulging bag of carrots or a toddler on your lap. But if you accept your burden with humor and equanimity, who knows what favors and blessings may flow to you in return.

Tickets, Seating, and Baggage

Oaxaca bus lines do not ordinarily publish schedules or fares. You have to ask someone (such as your hotel desk clerk) who knows, or call (or have someone call) the bus station. Only a few travel agents handle bus tickets. If you don't want to spend the time to get a reserved ticket yourself, hire someone trustworthy to do it for you. Another way of doing it all is to get to the bus station early enough on your traveling day to ensure you'll get a bus to your destination.

Although some lines accept credit cards and issue computer-printed tickets at their major stations, most reserved bus tickets are sold for cash and handwritten, with a specific *número de asiento* (seat number) on the back. If you miss the bus, you lose your money. Furthermore, airlines-style automated reservations systems have not yet arrived at the large majority of Oaxacan bus stations. Consequently, you can generally buy reserved tickets only at the *salida local* (local departure) station. (An agent in Tehuantepec, for example, cannot ordinarily reserve you a ticket on a bus that originates in Oaxaca city, a day's travel down the road.)

Request a reserved seat number, if possible, from numbers 1–25 in the *delante* (front) to *medio* (middle) of the bus. The rear seats are often occupied by smokers, drunks, and general rowdies. At night, you will sleep better on the *lado derecho* (right side) away from the glare of oncoming traffic lights.

Baggage is generally secure on Oaxaca buses. Label it, however. Overhead racks are often too cramped to accommodate airline-size carry-ons. Carry a small bag of your crucial items on your person; pack clothes and less essential items in your checked luggage. For peace of mind, watch the handler put your checked baggage on the bus and watch to make sure it is not mistakenly taken off the bus at intermediate stops.

If, somehow, your baggage gets misplaced, remain calm. Bus employees are generally competent and conscientious; if you are patient, recovering your luggage will become a matter of honor for many of them. Baggage handlers are at the bottom of the pay scale; a tip for their mostly thankless job would be very much appreciated.

On long trips, carry food, drinks, and toilet paper. Station food may be dubious and the sanitary facilities ill-maintained.

If you are waiting for a first-class bus at an intermediate *salida de paso* (passing station), you often have to trust to luck that there will be an empty seat. If not, your best option may be to ride a usually much more frequent second-class bus.

BY TRAIN

Improved highways, faster buses, and airplanes have put an end to passenger train service in Oaxaca.

BY CAR, TAXI, TOUR, OR HITCHHIKING

Getting around by car in Oaxaca has its pluses and minuses. On the minus side, cars are expensive to rent and roads are often narrow and usually shared with pedestrians, horses, cows, and burros. On the plus side, driving allows you to go where you want on your own schedule. For details on road conditions, mileage, and driving times, see the destination chapters. For tips on driving to Mexico from the United States, see the Getting There section.)

Car rental agents are usually on duty for flight arrivals. Just in case, make a reservation ahead of time and they will meet your flight: call **Budget** in Crucecita, tel. 958/587-0010, or **Alamo** in Santa Cruz, at the Hotel Castillo, tel. 958/587-0135. During the winter especially, make reservations in the United States and Canada prior to departure.

Rental Car

Car and jeep rentals are an increasingly popular transportation option for Oaxaca travelers. They offer mobility and independence for local sightseeing and beach excursions. In Oaxaca city, Huatulco and Puerto Escondido, the gang's at least partially there: **Hertz,** tel. 951/516-2434, fax 951/516-0009, hertz_oax@hotmail.com; **Budget,** tel./fax 951/511-5252; in Huatulco, tel. 958/587-0010, fax 958/587-0019; Puerto Escondido tel. 954/582-0312 or 954/582-0315, budget33@hotmail.com; and **Alamo** tel./fax 951/514-8534, fax 951/514-8686; Huatulco tel. 958/587-0135; Puerto Escondido tel. 954/582-3003, alamoescondido@hotmail.com.

Agencies generally require drivers to have a valid driver's license, passport, a major credit card, and may require a minimum age of 25. Some local companies do not accept credit cards, but offer lower rates in return.

Oaxaca car rentals are not cheap. They run more than in the United States, with a 15 percent or more "value added" tax tacked on. The cheapest possible rental car, usually a vintage stick-shift VW Beetle, runs $30–60 per day or $200–450 per week, depending on location and season. Prices are steepest during high Christmas and pre-Easter weeks. Before departure, use the international agencies' toll-free numbers to shop around for availability, prices, and reservations. During nonpeak seasons, you may save lots of pesos by waiting till arrival and renting a car through a local agency. Shop around, starting with the agent in your hotel lobby or the local yellow pages (under "Automóviles, renta de").

Car insurance that covers property damage, public liability, and medical payments is an *absolute must* and is required by Mexican law. Although it is customarily included in the price of your rental car, make certain that you're covered before signing the deal. **Collision insurance** is not usually included and costs extra. However, major credit cards, such as American Express, do usually furnish coverage that supplements your personal car insurance. Double-

check your coverage with both your auto insurance agent and your credit card company before leaving for Mexico.

If you get into an accident in Mexico without insurance, you will be in deep trouble, probably jail. Safe driving in Oaxaca requires more caution and less speed than back home. (For important car safety and insurance information, see the Getting There section.)

Taxis

The high prices of rental cars make taxis a viable option for local excursions. Cars are luxuries, not necessities, for most Oaxacan families. Travelers might profit from the local money-saving practice of piling everyone in a taxi for Sunday park, beach, and fishing outings. You may find that an all-day taxi and driver (who, besides relieving you of driving, will become your impromptu guide) will cost less than a rental car.

The magic word for saving money by taxi is *colectivo:* a taxi that you share jointly with other travelers. Your first place to practice getting a taxi will be at the airport, where *colectivo* tickets are routinely sold from booths at the terminal door.

If, however, you want your own private taxi, ask for a *taxi especial,* which will probably run about three or four times the individual tariff for a *colectivo.*

Your airport experience will prepare you for in-town taxis, which rarely have meters. *You must establish the price before getting in.* Bargaining comes with the territory in Mexico, so don't shrink from it, even though it may seem a hassle. If you get into a taxi without an agreed-upon price, you are letting yourself in for a more serious, potentially nasty hassle later. If your driver's price is too high, he'll probably come to his senses as soon as you hail another taxi.

After a few days, getting taxis around town will be a cinch. You'll find you don't have to take the high-ticket taxis lined up in your hotel driveway. If the price isn't right, walk toward the street and hail a regular taxi.

In town, if you can't seem to find a taxi, it may be because they are all hanging around waiting for riders at the local stand, called a taxi *sitio*. Ask someone to direct you to it: Say *"Excúseme. ¿Donde está el sitio taxi, por favor?"* ("Excuse me. Where is the taxi stand, please?").

Tours and Guides

For many Oaxaca visitors, locally arranged tours offer a hassle-free alternative to rental car or taxi sightseeing. Hotels and travel agencies, many of whom maintain front-lobby travel and tour desks, offer a bounty of sightseeing, water sports, bay cruise, fishing, and wildlife-viewing tour opportunities. (For details, see the destination chapters.)

Hitchhiking

Most everyone agrees hitchhiking is not the safest mode of transport. If you're unsure, don't do it. Hitchhiking doesn't make a healthy steady travel diet, nor should you hitchhike at night.

The recipe for trouble-free hitchhiking requires equal measures of luck, savvy, and technique. The best places to catch rides are where people are already arriving and leaving, such as bus stops, highway intersections, gas stations, RV parks, and on the highway out of town.

Male-female hitchhiking partnerships seem to net the most rides (although it is technically illegal for women to ride in commercial trucks). The more gear you and your partner have, the fewer rides you will get. Pickup and flatbed truck owners often pick up passengers for pay. Before hopping onto the truck bed, ask how much (*¿cuánto cuesta?*) the ride will cost.

Information and Services

PASSPORTS, TOURIST CARDS, AND VISAS

Your Passport

Your passport is your positive proof of national identity; without it, your status in any foreign country is in doubt. Don't leave home without one. United States citizens may obtain passports (allow 4–6 weeks) at local post offices. For-fee **private passport agencies** can speed this process and get you a passport within a week, maybe less.

Entry Into Mexico

For U.S. and Canadian citizens, entry by air into Mexico for a few weeks could hardly be easier. Airline attendants hand out *tarjetas turísticas* (tourist cards) en route and officers make them official by glancing at passports and stamping the cards at the immigration gate. Business travel permits for 30 days or less are handled by the same simple procedures.

Entry is not entirely painless, however. The Mexican government currently charges an approximate $20 fee per person for a tourist card. For air and bus travelers, this is no problem, since the fee is automatically included in the fare.

The entry fee can become a minor hassle for drivers, however. At this writing the government does not allow collection of the fee by border immigration officers. Instead, the officers issue a form that you must take to a bank, where you pay the fee. For multiple entries this can get complicated and time-consuming.

In addition to the entry fee, Mexican border immigration officials require that all entering U.S. citizens 15 years old or over must present proper identification—either a valid U.S. passport, an original (or a notarized copy of your) birth certificate, a military ID, or a state driver's license, while naturalized citizens must show naturalization papers (or a laminated naturalization card) or a valid U.S. passport.

Canadian citizens must show a valid passport or an original birth certificate. Nationals of other countries (especially those, such as Hong Kong, that issue more than one type of passport) may be subject to different or additional regulations. For advice, consult your regional Mexico Tourism Board office or consulate. For more Mexico-entry details, visit the Mexico Tourism Board's website, www.visitmexico.com, or call toll-free U.S. tel. 800/44-MEXICO (800/446-3942).

MEXICO TOURISM BOARD OFFICES

More than a dozen Mexico Tourism Board (Consejo de Promoción Turístico de Mexico) offices and scores of Mexican government consulates operate in the United States, Canada, Europe, and South America. Consulates generally handle questions of Mexican nationals abroad, while Mexico Tourism Boards serve travelers heading for Mexico.

For straightforward questions and Mexico regional information brochures, dial toll-free U.S./Can. tel. 800/44-MEXICO (800/446-3942) or Europe tel. 800/11-2266, or visit the website www.visitmexico.com. Otherwise, contact one of the North American regional or European or South American Mexico Tourism Boards for guidance:

IN NORTH AMERICA
From Arizona, California, Colorado, Hawaii, Idaho, Montana, Nevada, New Mexico, and Utah, contact **Los Angeles:** 2401 W. 6th St., 5th Floor, Los Angeles, CA 90057, tel. 213/351-2069, fax 213/351-2074, losangeles@visitmexico.com.

From Alaska, Idaho, Montana, Oregon, Washington, Wyoming and the Canadian Provinces of Alberta, British Columbia, Northwest Territories, Saskatchewan, and Yukon, contact **Vancouver:** 999 W. Hastings St., Suite 1110, Vancouver, B.C. V6C 2W2, tel. 604/669-2845, fax 604/669-3498, mgto@telus.net.

From Louisiana, Oklahoma, and Texas, contact **Houston:** 4507 San Jacinto, Suite 308, Houston, TX 77004, tel. 713/772-2581, fax 713/772-6058, houston@visitmexico.com.

From Alabama, Arkansas, Florida, Georgia, Mississippi, North Carolina, South Carolina, and Tennessee, contact **Miami:** 5975 Sunset Dr. #305, Miami, FL 33143, tel. 786/621-2809, fax 786/621-2907, miami@visitmexico.com.

From Illinois, Indiana, Iowa, Kansas, Michigan, Minnesota, Missouri, Nebraska, North Dakota, Ohio, South Dakota, and Wisconsin, contact **Chicago:** 300 North Michigan Ave., 4th Floor, Chicago, IL 60601, tel. 312/606-9252, fax 312/606-9012, chicago@visitmexico.com.

From Connecticut, Delaware, Kentucky, Maine, Maryland, Massachusetts, New Hampshire, New Jersey, New York, Pennsylvania, Rhode Island,

Vermont, Virginia, Washington D.C., and West Virginia, contact **New York:** 21 E. 63rd St., 3rd Floor, New York, NY 10021, tel. 212/821-0313 or 212/821-0314, fax 212/821-3067, newyork@visitmexico.com.

From Ontario and Manitoba, contact **Toronto:** 2 Bloor St. W, Suite 1502, Toronto, Ontario M4W 3E2, tel. 416/925-2753, fax 416/925-6061, toronto@visitmexico.com.

From New Brunswick, Newfoundland, Nova Scotia, Prince Edward Island, and Quebec, contact **Montreal:** 1 Place Ville Marie, Suite 1931, Montreal, Quebec H3B2C3, tel. 514/871-1052 or 514/871-1103, fax 514/871-3825, montreal@visitmexico.com.

IN EUROPE
In Europe, travelers may either use the all-Europe toll-free Mexico tourism information number 00800/11-2266, visit the website www.visitmexico.com, or contact the local offices directly:

London: Wakefield House, 41 Trinity Square, London EC3N 4DT, England, UK, tel. 207/488-9392, fax 207/265-0704, uk@visitmexico.com.

Frankfurt: Taunusanlage 21, 60325 Frankfurt-am-Main, Deutschland, tel. 0/6925-3509, fax 0/6925-3755, germany@visitmexico.com.

Paris: 4, rue Notre Dame des Victoires, 75002 Paris, France, tel. 1/425-896122 or 1/425-69213, fax 1/428-60580, france@visitmexico.com.

Madrid: Calle Velázquez 126, 28006 Madrid, España, tel. 91/561-3520 or 91/561-1827, fax 91/411-0759, spain@visitmexico.com.

Rome: Via Barberini 3, piso 7, 00187 Roma, Italia, tel. 06/487-4698, fax 06/487-3630 or 06/420-4293, italy@visitmexico.com.

IN SOUTH AMERICA
Contact the Mexico Tourism Board in either Argentina or Chile:

Buenos Aires: Av. Santa Fe 520, 1054 Buenos Aires, Argentina, tel. 1/4393-7070 or 1/4393-8235, fax 1/4393-6607, argentina@visitmexico.com.

Santiago: Bucarest 162, Providencia, Santiago, Chile, tel. 562/234-5899, fax 562/234-5898, chile@visitmexico.com.

More Options

For more complicated cases, get your tourist card early enough to allow you to consider the options. Tourist cards can be issued for multiple entries and a maximum validity of 180 days; photos are often required. If you don't request multiple entry or the maximum time, your card will probably be stamped single entry, valid for some shorter period, such as 90 days. If you are not sure how long you'll stay in Mexico, request the maximum. (One hundred eighty days is the absolute maximum for a tourist card; long-term foreign residents routinely make semiannual "border runs" for new tourist cards.)

Student and Business Visas

A visa is a notation stamped and signed on your passport showing the number of days and entries allowable for your trip. Apply for a student visa at the Mexican consulate nearest your home well in advance of your departure; the same is true if you require a business visa of longer than 30 days. One-year renewable student visas are available (sometimes with considerable red tape). An ordinary 180-day tourist card may be the easiest option, if you can manage it.

Entry for Children

Children under 15 can be included on their parents' tourist cards, but complications occur if the children (by reason of illness, for example) cannot leave Mexico with both parents. Parents can avoid the bureaucratic rigmarole by getting a passport and a Mexican tourist card for each of their children.

In addition to a passport or birth certificate, minors (under age 18) entering Mexico without parents or legal guardians must present a notarized letter of permission signed by both parents or legal guardians. Even if accompanied by one parent, a notarized letter from the other must be presented. Divorce or death certificates must also be presented, when applicable. Airlines will require the name, address, and telephone number of the person meeting unaccompanied minors upon arrival in Mexico.

Oaxaca travelers should hurdle all such possible delays far ahead of time in the cool calm of their local Mexican consulate rather than the hot, hurried atmosphere of a border or airport immigration office.

Entry for Pets

A pile of red tape can delay the entry of dogs, cats, and other pets into Mexico. Be prepared with veterinary-stamped health and rabies certificates for each animal. Contact your regional Mexico Tourism Board (see the sidebar "Mexico Tourism Board Offices"), call tel. 800/44-MEXICO (800/446-3942), or visit www.visitmexico.com for assistance.

Don't Lose Your Tourist Card

If you do, be prepared with a Xeroxed copy of the original, which you should present to the nearest federal Migración (Immigration) office (on duty long hours at the Oaxaca city, Huatulco, and Puerto Escondido airports) and ask for a duplicate tourist permit. Lacking this, you might present some alternate proof of your date of arrival in Mexico, such as a stamped passport or airline ticket. Savvy travelers carry a copy of their tourist card with them, while leaving the original secure in their hotel room or hotel desk safe.

Car Permits

If you drive to Mexico, you will need a permit for your car. Upon entry into Mexico, be ready with originals and copies of your proof-of-ownership or registration papers (state title certificate, registration, or notarized bill of sale), current license plates, and current driver's license. The auto permit fee runs about $25, payable only by non-Mexican bank MasterCard, Visa, or American Express credit cards. (The credit card–only requirement discourages those intending to sell a U.S.-registered car in Mexico without paying customs duties.) Credit cards must bear the same name as the vehicle proof-of-ownership papers.

The resulting car permit becomes part of the owner's tourist card and receives the same length of validity. Vehicles registered in the name of an organization or person other than the driver must be accompanied by a notarized affidavit authorizing the driver to use the car in Mexico for a specific time.

Border officials generally allow you to carry or tow additional motorized vehicles (motorcycle, another car, large boat) into Mexico but will probably require separate documentation and fee for each vehicle. If a Mexican official desires to inspect your trailer or RV, go through it with him or her.

Accessories, such as a small trailer, boat less than six feet, CB radio, or outboard motor, may be noted on the car permit and must leave Mexico with the car.

For updates and details on documentation required for taking your car into Mexico, call the Mexican government number in the United States, tel. 800/446-3942, or visit www.visitmexico.com. For many more details on motor vehicle entry and what you may bring in your baggage to Mexico, consult the AAA (American Automobile Association) *Mexico Travelbook*. (See Suggested Reading.)

Since Mexico does not recognize foreign automobile insurance, you must purchase Mexican automobile insurance. (For more information on this and other details of driving in Mexico, see the Getting There section.)

Crossing the Border and Returning Home

Squeezing through border bottlenecks during peak holidays and rush hours can be time-consuming. Avoid crossing 7–9 A.M. and 4:30–6:30 P.M.

Just before returning across the border with your car, park and have an *aduana* (customs) official remove and cancel the holographic identity sticker which you received on entry. If possible, get a *recibo* (receipt) or some kind of verification that it's been *cancelado* (canceled). Tourists have been fined hundreds of dollars for inadvertently carrying old uncanceled car entry stickers on their windshields.

At the same time, return all other Mexican permits, such as tourist cards and hunting and fishing licenses. Also, be prepared for Mexico exit inspection, especially for cultural artifacts and works of art, which may require exit permits. Certain religious and pre-Columbian artifacts, legally the property of the Mexican government, cannot lawfully be taken from the country.

If you entered Mexico with your car, by law you cannot leave Mexico without it except by permission from local customs authorities, usually the Aduana (Customs House) or the Oficina Federal de Hacienda (Federal Treasury Office). For local details, see the Information and Services section in the destination chapters.

All returnees are subject to U.S. immigration and customs inspection. These inspections have become generally more time-consuming since September 11, 2001. The worst bottlenecks are at busy border crossings, especially Tijuana and to a lesser extent, Mexicali, Nogales, Ciudad Juárez, Laredo, and Brownsville, all of which should be avoided during peak morning and (especially Sunday) afternoon hours.

United States law allows a fixed value (presently $400) of duty-free goods per returnee. This may include no more than one liter of alcoholic spirits, 200 cigarettes, and 100 cigars. A flat 10 percent duty will be applied to the first $1,000 (fair retail value, save your receipts) in excess of your $400 exemption. You may, however, mail packages (up to $50 value each) of gifts duty-free to friends and relatives in the United States. Make sure to clearly write "unsolicited gift" and a list of the value and contents on the outside of the package. Perfumes (more than $5), alcoholic beverages, and tobacco may not be included in such packages.

Improve the security of such mailed packages by sending them by **Mexpost** class, similar to U.S. Express Mail service. Even better (but much more expensive), send them by **Federal Express** or **DHL** international couriers, which maintain offices in Oaxaca city.

For more information on U.S. customs regulations important to travelers abroad, write for a copy of the useful pamphlet *Know Before You Go,* from the U.S. Customs Service, 1300 Pennsylvania Ave., Washington, DC 20229. You may also order by dialing the Customs Service at tel. 202/354-1000. For more information, log on to www.customs.gov.

Additional U.S. rules prohibit importation of certain fruits, vegetables, and domestic-animal and endangered-wildlife products. Certain live animal species, such as parrots, may be brought into the United States, subject to 30-day agricultural quarantine upon arrival, at the owner's expense. For more details on agricultural-product and live-animal importation, write for the free booklet *Travelers' Tips,* by the U.S. Department of Agriculture, Washington, D.C. 20250, tel. 202/720-2791.

For more information on the importation of endangered-wildlife products, contact the Fish and Wildlife Service, 1849 C. St. NW, Washington, DC 20240, tel. 202/208-4717.

MONEY
The Peso: Down and Up

Overnight in early 1993, the Mexican government shifted its monetary decimal point three places and created the "new" peso, which currently trades at around 11 per U.S. dollar. Since the peso value sometimes changes rapidly, U.S. dollars have become a much more stable indicator of Mexican prices; for this reason, they are used in this book to report prices. You should, nevertheless, always use pesos to pay for everything in Mexico.

Since the introduction of the new peso, the centavo (one-hundredth of a new peso) has reappeared, in coins of 5, 10, 20, and 50 centavos. Incidentally, the dollar sign, "$," also marks Mexican pesos. Peso coins *(monedas)* in denominations of 1, 2, 5, 10, and 20 pesos, and bills, in denominations of 20, 50, 100, 200, and 500 pesos, are common. Since banks like to exchange your traveler's checks for a few crisp large bills rather than the often-tattered smaller denominations, ask for some of your change in 50- and 100-peso notes. A 500-peso note, while common at the bank, may look awfully big to a small shopkeeper, who might be hard-pressed to change it.

Banks, ATMs, and Money Exchange Offices

Mexican banks, like their North American counterparts, have lengthened their business hours. Banco Internacional (BITAL), maintains the longest hours: as long as Mon.–Sat. 8 A.M.–7 P.M. Banamex (Banco Nacional de Mexico), generally

the most popular with local people, usually posts the best in-town dollar exchange rate in its lobbies; for example: *Tipo de cambio: venta 10.945, compra 11.022,* which means they will sell pesos to you at the rate of 10.945 per dollar and buy them back for 11.022 per dollar.

ATMs (*Cajeros Automáticos,* kah-HAY-rohs ahoo-toh-MAH-tee-kohs) are rapidly becoming the money source of choice in Mexico. Virtually every bank has a 24-hour ATM, accessible (with proper PIN identification code) by a swarm of U.S. and Canadian credit and ATM cards. *Note:* Some Mexican bank ATMs will "eat" your ATM card if you don't retrieve it within about fifteen seconds of completing your transaction. Retrieve your card *immediately* after getting your cash.

Since one-time bank charges, typically about $2 per ATM transaction, do not usually depend on the amount of cash you receive, it's cheapest to get the maximum amount (usually limited to about $300 daily) per transaction.

Even without an ATM card, you don't have to go to the trouble of waiting in long bank service lines. Opt for a less-crowded bank, such as Banco Internacional, Banco Inverlat, Bancomer, Banorte, Banco Serfín, or a private *casa de cambio* (money-exchange office). Often most convenient, such offices often offer long hours and faster service than the banks for a fee (as little as $.50 or as much as $3 per $100).

Keeping Your Money Safe

Traveler's checks, the traditional prescription for safe money abroad, are widely accepted in Oaxaca. Even if you plan to use your ATM card, purchase some U.S. dollar traveler's checks (a well-known brand, such as American Express or Visa) as an emergency reserve. Canadian traveler's checks and currency are not as widely accepted as U.S. traveler's checks, European and Asian even less. Unless you like signing your name or paying lots of per-check commissions, buy denominations of $100 or more.

In Oaxaca as everywhere, thieves circulate among the tourists. Keep valuables in your hotel *caja de seguridad* (security box). If you don't particularly trust the desk clerk, carry what you cannot afford to lose in a money belt. Pickpockets love crowded markets, buses, and airport terminals where they can slip a wallet out of a back pocket or dangling purse in a blink. Guard against this by carrying your wallet in your front pocket, and your purse, waist pouch, and daypack (which clever crooks can sometimes slit open) on your front side.

Don't attract thieves by displaying wads of money or flashy jewelry. Don't get sloppy drunk; if so, you may become a pushover for a determined thief.

Don't leave valuables unattended on the beach; share security duties with trustworthy-looking neighbors, or leave a secure bag with a shopkeeper nearby.

Tipping

Without their droves of visitors, Mexican people would be even poorer. Deflation of the peso, while it makes prices low for outsiders, makes it rough for Mexican families to get by. The help at your hotel typically get paid only a few dollars a day. They depend on tips to make the difference between dire and bearable poverty. Give the *camarista* (chambermaid) and floor attendant 20 pesos every day or two. And whenever uncertain of what to tip, it will probably mean a lot to someone—maybe a whole family—if you err on the generous side.

In restaurants and bars, Mexican tipping customs are similar to those in the United States and Europe: Tip waiters, waitresses, and bartenders about 15 percent for satisfactory service.

Credit Cards

Credit cards, such as Visa, MasterCard, and to a lesser extent, American Express and Discover, are widely honored in the hotels, restaurants, handicrafts shops, and boutiques that cater to foreign tourists. You will generally get better bargains, however, in shops that depend on local trade and do not so readily accept credit cards. Such shops sometimes offer discounts for cash sales.

Whatever the circumstance, your travel money will usually go much farther in Oaxaca than back home. Despite the national 15 percent ("value added" IVA) sales tax, local lodging, food, and transportation prices will often seem

like bargains compared to the developed world. Outside of the pricey high-rise beachfront strips, pleasant, palmy hotel-room rates often run $40 or less.

COMMUNICATIONS

Using Mexican Telephones

Although Mexican phone service has improved over the last decade, it's still sometimes hit-or-miss. If a number doesn't get through, you may have to redial it more than once. When someone answers (usually *"Bueno"*), be especially courteous. If your Spanish is rusty, say, *"¿Por favor, habla inglés?"* (¿POR fah-VOR, AH-blah een-GLAYS?). If you want to speak to a particular person (such as María), ask, *"¿María se encuentra?"* (¿mah-REE-ah SAY ayn-koo-AYN-trah?).

Since November 2001, when telephone numbers were standardized, Mexican phones have operated pretty much the same as in the United States and Canada. In Oaxaca city, for example a complete telephone number is generally written like this: 951/515-4709. As in the United States, the "951" denotes the telephone area code (*lada*, LAH-dah) and the 515-4709 is the number that you dial locally. If you want to dial this number long-distance (*larga distancia*), first dial "01" (like "1" in the United States), then 951/515-4709. All Mexican telephone numbers, with only three exceptions, begin with a three-digit *lada*, followed by a seven-digit local number. (The exceptions are Monterey, Guadalajara, and Mexico City, which have two digit *ladas* and eight-digit local numbers. The Mexico City *lada* is 55; Guadalajara's is 33; Monterey's is 81. For example, a complete Guadalajara phone number would read 33/6897-2253.)

In Oaxaca towns and cities, direct long-distance dialing is the rule—from hotels, public phone booths, and efficient private Computel telephone offices. The cheapest, often most convenient way to call is by purchasing and using a public telephone (Ladatel) card. Buy them in 20-, 30-, 50-, and 100-peso denominations at the many outlets—mini-markets, pharmacies, liquor stores—that display the blue and yellow Ladatel sign.

Despite the growing presence of card-operated street telephones, many folks still make their calls at the *larga distancia* (long-distance telephone office).

Calling Mexico and Calling Home

To call Mexico directly from the United States, first dial 011 (for international access), then 52 (for Mexico), followed by the Mexican area code and local number.

For station-to-station calls to the United States from Mexico, dial 001, then the area code and the local number. For calls to other countries, ask your hotel desk clerk or see the easy-to-follow directions in the local Mexican telephone directory.

Another convenient way (although a more expensive one) to call home is via your personal telephone credit card. Contact your U.S. long-distance operator by dialing 001-800/462-4240 for AT&T; 001-800/674-6000 for MCI; or 001-800/877-8000 for Sprint.

Yet another (although very expensive) way of calling home is collect. You can do this in one of two ways. Simply dial 09 for the local English-speaking international operator; or dial the AT&T, MCI, and Sprint numbers listed in the previous paragraph.

Beware of certain private "To Call Long Distance to the U.S.A. Collect and Credit Card" telephones installed prominently in airports, tourist hotels, and shops. Tariffs on these phones often run as high as $10 per minute (with a three-minute minimum), for a total of $30, whether you talk three minutes or not. Always ask the operator for the rate, and if it's too high, take your business elsewhere.

In small towns and villages, you must often do your long-distance phoning in the *larga distancia* (long-distance phone office). Typically staffed by a young woman and often connected to a café, the *larga distancia* becomes an informal community information and social center as people pass the time waiting for their phone connections.

Post, Telegraph, and Internet Access

Mexican *correos* (post offices) operate similarly, but more slowly and less securely, than their counterparts in the developed world. Mail services usually include *lista de correo* (for general delivery, address letters *"a/c lista de correo"*), *servicios filatelicas* (philatelic services), *por avión* (airmail), *giros* (postal money orders), and Mexpost secure and fast delivery service, usually from separate Mexpost offices.

Ordinary Mexican mail is sadly unreliable and pathetically slow. It's taken two or three weeks for some of my postcards to reach home from Oaxaca. If, for mailings within Mexico, you must have security, use the efficient, reformed government **Mexpost** (like U.S. Express Mail) service. For international mailings, check the local yellow pages for widely available **DHL** or **Federal Express** courier service.

Telégrafos (telegraph offices), usually near the post office, send and receive *telegramas* (telegrams) and *giros*. **Telecomunicaciones** (Telecom), the new high-tech telegraph offices, add telephone, public fax, and sometimes Internet connection to the available services.

Internet service, including personal email access, has arrived in Oaxaca's cities and larger towns. Internet cafés are becoming increasingly common, especially in Oaxaca city, the coastal resorts, and other larger towns, such as Tuxtepec in the North, Huajuapan and

Tlaxiaco in the Mixteca, and Juchitán and Salina Cruz in the Isthmus. Online rates average about $3 per hour.

Electricity and Time

Mexican electric power is supplied at U.S.-standard 110 volts, 60 cycles. Plugs and sockets are generally two-pronged, nonpolar (like the pre-1970s U.S. ones). Bring adapters if you're going to use appliances with polar two-pronged or three-pronged plugs. (A two-pronged polar plug has different-sized prongs, one of which is too large to plug into an old-fashioned nonpolar socket.)

The entire state of Oaxaca operates on central time, just like Mexico City and most of the rest of the country, except for the northwest states of Sinaloa, Nayarit, and Sonora, which operate on mountain time, and Baja California Norte, which operates on Pacific Time.

SPECIALTY TRAVEL

Bringing the Kids

Children are treasured like gifts from heaven in Mexico. Traveling with kids will ensure your welcome most everywhere. On the beach, take extra precautions to make sure they are protected from the sun.

A sick child is no fun for anyone. Fortunately, clinics and good doctors are available even in small towns. When in need, ask a storekeeper or a pharmacist, ¿Dónde hay un doctor, por favor?" (¿DOHN-day eye oon doc-TOHR por fah-VOHR?). In most cases, within five minutes you will be in the waiting room of the local physician or hospital.

Children who do not favor typical Mexican fare can easily be fed with always-available bananas, cakes, cheese, cookies, corn flakes, eggs, hamburguesas, milk, and oatmeal.

Your children will generally have more fun if they have a little previous knowledge of Mexico and a stake in the trip. For example, help them select some library picture books and magazines so they'll know where they're going and what to expect; or give them responsibility for packing and carrying their own small travel bag.

Be sure to mention your children's ages when making air reservations; child discounts of 50 percent or more are often available. Also, if you can arrange to go on an uncrowded flight, you can stretch out and rest on the empty seats.

For more details on traveling with children, check out *Adventuring With Children* by Nan Jeffrey. (See Suggested Reading.)

Travel for People with Disabilities

Mexican airlines and hotels are becoming increasingly aware of the needs of travelers with disabilities. Open, street-level lobbies and large, wheelchair-accessible elevators and rooms are available in most of Oaxaca's larger hotels.

U.S. law forbids travel discrimination against otherwise qualified people with disabilities. As long as your disability is stable and not liable to deteriorate during passage, you can expect to be treated like any passenger with special needs.

Make reservations far ahead of departure and ask your agent to inform your airline of your needs, such as boarding wheelchair or in-flight oxygen. Be early at the gate in order to take advantage of the pre-boarding call.

For many helpful details to smooth your trip, get a copy of *Traveling Like Everybody Else,* by Jacqueline Freedman and Susan Gerstein (see Suggested Reading). Get it from the publisher, Lambda Publishing, Inc., 3709 13th Ave., Brooklyn, NY 11218, tel. 718/972-5449. Also useful is the book *The Wheelchair Traveler,* by Douglas R. Annand. Yet another helpful publication is *New Horizons,* available from the U.S. Department of Transportation, or the Paralyzed Veterans of America, tel. 888/860-7244, www.pva.org.

Certain organizations both encourage and provide information about travel for those with disabilities. One with many Mexican connections is **Mobility International USA,** P.O. Box 10767, Eugene, OR 97440, tel. 541/343-1284 voice/TDD, fax 541/343-6812, www.miusa.org. A $35 membership gets you a semi-annual newsletter and referrals for international exchanges and homestays.

Similarly, **Partners of the Americas,** 1424 K St. NW, Suite 700, Washington, DC 20005, tel. 202/628-3300 or 800/322-7844, fax 202/628-3306, info@partners.net, with chapters in 45

U.S. states, works to improve understanding of disabilities and facilities in Mexico and Latin America. They maintain lists of local organizations and individuals whom handicapped travelers may contact at their destinations. For more information, visit www.partners.net.

Travel for Senior Citizens

Age, according to Mark Twain, is a question of mind over matter: If you don't mind, it doesn't matter. Mexico is a country where entire extended families, from babies to great-grandparents, live together. Elderly travelers will benefit from the respect and understanding Mexicans accord to older people. Besides these encouragements, consider the growing colony of retirees already in Oaxaca city, Puerto Escondido, and Huatulco, plus other Mexican havens, such as Puerto Vallarta, Guadalajara, Lake Chapala, Zihuatanejo, and Acapulco.

Certain organizations support senior travel. Foremost is **Elderhostel**, 11 Ave. de Lafayette, Boston, MA 02111-1746, tel. 877/426-8056, www.elderhostel.org. Elderhostel leads the senior field with an extensive international catalog of special tours, study, homestays, and people-to-people travel programs. (See Special Tours and Study options for Elderhostel Oaxaca programs.)

A number of newsletters publicize Mexico and Oaxaca vacation and retirement opportunities. Among the best is *Adventures in Mex-ico,* published six times yearly and filled with pithy hotel, restaurant, touring, and real estate information for independent travelers and retirees seeking the "real" Mexico. They presently offer two or three Oaxaca back issues for $2. For information, address Adventures in Mexico, P.O. Box 434, New Boston, NH 03070; or, in Mexico, P.O. Box 31–70, Guadalajara, Jalisco 45050; www.mexico-newsletter.com. One-year subscription runs $16, Canadian $22.

Equally worthy is the *Mexico File* monthly newsletter, which besides featuring pithy stories by Mexico travelers and news updates, offers an opportunity-packed classified section of Mexico rentals, publications, services, and much more. Ask for Oaxaca back issues and subscribe ($39/year) by contacting Simmonds Publications, 5580 La Jolla Blvd., #306, La Jolla, CA 92037, tel./fax 858/456-4419, tel. 800/563-9345 (voice mail), mf@mexicofile.com, www.mexicofile.com.

Houston-based Vacation Publications, Inc. offers yet more possibilities. Check out the book *Special Report for Discount Travelers,* which lists a plethora of air, credit-card, cruise, hotel, single, off-season, and travel-club discounts. Also useful is the magazine *Where to Retire.* To get information or a catalog, or to order, contact Vacation Publications, Inc., 1502 Augusta, Suite 415, Houston, TX 77057, tel. 713/974-6903, www.vacationsmagazine.com.

Health and Safety

STAYING HEALTHY

In Oaxaca as everywhere, *prevention* is the best remedy for illness. For those visitors who confine their travel to the beaten path, a few basic common sense precautions will ensure vacation enjoyment.

Resist the temptation to dive headlong into Mexico. It's no wonder that people get sick—broiling in the sun, gobbling peppery food, guzzling beer and margaritas, then discoing half the night—all in their first 24 hours. An alternative is to give your body time to adjust. Travelers often arrive tired and dehydrated from travel and heat. During the first few days, drink plenty of bottled water and juice, and take siestas.

Immunizations and Precautions

A competent physician can recommend the proper preventatives for your Oaxaca trip. If you are going to stay pretty much in Oaxaca city, your doctor will probably suggest little more than updating your basic typhoid, diphtheria-tetanus, and polio shots. If your trip is going to extend to the tropical south coast, best ask your physician about an antimalarial medication.

For camping or trekking in remote tropical

areas—below 4,000 feet or 1,200 meters—doctors usually recommend a gamma-globulin shot against hepatitis A and a schedule of chloroquine pills against malaria. While in backcountry areas, use other measures to discourage mosquitoes—and fleas, flies, ticks, no-see-ums, "kissing bugs" (see the Chagas' Disease and Dengue Fever section), and other tropical pests—from biting you. Common precautions include sleeping under mosquito netting, burning *espirales mosquito* (mosquito coils), and rubbing on plenty of pure DEET (n,n dimethyl-meta-toluamide) "jungle juice," mixed in equal parts with rubbing (70 percent isopropyl) alcohol. Although super-effective, 100 percent DEET dries and irritates the skin.

Sunburn

For sunburn protection, use a good sunscreen with a sun protection factor (SPF) rated 15 or more, which will reduce burning rays to one-fifteenth or less of direct sunlight. Better still, take a shady siesta-break from the sun during the most hazardous midday hours. If you do get burned, applying your sunburn lotion (or one of the "caine" creams) after the fact usually decreases the pain and speeds healing.

Safe Water and Food

Although municipalities have made great strides in sanitation, food and water remain potential sources of germs in some outlying parts of Oaxaca. While it's probably safe most everywhere, except in a few upcountry localities, it's still probably best to drink bottled water only. Hotels, whose success depends vitally on their customers' health, generally provide *agua purificada* (purified bottled water). If, for any reason, the available water is of doubtful quality, add a water purifier, such as "Potable Aqua" brand (get it at a camping goods stores before departure), or a few drops per quart of water of *blanqueador* (household chlorine bleach) or *yodo* (tincture of iodine) from the pharmacy.

Pure bottled water, soft drinks, beer, and fresh fruit juices are so widely available, it is easy to avoid tap water, especially in restaurants. Ice and *paletas* (iced juice-on-a-stick) may be risky, especially in small towns.

Washing hands before eating is a time-honored Mexican ritual that visitors should religiously follow. The humblest Mexican eatery will generally provide soap and a basin to *lavar las manos* (wash the hands). If it doesn't, don't eat there.

Hot, cooked food is generally safe, as are peeled fruits and vegetables. Milk and cheese these days in Mexico are generally processed under sanitary conditions and sold pasteurized (ask, "*¿Pasteurizado?*") and are typically safe. Mexican ice cream used to be both bad-tasting and of dubious safety, but national brands available in supermarkets are so much improved that it's no longer necessary to resist ice cream while in town.

In recent years, much cleaner public water and increased hygiene awareness have made salads—once shunned by Mexico travelers—generally safe to eat in tourist-frequented Oaxaca cafés and restaurants. Nevertheless, lettuce and cabbage, particularly in country villages, are more likely to be contaminated than carrots, cucumbers, green peppers, onions, and tomatoes. In any case, you can try dousing your salad in *vinagre* (vinegar) or plenty of sliced *limón* (lime) juice, the acidity of which kills some but not all bacteria.

First-Aid Kit

In the tropics, ordinary cuts and insect bites are more prone to infection and should receive immediate first aid. A first-aid kit with Ace bandage, acidophilus tablets, adhesive tape, antibiotic ointment, aspirin, Band-Aids, gauze, good tweezers, household chlorine bleach or iodine for water purifying, hydrocortisone cream, hydrogen peroxide, *manzanilla* (chamomile) tea bags for upset stomachs, mosquito repellent, Pepto-Bismol, rubbing alcohol, sharp pocket knife, swabs, and water-purifying tablets is a wise precaution for any traveler and mandatory for campers.

HEALTH PROBLEMS

Traveler's Diarrhea

Traveler's diarrhea (known in Southeast Asia as Bali Belly and in Mexico as turista or Montezuma's Revenge) sometimes persists, even among prudent vacationers. One can suffer turista for a week after simply traveling from California to Philadelphia or New York. Doctors say the familiar symptoms of runny bowels, nausea, and sour stomach result from normal local bacterial strains to which newcomers' systems need time to adjust. Unfortunately, the dehydration and fatigue from heat and travel reduce your body's natural defenses and sometimes lead to a persistent cycle of sickness at a time when you least want it.

Time-tested protective measures can help your body either prevent or break this cycle. Many doctors and veteran travelers swear by Pepto-Bismol for soothing sore stomachs and stopping diarrhea. Acidophilus, the bacteria found in yogurt, is widely available in the United States and Canada in tablets and aids digestion. Warm *manzanilla* (chamomile) tea, used widely in Mexico (and by Peter Rabbit's mother), provides liquid and calms upset stomachs. Temporarily avoid coffee and alcohol, drink plenty of *manzanilla* tea, and eat bananas and rice for a few meals until your tummy can take regular food.

Although powerful antibiotics and antidiarrhea medications, such as Lomotil and Imodium, are readily available over *farmacia* counters, they may involve serious side effects that consequently may become part of the problem themselves. They should not be taken in the absence of medical advice. If in doubt, consult a doctor.

Chagas' Disease and Dengue Fever
Chagas' disease, spread by the "kissing" (or, more appropriately, "assassin") bug, is a potential hazard in the Mexican tropics. Known locally as a *vinchuca*, the triangular-headed, three-quarter-inch (two centimeter) brown insect, identifiable by its yellow-striped abdomen, often drops upon its sleeping victims from the thatched ceiling of a rural house at night. Its bite is followed by swelling, fever, and weakness and can lead to heart failure if left untreated. Application of drugs at an early stage can, however, clear the patient of the trypanosome parasites that infect victims' bloodstreams and vital organs. See a doctor immediately if you believe you're infected.

Most of the precautions against malaria-bearing mosquitoes also apply to dengue fever, which does occur (although uncommonly) in outlying tropical areas of Mexico. The culprit here is a virus carried by the mosquito species *Aedes aegypti*. Symptoms are acute fever, with chills, sweating, and muscle aches. A red, diffuse rash frequently results, which may later peel. Symptoms abate after about 5 days, but fatigue may persist. A particularly serious, but fortunately rare, form, called dengue hemorrhagic fever, afflicts children and can be fatal. See a doctor immediately. Although no vaccines or preventatives, other than deterring mosquitoes, exist, you should nevertheless see a doctor immediately.

For more good tropical preventative information, get a copy of the excellent pamphlet distributed by the International Association of Medical Advice to Travelers (IAMAT). See the Medical Care section.

Scorpions and Snakes
While camping or staying in a *palapa* or other rustic accommodation, watch for scorpions, especially in your shoes, which you should shake out every morning. Scorpion stings and snakebites are rarely fatal to an adult but are potentially very serious for a child. Get the victim to a doctor calmly but quickly. For more snakebite details, see Reptiles and Amphibians in the Flora and Fauna section of the general Introduction.

Sea Creatures
While snorkeling or surfing, you may suffer a coral scratch or jellyfish sting. Experts advise you to wash the afflicted area with ocean water and pour alcohol (rubbing alcohol or tequila) over the wound, then apply hydrocortisone cream available from the *farmacia*.

Injuries from sea urchin spines and stingray barbs are painful and can be serious. Physicians recommend similar first aid for both: Remove the spines or barbs by hand or with tweezers, then soak the injury in as-hot-as-possible fresh water to weaken the toxins and provide relief. Another method is to rinse the area

MEDICAL TAGS AND AIR EVACUATION

Travelers with special medical problems might consider wearing a medical identification tag. For a reasonable fee, **Medic Alert,** P.O. Box 1009, Turlock, CA 95381, toll-free U.S. tel. 800/344-3226, www.medicalert.org, provides such tags, as well as an information hotline that will provide doctors with your vital medical background information.

For life-threatening emergencies, **Critical Air Medicine,** Montgomery Field, 4141 Kearny Villa Rd., San Diego, CA 92123, tel. 619/571-0482, toll-free U.S. tel. 800/247-8326 or (reachable from Mexico 24 hours) 800/010-0268, provides high-tech jet ambulance service from any Mexican locale to the United States. For a fee averaging about $15,000, they promise to fly you to the right U.S. hospital in a hurry.

Alternatively, for similar services, consider **Medjet Assistance,** toll-free U.S. tel. 800/963-3538. In emergencies worldwide, call U.S. tel. 205/595-6626 collect. For more information, visit www.medjetassistance.com.

with an antibacterial solution—rubbing alcohol, vinegar, wine, or ammonia diluted with water. If none are available, some relief may be achieved with urine, either your own or someone else's in your party. Get medical help immediately.

Tattoos

All health hazards don't come from the wild. A number of Mexico travelers have complained of complications from black henna tattoos. When enhanced by the chemical dye PPD, the tattoo can result in an itchy rash, which can lead to scarring. Best play it safe: If you must have a vacation tattoo, get it at an established, professional shop.

MEDICAL CARE

For medical advice and treatment, let your hotel (or if you're camping, the closest *farmacia*) refer you to a good doctor, clinic, or hospital. Mexican doctors, especially in medium-size and small towns, practice like private doctors in the United States and Canada once did before malpractice liability, group practice, and health insurance. They will come to you if you request it; they often keep their doors open even after regular hours; and, in general, charge modest fees.

You will receive generally good treatment at the vast majority of Oaxaca's hospitals and clinics, from the major tourist centers to small country towns and villages. If you must have an English-speaking, American-trained doctor, the **Interna-** tional Association for Medical Assistance to Travelers (IAMAT) publishes an updated booklet of qualified member physicians, two of whom practice in Oaxaca city and one in Huatulco. In Oaxaca, contact either Dr. Horacio Tenorio S. or Dr. Germán Tenorio V., at Clinica Hospital Carmen, Abasolo 215, tel./fax 951/516-0027. In Huatulco, contact general practitioner Dr. Andrés González Ayvar, tel. 958/587-0687, cell tel. 044-958/587-6065.

IAMAT also distributes a very detailed *How To Protect Yourself Against Malaria* guide, together with worldwide malaria risk and other communicable disease charts. For a copy, contact IAMAT, at 417 Center St., Lewiston, NY 14092, tel. 716/754-4883, or in Canada at 40 Regal Rd., Guelph, ON N1K 1B5, tel. 519/836-0102, or 1287 St. Clair Ave. W., Toronto, Ontario M6E 1B8, tel. 416/652-0137. You may also contact IAMAT at info@iamat.org or www.iamat.org.

For more useful information on health and safety in Mexico, consult Dr. William Forgey's *Traveler's Medical Alert Series: Mexico, A Guide to Health and Safety* (Merrillville, Indiana: ICS Books), or Dirk Schroeder's *Staying Healthy in Asia, Africa, and Latin America* (Emeryville, CA: Avalon Travel Publishing).

CONDUCT AND CUSTOMS

Safe Conduct

Mexico is an old-fashioned country where people value traditional ideals of honesty, family, fidelity, and piety. Crime rates are generally low; visitors are often safer in Mexico than in their hometowns.

Even though four generations have elapsed since Pancho Villa raided the U.S. border, the image of a Mexico bristling with *bandidos* persists. And similarly for Mexicans: Despite the century and a half since the *yanquis* invaded Mexico City and took half their country, the communal Mexican psyche still views gringos (and, by association, most foreign tourists) with revulsion, jealousy, and wonder.

Fortunately, the Mexican love-hate affair with foreigners does not usually apply to individual visitors. Your friendly *"buenos días"* ("good morning") or *"por favor"* ("please"),

when appropriate, is always appreciated, whether in the market, the gas station, or the hotel. The shy smile you will most likely receive in return will be your small, but not insignificant, reward.

Women

Your own behavior, despite low crime statistics, largely determines your safety in Oaxaca. For women traveling solo, it is important to realize that the double standard is alive and well in Mexico. Dress and behave modestly and you will most likely avoid embarrassment. Whenever possible, stay in the company of friends or acquaintances; find companions for beach, sightseeing, and shopping excursions. Ignore strange

MACHISMO

I once met an Acapulco man who wore five gold wristwatches and became angry when I quietly refused his repeated invitations to get drunk with him. Another time, on the beach near San Blas, two drunken campesinos nearly attacked me because I was helping my girlfriend cook a picnic dinner. Outside Taxco I once spent an endless hour in the seat behind a bus driver who insisted on speeding down the middle of the two-lane highway, honking aside oncoming automobiles.

Despite their wide differences (the first was a rich criollo, the campesinos were *indígenas*, and the bus driver, mestizo), the common affliction shared by all four men was machismo, a disease that seems to possess many Mexican men.

Machismo is a sometimes reckless obsession to prove one's masculinity, to show how *macho* one is. Men of many nationalities share the instinct to prove themselves. Japan's *bushido* samurai code is one example. Mexican men, however, often seem to try the hardest.

When confronted by a Mexican braggart, male visitors should remain careful and controlled. If your opponent is yelling, stay cool, speak softly, and withdraw as soon as possible. On the highway, be courteous and unprovocative; don't use your car to spar with a macho driver. Drinking often leads to problems. It's best to stay out of bars

or cantinas unless you're prepared to deal with the macho consequences. Polite refusal of a drink may be taken as a challenge. If you visit a bar with Mexican friends or acquaintances, you may be heading for a no-win choice of a drunken all-night *borrachera* (binge) or an insult to the honor of your friends by refusing.

For women, machismo also requires cautious behavior. In Mexico, women's liberation is long in coming. Few women hold positions of power in business or politics. Machismo requires that female visitors obey the rules or suffer the consequences. Keep a low profile; wear bathing suits and brief shorts only at the beach. Follow the example of your Mexican sisters: Make a habit of going out in the company of friends or acquaintances, especially at night. Mexican men believe an unaccompanied woman wants to be picked up. Ignore such offers; any response, even refusal, might be taken as a "maybe." If, on the other hand, there is a Mexican man whom you'd genuinely like to meet, the traditional way is an arranged introduction through family or friends.

Mexican families, as a source of protection and friendship, should not be overlooked—especially on the beach or in the park, where, among the gaggle of kids, grandparents, aunts, and cousins, there's room for one more.

men's solicitations and overtures. A Mexican man on the prowl will invent the sappiest romantic overtures to snare a gringa. He will often interpret anything but a firm "no" as a "maybe," and a "maybe" as a "yes."

Men

For male visitors, alcohol often leads to trouble. Avoid bars and cantinas; and if, given Mexico's excellent beers, you can't abstain completely, at least maintain soft-spoken self-control in the face of challenges from macho drunks.

The Law and Police

While Mexican authorities are tolerant of alcohol, they are decidedly intolerant of other substances, such as marijuana, psychedelics, cocaine, and heroin. Getting caught with such drugs in Mexico usually leads to swift and severe results.

Equally swift is the punishment for nude sunbathing, which is both illegal in public and offensive to Mexicans. Confine your nudist colony to private locations.

Although with decreasing frequency, traffic police in Oaxaca sometimes seem to watch foreign cars with eagle eyes. Officers seem to inhabit busy intersections and one-way streets, waiting for confused tourists to make a wrong move. If they whistle you over, stop immediately or you will really get into hot water. If guilty, say "Lo siento" ("I'm sorry") and be cooperative. Although the officer probably won't mention it, he or she is usually hoping that you'll cough up a $20 mordida (bribe) for the privilege of driving away.

Don't do it. Although he may hint at confiscating your car, calmly ask for an official boleto (written traffic ticket, if you're guilty) in exchange for your driver's license (have a copy), which the officer will probably keep if he writes a ticket. If, after a few minutes, no money appears, the officer will most likely give you back your driver's license rather than go to the trouble of writing the ticket. If not, the worst that will usually happen is you will have to go to the presidencia municipal (city hall) the next morning and pay the $20 to a clerk in exchange for your driver's license.

Pedestrian and Driving Hazards

Although Oaxaca's potholed pavements and holey sidewalks won't land you in jail, one of them might send you to the doctor if you don't watch your step, especially at night. "Pedestrian beware" is especially good advice on Oaxaca streets, where it is rumored that some drivers speed up rather than slow down when they spot a tourist stepping off the curb. Falling coconuts, especially frequent on windy days, constitute an additional hazard to unwary campers and beachgoers.

Driving Mexican country roads, where slow trucks and carts block lanes, campesinos stroll the shoulders, and horses, burros, and cattle wander at will, requires caution—and doubly so at night.

Socially Responsible Travel and Ecotourism

Latter-day jet travel has brought droves of vacationing tourists to developing countries largely unprepared for the consequences. As the visitors' numbers swell, power grids black out, sewers overflow, and roads crack under the strain of accommodating more and larger hotels, restaurants, cars, buses, and airports.

Worse yet, armies of vacationers drive up local prices and begin to change native customs. While visions of tourists as sources of fast money replace traditions of hospitality, television wipes out folk entertainment, Coke and Pepsi substitute for fruit drinks, and prostitution and drugs flourish.

Some travelers have said enough is enough and are forming organizations to encourage visitors to travel with increased sensitivity to native people and customs. They have developed travelers' codes of ethics and guidelines that encourage visitors to stay at local-style accommodations, use local transportation, and seek alternative vacations and tours, such as language-study and cultural programs and people-to-people work projects.

A number of especially active socially responsible travel groups sponsor tours all over the world, including Oaxaca. These include organizations such as **Global Exchange, Green Tortoise, Green Globe,** and **Third Eye Travel.** They all have websites that can be accessed via Internet search engines, such as Google and Yahoo, or the umbrella website www.sociallyresponsible.com.

The related **Ecotourism** movement promotes socially responsible tourism through the strategy of simultaneous enjoyment and enhancement of the natural environment. Oaxaca has become an ecotourism center partly because of the dedication of Oaxaca-based Ron Mader, founder and moving force behind the superb www.planeta.com website. Log on and you'll find virtually everything you need to know, from nature tour companies and village recycling projects to indigenous handicrafts cooperatives and international conferences, about Oaxaca-based ecotourism.

What to Take

"Men wear pants, ladies be beautiful" was once the dress code of one of the Mexican Pacific's classiest hotels. Men in casual Oaxaca can get by easily with just one jacket and no necktie, women with maybe one or two dressy outfits and the rest mostly simple skirts and blouses. Everyone bring a hat for sun and a light jacket or sweater for the occasional cool Oaxaca city winter evening.

Loose-fitting, hand-washable, easy-to-dry clothes make for trouble-free coastal tropical vacationing. Synthetic or cotton-synthetic-blend shirts, blouses, pants, socks, and underwear will fit the bill practically always on Oaxaca's balmy Pacific coast. For breezy nights, bring a lightweight windbreaker.

In all cases, leave showy, expensive clothes and jewelry at home. Stow items that you cannot lose in your hotel safe or carry them with you in a sturdy zipped purse or a waist pouch on your front side.

Packing

What you pack depends on how mobile you want to be. If you're planning on staying the whole time at a self-contained resort, you can take the two suitcases and one carry-on allowed by airlines. If, on the other hand, you're going to be moving around a considerable amount, it's best to condense everything down to one easily carried bag with wheels that doubles as luggage and soft backpack. Experienced travelers accomplish this by packing prudently and tightly, choosing items that will perform double or triple duty (such as a Swiss army knife with scissors).

Campers will have to be super-careful to accomplish this. Fortunately, camping along the tropical coast requires no sleeping bag. In the absence of bugs, simply use a hammock (buy it in Mexico) or, if sleeping on the sand or ground, a sleeping pad and a sheet for cover. In the winter, at most, you may have to buy a light blanket. If there are bugs, a compact tent that you and your partner can share is a must, as is mosquito repellent. A first-aid kit is absolutely necessary.

PACKING CHECKLIST

NECESSARY ITEMS
___ camera, film (expensive in Mexico)
___ comb
___ guidebook, reading books
___ inexpensive watch, clock
___ keys, tickets
___ lightweight clothes, hat
___ mosquito repellent
___ passport
___ prescription eyeglasses
___ prescription medicines and drugs
___ purse, waist-belt carrying pouch
___ sunglasses, sunscreen
___ swimsuit
___ toothbrush, toothpaste
___ tourist card, visa
___ traveler's checks, money
___ windbreaker

USEFUL ITEMS
___ address book
___ birth control
___ checkbook, credit cards
___ contact lenses
___ dental floss
___ earplugs
___ first-aid kit
___ flashlight, batteries
___ immersion heater
___ lightweight binoculars
___ portable radio/cassette player
___ razor
___ travel booklight
___ vaccination certificate

NECESSARY ITEMS FOR CAMPERS
___ collapsible gallon plastic bottle
___ dish soap
___ first-aid kit
___ hammock (buy in Mexico)
___ insect repellent
___ lightweight hiking shoes
___ lightweight tent
___ matches in waterproof case
___ nylon cord
___ plastic bottle, quart
___ pot scrubber/sponge
___ sheet or light blanket
___ Sierra Club cup, fork, and spoon
___ single-burner stove with fuel
___ Swiss army knife
___ tarp
___ toilet paper
___ towel, soap
___ two nesting cooking pots
___ water-purifying tablets or iodine

USEFUL ITEMS FOR CAMPERS
___ compass
___ dishcloths
___ hot pad
___ instant coffee, tea, sugar, powdered milk
___ moleskin (Dr. Scholl's)
___ plastic plate
___ poncho
___ short candles
___ whistle

ON THE ROAD

Oaxaca City

Oaxaca de Juárez (pop. 350,000, elev. 5,110 feet, 1,778 meters), the capital city of the state of Oaxaca, occupies the strategic intersection of the three great arms of the Valley of Oaxaca. From the city, the three sub-valleys diverge south, northwest, and east, like the thumb, index finger, and middle finger of a single hand. Aztec conquerors called that crucial hub, a hilltop above the present city, Huaxyacac (oo-AHSH-yah-kahk) (Point of the Guaje) for a forest of pod-bearing trees that once carpeted its slopes. The Spanish, who founded the city downhill, shifted that name to the more-pronounceable Oaxaca (wah-HAH-kah).

History

Before Columbus

As early as perhaps 20,000 years ago, small bands of people, whose ancestors had migrated from Asia, were gathering wild grains, vegetables, and fruits and hunting wild game in the present Valley of Oaxaca. They foraged from the bounty of forest and meadow while following the great herds—bison, camels, deer, horses, and mammoths—that roamed Ice Age America.

Later, around 8000 B.C., the climate had warmed, and the animal herds were gone. The people, no longer following the vast game migrations, settled into a more sedentary life. They began to sow and cultivate the fruits, vegetables, and grains they had originally gathered. By selection over generations they created more productive varieties. The remains of their handiwork litter cave floors from Tehuacán in present-day southern Puebla to Mitla in the valley west of Oaxaca city. Archaeologists have written of those remains: early varieties of corn and squash, woven fibers of cotton and maguey, stone arrow and ax heads, and stone seed-grinding implements.

The same experts believe that a few thousand years later many of those original humble fields and gardens had become productive fields supporting permanent settlements of thatched houses, not unlike many remote Oaxacan hamlets today. Later, perhaps by 2000 B.C., some of these villages had grown into towns, with proud columned stone houses for the upper classes, pyramids topped by temples, and small factories for producing jewelry, mirrors, and other specialized merchandise.

Finally, around 600 B.C., people speaking a Zapotec mother tongue founded Monte Albán on a mountaintop above the present city of Oaxaca. Monte Albán ruled the Valley of Oaxaca for more than a millennium, climaxing as a sophisticated metropolis of as many as 40,000, controlling a large and populous area of southern Mexico and enjoying diplomatic and trade relations with distant kingdoms. But for reasons unknown, Monte Albán declined to a shadow of its former glory by around A.D. 800.

Zapotec-speaking city-states, such as Zaachila, Dainzu, Mitla, and Lambityeco in the surrounding valleys, filled the power vacuum left by the decline of Monte Albán. They ruled small valley-floor kingdoms, each controlling a small flock of satellite towns. Later, Mixtec-speaking people from the northwest invaded the Valley of Oaxaca and took over Monte Albán, using it mostly as a burial ground. Their chiefs subjugated many of the Zapotec city-states and ruled as an upper-crust nobility over much of the Valley of Oaxaca, until the Aztecs invaded during the 1440s.

In 1456, after a dozen years of struggle against combined Mixtec and Zapotec forces, the victorious Aztecs established a garrison on the hill of Huaxyacac (now called El Fortín), overlooking the present city of Oaxaca. Although Aztec settlers had established a model colony by 1500 (including districts with well-known Valley of Mexico names that still exist, such as Xochimilco), their rule was brief. On December 25, 1521, after a token skirmish, conquistador Francisco de Orozco and his soldiers replaced them on the hill of Huaxyacac scarcely five months after the Spanish tide had flooded the Aztecs' Valley of Mexico homeland.

Conquest and Colonization

Spanish settlers began arriving soon after the conquistadores. Hernán Cortés, hearing of the beauty and bounty of the Valley of Oaxaca from both his lieutenants and emissaries from the Zapotec king, decided early on to stake out the Valley of Oaxaca as his personal domain. Time and again during the 1520s he ordered the settlers evacuated from Huaxyacac, only to find a year or two later that they had returned. During Cortés's absence on an expedition to Honduras, the settlers petitioned for and received a charter from King Carlos V for their town, which they christened Antequera after the old Roman city in Spain. Determined not to be outmaneuvered, Cortés personally went to Spain to plead his case and returned triumphant with the royal title of Marqués del Valle de Oaxaca. This included a grant of hundreds of thousands of acres and rights to the labor of thousands of indigenous subjects in a grand checkerboard domain stretching from the Valley of Mexico to the Isthmus of Tehuantepec. Cortés's lands surrounded the settlers' entire town of Antequera. In desperation, the townspeople petitioned the queen of Spain for land on which to grow vegetables: They were granted a one-league square in 1532, now the core of the modern city of Oaxaca.

For hundreds of years, Cortés's descendants reigned; the townspeople prospered; the church grew fat; and the natives toiled—in corn, cattle, cane, and cochineal.

Independence, Reform, and Revolution

In contrast to its neighbors in the state of Guerrero, conservative Oaxaca was a grudging player in the 1810–1821 War of Independence. But as the subsequent republican tide swept the country, local fervor produced a new state constitution, including a state legislature and governmental departments, such as public instruction and the Institute of Arts and Sciences.

By the 1850s, times had changed. Oaxacans were leading a new national struggle. Benito Juárez, a pure Zapotec native Mexican, was rallying liberal forces in the civil War of the Reforms against the oligarchy that had replaced colonial rule. Born in Guelatao, north of the valley, Juárez at age 12 was an orphan sheepherder. A Catholic priest, struck by the boy's intelligence, brought him to the city as a servant and taught him Spanish in preparation for the priesthood.

Instead, Benito became a lawyer. He hung out his shingle in Oaxaca, first as a defender of the poor, then state legislator, governor, chief justice, and finally the president of Mexico. In his honor, the city's official name was again changed—to Oaxaca de Juárez—in 1872.

In 1861, after winning the three-year civil war, Juárez's Reformista forces had their victory snatched away. France, taking advantage of the preoccupation of the United States with its own civil war, invaded Mexico and installed an Austrian Hapsburg prince as Emperor Maximilian of Mexico.

It took Juárez five years to prevail against Maximilian and his conservative Mexican backers. Although Maximilian and Juárez paradoxically shared many of the same liberal ideas, Juárez had Maximilian executed after his defeat and capture in 1867. Juárez bathed Mexico in enlightenment as he promulgated his "Laws of the Reform" (which remain essentially in force). Although the country rewarded him with reelection, he died of exhaustion in 1871.

Another Oaxacan of native Mexican descent, General Porfirio Díaz, vowed to carry Juárez's banner. Díaz, the hero who defeated the French in the battle of Puebla on Cinco de Mayo (May 5) of 1862, was elected president in 1876. "*No*

Reelección" was his campaign cry. He subsequently ruled Mexico for 34 years.

Under Díaz's "Order and Progress," Mexico, and to a lesser degree Oaxaca, was modernized at great human cost. As railroads, factories, and mines mushroomed, property ownership increasingly became concentrated among rich Mexicans and their foreign friends. Smashed protest marches, murdered opposition leaders, and rigged elections returned Díaz to office time and again.

But not forever. The revolt that ousted Díaz in 1910 has, in theory, never ceased. For the last three generations of the 20th century, the PRI, the Institutional Revolutionary Party, presided over a uniquely imperfect Mexican form of democracy. During that time the lives of native Oaxacans improved gradually. Although indigenous families now go to government health centers and more of their children attend government rural schools, the price for doing so is to become less indigenous and more Mexican.

Times in the Valley of Oaxaca nevertheless seem to be getting gradually better. In the late 1980s, UNESCO recognized Oaxaca as one of several world sites belonging to the "Cultural Patrimony of Mankind." The government took notice and began preparing Oaxaca for an influx of visitors. Museums were built, monuments refurbished, and the venerable buildings restored. Burgeoning tourism during the 1990s has visibly improved the economic well-being of many Oaxaca families.

Increased international and national awareness seems to have contributed to other improvements. Some long-standing grievances are being recognized. In 1995, moderate PRI governor Diodoro Carrasco Altamirano pushed through an unprecedented "Usos y Costumbres" law, which legalized Oaxacan native rights to their indigenous language and their traditional, town meeting form of government.

Nevertheless, by developed-world standards, most Oaxaca city families remain very poor. The political system, moreover, is far from perfect. But now, the victory of opposition presidential candidate Vicente Fox promises a new day for democracy in Oaxaca. Granted, Fox can't work miracles, but Oaxacans are hopeful that transgressions such as police brutality, bribes of public officials, vote buying, and murder of opposition community activists will quickly become things of the past.

Sights

Getting Oriented

The streets of Oaxaca still run along the same simple north-south grid the city fathers laid out in 1529. If you stand at the center of the old *zócalo* (town plaza) and look out toward the *catedral* across Avenida Hidalgo, you will be looking north. Diagonally left, to the northwest, you'll see the smaller plaza, **Alameda de León,** and directly beyond that, in the distance, the historic hill of Huaxyacac, now called **Cerro del Fortín.**

Along the base of that hill, the Pan American Highway (National Highway 190) runs generally east-west through the northern suburbs. Turn around and you'll see the porticoed facade of the **Palacio de Gobierno,** where Oaxaca's governor tends to the state's business. Half a mile (.8 km) behind that (although you can't see it from the *zócalo*), the *periférico* (peripheral boulevard) loops around the town's south end. There it passes the yawning but often dry wash of the **Río Atoyac** and the sprawling **Mercado Abastos,** a market and second-class bus terminal on the southwest. Finally, if you find a clear vantage point, you'll see the hill of **Monte Albán**

MARGARITA MAZA: A LIFE OF COURAGE AND CONVICTION

Calle M. Maza, a modest two-block lane on Oacaxa's northern downtown edge, memorializes Margarita Maza, both the wife of Mexico's revered president Benito Juárez and the heroine who gave her all for love and country. Her greatness and that of her husband were inextricably intertwined by their own strong liberal ideals and their collective fate. Years before Margarita was born, Benito, of pure Zapotec blood, came to Oaxaca city seeking both his sister and his fortune. He found his sister working as a cook in the household of Italian immigrant and merchant Antonio Maza and his wife, Petra Parada.

Benito also found refuge and warmth in the Maza household; through the Mazas, Benito got work and social connections that led to education and introduction into Oaxacan society. Benito was 20 years old when Margarita was born, the Mazas' youngest child. He bounced the baby on his knee and played with her like an older brother as she matured and while Benito's career as a lawyer, then Oaxaca state legislator, blossomed.

By the time Margarita was 17, their mutual affection had bloomed into love, and Benito, a successful attorney at 37, proposed marriage.

They were married in the church of San Felipe de Neri, in Oaxaca, on July 31, 1843. Even today such a match would be unusual; in the Oaxaca of 1843 it was unheard of. That he, a poor, dark brown Zapotec, and she, a lily-white daughter of a prominent merchant, were even able to associate, much less to marry, is testament to the Mazas' liberal views.

The same liberal views and their iron determination to do something about them scarred the last half of Benito and Margarita's 26 years of married life. From around 1854, when Benito was driven into exile in New Orleans, civil war, foreign invasion, and assassination attempts forced the family to be nearly always on the move, living in unfamiliar and trying circumstances, hounded and threatened by enemies, and continually lacking money.

One of the most dangerous episodes came in 1858, when Margarita, at the age of 32, had to move her brood of five children and entire household from Oaxaca to Veracruz, where Benito was running the liberal Mexican government-in-exile. Fearing spies and assassins, Margarita took the tortuous, roundabout route over the heart of the Sierra Madre, traveling at night, on foot beside looming 1,000 feet (300 meters) above the southwest horizon.

AROUND THE ZÓCALO

The venerable restored downtown buildings and streets, some converted to traffic-free malls, make a delightful strolling ground for discovering traditional Mexico at its best. The shady old *zócalo* basks at the heart of it all, a perfect place for taking a seat at one of many sidewalk cafés and watching the world glide by. Officially called Jardín Juárez, the *zócalo* was laid out in 1529. Its portals, clockwise from the west side, are named Flores, Clavería, Juárez, and Mercaderes.

Palacio de Gobierno

Give the guards at the front door of the statehouse a cheery *"buenos días"* or *"buenas tardes"* and step inside. City fathers first built a city hall on the same site in 1576. Repeated earthquakes led to reconstructions, until 1948, when the present building, a modernized and strengthened version of the previous 1884 structure, was finished.

Straight ahead, across the central patio and up the stairs, you'll see the main mural, by Arturo Bustos, completed during the 1980s. It depicts the struggles of Oaxaca's independence, reform, and revolutionary heroes. On the right, in his trademark bandanna, is *insurgente* José María Morelos y Pavón, who published the famous *El Correo del Sur* newspaper in Oaxaca during Mexico's War of Independence. In the center is Oaxaca's favorite son and Mexico's revered *presidente,* Benito Juárez, and his wife, Margarita Maza. Below them is Juárez's *reformista* cabinet (notice the young, restive General Porfirio Díaz with the sword on the right),

their burro-train, disguising herself in native *huipil* and sleeping by day in farmhouses of friendly Zapotec campesinos.

Later, Benito and Margarita enjoyed two years of peace together, beginning in 1861, after the liberal triumph in the civil War of the Reforms. Their marriage, although severely tried by hardship and separation, was a supremely happy one. Twelve children resulted; seven—six girls and a boy—outlived their parents. Two boys and three girls died when still young. Their love, although profoundly deep, had few pretensions. Benito called her his "old lady." She called him "Juárez" and, when asked, replied that "he is very homely but good."

Their peace together was short-lived. The French invasion forced Benito to travel the country, managing the government in a black carriage, one jump ahead of the French army. Margarita took the family on a hopscotch path into northern Mexico and finally to New York and Washington, DC. There, she reached the depths of despair when two of her three sons died. She wrote to Benito: "The loss of my sons is killing me. . . . I prefer death a thousand times more than life. . . . I do not blame persons who kill themselves. . . . If I had been braver I should have done it a year ago."

Eventually Margarita recovered her equilibrium, buoyed by the birth of her first grandchild, a baby girl, and the admiring attention of American society, including General Ulysses S. Grant and President Andrew Johnson.

On June 19, 1867, Juárez had the French-installed Emperor Maximilian executed. This was Margarita's signal to return home. A month later, with her party of 14, she arrived in Veracruz, showered by bouquets as she walked down the gangplank.

Reunited for three happy years with Margarita in Mexico City, Benito worked like a demon to turn his dreams for Mexico into reality. But overwork took its toll, and Benito suffered a stroke in October 1870. He recovered partially to discover that Margarita was fatally ill. She died on January 2, 1871, of cancer. Although weak, Benito strained with all of his strength and with tears in his eyes to lift her body into the coffin. All of Mexico, both friends and former enemies, joined in grief with their president for their beloved Margarita Maza, who had given as much as any heroine could for both love and country.

OAXACA CITY

To Mitla and Tehuantepec

To San Felipe de Agua

RESTAURANT LA TOSCANA

190

ANTEQUERA

CASA ARNEL

ALDAMA

ALIANZA

CONSTITUCIÓN

CURTIDURÍAS

CALZ. DE LA REPÚBLICA

AV. INDEPENDENCIA

M. DE TACUBAYA

EMILIO CARRANZA

CASA MARIA BED AND BREAKFAST

B. DOMÍNGUEZ

NEZTAHUALCÓYOTL

RESTAURANT COLIBRI

FIRST-CLASS BUS TERMINAL

HOTEL MISIÓN DE LOS ANGELES

LIBRES

CASA DE MIS RECUERDOS

PINO SUÁREZ

VINIGUELETZA LANGUAGE SCHOOL

ABASOLO

MURGUÍA

MORELOS

AMIGOS DEL SOL (SPANISH CLASSES)

AV. JUÁREZ

Juárez Park (El Llano)

HOTEL AND STUDIOS LA MARIPOSA

LENDING LIBRARY

CLINICA HOSPITAL CARMEN

PHOTOGRAPHY MUSEUM

SUITES LA FE

HOTEL DEL VIRREY

REFORMA

WINE SHOP

HOUSE OF DEPUTIES

HOTEL CASONA DEL LLANO

SEE DETAIL

TEMPLO SANTO DOMINGO

TOURIST YU'U OFFICE

M. MAZA DE JUÁREZ

GÓMEZ FARÍAS

HOTEL CONZATTI

HUMBOLDT

PARROQUIA CARMEN ALTA

BERRIOZABAL

MACEDONIA ALCALÁ

HOSPITAL SEGURO SOCIAL

CHAPULTEPEC

XÓLOTL

HÉROES DE

RUFINO TAMAYO

ARQUITOS

PORFIRIO DÍAZ

ARIPO (CRAFTS)

MUSEO DE JUÁREZ

G. VIGIL

CARRANZA

CASA OAXACA

LA BREW

CATHEDRAL

MARIANO MATAMOROS

PARROQUIA CARMEN BAJA

CALZADA NIÑOS HÉROES

QUETZALCÓATL

L. ALLENDE

GRASSROOTS/CENTER OF HOPE

TINOCO Y PALACIOS

HOTEL FORTÍN PLAZA

MARCOS PÉREZ

CRESPO

HOTEL LAS GOLONDRINAS

NICOLAS BRAVO

HOTEL VICTORIA

ESCALERA DEL FORTÍN

RESTAURANT LA MURALLA

HOTEL AITANA

RESTAURANT MANANTIAL VEGETARIANA

UNIVERSITY OF OAXACA SCHOOL OF FINE ARTS

AV. INDEPENDENCIA

COMONFORT

Cerro del Fortín

PLANETARIUM

GUELAGUETZA AUDITORIUM

CASA COLONIAL

HOTEL LOS REYES

BASÍLICA DE LA SOLEDAD

MUSEO

AV. HIDALGO

ASTRONOMICAL OBSERVATORY

190

To Etla, Pinotepa Nacional, and Mexico City

To Mex. 190

OAXACA CITY

To Mex 190

AV. HIDALGO

V. GUERRERO

CRISTÓBAL COLÓN

LA NORIA

J.L. RAYÓN

ARTEAGA

POSADA DE CHENCHO

G. ORTEGA

MANUEL DUBLADO

XICOTENCATL

KOCHITL

VEGA

PERIFÉRICO

SEE "OAXACA CITY CENTER" MAP

TEMPLO SAN AUGUSTIN

VILLA MARÍA

M. OCAMPO

M. FIALLO

U.N.O. LANGUAGE CENTER (SPANISH CLASSES)

ARMENTA Y LÓPEZ

5 DE MAYO

PLAZA DE ARMAS (ZÓCALO)

PALACIO DE GOBIERNO

MERCADO 20 DE NOVIEMBRE

BUSTAMANTE

MERCADO JUAREZ

MERCADO DE ARTESANÍAS

MIGUEL CABRERA

RESTAURANT EL NARANJO

20 DE NOVIEMBRE

J.P. GARCÍA

VALERIO TRUJANO

PAULINA YOUTH HOSTEL

LAS CASAS

L. ALDAMA

DIAZ ORDAZ

J. ZARAGOZA

HOTEL RINCÓN DEL PACIFICO

HOTEL MESÓN DEL ANGEL

MINA

TOURIST BUSES

MIER Y TERÁN

GALEANA

VICTORIA

PROL. DE VICTORIA

MERCADO ABASTOS

To Second-Class Bus Terminal

OAXACA CITY

To Airport, Coyotepec, Ocotlán, Puerto Angel, and Puerto Escondido

131

175

DETAIL

STAMP MUSEUM

HOTEL VILLA DE LEÓN

HOTEL MAELA

REFORMA

ETHNO-BOTANICAL GARDEN

GALERIA QUETZALLI

APTS. CASA DE LOS ABUELOS

HOTEL CASA VERTIZ

CASA BUGAMBILIAS

CAFE COFFEE BEANS

CAFE LA ANTIGUA

REST. LOS PACOS

MUSEO DE LAS CULTURAS DE OAXACA

TEMPLO SANTO DOMINGO

COINS AND ANTIQUES

5 DE MAYO

REST. EL CHE

CASA OLIVO

CINCO DE MAYO

MACEDONIA

ALCALÁ

PIZZA NOSTRONO

PLAZUELA LABASTIDA

REST. EL TOPIL

DEPARTMENTOS DEL FRAILE

SHOPPING PLAZA SANTA DOMINGO

ABASOLO

U.S. CONSUL

GALERIA INDIGO

ORO DE MONTE ALBÁN

PLAZA ALCALÁ

To Monte Albán

To Arrazola, Cuilapan, and Zaachila

© AVALON TRAVEL PUBLISHING, INC.

which struggled through two bloody wars, finally emerging, with Juárez, triumphant in 1867. On the mural's far left, you see Oaxaca's 1910 revolutionary hero in turn-of-the-century Marxian-style spectacles, Ricardo Flores Magón. Before exiting, take a look at Bustos's other two murals, on the left and right sides of the courtyard, which respectively depict Mexico's pre-Hispanic and conquest eras.

Mercado Juárez

The traditional Juárez market occupies the one-block square that begins just one block south and one block west of the *zócalo.* Stroll around for fun and perhaps a bargain in the honeycomb of traditional leather, textile, and clothing stalls.

While at the market, be sure to step to the southwest corner of 20 de Noviembre and Rayón for a history lesson in art inside the **Templo y Ex-convento de San Juan de Dios,** which stands on the site of Oaxaca's oldest church. The present structure, completed in 1703, replaced the former earthquake-damaged 1535 town cathedral, which itself replaced the original 1521 adobe structure.

OAXACA CITY CENTER

© AVALON TRAVEL PUBLISHING, INC.

Big paintings lining the nave walls depict landmarks in Oaxaca's religious history. Inside the front door, to the left, see Bishop las Casas protecting his native charges against soldiers and settlers. Farther inside is an oil of the Santa Cruz de Huatulco (see the Catedral de Oaxaca section); next comes Oaxaca's first mass, on the banks of the Río Atoyac, on November 25, 1521, and after that, the baptism of Cosijoeza, the last Zapotec king. Also, you'll find a series of oils showing the discovery, persecution, revolt, and reacceptance of the so-called "Idolators of Los Cajonos," whom Spaniards discovered worshiping their native gods on September 14, 1700.

Templo y Exconvento de San Agustín

Off-*zócalo* side streets are studded with Oaxaca's old church gems. One of the most precious and most accessible is the San Agustín church and ex-convent one block due east from the Palacio de Gobierno along Calle Guerrero. One of the few Oaxacan works of the Augustinian order, the original adobe church on this site was finished in 1596, but it was seriously damaged by subsequent earthquakes. The present church, finished in 1722, replaced the original. A generation after the Augustinians were expelled in the 1860s, Bishop Gillow of Oaxaca acquired and reactivated the church in 1893 and started the Casa de Cuna, a children's home and school, which still exists next door.

San Agustín's baroque facade blooms with a pious pastoral sculpture of a bearded San Agustín, fifth-century Bishop of Hipona, North Africa, above the entrance arch. Below, flanking the entrance portal, stand sculptures of Augustinian Saints Alipio, on the left, and Thomas of Valencia, on the right.

Inside, the same saints grace the grand, gilded main altarpiece, with the addition of Augustinian founding fathers San Juan Sahagún and San Fulgencio. The gilded south (right) transept altarpiece displays a heavenly image of Santa Monica, mother of San Agustín. Finally, look below the pulpit for the glass capsule that contains a bone-fragment relic of San Agustín, gift from the Roman Augustinians.

Catedral de Oaxaca

Return to the *zócalo*'s opposite, north side, for a look at the present cathedral. It replaced the 1550 original, demolished by an earthquake in 1696. Finished in 1733, with appropriately burly twin bell towers, the present cathedral is distinguished

Visitors enjoy the Oaxaca *zócalo*-front view.

© BRUCE WHIPPERMAN

OAXACA CITY

by its Greek marble main altar, where a polished Italian bronze Virgin of the Ascension is being drawn upward to the cloud-tipped heavenly domain of the Holy Spirit (the dove) and God (the sunburst). Flanking opposite sides of the altar, notice the glass images of noble, bearded St. Peter and St. Paul.

Of considerable historical interest is the **Santa Cruz de Huatulco** (Holy Cross of Huatulco), enshrined in a chapel at the middle, south (right) side of the nave. The cross, about two feet high, is one of four made in 1612 by Oaxaca bishop Juan Cervantes from the original mysterious cross worshipped by the natives on the southern Oaxaca coast long before the conquest. An explanation, in Spanish, gives three versions of the story of the cross, which, the natives reported to the conqueror Pedro Alvarado in 1522, was erected long before by a strange, white-robed holy man, who soon departed and never returned. Bishop Cervantes sent the three other copies of the cross, respectively, to authorities at Santa María Huatulco town, Mexico City, and Rome. (For more details of the Holy Cross of Huatulco, see the Bahías de Huatulco history section of the Pacific Resorts and Southern Sierra chapter.)

The basilica of Oaxaca's patron, La Señora de la Soledad, usually quiet, is awash with celebrants during the patronal festival in the second week of December.

NORTHWEST OF THE ZÓCALO

Templo de San Felipe Neri

Just two blocks west of the cathedral, along Independencia, at the corner of Tinoco and Palacios, rises the distinguished facade of the Templo de San Felipe Neri. The building is immediately notable, for it faces south, unlike the great majority of Oaxaca's churches, which face west.

Its builders finished the structure, once a convent of the order of San Felipe Neri and dedicated it to the Virgin of Patrocinio, in 1773. The subsequent 1795 earthquake caused extensive damage, which was not completely repaired until the 20th century. Unfortunately, more earthquakes, in 1928 and 1931, inflicted additional destruction. The present restoration was completed in 1985.

The result appears well worth the effort. Original builders crafted the facade in the 17th-century "plateresque" tradition, so-named for the designs,

similar to those of fine silverware, using muted green volcanic *cantera* stone. The sole exception is the noble statue of San Felipe Neri, carved of contrasting yellow *cantera,* in clerical hat and bishop's cape, that presides above the front door.

Walk inside to admire the temple's glorious golden *retablo* (altarpiece). It towers three stories, inhabited by a host of apostles, saints, angels, and cherubs, all reigned over by the Virgin and finally San Felipe de Neri at the very top.

Museo Arte Prehispánico de Rufino Tamayo

Just one block farther north, this museum, at 503 Morelos, tel. 951/516-4750, exhibits the brilliant pre-Columbian artifact collection of celebrated artist Rufino Tamayo (1899–1991). Displays include hosts of animal motifs—Colima dogs, parrots, ducks, snakes—whimsically crafted into polychrome vases, bowls, and urns. Open Mon. and Wed.–Sat. 10 A.M.–2 P.M. and 4–7 P.M., Sun. 10 A.M.–3 P.M.

Continue three blocks west, past the University of Oaxaca School of Fine Arts and the airy Plaza of Dances, to the baroque **Basílica de Nuestra Señora de la Soledad.** Inside, the Virgin of Solitude, the patron of Oaxaca, stands atop the altar with her five-pound solid golden crown, encrusted with 600 diamonds.

Step into the **Museo de la Soledad,** at the downhill side of the church, rear end. A multitude of objects of adornment—shells, paintings, jewelry—crowd cabinets, shelves, and aisles of musty rooms. Large stained-glass panels tell of the images of Jesus and the Virgin that arrived miraculously in 1620, eventually becoming Oaxaca's patron symbols. Open daily except Wednesday, 10 A.M.–2 P.M. and 4–6 P.M., tel. 951/516-5076.

ANDADOR DE MACEDONIO ALCALÁ

The tranquil Andador de Macedonio Alcalá pedestrian mall, named after the composer of the Oaxacan hymn "Dios Nunca Muere" ("God Never Dies"), leads north from the *zócalo*. Paved with Oaxaca green stone in 1985 and freed of auto traffic, the mall connects the *zócalo* with a number of unmissable Oaxaca sights.

Teatro Alcalá

Among them is the Alcalá theater at 900 Independencia, tel. 951/516-3387 (from the back of the cathedral head right one block along Independencia to the corner of Independencia and 5 de Mayo). Christened by a 1909 opening performance of *Aida,* the Alcalá houses a treasury of Romantic-era art. Above the foyer, a sumptuous marble staircase rises to a bas-relief medallion allegorizing the triumph of art. Also take a look around the theater's gallery of paintings of Miguel Cabrera (1695–1768), a native Zapotec who rose to become New Spain's renowned baroque painter.

Before you leave, you might take a look inside the **Galería Nancy Canseco,** on the 5 de Mayo side, ground floor, which showcases the work of local and nationally recognized artists.

Open Mon.–Sat. 10 A.M.–2 P.M. and 4–8 P.M., Sun. 4–8 P.M.

Museo de Arte Contemporaneo de Oaxaca

Continuing north along the Alcalá street mall, you soon pass the so-called **Casa de Cortés,** now the **Museo de Arte Contemporaneo de Oaxaca,** Macedonio Alcalá 202, tel. 951/514-2818 or 951/514-2228, open daily except Tues. 10:30 A.M.–8 P.M. Past the bookstore (mostly Spanish but some English-language history, art, and guidebooks), exhibitions feature works of local and nationally known modern artists. Although named popularly for Hernán Cortés, the building is at least a hundred years too new for Cortés to have lived there. The coat of arms on the facade above the door reveals it to have been the 17th-century home of a different Oaxaca family.

Exconvento de Santa Catalina

Continue uphill and, at Murguia, detour right again, to the **Exconvento de Santa Catalina,** the second-oldest women's convent in New Spain, founded in 1576. Although the quarters of the first novitiates were spare, the convent grew into a sprawling chapel and cloister complex decorated by fountains and flower-strewn gardens. Juárez's reforms drove the sisters out in 1862; the building has since served as city hall, school, and movie theater. Now, it stands beautifully restored as the Hotel Camino Real. Note the native-motif original murals that the renovation revealed on interior walls.

Centro Cultural de Santo Domingo

Return to the Alcalá street mall and continue another block uphill to Oaxaca's pride, the **Centro Cultural de Santo Domingo,** which contains two main parts, side by side: the **Museum of the Cultures of Oaxaca** and the **Church and Ex-convent of Santo Domingo,** both behind the broad Plaza Santo Domingo maguey garden and pedestrian square.

Inside, Santo Domingo church (open daily 7 A.M.–1 P.M. and 5–8 P.M.) glows with a wealth of art. Above the antechamber spreads the entire genealogical tree of Santo Domingo de Guzmán, starting with Mother Mary and weaving through a score of noblemen and women to the saint himself over the front door.

Continuing inside, the soaring, Sistine Chapel–like nave glitters with saints, cherubs, and Bible-story paintings. The altar climaxes in a host of cherished symbols—the Last Supper, sheaves of grain, loaves and fishes, Jesus and Peter on the Sea of Galilee—in a riot of gold leaf.

Continue next door to the museum, open daily except Mon. 10 A.M.–7:30 P.M., tel. 951/516-2991, which occupies the completely restored convent section of the Santo Domingo church. Exhibitions begin on the bottom floor in rooms adjacent to the massive convent cloister, restored in 1998 to all of its original austere beauty. A downstairs highlight is the long-neglected but now safely preserved **Library of Francisco Burgoa,** which you can walk right through and examine some of the more important works on display. The collection, 23,000 titles in all, includes its earliest work, a 1484 commentary on the works of Aristotle by Juan Versor.

A Museo sign points you upstairs via a glitteringly restored, towering domed chamber, adorned overhead with the Dominican founding fathers, presided over by Santo Domingo de Guzmán himself.

It's hard not to be impressed by the seeming miles of meticulously prepared displays divided into about a dozen long rooms covering various historical periods. One room exhibits priceless Monte Albán–era artifacts, including one of the most important of the original so-called *danzantes,* with the typically mutilated sex organs. The climax comes in the Tesoros of Tomb 7 room, where the entire gilded treasure discovered at Monte Albán Tomb 7 is on display. Besides a small mountain of gold and turquoise ornaments, notice the small but masterfully executed golden head of Ecéchatl, god of the wind, made eerie by the omission of facial skin over the jaw, to produce a nightmarishly skeletal piece of jewelry.

The museum has recently established an **ethno-botanical garden** in its big backyard. Staff customarily conduct tours (at this writing, in Spanish only, Tues., Thurs. and Sat. 10 A.M.

and 5 P.M.). Inquire at the museum front desk or by tel. 951/516-2991 or 951/516-7915 for updated tour information.

A Trove of Small Museums

Back outside, step across Alcalá, a few doors uphill, into the rust-colored old building, now tastefully restored as the museum of the **Instituto de Artes Gráficos de Oaxaca,** tel. 951/516-6980. Inside, displays exhibit mostly contemporary etchings, wood-block prints, and paintings by artists of both national and international renown. Exhibits change approximately monthly; open daily except Tues. 9:30 A.M.–8 P.M.

Head west one block (along the Plazuela Carmen mall, off Alcalá across from the museum) to the **Casa de Juárez** museum, 609 Garcia Vigil, tel. 951/516-1860. The modest but beautifully restored house was the home of Juárez's benefactor, priest and bookbinder Father Antonio Salanueva. Rooms decorated with homey mid-19th-century furnishings realistically illustrate the life and times of a man as revered in Mexico as his contemporary, Abraham Lincoln, north of the border. Open daily except Mon., 10 A.M.–6 P.M.

Later, if you have time, return to the Santo Domingo church plaza and continue east past the church along Constitución to the new **Museo Philatelica de Oaxaca,** at Reforma 504, tel. 951/516-8028, just uphill from the corner of Constitución, open daily except Mon., 9 A.M.–7 P.M. Inside, showcases display the noted collection of José Cosino y Cosio, a library of international postal paraphernalia. Planners project that the museum's collection, of mostly Mexican and Oaxacan postage stamps, will grow steadily during succeeding decades.

Continue a few blocks down Reforma, turn left at Murguia, and continue half a block to the **Centro de Fotografía Alvarez Bravo,** Murguia 302, tel. 951/514-1933, open daily except Tues., 9:30 A.M.–8 P.M. Here, front galleries display the work of both locally prominent and internationally acclaimed photographers, while instructors in back courtyard rooms conduct photography classes for children, adult beginners, and professionals.

NORTH END

Arquitos and San Felipe del Agua Village

Long ago, Oaxaca's city fathers provided for a permanent town water supply. They tapped the bountiful natural springs flowing from the mountains rising directly north of the city, topped by the towering Cerro San Felipe (elev. 10,200 feet, 3,100 meters). The aqueduct they built gave rise to the name San Felipe del Agua, the foothill village where the aqueduct begins. Although now replaced by underground steel pipes, the original 18th-century aqueduct still stands, paralleling the downhill road from San Felipe and ending in a quaint string of arches, called **Los Arquitos,** in the city neighborhood several blocks northwest of Santo Domingo church.

Starting from Plaza Santo Domingo, walk uphill four blocks north, along Alcalá; turn left at Xolotl (show-LOH-tuhl) and continue for three blocks to Tamayo, which runs uphill, paralleling the arches. The most entertaining thing about the Los Arquitos neighborhood is the way the residents have adapted to the aqueduct, ingeniously tucking their individual home and store doorways beneath the arches. Don't miss the little shrine built beneath one arch, at Tamayo 802, and also the tiny restaurant, El Pavito (The Little Peacock), beneath another. Also notice the colorfully picturesque contrast between the arches' red brick and light green *cantera* stone construction. Finally, be sure to explore some of the side lanes, such as the one opposite Tamayo 818 that heads beneath an arch and opens into a tiny plaza presided over by Archangel Gabriel. Afterward, stop for a drink or a bite to eat at the inviting Fonda de la Cruz, corner of Tamayo and Xolotl.

Next, take a taxi or a bus (near the *zócalo,* catch one labeled "San Felipe," north, from the corner of Independencia and Reforma, or uphill along Pino Suárez) or drive the few miles uphill to the source, suburban **San Felipe del Agua** village. The jumping-off point is Avenida Netzahualcoyotl (nay-tzah-oo-wahl-coh-YOH-tuhl), which heads uphill at the big green "San Felipe" sign from its intersection with Highway 190 (Avenida

Archangel Gabriel presides over a quiet corner in the Los Arquitos district.

Niños Héroes), one block east of the Pemex station. Drivers, continue about two-thirds of a mile (1 km), bear left at the hotel sign, then right one block, left one long block, and right again. You'll be on your way uphill, heading along Calzada San Felipe, which parallels the old stone aqueduct on your left. In a few miles the road becomes San Felipe's Calle Hidalgo, which, in turn, will lead you all the way to the bus turnaround at the foot of Cerro San Felipe.

Here the air is fresh and cool, and the view, both uphill and down, is inspiring. Below spreads the city and valley both left and right, while uphill rises the green, pine-tufted massif of Cerro San Felipe.

Continue uphill about a quarter mile (.4 km) to **Parque Comunal de San Felipe** trailhead and guard station. See the map at the guard station for trails that lead uphill through pine-shadowed glens and past waterfalls, all the way to the top of the mountain. It's a stiff, all-day 4,000-foot (1,200-meter) uphill hike. If clouds don't gather, and you start hiking early enough (preferably before 9 A.M.), the stupendous mountaintop view will be your reward.

Or ask for a guide at the guard station. Under any conditions, take a hat, water, lunch, and strong shoes.

Travelers who want more leisure can have it poking around the diminutive town plaza and

San Felipe Apóstol church a few blocks downhill. Stop by for at least a drink at the showplace **Restaurant Las Campañas** (with patio-bar **La Ermita** in the back), on the plaza corner adjacent to the church, tel. 951/515-3178.

Accommodations

Oaxaca offers a wide range of good lodgings. Air-conditioning is not particularly necessary in temperate Oaxaca, although hot-water showers (furnished by all lodgings listed below) feel especially comfy during cool winter mornings and evenings. The less expensive hotels, which generally do not accept credit cards, are mostly near the colorful, traffic-free *zócalo*. With few exceptions, Oaxaca's plush, resort-style hostelries dot the northern foothill edge of town. During holidays and festivals (Easter week, July, August, late October–early November, December 15–January 4), many Oaxaca hotels raise their prices 20–30 percent above the numbers listed below. (Note: Many of the following lodgings and much more are advertised on websites, notably **www.mexonline.com** and others listed in Internet Resources.)

For other lodging options, see the Bed-and-Breakfasts, Homestays, and Apartments section.

HOTELS

Near the Zócalo

Under $50: For economy, consider the nine-room **Hotel Salvador,** 20 de Noviembre 204, tel. 951/516-4008, a block west of the *zócalo,* next door north of the Hotel Francia. Here, you can get a plain but decent upstairs room with bath for about $30 s, $35 d, $40 t, with the plus of a good restaurant downstairs.

Even closer to the *zócalo* is the petite and popular **Hotel Las Rosas,** Trujano 112, Oaxaca, Oaxaca 68000, tel. 951/514-2217, just half a block west of the *zócalo*. Climb a flight of stairs to the small lobby, relatively tranquil by virtue of its second-floor location. Beyond that, a double tier of rooms surrounds a homey inner patio. Adjacent to the lobby is a cheery sitting room with a

big, beautiful tropical aquarium and a TV, usually kept at subdued volume. In the rear, guests enjoy an airy terrace for reading and relaxing.

The rooms themselves, although plainly furnished, are clean and tiled (except some bathrooms, which could use an extra scrubbing). Prices, at about $30 s, $38 d, $47 t, while not the bargain they once were, are relatively reasonable for such a well-located hotel. No credit cards, parking, or wheelchair access.

Conveniently situated just east of the *zócalo's* northeast corner, the newly polished up colonial-era **Hotel Real de Antequera,** Hidalgo 807, Oaxaca, Oaxaca 68000, tel. 951/516-4635, tel./fax 951/516-4020, ara5109@prodigy.net.mx, offers plenty for reasonable rates. The 29 comfortable rooms around an inviting old world–style restaurant-patio rent for $40 s or d, all with bath, fans, cable TV, phones, parking, and credit cards accepted.

Back half a block west of the *zócalo,* find the **Hóstal Santa Rosa,** at Trujano 201, Oaxaca, Oaxaca 68000, tel. 951/514-6714 or 951/514-6715. The streetside lobby leads past an airy restaurant to the rooms, recessed along a meandering inner passageway and courtyard. Inside, the rooms are very clean, comfortably furnished, and decorated in pastels. Rents, although raised, continue to be reasonable, usually at $35 s, $42 d, except during festivals and holidays, when they might rise as much as 40 percent. It offers TV, phones, parking, limited wheelchair access, and an in-house travel-tour agency, but no credit cards are accepted.

Just half a block north, find the longtime **Hotel Francia,** 20 de Noviembre 212, Oaxaca, Oaxaca, 68000, tel. 951/516-4811 or 951/516-4120, fax 951/516-4251, safer@prodigy.net.mx. Savvy new managers have brightened up the Francia with fresh white paint, a bright chandelier, potted palms, shiny lobby tile, and a new restaurant. They have also added a renovated colonial-era section (once a separate hotel next door) built around an invitingly traditional interior patio. Rooms are clean and spacious, with high ceilings and old-world dark wood furniture. Rates for the 62 rooms are $42 s or d, $55 t, all with baths, hot water, fans, TV, phones, and credit cards accepted; parking $4/day.

Go a block north of the zócalo to the leafy Alameda de León square in front of the cathedral and the very popular **Hotel Monte Albán**, Alameda de León 1, Oaxaca, Oaxaca 68000, tel. 951/516-2777 or 951/516-2330, fax 951/516-3265, montealban@prodigy.net.mx. This longstanding hostelry encloses a big patio/restaurant that hosts folk-dance shows nightly 8:30–10 P.M. During the first evening this could be understandably exciting, but after a week you might feel as if you were living in a three-ring circus. The 20 rooms, which surround the patio in two floors, are genuinely colonial, with high beamed ceilings and big bedsteads. Rates, at about $30 s, $45 d, $53 t, are reasonable for such a nicely located hotel; no parking, but credit cards are accepted.

Continue northeast a few blocks to the busy, traveler-favorite, 39-room **Posada del Virrey**, 1001 Morelos, Oaxaca, Oaxaca 68000, tel. 951/516-5555 or 951/516-5141, fax 951/516-2193, posadavirrey@hotmail.com, www.geocities.com/posadavirrey. Yet another converted 19th-century house, the hotel's two floors of rooms surround a spacious inner restaurant patio, mornings and evenings often half-filled with mostly foreign travelers, reading, conversing, and relaxing.

The rooms are clean and comfortably furnished, including one, two, or three double beds, with attractive brown and bright orange bedspreads and handsome rustic handmade wooden furniture. Rentals run about $35 s, $40 d (in one bed), and $45 d or t (in two beds), with cable TV, phone, fan, parking 9 P.M.–9 A.M., and credit cards accepted. Get your reservations in early, especially during holidays.

(For quieter, more refined ambience, consider the bed-and-breakfast **Casa Luz María,** across the street. See the Bed-and-Breakfasts section for more details.)

$50–100: Just a few doors south of the zócalo's southeast corner, consider the popular 1980s-mod **Hotel Gala**, Bustamante 103, Oaxaca, Oaxaca 68000, tel. 951/514-2251 or 951/514-1305, fax 951/516-3660, galaoax@prodigy.net.mx, www.terranova-oaxaca.com.mx/gala.html. Here, guests enjoy comfortable, modern, deluxe accommodations at relatively moderate prices right in the middle of the zócaló action. Rooms, although tastefully decorated and carpeted, are smallish. Get one of the quieter ones away from the street. The 36 rooms rent for about $41 s, $55 d, and $71 for junior suite; credit cards are accepted. It offers phones, TV, fans, and a restaurant, but parking is not included.

For a touch of class and breakfast at moderate rates, continue east and around the corner north to **Hotel Anna Sofia**, at Armenta y López 104, Oaxaca, Oaxaca 68000, tel./fax 951/514-8866, annasofia@oaxaca.com.mx. Owners have renovated a patrician, two-story colonial family house that gracefully enfolds a pair of tranquil, leafy interior courtyards. The 19 surrounding rooms are clean, carpeted, and comfortably furnished with shiny tiled baths. Some interior rooms are dark, however, lacking windows. Look at more than one before choosing. Considering the refinement, rates are very reasonable: about $48 s, $55 d, $70 t, with fans, cable TV, phone, parking, and American breakfast every morning except Monday.

Along with an enviable zócalo location, the **Hotel Señorial**, Portal de Flores 6, Oaxaca, Oaxaca 68000, tel. 951/516-3933, fax 951/516-3668, provides clean rooms, efficient management, a reliable restaurant, and an inviting (but unheated) swimming pool and patio. The hotel's only drawback is that some (but not all) of its rooms have louvered (not soundproof) communal air shaft windows and hallway transoms. This, especially during high fiesta seasons, results in noise that can't be shut out. Light sleepers should bring earplugs, especially on weekends and holidays, when the popular Señorial will be brimming with guests. The 107 rooms rent for about $60 s or d, $65 t, with TV, limited wheelchair access, phones, and parking, and credit cards are accepted.

Jump six blocks (three south, three west) from the *zócalo,* to **Hotel Rivera del Ángel,** Mina 518, Oaxaca, Oaxaca 68000, tel. 951/516-6666, fax 951/514-5405, www.riveradelangel.com, which offers several advantages, including secure parking. Downstairs, an airy, shiny, but busy lobby and restaurant area offers nothing special, but through the lobby windows, feast your eyes on the inviting big blue pool and sunny central patio. Upstairs, you'll find the rooms semi-deluxe, clean, spacious, and comfortable, many with private terraces overlooking the pool patio. The hotel's main drawback, besides the questionable neighborhood (streetwalkers, low-life bars, and drunks at night), is street noise, from buses along Mina. Ask for a *tranquilo* off-street room, next to, or above the inner pool-patio. Asking rates run a reasonable $39 s, $53 d, low season, $60 and $70 high, with TV, fans, phones, restaurant, parking, travel agency, and tour buses to Mitla and Monte Albán. Credit cards not accepted.

Return just two blocks west of the *zócalo,* to the class-act **Parador San Miguel,** Av. Independencia 503, Oaxaca, Oaxaca 68000, tel./fax 951/514-9331, sanmigueloaxaca@hotmail.com, www.mexonline.com/paradorsanmiguel.htm. Here, little seems to have been spared in transforming a colonial-era home into a lovely hotel. Inside, a plethora of old-world details—leafy, tranquil inner patio, sunny upstairs corridors, brilliant stained glass–decorated staircase, scrolled wrought-iron railings, handsome hand-carved wooden doors—are bound to please lovers of traditional refinement. A correspondingly elegant restaurant, the Andariega, completes the gorgeous picture.

The 19 rooms and four suites are no less than you'd expect, attractively furnished with custom-woven bedspreads and curtains, handcrafted bamboo and leather furniture, elegantly tiled shower baths, and a choice of king, single, or double beds. (If the Parador San Miguel has a drawback, it's the traffic noise from busy Calle Independencia just outside the front door. Ask for a room away from the street.)

But never mind, the place is simply exquisite

and prices are reasonable: $85 s or d, $95 t; add about 30 percent during festivals and holidays. All with a/c, cable TV, and credit cards accepted. Reserve by telephone or email.

Alternatively, check out the queen of *zócalo*-front hotels, the long-time **Hotel Marques del Valle** on the north side of the *zócalo,* Portal Clavería, P.O. Boxes 13 and 35, Oaxaca, Oaxaca 68000, tel. 951/514-0688 or 951/516-3474, fax 951/516-9961, hmarques@prodigy.net.mx. Guests enter to enjoy a restored lobby, with bright chandeliers, mirrors, and shiny dark-wood paneling. Upstairs, however, massive wrought-iron fixtures cast gloomy nighttime shadows through the soaring, balconied central atrium. The 96 rooms, nevertheless, retain their original 1940s polish, with handcrafted cedar furniture and marble-finished baths. Deluxe rooms have TV, carpets, and some balconies looking out onto the *zócalo.* Standard rooms rent for about $80 s, $100 d, $120 t, with restaurant/bar, limited wheelchair access, and credit cards accepted.

North of the Zócalo

Under $50: The most economical north-side option, **Casa Arnel,** is also farthest north (actually, under a mile) from the *zócalo,* at Aldama 404, Colonia Jalatlaco, Oaxaca, Oaxaca 68080, tel./fax 951/515-2856, casa.arnel@spersaoaxaca.com.mx, www.casaarnel.com.mx. Casa Arnel stands at the edge of downtown, so removed from the urban bustle that it feels as if it's embedded in another era. As one person explained, Jalatlaco, the formerly separate village, is "old, with stone streets. . . . It's *so* Oaxaca." In front of Casa Arnel, the streets are indeed cobbled with stone, and across from it stands the ancient village church, San Matias Jalatlaco, beside its shady neighborhood plaza.

Casa Arnel is a family home that grew into a hotel, with about 20 rooms around a jungly garden blooming with birdcalls, flowers, and big, leafy plants, with a monument of a library in the middle of it all. Additional amenities include a broad roof deck with umbrellas, tables, and chairs for sunning and relaxing. Old-style rooms, all with bath, are clean but bare-bulb plain. A new crop of renovated rooms is more attractive, with new bedspreads, curtains, and shiny furniture and fixtures. Prices, however, are reasonable: old-style $22 s, $27 d; new-style $30 s, $35 d; suite for four or more, $54. Rock-bottom shared-bath rooms go for $10 s, $20 d; breakfast extra, but with restaurant (sometimes unexpectedly closed) and travel agency, and just three blocks from big, shady El Llano park with its good restaurants and services. Bargain for a cheaper long-term rate. Reserve via telephone or email.

Several blocks south, back toward the zócalo, budget-minded travelers should also consider the petite **Hotel Maela**, a block east of the Santo Domingo church compound, at Constitución 206, Oaxaca, Oaxaca 68000, tel. 951/516-6022. Inside, just past the small reception, the hall tiles shine, the ceilings are gracefully high, and the 11 rooms, mostly upstairs, are spacious, with private shower baths and attractive handmade wood dressers, beds, and end tables. Ceiling lights are bare-bulb, but nighttime reading lamps are shaded. Tariffs run about $22 s, $28 d, $32 t, with TV and parking.

Nearby is another well-located budget choice, the **Hotel Villa de León**, adjoining the Santa Domingo church grounds, Reforma 405, Oaxaca, Oaxaca 68000, tel. 951/516-1958, fax 951/516-1977. Don't be put off by the lackluster reception area; rather, notice the light, airy courtyard cafeteria, encircled by an upstairs balcony of rooms. Step into one of them and you'll find it clean, carpeted, and thoughtfully decorated with rustic hand-hewn wooden beds, tables, lamps, and attractive brown bedspreads. Ask for a room away from the noisy street front. Prices run about $20 s, $29 d, and $39 t, and $47 q, all with hot-shower baths; credit cards accepted.

Farther south, halfway between the zócalo and Santo Domingo church, right in the middle of the tranquil 5 de Mayo restaurant and shopping district, find the old-fashioned, **Hotel Principal**, 5 de Mayo 208, Oaxaca, Oaxaca 68000, tel./fax 951/516-2535, like a slice out of the 1940s. Past the entry, the two stories of 16 rooms surround a quiet, geranium-decorated interior patio. A few sofas for sitting line the patio and upstairs corridor. The rooms are clean, high ceilinged and tile floored, with shaded bed lamps. No TV, no

phones, but with hot-water baths all day. Rentals of three smaller-grade rooms run about $26 s, $30 d; larger, superior rooms are $36 s or d, all with private shower baths and fans.

On the west side, about three blocks west of the Santo Domingo church is the very inviting and super-popular **Hotel Las Golondrinas**, at Tinoco y Palacios 411, Oaxaca, Oaxaca 68000, tel. 951/514-3298 or tel./fax 951/514-2126, lasgolon@prodigy.net.mx. Rooms enfold an intimate garden, lovingly decorated with festoons of hothouse verdure. Leafy bananas, bright bougainvillea, and platoons of potted plants line pathways that meander past an intimate fountain patio in one corner and lead to an upstairs panoramic vista sundeck on the other. The care also shows in the rooms, which are immaculate and adorned with spartan-chic, pastel earth-toned curtains and bedspreads and natural wood furniture. Guests additionally enjoy use of laundry facilities, a TV sitting room, a shelf of paperback books, and a breakfast restaurant open 8–10 A.M. All this for only about $31 s, $40 d, and $47 t. In addition to the 27 regular rooms, two honeymoon suites rent for about $50 each.

For yet another economical and highly recommended north-side lodging option, see the **Hotel and Studios Las Mariposas** in the Apartments section.

$50–100: Walk several blocks north of Santo Domingo church to the **Hotel Casona de Llano,** Av. Juárez A701, Oaxaca, Oaxaca 68000, tel. 951/514-7719 or 951/514-7703, fax 951/516-2219, a favorite of visitors who enjoy the shady, untouristed ambience of Oaxaca's big Sunday park, officially Parque Paseo Juárez, but popularly **El Llano** (YAH-noh) (Plain or Flat Place). The memorable time to arrive is in the evening, when the hotel puts on its most impressive face: You enter the lobby, crowned with high ceilings hung with gleaming chandeliers, continue past polished mahogany Doric columns, and enter a graceful Porfirian dining room, where guests often linger after dinner. You hear music, investigate, and find someone playing a tune on a handsomely preserved and polished upright piano in a side parlor. Your room, by contrast,

OAXACA CITY

is modern, comfortably furnished, and very clean. In the morning, you open your door and look out upon a tranquil, grassy, inner tropical garden. The 28 rooms rent for a moderate $42 s, $54 d, and $66 t; with fans, TV, phones, parking, and credit cards accepted. Reserve ahead.

On the other side and south of El Llano, step into **Hotel Casa Vertíz,** arguably the most inviting small hotel in Oaxaca, at Reforma 404, Oaxaca, Oaxaca 68000, tel. 951/516-2525, reservaciones@hotelvertiz.com.mx, www.hotelvertiz.com.mx. Here you find a masterfully rebuilt former colonial house with air, light, and space that invites lingering. Past the reception, guests enjoy a refined, airy patio restaurant and an exquisitely naturalistic tropical rear garden. Upstairs, rooms open on to a spreading upstairs terrace shaded on one side by a grand old tree.

The inner garden patios of the ex-convent of Santa Catalina (now the Hotel Camino Real) are havens of old-world calm.

© BRUCE WHIPPERMAN

The 14 rooms, both upstairs and down, open directly to all these graceful amenities. Rooms are luxuriously appointed with designer-rustic tile floors, earth-toned bedspreads and curtains, deluxe tiled baths (four rooms have tubs), and queen-sized beds. Rentals run $95 s or d, with cable TV, phone, in-room Internet connection, parking, and credit cards accepted. Upstairs rooms have a/c; downstairs have fans.

Farther south, just two blocks uphill from the *zócalo* stands the **Hotel Calesa Real,** Garcia Vigil 306, Oaxaca, Oaxaca 68000, tel. 951/516-5544, fax 951/516-7232, www.mexicohotels.com /hotelcalesareal.html. Here, owners have packed a converted 18th-century mansion with a host of facilities and 70 rooms, an amazing number that you don't suspect as you enter its attractive colonial-style lobby and continue past a small but inviting palm-enfolded tropical pool patio. Upstairs, rooms are 1980s-standard deluxe, carpeted and pleasingly decorated in beige and pastels. They rent for $80 s, $100 d, and $120 t, with fans, TVs, phones, restaurant, coffee shop, small pool, sauna, whirlpool tub, travel agency, and parking. Credit cards are accepted.

Over $100: Oaxaca's classiest downtown hotel, the **Camino Real,** Calle 5 de Mayo 300, Oaxaca, Oaxaca 68000, tel. 951/516-0611 or toll-free U.S./Can. tel. 800/7-CAMINO (800/ 722-6466), fax 951/516-0732, oax@camino-real.com, occupies the lovingly restored former convent of Santa Catalina, four blocks north, one block east of the *zócalo*. Flowery secluded courtyards, massive arched portals, soaring beamed ceilings, a big blue pool, and impeccable bar and restaurant service combine to create a refined but relaxed old-world atmosphere. Rooms are large, luxurious, and invitingly decorated with antiques and folk crafts and furnished with a plethora of modern conveniences. If street noise is likely to bother you, get a room away from bustling Calles Abasolo and 5 de Mayo; if not, bring earplugs. The hotel entertains guests and the paying public (about $35 per person) with a weekly class-act in-house buffet and folkloric dance performance. Room rates run about $215 s, $250 d; with phones and TV, but parking not included; credit cards are accepted.

North-Side Suburban Luxury Hotels

$50–100: Hotel Misión de Los Angeles, Calz. Porfirio Díaz 102, Oaxaca, Oaxaca 68050, tel. 951/502-0100, fax 951/515-0111, inquiries@ hotel-mision-oaxaca.com, www.hotel-mision-oaxaca.com, rambles like a hacienda through a spreading oak- and acacia-decorated garden-park two blocks uphill from Hwy. 190, about a mile north of the city center. After a rough few days on the sightseeing circuit, it's an ideal place to kick back beside the big pool or enjoy a set or two of tennis. The rooms and suites are spacious and comfortable, decorated in earth tones and pastels and have big garden-view windows or balconies. Upper rooms are quieter and more private. (Some rooms, however, may not be as favorably located; look at more than one before deciding.) The 162 rooms and suites rent from about $83 d, $130 d for junior suite; with phones, parking, disco, and restaurant; credit cards accepted.

Also near Highway 190, a few blocks west, the **Best Western Hotel Fortín Plaza,** Av. Venus 118, Colonia Estrella, Oaxaca, Oaxaca 68040, tel. 951/515-7777, toll-free U.S./Can. tel. 800/528-1234, fax 951/515-1328, fortin@prodigy.net.mx, www.bestwestern.com, is hard to miss, especially at night. Its yellow-lit six-story profile tops everything else in town. The hotel offers the usual modern facilities—restaurant/bar, pool, live music Tues.–Sat., disco, and parking—in a compact, attractively designed layout. Upstairs, guests enjoy deluxe, clean, and comfortable rooms with private-view balconies (whose tranquility is reduced, however, by considerable highway noise—ask for a more *tranquilo* mountain-view room). Room rates run about $82 s and $96 d, with phones, TV, wheelchair access, and parking; credit cards accepted. Ask for a discount or a *paquete* (package), especially during weekdays and the low-occupancy months of January, May, June, and September. Reserve by phone or through the website.

Over $100: Just two blocks west, uphill, from the Fortín Plaza, the **Hotel Victoria,** Km 545, Carretera Panamericana, Oaxaca, Oaxaca 68070, tel. 951/515-2633, fax 951/515-2411, ventas@hotelvictoria.com.mx, www.hotelvictoriaoax .com.mx, spreads over a lush hillside garden of panoramic vistas and luxurious resort ambience.

The 1960s-modern lobby extends from an upstairs bar downhill past a terrace restaurant to a flame tree and jacaranda-decorated pool patio. As for rooms, the most luxurious are in the newer wing detached from the lobby building. There, the junior suites are spacious, comfortable, and sumptuously appointed, with double-size bathrooms and private-view balconies. The 150 rooms, junior suites, and villas rent for about $100, $140, and $180 d, respectively; with TV, phones, a/c, tennis court, live music Tues.–Sat. evenings, handicrafts shop, parking, and wheelchair access; credit cards accepted.

Cooler, breezier **San Felipe village,** in the foothills north of Oaxaca town has recently become home to a number of restful luxury lodgings. Choice among them, **Hacienda Los Laureles,** at Hidalgo 21, San Felipe del Agua, Oaxaca 68020, tel. 951/501-5300, is the labor of love of personable German expatriate owner-managers Ligia and Peter Kaiser. After a career of managing hotels in Europe, Africa, and the United States, Peter and Ligia decided to create their version of heaven in Oaxaca. During the late 1990s they rebuilt a

Hotel Victoria's folkloric dance show for guests

venerable hacienda, tenaciously preserving its rustic old-world essence, while installing the best of the new. Now, Hacienda Los Laureles's centerpiece is its lush interior garden of grand tropical trees and climbing vines that, at night, shadowed lighting and the serenades of crickets and tree frogs transform into an enchanted forest.

The Hacienda's 25 rooms, which all open onto this precious scene, are decorated in elegant simplicity, with high ceilings, handsome tile floors, and hand-hewn mahogany furniture. Bathrooms are likewise luxurious and comfortable. Rentals run about $225 s or d for deluxe and $250 s or d for superior deluxe. Suites for 3–6 or more are also available. All come with a/c, cable TV, pool with whirlpool tub, and an excellent terrace restaurant. *Temazcal* therapeutic hot room and spa services are also available at an extra cost. For information and reservations call tel./fax 951/501-5301 or 951/520-0890, email pkaiser@prodigy .net.mx, or log on to www.hotelhaciendaloslaureles.com. (You may also reserve through booking agent Mexico Boutique Hotels' toll-free U.S. tel. 877/278-8018, toll-free Can. tel. 866/818-8342, or www.mexicoboutiquehotels.com.)

BED-AND-BREAKFASTS, HOMESTAYS, AND APARTMENTS

Many Oaxacans offer either lodging in their homes or apartment and house rentals. If you're interested in such options in Oaxaca now (or are going to be in Oaxaca looking), be sure to see the classified sections of the English-language newspapers, *Oaxaca Times*, and *Oaxaca*, which usually advertise a number of non–hotel-style rentals. Both papers are routinely available at hotels, shops, or at the federal tourist information office, north side of the *zócalo*, corner of Independencia and Hidalgo. Alternatively, find a copy at the *Oaxaca Times* office, 307 Alcalá. For *Oaxaca Times* information and subscriptions, call tel. 951/516-3443, fax 951/516-3265, email info@oaxacatimes.com, or log on to www.oaxacatimes.com. Likewise, find the *Oaxaca* office, at Catalina 210, San Felipe del Agua; for information and subscriptions, dial tel./fax 951/520-

2463, email info@go-oaxaca.com, or log on to www.go-oaxaca.com.

Websites, such as **www.mexonline.com,** customarily advertise a number of Oaxaca lodgings. See the Internet Resources section. Moreover, the downtown **tourist information office,** see the Information section, lists a number of economical home-style lodgings. Also, **language schools** (see Language Instruction and Courses) arrange homestays with families.

Meanwhile, read on to find out about a number of promising lodging options sprinkled around town. Unless otherwise stated, prices given below are daily rates, often subject to healthy discounts for long-term stays.

Bed-and-Breakfasts North and East of the Zócalo

Oaxaca bed-and-breakfast lodgings as a group are not particularly economical, since they are a North American transplant that appeals to foreign visitors who are accustomed to paying somewhat elevated prices.

Under $50: One of the more attractive Oaxaca bed-and-breakfasts is homey but exclusive **Casa Luz María,** 1002 Morelos, Oaxaca, Oaxaca 68000, tel. 951/516-2378, f_faqoaga @hotmail.com. Since it's her home, the owner chooses her clients carefully. If you qualify, your reward will be one of her five comfortable, immaculate, modern rooms (or her one kitchenette apartment), all built around a pair of flowery, sunny interior patios. Two of the rooms have private baths, three are shared; with hot water, fans, no phone nor TV, no credit cards accepted. Rentals include a hearty breakfast, with coffee, tea, fruit, bread, eggs, and sweet rolls. The owner assured me that her prices, which she declined to state, are both flexible and moderate.

(For a very economical hostel-style, but with private rooms, bed-and-breakfast option, see **Paulina Youth Hostel** in the Hostel section.)

$50–100: Two blocks, one east and one north, from the *zócalo* is the **Hotel Anna Sofia,** Armenta y López 104, tel./fax 951/514-8866. Check out this charming bed-and-breakfast lodging, by returning to the Hotels Near the *Zócalo*, section.

Behind ex-convent Santo Domingo, find

Casa Las Bugambilias, Reforma 402, Oaxaca, Oaxaca 68000, tel./fax 951/516-1165, bugambilias@infosel.net.mx, www.lasbugambilias.com, with seven rooms artfully tucked behind its good restaurant. The rooms, immaculate and thoughtfully appointed with art and handicrafts, are all different. Some open onto a lovely rear garden. Take a look at as many as possible before choosing. Rules include minimum three-night stay, children over 12 only, no pets, and no smoking. Rates run from $42 s, $54 d to $72 s, $84 d for the largest. All include private bath and breakfast in the attractive adjacent restaurant, La Olla.

Continue east two blocks and turn north a block to the bed-and-breakfast gem **Casa de Mis Recuerdos** (House of My Memories), Pino Suárez 508, Oaxaca, Oaxaca 68000, tel. 951/515-5645, fax 951/515-8483, misrecue@prodigy.net.mx, www.misrecuerdos.net. Enter the front gate and continue through a blooming, bougainvillea-festooned garden to the private home of the Valenciana family, which has been accommodating students and foreign visitors for years. The rented rooms occupy rear and front sections. The four front rooms, immaculate, spacious, and lovingly decorated with folk art and furnished with handmade wooden furniture, have two bathrooms between them. They are closer to the busy street front than the five similarly furnished rear rooms, which, although they have private baths, are smaller. Guests also have the use of an airy, shaded rooftop gazebo for reading and relaxing. Breakfast, included with rentals, is served in the inviting downstairs family dining room. Rooms normally rent for about $42 s, $55 d, rising to around $70 s, $95 d during festivals and holidays, with all linens and cleaning service included. Discounts are negotiable for long-term stays. You may also book via a second email address, B521955@hotmail.com. For more information, log on to www.mexonline.com/valencia.htm.

Continue north, two blocks uphill past Boulevard Niños Héroes-Highway 190, and your reward will be **Casa María,** Belasario Domínguez 208, Colonia Reforma, Oaxaca, Oaxaca, tel./fax 951/515-1202, maria@oaxacalive.com, life project of welcoming owner María Luz Díaz. Her 18-room abode basks behind a flowery, spacious green garden, perfect for reading and relaxing. Past the inviting terrace and dining-living area, the rooms, several upstairs, are clean, modern, and comfortably furnished. A separate kitchen is available for guest use. Breakfast is hearty American-style, but served only between 8 and 9 A.M.

María usually has many guests, who often head out in the morning, but linger on the terrace and in the living room during the evenings, comparing their experiences of the day over coffee and tea. Room prices begin at about $40 s, $50 d with one double bed. Bungalows (kitchenette apartments) run about $60 d, breakfast not included. More luxurious suites are about $80. A large family apartment for five costs about $115. Prices rise about 25 percent during festivals and holidays. All with private shower baths and fans; some parking in her four-car garage. Massage and traditional *temazcal* hot-room treatments are available at an extra cost.

Over $100: Elegant **Casa Oaxaca,** Garcia Vigil 407, Oaxaca, Oaxaca 68000, tel. 951/514-4173, fax 951/516-4412, casaoax@prodigy.net.mx, www.casa-oaxaca.com, is straight uphill four blocks and a world apart from the *zócalo*. Its sky-blue colonial facade reveals nothing of its singularly unique interior. The lobby, which appears more like an art museum foyer than a lodging entrance, provides the first clue. Past that, you enter a spacious, plant-decorated courtyard, with the wall plaster artfully removed here and there to reveal the brick underlay. Continue to a rear courtyard, which centers on a blue designer pool and a *temazcal* traditional native hot room. All six rooms, which border the courtyards, are luxuriously austere and uniquely appointed with antiques, crafts, and contemporary wall art. Rates are $125 s or d for the four smallest, yet spacious units; $165 s or d for a larger suite, and $250 for a two-story apartment above the rear courtyard. Rates include airport transfers, breakfast in the exclusive Casa Oaxaca restaurant; credit cards are accepted. *Temazcal* treatments, complete with native healer, run about $50 per person. (Casa Oaxaca is also bookable through Mexico Boutique Hotels' toll-free U.S. tel. 877/278-8018 or toll-free Can. tel. 866/818-8342. For more

OAXACA CITY

information, log on to www.mexicoboutique-hotels.com.)

Bed-and-Breakfasts South and West of the Zócalo

$50–100: Only a few bed-and-breakfast lodgings dot the south and west sides of town. Here are two gems, however:

Start with **Posada de Chencho,** several blocks southeast of the *zócalo,* at 4 Privado Noria 115, tel./fax 951/514-0043, pchencho@prodigy.net.mx, www.mexonline.com/chencho.htm. Part of the attraction here is the spark-plug owner, Inocencio "Chencho" Velasco, a friendly Mixtec version of Santa Claus. Such a stream of visitors from all over the world stay at his place that he seems to know someone everywhere. Moreover, very well-informed, English-speaking Chencho is a treasury of information about Oaxaca, both local and statewide. His compound, 22 immaculate rooms in two stories, surrounds an inviting, green garden patio. The rooms themselves are comfortably and thoughtfully decorated, with Western-standard baths. Downstairs, guests enjoy a dining room and a big sitting room/library, besides patio nooks for reading and relaxing. Some rooms in the sun might get hot during the summer. If heat bothers you, be sure to select one in the shade, with a ceiling fan. If your room has no fan, ask Chencho to supply one. Rates run about $42 s, $55 d, including breakfast. A full-board single costs $60. Ask for a cheaper long-term rate.

Get to Chencho's by walking east, along Guerrero, from the southeast corner of the *zócalo.* After four blocks, at Xicotencatl (shee-koh-tayn-KAH-tuhl), turn right and continue another four blocks south to Calle La Noria; 4 Privado La Noria is one of the one-block streets to your left that run south from La Noria.

On the west edge of downtown, about 10 blocks due west of the *zócalo,* stands **Casa Colonial,** Calle Miguel Negrete 105, tel./fax 951/516-5280, toll-free U.S./Can. tel. 800/758-1697 (reservations), colonial@spersaoaxaca.com.mx or karensue@jeffnet.org, www.mexonline.com/colonial.htm. Personable owners Jane and Thornton Robison, who seem to know everyone in town, call their domain the "posada with no sign," because they don't advertise and only accept guests with reservations. Upon arrival, you immediately see why Casa Colonial is such a favorite among savvy visitors. Low-rise rooms and apartments enfold a spacious, gracefully lovely inner garden. Rooms vary from high-ceilinged, antique-decorated Victorians to smaller, one-person garden-side units. Besides the leisurely tropical ambience, guests enjoy the use of a spacious, refined but homey living room with a fine library and Internet connection. Room prices vary according to size and elegance from $50 s to about $95 d. They welcome long-term guests at a discount, April–October. For information on their Casa Colonial Tours, visit www.mexonline.com/casacolonialtours.htm.

Apartments

An increasing number of visitors are opting for longer Oaxaca stays, and a number of recommendable small apartment complexes are ready to accommodate them.

Under $50: In the southeast quarter, an easy five-block walking distance to the *zócalo,* you'll find the attractive **Villa María,** Arteaga 410 A, tel. 951/516-5056, fax 951/514-2562. Villa María is the labor of love of trilingual (English, French, Spanish) owner-manager María Garcia, so welcoming that you immediately feel at home. Step inside her domain and you'll see the other reason for Villa María's popularity: about 15 apartments surrounding an inviting, plant-adorned inner patio, where stairways rise to rooftop sundecks furnished with comfortable chairs and shady umbrellas. The immaculate, thoughtfully decorated all one-bedroom housekeeping apartments, with themes such as "Mixteco," are completely furnished, including dishes, silverware, and maid service. Apartments vary in cost, from $45 to $65 d per night, $400–600 per month, depending on location, size, and amenities.

About five blocks north of the *zócalo,* right in front of Santo Domingo church and plaza, is **Departmentos del Fraile,** Macedonio Alcalá 501, Oaxaca, Oaxaca 68000, tel./fax 951/516-4310, cell tel. 044-951/5070, goodwood@prodigy.net.mx, www.ladelosabuelos.com.mx. Family owner-managers offer four compact, modern, rustic-chic apartments, hidden behind a street-front wall, and tucked within a quiet leafy inner courtyard. The renovated units have one bedroom, bathroom, and kitchenette. Rent, monthly only, runs about $600/month.

Behind (east of) the Santo Domingo church block, find **La Casa de los Abuelos,** Reforma 410, Oaxaca, Oaxaca 68000, tel. 951/516-1982, lacasadelosabuelos@hotmail.com. This charmingly quirky colonial-era complex is the life project of personable owner-builder Luis Arroyo Nunez, who inherited it from his *abuelos* (grandparents). This former priests' residence for Santo Domingo church was confiscated by the government after the *cristero* revolt of the late 1920s.

Luis's six completely renovated apartments, built around two quiet inner patios, are replete with unique details, such as exposed original brick walls, old family photos, bric-a-brac, and sturdy wooden staircases leading up to bedroom lofts. Rentals include invitingly furnished living-dining rooms, kitchenettes, queen-sized beds, and shower baths. Asking rates are $50/day, $300/week, $750/month, with fans, TV, purified bottled water, and Internet connection.

Nearby, a block east and a block north, just south of Los Llanos park, **Hotel and Studios Las Mariposas,** Pino Suárez 517, tel. 951/515-5854, viut@prodigy.net.mx, www.mexonline.com/mariposas.htm, is strongly recommended by ex-customers for either short or long-term stays. Welcoming and knowledgeable owner Teresa Dávila offers five comfortable studio kitchenette suites with private baths, for about $35 s, $45 d in her restored 19th-century family house. In addition, four rooms with bath rent for about $25 s, $35 d. Ask for a discount for a long-term stay. Besides the happy customers, pluses include use of fax machine, Internet connection, coffee, and optional breakfast and TV.

(You might also consider the good long-term rental possibilities at **Casa Luz María, Casa María, Posada de Chencho,** and **Casa Colonial,** described in the Bed-and-Breakfast section.)

HOSTELS

Oaxaca offers at least two hostel-style lodgings:

Plaudits are due to the beautifully restored **Paulina Youth Hostel,** V. Trujano 321, Oaxaca, Oaxaca 68000, tel. 951/516-2005, reservations@paulinahostel.com, www.paulinahostel.com, just three blocks west of the *zócalo*. Here, owners have created the best of all possible hosteling worlds, with a good cafeteria and inviting, spacious common areas, all within attractive garden grounds. The comfortable, squeaky-clean rooming options include separate male and female dorms for $10 per person and private rooms with shower baths for $21 s, $23 d, all with orthopedic mattresses, roof terrace, hot water, and hearty breakfast thrown in for free. Get your reservations in early.

Distant second choice goes to artsy-scruffy **Plata Gelatina,** 503 Independencia, Oaxaca, Oaxaca 68000, tel. 951/514-9391, platagelatina@hotmail.comhostel, just a block west of the *zócalo*. Location, right in the middle of the downtown action, is the major advantage of Plata Gelatina (Gelatin Plate), so-named by the photographer-owner, whose black-and-white gelatin silver plate prints decorate the reception. Upstairs, two dorms ($6 per person)—one mixed 10-bed and one female seven-bed—and four stuffy rooms ($16 d) with shared baths provide the lodging options. A pizza oven at street level downstairs also cooks at least one of the rooms upstairs. The bathroom-shower room is decently clean, but is small and probably crowded during times of high occupancy.

TRAILER PARKS AND CAMPING

Oaxaca has two, possibly three, trailer-camping parks. The best choice for tenting and for rigs 25 feet (7.5 meters) or under is **San Felipe del Agua Trailer Park,** Camino de la Chigolera 10, San Felipe del Agua, Oaxaca, Oaxaca 68020. It perches atop a valley-view knoll in foothill San Felipe del Agua village, about three miles (5 km) north of downtown.

The San Francisco, California expatriate owner (and former Oaxaca consular agent) Roberta

French and her son Doug French offer all hookups for about 10 rigs in a large country lot with few trees, but plenty of room for tent space. A small clubhouse with kitchenette, shower, and toilet is also available for resident use. Owners charge about $5 per party for camping, $10 for RVs, including water, electricity, and drainage. For reservations (probably not necessary), write P.O. Box 252, Oaxaca, Oaxaca 68000, or call tel. 951/520-0947, or fax 951/516-4239, or email info@oaxacanstuff.com. For more information, log on to their interesting (weaving, mezcal) website, www.oaxacanstuff.com.

Their hilltop location, at the jumping-off point for hiking trails, past waterfalls and meadows, en route to the summit of towering, pine-tufted Cerro San Felipe (elev. 10,300 feet, 3,140 meters), appears ideal for hikers and backpackers. Look at the map at the community park guard station a quarter mile (.4 km) uphill from the San Felipe bus turnaround for trail information. The trailer park manager, who also rents horses, might serve as your guide; figure on paying him about $30 for a day's outing.

Get there by bus, taxi, or car to San Felipe del Agua village. By bus, ride San Felipe–marked Choferes del Sur bus from the corner of Independencia and Reforma, two blocks east of the *zócalo,* thence following Pino Suárez uphill, past El Llano park. Get off at the San Felipe del Agua village plaza (see the old church on the right) and follow the drivers' directions below. (Note: The end-of-the-line bus turnaround is a few blocks farther uphill from the village plaza. From there, you can hike a quarter mile (.4 km) to the **Parque Comunal San Felipe** guard station and trailhead.)

For drivers, the jumping-off point for San Felipe del Agua is Avenida Netzahualcoyotl (nay-tzah-oo-wahl-coh-YOH-tuhl), which heads uphill at the big green San Felipe sign from its intersection with Highway 190

(Avenida Niños Héroes), one block east of the Pemex station. Continue uphill about two-thirds of a mile (1 km), bear left at the hotel sign, then right one block and left one long block, and right again. You'll be on your way, heading uphill along Calzada San Felipe, which parallels the old stone aqueduct (on your left). In a few miles the road becomes San Felipe village's Calle Hidalgo. Just before the San Felipe plaza, at the restaurant on the right, turn left (west) on to Calle Iturbide, then right again at the first street, Morelos, then another quick left onto the "Prologation of Iturbide." After another long block or two downhill, at the arroyo bottom, turn right onto Chigolera; continue, winding uphill .4 mile (.6 km) to the trailer park sign and gate on the left.

More accessible is the run-down **Oaxaca Trailer Park,** 900 Av. Violetas, Oaxaca, Oaxaca 68000, at the far northeast side of town. Once an excellent, popular facility, the Oaxaca Trailer Park has been allowed to deteriorate and was being (at least partly) converted into bungalows or apartments at this writing. Still, dozens of all-hookup spaces will probably remain, including showers, toilets, and security fence. Get there by turning left at Violetas, marked by the big green Colonia Reforma sign over the highway, several blocks east of the first-class bus terminal on Highway 190. Continue uphill six long blocks to the trailer park on the left.

On the way into town, from the north along Highway 190, RVers might check to see if the old **Rosa Isabel Trailer Park** is open. The owner, Elia Hernandez, tel. 951/515-3143, mimimonroy@hotmail.com, assured me that she was going to keep it running and rent RV spaces with all hookups for about $10. Find it by looking along the right (south) side of Highway 190, heading southeast into town, about a half mile (1 km) past the big Hotel Villas Del Sol sign.

Food

SNACKS, FOOD STALLS, AND COFFEEHOUSES

During fiestas, snack stalls along Hidalgo at the cathedral-front Alameda de León square abound in local delicacies. Choices include *tlayudas*, giant crisp tortillas loaded with avocado, tomato, onions, and cheese, and *empanadas de amarillo*, huge tacos stuffed with cheese and red salsa. For dessert, have a *buñuelo*, a crunchy, honey-soaked wheat tortilla.

At non-fiesta times, you can still fill up on the sizzling fare of taco, *torta*, hamburger, and hot dogs (eat 'em only when they are served hot) at stands that set up in the same vicinity.

For very economical, wholesome local fare, go to the acre of food stalls inside the **Mercado 20 de Noviembre**, two blocks south of the *zócalo's* southwest corner. Adventurous eaters will be in heaven among a wealth of succulent *chiles rellenos;* piquant *moles* (moh-LAYS); fat, banana leaf–wrapped *tamales Oaxaqueños;* and savory *sopas* (soups) and *guisados* (stews). Insist, however, that your selection is served hot.

The airy, tranquil interior patio of **Hostería Alcalá** Alcalá 307, open daily 8:30 A.M.–11 P.M., four blocks north of the *zócalo*, is ideal for a relaxing refreshment or lunch break from sightseeing along the Alcalá pedestrian mall.

For coffee and dessert, you have a number of additional downtown choices, notably **Coffee Beans**, Cinco de Mayo 400, five blocks north of the *zócalo;* or nearby **Restaurant La Antigua**, a block east at Reforma 401, just uphill from Abasolo; or mini-café **La Brew**, Garcia Vigil 304, tel. 951/514-6973, on the west side, next door to the Hotel Calesa Real. La Brew, owned and operated by knowledgeable local resident Susan McGlynn, is open Mon.–Sat. 8 A.M.–8 P.M., Sun. 8 A.M.–2 P.M.

For baked goods, a quartet of good carryout bakeries stand within a stone's throw of the *zócalo*. First, try the sweet offerings of **Tartamiel Pastelería Frances,** on Trujano, half a block west from the southwest corner of the *zócalo;* open Mon.–Sat. 7 A.M.–8 P.M., Sun. 11:30 A.M.–7 P.M. Continue clockwise, north of the *zócalo* a block,

to **Panadería Bamby,** at the northwest corner of G. Vigil and Morelos; open Mon.–Sat. 6 A.M.–9 P.M. A block east of the *zócalo*, stop by either the **Pastelería and Café La Vasconia,** Independencia 907, tel. 951/516-2677, between Cinco de Mayo and Reforma, open daily 7 A.M.–9:30 P.M. or **Pastelería Quemen**, across the street; open daily, 8 A.M.–9 P.M.

CAFÉS AND RESTAURANTS

Around the Zócalo

Oaxaca visitors enjoy many good eateries right on or near the *zócalo*. In fact, you could spend your entire Oaxaca time enjoying the fare of the several *zócalo*-front sidewalk cafés. Of the seven cafés, six offer recommendable food and service. Moving counterclockwise from the northwest corner, they are **Primavera, La Cafetería, Del Jardín, Terranova, Amarantos,** and relative newcomer, **Sabor y Tradición.** First place overall goes to the pricier, upper-class **Terranova**, at the southeast corner, for its professionally prepared and served lunch and dinner entrées. For the best breakfasts, however, go to **Primavera**, at the diagonally opposite corner. **La Cafetería** and **Del Jardín** (with loud marimba music most nights) rate generally good for food (notably Del Jardín's tummy-warming apple strudel), but their service can be spotty. While service at **Amarantos** is usually good, its food is only fair. They all are open long hours, about 8 A.M.–midnight, and serve from very recognizable menus.

Note: The *zócalo's* west side is generally shadier, cooler and more pleasant during the warm March, April, and May dry season. On the other hand, the east side, which gets the afternoon sun, is the warmer and often the more pleasant side during the cooler months of November, December, and January. As for *zócalo*-front seating, nonsmokers can escape to the open-air tables, thus avoiding the cigarette and cigar smoke beneath the portal.

The one drawback of *zócalo*-level eating is the persistent flow of vendors, which can be

A OAXACAN MENU

Oaxacan food adds another layer to the already rich Mexican food tradition. Oaxacan menus start off with appetizers, such as *quesillo a la plancha,* Oaxaca's famous white cheese, served melted, with guacamole and black beans. An appetizer list wouldn't be truly Oaxacan without *chapulines,* small grasshoppers grilled with minced onion in oil until crunchy.

Next come the Oaxacan *sopas* (soups), such as *sopa de guias,* a delicious stewed medley of squash flowers, tender baby squash, small corn dumplings, corn, and tender vine shoots. Other typically served soups include *caldillo de nopales,* a broth of fleshy cactus leaves, often cooked with bits of pork, chicken, or small shrimps, and *sopa de frijoles,* black bean soup, with cheese chunks and tortilla chips.

Main courses must include *moles* (MOH-lays), the most Oaxacan of all dishes. Very typical is *mole negro* (black *mole*), a spicy-sweet mixture of chocolate, chilies, garlic, peanuts, and a score of spices and other flavorings, cooked to a sauce, then baked with chicken or turkey. The turkey variation, called *mole de pavo,* is so *típica* that it's widely regarded as the national dish.

The *mole* list goes on, through *mole amarillo* (yellow *mole*) to *mole colorado* (red *mole*), a sauce of chilies, sesame seeds, almonds, raisins, bananas, tomatoes, and spices, served over chicken with rice seasoned with *chepil,* a wild local herb.

Oaxacan main-dish sauces are not necessarily chili based. Some menus feature fruit- and nut-based sauces, such as *almendrado,* an almond sauce spiced with tomatoes, green olives, and herbs and served over chicken.

Oaxacans also enjoy local variations on the usual Mexican *antojitos,* such as *chiles rellenos de picadillo.* Here the cook replaces the usual *chiles rellenos* cheese stuffing with minced, spiced pork, beef, or chicken and serves them with guacamole, grilled onion, and refried black beans.

Menu meat selections often include *cecina* (say-SEE-nah), thin slices of spicy cured pork, frequently served with bean sauce and cheese, or *tasajo,* thinly sliced grilled beef, often dished up with *chilaquiles* (tortillas cooked in chili-tomato sauce).

Finally, top off your meal with a local dessert, such as flan (egg custard), and a drink, such as *té de poleo,* a tea brewed from *poleo,* a local, mint-like herb, or *café de la olla,* a rich regional coffee sweetened with *panela,* the dark brown sugar that market vendors sell by the chunk.

unnerving. If, however, you refuse (or bargain for) their offerings gently and with humor, you might begin to accept and enjoy them as part of the entire colorful scene. (If they really get to you, best take an inside table or retreat to the one restaurant that shoos them away, the Terranova.)

As for *zócalo*-front restaurants, serious-eating longtimers return to **El Asador Vasco,** Portal Flores 10A, tel. 951/514-4755, on the second-floor balcony above the Restaurant Jardín. The menu specializes in hearty Basque-style country cooking: salty, spicy, and served in the decor of a medieval Iberian manor house. Favorites include fondues (bean, sausage, and mushroom), garlic soup, salads, veal tongue, oysters in hot sauce, and the *carnes asadas* (roast meats) house specialties. Expect to pay $25–35 per person. Open daily 1–11 P.M.

Longtimers also swear by the Oaxacan specialties at **Casa de la Abuela** (Grandmother's House), at the *zócalo*'s northwest corner, above the Primavera café, tel. 951/516-3544. Here you can enjoy tasty, professionally prepared regional dishes and airy *zócalo* vistas from the balcony. Open daily 11 A.M.–10 P.M. Call for reservations and a table with a view. Entrées run $5–15.

For a tasty regional-style meal or snack, try **Restaurant Balcón de la Alameda,** Hidalgo 612, tel. 951/516-2917, around the corner and upstairs, at the plaza Alameda de León. You can choose a hearty *comida corrida* four-course lunch ($6), a chicken *mole* ($6), or maybe a savory *sopa de guias* (squash flower soup) ($4); open daily 8 A.M.–11 P.M.

For fine Oaxacan specialties in a graceful, old-world setting, try **Andariega Restaurant,** Independencia 503, in the Hotel Parador de San

Miguel, two blocks west of the cathedral. Here's one of your best chances to try some of Oaxaca's *moles*, such as *almendrado* (almond), *verde* (green), *amarillo* (yellow), or *negro* (black), over chicken, beef, or pork ($8–10). Other favorites are *chiles rellenos*, stuffed with cheese and *picadillo* (spiced meat) ($8), and red snapper in orange sauce ($8). An excellent daily four-course *comida* lunch also runs about $8.

For many loyal local upper-class patrons, **Restaurant Catedral,** García Vigil 105, tel. 951/516-3285, two blocks north of the *zócalo*, at the corner of Morelos, serves as a tranquil refuge from the street hubbub. The refined ambience—music playing softly in the background, tables set around an airy, intimate fountain patio crowned by the blue Oaxaca sky above—is half the show. The finale is the very correct service and quality food for breakfast, lunch, or supper. The Aguilar family owners are especially proud of their *moles*, sauces that flavor their house spe-

© BRUCE WHIPPERMAN

Time seems to pass leisurely from the vantage of a *zócalo*-front café.

cialties. These include fillets, both meat and fish ($8–15) and regional dishes, such as banana leaf–wrapped *tamales Oaxaqueños* ($8). It's open daily 8 A.M.–midnight.

Back on Hidalgo, just past the *zócalo*'s northeast corner, the spotless little *fonda* **El Mesón,** Hidalgo 805, tel. 951/516-2729, specializes in buffet food. For about $4, you can select your fill of fresh fruit, salads, *frijoles charros* (chili beans), and several entrées, including roast beef and pork, chicken, *moles*, tacos, tamales, and enchiladas. Open daily 8 A.M.–11:30 P.M.

More good eating, in a genteel, relaxed atmosphere, awaits you at the very popular **Restaurant El Sagrario,** 120 Valdivieso, tel. 951/514-0303 or 951/514-3319, around the corner behind the church. Mostly local, youngish upper-class customers enjoy either a club/bar atmosphere (lower level), pizza parlor booths (middle level), or restaurant tables (upper level). At the restaurant level during the evening, you can best take in the whole scene around you—chattering, upbeat crowd, live guitar, flute, jazz, or salsa melodies, and elegantly restored colonial details. Then, finally, comes the food, beginning, perhaps, with an appetizer, continuing with a soup or salad ($4), then an international or regional specialty ($6–10), which you top off with a light dessert and a savory espresso coffee. Open daily 8 A.M.–midnight. Music volume goes up later in the evening. Credit cards accepted.

On the other hand, a legion of American, Canadian, and European budget travelers swear by the no-nonsense budget **Restaurant Quickly,** 100 Alcalá, tel. 951/514-7076, half a block farther from the *zócalo*, on the Alcalá pedestrian mall. Once you taste the giant hamburgers ($3), chocolate milkshakes ($3), or pancakes ($3) (or veggies, if you prefer), you'll understand why. Open daily 8 A.M.–11 P.M.

North of the Zócalo

Devotees of light, vegetarian-style cuisine get what they're hungering for at **La Manantial Vegetariana,** at two locations. The original branch is at Tinoco y Palacios 303, tel. 951/514-5602 (west side of street, just above Matamoros, two blocks west and three blocks north of the *zócalo*); the new branch is inside the Santo Domingo shopping plaza diagonally across Alcalá, from the Santo Domingo church. The tranquil patio ambience sets the tone for the house specialty, a set lunch *comida.* Typically they might offer soup (onion or cream of zucchini), salad (mixed greens or tomato cucumber), stew (mushroom or soya steak), bread, fruit drink, dessert, and coffee or tea. About $5 until 7 P.M., $7 after that. Open daily 9 A.M.–9:30 P.M.

Although **Restaurant La Muralla** (The Wall), Bravo 510, corner of Crespo, tel. 951/514-2239, is a seven-block walk or taxi ride (four north, three west) from the *zócalo,* your effort will be amply rewarded. Enter the door and immediately it appears as if you've been transported to a foreign realm, perhaps somewhere in the country outside Xian or Guangzhou. Besides relishing the standard but tastily prepared dishes, such as wonton soup ($6), chicken chow mein ($7), and barbecued spareribs ($7), you will be entertained by the occupants of a big mid-room tropical aquarium. Open daily 1–8 P.M.; Visa accepted.

Go to the Santo Domingo church plaza-front, and enter the equally palate-pleasing **Pizza Nostrana Spaghettería,** corner of G. Vigil and Allende, across from Santo Domingo church, tel. 951/514-0778, where the friendly Abruzzo-born owner makes certain of the correctness of her cuisine. How she manages to assemble a proper meal of, say, *prosciutto e melone, pasta boscaida al dente, zucchine dorate,* and *flan napolitane* (about $20 total) in this far corner of Mexico is a secret that I'm pleased to leave with her. Top it all with a good bottle of old-world Tuscan Chianti and a request that they play Luciano for you. She's open daily 1–11 P.M.

Four blocks farther east, behind Santo Domingo, half a block north of Abasolo, **Café La Olla,** Reforma 402 (front of Casa Bugambilias bed-and-breakfast), tel. 951/516-6668, enjoys a loyal following of longtime North American expatriates. Here, the dark-beamed ceiling, subdued spotlighting of the art-decorated walls, quiet music, and candlelight set the refined, romantic tone. Select from a long but light menu of skillfully prepared and presented soups (Aztec soup is nearly a meal in itself), salads, Oaxacan specialties,

and meats. La Olla's main drawback is street noise, which you can minimize by taking an upstairs table. Open daily except Sun., 8 A.M.–11 P.M.

Right across the street is **Café La Antigua,** Reforma 401, tel. 951/516-5761, enjoyed by a long list of loyal patrons for entirely different reasons. Here, the main course is conversation and fine on-site roasted "Pluma" (from the mountains above Puerto Escondido) Oaxaca coffee. Along with their savory lattes, cold cappuccinos, and mocha frappés, patrons can enjoy fresh baked goods, crepes, sandwiches, eggs, and juices ($2–6). The prime mover behind all this is friendly coffee grower and owner Diego Woolrich Ramírez, who keeps La Antigua open Mon.–Sat. 9 A.M.–10 P.M.

Continue east two blocks and north two more, to the relaxing garden of **Mariscos Jorge,** on Pino Suárez, across from El Llano park, tel. 951/513-4308, standout standby of local middle- and upper-class patrons. Choose from a long menu of seafood (14 cocktail selections, including, shrimp, squid, and clam) ($3–5), salads and soups ($4), and entrées, including fish fillets, from breaded and baked to *a la diabla,* octopus, and much more ($6–12). Also pleasant for breakfast. Open daily 8 A.M.–6:30 P.M.

South of the Zócalo

Only a few good sit-down restaurants sprinkle the neighborhoods south of the *zócalo.* A trio of them, well known for Oaxacan cuisine, stand out.

Local folks strongly recommend the no-nonsense, country-style (but refined) **La Flor de Oaxaca,** Armenta y López 311, tel. 951/516-5522, a block east and half a block south from the *zócalo's* southeast corner. Along with spotless linen and very correct service, you'll get the customary bottomless plate of warm corn tortillas to go with your entrée. The *mole*-smothered regional specialties come mostly in four styles, *con tasajo* (thin broiled steak), *con pollo* (chicken), *con cecina* (roast pork) (all about $7), or *sola* (without meat, $5). Besides those, you can choose from an extensive menu of equally flavorful items, such as *tamales Oaxaqueños* (wrapped in banana leaves, $4), pork chops ($7), several soups, spaghetti, and much more. Vegetable lovers get started off right with their crisp *ensalada mixta* (sliced tomato, cucumber, onion, avocado, and lettuce with vinegar and oil dressing, $4). Open Mon.–Sat. 7:30 A.M.–10 P.M., Sun. 7:30 A.M.–3 P.M. Credit cards accepted.

If, however, you hanker for some nouveau variations on the Oaxaca regional theme, head to **Restaurant El Naranjo** (The Orange Tree), Trujano 203, tel. 951/514-1878, two blocks west of the *zócalo's* southwest corner. Here, the quiet, genteel patio atmosphere sets the tone, and the long, inviting menu tempts the palate. Choose among soups ($4), salads ($4), and Oaxaca's seven *moles,* one for each day of the week. Use them to flavor any one of a host of stuffed chilies ($6), tamales ($5), stewed chicken ($7), roast pork ($8), and much more. Open Mon.–Sat. 9 A.M.–9 P.M. (If you want to learn more, ask friendly owner Iliana de la Vega about her exceptional hands-on cooking classes.)

For yet another treat, try **Restaurant Los Angeles** in the Hotel Parador San Agustín, at Armenta y López 215, tel. 951/516-2022, one block east and half a block south of the *zócalo's* southeast corner. Here again the specialty is nouveau food with a Oaxacan twist. If possible, arrive with a party of three or four so you can taste as many of their delicacies as possible: squash flower stuffed with cheese, with mild chili sauce ($6); lettuce festival salad with white cheese, red bell pepper, avocado, and sesame ($5); cream of broccoli soup ($4); and fettuccine with spinach and cheese sauce with ham ($8). Open daily 7 A.M.–11 P.M. (During times of low occupancy, the restaurant serves only breakfast. Call ahead to double-check.)

Splurge Restaurants

The Oaxaca visitor influx during the 1990s has nurtured a crop of fine restaurants. One of the classiest is the elegantly upscale **El Che,** 5 de Mayo 413, tel. 951/514-2122, fax 951/514-2211, where everything seems designed for perfection. In a luxuriously spacious and high-ceilinged dining room, tuxedoed waiters scurry with plates of delicacies, replacing your embroidered white tablecloth with another halfway through dinner, while light classical music plays in the background. The continental-style specialties—Roquefort salad, French onion soup, fillet with mushrooms and cannelloni, fine wine list—please the palates of their well-to-do clientele. Figure a minimum of $35 per person, including wine. Find them on the corner across the street from the south side of Santo Domingo church; open daily, about 1–11 P.M. Reservations are necessary.

Hotel manager and chef Alejandro Ruiz of **Casa Oaxaca,** Garcia Vigil 407, tel. 951/514-4173, puts his all into blending the best of old and new cuisine. For example, start off with duck paté ($7), continue with *flor de calabaza,* stuffed with cheese and accompanied by *tostaditas* (toasted corn) and guacamole ($6). Follow through with broiled shrimp in their juice, with lentils ($15), or baked *robalo* (snook), with lemon ($18), all accompanied with a bottle of Concha Toro Chilean Sauvignon Blanc. Finish off with either baby coconut custard, mango pie, or *guanabana* mousse, or a sampling of all three ($8). Open daily 6–10 P.M.; reservation required.

In the far northeast corner of downtown, showplace **Restaurant La Toscana,** at the corner of 5 de Mayo and Alianza (in the old Jalatlaco neigborhood), tel. 951/513-8742, offers a long, elegant Mediterranean menu, spiced with a dash of traditional Oaxaca. Although it would be hard to go wrong with most anything here, I enjoyed the lettuce and tomato salad with goat cheese ($6), shrimp fettucine ($6), leg of *jabali* (wild pig) ($12), and, for dessert, croquettes of coconut and banana ($6). Open daily 9 A.M.–11 P.M.; reservations recommended.

Entertainment and Recreation

ENTERTAINMENT AND EVENTS

Around the Zócalo

The Oaxaca *zócalo,* years ago relieved of traffic, is ideal ground for spontaneous diversions. Regular concerts serenade from the *zócalo* band kiosk at 7 P.M. nearly every evening: the Oaxaca state band, Tuesday and Thursday; Marimba band, Monday, Wednesday, and Friday; and the Oaxaca orchestra, Sunday. At other times, divert yourself by running like a kid over the plaza, bouncing a 10-foot-long *aeroglobo* into the air. (Get them from vendors in front of the cathedral.) If you're in a sitting mood, watch the world go by from a *zócalo* sidewalk café. Later, take in the folk dance performance at the Hotel Monte Albán on the adjacent Plaza Alameda de León, nightly 8:30–10 P.M., for about $3.

After that, return to a *zócalo* café and enjoy the musicians who entertain most every evening until midnight.

Fiestas

There seems to be a festival somewhere in the Valley of Oaxaca every week of the year. Oaxaca's wide ethnic diversity explains much of the celebrating. Each of the groups celebrates its own traditions. Sixteen languages, in dozens of dialects, are spoken within the state. Authorities recognize around 500 distinct regional costumes.

All of this ethnic ferment focuses in the city during the July **Lunes del Cerro** festival. Known in pre-Hispanic times as the **Guelaguetza** (gay-lah-GAY-tzah) (Offering), tribes reunited for rituals and dancing in honor of Centeotl, the god of corn. The ceremonies, which climaxed with the sacrifice of a virgin who had been fed hallucinogenic mushrooms, were changed to tamer, mixed Christian-native rites by the Catholic Church. Lilies replaced marigolds, the flower of death, and saints sat in for the indigenous gods.

For the weeks around the two Mondays following July 16, the **Virgin of Carmen** day, Oaxaca is awash with native Mexicans in costume from all seven traditional regions of Oaxaca. The festivities, which include a crafts and agricultural fair, climax with dances and ceremonies at the Guelaguetza amphitheater on the Cerro del Fortín hill northwest of the city. Entrance to the Guelaguetza dances runs about $30; bring a hat and sunglasses. Make hotel reservations months ahead of time. For more Guelaguetza tickets ($35 per person), contact local tourist information office, at the north edge of the *zócalo,* corner of Independencia and Garcia Vigil, tel. 951/515-2510 or 951/518-5535, info@oaxaca.gob.mx.

Note: If the first Monday after July 16 happens to fall on July 18, the anniversary of Benito Juárez's death, the first Lunes del Cerro shifts to the succeeding Monday, July 25.

© BRUCE WHIPPERMAN

The July "Mondays on the Hill" dance performances, also known as the Guelaguetza, are an unmissable Oaxaca event.

The *zócalo* is Oaxaca's prime venue for spontaneous entertainment.

© BRUCE WHIPPERMAN

OAXACA CITY

On the Sunday before the first Lunes del Cerro, Oaxacans celebrate their history and culture at the Plaza de Danzas adjacent to the Virgen de la Soledad church. Events include a big sound, light, and dance show and depictions in tableaux of the four periods of Oaxaca history.

Besides the usual national holidays, a number of other locally important fiestas liven up the Oaxacan calendar. The first day of spring, March 21, kicks off the **Juegos Florales** (Flower Games). Festivities go on for 10 days, including crowning of a festival queen at the Teatro de Alcalá, poetry contests, and performances by renowned artists and the National Symphony.

On the second Monday in October, residents of Santa María del Tule venerate their ancient tree in the **Lunes del Tule** festival. Locals in costume celebrate with rites, folk dances, and feats of horsemanship beneath the boughs of their beloved great cypress.

As in many southern-Mexico locales, Oaxaca folks celebrate a robust **Day of the Dead** (Día de los Muertos) November 1 and 2. Families gather at cemeteries, where they decorate the graves of their departed with the favorite foods of the deceased and lights to guide their beloved ancestors to reunite with the family (albeit temporarily) once again.

Oaxacans venerate their patron, the Virgen de Soledad, December 16–18. Festivities, which center on the Virgin's basilica (on Independencia six blocks west of the *zócalo*), include fireworks, dancing, food, and street processions of the faithful bearing the Virgin's gold-crowned image decked out in her fine silks and satins.

For the **Fiesta de los Rábanos** (Festival of the Radishes) on December 23, celebrants fill the Oaxaca *zócalo*, admiring displays of plants, flowers, and figures crafted of giant radishes. Ceremonies and prizes honor the most innovative designs. Food stalls nearby serve traditional delicacies, including *buñuelos* (honey-soaked fried tortillas), plates of which are traditionally thrown into the air before the evening is over.

Oaxaca people culminate their *posada* week on **Nochebuena** (Christmas Eve) with candle-lit processions from their parishes, accompanied by music, fireworks, and floats. They converge on the *zócalo* in time for a midnight cathedral mass.

Folkloric Dance Shows

If you miss the Lunes del Cerro festival, some towns and villages stage smaller Guelaguetza celebrations year-round. So do a number of hotels, the most reliable of which occurs nightly at 8:30 P.M. at the Hotel Monte Albán, on Plaza Alameda de León, tel. 951/516-2777, adjacent to the *zócalo*. At other hotels, days may change, so call ahead to confirm: Hotel Camino Real, tel. 951/516-0611, Friday, $35 show with dinner, not including drinks; Restaurant Casa de Cantera, Murguia 102, at 8:30 P.M., $10 per person, varied schedule, tel. 951/514-7585.

Performing Arts and Fine Arts

Many Oaxaca institutions, such as the **Museo de Arte Contemporaneo de Oaxaca,** the **Teatro Macedonio Alcalá,** the **Instituto de Artes Graficos de Oaxaca,** the art film **Cinema El Pochote** (817 Garcia Vigil, tel. 951/514-1194), and others, sponsor first-rate cultural events. See the excellent monthly calendars of events in the English-language newspapers *Oaxaca Times* and *Oaxaca* for details on films, theater, music, dance, and art exhibits.

Nightlife

When lacking an official fiesta, you can create your own at a number of nightspots around town.

The big hotels are reliable for live dance music and discotheques. Call to confirm programs: Camino Real, tel. 951/516-0611; Fortín Plaza, tel. 951/515-7777; and the Victoria, tel. 951/515-2633.

Besides many of the sidewalk cafés around the *zócalo*, a number of restaurants also offer live music seasonally. Try the El Sagrario, on Valdivieso behind the cathedral, tel. 951/514-0303, evenings beginning about 9 P.M., and the Hotel Marques del Valle restaurant on the *zócalo*, tel. 951/516-3474.

Perhaps the most intense in-town nightspot is **Candela,** Murguia 413, corner of Pino Suárez, tel. 951/514-2010, which jumps with hot salsa and African-Latin rhythms from about 10 P.M. Thurs.–Sat. Call to confirm. (Women, be aware that a well-known cadre of local Romeos regularly frequents this and other such downtown spots.)

SPORTS AND RECREATION

Jogging, Walking, and Horseback Riding

For jogging, try the public **Ciudad Deportiva** (Sports City) fields on the west side of Highway 190 about two miles (3 km) north of the town center. Closer in, you might also jog around the big **Juárez Park** (El Llano), on Avenida Juárez, three blocks east and about 10 blocks north of the *zócalo*.

For an invigorating in-town walk, climb the **Cerro del Fortín** hill. Your reward will be a breezy city, valley, and mountain view. The key to getting there through the maze of city streets is to head to the **Escalera del Fortín** (staircase), which will lead you conveniently to the instep of the hill. For example, from the northeast *zócalo* corner walk north along the Alcalá mall. After five blocks, in front of the Santo Domingo church, turn left onto Allende, continue four blocks to Crespo, and turn right. After three blocks, you'll see the staircase on the left. Continue uphill, past the Guelaguetza open-air auditorium, to the road (Avenida Nicolas Copernicus) heading north to the **Planetarium.** After that, enjoying the panorama, you can keep walking along the hilltop for at least another mile. Take a hat and water. The round-trip from the *zócalo* is a minimum of two miles (3 km); the hilltop rises only a few hundred feet. Allow at least a couple of hours.

Sierra Madre Horse Trails offers horseback tours (around $11/hour) in the wooded, panoramic-view foothills above San Felipe del Agua village north of town. For more information and reservations (at least one day in advance), call tel. 951/520-0947 or 951/515-6864, info@oaxacastuff.com.

Swimming, Tennis, and Sporting Goods

Swimmers do their thing at multi-pool **Balneario La Bamba,** tel. 951/514-0925, about 2.5 miles (4 km) south of town along Hwy. 175 before the airport, on the left side, just past the big green Experimental sign over the highway. The pools are open daily except Mon. 10 A.M.–5 P.M.; entrance is about $3 for adults, kids $2. Serious lap swimmers should choose days and hours in order to avoid crowds, Sunday afternoon being the most crowded.

For tennis, stay at either the **Hotel Victoria** or the **Misión de los Angeles,** which have courts. Otherwise, call the **Club de Tenis Brenamiel,** next to the Hotel Villas del Sol, Km 539.5 on Hwy. 190, tel. 951/512-6811, about three miles

north of the center of town, and reserve a court; about $6 an hour.

A modest sporting goods and clothing selection is available at **Deportes Ziga,** on the southwest corner of Alcalá and Matamoros, next to La Mano Mágico handicrafts shop. Open Mon.–Sat. 9 A.M.–3 P.M. and 4–9 P.M., Sun. 11 A.M.–2 P.M.

Shopping

The city of Oaxaca is renowned as a handicraft shopper's paradise. Prices are moderate, quality is high, and sources—in both large traditional markets and many dozens of private stores and galleries—are manifold. In the city, however, vendors do not ordinarily make the merchandise they sell. They buy wholesale from family shops in town, the surrounding valley, and remote localities all over the state of Oaxaca and Mexico in

general. If your time is severely limited, best buy from the good in-town sources, many of which are listed below.

If, on the other hand, you have the time to benefit (both because of lower prices and person-to-person contact with the artisans) by going to the villages, consult the Valley of Oaxaca chapter for sources of local village handicrafts.

Traditional Markets

The original town market, **Mercado Juárez,** covers the entire square block just one block south and one block west of the *zócalo.* Many dozens of stalls offer everything; cotton and wool items—such as dresses, *huipiles,* woven blankets, and serapes—are among the best buys. Despite the overwhelming festoons of merchandise, bargains are there for those willing to search them out.

Before diving into the Juárez market's cavernous interior, first orient yourself by looking over the lineup of stalls on the market's west side, along the block of 20 de Noviembre, between Las Casas and Trujano. Here, you'll be able to select from a reasonably priced representative assortment—*alebrijes* (fanciful wooden animals), black and green pottery, cutlery, filigree jewelry, *huipiles,* leather goods, pewter, tinware—of much that Oaxaca offers.

After your Juárez market tour, walk a block west, to J.P. Garcia, and three and a half blocks south, between Mina and Zaragoza, for a look inside the **Mercado de Artesanías** handicrafts market. Here, you'll find more of the same—a ton of textiles—*huipiles, camisas* (shirts), *blusas* (blouses), and *tapetes* (carpets), plus *alfarería* (pottery), *alebrijes,* and some for-tourist masks.

© BRUCE WHIPPERMAN

Piles of polished wooden utensils, imported from the Oaxaca coast, are offered at *zócalo* **holiday handicrafts stands.**

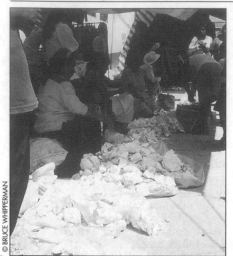

© BRUCE WHIPPERMAN

OAXACA CITY

Oaxaca market vendors offer many old-fashioned items, including *cal* (solid mineral lime) for limewater to soak corn for tortillas.

Private Handicrafts Shops

Although pricier, the private shops generally offer the choicest merchandise. Here you can select from the very best: *huipiles* from San Pedro de Amusgos and Yalalag, richly embroidered "wedding" dresses from San Antonino Castillo Velasco, rugs and hangings from Teotitlán del Valle; pottery—black from San Bártolo Coyotepec and green from Atzompa; carved *alebrijes* animals from Arrazola; whimsical figurines by the Aguilar sisters of Ocotlán; mescal from Tlacolula; and masks from Huazolotitlán.

Most of the best individual shops lie scattered along three streets—5 de Mayo, Macedonio Alcalá, and Garcia Vigil, which run uphill, north of the *zócalo.*

A good place to get prices and selection in perspective is the crafts shop in the federal tourist information center, 607 Independencia, tel. 951/516-0123, off the *zócalo,* diagonally north of the cathedral. It's open Mon.–Sat. 9 A.M.–8 P.M.

Next, head north along the Alcalá mall; two blocks north of Independencia, you'll arrive at a Oaxaca favorite, the **Palacio de las Gemas,** corner of Morelos and Alcalá, tel. 951/514-4603. Al-

though specializing in semiprecious stones and jewelry, it has much more, including a host of charming hand-painted tinware Christmas decorations, Guerrero masks, and pre-Columbian reproductions in onyx and turquoise. Open Mon.–Sat. 10 A.M.–3 P.M. and 5:30–9 P.M.

Head a block east to Cinco de Mayo, turn left (north) half a block to the big house on the right, headquarters of MARO, **Mujeres Artesanías de las Regiones de Oaxaca** (Craftswomen of the Regions of Oaxaca), 204 Cinco de Mayo, Oaxaca, Oaxaca 68000, tel./fax 951/516-0670. Here a remarkable all-Oaxaca grass-roots movement of women artisans has gotten the government to stake them to a building, where they sell their goods and demonstrate their manufacturing techniques. The artisans are virtually pure native Mexicans from all parts of Oaxaca, and their offerings reflect their unique effort. Hosts of gorgeous handicrafts—wooden masks, toys, carvings; cotton *traje* native clothing, such as *huipiles, pozahuancos, quechquémitles;* wool serapes, rugs, and hangings; woven palm hats, mats, and baskets; fine steel knives, swords, and machetes; tinplate mirrors, candlesticks, and ornaments; leather saddles, briefcases, wallets, and belts—fill the shelves of several rooms. It's open daily 9 A.M.–8 P.M. Don't miss it; better still, do a major part of your Oaxaca shopping at this store.

Return a block west via Murguia back to Alcalá and step into **La Mano Mágico** on the west side, just below the corner of Murguia, at Alcalá 203, tel./fax 951/516-4275. The shop offers both a colorful exposition of crafts from all over Mexico and a patio workshop, where artisans work, dyeing wool and weaving examples of the lovely, museum-quality rugs and serapes that adorn the walls. Open Mon.–Sat. 10:30 A.M.–3:00 P.M. and 4–7:30 P.M.

Across the street, step into **Cuchillos Alcalá,** Alcalá 206, tel. 951/514-7943, for an interesting selection of cutlery—knives, swords, scissors—and much more from a longtime Oaxacan tradition. Open Mon.–Sat. 10 A.M.–8 P.M.

Continue uphill on Alcalá, a block farther north, to the **Plaza Alcalá** complex, southwest corner of N. Bravo, which has both a tranquil courtyard restaurant and some good shops. Outstanding among them is the excellent **Librería Amate** bookstore, tel. 951/616-6960, fax 951/516-7181, corazon@spersaoaxaca.com.mx, on the lower level. Personable owner Henry Wangeman stocks an expertly selected library of English-language books about Mexico, including archaeology, cookbooks, ethnography, guides, history, literature, maps, postcards, and much more. Upstairs, Librería Amate's brother shop, **Corazón del Pueblo** (Heart of the People), Alcalá 307, tel. 951/514-1808, accomplishes the same with a fine, eclectic collection of Mexican handicrafts. Open Mon.–Sat. 10:30 A.M.–2:30 P.M. and 3:30–7:30 P.M.

If you're interested in weaving, step directly across Alcalá, to the **Tapetes de Teotitlán** shop of the Martínez family of the famous Teotititlán del Valle weaving village. (See the Around the Valley of Oaxaca chapter.) Here, you're looking at the real thing: fine, mostly traditional designs, made of all-natural dyes. Open Mon.–Sat. 11 A.M.–7:30 P.M. and Sun. 1–7 P.M.

Half a block farther uphill, be sure to look inside **Oro de Monte Albán** jewelry store, Alcalá 403, tel. 951/514-3183, just downhill from the Santo Domingo church front. This extraordinary family-run enterprise carries on Oaxaca's venerable goldsmithing tradition as the sole licensed manufacturer of replicas from the renowned treasure of Monte Albán Tomb 7. Besides the luscious, museum-quality reproductions, Oro de Monte Albán offers a fine assortment of in-house silver and gold earrings, charm bracelets, necklaces, brooches, and much more. Open Mon.–Sat. 10 A.M.–8 P.M., Sun. noon–8 P.M.

Rewards await shoppers who are willing to walk a few long blocks farther uphill, to the state-run **ARIPO** (Artesanías y Industrias Populares de Oaxaca), 809 Garcia Vigil, tel. 951/514-4030 or 951/514-0861. You can pick from a broad, authentic, and very traditional selection of carved animals, ceramics, *huipiles,* masks, tinware, wedding dresses, and much more. Prices vary: cheap on some items and high on others. Open Mon.–Sat. 9 A.M.–7 P.M., Sun. 11 A.M.–4 P.M.

Fine Arts Galleries

The tourist boom has stimulated a Oaxaca fine arts revival. Several downtown galleries bloom with the sculpture and paintings of masters, such as Rufino Tamayo, Rudolfo Morales, Francisco Toledo, and a host of up-and-coming local artists. Besides La Mano Mágica, listed in the Private Handicrafts Shops section, a number of galleries stand out. Foremost among them is **Arte de Oaxaca,** the gallery of the Rudolfo Morales Foundation, Murguia 105, between Alcalá and 5 de Mayo, tel. 951/514-2324 or 951/514-0910, open Mon.–Fri. 10 A.M.–2 P.M. and 5–8 P.M. and Sat. 10 A.M.–2 P.M.

Also outstanding is **Galería Quetzalli,** Constitución 104, between Reforma and 5 de Mayo, tel. 951/514-2606, fax 951/514-9407, local outlet for celebrated artist Francisco Toledo. Opposite the south wall-flank of Santo Domingo church, it's open Mon.–Sat. 10 A.M.–2 P.M. and 5–8 P.M.

Also well worth visiting is **Galeria Arte Mexicano,** in the Santo Domingo shopping complex, southwest corner of Alcalá and Allende, diagonally across Alcalá from the Santo Domingo church. It's open Mon.–Sat. 10 A.M.–8 P.M. and Sun. 11 A.M.–5 P.M.

For something new and unusual, go to **Galería Indigo,** Allende 104, corner of Alcalá, tel./fax 951/514-3889, info@indigo.org.mx, across from Santo Domingo church. Inside, several spacious rooms contain dramatic displays of modern paintings and exquisite one-of-a-kind handicrafts, both traditional and innovative, from Mexico, Central America, and Asia. They're open Mon.–Sat. 10 A.M.–8:30 P.M. (except closed Wed. 2–4:30 P.M.) and Sun. noon–6 P.M.

Completely different but just as fascinating is the longtime coin, antique bric-a-brac, and art store **Monedas y Antiguidades,** Abasolo 107, between the upper end of Cinco de Mayo and Reforma, tel. 951/516-3935. Browsers enjoy a potpourri of art, from kitsch to fine, plus a for-sale museum of dusty curios, from old silver coins and pioneer clothes irons to revolutionary photos and Porfirian-era tubas. Open Mon.–Sat. 10 A.M.–2 P.M. and 5–9 P.M., Sun. noon–3 P.M.

Cutlery and Metalwork Shops

Oaxaca is well known for its fine metal crafts. A few families produce nearly everything, which at least three of them sell from their own shops.

While in Mercado Juárez, stop by stall #5 to see the fine swords, knives, and scissors of Miguel Martínez and family, tel. 951/514-4868. Walk a few blocks west and south to see an even wider selection, plus artisans at work, at Guillermo Aragon's street-front shop at J.P. Garcia 503, tel. 951/516-2658, open Mon.–Sat. 9 A.M.–3 P.M. and 4–8 P.M. Finally, to select from a charming host of old-fashioned molded and painted tin figures, from soldiers and airplanes to horses and hockey players, stop by the González family shop, at north-side Porfirio Díaz 503, #4, tel. 951/516-5432, fax 951/514-7052.

Groceries, Wine, and Natural Food
For fruits and vegetables, the cheapest and freshest are in the Juárez market, which takes up the square block immediately southwest of the zócalo.

For simpler, straightforward grocery shopping, stop by **Abarrotes Lonja** on the zócalo next to the Hotel Señorial; open daily 8 A.M.–9:30 P.M.

Lovers of fine wine needn't go without in Oaxaca any longer. Head for **La Esquina** wine and mescal shop, at the north end at Gómez Farías 212B, tel. 951/515-2335, three blocks uphill, one block right, from the Santo Domingo church front. Find it open Mon.–Sat. 11 A.M.–3 P.M. and 5–9 P.M.

Local natural-food devotees get their heart's content of teas—arnica, anise, manzanilla—and ginseng, organic grains, granola, and soy burgers at **Tienda Naturista Trigo Verde,** J.P. Garcia 207, tel. 951/516-2369, two blocks west of the zócalo. Open Mon.–Sat. 8:30 A.M.–9 P.M., Sun. 9 A.M.–6 P.M.

Photography and Cameras
Downtown has some good photo shops, most on 20 de Noviembre, a block west of the zócalo. Best of all is **Oaxakolor,** 20 de Noviembre 108, tel. 951/516-3487, perhaps the best-stocked photo store in Oaxaca. It carries dozens of cameras—35 mm point-and-shoot, SLRs, professional medium format—as well as an abundance of film, including popular and professional color, slides, sheet, black and white, and a host of accessories. Open Mon.–Sat. 9 A.M.–9 P.M.

More ordinary, but still well stocked, is **Foto Figueroa,** Hidalgo 516, corner 20 de Noviembre, tel. 951/516-3766. With plenty of Kodak film and accessories, it offers quick develop-and-print service. Open Mon.–Sat. 9 A.M.–8 P.M.

Express Kolor, half a block farther down at 20 de Noviembre 225, tel. 951/516-1492, is better stocked, with scores of point-and-shoot cameras and many Minolta, Vivitar, and Olympus accessories. It also stocks Konica, Fuji, Kodak, and Agfa films in color and black and white, both roll and sheet. Open Mon.–Sat. 9 A.M.–8 P.M.

Other Practicalities

INFORMATION
Tourist Information
The state-federal governments maintain a good information office, which includes a handicrafts shop, at the zócalo's north edge, at 607 Independencia, corner G. Vigil, tel. 951/516-0123, fax 951/516-0984, info@oaxaca.gob.mx, open daily 9 A.M.–8 P.M.

Publications
One of Oaxaca's best sources of new English-language books about Mexico is the **Librería Amate** store on the ground floor of Plaza Alcalá, Alcalá 307, four blocks north of the zócalo, tel. 951/516-6960; open Mon.–Sat. 10 A.M.–2:30 P.M. and 3:30–7 P.M.

Another good source is bookstore **Librería Universitaria,** at Guerrero 104, half a block east of the zócalo, tel. 951/516-4243. It has English paperbacks, both used and new, a number of indigenous language dictionaries, and guides, cookbooks, art, and history books. Open Mon.–Sat. 9:30 A.M.–2 P.M. and 4–8 P.M.

The interesting **Librería de Bibliofiles de Oaxaca** (Bibliophiles' Bookstore of Oaxaca), M. Alacalá 104, tel. 951/516-9901, offers a big collection of new, mostly Spanish books, but with a good number of art, crafts, archaeology, and cultural books in English. Find them just downhill from the Santo Domingo church; open daily 10 A.M.–9 P.M.

Oaxaca's largest general book source (nearly completely in Spanish, however) is **Proveedora Escolar,** Independencia 1001, tel. 951/516-0489, fax 951/514-5655, which, as its name implies, is especially useful for those seeking a wealth of detailed, historical, geographical, touristic, cultural, and archaeological information about Oaxaca. It's a cultural experience in itself to visit the place; open Mon., Sat. 9 A.M. 2 P.M. and 4–8 P.M. The materials you'll probably most want to peruse are on the upper floors.

The daily English-language *Miami Herald* is usually available late mornings at the stand beneath the portal at southwest corner of the *zócalo*. If not, try the small news shop west from the same corner at Trujano 106A, open daily 8 A.M.–9:30 P.M.

Pick up a copy of the informative tourist newspaper, the *Oaxaca Times*, at your hotel, the tourist information office, or at the publisher, the Instituto de Comunicación y Cultura, 307 Alcalá, second floor, tel. 951/516-3443, www.oaxacatimes.com. The *Oaxaca Times* prints cultural and historical features, tourist hints, and a list of local events.

Also useful is the commonly available alternative trilingual tourist newspaper *Oaxaca* (published in English, Spanish, and French), Catalina 210, San Felipe del Agua, Oaxaca, tel./fax 951/520-2463, info@go-oaxaca.com, www.go-oaxaca.com.

Libraries

The city *biblioteca* (public library), at the corner of Morelos and Alcalá, two blocks north of the *zócalo*, tel. 951/516-5681, in a lovingly restored former convent, is worth a visit, if only for its graceful, cloistered Renaissance interiors and patios. Open Mon.–Fri. 9 A.M.–8:30 P.M.

Visitors starving for a good read will find satisfaction by borrowing at least one of the thousands of volumes at the **Oaxaca Lending Library,** at 519 Pino Suárez, about five blocks north of the *zócalo* on east side of Juárez park. Open approximately Mon.–Fri. 10 A.M.–1 P.M. and 4–7 P.M., Sat. 10 A.M.–1 P.M.

Volunteer Work and Donations

Local residents and visitors have bonded together to provide self-help for Oaxaca's street children and poor single-parent families. Two organizations, **Grassroots** and **Food Harvest,** operate cooperatively out of their headquarters, the **Center of Hope,** 308 Crespo, tel. 951/501-1069, about four blocks north, three blocks west of the *zócalo*.

The all-volunteer organizations raise money for food, schoolbooks and uniforms, housing, foster care, and much more for homeless children and destitute single mothers and their children. They welcome donations and volunteers, and visitors are always welcome, Mon.–Fri. 9 A.M.–7 P.M., Sat. 10 A.M.–3 P.M.

Outside of Oaxaca, you can send contributions to both organizations: Mail checks, addressed and written to the order of "Oaxaca Street Children Grassroots," 449 Crane Ave. S, Taunton, MA

A pair of make-believe soldiers guard a pre-Easter street shrine.

OAXACA CITY

© BRUCE WHIPPERMAN

02780. Get more information from Frank Vannini, tel. 508/884-8207, vannini@mediaone.net.

SERVICES

Money Exchange

Several banks, all with ATMs, dot the downtown area. (Note: Remove your ATM card promptly, for some local machines are known to "eat" them if left in more than about 15 seconds after the transaction is finished.) The most convenient (ATM only) is **Banamex** on Valdivieso, directly behind the cathedral.

The best-bet, full-service bank is long-hours **Banco Internacional** (Bital), a block north, a block east of the *zócalo*, at the corner of Guerrero and Armenta y López, open Mon.–Sat. 8 A.M.–7 P.M., tel. 951/516-5010 or 951/516-9753.

A full-service **Banamex** branch nearby serves customers just one block due east of the *zócalo*, at Hidalgo at Cinco de Mayo, tel. 951/516-5900, open Mon.–Fri. 9 A.M.–4 P.M., Sat. 10 A.M.–2 P.M. If Banamex is too crowded, go to **Banco Serfin** on the Independencia corner just north of the Cathedral, tel. 951/516-1100. Open Mon.–Fri. 9 A.M.–4 P.M., Sat. 10 A.M.–2 P.M.; U.S., Canadian, Japanese, and many European currencies and traveler's checks; or Serfin's neighbor, **Banco Santander Mexicano,** Independencia 605, tel. 951/516-2526, just northwest of the cathedral, a few doors west of the Garcia Vigil corner. Open Mon.–Fri. 9 A.M.–4 P.M., Sat. 10 A.M.–2 P.M.

After bank hours, go to **Casa de Cambio Internacional de Divisas,** tel. 951/516-3399, on the Alcalá street mall just north of the *zócalo*, behind the cathedral. Although it may pay about a percent less than banks, it changes as many major currencies and traveler's checks. Open Mon.–Sat. 8:30 A.M.–7:30 P.M., Sun. 9 A.M.–5 P.M.

Although the former **American Express** agency, Viajes Mexico Istmo y Caribe (MICSA), no longer operates as such, the adjacent money exchange booth cashes American Express traveler's checks and replaces lost traveler's checks if you have a police report and your receipt in hand. Located behind the cathedral, at Valdivieso 2;

money service hours Mon.–Fri. 9 A.M.–2 P.M. and 4–6 P.M., Sat. 9 A.M.–1 P.M.

Travel and Tour Agencies and Guides

Viajes Mexico Istmo and Caribe, tel. 951/516-2700 or 951/516-2919, fax 951/516-7475, conveniently located a block northeast of the *zócalo* behind the cathedral at the corner of Valdivieso and Independencia (hours cited in the previous paragraph), is a good source for most travel services, especially air tickets.

Other agencies are more experienced at tours. Among these are **Viajes Xochitlán,** Bravo 210 A, tel. 951/514-3271 or 951/514-3628, fax 951/514-2556, oaxaca@xochitlan-tours.com.mx, www.xochitlan-tours.com.mx. Go in comfort to all and any Oaxaca city and Valley sites and villages, such as Monte Albán, Mitla, Teotitlán del Valle, Tlacolula, and much, much more. They specialize in both individual and groups, tourist and business services, and travel agent services, such as air and bus tickets and hotel bookings.

Oaxaca Tours at the Santo Domingo Plaza, 417 Alcala, upper floor, tel. 951/516-1005, fax 951/514-6699, www.oaxacatours@oaxacatours.com, offers a number of promising alternatives. One of the most unique of its offerings includes guided visits to a number of Oaxaca Valley and Mixteca communities off the tourist track. In the Valley, these include, besides the well-known Teotitlán del Valle, the very interesting small towns of Santa Ana del Valle, San Jose Mogote, Santiago Suchilquitongo, San Pablo Huitzo, and San Pablo Huixtepec. For more details, see Guided Tours in the Around the Valley of Oaxaca chapter.

Also experienced in Oaxaca Valley tours is **Agencia de Viajes Pitao,** at the Hotel Calesa Real, Garcia Vigil 306, tel. 951/514-3662. Beside regular departures including Monte Albán, El Tule and Mitla, and Cuilapan and Zaachila, they also schedule individual tours, for up to 4 persons, including guide and auto transportation for about $20 per hour.

Another reliable travel and tour agent is longtime **Viajes Turisticos Mitla,** branch office at Hóstal Santa Rosa, Trujano 201 (a block west of the plaza's southwest corner), tel. 951/514-7800 or 951/514-7806. They offer tours, usually around the Valley of Oaxaca, including guide and transportation, for small or medium-sized groups. Their main office is at the Hotel Rivera del Ángel, at F.J. Mina 518 (two blocks south, three blocks west of the plaza), tel. 951/514-3152, fax 951/516-6175. They also provide very economical bus-only tourist transportation to a plethora of Oaxaca Valley sites, with multiple daily departures to Monte Albán. For more information and reservations, contact the bus departure ticket desk at the Hotel Rivera del Ángel, tel. 951/516-5327 or 951/514-3161.

A Oaxaca regiment of **private individual guides** also offer tours. Among the most highly recommended is English-fluent **Juan Montes Lara,** backed up by his wife Karin Schutte. Besides cultural sensitivity and extensive local knowledge, they can also provide comfortable transportation in a GMC Suburban wagon. Contact them at their home, at Prol. de Eucaliptos 303, Colonia Reforma, Oaxaca, Oaxaca 68050, tel. 951/513-0126, fax 951/515-0126, jmontes-lara@yahoo.com.

More athletic travelers might enjoy the services of **Bicicletas Bravo,** Garcia Vigil 409 C, five blocks due north of the *zócalo,* tel. 951/516-0953, roger@bikeoaxaca.com, www.bikeoaxaca.com, which both rents bikes and conducts bike tours into the countryside.

For even more extensive backcountry adventure bicycling, hiking, and camping in the mountains north of Oaxaca city (see the Northern Oaxaca chapter, first destination section), contact **Expediciones Sierra Norte,** 201 M. Bravo, tel. 951/514-8271, fax 951/516-7745, sierranorte@oaxaca.com, www.sierranorte.org.

For other more diversified and farther-ranging guide and tour recommendations, see the Getting Around section of the Around the Valley of Oaxaca chapter. Also, you might inquire for a guide recommendation at the government tourist information office, north side of the *zócalo,* at Independencia 607, corner of G. Vigil, tel. 951/516-0123, info@oaxaca.gob.mx.

Car Rentals

Car rentals offer another convenient means of ex-

ploring Oaxaca city and environs. Although town and valley roads present no unusual hazards, drive defensively, anticipate danger, and keep a light foot on the accelerator. Also be aware that road hazards—animals, people, potholes, barricades, rocks—are much more formidable at night.

To rent a car, all you need is a current driver's license and a credit card. However, car rentals, which by law must include adequate Mexican liability insurance, are expensive, running upward of $40 per day. Save *mucho dinero* by splitting the tariff with others.

Get your rental through either a travel agent or, before departure, through U.S. and Canadian toll-free car rental numbers, or in Oaxaca locally: **Budget,** tel./fax 951/511-5252 or 951/516-4445; **Hertz,** tel. 951/516-2434, fax 951/516-0009, hertz_oax@hotmail.com; and **Alamo,** tel./fax 951/514-8534, fax 951/514-8686.

Communications

The Oaxaca *correo* (post office), across from the cathedral at the corner of the Alameda de León square and Independencia, tel. 951/516-2661, is open Mon.–Fri. 8 A.M.–7 P.M., Sat. 9 A.M.–1 P.M.

Telecomunicaciones, at the next corner of Independencia and 20 Noviembre, tel. 951/516-4902, offers money orders, telephone, and public fax. Hours are Mon.–Fri. 8 A.M.–7:30 P.M., Sat. 9 A.M.–4 P.M., Sun. 9 A.M.–noon.

For long-distance and local telephone service, buy a Ladatel phone card (widely available in stores; look for the yellow Ladatel sign) and use it in public street telephones. Lacking that, take advantage of the efficient **Computel** long-distance phone and public fax office on Independencia, across from the Plaza Alameda de León, tel. 951/514-8084, open 7 A.M.–10 P.M.

Answer your email and connect to the **Internet** at any one of a number of downtown spots. For example, try the warren of small stalls and telephone booths, at Alcalá 100, tel. 951/516-6510, behind the cathedral, a block north of the *zócalo;* open daily 7 A.M.–11 P.M.; alternatively, go to **Desvan,** on the *zócalo*'s east side, open daily 9:30 A.M.–10 P.M.; or walk three blocks west to

Comunitel, at 20 de Noviembre 208, open daily 7 A.M.–10 P.M.

Health and Emergencies

If you get sick, ask your hotel desk to recommend a doctor. Otherwise, go to **Clinica Hospital Carmen,** Abasolo 215, tel./fax 951/516-0027, staffed by English-speaking IAMAT Doctors Horacio Tenorio S. and Germán Tenorio V.

For routine medicines and drugs, go to one of many pharmacies, such as the **Farmacias Ahorro** on Cinco de Mayo, near the northeast corner of Murguia, one block east, two blocks north of the cathedral. Open daily 7 A.M.–11 P.M. After hours, call Farmacia Ahorros' 24-hour free-delivery service, tel. 951/515-5000.

For police emergencies, call the emergency number 066, or get a taxi to the **Dirección de Seguridad,** at Aldama 108, just north of the *zócalo.* For fire, call the *bomberos,* tel. 951/516-2231, 951/511-5252, or 951/516-4445.

Consulates and Immigration

The U.S. Consul, Alcalá 407, tel./fax 951/514-3054, five blocks north of the *zócalo,* is open Mon.–Fri. 10 A.M.–3 P.M. At other times, in true emergencies only, call the consul at home, tel. 951/540-8029.

The Canadian Consul does the same for Canadian citizens Mon.–Fri. 11 A.M.–2 P.M., at 700 Pino Suárez, local 11B, tel. 951/513-3777, fax 951/515-2147. After hours, call toll-free Mex. tel. 800/706-2900.

Other consuls customarily available in Oaxaca are the French, at Vicente Guerrero 105, tel. 951/514-1900; Italian, Alcalá 400, tel. 951/516-5058; and Spanish, Porfirio Díaz 340, tel. 951/515-3525. For more information, look for consulate contact numbers in the *Oaxaca Times* or the telephone directory yellow pages, under *"Embajadas, Legaciones, y Consulados,"* or call the U.S. or Canadian Consuls above.

If you lose your Mexican tourist permit, make arrangements with **Migración** well before your departure from Mexico. Take proof of arrival date in Mexico—stamped passport, airline ticket, or copy of lost permit—to the airport Migración,

tel. 951/511-5733, a day (or at least three hours) before your scheduled departure.

Language Instruction and Courses

A long list of satisfied clients attests to the competence of the **Becari Language School,** N. Bravo 210, tel./fax 951/514-6076, becarioaxaca@rpodigy.net.mx, www.mexonline.com/becari.htm. Offerings include small group Spanish instruction, as well as cooking and dancing classes. If you desire, the school can arrange homestays with local families. Its modest downtown facility includes, besides classrooms, a social area for sitting and getting to know other students.

A number of readers have strongly recommended **Instituto Cultural de Oaxaca,** P.O. Box 340, Oaxaca, Oaxaca 68000, tel. 951/515-3404 or 951/515-1323, fax 951/515-3728, inscuoax@prodigy.net.mx, www.instculturaloax.com.mx, for both cultural activities and excellent academic-level Spanish instruction. Their campus, in former mansion grounds, surrounded by tranquil green gardens, is ideal for relaxed study. Find them on the north side, at Juárez 909, near the corner of Niños Héroes (Highway 190).

Similarly highly recommended is the **Vinigúlaza Language and Tradition** *(Vinigúlaza Idioma y Tradición)* school, associated with the local English-language Cambridge Academy, at Abasolo 503 (about five blocks east, four blocks north, of the plaza), tel. 951/513-2763, director@vinigulaza.com, www.vinigulaza.com. Spanish instruction is either in small groups, or individual. Schedules are flexible, and prices are reasonable. Social activities often include no-host dinners at local restaurants and a small on-site café where students can enjoy tea, coffee, and conversation.

Alternatively, for more lightweight instruction, try **Español Interactivo** (Interactive Spanish) language school at Armenta y López 311 B, Oaxaca, Oaxaca 68000, tel./fax 951/514-6062, interacc@prodigy.net.mx, www.mexonline.com/esp-interactivo.htm. One block east and half a block south of the *zócalo,* by San Agustín church, the school offers three levels: regular and intensive levels with 2–4 students per class and private one-on-one instruction. Also offered are homestays with Oaxaca families and classes in folkloric and salsa dancing, weaving, and painting on clay and wood.

Informal, minimal-fee Spanish instruction is sometimes available by volunteers at the **Oaxaca Lending Library,** M. Alcalá 305, corner of Murguia; open Mon.–Fri. 10 A.M.–1 P.M. and 4–7 P.M., Sat. 10 A.M.–1 P.M.

Oaxacan Cooking and Culture

Susana Trilling, Oaxaca resident and author of *My Search for the Seventh Mole* (as in MOHlay), offers an unusual mix of Oaxacan culture, cooking, and eating, with a lodging option, at her rancho cooking school in the Etla Valley, north of the city, Rancho Aurora, P.O. Box. 42, Admon. 3, Oaxaca, Oaxaca 68101, tel./fax 951/518-7726, seasons@spersaoaxaca.com.mx, www.seasonsofmyheart.com. The simplest choice is a one-day cooking adventure, including a morning trip to a local native market to buy food, then preparing and eating later at Susana's rancho. Other options are a long Thursday–Tuesday cooking and cultural adventure, or an extended one-week version of the same thing. Farther-ranging cooking excursions regularly include outlying parts of Oaxaca, such as the Isthmus of Tehuantepec or northern Oaxaca, around Tuxtepec.

Alternatively, downtown, contact **Iliana de la Vega,** 203 Trujano, tel. 951/514-1878, iliana@elnarajo.com.mx, owner of popular Restaurant El Naranjo, about her highly recommended cooking classes. Iliana's one-day three-hour ($40) class ordinarily starts in the morning. Call or drop in at the restaurant, two blocks west of the *zócalo*'s southwest corner.

GETTING THERE AND AWAY
By Air

The **Oaxaca Airport** (code-designated OAX) has several daily flights that connect with Mexico City and other Mexican destinations. Many of the Mexico City flights allow same-day connections between Oaxaca and many U.S. gateways.

Mexicana Airlines flights connect a number of times daily with Mexico City. For reservations or flight information, call tel. 951/516-8414 or 951/514-7253.

Aeroméxico flights also connect several times daily with Mexico City. For reservations, call tel. 951/516-3765 or 951/516-1066; for flight information, call tel. 951/511-5055.

Mexicana Airlines affiliate **Aerocaribe** flights connect daily with Huatulco and Puerto Escondido; and also daily with Cancún, via Tuxtla Gutiérrez, Villahermosa, and Mérida. For reservations, call tel. 951/516 0266 or 951/516-0229; for flight information, call tel. 951/511-5247.

Aviacsa airlines connects once daily with Mexico City and once daily with Tijuana via Mexico City. For information and reservations, call tel. 951/514-5123.

Alternatively, charter airlines connect Oaxaca city with various points within Oaxaca. **Aerotucan,** Alcalá 201, upper floor, suite 204, tel. 951/501-0530, or 951/501-0532, regularly connects Oaxaca city with both Puerto Escondido and Huatulco. For many more details, visit www.aerotucan.com or contact a travel agent.

Moreover, **Aerovega,** the dependable local air-taxi service routinely connects Oaxaca city with Puerto Escondido and other Oaxaca destinations. For information and reservations, call tel. 951/515-4982.

The Oaxaca airport provides a modicum of services, such as a good upstairs restaurant with a view; several shops; an international newsstand; car rentals; a helpful tourist information office (that will call hotels for you free), open daily 7 A.M.–8 P.M., tel. 951/511-5040; a bank, open Mon.–Sat. 8 A.M.–7 P.M., tel. 951/503-3188; and an ATM.

Arrival transportation for the six-mile (10-km) trip into town is easy. Fixed-fare collective taxi tickets run about $3 per person for downtown ($5 to north-side Hotels Misión de los Angeles, Fortín Plaza, and Victoria). For the same trip, a *taxi especial* (private taxi) ticket runs about $10 for four persons; larger GMC Suburbans, $19 for up to 8 persons. No public buses run between the airport and town.

Car rental agents stationed regularly at the

Oaxaca Airport are **Budget,** tel./fax 951/511-5252, 951/516-4445; **Hertz,** tel. 951/516-2434, fax 951/516-0009, hertz_oax@hotmail.com; and **Alamo,** tel./fax 951/514-8534, fax 951/514-8686.

For **departure,** save taxi money by getting your *colectivo* airport transportation ticket ahead of time, at Transportacion Terrestres on the west side of Plaza Alameda de León, across from the cathedral, tel. 951/514-4350, open daily 9 A.M.–2 P.M. and 5–8 P.M.

Furthermore, keep enough dollars or pesos for your $12 international departure tax (which may be collected in Mexico City) if your air ticket doesn't already cover it. If you lose your tourist permit, make arrangements with **Migración** several hours prior to departure from Mexico. Take proof of arrival date in Mexico, such as a stamped passport, airline ticket, or copy of lost permit, to airport Migración, tel. 951/511-5733.

By Car or RV

Paved (but long, winding, and sometimes potholed) roads connect Oaxaca city with all regions of Oaxaca and neighboring states.

Four alternative routes connect Oaxaca city south with the Pacific Coast: Two of them, via Highways 175 and 131, connect directly south over the super-scenic, but rugged Sierra Madre del Sur. Especially during the June–October rainy season, travelers are subject to landslides and bridge washout delays. The longer, but less rugged and more dependable route connects via Highway 190 southeast with Tehuantepec, thence Pacific coast Highway 200 west. The fourth route, also less direct, but still rugged, connects west via Highway 190, thence south with the Pacific coast, via Highway 125.

Narrow national **Highway 175** connects along 148 winding, sometimes potholed miles (238 km) with its junction with coast Highway 200 at Pochutla (thence six miles, 10 km to Puerto Ángel). The road climbs to more than 9,000 feet (2,700 meters) through winter-chilly pine forests and indigenous Chatino and Zapotec villages. Fill up with gas at the last-chance Pemex in Mihuatlán heading south and at Pochutla (north edge of town) heading north; carry water and blankets and be prepared for emergencies. Under dry, daylight conditions, count on about seven hours at the wheel, south from Oaxaca to Puerto Ángel, about eight hours in the opposite direction.

About the same is true for the paved **National Highway 131** route south from Oaxaca, which splits off of Highway 175 two miles (3 km) south of San Bártolo Coyotepec. On your way out of town, fill up with gasoline at the Oaxaca airport Pemex. Continue, via Zimatlán and Sola de Vega (fill up with gas again), over the pine-clad Pacific crest, a total of 158 miles (254 km) to Puerto Escondido. Under dry, daylight conditions, allow about seven hours southbound, about eight hours in the opposite direction. Unleaded gasoline is regularly available mid-route at the Sola de Vega Pemex only.

Highway 190 connects Oaxaca city southeast with Tehuantepec along 155 miles (250 km) of well-maintained but winding highway. Allow about 4.5 hours Tehuantepec direction (downhill), 5 hours in the opposite direction.

At Tehuantepec, connect west with Highway 200, via Salina Cruz (nine miles, 15 km), to the Oaxaca Pacific Coast, and Bahías de Huatulco (100 miles, 161 km, three hours), Pochutla–Puerto Ángel (124 miles, 200 km, four hours), and Puerto Escondido (170 miles, 274 km, five hours) of paved, lightly traveled, but secure highway.

The 229-mile (368-km) **Highway 190–Highway 125** route connects Oaxaca southwest with coastal Pinotepa Nacional, via the Mixtec country destinations of Yanhuitlán, Teposcolula, and Tlaxiaco. Although winding most of the way, the generally uncongested road is safely drivable (subject to some potholes, however) from Oaxaca in about eight driving hours if you use the *cuota* (toll) *autopista* northwest of Oaxaca city (exit to old Highway 190 at Nochixtlán). Add an hour for the 7,000-foot (2,100-meter) climb in the opposite direction.

The 350-mile (564-km) winding **Highway 190-160** from Oaxaca to Cuernavaca, Morelos, and Mexico City via Huajuapan de León requires a very long day, or better two, for safety. Under the best of conditions, the Mexico City–Oaxaca driving time runs 11 hours either way. Take it easy and stop overnight en route.

(Make sure you arrive in Mexico City on a day when your car is permitted to drive. See the sidebar "Mexico City Driving Restrictions.")

Alternatively, you can cut your Mexico City–Oaxaca driving time significantly via the Mexico City–Puebla–Oaxaca *autopista,* combined 150D-131D, which, southbound, takes off from the southeast end of Mexico City's Calz. General Ignacio Zaragoza. Northbound, follow the signs on Highway 190 a few miles north of Oaxaca. Allow about six hours driving time at a steady 60 mph (about 100 kph). Tolls, which are worth the increased speed and safety, run about $30 for a car, much more for a big RV.

By Bus

Luxury and First Class: Cristóbal Colón (CC) and Autobuses del Oriente (ADO), Oaxaca's major luxury- and first-class carriers, and their associated minor carriers operate out of the modern terminal on Highway 190, Calz. Héroes de Chapultepec 1036, at Carranza, on the north side of town. All bus lines accept credit cards and are bookable via the information and reservation line, toll-free Mex. tel. 800/702-8000. At the terminal, passengers enjoy a squad of public telephones out in front, snack stands, luggage lockers, and cool, refined Restaurant Colibrí, across the street.

Moreover, all of the carriers that use the Héroes de Chapultepec terminal cooperate through the joint agency, **Ticket Bus,** which sells tickets at a convenient downtown office. Find it a block west of the *zócalo,* at 20 de Noviembre 103 D, tel. 951/514-6655 or toll-free Mex. tel. 800/702-8000.

Cristóbal Colón (CC) offers service to most major Oaxaca destinations. Buses connect northwest with Mixteca destinations of Nochixtlán, Tamazulapan, and Huajapan de León, continuing to Puebla and Mexico City. Westerly, they connect with the Mixteca Alta, via Teposcolula, Tlaxiaco, Juxtlahuaca, Putla de Guerrero, and Pinotepa Nacional on the coast. Southerly, they connect (via the surer, but long, Isthmus route) via Salina Cruz, with Huatulco, Pochutla, Puerto Ángel, and Puerto Escondido; southeasterly, with Tehuantepec, Chiapas, and Guatemala; and northerly, with Villahermosa.

Autobuses del Oriente (ADO), offers limited Oaxaca connections, mostly along the Highway 190 corridor, connecting northwest with Mexico City (Tapo and Norte stations), via Nochixtlán and Huajuapan de León, and southeast, with Tehuantepec and Salina Cruz, and northeast to the U.S. border, at Reynosa. Other departures connect northwest with Veracruz, Coatzacoalcos, Villahermosa, Palenque, and Mérida.

Regional **Cuenca** buses connect with northern Oaxaca points along Highway 175, including Ixtlán de Juárez, Valle Nacional, and Tuxtepec, continuing all the way to Veracruz.

Sur departures connect with Mexico City Tapo station, along old Highways 190 and 160, via Huajuapan de León, Izucar de Matamoros, Puebla, and Cuatla, Morelos.

Autobuses Unidos (AU) departures connect with Mexico City along the fast *autopista* expressway, via Nochixtlán, Coixtlahuaca, and Puebla; or along the old Highway 131 via Cuicatlán, Teotitlán del Camino, Tehuacán, and Puebla.

Second Class: A swarm of long-distance second-class buses runs from the *camionera central segunda clase* southwest of downtown, just north of the Abastos market. Get there by taxi or by walking due west about eight blocks from the *zócalo* to the west end of Calle Las Casas. Take care crossing the busy *periférico* (peripheral boulevard) straight across the railroad tracks. Keep walking the same direction, along the four-lane street for two more blocks, to the terminal gate on the right. Inside, you'll find an orderly array of snack stalls, a cafeteria, luggage lockers, a long-distance telephone and fax, and a lineup of *taquillas* (ticket booths).

With one exception (see the last paragraph of this section) all ticket booths line up along the terminal, to your left as you enter. **Fletes y Pasajes,** tel. 951/516-2270, dominates the terminal, with three separate ticket booths. All three Fletes y Pasajes booths sell tickets to most of their destinations. They offer very broad second-class service, connecting with nearly everywhere in Oaxaca: westerly, with Mixteca destinations of Nochixtlán, Tamazulapan, Huajuapan, and Tlaxiaco, connecting all the

OAXACA CITY

way via Highway 125 to Pinotepa Nacional on the coast; northerly, via Teotitlán del Camino and Mazateca destinations around Huatla de Jiménez; easterly, with Mitla and Mixe destinations of Ayutla, Zacatepec, and Juquila Mixes; and southeasterly, with Isthmus destinations of Tehuantepec, Juchitán, and Salina Cruz. Besides all of the above, Fletes and Pasajes offers luxury-class "super" expressway connections with Mexico City.

In approximate consecutive order, moving left, from the entrance, first find **Transportes Oaxaca Istmo,** tel. 951/516-3664. Departures connect with dozens of destinations east and south. These include east Valley of Oaxaca destinations of Tlacolula and Mitla, continuing to the Isthmus destinations of Tehuántepec, Juchitán, and Salina Cruz. From Tehuántepec and Salina Cruz, they connext west, with Pacific Coast destinations of Huatulco, Pochutla (Puerto Ángel), and Puerto Escondido.

Cooperating Auto Transportes Oaxaca-Pacífico, tel. 951/516-2908, and **Autobuses Estrella del Valle,** tel. 951/516-5429, travel the Highway 175 north-south route between Oaxaca and Pochutla–Puerto Ángel. Both lines continue, connecting along east-west coastal Highway 200 with Bahías de Huatulco, Puerto Escondido, and Pinotepa Nacional.

Estrella Roja del Sureste and **Trans Sol** (with some first-class) buses, tel. 951/516-0694, connect directly with Puerto Escondido along Highway 131 north-south via Sola de Vega (with side trip to Juquila pilgrimage shrine). From Puerto Escondido, you can make coastal connections with Pochutla–Puerto Ángel, Bahías de Huatulco, and Pinotepa Nacional.

Several other semi-local lines connect mostly with Oaxaca Valley points: **Choferes del Sur,** with the northwest Oaxaca Valley, ranging from San Felipe del Agua north of the city to Etla northwest. **Autobuses de Oaxaca** connects south with Cuilapan and Zaachila. **Sociedad Cooperativa Valle del Norte** connects west with Teotitlán del Valle and Tlacolula. Finally, if you hanker for a long, sometimes rough but scenic back-roads adventure, ride **Flecha de Zempoatepetl** northeast to remote Zapotec mountain native market towns of Villa Alta and Yalalag, via Tlacolula and Cuajimoloyas.

Finally, to the right of the entrance as you enter, **Pasajeros Benito Juárez** buses climb the mountains edging the Oaxaca Valley's north side, to the cool, pine-shadowed mountain-top communities of Benito Juárez and Cuajimoloyas (Koo-ah-hee-moh-LO-yahs). (See the Northern Oaxaca chapter.)

Around the Valley of Oaxaca

A feast of old-Mexico sights and experiences awaits travelers willing to venture outside of the city of Oaxaca. The list—colorful country markets, crafts villages, archaeological sites, venerable churches, natural wonders—goes on and on. The towns themselves help you set your itinerary. They each have their market day, when local color is at a maximum and prices are at a minimum. Moving clockwise, the prime market destinations (in addition to Oaxaca city, where the big markets are the Juárez every day and the Abastos on Saturday) are Tlacolula, 45 minutes east, Sunday; Ocotlán, 45 minutes south, Friday; Ejutla, an hour south, Thursday; Miahuatlán, 90 minutes south, Monday; Zaachila, 30 minutes southwest, Thursday; Zimatlán, 45 minutes southwest, Wednesday; and Etla, 30 minutes northwest, Wednesday.

These market visits can be conveniently combined with stops at handicrafts villages and ruins. Notable handicrafts villages include Teotitlán del Valle and Santa Ana del Valle, on the east side; San Bartolo

Coyotepec and Ocotlán to the south; Arrazola toward the southwest; and Atzompa on the west. Among the premier archaeological sites are Mitla and Yagul, on the east side; Zaachila, southwest; Monte Albán, west; and Suchilquitongo and San José El Mogote, northwest.

GETTING AROUND

On Your Own: Buses and Rental Cars

Droves of buses from the west-side Abastos *camionera segunda clase* (second-class bus terminal) run everywhere in the Valley of Oaxaca and beyond. Arrive early any day and you could cover most major valley destinations in about a week that way: two days east

(Teotitláan, Tlacolula, Mitla), two days south (crafts villages, Ocotlán market), two days southwest and west (Zaachila market and archaeological site, Cuilapan, Arrazola, Monte Albán, and Atzompa), and one day northwest (Etla market and San José Mogote). For second-class bus destination details, see By Bus in the Getting There and Away section of the Oaxaca City chapter.

Get to the second-class bus terminal by walking one block south from the *zócalo,* turn right at Las Casas, and keep walking about 10 blocks. With caution, cross the *periférico* boulevard. The big terminal is two blocks farther, on the right.

More leisurely options would be to rent a

car or take a tourist bus or both. Get your car rental through either a travel agent or through U.S. and Canadian toll-free car rental numbers or in Oaxaca locally: **Budget**, tel./fax 951/511-5252, 951/516-4445; **Hertz**, tel. 951/516-2434, fax 951/516-0009, hertz_oax@hotmail.com; and **Alamo**, tel./fax 951/514-8534, fax 951/514-8686.

For tourist buses, a good bet is to go with Viajes Turísticos Mitla, which offers economical tourist bus transportation to a number of Oaxaca Valley sites, with multiple daily departures to Monte Albán. For more information and reservations, contact the bus departure ticket desk at the Hotel Rivera del Ángel, tel. 951/516-5327 or 951/514-3161.

Alternatively, other agencies offer similar arrangements. For example, try **Agencia de Viajes Pitao**, at the Hotel Calesa Real, Garcia Vigil 306, tel. 951/514-3662. Their regular departures include Monte Alban, El Tule-Mitla, and Cuilapan-Zaachila-Arrazola. Many hotels also have economical tourist bus arrangements. See your desk clerk or lobby travel agency.

Guided Tours

Many private individual guides offer tours. Among the most highly recommended is English-fluent **Juan Montes Lara**, backed up by his wife Karin Schutte. Besides cultural sensitivity and extensive local knowledge, they can also provide comfortable transportation in a GMC Suburban wagon. Contact them at their home, at Prol. de Eucaliptos 303, Colonia Reforma, Oaxaca, Oaxaca 68050, tel. 951/513-0126, fax 951/515-0126, stmn-ayt@rocketmail.com.

Oaxaca Tours at the Santo Domingo Plaza, 417 Alcala, upper floor, tel. 951/516-1005, fax 951/514-6699, offers a number of promising alternatives. One of the most unique of its offerings includes guided visits to a number of Oaxaca Valley and Mixteca communities off the tourist track. In the valley, these include, besides the well-known Teotitlán del Valle, the very interesting small towns of Santa Ana del Valle, San Jose Mogote, Santiago Suchilquitongo, San Pablo Huitzo, and San Pablo Huixtepec. All of these towns welcome visitors upon arrival at their community museums for an overview; tours continue to local handicrafts factory shops, archaeological sites, and other points of interest, such as historic churches, springs, mountain summits, caves, sacred sites, hikes and viewing of wildlife and medicinal plants, and more. For more information, visit their office or the Oaxaca Tours website, www.oaxacaoaxaca.com (click on museums), oaxacatours@oaxaca-tours.com, or, outside of Mexico, call their U.S. agent, Zapotec Tours, toll-free U.S. tel. 800/446-2922. (The Mixteca museum communities that Oaxaca Tours customarily visits include San Martín Huamelulpan, San Miguel Progreso, San Miguel Tequixtepec, Huajuapan de León, San Pedro y San Pablo Tequixtepec, and San Juan Mixtepec. For details on these, see the Mixteca chapter.)

Another promising alternative is **Judith Reyes López**, who operates through her **Art and Tradition** tours. Judith offers options, ranging from half-day city tours and whole-day Oaxaca Valley archaeological and crafts village outings, to farther-reaching explorations of the art and architecture of venerable Dominican churches in the Mixteca. Contact her at Priv. De Marte 109, Colonia Estrella, Oaxaca, Oaxaca 68140, tel./fax 951/515-1182, judithreyes37@hotmail.com, www.mexonline.com/tradicion.htm.

On the other hand, folks interested in the exceedingly diverse natural world of Oaxaca might appreciate a tour led by biologist **Fredy Carrizal Rosales**, owner-operator of **Tourism Service in Ecosystems**. Fredy offers customized explorations of many Oaxaca locations—pine-oak woodlands, coastal mangrove wetlands, semi-desert highlands, lush coastal foothill forest coffee plantations—viewing and identifying plants and animals and enjoying nature in general. Contact him at his Oaxaca office, at Garcia Vigil 406, Interior, tel. 951/515-3305, cell tel. 044-951/51103-3175, fredymar@prodigy.net.mx, www.mexonline.com/ecoax.htm.

Customized explorations of Oaxaca's indigenous communities and traditions and natural treasures are the specialty of native Zapotec guide **Florencio Moreno**, who operates **Academic Tours in Oaxaca**, tel./fax 951/518-4728, cell tel. 044-951/510-2244. Florencio's tours reflect

COMMUNITY MUSEUMS

Oaxaca's many community museums *(museos comunitarios)* provide visitors with a potentially rewarding alternative to getting to know local people. The museums, which now number about 20, sprinkle the Valley of Oaxaca and the Mixteca. The first community museums began as a result of archaeological digs. Later museums arose from the local need to house historic community documents and the myriad of artifacts that folks have been digging up on their own all over the state for centuries.

During the 1980s and 1990s, the government funded a number of communities for a building and expertise for installing exhibits. Now, excellent small museums in the communities of Teotitlán del Valle and Santa Ana del Valle in the east Valley of Oaxaca and San José El Mogote and Suchilquitongo in the northwest valley welcome visitors during regularly maintained hours. See the individual communities' sections in this chapter for more information.

The same is more or less true for the well-organized Mixteca museums in Huajuapan de León, San Pedro y San Pablo Tequixtepec, Yucunama and Huamelulpan. See the communities' sections in the Mixteca chapter for details.

A number of other small communities also have established museums but do not yet maintain regular hours. Nevertheless, local contact persons are available to open their museums for visitors. In the Oaxaca Valley, such museums exist, at San Pablo Huixtepec (on Highway 131, south of Zimatlán), and San Pablo Huitzo (northeast, off of Highway 190); see the Valley of Oaxaca map. The same is true, in the Mixteca, for the communities of Yucuita, near San Miguel Tequixtepec, Tepelmeme de Morelos, San José Progeso, San Juan Mixtepec, Santa Maria Cuquila, and Santa Maria Yucuhiti. See the Mixteca chapter

Local community museum guide pauses at a valley-view overlook above Santa Ana del Valle.

© BRUCE WHIPPERMAN

for map locations and museum details for most of these communities.

REACHING OUT

By establishing museums for public viewing, the communities are reaching out as never before. Your interest in visiting them will most likely be seen as a compliment by the local people. If you're interested in seeing more than just the museum, ask the museum attendant to suggest a guide who can show you around. Most of these museums have regular guides who are available to lead visitors to notable local sites, such as ruins, sacred caves, lakes, springs, mountain summits, and artisans' shops.

Always volunteer to pay ("donate to the museum": *donar al museo*) for such services. If necessary, be sure to bring along your own English-speaking guide or friend to interpret.

A convenient option is being offered by **Oaxaca Tours,** headquartered in Oaxaca city, at Santo Domingo Plaza, 417 Alcala, upper floor, tel. 951/516-1005, fax 951/514-6699. For a fee, they furnish a guide and transportation to the museum communities, especially those in the Oaxaca Valley, and also to some in the Mixteca. For more details, see the Guided Tours section.

his broad qualifications: fluency in native dialects, historical knowledge and cultural sensitivity, personal connections with indigenous crafts communities, and expertise in wildlife viewing and identification. His excursions can be designed to last a day or a week and include any region of Oaxaca, exploring anything from folk art and hidden archaeological sites to the colorful indigenous markets and festivals of the Mixteca or the Isthmus. For more information, write Florencio at home, at Nieve 208A, Colonia Reforma, Oaxaca, Oaxaca 68040, coquita @prodigy.net.mx, or log on to www.mexonline .com/academictoursinoaxaca .htm.

For more guide recommendations, ask at the state-federal governments' tourist information office, at the *zócalo's* north edge, at 607 Independencia, corner G. Vigil, tel. 951/516-0123, fax 951/516-0984, info@oaxaca.gob.mx, open daily 9 A.M.–8 P.M.

Higher up the economic scale, **commercial guided tours** also provide a hassle-free means of exploring the Valley of Oaxaca. Travel agencies, such as **Viajes Turísticos Mitla, Viajes Xochitlán** and others offer such tours. See the Services section in the Oaxaca City chapter.

TOURIST YU'U COMMUNITY LODGING

Several Oaxaca Valley communities invite visitors

to stay in their community tourist lodging: Yu'u in Zapotec (say "You"). The Yu'u are government-built, but locally managed and generally well-maintained, modern-standard kitchenette bungalows, typically sleeping four, with private hot-water shower bath and toilet. Yu'u are located, on the east side of the Valley of Oaxaca (moving eastward), at **San Sebastián Abasolo, Santa Ana del Valle,** and **Hierve El Agua.** Another Yu'u, at the southwest edge of the Valley of Oaxaca, at idyllic **San Sebastian de las Grutas** (cave and lovely tree-shaded, spring-fed river) also offers accommodation.

In addition, although not strictly in the Valley of Oaxaca, the easily accessible (atop the north-valley mountain range 10–15 miles or 16–24 km by car or bus from Tlacolula) communities of **Benito Juárez, Cuajimoloyas,** and **Llano Grande** (see the Northern Oaxaca chapter) offer rustic Yu'u accommodations. Other Yu'u-style accommodations are available, in the Mixteca, at Apoala, San Miguel Tequistepec, and Huamelulpan. (See the Mixteca chapter.) For more Yu'u information and reservations, stop by the government alternative tourism office, at Murguia 206 (up the driveway, in the back), tel. 951/516-4828, sedetur5@oaxaca .gob.mx. (If somehow you are not able to make contact with the Yu'u office, try Oaxaca government tourism, tel./fax 951/516-0123, info@oaxaca.gob.mx.)

East Side: The Textile Route

The host of colorful enticements along this path could tempt you into many days of delightful exploring. For example, on Saturday you could head out, visiting the great El Tule tree and the weavers' shops in Teotitlán del Valle and continuing east for an overnight at Mitla. Next morning, explore the Mitla ruins, then return, stopping at the hilltop Yagul archaeological site and the Sunday market at Tlacolula. In either direction, going or coming from the city, you could pause for a brief exploration at the Dainzu and Lambityeco roadside archaeological sites.

One more day would allow more time to venture past Mitla to the remarkable mountainside springs and limestone mineral deposits at Hierve de Agua. Stay longer and have it all: a two- or three-day stay in a colorful market town, such as Tlacolula, with a side trip to a quiet backcountry village, such as San Bartolomé Quialana or San Marcos Tlapazola.

EL TULE AND TLACOCHAHUAYA

Santa María del Tule

El Tule is a gargantuan Mexican *ahuehuete* (cypress), probably the most massive tree in Latin America. Its gnarled, house-size trunk divides into a forest of elephantine limbs that rise to bushy branches reaching 15 stories overhead. The small town of Santa María del Tule, nine miles (14 km) east of the city on Highway 190, seems built around the tree. A crafts market, a church, and the town plaza, where residents celebrate their El Tule with a fiesta on October 7, all surround the beloved 2,000-year-old living giant.

Note: Eastbound, the highway funnels through traffic to a right-hand bypass before the El Tule tree itself. Stay in the left, local lane if possible. If not, park along the bypass and walk a block north to El Tule.

Tlacochahuaya

At San Jerónimo Tlacochahuaya (tlah-koh-chah-WYE-yah), about four miles (7 km) west of El Tule, stands the village's pride and joy, the venerable 16th-century **Templo y Exconvento de San Jerónimo.** Dominican padres and their native acolytes, under the guidance of Father Jordán de Santa Catalina, began its construction in 1586 and completed it a few decades later.

Tlacochahuaya is usually a quiet little town except during holidays, notably the eight days of processions, dances, fireworks, and food, climaxing on September 30, the feast day of San Jerónimo.

The church's relatively recent 1991 restoration glows so brilliantly, especially from the white baroque facade, that, standing beneath the

El Tule, Latin America's most massive tree, is the usual first stop on valley tours east of Oaxaca city.

spreading wild fig tree in the courtyard (or more precisely, atrium), you can feel the facade reflecting the warmth of the late afternoon sun. The atrium appears big enough to assemble a crowd of about 5,000 folks, probably the number of local *indígenas* the padres hoped to convert during the 16th century. At the atrium's corners stand the three open-air but arch-roofed chapels, or *pozas,* where the conversions took place.

Above the entrance portal, see San Jerónimo standing piously, his left hand on a skull, listening for the voice of God. Inside, glance upward at the lovely nave ceiling and appreciate the still-vital spirit of those long-dead artists who created its flowery, multicolored swirls. Look for the group of oil paintings depicting the legend of the **Virgin of Guadalupe,** with the last showing the roses miraculously tumbling from Juan Diego's cape, emblazoned with her image.

Once when I visited, near the entrance was the pledge of the Sacerdote de Cristo (Priest of Christ), which, translated, reads:

The priest of Christ offers
THIS MASS
As if it were your
FIRST MASS
As if it were your
ONLY MASS
As if it were your
LAST MASS

Get there by car, guide, or by the Sociedad Cooperativa Valle del Norte or Fletes y Pasajes local bus from the Camionera Central Segunda Clase.

DAINZU AND LAMBITYECO ARCHAEOLOGICAL SITES

Among the several Oaxaca Valley buried cities, Dainzu and Lambityeco, both beside the highway, are the most accessible. Dainzu comes first, on the right about six miles (9 km) east of El Tule.

Dainzu

Dainzu (in Zapotec, Hill of the Organ Cactus), open daily 10 A.M.–5 P.M., spreads over an approximate half-mile square, consisting of a partly restored ceremonial center surrounded by clusters of unexcavated mounds. Beyond that, on the west side, a stream runs through fields, which at Dainzu's apex (around A.D. 300) supported a town of about 1,000 inhabitants.

The major excavation, at the foot of the hill about a hundred yards south of the parking lot, reveals more than 30 bas-reliefs of ball players draped with leather head, arm, and torso protectors. Downhill, to the west, lies the partly reconstructed complex of courtyards, platforms, and stairways. The northernmost of these was excavated to reveal a tomb, with a carved door supporting a jaguar head on the lintel and arms—note the claws—extending down along the stone doorjambs. The jaguar's face, with a pair of curious vampire teeth and curly nostrils, appears so bat-like that some investigators have speculated that it may represent a composite jaguar-bat god.

A couple of hundred yards diagonally southwest you'll find the ball court running east-west in the characteristic I-shaped layout, with a pair of "scoring" niches at each end and flanked by a pair of stone-block grandstand-like seats. Actually, archaeologists know that these were not seats, because the blocks were once stuccoed over, forming a pair of smooth inclined planes (probably used for glancing shots) flanking the central playing area.

Lambityeco

Six miles (10 km) farther, Lambityeco, open daily 10 A.M.–5 P.M., is on the right, a few miles past the Teotitlán del Valle side road. The excavated portion, only about 100 yards square, is a small but significant part of Yegui (Small Hill, in Zapotec), a large buried town dotted with hundreds of unexcavated mounds, covering about half a square mile. Salt-making appears to have been the main occupation of Yegui people during the town's heyday, around A.D. 700. The name "Lambityeco" may derive from the Arabic-Spanish *alambique,* the equivalent of English "alembic," or distillation or evaporation apparatus. This would explain the intriguing presence of the more than 200 local mounds. It's tempting to speculate that they are the remains of *cujetes,* raised leaching beds,

VALLEY OF OAXACA

TOWN NAMES

Town names in Oaxaca (and in Mexico) generally come in two pieces: an original native name, accompanied by the name of the town's patron saint. Very typical is the case of San Jerónimo Tlacochahuaya, a sleepy but famous little place covered in this chapter. Combining both the saint's name (here, San Jerónimo) and the native name often makes for very unwieldy handles, so many towns are known only by one name, usually the native name. Thus, in the Oaxaca Valley, west side, San Jerónimo Tlacochahuaya, Santa María del Tule, Tlacolula de Matamoros, and San Pablo Villa de Mitla, for example, are commonly called Tlacochahuaya, El Tule, Tlacolula, and Mitla, respectively.

Nevertheless, sometimes a town's full name is customarily used. This is especially true when a single name—such as Etla, northwest of Oaxaca city—identifies an entire district, where many towns, such as San Agustín Etla, San Sebastián Etla, and San José Etla must necessarily be identified with their full names. In this book, although we may mention the formal name once on a map or in the text, we generally conform to local, customary usage for town names.

still used in Mexico for concentrating brine, which workers subsequently evaporate into salt.

In the present small restored zone, archaeologists have uncovered, besides the remains of the Valley of Oaxaca's earliest known *temascal* (ritual steam house), a number of fascinating ceramic sculptures. Next to the parking lot, a platform, mound 195, rises above ground level. If, after entering through the gate, you climb up its partially restored slope and look down into the excavated hollow in the adjacent east courtyard, you'll see stucco friezes of a pair of regal, lifelike faces, one male and one female, presumably of the personages who were found buried in the royal grave (Tomb 6) below. Experts believe this to be the case, because the man was depicted with the symbol of his right to rule—a human femur bone, probably taken, as was the custom, from the grave of his chieftain father.

Mound 190, sheltered beneath the adjacent large corrugated roof about 50 yards to the south, contains a restored platform decorated by a pair of remarkably lifelike, nearly identical divine stucco masks. These are believed to be of Zapotec rain god Cocijo (see the water flowing from the mouths). Notice also the rays in one hand, perhaps lightning, representing power, and flowers, for fertility, in the other.

TEOTITLÁN DEL VALLE

Teotitlán del Valle, pop. 5,000, nine miles (14 km) east of El Tule, at the foot of the northern Sierra, means "Place of the Gods" in Nahuatl; before that, it was known, appropriately, as Xa Quire (shah KEE-ray) or "Foot of the Mountain," by the Zapotecs who settled it, archaeologists estimate, at least 2,000 years ago. From the age of artifacts uncovered beneath both the present town and at nearby sites, experts estimate that approximately 1,000 people were living in Teotitlán by A.D. 400.

Teotitlán people are relatively well off, not only from sales of their renowned *tapetes* (woven wool carpets), but from their rich communal landholdings. Besides a sizable swath of valley-bottom farmland and pasture, which every Teotitlán family is entitled to use, the community owns a dam and reservoir and a small kingdom of approximately 100,000 acres of sylvan mountain forest and meadow, spreading for about 20 miles (32 km) along the Valley of Oaxaca's lush northeastern foothills.

Getting Oriented

Teotitlán del Valle has two principal streets: Juárez, the entrance road, which runs northerly about 2.5 miles (4 km) from the highway, and Hidalgo, which intersects it at the center of town. Turn right at Hidalgo (where the pavement becomes cobbled) and you'll be looking east, toward the town plaza and, behind it, the 17th-century town church.

Textile Shops

Nearly every Teotitlán house is a mini-factory where people card, spin, and color wool, often using hand-gathered natural dyes. Each step of wool preparation is laborious; pure water is even a chore—families typically spend two days a week collecting it from mountain springs. The weaving, on traditional hand looms, is the final, satisfying part of the process.

Visiting the workshop stores should be first on your itinerary. Be sure not to miss the shop of renowned master Isaac ("Bug in the Rug") Vasquez, at Hidalgo 30, open daily 10 A.M.–6 P.M., tel. 951/514-4122. Also, be certain to look inside the store of the skilled Cooperativa Mujeres Tejedoras (Women Weavers' Cooperative). The cooperative shop, Casa Santa Cecilia, managed by Josefina Jiménez, displays the fine, for-sale woven products of 28 women weavers. Find it on the road into town, on the right side, about a quarter mile (half a kilometer) from Oaxaca Highway 190.

The best weaving is generally the densest, typically packing in about 45 strands per inch (18 strands per centimeter); ordinary weaving incorporates about half that. Please don't bargain too hard. Even the highest prices typically bring the weavers less than a dollar an hour for their labor.

Community Museum

Reserve enough time to visit the community museum, **Balaa Xtee Guech Gulal,** whose name translates from the local Zapotec as "Shadow of the Old Town." It's on the north side of Hidalgo, about a block east of Juárez. Step inside (open daily except Mon. 10 A.M.–6 P.M.) and enjoy the excellent exhibits that illustrate local history, industry, and customs. One display shows the wool-weaving tradition, introduced by the Dominican padres, including sources of some natural dyes—*cochinilla* (red cochineal), *musgo* (yellow moss and lichens), *anil* (dark blue indigo), and black *quizache* bean. Another exhibit shows the local practice of service to the bride's parents by a prospective groom, with a house mock-up showing the prospective bride making tortillas for him. Be sure to get a copy of the good English-language explanatory pamphlet.

A Walk Around Town

If you ask, a community museum volunteer may be available to lead you on a walking tour of the town and environs. Highlights often include visits to weavers' homes, the church, a traditional

© BRUCE WHIPPERMAN

VALLEY OF OAXACA

Master weaver Isaac Vasquez demonstrates his technique on the spinning wheel in his Teotitlán del Valle shop.

temascal (ritual steam house), the recently reconstructed foundation stones of the ancient town, the dam and lake, and the hike to Picacho, the peak above the town's west side.

Lacking a guide, simply stroll out on your own self-guided tour. Head east on Hidalgo. If you haven't already, take a look around the plaza-front textile stalls, then continue to the church, **Templo de la Preciosa Sangre de Cristo** (Church of the Precious Blood of Christ). Here, community adoration focuses during both the July 1–15 patronal festival and the September 7–9 Fiesta del Señor de La Natividad (Festival of the Lord of the Nativity), which include processions, fireworks, and the spectacular Danza de las Plumas (Dance of the Feathers).

The church itself, built over an earlier Zapotec temple, contains many interesting pre-Columbian stones, which the Dominican friars allowed to be incorporated into its walls. Notice the corn motif carved into the front doorway arch, similar in style to the monolith built into the outside wall at the right of the church entrance steps. Inside, admire the nave's flowery overhead decorations and the colorful Bible-story paintings. Continue from the nave into the intimate *claustro* (cloister) and see the Zapotec god of the wind, with stone curls carved to represent the wind (in the southwest corner, to the right as you enter from the nave).

Outside, behind the church, continue to the reconstructed foundation corner of the original **Zapotec temple.** Notice the uniquely Zapotec stone fretwork, similar to the famous *greca* remains at Mitla, 20 miles (32 km) farther east.

If you have time, you can venture even farther afield. One option is to walk or drive along the bumpy but passable uphill gravel continuation of main street Calle Juárez about a mile (1.6 km) to the **town dam.** After the summer rains, the reservoir fills and forms a scenic lake, good for swimming, picnicking, and even possibly camping, along its pastoral mountain-view shoreline. If you plan to camp at the Teotitlán reservoir, first ask for permission at the museum or the *presidencia municipal.*

Travelers can extend their Teotitlán adventure all the way into the mountains. From the Teotitlán reservoir, hike (be prepared with water, good shoes, and a hat), hitchhike, taxi, or drive about 12 more miles (19 km) uphill (with an elevation gain of 5,000 feet, 1,500 meters) along the good gravel road to pine-shadowed **Benito Juárez** and **Cuajimoloyas** mountain hamlets. (See the Northern Oaxaca chapter for details.)

Back at the Teotitlán reservoir, you can also adventure up the slope of **Picacho,** the steep, peaked hill a mile (1.6 km) west of town. The usual route from town is along Calle 2 de Abril, which heads west, bridging the west-side arroyo. Continue uphill, bearing right at the fork at the base of the hill. First you pass some houses, then continue, curving left around the hillside. Eventually, before the summit, you pass some *cuevitas* (small caves), a holy site where local folks have been gathering for sacred ceremonies each New Year's Day since before anyone can remember.

Food

Sample Teotitlán's best, at the charmingly traditional **Tlamanalli** restaurant, on Juárez, about a block south of Hidalgo. Their menu of made-to-order Zapotec specialties, such as *sopa de calabaza* (squash soup) and *guisado de pollo* (chicken stew) is limited, but highly recommended by Oaxaca city chefs. Open daily 1–4 P.M., longer hours when more people stop by.

Getting There

You can go to Teotitlán by car, tour, taxi, or bus. Drivers, simply turn left from Highway 190 at the signed Teotitlán del Valle side road, nine miles (14 km) east of El Tule. By bus, ride a Fletes y Pasajes Tlacolula- or Mitla-bound bus from the *camionera central segunda clase* (second-class bus station) by the Abastos market at the end of Las Casas, past the *periférico* west of downtown. Get off at the signed bus stop, and walk, taxi, or hitchhike the 2.5 miles (4 km) into town.

SANTA ANA DEL VALLE

This is a sleepier version of Teotitlán, where virtually every family speaks the Zapotec tongue at home and earns at least part of its living through weaving. Many older folks understand Spanish

© BRUCE WHIPPERMAN

Visits to home factory shops are a part of the community museum tour at Santa Ana del Valle.

only with difficulty. Santa Ana del Valle, like Teotitlán, has thousands of acres of communal lands in the valley bottom and mountains north of the town. Nearly all households tend plots of corn, beans, and vegetables. Most also graze cattle, sheep, and goats in specified communal areas. These lands have been traditionally held by the town since before the conquest. Families may buy or sell shares of their allotted land, but only within the Santa Ana del Valle community.

Community Museum

Your first stop should be the excellent community museum, **Shan Dany,** on the town plaza, opposite the *presidencia municipal,* open Mon.–Sat. 10 A.M.–2 P.M. and 3–6 P.M. The exhibits include an archaeological section with pre-conquest remains found during a recent plaza-front construction project. Also notice the ponderous monolith, brought from the mountain above town, carved with the visage of Cocijo, the god of

lightning and rain. Another museum section details 1910–1917 revolutionary history, when townsfolk had to flee to the hills and wage a guerrilla war against rampaging forces of "Primer Jefe" General Venustiano Carranza.

Toward the rear of the museum, a pair of excellent displays illustrate more community lore: One shows many of the naturally occurring dyes, including avocado seeds, *guaje* bark, and *copal* bark, that local weavers gather and use; the other explains the Danza de la Pluma (Dance of the Feathers), in which a dozen young men dance and brighten the town plaza with their huge, round feathered hats. This dance takes place during the July 26 and August 14–16 split-date festival in honor of Santa Ana.

A Walk Around Town

Ask and a museum volunteer staff may be able to find a guide (offer to pay) to lead you on a two- or three-hour *recorrido* (tour) around town, including the *presa* (dam and small reservoir), a creek (where you can cool off during the summer rainy season—bring your bathing suit), a breezy *mirador* (viewpoint) for a spectacular valley vista, and an old gold, silver, and copper mine. During the walk, your guide might identify and explain the uses of the many medicinal plants along the path. Be sure to ask them to point out the poison oak–like *mala mujer* (bad woman) bush to you. Finally, ask them to take you to shops of outstanding local weavers for demonstrations and possible purchases of their work.

If you can't get a guide, you can still do most of the walk on your own. The path to the dam takes off from Calle Plan de Ayala, on the east, uphill side of town. It's only about half a mile (.8 km); bear left, around the hill. If you get confused, ask a younger person (most likely to understand Spanish) *"¿Donde está la presa"* (PRAY-sah), *"por favor?"* The viewpoint, the big moss-mottled rock about halfway up the steep, left-hand slope, sticks out of the hillside to the left and above the path to the dam.

Accommodations

The comfortable Santa Ana tourist Yu'u is on the entrance road to town. It is well situated for

VALLEY OF OAXACA

exploring, being just a few blocks from the center of town. Reserve a spot here through the state-federal alternative tourism office, Murguia 206 (up the driveway, in the back), tel. 951/516-4828, sedetur5@oaxaca.gob.mx, www.oaxaca.gob.mx/sedetur/alte.

Shopping

Although Santa Ana weavers sell much of their work through shops in Teotitlán del Valle and Oaxaca, they also sell directly in town, from both the **Mercado de Artesanías** on the town plaza and their home workshops. For suggestions of whom to visit, ask at the museum, or go directly to **Casa Martínez,** the house of personable master weaver Ernesto Martínez, at Matamoros 3, corner of V. Carranza, tel. 951/562-0366, around the corner a few doors downhill from the town plaza. You'll also be welcome at the home shop of the friendly weaving family of Alberto Sánchez Garcia, at Sor Juanes Inés de la Cruz 1, a few blocks from the town plaza, tel. 951/562-0655 or 951/562-0499.

Sombreros (literally "shade makers") are plentiful at the Sunday Tlacolula market.

© BRUCE WHIPPERMAN

VALLEY OF OAXACA

Getting There

You can go by car, tour, taxi, or bus. Drivers, turn left at the fork across Highway 190 from the Tlacolula Pemex *gasolinera* (24 miles, 38 km) east of Oaxaca city. After half a mile (.8 km), turn left again at the signed Santa Ana del Valle side road. Continue another few minutes; pass the tourist Yu'u, on the right, and arrive at the town plaza a few blocks farther. By bus, you can ride a Tlacolula- or Mitla-bound bus from the second-class bus station by the Abastos market, end of Las Casas, west of downtown. Get off at the Tlacolula stop on Highway 190 by the Pemex station. Cross to the side road on the north side of the highway and either take a taxi, ride the Transportes Municipal del Santa Ana del Valle local bus, or hike the four miles (6.4 km) from the highway—walk the side road half a mile (.8 km) to a signed Santa Ana fork; go left and continue for two more miles (3.2 km), passing the tourist Yu'u on the right, and then on to the town plaza a few blocks farther.

TLACOLULA

The Zapotec people who founded Tlacolula (pop. 15,000; 24 miles, 38 km east from Oaxaca) around A.D. 1250 called it Guichiibaa (Place between Heaven and Earth). Besides its beloved church and chapel and famous Sunday market, Tlacolula is also renowned for *mescal.* Get a good free sample at friendly **Pensamiento** shop, on main street Juárez no. 9, as you head from the highway toward the market. Besides many hand-embroidered Amusgo *huipiles* and Teotitlán weavings, Pensamiento offers *mescal* in more than 20 flavors, with many more for women than men.

Just before the market, take a look inside the main town church, the 1531 **Parroquia de la Virgen de la Asunción.** Although its interior is distinguished enough, the real gem is its attached chapel, **Capilla del Señor de Tlacolula,** which you enter from the nave of the church. Every inch of the chapel's interior gleams with sculptures of angels and saints, paintings, and gold scrollwork. Notice the pair of floating angels, each holding a great pendulous solid silver censer, on opposite sides of the altar; also, admire the solid silver fence in front of the altar. Saints seem to live on in every corner of the chapel. Especially graphic are the martyrs, who reveal the way they died, such as a sorrowful San Sebastián, his body shot full of arrows, and a decapitated San Pablo, his head on the ground.

Ordinarily tranquil, the church grounds seem to nearly burst with faithful during the five-day **Fiesta del Santa Cristo de Tlacolula,** climaxing on the second Sunday of October, when the plaza is awash with merrymakers. It is then that folks enjoy their favorites, the **Danza de los Jardineros** (Dance of the Gardeners) and the spectacular **Danza de las Plumas** (Dance of the Feathers) along with a *pelota mixteca* (traditional Mixtec ball game) tournament.

The big gate bordering the church grounds leads you to the Tlacolula market. One of Oaxaca's biggest and oldest, the Tlacolula market draws tens of thousands from all over the Valley of Oaxaca every Sunday. Wander around and soak it all in—the diverse crowd of buyers and sellers, and the equally manifold galaxy of merchandise. How about a hand-hewn yoke for your oxen or a new stone *mano* and *metate* for your kitchen? If not, perhaps some live (or ground) *chapulines* (grasshoppers), maybe a live turkey for dinner tomorrow, or a hunk of sugarcane to chew on while you stroll along?

For **accommodations,** try the basic but clean downtown Tlacolula lodging, the **Hotel and Restaurant Calenda,** at Juárez 40, Tlacolula Oaxaca 70400, tel. 951/562-0660. They offer about 30 rooms with hot-water shower baths and fans in three floors around an interior restaurant courtyard. Rentals run about $10 s, $15 d, and $25 t. Their restaurant serves a wholesome country menu that, although specializing in barbecue *(barbacoa)* chicken *(pollo)*, goat *(chivo)*, or lamb *borrego*, offers many more hearty choices, such as pork chops, spaghetti, eggs, fish, and *chiles rellenos.*

YAGUL ARCHAEOLOGICAL ZONE

The regal remains of Yagul (Zapotec for Old Tree), open daily 10 A.M.–5 P.M., preside atop their volcanic hilltop, 28 miles (45 km) east of Oaxaca city. Although only six miles (10 km) from Mitla and sharing architectural details, such as Mitla's famous *greca* fretwork, the size and complexity of its buildings suggest that Yagul was an independent city-state in its own right. Local folks call the present ruin the Pueblo Viejo (Old Town) and remember it as the forerunner of the present town of Tlacolula. Archaeological evidence, which indicates that Yagul was occupied for about a thousand years, at least until around A.D. 1100 or 1200, bears them out.

One of Yagul's major claims to fame is its **Palace of Six Patios,** actually three nearly identical but separate complexes of two patios each. In each patio, rooms surround a central courtyard. The northerly patio of each complex is more private and probably was the residence, while the other, more open, patio served administrative functions.

South of the palace sprawls Yagul's huge **ball court,** the second largest in Mesoamerica, shaped in the characteristic Oaxaca I configuration. Southeast of the ball court is Patio 4, consisting of four mounds surrounding a courtyard. A boulder sculpted in the form of a frog lies at the base of the east mound. At the courtyard's center, a tomb was excavated; descend and explore its three *greca*-style, fretwork-decorated chambers.

If it's not too hot, gather your energy and climb to the hilltop above the parking lot for a fine view of the ruin and the entire Valley of Oaxaca. The name for this prominence, the Citadel, probably was accurately descriptive, for Yagul's defenders long ago added rock walls to enhance the hilltop's security.

The airy *palapa* **Restaurant Centeotl,** tel./fax 951/516-6186, tel. 951/512-0289, on the Yagul archaeological zone entrance road may be worth a stop, if only for a drink and a rest in the shade. Although once well-known for excellent cuisine, the restaurant seems to have fallen on hard times, and food freshness sometimes suffers. Open daily 11 A.M.–7 P.M.

As you leave, take a look at the pre-Columbian ball-game ring mounted by the restaurant entrance. Although the ring is interesting all by itself, the cannonball-size stone sphere perched atop the ring doubles the intrigue, since (if it's authentic, as the owner claims) a stone ball is in variance with general archaeological opinion that the pre-Columbian ball game was played with a rubber, rather than a rock ball. (Pity the pre-Columbian ball players who had to bat such a hard, heavy missile around with their arms, shoulders, and torsos.)

SAN BARTOLOMÉ QUIALANA AND SAN MARCOS TLAPAZOLA

For travelers hankering to explore beyond the usual tourist track, this pair of country villages makes for an interesting excursion, out from Tlacolula. These little places (which, on foot, are about two miles or 3.2 km apart) have their own unique set of enticements. Tlapazola women (not men) make attractive *barra rojo* (red pottery). Locally handcrafted textiles include characteristic black-and-white wool *cobijos* (blankets) and multicolored embroidered dresses and blouses. Other available handicrafts are reed baskets and *ixtle* (maguey fiber) nets. Local sights include Calvario, an unexcavated hilltop pyramid, and venerable village churches. The sylvan, oak-studded canyons of towering Cerro Piedra del Sol (elev. 9,600 feet, 2,850 meters) beckon, with hikes to a *cascada* (waterfall) and *manantiales* (springs).

Moreover, if you schedule your visit right, you'll get in on the country color and merrymaking of Quialana's **Fiesta de San Bartolomé** (four days around August 27) or Tlapazola's **Fiesta de San Marcos** (November 13).

For accommodations, you might check around to see if the local Yu'u (which at this writing were closed) have reopened. Guests at both the Quialana and Tlapazola Yu'u have enjoyed breezy hillside cornfield locations. The best time to stay is during the summer rains, when it's not too hot. The green corn rustles in the breeze, dogs bark faintly in the distance, clouds billow up over the lush valley and somber dark green mountains, and now and then a truck (or a loaded burro or oxcart) passes by. For more Yu'u information and reservations, contact the government alternative tourism office, at Murguia 206 (up the driveway, in the back), tel. 951/516-4828, sedetur5@oaxaca.gob.mx. (For more details, see Tourist Yu'u Community Lodging.)

Get to Quialana (pop. 2,500) by car, taxi, or bus and to Tlapazola (pop. 1,500) by either car, taxi, or passenger truck, all via Tlacolula. The route is via Calle Matamoros, which heads south from the middle of Tlacolula to both Quialana and Tlapazola. For Quialana, catch a taxi or the Transportes Municipal Quialana bus; for Tlapazola, catch the Servicios Mixto de Pasaje y Cargo small truck. If you catch the truck, be prepared to stand with the rest of the folks. For more comfort, splurge (maybe $3 or $4) for a taxi.

Drivers, turn into Tlacolula from Highway 190 at the Pemex gas station. Continue south, probably having to detour around the market. You will eventually reach the railroad tracks. Find Calle Matamoros, which crosses the tracks near the west end of town. Mark your odometer as you cross the tracks. Continue south for two miles (3.2 km) to a crossroads. For Quialana, continue straight ahead almost another mile (1.4 km) to the Quialana Tourist Yu'u. The town church and plaza are just short of a mile ahead uphill. For Tlapazola, turn right at the dirt crossroads at mile two (3.2 km) and continue another 2.8 miles (4.5 km) to the Tlapazola Tourist Yu'u, and another half mile (.8 km) past that to the town church and plaza.

MITLA

The ruins at Mitla, open daily 10 A.M.–5 P.M., about 31 miles (50 km) from Oaxaca city, are a "must" for Valley of Oaxaca sightseers. Mitla ("Liobaa" in Zapotec, the Place of the Dead) flowered late, reaching a population of perhaps 10,000 during its apex around A.D. 1350. The old city remained occupied and in use for generations after the conquest.

During Mitla's heyday, several feudalistic, fortified city-states vied for power in the Valley of Oaxaca. Concurrently, Mixtec-speaking people arrived from the north, perhaps under pressure from Aztecs and others in central Mexico. Evidence suggests that these Mixtec groups, interacting with the resident Zapotecs, created the unique architectural styles of late cities, such as Yagul and Mitla. Archaeologists believe, for example, that the striking *greca* (Greek-like) frets

MITLA ARCHAEOLOGICAL ZONE

CHURCH GROUP

MITLA CHURCH

PARKING

HANDICRAFTS STALLS

GATE

PALACE

ADOBE GROUP

COLUMN OF LIFE

SHRINE

COLUMNS GROUP

TOMBS

ARROYO GROUP

Arroyo

Mitla River

HOTEL AND RESTAURANT LA ZAPOTECA

SOUTH GROUP

FRISSELL MUSEUM

MITLA TOWN PLAZA

HOTEL AND RESTAURANT MITLA

To Mex. 190, Oaxaca, and Tehuantepec

0   100 yds
0   100 m

VALLEY OF OAXACA

© AVALON TRAVEL PUBLISHING, INC.

© BRUCE WHIPPERMAN

Archaeologists believe that the fretwork designs that decorate the monumental ruins at Mitla represent a fusion of Mixtec and Zapotec motifs.

that honeycomb Mitla facades resulted from the Mixtec influence.

Exploring the Site

In a real sense, Mitla lives on. The ruins coincide with the present town of San Pablo Villa de Mitla, whose main church was built on top of and still occupies the northernmost of five main groups of monumental ruins. Virtually anywhere archaeologists dig within the town they hit remains of the myriad ancient dwellings, tombs, and plazas, which connected the still-visible landmarks.

Of the five ruins clusters, the best preserved is the fenced-in **Columns Group.** Its exploration requires about an hour. The others—the Arroyo and Adobe Groups beyond an arroyo and the South Group across the Mitla River—are rubbled, unreconstructed mounds. Although the **North Group** has suffered due to past use by the local parish, it's well worth a visit. Evidence indicates the Adobe and South Groups were ceremonial compounds, while the Arroyo, North, and Columns Groups were palaces.

The public entrance to the Columns Group leads from the parking lot past a tourist market

and through the gate (open daily 9 A.M.–5 P.M.). Inside, two large patios, joined at one corner, are each surrounded on three sides by elaborate apartments. A shrine occupies the center of the first patio. Just north of this stands the **Palace of Columns,** the most important of Mitla's buildings. It sits atop a staircase inaccurately reconstructed in 1901.

Inside, a file of six monolithic columns supported the roof. A narrow **"escape" passage** exits out the right rear side to a large patio enclosed by a continuous narrow room. The purely decorative *greca* facades, which required around 100,000 cut stones for the entire complex, embellish the walls. Remnants of the original red and white stucco that decorated the entire complex hide in niches and corners.

Walk south to the second patio, which has a similar layout. Here, the main palace occupies the east side, where a passage descends to a **tomb,** beneath the front staircase. Both this and another tomb beneath the building at the north side of the patio are intact, preserving their original crucifix shapes. (The guard, although he is not supposed to, may try to collect a tip for letting you descend.) No one knows who or what were buried in these tombs, which were open and empty at the time of the conquest.

The second tomb is similar to the first, except that it contains a stone pillar called the **Column of Life;** by embracing it, legend says, you will learn how many years you have left.

The interesting **Church Group** (notice the church domes) is on the far north side of the Palace of Columns. Builders used the original temple stones to erect the church here. On its north side is a patio leading to another interior patio surrounded by another *greca*-decorated palace.

The Frissell Museum

The Frissell Museum, a block west of the town entrance road, by the Mitla town plaza, has been closed for several years due to earthquake damage. Thankfully, it is slated to be repaired and re-opened in the near future. Perhaps by the time you read this, its exceptionally fine artifact collection, including a host of finely preserved ceramic figurines, yet-to-be-deciphered Zapotec glyphs, and a Zapotec marriage certificate in stone, will again be on display.

Besides its collection, the museum's historic venerable hacienda-style home is notable in its own right. From the mid-19th century, as the **Posada La Sorpresa,** it served as a lodging, owned and operated by the longtime local Quero family. In 1950, they sold it to American artifact collector Ervin R. Frissell, who turned the hotel into both his home and a repository for his growing collection and that of his friend, Howard Leigh, noted scholar of Mixtec language and culture. Upon their deaths, the entire building and artifact collection passed to the University of the Americas.

Fiesta del Apóstol de San Pablo

Mitla (pop. 15,000), although famous, is a quiet town where tranquillity is disturbed only by occasional tourist buses along its dusty, sun-drenched main street. A major exception occurs during Mitla's key fiesta, which centers on the town's venerable 16th-century church, dedicated to San Pablo Apóstol (St. Paul the Apostle). If you plan

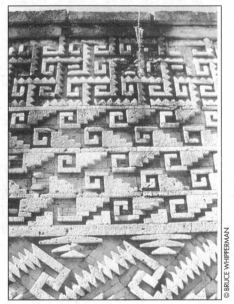

© BRUCE WHIPPERMAN

The unique stone fretwork at Mitla and other Oaxaca Valley archaeological sites is called *greca* for its resemblance to certain traditional Greek designs.

your visit during the eight days climaxing around January 25 (or also around June 29, the day of San Pablo and San Pedro), you can join with the townsfolk as they celebrate their *patrón* with masses, processions, a feast, fireworks, *jaripeo* (bull roping and riding), and dancing.

Accommodations and Food

Directly across the street from the Frissell Museum, stop for a refreshment at the homey **Hotel and Restaurant Mitla,** Benito Juárez 6, Mitla, Oaxaca 70430, tel. 951/568-0112, domain of the sparkplug mother-daughter team of Teresa and Gloria González de Quero. Here you can enjoy Mexico as old-timers remember it, in a charmingly ramshackle hacienda-style farmhouse, where roosters crow, dogs snooze, and where guests can have their seasonal fill of bananas, avocados, mandarins, and papayas from a shady backyard *huerta* (orchard). Their 16 rooms vary.

VALLEY OF OAXACA

Most rooms in the upstairs tier—plain but clean, with the essentials, including hot water—are acceptably rustic. Overnight rates run about $10 s, $17 d, with parking.

Alternatively, about five blocks north, closer to the archaeological zone, try the also family-run **Hotel and Restaurant La Zapoteca**, 5 de Febrero 12, Mitla, Oaxaca 70430, tel. 951/568-0026, open daily 7:30 A.M.–7 P.M., on the right just before the Mitla River bridge. The spic-and-span restaurant (praised by locals for "the best *chiles rellenos* in Oaxaca") is excellent for meals, and the 20 clean, reasonably priced rooms are fine for an overnight. Rentals run about $15 s, $20 d, $27 t, with hot water and parking.

Shopping

Instead of making handicrafts, Mitla people concentrate on selling them, mostly at the big **handicrafts market** adjacent to the archaeological zone parking lot. Here you can sample from a concentrated all-Oaxaca assortment, especially textiles: cotton *huipiles*, wool hangings and rugs, onyx animals and chess sets, fanciful *alebrijes*, and leather huaraches, purses, belts, and wallets.

Other Practicalities

High finance has come to Mitla via the Banco Internacional and ATM. Find them open approximately Mon.–Fri. 8 A.M.–7 P.M., Sat. 8 A.M.–3 P.M., on the main ingress street, 5 de Febrero, left side, on the way to the Mitla ruins.

Bus travelers can get to Mitla from Oaxaca by Fletes y Pasajes bus from the second-class bus terminal. Drivers get there by forking left from main Oaxaca Highway 190, at the big Mitla sign, onto Highway 176. Continue about two miles (3.2 km) to the Mitla town entrance, on the left. Head straight through town, pass the town plaza, continue across the (usually dry) Mitla River bridge, and after about a mile (1.6 km), arrive at the site.

HIERVE EL AGUA MINERAL SPRINGS

Although the name of this place translates as boiling water, the springs that seep from the side of the limestone mountain less than an hour's drive east of Mitla aren't hot. Instead, they are loaded with minerals. These minerals over time have built up into rock-hard deposits, forming great algae-painted slabs in level spots and, on steep slopes, accumulating into what appear to be grand frozen waterfalls.

The Springs

Although the springs may be crowded on weekends and holidays, you'll probably have Hierve el Agua nearly to yourself on weekdays. The first thing you'll see after passing the entrance gate is a lineup of snack and curio stalls at the cliff-side parking lot. A trail leads downhill to the main spring, which bubbles from the mountainside and trickles into a huge basin that the operators have dammed as a swimming pool. Bring your bathing suit.

Part of Hierve el Agua's appeal is the panoramic view of mountain and valley. On a clear day, you can see the tremendous massif of **Zempoatepetl** (saym-poh-ah-TAY-pehtl), the grand holy mountain range of the Mixe people, rising above the eastern horizon.

From the ridge-top park, agile walkers can hike farther down the hill, following deposits curiously accumulated in the shape of miniature limestone dikes that trace the mineral water's downhill path. Soon you'll glimpse a towering limestone formation, like a giant petrified waterfall, appearing to ooze from the cliff downhill straight ahead, on the right.

Back uphill by the parking lot, operators have augmented the natural springs with a resort-style swimming pool where, along with everyone else, you can frolic to your heart's content.

Hikers can also enjoy following a *sendero peatonal* (footpath) that encircles the entire zone. Start your walk, either from the trailhead beyond the bungalows past the pool or at the other end, at the cliff edge between the parking lot and the entrance gate. Your reward will be an approximately one-hour, self-guided tour, looping downhill past the springs and the great frozen rock cascades and featuring grand vistas of the gorgeous mountain and canyon scenery along the way.

The Hierve de Agua zone and surrounding country is habitat for a hardy dry-country **palm** you'll probably see plenty of while strolling around. Lack of winter-spring moisture usually keeps the palms small, sometimes clustering in great gardens, appearing like regiments of desert dwarfs. Local people gather and weave their fronds into *tenates* (baskets), *petates* (mats), *escobas* (brooms), and more, which they sometimes sell in the stalls by the parking lot.

Accommodations and Food
The Hierve el Agua Tourist Yu'u lodging provides the key for a restful one- or two-night stay. The several clean and well-maintained housekeeping bungalows, with shower baths and hot water, rent for about $7 per person, or around $40 for up to six in a bungalow, with refrigerator, stove, and utensils. Make reservations through the alternative tourism office in Oaxaca, Murguia 206 (up the driveway, in the back), tel. 951/516-4828, sedetur5@oaxaca.gob.mx, www.oaxaca.gob.mx/sedetur/alte.

For food, you can bring and cook your own in your bungalow or rely upon the strictly local-style beans, *carne asada* (roast meat), tacos, tamales, and tortillas offered by the parking-lot food stalls. In any case, fruit and vegetable lovers should bring their own from Oaxaca. Produce selection in local San Lorenzo village stores will most likely be minimal.

Getting There
Get there by riding an Ayutla-bound Fletes y Pasajes bus east out of either Oaxaca city (second-class terminal) or Mitla on Highway 179 just south of town. Get off at the Hierve el Agua side road, about 11 miles (18 km) past Mitla. Continue the additional five miles (8 km) by the local "San Lorenzo–Hierve el Agua"–marked bus.

Drivers, head east from Mitla along Highway 179, the road that branches east at the Mitla sign from Highway 190, two miles (3.2 km) before Mitla town. After another approximately 11 miles (18 km), follow the signed gravel side road that forks right another five miles (8 km), through San Lorenzo village to Hierve el Agua. *Warning:* Until they get around to paving it, the clay roadbed through San Lorenzo village and beyond is *extremely slippery* when wet with rain. Under such conditions, unless you're driving a good-traction four-wheel-drive vehicle, park your car in the village and walk the final quarter mile (.4 km), which steeply descends to the Hierve de Agua entrance.

South Side: The Crafts Route

Travelers who venture into the Valley of Oaxaca's long, south-pointing fingers, sometimes known as the Valleys of Zimatlán and Ocotlán, can discover a wealth of crafts, history, and architectural and scenic wonders. These are all accessible by day trips from the city by car or combinations of bus and taxi. Most reachable are the renowned crafts villages of Coyotepec, Tilcajete, Jalieza, and others along Highway 175, between the city and the colorful market town of Ocotlán (best to plan a visit to all on Friday, Ocotlán's market day). Another day, you can either continue farther south, off the tourist track, to soak in the feast of sights at the big market in Ejutla or fork southwest, via Highway 131 through Zimatlán, to the idyllic groves, crystal springs, and limestone caves hidden around San Sebastián de las Grutas.

SAN BARTOLO COYOTEPEC
San Bartolo Coyotepec (Hill of the Coyote), on Highway 175 14 miles (23 km) south of the city, is famous for its pottery and its August 24–27 festival. During the Fiesta de San Bartolomé, masked villagers costumed as half-man, half-woman in tiaras, blond wigs, tin crowns, and velvet cloaks dance in honor of their patron.

The town's black pottery, the renowned *barro negro* sold all over Mexico, is available at the signed pottery Mercado on the right and at a number of cottage factory shops (watch for signs) off the highway, scattered along (east side) Juárez Street. **Doña Rosa,** who passed away in 1980, pioneered the technique of crafting lovely, big, round jars without a potter's wheel. With their local clay, Doña Rosa's descendants and neighbor families regularly turn out acres of glistening black plates, pots, bowls, trees of life, and fetching animals for very reasonable prices. (Figure on about $20 for a pearly black, three-gallon vase, and perhaps $2 for a cute little black rabbit.)

Cochineal Farm

On your way either to or from Coyotepec and Ocotlán, you might want to stop at the small demonstration cochineal farm and museum, just off the highway at San Bartolo Coyotepec, a few miles south of the Oaxaca airport. The farm, officially the **Centro de Difusión del Conocimiento de la Grana Cochinilla Tlapanochestli,** is the labor of love of retired chemical engineer Ignacio J. del Río Dueñas. Señor Dueñas graciously welcomes all visitors—schoolchildren, visiting scholars, neighbors, tourists—to his rancho for the purpose of breathing life into the ancient Oaxaca tradition of cochineal dye, the source of the bright reds in many of the Oaxaca weavings. (See the sidebar "Cochineal—Nature's Richest Red Dye" in the Introduction.)

Others besides Señor Dueñas believe in cochineal and support its use as a natural dye. It is produced from the bodies of the scale insect, *Dactylopius coccus,* which thrives on the thick leaves of the nopal (prickly pear) cactus, found all over Mexico and much of the western United States. Precisely *because* cochineal is a natural (as opposed to synthetic) product, it is gaining favor as a natural food and cosmetic (lipstick) coloring. The small amount of cochineal that Señor Dueñas produces sells for about $200 per kilogram (compared with silver, at about $100).

He'll be happy to show you around his acre of cactus, demonstrate how the insects are harvested, and explain his several interesting museum exhibits, which illustrate the history and uses of cochineal. For more information, contact Señor Dueñas at Rancho La Nopalera, Km 10.5 Carretera Oaxaca–Puerto Ángel, Santa María

Coyotepec, Oaxaca, tel./fax 951/551-0003, tlapanochestli@infosel.net.mx.

Get there by bus from the *camionera segunda clase,* via regional buses Estrella del Valle, Oaxaca Pacifico, or Estrella Roja del Sureste, or more local Choferes del Sur buses.

By car, turn right, southbound, at the small red roadside sign Grana Cochineal Tlapanochestli at the southern edge of Santa María Coyotepec village, on Highway 175 4.7 miles (7.5 km) south of the Oaxaca airport. After a few hundred yards westbound on a dirt road, another sign directs you left to the rancho.

CRAFTS VILLAGES ON THE ROAD TO OCOTLÁN

Each of the three little crafts villages not far north of Ocotlán has something unique to offer. In order to visit all of them, plus Coyotopec and Ocotlán, on Friday, you'll need to get an

San Antonino Castillo Velasco women embroider the famous "Oaxaca wedding dresses."

early start. If you're inclined to linger, it's best to allow two days for your visit. Under any circumstances, visit **San Antonino Castillo Velasco** on the same Friday that you visit Ocotlán, because it also has its *tianguis* (indigenous market) on Friday. Two things to look for are the wonderful **breads,** fresh and yummy, as you come into town, and the famous *vestidos de San Antonino,* sometimes known as "Oaxaca wedding dresses," marked by their elaborately fancy and colorful animal and floral embroidery. On Friday, a few women sell them in the regular market (turn left at the first block after the bread stalls). If you arrive and no one seems to be selling any dresses, mention *"vestidos de San Antonino,"* and someone will lead you to a woman who makes them. Alternatively, ask for friendly Rosa Canseco Godines (go-DEE-nays) (Calle Guerrero 33), one of the local *maestras* of the craft. If she's home, she'll gladly show you examples of her beautiful work.

Bus passengers, take a taxi or walk the mile (1.6 km) from Ocotlán. Drivers, turn west (left, northbound) at the San Antonino sign just at the northern (Oaxaca) edge of Ocotlán.

San Martín Tilcajete, about 21 miles (37 km) south of Oaxaca (not far north of the Highway 131 fork), and **Santo Tomás Jalieza** (south of the Highway 131 fork) a mile or two farther south, can be visited as a pair on any day. San Martín is one of the sources (besides Arrazola) of the *alebrijes,* fanciful wooden creatures occupying the shelves of crafts stores the world over.

Dozens of factory-stores sprinkle the whole town. Start on the front main street, but also be sure to wander the back lanes and step into several cottage workshops, whose occupants will be happy to show you what they have and demonstrate how they make them. You'll find lots more than funny animals. Artisans have branched out to plants, such as purple palm trees and yellow cactus. Some items, such as imaginatively painted jewel boxes and picture frames, are practical, while others, such as miniature sets of tables and chairs, are for kids 3–90.

Jalieza, on the other hand, is known as the town of embroidered *cinturones* (belts). Townsfolk, virtually all of whom practice the craft,

pots on display at the market in Ocotlán

concentrate all of their selling in a single many-stalled market in the middle of town. Step inside and you'll be tempted, not only by hundreds of hand-embroidered leather belts, but by a wealth of lovely hand-loomed and embroidered purses, shawls, small backpacks, and much more. Furthermore, asking prices are very reasonable. Open daily about 10 A.M.–6 P.M.

OCOTLÁN

Your first stop in district capital Ocotlán (pop. 20,000; 26 miles, 42 km south of Oaxaca) should probably be the interesting trio of shops run by the Aguilar sisters, Irene, Guillerma, and Josefina. Watch for their signs, on the right, on the outskirts, about a quarter mile (.4 km) on the Oaxaca side from the town plaza. Their creations include a host of fanciful figures in clay: vendors with big ripe strawberries, green and red cactus, goats in skirts, and bikini-clad blondes.

VALLEY OF OAXACA

BUILDING CHURCHES

Although European architects designed nearly all of Mexico's colonial-era churches, embellishing them with old-world Gothic, Renaissance, baroque, and Moorish decorations, native artists blended their own geometric, floral, and animal motifs. The result was a hybrid that manifested in intriguing variations all over Mexico. This was especially true in Oaxaca, where droves of faithful worship before gilded altars and flowery ceilings built and decorated by their long-gone ancestors. Local materials further distinguish Oaxacan churches from others in Mexico. The spectrum of soft pastels of local *cantera* volcanic stone, from yellow through gray, including green in Oaxaca city, marks Oaxacan walls and facades.

Sometimes the native influence led to poor ("provincial") versions of European designs; other times (notably, the Templo y Exconvento de Santo Domingo in Oaxaca city), artists merged brilliant native decorations with the best of European-style vaults, arches, and columns.

THE LAYOUT

Mexican church design followed the Egypto-Greco-Roman tradition of its European models. Basically, architects designed their churches beginning with the main space of the **nave,** in the shape of a box, lined with high lateral windows. Depending on their origin and function, the churches fit into three basic groups—the monk's **monastery or convent** *(convento),* the bishop's **cathedral** *(catedral),* and the priest's parish church *(templo, parroquia).* Most Oaxacan monastic churches (nearly all now ex-convents) were begun during the 16th and 17th centuries by the missionary orders—a handful by the Franciscans, Jesuits, and Augustinians, and the overwhelming remainder by the Dominicans.

In Oaxaca, faced with the constant threat of earthquake, the Dominican padres built massively

Solomonic columns are attractive but unusual embellishments in the facades of colonial-era Oaxacan churches, such as the Templo de Santa Catarina in Santa Catarina Ixtepeji.

thick walls supported on the exterior with ponderous buttresses. Key elements were naves, with or without **transepts** *(cruceros),* cross spaces separating the nave from the altar, making the church layout resemble a Christian cross. They placed the **choir** *(coro)* above and just inside the entrance arch.

At the opposite, usually the east (or sunrise) end of the church, builders sometimes extended the nave beyond the transept to include a **presbytery** *(presbiterio),* which was often lined with seats where church officials presided. The building ended past that at the **apse** *(ábside)*, the space behind the altar, frequently in semi-circular or half-octagonal form. Within the apse rose the gilded **retable** *(retablo)* adorned with sacred images, attended by choirs of angels and cherubs.

Larger churches usually incorporated side altars presided over by images of locally popular saints, nearly always including the Virgin of Guadalupe.

THE FACADE

Outside, in front, rises the facade *(fachada)*, sometimes in a uniform style, but just as often a mixture of Renaissance, Gothic, and baroque, with some Moorish *(mujedar)* worked into the mix. A proliferation of columns nearly always decorates Oaxacan church facades, from the classic Etruscan, Doric, Ionic, and Corinthian *(Toscano, Dórico, Jónico, Corintio)* pillars to spiraled Solomonic *(Salomónico)* barber's poles and bizarre *estipites*. *Estipite* columns, a baroque feature of Plateresque facades (so-named for their resemblance to elaborate silverware designs), usually begin with a classical capital (base) but rise, curiously, like an inverted obelisk, widening to a pair or trio of elaborately carved prismatic blocks and narrowing quickly again to an identical capital at the top.

CONVENTS

The monastery- (or convent-) style churches, besides all of the above, included living and working quarters for the members of the order, typically built around a columned patio called the **cloister** *(claustro)*. A corridor through an arched porch *(portería)* adjacent to the nave usually leads to the cloister, from which monks and nuns could quickly reach the dining hall, or **refectory** *(refectorio)*, and their private rooms, or cells *(celdas)*.

The Oaxacan missionary fathers always designed their churches with an eye to handling the masses of natives whom they hoped to convert. For them, padres included an **atrium** *(atrio)*, a large exterior courtyard in front of the facade. For the partly initiated natives, they often built an open chapel *(capilla abierta)* on one side of the atrium. Conversions also occurred at smaller open chapels *(pozas)*, built at the corners of the atrium.

OAXACA STANDOUTS

Outstanding examples (nearly all Dominican) of Oaxaca church architecture are scattered throughout the state, notably, in the following locations:

Oaxaca City
Church and Ex-convent of Santo Domingo
Church and Ex-convent of San Agustín
Church of San Felipe Neri
Cathedral of Oaxaca
Basilica and Ex-convent of Nuestra Señora de la Soledad

Valley of Oaxaca
Cuilapan
Tlacochahuaya
Tlacolula
Ocotlán

Mixteca
Teotongo
Tamazulapan
Tejupan
Coixtlahuaca
Teposcolula
San Juan Teposcolula

Northern Oaxaca
Ixtlán de Juárez
Calpulalpan
Santa Catarina Ixtepeji

Isthmus
Tehuantepec
Juchitán

The main Ocotlán attraction (unless you're lucky enough to arrive for the big fiesta on the third Sunday of May) is the huge Friday market. Beneath a riot of colored awnings, hordes of merchandise—much modern stuff, but also plenty of old-fashioned goodies—load a host of tables and street-laid mats. How about a saddle for your donkey? If not that, why not four or five turkeys, a goat, or perhaps half a dozen bags of hard-to-get wild medicinal plants? And be sure to pick up a kilo or two of *cal* (lime or quicklime) for soaking your corn. If you're looking for lots of native costumes, you'll have to head for the mountains, because few women (except for their ribbon-decorated braids) and virtually no men wear *traje*. You'll hear plenty of Zapotec, however. At least half of the local people are native speakers.

Since markets are best in the morning, best make Ocotlán your *first* Friday stop. Drivers could get there by heading out straight south from the city, arriving in Ocotlán by midmorning. Spend a few hours, then begin your return in the early afternoon, stopping at the several crafts villages along the road back to Oaxaca. Gasoline is available at the Pemex *gasolinera*, on the highway, on the north edge of Ocotlán.

Bus travelers could hold to a similar schedule by riding an early Autobuses Estrella del Valle or Autotransportes Oaxaca-Pacífico from the second-class Abastos bus terminal, then returning, in steps, by bus, or more quickly by taxi, stopping at the crafts villages along the way.

The late celebrated artist Rudolfo Morales financed the renovation of many Oaxaca public buildings, including the 16th-century Templo de Santo Domingo in his hometown, Ocotlán.

© BRUCE WHIPPERMAN

VALLEY OF OAXACA

Casa de Cultura Rudolfo Morales

During the 1980s and 1990s, Ocotlán came upon good times, largely due to the late Rudolfo Morales, the internationally celebrated but locally born artist, who dedicated his fortune to improving his hometown. The Rudolfo Morales Foundation has been restoring churches and other public buildings, reforesting mountainsides, and funding self-help and educational projects all over Ocotlán and its surrounding district. The bright colors of the plaza-front *presidencia municipal* and the big church nearby result from the good works of Rudolfo Morales.

Morales Foundation's local efforts radiate from the Casa de Cultura Rudolfo Morales, in the yellow-painted mansion at Morelos 108, three doors north from the Ocotlán plaza's northwest corner, tel. 951/571-0198. In the Casa Cultura's graceful, patrician interior, the Morales family and staff manage their foundation's affairs, teach art and computer classes, and sponsor community events.

The Foundation staff also welcome visitors, Mon.–Fri., 10 A.M.–2 P.M. and 4–8 P.M. For advance information, log on to www.artedeoaxaca.com, or contact the foundation's headquarters in Oaxaca city, at Murguia 105, Oaxaca, Oaxaca 68000, between Alcalá and 5 de Mayo, open Mon.–Fri. 10 A.M.–2 P.M. and 5–8 P.M. and Sat. 10 A.M.–2 P.M., tel. 951/514-2324 or 951/514-0910, galeria@artedeoaxaca.com.

Templo de Santo Domingo

Local people celebrate Rudolfo Morales's brilliant restoration of their beloved 16th-century Templo de Santo Domingo. Gold and silver from the infamous mines at Santa Catarina Minas, in the mountains east of Ocotlán, financed the church's initial construction. When overwork and disease had tragically decimated the local native population by around 1600, the mines had to be abandoned, and work on the church stopped. Although eventually completed over the succeeding three centuries, it had slipped into serious disrepair by the 1980s.

Fortunately, the Templo de Santo Domingo is now completely rebuilt, from its bright blue, yellow, and white facade to the baroque gold glitter of its nave ceiling. Inside on the right side, you'll pass a pious Saint John the Baptist, with Mary Magdalen at his feet. Up front, above the main altar, a white-haired, bearded Creator reigns, resembling an indigenous Father Sun, with a halo of golden rays bursting from behind his head. Below him, Jesus hangs limply on the cross, flanked below by Mother Mary with a knife in her breast and St. John the Baptist lamenting at Jesus' feet.

Walk to the nave's south (right) side, to a gilded chapel, dedicated to the Lord of the Sacristy, the image above the altar. Also notice the adjacent oil painting of the Virgin of the Rosary, singular for her mestizo facial features. The Lord of the Sacristy (Señor de la Sacristía) is the object of community adoration in a festival of food, fireworks, processions, high masses, and dances climaxing on the third Sunday in May.

EJUTLA

Tour buses usually skip Ejutla de Crespo (pop. 20,000) because of its distance, about 36 miles (59 km) from Oaxaca city. This is a pity, because Ejutla (ay-HOOT-lah) hides some surprises, not the least of which is its huge, colorful **Thursday market.** Folks troop in from country villages all over the huge Ejutla governmental district and farther, to haggle over everything from *hamacas* and huaraches to radios and refrigerators.

Sights

Take a walk around Ejutla's shady plaza to get your bearings. The portico-fronted *presidencia municipal* stands on the plaza's south side; the market is on the north; and the big, proud **Templo de la Natividad** stands on the west. Sometime around 1750, the present church replaced the 16th-century original (which itself replaced a big pre-conquest Zapotec pyramid). Over the years, earthquakes took their toll; it was extensively restored around 1900.

Several large hieroglyph-decorated stones built into the church's walls attest to the fact that the entire town remains an unexplored archaeological zone. You can find more evidence of this about two blocks north and two blocks east of the church, near the corner of Calles Altimirano and 16 de Septiembre. A big house compound encloses what appears to be a small hill, which is actually a buried temple-topped pyramid. Look for the several hieroglyph-decorated pre-conquest stones that have been incorporated into modern walls.

Since the church is usually open, you might as well step into the cool interior and contemplate the town's patron, the **Virgin of the Nativity,** presiding above the altar in what at first glance appears to be a bridal gown. In the lovely transept chapel on the right of the nave, you'll see another image of the same patron. Local people celebrate both, with a big fiesta centering around December 8.

For something else interesting, step over to the *presidencia* and look on the wall for Ejutla's official *escudo* (coat of arms), which incorporates no arms at all. It's a portrait in tile of a bean vine, encircling a view of the sun rising from behind a likeness of Cerro El Labrador, the town's sacred mountain, towering in the east. A poem, in praise of the "SUN, which rises here earlier than other lands . . . the source of life . . . without which there would be nothing" is included at the base of the *escudo*.

Practicalities

Another of Ejutla's surprises is the **Hotel 6,** Km 61.5 Carretera Oaxaca-Puerto Ángel, Ejutla de Crespo, Oaxaca, tel. 951/573-0350, "probably the best in North America," claims the

VALLEY OF OAXACA

owner-operator, friendly former Olympic wrestler and civil engineer Mario E. Corres. A sign, which strikingly resembles Motel 6 signs all over the United States and Canada, draws you into the parking lot. You know you're in for something unique when you pull up to a portaled, old hacienda as big as a baseball field, with a jungle on one side, complete with tree house and a swinging rope walkway.

Inside, you'll find everything completely in order, from three spreading courtyards, a pool, and two big function rooms to a huge living room, a dining room, and a spotless, shining, old-fashioned kitchen. The climax to all this is Señor Corres's museum, complete with his family tree, which he gladly explains to visitors.

The 14 rooms, which after everything else seem an afterthought, are plain but clean. Some are more inviting than others. Take a look at two or three, small and large, before choosing. If the weather's warm, you'll need a fan, which some rooms have. For all this, rates are only $20 s or d, $30 t, with parking, hot-water shower baths, and an elegantly homey dining room.

You'll encounter most of Ejutla's services during your stroll around town—most of the available stores and institutions are right on or near the plaza. Starting at the *presidencia municipal,* on the south and moving clockwise, first comes **Telecomunicaciones,** which offers telegraph, money order service, and fax, under the portal just west of the *presidencia.*

On the southwest plaza corner is the town's best, **Restaurant Mary,** where a squad of hardworking teenage girls serve hearty country food daily 8 A.M.–7 P.M.

From there, down the street south, at the first corner away from the plaza, is the **bus station** where first- and second-class Autotransportes Oaxaca-Pacífico and Autobuses Estrella del Valle will take you anywhere along Highway 175 between Puerto Ángel and the City of Oaxaca. On the same street, a short block west from the bus station is the *correo* (post office). Switch back to the Restaurant Mary and walk west away from the plaza to **Farmacia San Antonio and Clínica Urgencias** with Dr. Lorenzo Antonio Elorza. Go to the northwest plaza corner and you'll see the Casa

Altamirano **grocery store** *(abarrotería)* and half a block east of that, the open-air **market,** where you can get the fresh items that the grocery store doesn't have. Continuing north, at the street corner, is the *huarachería* **La Principal,** with a huge assortment of down-home footwear, nearly all made on-site by the owner's daughter. One short block behind (north) that is the **Clínica San Gabriel,** with a gynecologist and a general practitioner-surgeon on call 24 hours, tel. 951/573-0244. If you need another *farmacia* (pharmacy) you have your choice of the Santa Fe, on the northeast side, and the Liliana, east of the plaza, next to the church. **Gasoline** is available at the highway Pemex *gasolinera* at the north edge of town.

DOWN HIGHWAY 131
Zimatlán
Travelers who head far enough along Highway 131, which branches west about 22 miles (35 km) south of the city through the Oaxaca Valley's southwest side, are in for more than just one treat. They pass some of Oaxaca's most productive farmland: lush fields and pastures that in summer and fall appear like a verdant carpet reaching to the foot of pine- and oak-studded mountains.

Zimatlán (pop. about 25,000), the capital of all this, appears simply as a workaday agricultural town, with a modicum of strictly local-style services. Zimatlán's pace quickens, however, on Wednesday, when the town market overflows with a flood of Zapotec buyers and sellers from the surrounding mountains. Excitement peaks during the eight days around January 15, when folks celebrate the unique **Fiesta del Dulce Nombre de Jesús.** Keeping by their traditional ways, townspeople enjoy old-fashioned events, including processions, a big everyone-invited barbecue, *jaripeo* (bull mounting), and the Danza de las Plumas (Feathers) and Danza de los Jardineros (Gardeners), plus a *pelota mixteca* pre-conquest ball-game tournament.

San Sebastián de las Grutas
It's hard not to fall in love with this idyllic hidden corner of the Valley of Oaxaca. Don't be put off by the scruffy, tourist-*comedor*-cluttered

Highway 131 right turnoff intersection, 45 miles (73 km) south of Oaxaca city. After a quarter mile (.4 km) toward the *grutas* (caves), the road becomes a gently winding, sylvan creekside drive. The jade-green brook (sometimes muddy in wet season) gurgles downhill over little rocks and giant boulders, pausing here and there in picture-perfect swimming holes. Meanwhile, from overhead, a regal host of towering, gnarled *sabinos (tules* or *ahuehuetes)* shades the creek, appearing every bit as ancient and grand as their northern cousins, the California redwoods. Now and then, you pass by the rustic wooden homes and the cornfields of the local farm families. Or you might glimpse the big cylindrical fermentation vats of a rough-and-ready roadside *mescal* factory.

About eight miles (13 km) past San Sebastián de las Grutas town (pop. 2,000) you reach the caves. The creek emerges clear and pristine, as if by magic, from beneath a big rock at the foot of a mountain. There are modern-standard tourist Yu'u cabins.

A hundred yards uphill are the caves, which you can tour for a fee of about $1. A guide with a pair of strong flashlights will lead you on an easy, mostly level walk through the cave's several chambers, which vary from about 20 feet (six meters) to more than 200 feet (60 meters) in height. He's used to getting a tip of about $2 per person.

The cave you will see is only one of the several partly explored caves honeycombing the mountain, Cerro Cruz del Lado. Its five or six main chambers stretch about 500 yards (about .5 km) into the mountain. Inside, the formations, which include many towering stalagmites and plenty of bulging stalactites, initially appear, in the semi-darkness of the flickering flashlights, to be gargantuan mounds and columns of half-melted vanilla-chocolate-swirl ice cream. However, when your eyes get accustomed to the darkness, most of the formations, more than any cave I've ever seen, take on fanciful shapes. Bring your own flashlight and have fun dreaming up your own interpretations instead of merely seeing the guide's camel, turtle, shark, alligator (which looked like a seal to me), or tiger.

© BRUCE WHIPPERMAN

Spectacular stalagmites and stalactites adorn the limestone caves that honeycomb the mountains near San Sebastián de las Grutas.

Practicalities: One could spend several enjoyable days hiking, bird-watching, swimming in the creek, sitting in the town plaza, and getting to know the local people. They're generally friendly, having seen enough visitors so that they're not afraid and don't think you're too strange. The shady streamside, moreover, appears ripe for camping, either in your tent or (self-contained) RV. Get permission first from the tourist Yu'u manager or the municipal authorities at the presidencia in San Sebastián de las Grutas, a mile (1.6 km) downstream from the cave parking lot.

Alternatively, you can stay in one of the three clean, six-person tourist Yu'u units, for about $6 per person per night, with beds, blankets, showers, hot water, and furnished kitchenette. Bring your own towels, soap, and food from Oaxaca city or Zimatlán. Local supplies may be severely limited. Although reservations are not generally necessary, best reserve anyway, through the government alternative tourism office,

VALLEY OF OAXACA

Murguia 206 (up the driveway, in the back), tel. 951/516-4828, sedetur5@oaxaca.gob.mx, www.oaxaca.gob.mx/sedetur/alte.

A number of downscale eating stands near the caves sell basic local meals, which, if hot, should be wholesome. Water, drinkable directly from the pristine spring source by the caves, is not a problem here.

Get there by bus via the Solteca or Estrella Rojo del Sureste bus from the *camionera central segunda clase* (second-class bus terminal) next to the Abastos market on the southwest side of Oaxaca city. The Solteca buses, some of which go right to the caves, leave several times a day, beginning around 6 A.M. The Estrella Rojo del Sureste may only drop you at the intersection, eight miles (13 km) from the caves. Walk or take a taxi from there. Drivers, follow Highway 131, a total of 53 miles (76 km) south of Oaxaca city. Allow about two hours' driving time. In the reverse, north direction, the *grutas* are 119 miles (190 km) north of Puerto Escondido. For safety, under the best of conditions, allow about four hours of daylight driving time.

Sola de Vega

San Miguel Sola de Vega (pop. 13,000), diminutive capital of the remote, sprawling governmental district of the same name, is the main service stop on Oaxaca–Puerto Escondido Highway 131. The town, 59 miles (95 km) south of Oaxaca (99 miles, 159 km, north of Puerto Escondido), presides over a lush mountain valley checkerboard of corn, cane, and cattle. The lovely *sabino*-shaded Sola de Vega river ripples right past the town, crossed by quaint but practical suspension footbridges. It looks as if the people have plenty of fun, spending about half their time in the water. Camping by tent or RV appears promising in shady spots by the river. Get permission from authorities at the *presidencia municipal* at the town plaza, about three blocks north from the highway.

If you arrive on Sunday, Sola de Vega's traditional market day, be sure to visit the local *tianguis* (native market) around the town plaza, three blocks north of the highway.

Practicalities: A few stores near the plaza can supply basic groceries. For cooked food, try one of the many country comedores by the highway or, if you prefer, the dining room of the plain but clean Hotel Aguirre, on the highway. Its 15 rooms, in three floors, rent for about $12 s, $15 d, $25 t, with hot-water showers. Although you will not generally need a reservation, you can contact the hotel at tel. 951/574-0046 or 951/574-0047.

Drivers, fill up with gasoline at the Pemex station on the north side of town, since gasoline is likely to be scarce between Puerto Escondido and Oaxaca. For other essential services, you have the *correo* and *telégrafo* by the plaza, a *centro de salud* on Independencia, off the plaza, and a private physician, Dr. Vicente Mendoza Martinez, also on Independencia. For nonprescription medicines and phone calls, go to the *farmacia-caseta larga distancia* San Miguel, right on the highway at the south (Puerto Escondido) end of town. Also on the highway you'll find the Solteca and Estrella Roja del Sureste bus stations.

SOUTHWEST SIDE

Zaachila

About 10 miles (16 km) south of Oaxaca, Zaachila (pop. 30,000), like Mitla, overlies the ruins of its ancient namesake city, which rose to prominence after the decline of Monte Albán. Although excavations have uncovered many Mixtec-style remains, historical records nevertheless list a number of Zapotec kings who ruled Zaachila as a virtual Zapotec capital. On the eve of the conquest, a Mixtec noble minority dominated the Zapotec-speaking inhabitants, whose leaders the Mixtec warriors had sent fleeing for their lives to Tehuantepec.

The big forested hill that rises north of the market plaza is topped by a large, mostly unexplored pyramid. Several unexcavated mounds and courtyards dot the hill's north and south flanks. The site parking lot and entrance gate are adjacent to the colonial church just north of the plaza.

In 1962, archaeologist Roberto Gallegos (guarded from hostile residents by armed soldiers) uncovered a pair of unopened tombs beneath the summit of the Zaachila pyramid. They yielded a trove of polychrome pottery, gold jewelry (including a ring still on a left hand), and jade fan handles. Tomb 1, which is open for public inspection, descends via a steep staircase to an entrance decorated with a pair of cat-motif heads. On the antechamber walls a few steps farther on are depictions of owls and a pair of personages (perhaps former occupants) inscribed respectively with the name-dates 5-Flower and 9-Flower. Do not miss the bas-reliefs on the tomb's back wall (take a flashlight), which depict a man whose torso is covered with a turtle shell and another whose head is emerging from a serpent body.

Hint: The narrow tomb staircase is negotiable by only a few persons at a time and often requires an hour for a tour-bus crowd to inspect it. Rather than waste your market time standing in line, go downhill, stroll around the market, and return when the line is smaller. If driving, arrive early, around 9 A.M. on Thursday, to avoid tour-bus crowds. Return in early afternoon, allowing time to visit Cuilapan and Arrazola.

As for food, perhaps the most highly recommended restaurant in town is **Restaurant La Capilla.** Alternatively, wholesome (make sure you get it served hot) country fare is available at the regiment of permanent *fondas* (food stalls) in the market.

Get to Zaachila by second-class **Autobuses de Oaxaca** bus, from the second-class bus terminal, or by private tourist bus. (See the Getting Around section for details.)

By car from Oaxaca city, head south from downtown to the *periférico* (peripheral boulevard). Do not continue south via the airport Highway 131-175. Instead, from the *periférico* a block west of the airport highway intersection, follow the four-lane boulevard that angles left, away from the *periférico,* in a westerly direction, across the Atoyac River bridge. Just after crossing the bridge, do not continue straight ahead toward Monte Albán, but fork left (south) onto the Zaachila road.

Cuilapan de Guerrero and Arrazola

Southwest of Oaxaca city, between Zaachila and Arrazola, Cuilapan de Guerrero is famous for its elaborate but unfinished **Exconvento de Santiago,** or Saint James (visible from the highway), where Vicente Guerrero, father of the Mexican republic, was infamously executed in 1831. Although begun in 1535, the cost of the basilica and associated monastery began to balloon. In 1550, King Philip demanded humility and moderation of the builders, whose work was finally ended by a 1570 court ruling. The extravagances—the soaring, roofless basilica, magnificent baptismal font, splendid Gothic cloister, and elaborate frescoes—remain as national treasures.

Arrazola, a few miles farther north, toward Oaxaca, is one of the sources of the intricately painted *alebrijes* (ah-lay-BREE-hays)—fanciful wooden creatures that decorate the shelves of handicrafts shops all over Mexico and foreign countries. Bus travelers, get there either by second-class bus or by tourist bus from the city. Drivers, turn west (left) onto signed Highway 145 a few miles north of Cuilapan or, traveling south, 3.2 miles (5.1 km) south of the Atoyac River Bridge in Oaxaca city. Pass through San Javier village and continue from the turnoff a total of three miles (5 km) to the Arrazola town plaza. Turn right immediately before the plaza onto Calle E. Zapata and turn left after one block, at Independencia. After one more block you will be at Calle Obregón, where everyone seems to be making *alebrijes.* Although you should visit a number of family workshops along the street, be sure to visit **Pepe Santiago** and his Santa's workshop of craftspeople. Inside the Santiago compound (on the right, just below the hilltop), men saw and carve away while a cadre of young women painstakingly add riots of painted brocade to everything from whimsical dragons and gargoyles to armadillos, giraffes, and rabbits.

West Side: The Archaeological Route

Although all of these interesting destinations are readily reachable from Oaxaca city, they are far too rich to be visited in a single day. As a minimum, be sure to visit Monte Albán, which can be conveniently combined with a side trip to Atzompa. On another day, preferably a Wednesday, visit the Etla market, with stops at the community museums and key archaeological sites at El Mogote and Suchilquitongo nearby.

MONTE ALBÁN

Monte Albán ranks among Mesoamerica's most regal and spectacular ruined cities. The original Zapotec name was Danni Dipaa. The lable "Monte Albán" was probably coined by a local Spaniard because of its resemblance to a similarly named Italian hilltop town.

Monte Albán's original inhabitants cultivated beans, chilies, corn, fruits, and squash on the hillsides and in adjacent valleys, occasionally feasting on meat from deer, small game, and perhaps (as did other pre-conquest Mexicans) domesticated dogs. Tribute from surrounding communities directly enriched Monte Albán's ruling classes, and, by extension, its artisans and farmers.

The great city atop the hill reigned for at least 1,200 years, between 500 B.C. and A.D. 750, as the capital of the Zapotecs and the dominant force between Teotihuacán in the Valley of Mexico and the Maya empires of the south. Archaeologists have organized the Valley of Oaxaca's history from 500 B.C. to the conquest into five periods, known as Monte Albán I–V. Over those centuries, the hilltop city was repeatedly reconstructed with new walls, plazas, and staircases, which, like layers of an onion, now overlie earlier construction.

Remains from Monte Albán Period I (500 B.C.–A.D. 1) reveal an already advanced culture, with gods, permanent temples, a priesthood, a written language, numerals, and a calendar. Sharply contrasting house styles indicate a differentiated, multilayered society. Monte Albán I ruins abound in graceful polychrome ceramics of uniquely Zapotec style.

Concurrent Olmec influences have also been found, notably in the buildings known as the Danzantes (Dancers), decorated with unique bas-reliefs similar to those unearthed along the Veracruz and Tabasco coasts.

Monte Albán II people (A.D. 1–300), by contrast, came under heavy influence from Chiapas and Guatemala in the south. They built strange, ship-shaped buildings, such as Monte Albán's Building J, and left unique remains of their religion, such as the striking jade bat-god now on display in the Anthropology Museum in Mexico City.

Monte Albán reached its apex during Period III (A.D. 300–800), attaining a population of perhaps 40,000 in an urban zone of about three square miles (eight sq. km), which spread along hilltops (including the El Gallo and Atzompa archaeological sites) southwest of the present city of Oaxaca.

Vigorous Period III leaders rebuilt the main hilltop complex as we see it today. Heavily influenced by the grand style of the Teotihuacán structures in the Valley of Mexico, the buildings were finished with handsome sloping staircases, corniced walls, monumental carvings, ball courts, and hieroglyph-inscribed stelae depicting gods, kings, and heroic scenes of battle.

By A.D. 750, few foreign influences were continuing to enrich Monte Albán's uniquely Zapotec pottery styles. Quality declined until they seemed like mere factory copies. Concurrently, the Zapotec pantheon expanded to a horde of gods, as if mere numbers could protect the increasingly isolated Valley of Oaxaca from the outside world.

In A.D. 800, Monte Albán, mysteriously cut off from the rest of Mesoamerica, was declining in population and power. By A.D. 1000, the city was virtually abandoned. The reasons—whether drought, disease, or revolt—and the consequent loss of the necessarily imported water, wood, salt, and food supplies remain an enigma.

During Periods IV and V, Mixtec peoples from the north invaded the Valley of Oaxaca. They warred with valley Zapotecs and despite their relatively small numbers, became a ruling class in a number of valley city-states. The blend of Mixtec and Zapotec art and architecture sometimes led to new forms, especially visible at the west valley sites of Yagul and Mitla.

Monte Albán, meanwhile, although abandoned, was not forgotten. It became both a refuge and a venerated burial place. In times of siege, local people retreated within the walls of a fortress built around Monte Albán's South Platform. At other times, Mixtec nobles opened tombs and reused them as burial vaults right up until the eve of the conquest.

Exploring the Site

Visitors to Monte Albán enjoy a panoramic view of green mountains rising above the checkerboard of the Valley of Oaxaca. Monte Albán is fun for a picnic; alternatively, it is an auspicious place to perch atop a pyramid above the grand Main Plaza, etched by lengthening afternoon shadows, and contemplate the ages. Allow at least two hours for your visit. The site opens daily at 8 A.M. and closes promptly at 6 P.M. daily.

As you enter past the visitor center, north is on your right, marked by the grand **North Platform,** topped by clusters of temples. The **Ball Court** will soon appear below on your left. Twenty-foot-high walkways circumscribe the sunken I-shaped playing field. To ensure true bounces, builders spread smooth stucco over all surfaces, including the slopes on opposite sides (which, contrary to appearances, did not seat spectators). This, like all Oaxacan ball courts, had no stone ring (for supposed goals), but rather four mysterious niches at the court's I-end corners.

The **Main Plaza,** 1,000 feet long and exactly two-thirds that wide, is aligned along a precise north-south axis. Probably serving as a market and civic/ceremonial ground, the monumentally harmonious Main Plaza was the Zapotec "navel" of the world.

Monte Albán's oldest monumental construction, the **Danzantes** building (surmounted by newer Building L, on the west side of the plaza between Buildings M and IV), dates from Period I. Its walls are graced with a host of personages,

known commonly as the *danzantes* (dancers) from their oft-contorted postures—probably chiefs vanquished by Monte Albán's armies. Their headdresses, earplugs, bracelets, and necklaces mark them among the nobility, while glyphs around their heads identify each individual.

Building J (circa A.D. 1), one of the most remarkable in Mesoamerica, stands nearby in mid-plaza at the foot of the South Platform. Speculation has raged since excavators unearthed its arrow-shaped base generations ago. It is not surprising that Alfonso Caso, Monte Albán's principal excavator, theorized it was an astronomical observatory. In the mind's eye, it seems like some fantastic ocean (or space?) vessel, being navigated to some mysteriously singular southwest destination by a ghostly crew oblivious of its worldly, earthbound brother monuments.

The **South Platform,** especially during the late afternoon, affords Monte Albán's best vantage point. Starting on the right-hand, Palace-complex side, **Building II** has a peculiar tunnel on its near side, covertly used by priests for privacy or perhaps some kind of magical effect. To the south stands Building P, an undistinguished, albeit multiroom palace.

The South Platform itself is only marginally explored. Looters have riddled the mounds on its top side. Its bottom four corners were embellished by fine bas-reliefs, two of which had their engravings intentionally buried from view. You can admire the fine sculpture and yet-undeciphered Zapotec hieroglyphs on one of them, along with others, at the South Platform's plaza-edge west side.

Still atop the South Platform, turn southward, where you can see the 7-Deer complex, a few hundred yards away, labeled for the name-date inscribed on its great lintel.

Turning northward again, look just beyond Building J to Buildings G, H, and I at plaza center, erected mostly to cover a rocky mound impossible to remove without then-unavailable dynamite. Between these buildings and the palace complex on the right stands the small chapel where the remarkable bat-god jade sculpture was found.

On Monte Albán's northern periphery stand

To Tomb 172

To Tomb 72

TOMB 103

TOMB 104

TOMB 7

CAFÉ

PARKING AREA

BUILDING X

VISITOR CENTER
(SHOP AND MUSEUM)

NORTHWEST
MOUND

NORTH PLATFORM

BUILDING D

PATIO OF THE
GEODESIC VERTEX

SUNKEN
PATIO

BUILDING E

NORTH
PLATFORM

MAIN PLAZA

MAIN
BALL COURT

BUILDING N

BUILDING IV

BUILDING II

BUILDING G

THE
CHAPEL

BUILDING H

BUILDING P

BUILDING I

BUILDING L

THE PALACE
COMPLEX

BUILDING OF
THE DANCERS

BUILDING J

BUILDING M

BUILDING Q

BUILDING O

SOUTH PLATFORM

MOUND III

To 7-Deer Complex (250 m)

VALLEY OF OAXACA

To Oaxaca

SMALL BALL COURT

TOMB 105

MONTE ALBÁN ARCHAEOLOGICAL ZONE

0   100 yds

0   100 m

© AVALON TRAVEL PUBLISHING, INC.

a number of tombs that, when excavated, yielded a trove of artifacts, now mostly housed in museums. Walking west from the Northern Platform's northeast base corner, you will pass Mound X on the right. A few hundred yards farther comes the **Tomb 104** mound, presided over by an elaborate ceramic urn representing Cocijo, the Zapotec god of rain. Just north of this is **Tomb 172,** with the skeletons and offerings left intact.

Heading back along the northernmost of the two paths from Tomb 104, you will arrive at **Tomb 7** a few hundred feet behind the visitor center. Here, around 1450, Mixtec nobles removed the original 8th-century contents and reused the tomb, burying a deceased dignitary and two servants for the netherworld. Along with the bodies, they left a fabulous treasure in gold, silver, jade, alabaster, and turquoise, now visible at the museum at the Centro Cultural de Santo Domingo in Oaxaca city.

A few hundred feet toward town on the opposite side of the road from the parking lot is a trail leading past a small ball court to the Cerro de Plumaje (Hill of Plumage), site of **Tomb 105.** A magnificent entrance door lintel, reminiscent of those at Mitla, welcomes you inside. Past the patio, descend to the mural-decorated tomb antechamber. Inside the cruciform tomb itself, four figures walk in pairs toward a great glyph, flanked by a god and goddess, identified by their name-dates.

Visitor Center

The Monte Albán Visitor Center, open daily 8 A.M.–6 P.M., tel. 951/516-1215, has an excellent museum, good café with airy terrace, and information counter. Also, a well-stocked store offers many books—guides, histories, art, folklore—on Mesoamerica. First, take a look inside the museum, which displays a number of Monte Albán's famous finds. Most notable are several of the original *danzantes* monolith reliefs, recognizable by their mutilated genitals.

In the bookstore, look for one of the most useful Oaxaca archaeological guides, Professor Ignacio Bernal's *Official Guide of the Oaxaca Valley,* which includes Cuilapan, Dainzu, Lambityeco,

VALLEY OF OAXACA

THE TRAGIC STORY OF PRINCESS DONAJI

The fabled marriage of King Cosijoeza of the Zapotecs to Coyollicatzin, daughter of Emperor Moctezuma II of the Aztecs, around 1490 was a happy one. It resulted in five children, the youngest of whom was a charming little girl.

The king asked his soothsayers what their divinations told of his little daughter's future. They replied that her life would be filled with tragic events and that she would finally sacrifice herself for her people. The king, saddened by the news, but happy that she would turn out to be so selfless, named her Donaji (Great Soul).

Earlier, Cosijoeza (koh-see-ho-AY-zah), who ruled the Zapotec Isthmus domains from his capital at present-day Tehuantepec, had been an uneasy ally of his old enemy, King Dzahuindanda (zah-ween-DAHN-dah) of the Mixtecs. In 1520, with the Aztec threat diminished by the Spanish invasion, Cosijoeza recklessly attacked the fierce Mixtecs, losing the initial battle and then nearly his life as the Mixtecs pressed their advantage.

However, the Spanish, in the person of Hernán Cortés's lieutenant, Francisco Orozco, soon imposed a Mixtec-Zapotec treaty in which Dzahuindanda received Princess Donaji as a hostage to guarantee the peace.

Having Donaji as a prisoner at Monte Albán (known as Danni Dipaa in those days) was not exactly an advantage to Dzahuindanda, for he suspected that she was as much a spy as a hostage. His guess was right. Donaji gleaned intelligence vital to the Zapotec counterattack her father Cosijoeza was planning. At the moment Dzahuindanda's forces were most vulnerable, she sent her father a secret message to attack, which he did, with complete success, except for one thing.

With the treaty broken, the outraged Mixtecs decided to do away with Donaji. They decapitated her and buried her body before her father could rescue her. Later, some Zapotecs found Donaji's remains on the bank of the Atoyac river. They were surprised to see a lovely violet wild iris blossoming from her blood. Even more surprising, they found the flower's roots growing around her head, which was without any sign of decomposition.

Three hundred years later, the Oaxaca government decided to honor the heroine who sacrificed herself for her people by adding an image of Donaji's head to the Oaxacan coat of arms, where it remains to the present day.

Mitla, Monte Albán, Yagul, and Zaachila. (Unfortunately, it has been lately out of print.) Alternatively, covering the same territory, in more depth, is *Oaxaca, the Archaeological Record,* by archaeologist Marcus Winter. (See Suggested Reading.)

Getting There

To get to Monte Albán by driving, follow the big Monte Albán sign on the *periférico,* at the south edge of downtown. Immediately cross over the Atoyac River bridge, then bear right, and continue about four miles (6 km), heading uphill, to the summit.

Alternatively, go by economical **tourist bus,** departing from your hotel or downtown Hotel Rivera del Ángel at Mina 518, five blocks west of the *zócalo.* For more details, see the Getting Around section.

SANTA MARÍA ATZOMPA

The modern town of Santa María Atzompa (pop. 5,000) spreads over the western end of the greater Monte Albán archaeological complex, overlying hundreds of acres of unexplored ancient remains. The majority of modern Atzompans, however, have little time for the past. They are busy producing their distinctive pottery creations—fetching emerald green–glazed cooking pots, bowls, baking dishes, plates, and more—famous all over Mexico and the world.

Now, however, they make much more than these, having developed a host of new styles. These include multicolored vases, some with artfully cut holes for placing dried or fresh flowers, as well as lily-adorned crosses, vases, plates, and red pottery, inscribed with fetching floral motifs.

Atzompa's artists, moreover, make it very easy to select from their wares, with an inviting Mercado de Artesanías (Handicrafts Market) and restaurant on the entrance road (right side) after a long initial lineup of private stores. Each of the *mercado* displays contains the name and address of the artist, whom you can contact nearby in town. (Note: Recently, some artists have been trying harder, building individual stores on the road before the official Handicrafts Market. For the best selection however, pass these and go straight to the official market.)

Get to Atzompa by driving or by bus, from the Abastos second-class bus terminal. Drivers head northwest out of town, along the *periférico* in the direction of Mexico City. After about a mile (1.6 km), follow the Monte Albán sign, bearing left around the traffic circle, which heads you momentarily back toward town. Immediately turn right, cross the Atoyac River bridge, and continue for about half a mile (.8 km), turning right at an intersection toward Atzompa.

Continue another 2.5 miles (4 km) to the Mercado de Artesanías and restaurant on the right.

SAN JOSÉ EL MOGOTE

Finds uncovered at San José El Mogote have shed considerable light on Valley of Oaxaca prehistory, especially during the thousand-year period preceding the founding of Monte Albán, around 500 B.C. Remains reveal that El Mogote was founded around 1500 B.C. and developed into a sophisticated center, with factory workshops supervised by elite merchants, which manufactured mica mirrors and jewelry for local and regional trade.

Old San José El Mogote lives on, literally, in the backyards of its present Zapotec residents. The people had forgotten what was buried in the seven or eight *mogotes* (mounds) dotting their village. From the pottery shards littering their fields, however, they suspected something was buried beneath the mounds. Archaeologists came and dug up the treasures now displayed

After 2,000 years, the ball court at San José El Mogote still waits to be excavated and perhaps someday reconstructed.

in the community museum, the restored **Hacienda del Cacique.**

Museum

El Mogote people take justifiable pride in their museum, housed in a gorgeously restored old hacienda, the former rancho home of a local founding *cacique* (political boss) family. Its intriguing displays include shell jewelry, ceramic and stone burial offerings, a reconstructed tomb, a pre-Columbian adobe wall, a photo of a *danzante* monolith (still situated in the ruins) like those found at Monte Albán, and exquisite ceramic sculptures. Outstanding among these is the amazing *diablo enchilado,* with a half-scowling, devilish grin, exactly like a scary red Halloween demon. *Note:* If you arrive unannounced and find the museum closed, ask across the street at the house of husband-wife jewelers, personable Hector Joel Cruz and Victoria Jiménez.

Exploring the Site

The site consists in all of eight mounds that extend over a local half-mile square. Only one of them, the biggest, immediately behind the museum, has been extensively investigated. Climb its reconstructed stone staircase to a broad courtyard. On the courtyard's north side is an excavated shaft, customarily locked, with the *danzante* monolith at its bottom. Climb the regal, stair-stepped pyramid adjoining the courtyard. At the summit, you can glimpse the other mounds, scattered near and far. Most notable among these is a partly excavated ball court, a five-minute walk to the northwest, once used for the *pelota mixteca* ball game, still played locally.

Farther afield, a 10-minute walk to the southwest side of the zone past a modern but now unused stone *era* (threshing circle), local people can lead you to a corrugated iron roof that shelters the stone foundation of what archaeologists believe to be an elite family house.

While exploring the site, you may see a scattering of tiny yellow daisies. Local folks call this *yerba de conejo* (herb of the rabbit). They take it as a tea, or mixed with beans, for *comida,* especially before siestas. Some say that its aphrodisiac effect is potent indeed.

Festival of San José

Arrive during the third week in March and join in the fun of the patronal festival of San José, which climaxes on the weekend closest to March 19. Festivities include processions, fireworks, dances of giant figures (called *monos* or *marmotas*), and a *pelota mixteca* tournament. While at the museum, ask the volunteers to show you the *hule* (natural rubber) ball and the leather mitts currently used to play the game.

Getting There

You can reach El Mogote a number of ways. Easiest is to go by tour or taxi from downtown. You can also go solo by second-class bus from the *camionera central segunda clase,* just north of Abastos market. Catch a Nazarena bus, run by the Choferes del Sur Cooperative. Alternatively, you can catch a *colectivo* (collective microbus taxi) on the prolongation of V. Trujano, which runs along the north side of the bus station.

Drivers, head north along Highway 190 out of town. About 7.5 miles (12 km) from downtown, at the fork to the new *cuota* (toll) expressway, stay on the *libre* (free) old route. After less than a mile (one and a half km), turn left (west) at the San José Mogote side road (marked by the pyramid archaeological symbol sign). Pass over the railroad tracks, continue about half a mile (.8 km), and at the bus stop shelter, turn left. Continue to the museum just past the water towers on the left.

ETLA

Although Etla's Wednesday market invariably has stalls overflowing with its famous white cheese, vendors offer plenty of other old-fashioned merchandise. How would you like, for example, some fresh sheepskins, burro pack frames, green Atzompa pottery, or red Oaxaca tamales?

The market's main attraction, however, is the battalion of native country women offering mounds of carrots, forest-gathered herbs, nopal cactus leaves, onions, and much more.

For food, head to country-style comedor **La Fonda** of elderly Señora Julia Angulo, adjacent to the Market's east side. Alternatively, try **Restaurant Chefy,** for a wholesome, home-style breakfast or lunch, on the left side of the main street as you enter town from the highway.

Get to Etla much as you would get to Mogote. Preferably arrive at the market by about 10 A.M. to allow time for visits to El Mogote and/or Suchilquitongo later. By bus, ride a Choferes del Sur Etla–marked bus from the second-class bus station. By car, head north along old *(libre)* Highway 190 about nine miles (15 km) from the city center and turn left at the big green Etla highway sign. The market is the prominent stone building on the right before the rail station, about a quarter mile (.4 km) from the highway.

SUCHILQUITONGO AND CERRO DE LA CAMPANA ARCHAEOLOGICAL ZONE

Suchilquitongo

Before heading uphill to investigate the important Cerro de la Campana archaeological zone, look around the nearby Suchilquitongo town plaza. Suchilquitongo ("Place of Flowers" in the Mixtec language; pop. about 5,000) is the seat of the surrounding Suchilquitongo *municipio,* a rich domain of hills and mountains enclosing the emerald vale of the upper Río Atoyac. Using irrigation, bottomland farmers routinely bring in three crops per year, achieving some of Mexico's highest yields per acre in corn, beans, alfalfa, and squash. If only the rest of Oaxaca were so productive. Although virtually all of the bottomland is privately owned, much of the surrounding hills and mountains is undeveloped town communal pastureland.

The Suchilquitongo **Museo Comunitario** (open daily 10 A.M.–3 P.M. and 5–7 P.M.), on the town plaza, is one of the network of community museums sprinkled around the state.

The museum displays artifacts, reproductions, and a actual-sized mock-up model of the famous Tomb 5, discovered in the Cerro de la Campana (formerly Huijazoo) archaeological zone in 1985. A glance at the archaeological displays reveals why it's considered the most important Zapotec city-state tomb uncovered to date. It was literally a house of the dead, with the remains of at least 20 noble personages of at least three generations,

Suchilquitongo baskets begin with the bamboo-like local *carrizos* (reeds) in the hands of a skilled craftsperson.

© BRUCE WHIPPERMAN

with calendric birth-names, such as 5-Earth, 5-Serpent, and 12-Monkey. Before the excavation, they lay at rest in a massive three-room, 15-foot-deep crypt complex among piles of jewelr, supplied with elaborate goods for the afterlife and surrounded by bright murals of ceremonial scenes, including a grand procession of feathered and helmeted ball players. Before you leave the Tomb 5 mock-up, be sure to see the **sphere of day and night,** and the richly engraved columns and tomb entrance door, both embossed with as yet-untranslated Zapotec glyphs.

Another museum room illustrates the Spanish-Mexican custom of *mayordomía,* as acted out by Suchilquitongo people for their major fiesta, the July 22–27 fiesta of Santiago (St. James). Everyone participates—cooking food, making costumes, rehearsing for the dancing, setting up *ramadas* for shade, spiffing up the church, donating money—especially the *mayordomo,* the man or woman nominated by the

VALLEY OF OAXACA

presidente municipal and approved by a grand church meeting of the entire community to head all this up. The *mayordomo,* nearly always a person of means, usually ends up his or her term of office poorer, but rich with community affection and prestige.

Before you leave Suchilquitongo, you might want to visit one of the town's **basket weavers** at work. For a small fee, maybe the equivalent of a couple of dollars, the person at the museum desk may be able to guide you (or find someone who can) to one of their workshops.

Suchilquitongo's other significant craft is **stonemasonry.** Local quarries mine three types—*morada* (pink), white *blanco* (meaning white, but actually a pale green), and *amarillo* (pale yellow)—of the soft *cantera* (volcanic tufa) for which Oaxaca is famous. As you exit at the highway, go left a few hundred yards, and on the right you'll see the covered workshop of master stonemason **Cenobio Ausencio Pinelo Martínez,** who's teaching his sons his disappearing craft.

Exploring Cerro de la Campana

From the town plaza, you can see the Cerro de la Campana cluster of hilltops above the northern horizon. The site is about a two-mile (three-km) 500-foot (150-meter) climb. If it's hot, hire a taxi. If not, be sure to wear a hat, sturdy shoes, and take water. Atop the hill, you'll find Tomb 5 (hopefully open to the public after years of restoration), a ball court, three courtyards, and three partly restored pyramids.

After you arrive atop the hill, look closely at the knolls in the immediate vicinity and you'll see that they too are topped by pyramids, approximately 20 in all. Also, as you walk next to a road-cut section of hillside; look carefully and you'll be able to spot and examine 1,500-year old pottery shards.

Climb to the highest—the cross-topped—pyramid, and your reward will be a breezy view of the entire Etla Valley and mountain panorama. Notice the dark Monte Albán ridge, far to the southeast, to the right of distant Oaxaca city (below the Cerro San Felipe massif on the left). You can immediately see Cerro de la Campana's advantages: direct signal-fire communication with its contemporary, Monte Albán; a strong defensive position; and fertile riverbank fields. Why it was abandoned, like Monte Albán and many other Oaxacan cities around A.D. 800, remains a puzzle for future generations of archaeologists to decipher from the bones, stones, and the mute, mysterious glyphs Cerro de la Campana's builders have left behind.

Getting There

Get there by bus via one of the Cooperativo de Autobuses Suchilquitongo buses, which leave from the second-class bus terminal just north of the Abastos market, west of the *periférico.* Alternatively, you can go by a Suchilquitongo-bound **colectivo** (collective taxi van) on the prolongation of V. Trujano, which runs along the bus station's north side.

Drivers, head out of town along Highway 190, in the direction of Mexico City, northwest. Bear right onto Highway 190 *libre* (free) at the *cuota* (toll) expressway entrance, about 7.5 miles (12 km) from the city center. Continue another several miles; pass an industrial park entrance on the left and, within a few minutes, turn left 17 miles (27 km) from the city center at the big Suchilquitongo entrance arch on the left. Continue to the railroad tracks. On the right just before the tracks, notice Calle Victoria, which heads uphill, passing the church, about 1.5 miles (2.5 km), to the Cerro de la Campana archaeological zone. Continue another half mile (.8 km) to the town plaza. Climb the plaza stairway on the right to the museum.

Pacific Resorts and Southern Sierra

Historically, Oaxaca's southern coastal residents have both earned their livelihoods and sought their connections with the outside world by the Mar del Sur, the Southern Sea, the traditional Mexican name for the Pacific Ocean. Before roads were built, the Oaxaca coast slumbered, every bit like an isolated South Seas island, dependent upon occasional ships for trade and news from the exterior world.

The major cause of the isolation was the towering, cloud-capped wall of the Sierra Madre del Sur (Mother Range of the South).

Oaxaca's high southern Sierra, always remote and mysterious, was finally unveiled in its majesty only in the 1980s, when satellite photo measurements revealed that Cerro Quiexobra, at 12,300 feet (3,750 meters), was by far Oaxaca's tallest mountain massif, a scarce 50 miles (80 km) due north of the Bahías de Huatulco.

From such high, cool, pine-crested summits along its entire 200-mile (320-km) rampart, the Sierra Madre del Sur plunges precipitously downward more than two miles (3 km), through lush vine-hung canyon and foothill forest to the Pacific shore, an acacia-tufted expanse of endless summer.

There, as if forced southward by the weight of the high mountains, the coastline bulges to Oaxaca's (and nearly the entire country's) most southerly point, near the petite bay and resort of Puerto Ángel. From there, the Oaxaca coastline bends northerly—on its east side, northeast toward the Isthmus, and on its west side, northwest toward the Mixtec Coast, often called the Costa Chica (Little Coast) in southern Mexico.

During the 1970s and 1980s paved highways and airlines ended the Oaxaca coast's iso-

lation and brought a trickle of Mexican and foreign visitors to the region. The government recognized the area's potential and began developing a new, ecologically correct vacation land at the Bahías de Huatulco. Meanwhile, visitors were discovering the South Seas village resorts of Puerto Ángel and Puerto Escondido.

Now the steady stream of vacationers can choose from a growing menu of outdoor diversions, from strolling the sand and snorkeling in hidden coves to rescuing sea turtle eggs, splashing in upland waterfalls, and lodging comfortably overnight at rustic jungle coffee farms.

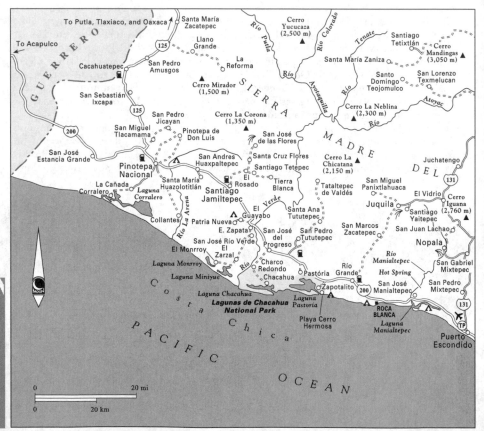

Puerto Ángel and Vicinity

During his three presidencies, Oaxaca-born Benito Juárez shaped many dreams into reality. One such dream was to better the lot of his native brethren in the isolated south of Oaxaca by developing a port for shipping the lumber and coffee they could harvest in the lush Pacific-slope jungles of the Sierra Madre del Sur. The small bay of Puerto Ángel, directly south of the state capital, was chosen, and by 1870 it had become Oaxaca's busiest port.

Unfortunately, Benito Juárez died two years later. New priorities and Puerto Ángel's isolation soon wilted Juárez's plan, and Puerto Ángel lapsed into a generations-long slumber.

In the 1960s, Puerto Ángel was still a sleepy little spot connected by a single frail link—a tortuous cross-Sierra dirt road—to the rest of the country. Adventure travelers saw it at the far south of the map and dreamed of a South Seas paradise. They came and were not disappointed. Although that first tourist trickle has grown steadily, it's only enough to support the sprinkling of modest lodgings and restaurants that now dot the beaches and

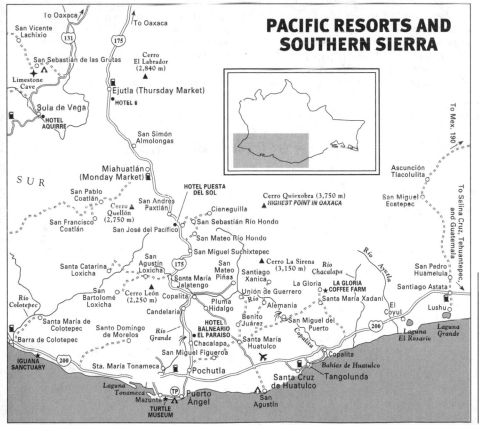

PACIFIC RESORTS AND SOUTHERN SIERRA

PACIFIC RESORTS

© AVALON TRAVEL PUBLISHING, INC.

hillsides around Puerto Ángel's tranquil little blue bay.

BEACHES AND SIGHTS

Getting Oriented

Puerto Ángel is at the southern terminus of High-way 175 from Oaxaca, about six miles (9 km) downhill from its intersection with Highway 200. It's a small place, where nearly everything is within walking distance along the beach, which a rocky bayfront hill divides into two parts: Playa Principal, the main town beach, and sheltered west-side Playa Panteón, the tourist favorite. A scenic boulder-decorated shoreline *andador*, or walkway (watch out for gaps and holes in the concrete), connects the two beaches.

A paved road winds west from Puerto Ángel along the coastline a couple of miles to Playa Zipolite, lined by a colony of hammock-and-bamboo beachfront cabanas, popular with an international cadre of budget-minded seekers of heaven on earth. Continuing west, the road

passes the former turtle-processing village beaches of Playa San Agustinillo and Playa Mazunte. From there, it goes on another four miles (6.4 km), joining with Highway 200 (and thence Puerto Escondido) at San Antonio village at Km 198.

The major local service and transportation center is **Pochutla** (pop. 35,000), a mile (1.6 km) north along Highway 175 from its Highway 200 junction.

Getting Around

Local *colectivos* ferry passengers frequently between Pochutla and Puerto Ángel (fare, about $.50) from about 7 A.M. until 8 P.M., stopping at the Highway 200 intersection. Some buses continue on to Zipolite and Mazunte after stopping on Boulevard Uribe, Puerto Ángel's main bayfront street. Also from Boulevard Uribe, a local shuttle bus connects frequently with Zipolite, San Agustinillo, Mazunte, and back about every half hour during daylight hours, stopping everywhere en route. Taxis also routinely make runs between

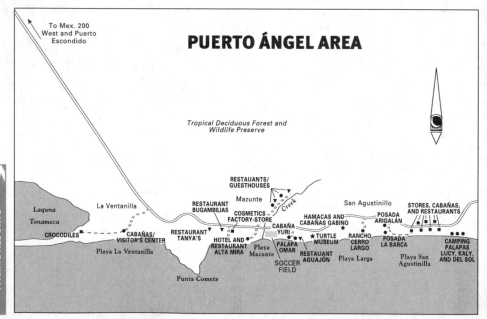

PUERTO ÁNGEL AREA

Puerto Ángel and either Zipolite or Pochutla for about $5.

You can also get around by boat. Captains routinely take parties of up to eight for sightseeing, snorkeling, and picnicking to a number of nearby beaches. Bargain at the Puerto Ángel pier (rate should run about $15/hour), or contact the local travel agent, **Agencia de Viajes Gambusino,** tel. 958/584-3080 or 958/584-3038.

Playas Principal, Panteón, and Estacahuite

Playa Principal's 400 yards of wide golden sand decorate most of Puerto Ángel's bayfront. Waves can be strong near the pier, where they often surge vigorously onto the beach and recede with some undertow. Swimming is more tranquil at the sheltered west end, toward Playa Panteón. The clear waters are good for casual snorkeling around the rocks, on both sides of the bay.

Sheltered Playa Panteón (Cemetery Beach) is Puerto Ángel's sunning beach, lined with squadrons of beach chairs and umbrellas in front of beachside restaurants. **Playa Oso** (Bear Beach) is a little dab of sand beside a rugged seastack of rock beyond Playa Panteón, fun to swim to from Playa Panteón.

Playa Estacahuite, just outside the opposite (east) side of the bay, is actually two beaches in one: a pair of luscious coral-sand nooks teeming with fish grazing the living reef just offshore. (Don't put your hands in crevices; a moray eel may mistake your finger for a fish and bite.) A pair of *palapa* restaurants perched picturesquely above the beaches provides food and drinks. Get there in less than a mile by taxi or on foot via the dirt road that forks right off the highway, about 400 yards uphill from beachfront Boulevard Uribe.

Playa Zipolite

Playa Zipolite is a wide, one-mile (1.6-km) strand of yellow-white sand enfolded by headlands and backed by palm groves. It stretches from the intimate little cove and beach of **Playa del Amor** tucked on its east side to towering seaside cliffs rising behind the new-age Shambhala retreat on

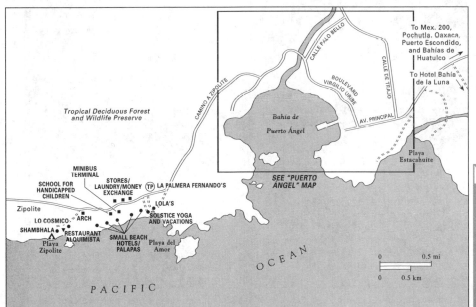

© AVALON TRAVEL PUBLISHING, INC.

the west end. The Playa Zipolite surf, although usually tranquil in the mornings (but always with significant undertow), can turn thunderous by the afternoon, especially when offshore storms magnify both the swells and the undertow. Experienced surfers love these times, when everyone but experts should stay out.

Good surfing notwithstanding, Zipolite's renown stems from its status as one of the very few nude beaches in Mexico. Bathing au naturel, practiced nearly entirely by visitors and a few local young men, is tolerated only grudgingly by local people, many of whose livelihoods depend on the nudists. If you're discreet and take off your clothes at the more isolated west end (behind the big rock), no one will appear to mind (and women will avoid voyeuristic attentions of Mexican boys and men).

Visitors' nude sunbathing habits may be contributing to the gruffness of some local people. Many of them probably prefer their former occupations in turtle fishing rather than serving tourists, who often seem to be in short supply compared to the battalion of beachfront *palapas* competing for their business.

Most Zipolite visitors stay in the palm-shaded east-end trailer park or in one of the score of basic hammock-equipped beachfront cabana hotels. Often with fans and outside cold-water showers and privies, cabanas rent for $10–15 d per night, depending upon amenities. Although many are indifferently managed, some, such as Lola's, Lo Cósmico, and Shambhala (see Zipolite Accommodations), are unique.

Playas San Agustinillo and Mazunte

About a mile (1.6 km) west of Zipolite, a wide, mile-long, yellow-sand beach curves past the village of San Agustinillo. On the open ocean but partly protected by offshore rocks, its surf is much like that of Zipolite, varying from gentle to rough, depending mostly upon wind and offshore swells. Small village groceries and beachside *palapa* restaurants supply food and drinks to the occasional Zipolite overflow and local families on weekends and holidays.

Afternoons at tourist favorite Playa Panteón offer palm-shaded sand, super-fresh seafood, and vistas of Puerto Ángel's petite blue bay.

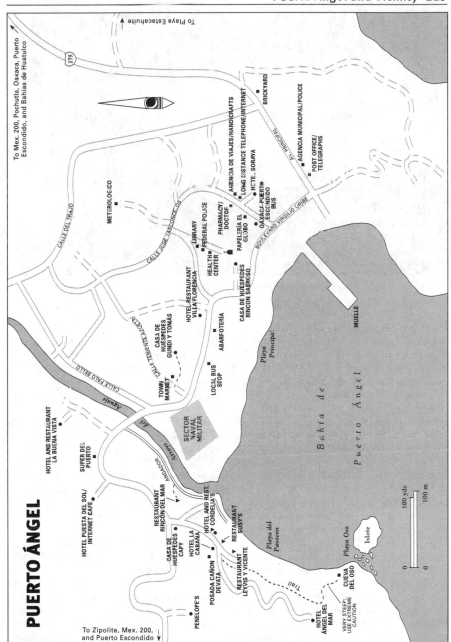

PUERTO ÁNGEL

To Mex. 200, Pochutla, Oaxaca, Puerto Escondido, and Bahías de Huatulco

To Playa Estacahuite

175

METEOROLOGICO

CALLE DEL TRAJO

CALLE JOSE VASCONCELOS

LIBRARY

FEDERAL POLICE

PHARMACY/
DOCTOR

PAPELERIA EL
GLOBO

HEALTH
CENTER

HOTEL-RESTAURANT
VILLA FLORENCIA

CASA DE
HUÉSPEDES
GUNDI Y TOMAS

CALLE TENIENTE AZUETA

CASA DE HUÉSPEDES
RINCON SABROSO

ABARROTERIA

TOWN
MARKET

LOCAL BUS
STOP

CALLE PALO BELLO

Arroyo

Arroyo del

SECTOR
NAVAL
MILITAR

AGENCIA DE VIAJES/HANDICRAFTS

LONG DISTANCE TELEPHONE/INTERNET

HCTE. SORAYA

OAXACA-PUERTO
ESCONDIDO
BUS

BRICKYARD

AGENCIA MUNICIPAL/POLICE

POST OFFICE/
TELEGRAPHS

BOULEVARD VIRGILIO URIBE

AV. PRINCIPAL

MUELLE

Playa
Principal

Bahía de

Puerto Ángel

HOTEL AND RESTAURANT
LA BUENA VISTA

SUPER DEL
PUERTO

HOTEL PUESTA DEL SOL/
INTERNET CAFE

RESTAURANT
RINCÓN DEL MAR

CASA DE
HUÉSPEDES
CAPY

HOTEL LA
CABAÑA

HOTEL AND REST.
CORDELIA'S

RESTAURANT
SUSY'S

RESTAURANT
LEVIS Y VICENTE

POSADA CAÑON
DEVATA

Andador

Arroyo

Playa del
Panteon

Playa Oso

Islote

CUEVA
DEL OSO

Trail

VERY STEEP:
USE EXTREME
CAUTION

HOTEL
ANGEL DEL
MAR

PENELOPE'S

To Zipolite, Mex. 200,
and Puerto Escondido

100 yds

100 m

0

0

N

Sun, sand, and surf are at their golden best at Playa Mazunte.

Fishing is excellent, either in the surf, from nearby rocks, by rented *panga,* or from your own boat launched from the beach. Beach camping is customary in San Agustinillo, especially at the roadside *ramadas* at the east (Zipolite) end of the beach.

Remnants of the local turtle industry can be found at the rusting former processing factories on Playa San Agustinillo (west end) and Playa Mazunte two miles (3 km) farther west.

The half-mile-long (.8 km), yellow-sand Mazunte Beach, like San Agustinillo, is semi-sheltered and varies from tranquil to rough. Fishing is likewise good, beach camping is customary (as a courtesy, ask nearby business owners if it's okay), and local stores and seafood *palapa* restaurants sell basic supplies and food.

Mazunte people have also been renovating their houses and building **cabanas** in order to accommodate an increasing number of visitors. Some have even begun to advertise on the Internet. Signs along the road and at the beach advertise their homespun lodgings and restaurants. For more information, see Mazunte Accommodations.

Turtle Museum

The former turtle processing plant at Mazunte lives on as a turtle museum, including aquarium, study center, and turtle hatchery. Here, you can peruse displays illustrating the ongoing turtle research and conservation program and see members of most of Mexico's turtle species paddling in tanks overlooking the beach where their ancestors once swarmed. The center, on the main road, east end of village, is open Wed.–Sat. 10 A.M.–4:30 P.M., Sun. 10 A.M.–2:30 P.M. For more information contact the Centro Mexicano de la Tortuga, P.O. Box 16, Puerto Ángel, Oaxaca 70902, tel. 958/584-3055, fax 958/584-3063, www.tomzap.com/turtle.html.

Cosmetics Factory and Store

About half a mile (.8 km) farther west along the main road through Mazunte village, stop by the store and works of the **Fábrica Ecológia de Cosmeticos Naturales de Mazunte.** Initially funded mostly by the Body Shop Foundation, spearheaded by the local chapter of ecology corps **Ec Solar,** and supported by an international government-university consortium, the factory

A TURTLE ARRIVES AT PLAYA LA VENTANILLA

It was raining, and the wind, although not cold, was driving the surf high on Playa La Ventanilla. On the rocky headland above the beach, a small hole, like a round window, appeared to have been carved in the rock. Our guide, Pedro, who had just rowed us through the community wetland-ecological preserve, explained.

"That's why we call this La Ventanilla. Because of that hole that the sea and wind have carved out."

"It's like a little window, a *ventanilla.*"

"Yes, that's right."

He then went on to tell us something we didn't expect.

"We are waiting for the turtles to arrive. They come this time of year, especially when the wind blows toward shore like this. Yesterday afternoon and night nearly 80 turtles came and laid about 8,000 eggs."

It seemed too many.

"Eight thousand? Are you sure?"

"Yes . . . and they're buried right here."

He pointed to a fenced-off area in the sand, laid out in a grid of several dozen stakes.

"Each turtle lays about 100 eggs, and we buried each one's eggs separately under each of these stakes."

Before I could answer, a lookout atop the headland yelled something.

"A turtle has come ashore."

We scanned the beach. A black, pointed silhouette showed at the edge of the sand.

"There it is."

Two or three young male villagers raced toward the beach. They stopped several steps short of the turtle, however.

"We don't want to interfere with its egg-laying."

For several minutes, we watched the turtle, not large, perhaps 50 pounds and two feet long, strug-

gle to climb one last small sand ridge before reaching the flat part of the beach. We asked what kind of turtle it was.

"It's a *golfina* turtle," Pedro explained. "Two other kinds arrive here. The *laut,* and the *sacasillo.* The *laut* can be big, maybe as much as a ton. They arrive in February."

After watching the turtle struggle for a few minutes longer, Pedro decided to help. He picked it up by the shell and placed it on level sand a dozen feet farther inland. He sympathized with the turtle's plight.

"The turtle seems very tired. It's small and weak."

The boost seemed to encourage the turtle. It immediately began digging with its flippers. After 10 minutes it began depositing its eggs in a foot-deep hole. Pedro promptly removed the eggs and placed them in a bucket. After a few minutes, the seemingly near-exhausted turtle was finished. Pedro had kept count.

"Seventy-five eggs. Not many."

"But it's better than nothing."

Pedro nodded his head in agreement.

He let the turtle cover up the empty hole. After doing so, it packed down the sand over where it had deposited the eggs, rocking its body back and forth with its flippers. Then it turned and headed back toward the waves. Pedro gently lifted it up and placed it near the water. Soon the turtle was gone, beneath the surf.

Pedro took the bucket of 75 eggs and buried them beneath a new marker alongside the other 80 markers.

"You are the turtle papa," we said. He laughed.

"Soon these eggs will hatch into thousands of little turtles, which we will return to the sea."

"And maybe many of them will return here."

"Yes, we hope so."

and store employ local workers to make and sell all-natural shampoo, skin cream, hair conditioner, and more. Staff are working hard to assure that the effort catches on, so that locally-grown products, such as coconut, corn, and avocado oils, and natural aromatics will form the basis for a thriving cottage cosmetics industry.

Playa La Ventanilla

Continue about a mile and a half (two and a half km) west along the main road over the low hill west of Mazunte and turn left at the signed dirt road to pristine wildlife haven Playa and Laguna la Ventanilla. Now protected by local residents, swarms of birds, including pelicans, cormorants, and herons, nest there, and a population of wild *cocodrilos* and *lagartos* is making a comeback in a bushy mangrove wetland. Boatmen headquartered at the *palapa* beach village at road's end guide visitors on a two-hour eco-tour ($4 per adult, kids half price), which includes a stop for refreshment at a little mid-lagoon island. The boatmen are known for their wildlife-sensitivity and allow no motor vehicles within 100 yards (91 meters) of their communally owned lagoon-sanctuary.

The Playa La Ventanilla community has also taken responsibility for protecting the turtles that arrive on their beach against poachers. During both February and June–October, hundreds of sea turtles come ashore to lay eggs. If necessary, community volunteers help the exhausted turtles up the steep beach, where they lay their eggs. Volunteers then gather the eggs and rebury them in a secure spot. After the hatchlings emerge about a month and a half later, volunteers nurture them for about three months and release them safely back into the ocean.

Moreover, the La Ventanilla *ejido* invites visitors to stay in their rough-and-ready, rustic but sturdy, concrete-floored cabanas with beds. (Bring your own mosquito net.) For more information, log on to www.tomzap.com/ventanil.html.

ACCOMMODATIONS

Although only the newest of Puerto Ángel's dozens of lodgings (nearly all modest, home-grown guesthouse-style accommodations) is directly on the beach, most of them are within a stone's throw of it. The successful lodgings have given their legion of savvy repeat customers what they want: clean, basic, tepid-water accommodations in tranquil, television-free settings where Puerto Ángel's natural isolation and tropical charm set the tone for long, restful holidays.

Visitors have their choice of two accommodations neighborhoods in Puerto Ángel, the main town and Playa Panteón. The main town lodgings dot the hillside above the main town beach, the pier, and the single business street. The Playa Panteón (Cemetery Beach) lodgings, by contrast, are on the sleepier west side of the bay,

above the homey lineup of *palapa* restaurants that line petite Playa Panteón. There are also many other lodging choices available outside of Puerto Ángel, in nearby Bahía de la Luna, Zipolite, and Mazunte.

Main Town Accommodations

Under $50: At the splendidly isolated **Casa de Huéspedes Rincón Sabroso,** Puerto Ángel, Oaxaca 70902, tel. 958/584-3095, atop a bay-vista hill, guests enjoy lodgings that open onto a hammock-hung breezeway adorned by luscious tropical greenery. Inside, rooms are very clean (but dark), with white walls, tile floors, shiny bathrooms, and natural wood furnishings. Guests have the additional option of good food and each other's company in an airy café, perched above a heavenly bay and sunset panorama. Rates for the eight rooms run about $14 s, $16 d, $19 t low season, about $18, $22, and $24 high, with fans. Owners have added a pair of more private, deluxe rooms (Nos. 9 and 10), with hot water, for about $20 d low season, $30 high.

Equally exceptional on the hill two blocks west is **Casa de Huéspedes Gundi y Tomás,** address simply Puerto Ángel, Oaxaca 70902, tel. 958/584-3068, gundtoma@hotmail.com, the life project of friendly German expatriate Gundi López. Her homey, rustic-aesthetic complex rambles up a leafy hillside to a breezy bay-view *palapa* where patrons relax, socialize, and enjoy food and drink from Gundi's kitchen. Just above that, guests enjoy a double row of several clean, simply furnished (although dark) rooms, shaded by a shared hammock-hung porch with a view. Besides all this, Gundi is happy to volunteer information about local sights and activities and arrange excursions for her guests. Rooms with shared showers and toilets cost about $14 d low season, $17 high; larger rooms with private shower and toilet run about $17 d low season, $20 high, all with fans. Get there by walking uphill along the little alley adjacent to the town market and just opposite the beachfront naval compound.

Another Puerto Ángel gem is **Hotel La Buena Vista,** P.O. Box 48, Puerto Ángel, Oaxaca 70902, tel./fax 958/584-3104, U.S. tel. 415/388-9067, reservations@labuenavista.com, www.labuenavista.com, tucked on the hillside that rises just west of the Arroyo del Aguaje. The hotel's four tiers stairstep artfully up the jungly slope. First- and second-level rooms open to shady, hammock-hung porches that offer lovely views. On the third level, a luxuriously airy restaurant *palapa* opens to a picture-perfect bay vista. The climax is a pair of large onyx tile–floored fourth-floor rooms that share an entire private patio with hammocks. Above that, owners have added a luxurious pool-patio for guest enjoyment.

All rooms are immaculate, light, and simply but tastefully furnished, with spotless bathrooms. Low-season rates for the approximately 20 rooms run about $30 s, $33 d for standard, $35 s or d for deluxe room with private balcony, and $45 d for the top-floor deluxe room with double-size onyx bathtub; high season, the same go for about $38, $40, and $46, all with fans, an excellent restaurant, and hot water in the deluxe rooms.

Travelers who enjoy being right in the middle of the Puerto Ángel beachfront street scene choose the worthy **Hotel Villa Florencia,** Blv. Virgilio Uribe s/n, Puerto Ángel, Oaxaca 70902, tel./fax 958/584-3044, villaserenaoax@hotmail.com. Here, in the shady interior lobby-patio, past the excellent street-front restaurant, tranquility reigns as soft classic songs and instrumental music play in the background, while guests read and relax on comfortable chairs and couches. Upstairs, the approximately 15 rooms, with bath, are immaculate and thoughtfully decorated with local art and handicrafts. Rates run about $25 s, $35 d, $40 t year-round, add $3 for a/c.

On the east side, find 1960s motel–style **Hotel Soraya,** perched on the bluff above the pier, at Priv. José Vasconcelos 2A, Puerto Ángel, Oaxaca 70902, tel./fax 958/584-3009. Well managed by personable owner Hortencia Tanus, the hotel includes a restaurant with an airy bay view, fine for bright morning breakfasts and sunset-glow dinners. Outside, two tiers of spartan but light and comfortable rooms enclose a parking patio. Although some rooms have a/c, the fan-only ones are generally better. Rent on

the upper tier for more privacy. The 32 rooms rent for about $35 s or d, and $40 t high season, ask for a discount during low season.

Playa Panteón Accommodations

Under $50: Heading around the curve of the bay to the Playa Panteón neighborhood, you'll find one of Puerto Ángel's old standby budget lodgings, **Casa de Huéspedes Capy,** Playa Panteón, P.O. Box 44, Puerto Ángel, Oaxaca 70902, tel./fax 958/584-3002, hotel_capy@hotmail.com, sitting on the bay-view hillside by the road fork to Zipolite. Rooms, in two tiers with views toward Playa Panteón, are basic but clean with fans and cool-water private baths. Good family management is the Capy's strong suit. This shows in the shady restaurant, Arcely, also with a view, where good food in a friendly atmosphere encourages guests to linger, reading or talking, for hours. The family also watches the community TV at night; if it bothers you, ask them to turn it down. The 10 rooms rent for about $10 s, $15 d low season, $12 and $16 high. Rooms with two beds go for $18 d, $19 t low season, $19 and $20 high.

Not far away, about 100 yards uphill past the road fork to Zipolite (watch for the sign at the hilltop driveway on the left), consider the guesthouse **Penelope's** (of Homeric legend), P.O. Box 49, Puerto Ángel, Oaxaca 70902, tel. 958/584-3073. With only a few rooms but benefiting from a breezy, quiet hilltop setting, Penelope's features comfortably furnished rooms with hot water showers, and porches with hammocks and fans. Owner Patricia enjoys sharing her home with guests, taking special pleasure in serving her uniquely delicious margarita cocktails. Rentals run about $15 s, $15–32 d. Add about $4 per person for breakfast, $7 for dinner.

Downhill, new **Hotel Cordelia,** Puerto Ángel's first beachfront lodging, stands right on Playa Panteón, Puerto Escondido, Oaxaca 70902, tel. 958/584-3109, azul_profundomx@hotmail.com. The Cordelia's seven rooms, most with bay views, are sparely but pleasingly decorated with rustic whitewashed walls, attractive native floor tiles, natural wood furniture and artful tile touches in the modern-standard baths. No phone, no TV, just the murmur of the gentle Playa Panteón surf to lull you to sleep. Rooms have fans and rent for about $25 s or d, $50 t or q low season, $30 and $60 high. There's a good restaurant downstairs.

This trip I was happy to discover that the family-operated Puerto Ángel gem, **Posada Cañon Devata,** P.O. Box 10, Puerto Ángel, Oaxaca 70902, tel. 958/584-3048, tel./fax 958/584-3137, posadacanon@yahoo.com, has reopened. Owner and artist Mateo López and his son Dashan have resumed management after a two-year hiatus. During the 1980s, Mateo and his former spouse Susana restored their deforested canyon to health, artfully placing about a dozen charmingly petite, art-decorated guest cabanas along leafy hillside paths. Low-season rentals (with fans) run about $30 s, $35 d low season; $45 and $50 high. The hotel features a good macrobiotic restaurant.

Atop the hill via the adjacent steep road, the **Hotel Ángel del Mar,** Puerto Ángel, Oaxaca 70902, tel. 958/584-3008, fax 958/584-3014, offers 42 rooms at about $20 s, $30 d low season; $35 and $48 high. Credit cards are accepted (but you'll get a discount if you pay cash). Guests enjoy a big, open-air dining room, swimming pool, and large light rooms with private balconies looking down upon a panoramic bay vista. Mornings, guests can enjoy sunrises over the bay and evening sunsets over the ocean. Revitalized management has recently brightened the place up with new paint everywhere and new bedspreads and lampshades to go with the venerable polished wood furniture in the rooms.

Far East Side: Bahía de la Luna

Vacationers hankering for splendid isolation can have it at Bahía de la Luna, on the coast about three small bays east of Puerto Ángel, at P.O. Box 90, Pochutla, Oaxaca 70900, tel./fax 958/584-6186, bahia-de-la-lu@usa.net, www.totalmedia.qc.ca/bahiadelaluna. Here, owner Ivan Wastchenko shares his paradise with visitors. His approximately 15 rustic-chic adobe, palm-thatched cabanas cluster on a lovely, isolated crescent of golden sand. No phones, TV, or traffic; simply sun, sea, sand, and catch-of-the-day home-cooked seafood. Cabanas, thoughtfully and comfortably furnished, rent for about $40 s, $45 d

low season, $50 and $55 high, including three meals, fans, but room-temperature water. Ivan also offers a beachfront house, sleeping five, with kitchen, for $180 low season, $200 high.

Get there by boat from Puerto Ángel or the rugged jeep road, signed Bahía de la Luna, which forks east about four miles (6.4 km) uphill from Puerto Ángel. Not far after the highway, follow the first fork right, along a ridge, then steeply (and ruggedly) downhill to the picture-perfect cove and beach.

Zipolite Accommodations

Zipolite's line of rustic (all under $50 d; bring your own towel and soap) lodgings starts at **Lola's,** on the east end of the beach, Playa Zipolite, Puerto Ángel, Oaxaca 70902, tel. 958/584-3201 or 958/584-3203. The friendly, elderly owner continues her decades-long good management (although her equally personable daughter now does most of the day-to-day work) of her thatch-shaded restaurant and beach cabanas. For customers who hanker for a bit better lodging, Lola has broken new ground with Zipolite's first permanent units, eight new rooms with private baths (but only room-temperature water) and ceiling fans. The best are two front, top-floor units overlooking the gorgeous beach and sunset vista. The scene at Lola's resembles a mini-resort, with the restaurant right on the beach, where guests enjoy late breakfasts, stroll out for swims, read thick novels, and kick back and enjoy convivial conversation with mostly North American and European fellow vacationers. Although past hurricanes wiped out the rustic wood cabanas, they've been rebuilt with modern-standard stucco units that rent for about $15 s, $20 d, $25 t year-round, with fan and private shower baths.

Alternatively, consider **Solstice Yoga and Vacations,** P.O. Box 18, Puerto Ángel, Oaxaca 70902, fax 958/584-3070, www.solstice-mexico.com, next door (west) to Lola's, at Playa Zipolite. Friendly European expatriate owners Brigette Longueville and Guy Hamaekers have built an inviting, authentically rustic mini-colony of two-story cabanas on the gorgeous Zipolite beachfront. Accommodations are in Robinson Crusoe–, south sea islands–, open-style in all natural wood, with ladders leading to upstairs sleeping-lounging areas, where serape-draped beds are hung with gauzy mosquito nets. Guests are about evenly divided between beach vacationers and yoga devotees, who attend sessions in the in-house studio.

Accommodations rent for about $20 d low season, $30 high, for the one smaller unit, and about $25 low, $35 high for the three larger units; $5 per extra person, with private bathroom with toilet and tepid-water shower baths and breakfast included. Dormitory accommodations are also available, for $8 per person low season, $10 high. Brigette and Guy offer Hatha yoga classes for $5 per 1.5 hours.

The **Lo Cósmico,** Playa Zipolite, P.O. Box 36, Pochutla, Oaxaca 70900, locosmico@hotmail .comcabanas, www.locosmico.com, nestle on a cactus-decorated rocky knoll at the opposite (west) end of the beach. White spheres perched on their thatched roof peaks lend a mystical Hindu-Buddhist accent to the cabanas' already picturesque appearance. In the restaurant atop the knoll, you're likely to find Regula and Antonio Nadurille, Lo Cósmico's European-Mexican owners. Regula manages the restaurant, specializing in a dozen varieties of tasty crepes, while Antonio supervises the hotel. Their hillside and beach-level cabanas are clean, candle-lit, and equipped with hammocks and concrete floors, for about $12–17 d, with outside showers and toilets. Recently, Antonio has built a number of sturdy, rock-walled, hurricane-proof designer rooms on his hillside. Figure about $20 d for these, including private baths.

Shambhala, Puerto Ángel, P.O. Box 68, Pochutla, Oaxaca, 70900, fax 958/584-3151 or 958/584-3152, www.advantagemexico.com/ shambhala/index.html, on the adjacent forested hillside, is as it sounds—a tranquil Buddhist-style retreat. Shambhala's driving force is the friendly owner/community leader Gloria Esperanza Johnson, who arrived in Zipolite by accident in 1970 and decided to stay, eventually adopting Mexican citizenship.

Shambhala is a quiet, alcohol-free haven for lovers of reading, sunbathing, hiking, yoga, and meditation. It sits atop an enviable few acres at the edge of a sylvan hinterland. Adjacent cactus-studded cliffs plummet spectacularly to surf-splashed rocks below, while trails fan out through lush tropical deciduous forest. An excellent macrobiotic restaurant with panoramic vista completes the attractive picture.

Gloria has built Shambhala from the ground up and now offers a number of clean, basic accommodations. In nearly all cases, toilets and (room temperature-tepid) showers are shared. Simplest are dorm rooms for $3 per person; next come shared bunk-bed rooms for $4 per person; small individual rooms for two go for $6; small cabana for two, with bath, $18; and large beachfront cabana for four with two double beds, $20. Work exchange for room and board is negotiable. For reservations from the U.S., call Daniel R. Ortega, 402 Market St., Suite 226, San Diego, CA 92101, fax 347/214-2533, cell tel. 619/549-5300.

Get to both Shambhala and Lo Cósmico by turning from the main road onto the dirt driveway just west of the arch at Zipolite's west end. Bear right at the first fork, then left at the next for Lo Cósmico, right for Shambhala.

Posada Arigalan and Posada Rancho Cerro Largo

About half a mile (1 km) west of San Agustinillo, **Posada Arigalan** basks atop its ocean-view forested hilltop. Owner Rose Guillen offers several (all nonsmoking) comfortable suites and rooms, featuring views, your choice of double or king sized beds, and fans or a/c. Rentals run around $55 d for the suites, about $45 for the rooms. All accommodations have private shower baths, but at this writing, with room temperature (tepid, not cold) water only. The beach and restaurants at San Agustinillo are reachable within minutes by path or the highway.

The same owner also offers similar accommodation at the four-room beachfront **Posada La Barca** nearby. Reserve by mail, at P.O. Box 882, Comfort, TX 78013, call tel. 830/995-4233, or email arigalan@hotmail.com.

For more information, log on to www.tomzap .com/arigalan.html and/or www.arigalan.com.

Outstandingly innovative **Posada Rancho Cerro Largo,** P.O. Box 121, Pochutla, Oaxaca 70900, fax 958/584-3063, ranchocerro-largomx@yahoo.com, half a mile (1 km) farther west, is the creation of eco-activist Mario Corella, descendant of a longtime Hermosillo, Sonora, hotel family. After knocking around in the hospitality trade for several years, Mario decided to create his own version of utopia. Mario says that he wanted to "be in contact with nature and live among the community with as little impact as possible. I would welcome guests as friends, to share the dinner table with me and the hotel staff."

He's done it, with a reception-restaurant and several rustically charming tile-floored, wood-and-adobe cabanas, furnished with hand-loomed bedspreads and opening to hammock-hung ocean-view verandas. The entire complex nestles in a cactus-dotted, leafy hillside forest, linked by a path that meanders, between panoramic ocean viewpoints, to a gorgeously isolated, wave-washed sandy beach below. Rates run a reasonable $60 s, $70 d, add $18 per person for breakfast and dinner. Reservations are mandatory in winter, highly recommended anytime. Look for the signed driveway on the Puerto Ángel–Mazunte road, four miles (6.4 km) from the Puerto Ángel bus stop.

Mazunte Accommodations

Mazunte folks offer a number of lodgings, from rough beachfront cabanas to semi-deluxe, architecturally designed thatched *palapas*. Although the humblest of these accommodations are low on luxury, they are high on gorgeous blue water, lazy hammocks, yellow sand, palmy shade, and balmy breezes.

Many of the more basic lodgings cluster on or near the Mazunte main beach. Highest marks go to **Palapa Omar,** tel. 954/588-3245, which offers six simple cabanas, with double beds, fans, shared toilet with room-temperature shower, and beachfront restaurant. Rentals cost about $20 for two.

Second choice next door goes to **Cabañas Yuri,** no phone, with about six wooden-floored, thatched *palapas,* for about $15 d with shared bath, $25 d with private room-temperature bath. No fans (a minus, especially during the hot spring) at this writing. Make sure that everything works before you move in. Get to Mazunte Beach from the main through-town road via

the side road to the beach, just east of the town soccer field.

The fanciest accommodation in Mazunte is the lovely hillside **Alta Mira Bungalows,** sister lodging of Hotel La Buena Vista in Puerto Ángel. Guests enjoy a lovely hillside ocean-view setting with a good restaurant, the murmur of the waves, and a stepped path down to glorious Mazunte Beach. The approximately 10 rooms are comfortable rustic-chic, with handcrafted furniture and soft beds. Rentals begin at about $35 d. At this writing, the Alta Mira's main drawback is lack of electricity. Reserve via the Buena Vista in Puerto Ángel: P.O. Box 48, Puerto Ángel, Oaxaca 70902, tel./fax 958/584-3104, mail@buenavista.com. For more information, log on to www.labuenavista.com, where you can link with the Alta Mira (High Sight) Bungalows' page.

Get to Alta Mira Bungalows from the main through-town road. A block west of the bridge, go left at the side road, Calle Rinconcito. Continue about a block to the signed uphill side road on the right.

Several other inviting accommodations dot the Mazunte beaches and tropical forest environs. Especially attractive is **Posada Las Mazuntinas,** P.O. Box 87, Pochutla, Oaxaca 70900, tel. 958/583-9709, mazuntinas@hotmail.com, which nestles in the forest about five minutes from the beach. Owner Yolanda Quintana offers four comfortable, architecturally designed thatched-*palapa* suites and rooms, with hot water, and a three-car garage. For more information, including photos, log on to www.tomzap.com/mazunteb .html#hotels. (This website also lists a number of other accommodations possibilities in Mazunte.)

Trailer Parks and Camping

The homey **Trailer Park La Palmera Fernando's** and café has about 20 parking (big rigs possible) or camping spaces beneath a shady, tufted grove by the road at the east end of Playa Zipolite. Reserve by writing friendly owner Fernando Torres at Carretera Playa Zipolite–Puerto Ángel, Oaxaca 70902. A spirit of camaraderie often blooms among the tents and assorted RVs of travelers from as far away as Miami, Medicine Hat, and Murmansk. About $8 for small RV,

$12 large, $20 very large, gets you a space for two persons, including electricity; shared dump station, shower, and toilets. Tent spaces cost $6 for two persons.

One of Zipolite's best tenting spots is on the beach below Shambhala (with fine food from neighboring Restaurant Alquimista or Shambhala's restaurant uphill). The friendly owner, Gloria Johnson, will probably allow you to use Shambhala's showers and toilets for a small fee. Ask at the Shambhala office, tel./fax 958/584-3151 or 958/584-3152, for permission to camp.

Beach camping is customary in San Agustinillo, especially at the rustic, hammock-hung roadside *ramadas* **Palapa Lucy, Palapa Kaly,** and **Palapa Sol Mar** at the east (Zipolite) end of the beach. Camping is also customary in **Mazunte** on the beach, in front of Palapa Omar and Cabañas Yuri.

FOOD

For a country place, Puerto Ángel has surprisingly good food, starting with the **Hotel Villa Florencia,** right on the main beachfront street. Lulu, the wife of the late Italian-born owner/chef carries on his tradition, specializing in antipasti and salads ($3–5), and meat and seafood pastas ($5–15). Like any good country Italian restaurant, service is crisp and presentations are attractive. The modest wine list has, in the past, included some good old-country imports, and the pastas al dente and cappuccino are among the best on the coast. Open daily 8 A.M.–11 P.M. (If you're in need of lodging, ask at the hotel desk in back to see some of their clean, comfortable rooms.)

The unpretentiously elegant *palapa* restaurant at the **Hotel La Buena Vista,** tel. 958/584-3104, is the best spot in town for a leisurely, intimate dinner and a *buena vista* (good view). Here, the prodigious effort that owner/managers Lourdes and Carrie Díaz have invested in their kitchen and staff comes together beautifully. The servers, fetchingly attired in colorful Oaxaca *huipiles,* glide gracefully between kitchen and tables with a bounty of crisp salads and savory soups ($3–6), tender pastas ($4–7), and fresh broiled fish and meats ($7–15). It's open

7:30–11 A.M. for breakfast, closed afternoons, then open for supper 6–10 P.M.

Four or five *palapa* restaurants line Playa Panteón. Here, the charming beach scene is an extra added to the already good food, especially at **Restaurant Cordelia** (on the far left as you approach the beach). Although seafood is the best choice in general, Cordelia offers an inviting list of good salads, pastas, meats, and poultry to boot ($3–15). Open daily 8 A.M.–10 P.M. low season, 8 A.M.–midnight high.

If you appreciate vegetables, don't miss the open-air restaurant of the Hotel Cañón Devata, tel./fax 958/584-3137, tucked in the canyon uphill from Playa Panteón. Here, hearty macrobiotic vegetarian fare is the theme. During the low season, the restaurant is open for breakfast only, daily 7 A.M.–2 P.M. High season, they're open for breakfast ($3–5), lunch ($5–8), and dinner ($7–12), daily 7 A.M.–9 P.M.

For a spectacular view with late lunch or early dinner (or even just a drink), go to the family-run **Restaurant Rincón del Mar,** which clings to the west-side headland overlooking the bay. (Follow the *andador* toward the beach from the beachfront Avenida Uribe bridge, just west of the naval compound. At the restaurant sign, follow the stairway up the rocky headland.) The star of the show (aided by a husband-daughter team) is the wife Mari, who crafts a short but tasty menu of soups and salads ($3–5), pastas ($4–7), and seafood and meats ($5–12). Open daily 4–10 P.M.

Zipolite and Mazunte Restaurants

Zipolite also has some good eateries. For hearty macrobiotic-style fare and a breezy beach view, go to the restaurant at **Shambhala** on the Playa Zipolite west-end headland above the beach. Personable owner Gloria Johnson runs a very tidy kitchen, which serves good breakfasts ($3–6), soups and salads ($3–4), and sandwiches ($3–5). Open daily 8 A.M.–8 P.M. No alcohol.

Regula, the European co-owner of **Lo Cósmico** on the knoll just east of Shambhala, cooks from a similar macrobiotic-style menu, although she specializes in several variations of crepes, including egg, meat, cheese, and vegetable ($3–6). Open daily, high season, from around 8 A.M. to about 7 P.M. Shorter hours and closed Monday during the low season.

Right on the Shambhala–Lo Cósmico beachfront, a regiment of satisfied patrons of **Restaurant Alquimista** choose from a seeming mile-long menu of appetizers (hummus, guacamole, $3–5), soups (onion, cream of carrot, $3–6), salads (Greek, romaine, $4–6), *tortas* (egg, ham, cheese, $3–5), fish (10 styles of fillet, $6–12), pastas (al burro, cream, Bolognese, $4–8), hamburgers (fish, beef, chicken, $4) and much, much more. Open daily, 4–10 P.M. low season; noon–midnight high season.

For homey elegance, continue past Zipolite to the restaurant at **Posada Rancho Cerro Largo.** Here, friendly eco-activist owner Mario Corella invites guests to share a meal ($8–20) and the beautiful view with him and the hotel staff. Don't show up unannounced; fax 958/584-3063 or email ranchocerrolargomx@yahoo.com a few days ahead of time and ask for a reservation. For access directions, see Posada Rancho Cerro Largo under Accommodations.

Mazunte visitors enjoy a number of recommendable home-grown restaurants. On the beach, try **El Aguajon** seafood *palapa*. The hardworking (he's Mexican, she's French) owners put out a tasty menu that specializes in catch-of-the-day seafood ($5–10), but also features savory wood-oven pizza ($6–8) and home-style lasagna ($5).

Tasty vegetarian-style goodies are the specialty at **Tanya's,** on the west side, uphill, above the cosmetics factory-store. Besides super-fresh seafood ($5–10), Tanya offers plenty of hearty juices ($2–3), salads ($3–5), and soy burgers ($3–4).

On the main street, about a block west from the cosmetics factory-store, try restaurant **Bugambilias,** with a likewise hearty menu, featuring seafood ($5–10), spaghetti ($4–6), hamburgers ($3–5), salads ($3–4), and fish tacos ($2–4).

Perhaps the most elegant dining spot in Mazunte is Doña Rosa's, at the **Hotel Alta Mira.** Although the ocean view is justification enough, the Japanese, Italian, and vegetarian cuisine of Doña Rosa provides the strongest reason for a meal there. Open for breakfast ($5–8) and dinner ($5–15) during high season, late fall–winter–spring. During summer–fall low season,

be sure to call ahead (tel. 958/584-3104) to see if she's open.

ENTERTAINMENT AND RECREATION

Puerto Ángel's entertainments are mostly spontaneous. If anything exciting is going to happen, it will most likely be on the beachfront Boulevard Uribe, where people tend to congregate during the late afternoon and evenings. A small crowd may accumulate in the adjacent restaurant Villa Florencia for coffee, talk, or something from the bar.

The town's major scheduled event is the big **Fiesta de San Miguel Arcangel** on October 1 and 2. Then the *mascaritas* (masked children) dancers romp, carnival games, and rides light up the street-front, and a regatta of fishing boats parades around the bay.

Sunsets

Sunset-watchers get their best chance from the unobstructed hilltop perch of the Hotel Ángel del Mar, or Lola's, on the beach in Zipolite, where the bar and restaurant at each place can provide something to enliven the occasion even if clouds happen to block the view.

Hotel Ángel del Mar sometimes provides music for dancing during the highest seasons, most likely between Christmas and New Year and the week before Easter.

For additional diversions, head west to Puerto Escondido or east to Bahías de Huatulco, each about an hour by car, for more and livelier entertainment.

Jogging

Potholed streets, rocky roads, and lack of grass sharply curtail Puerto Ángel jogging prospects. The highway, however, which runs gradually uphill from near the pier, does provide a continuous, more or less smooth surface. Confine your jogging to early morning or late afternoon, and take water along.

Swimming and Surfing

Swimming provides better local exercise opportunities, especially in the sheltered waters off of Playa Panteón. Bodysurfing, boogie boarding, and surfing can be rewarding, depending on wind and swells, off Playa Zipolite. Be super-careful of undertow, which is always a threat, even on calm days at Zipolite. If you're inexperienced, don't go out alone. Novice and even experienced swimmers sometimes drown at Zipolite. If you get caught in a current pulling you out to sea, don't panic. Experts advise that you simply float and paddle parallel to the beach a hundred yards or so, to a spot where the offshore current is not so severe (or may even push you back toward the beach). Alcohol and surf, moreover, don't mix. On rough days, unless you're an expert, forget it. Bring your own board; few, if any, rentals are available.

Sailing and Windsurfing

If you have your own carryable boat or windsurfing gear, sheltered **Playa Panteón** would be a good place to put it into the water, although the neighboring headland may decrease the available wind. Calm mornings at **Playas Zipolite, San Agustinillo,** or **Mazunte** (see under Beaches and Sights), or afternoons, with more wind but rougher waves, are the most promising times.

Snorkeling and Scuba Diving

Rocky shoals at the edges of Puerto Ángel Bay, especially just off **Playa Panteón,** are fine for casual snorkeling. **Playa Estacahuite,** on the open ocean just beyond the bay's east headland, is even better. Best bring your own equipment. If you don't, you can rent a snorkel and mask from restaurants Cordelia or Leyvis y Vicente, on Playa Panteón, for about $3 an hour.

Puerto Ángel now has a **professional scuba diving shop,** run by the owner-builder of Hotel Cordelia, at Playa Panteón, tel. 958/584-3109, azul_profundomx@hotmail.com.

Alternatively, beginners can contact the well-equipped and certified dive instructors of **Buceos Triton** dive shop, tel./fax 958/587-0844, or **Hurricane Divers,** tel. 958/587-1107, hurricanedivers@hotmail.com, www.hurricanedivers.com, both at the Santa Cruz de Huatulco marina. (For more details, see Swimming, Surfing,

Snorkeling, and Scuba Diving in the Bahías de Huatulco section.)

Fishing

The bayfront pier is the best place to bargain for a boat and captain to take you and your friends out on a fishing excursion. Prices depend on season, but you can figure on paying about $20 an hour for a boat for four or five persons with bait and two or three good rods and reels. During a three-hour outing, a few miles offshore, a competently captained boat will typically bring in three or four big, good-eating *robalo* (snook), *huachinango* (snapper), *atún* (tuna), or pompano. If you're uncertain about what's biting, go down to the dock around 2 or 3 P.M. in the afternoon and see what the boats are bringing in.

Vicente, of Leyvis y Vicente restaurant on Playa Panteón, takes out fishing parties of up to six persons for around $20 an hour, bait and tackle included. You can also arrange fishing trips through the **Gambusino Travel Agency,** tel. 958/584-3038, fax 958/584-3070, open Mon.–Sat. 9 A.M.–2 P.M. and 4–8 P.M., in the office across the street from the doctor and pharmacy on Av. Teniente Vasconcelos, just uphill from Uribe.

SHOPPING
Market

The biggest local market is the Monday *tianguis,* which spreads along the Pochutla main street, Highway 175, about seven miles (11 km) from Puerto Ángel, one mile (1.6 km) inland from the Highway 200 junction. It's mostly a place for looking rather than buying, as throngs of vendors from the hills line the sidewalks, even crowding into the streets, to sell their piles of carrots, cilantro, forest herbs, *jícama,* mangoes, and onions.

On other days, vendors confine their displays to the permanent Mercado 5 de Octubre, on the east side of the main street, between Calles 1 and 2 Sur.

Groceries

The best-stocked Puerto Ángel local store is the

Super Del Puerto at the west end of beachfront street Uribe, uphill past the arroyo bridge. Also, a few little-bit-of-everything stores in Zipolite and on Uribe in the middle of Puerto Ángel sell bread, cheese, milk, some vegetables, and other essentials.

Handicrafts

For fine custom-made hammocks, visit local craftsman Gabino Silva at his country shop, off a jungly stretch of the road between Zipolite and San Agustín. He also rents a cabana. Watch for the sign labeled Hamacas and Cabaña on the beach side of the road, 4.2 miles (6.7 km) from the Puerto Ángel bus stop.

A handful of handicrafts have arrived in Puerto Ángel, at new La Primavera beachware store, on Vasconcelos, directly uphill from the pier, tel. 958/584-3251, open daily 9 A.M.–10 P.M.

A few stores sell some unique handicrafts in Pochutla. **Foto Garcia,** on main street Lázaro Cárdenas 76 (west side), tel. 958/584-0735, offers many whimsical coconut carvings by a local craftsman. It's open Mon.–Sat. 8 A.M.–2 P.M. and 4–8 P.M.

Additionally, the Pochutla *larga distancia,* **Caseta Cybeltel,** between Calles 1 and 2 Norte (across the street from the Hotel Izola), open daily 7 A.M.–10 P.M., customarily offers a varied collection of mostly Guatemalan hand-embroidered purses, *huipiles,* shirts, vests, and 1960s-style tie-dyed apparel.

INFORMATION AND SERVICES

Money Exchange

The only regular local money exchange in Puerto Ángel is the Gambusino Travel Agency, on Vasconcelos, the street that runs from the Puerto Ángel pier uphill. Otherwise, go to **Banco Internacional** (Bital) on the Pochutla main street, Lázaro Cárdenas, tel. 958/584-0698, open Mon.–Fri. 8 A.M.–7 P.M., Sat. 8 A.M.–3 P.M. Alternatively, try **Bancomer,** corner of Lázaro Cárdenas and Av. 3A Norte, tel. 958/584-0259, open Mon.–Fri. 8 A.M.–5 P.M., Sat. 9 A.M.–1 P.M. Another option is **Bancrecer,** next door to Bancomer, tel. 958/584-0763, open Mon.–Fri.

9 A.M.–5 P.M., Sat. 10 A.M.–2 P.M. Call to confirm money-changing hours.

Communications and Travel Agent

The Puerto Ángel *correo* and *telecomunicaciones* stand side by side at the Agencia Municipal at the foot of Hwy. 175. Both are open Mon.–Fri. 9 A.M.–3 P.M.

The Puerto Ángel *larga distancia* telephone, fax office, and **Gela net** Internet access is on Calle José Vasconcelos, just uphill from main street Uribe, tel. 958/584-3046 or 958/584-3054, fax 958/584-3070, shenalo@hotmail.com. Hours are daily 7 A.M.–10 P.M.

Internet access is also available at **Hotel Puesta del Sol and Cyber café,** about half a block west of the Blvd. Uribe bridge, or **Caseta Cybeltel,** in Pochutla, main street, across from the Hotel Izola. Caseta Cybeltel also maintains a *lista de email* of email messages, like a *lista de correo.*

Puerto Ángel's travel agent, friendly Mati Velasco (who also runs the *larga distancia* and Internet access) of **Agencia de Viajes Gambusino,** tel. 958/584-3080 or 958/584-3038, arranges tours and fishing trips and sells reserved air and bus tickets at her small office on Vasconcelos, next door and uphill from the *larga distancia.*

Health and Police

Puerto Ángel's kindly and respected private **doctor,** Dr. Constancio Aparicio Juárez, holds consultation hours Mon.–Sat. 7 A.M.–2 P.M. and 5–9 P.M. and also runs the **pharmacy,** on Av. Vasconcelos, tel. 958/584-3058, across from the *larga distancia.* For serious illness requiring diagnostic specialists, Dr. Juárez recommends you go to the government Hospital Regional in Pochutla, tel. 958/584-0204, or the Seguro Social in Crucecita (Bahías de Huatulco), tel. 958/587-0124 or 958/587-0264.

Another option is to go to the small government **Centro de Salud** health clinic, on the hill behind the church, which concentrates on preventative rather than diagnostic medicine. Go up Vasconcelos a long curving block, go left at the first corner, and continue another block to the health center.

For police emergencies, contact the **federal**

police *(preventiva)*, at the *agencia municipal,* tel. 958/584-3207, end of Blvd. Uribe, or call the **policía preventiva,** at the Presidencia Municipal, in Pochutla, on the town plaza, one block east of the main north-south town thoroughfare, tel. 958/584-0273.

Ecological Project

Ecological activism has spread to Mazunte, where the **Asociación de Comuneros de Mazunte** has picked up the green banner. Led by their earnest activist-president Ermilo López Bustamante, the association is building an ecologically correct time-share development and encouraging waste composting and water and forest conservation. Partly as a result of their efforts, cutting trees around Zipolite, San Agustín, and Mazunte has become a definite community no-no. Consequently, the tropical deciduous forest zone between Zipolite and Mazunte is rapidly becoming a luxuriantly healthy eco-preserve. A good place to contact Bustamante might be through the turtle museum, where he's well known.

GETTING THERE AND AWAY

By Air

Scheduled flights to Mexican destinations connect daily with airports at **Huatulco,** 19 miles (30 km) east, or **Puerto Escondido,** 44 miles (71 km) west, by road from Puerto Ángel.

By Car or RV

Good roads connect Puerto Ángel to the west with Puerto Escondido and Acapulco, north with Oaxaca, and east with the Bahías de Huatulco and the Isthmus of Tehuantepec.

Highway 200 connects westward with Puerto Escondido in an easy 44 miles (71 km), continuing to Pinotepa Nacional (135 miles, 217 km, three hours) and Acapulco in a total of seven hours (291 miles, 469 km) of driving. In the opposite direction, Bahías de Huatulco (actually Crucecita town), 22 miles (35 km) is reachable in about 45 minutes. The continuation to Salina Cruz stretches another 92 miles (148 km), or around 2.5 additional hours of driving time.

North to Oaxaca, paved but narrow and winding National Highway 175 connects 148 miles (238 km) over the Sierra Madre del Sur from its junction with Highway 200 at Pochutla. The road climbs to around 9,000 feet through cool (chilly in winter) pine forests and hardscrabble Chatino and Zapotec native villages. Fill up with gas in Pochutla. Unleaded gasoline is available at the Pochutla Pemex stations, both on through-town Highway 175: about 300 yards toward town from Highway 200, and on the north, uphill, edge of town. Carry water and blankets, and be prepared for emergencies. The first gas station after Pochutla is at Miahuatlán, 90 miles (144 km) north. Allow about eight hours behind the wheel from Puerto Ángel to Oaxaca, about seven in the opposite direction.

By Bus

One long-distance bus line, second-class **Estrella del Valle,** connects Puerto Ángel directly to Oaxaca and Pochutla, where many long-distance connections may be made. Buses depart from the main-street corner of Uribe and Vasconcelos. The Pochutla-bound buses depart hourly during daylight hours, the Oaxaca bus once, nightly, at 10 P.M. Double check the schedule at the adjacent Papelería El Globo, which serves as the information and ticket office.

In Pochutla, from three separate stations, many other long-distance buses connect with points west, east, and north. The stations cluster less than a mile (1.6 km) north from the Highway 200 junction along Avenida Lázaro Cárdenas, the Highway 175 main street into Pochutla.

As you enter the Pochutla business district, first you'll see first-class **Cristóbal Colón** station on the left (at L. Cárdenas 84, tel. 958/584-0274). Several departures per day connect east with Crucecita. Some continue east, connecting with Salina Cruz and Tehuantepec, and continuing to Chiapas destinations of Tuxtla Gutiérrez San Cristóbal and Tapachula, at the Guatemala border. A few buses connect north with Oaxaca via the long, relatively level, Isthmus route, via Salina Cruz and Tehuantepec. During the dry season, buses also connect with the trans-Sierra but shorter Highway 175. One bus connects daily with Puebla and Mexico City. A few buses also connect daily west with Puerto Escondido. Next, a few doors farther north, at L. Cárdenas 94, tel. 958/584-0380, **Estrella Blanca** subsidiary-line buses (such as first-class Elite, luxury-class Turistar, Flecha Roja, and Autotransportes Cuauhtémoc) connect west daily with Puerto Escondido, continuing to Acapulco and Lázaro Cárdenas in Michoacán, there continuing along the entire Mexican Pacific coast, all the way to the U.S. border. They also connect east (many per day) with Bahías de Huatulco destinations of Crucecita and Santa Cruz de Huatulco and Salina Cruz on the Isthmus. A few "plus" (say "ploos") luxury-class buses connect daily, all the way to Mexico City.

About a block farther, across the main street, **Autobuses Estrella del Valle, Autobuses Oaxaca Pacífico,** and **Fletes y Pasajes** (tel. 958/584-0138 or 958/584-0349) operate out of their joint central bus station *central de autobus.* Frequent second-class and some first-class service is offered, connecting west with Puerto Escondido and Pinotepa Nacional; north with Oaxaca and Mexico City; and east with Huatulco, Salina Cruz, and the Chiapas border.

UPLAND EXCURSIONS FROM PUERTO ÁNGEL

Highway 175 curves its way from Puerto Ángel north, rising from the coast, continuing past a scattering of villages set in luxuriant forests, and finally climbing to cool, pine-tufted heights, where on a clear day the shining blue Pacific far below seems half a world away.

Travelers who hurry along this route find little; many of those who linger discover pleasant surprises along the way.

San Pedro Pochutla

The capital of the Pochutla governmental district was founded around 1600. One look along the busy, cluttered main street of Pochutla (pop. about 30,000) reveals that it's a market town. This is most apparent on Monday, when the side streets off the main street (Highway 175, locally known as Avenida Lázaro Cárdenas) bloom with colorful *tianguis* (awnings) of vendors offering a collective mountain of merchandise.

On other days, vendors confine their piles to the formal indoor market, the **Mercado 5 de Octubre,** between Calles 1 and 2 Sur at the downtown center, on the east side of Lázaro Cárdenas.

Although most people come to Pochutla for business or to catch a bus, this town offers more than the merely perfunctory. A closer look reveals that Pochutla is really two towns rolled into one—the busy main street and the spacious, completely automobile-free central plaza and mall just one block downhill to the east.

The perfect perch for taking it all in is the upstairs plaza-view **Restaurant San Ángel** on the plaza's west side, open daily 9 A.M.–11 P.M. You can start off the day with a good breakfast or enjoy a fresh seafood lunch or dinner while being entertained by the plaza scene below. Directly east, across the plaza, spreads the *presidencia municipal,* and to the right (south) rise the baroque domes of the town church, the **Templo de San Pedro.**

On the west side of the plaza, the townsfolk have planted a living reminder of Pochutla, whose name comes from the Aztec-language label Pochtlán (Land of the Pochotes) for the locally plentiful *pochote* tree. You'll see a young specimen with small green leaves, five to a bunch, and spines on the trunk. People say that the *pochote* tree's edible roots sustained many starving families during times of drought and war.

Excitement mounts in Pochutla during the June 21–28 **Fiesta de San Pedro y San Pablo.** Celebrations begin with early morning masses and religious processions, then carnival rides and games, food, and fireworks. Finally, a parade of floats carries a gaggle of mysterious masked characters who climax the festivities with a traditional dance.

Even during non-festival times the nighttime plaza, illuminated with Porfirian-era streetlight globes, is doubly interesting, so much so that you may decide to stay overnight. If so, Pochutla can accommodate you with the invitingly traditional **Hotel Pochutla,** Madero 102, Pochutla, Oaxaca 70900, tel./fax 958/584-0033, at the plaza's northwest corner. Owners offer 34 rooms arranged around an intimate, plant-decorated inner patio. Although many downstairs rooms are musty, upstairs they are invitingly quaint, with old-world louvered tropical-style doors, some of which open to balconies overlooking the colorful plaza scene. Rates run about $16 s, $20 d, $24 t, with fan and private hot-water shower bath.

Chacalapa

About nine miles (14 km) uphill from Pochutla along Highway 175, the village of San José Chacalapa nestles in the tropical foothill forest. The village's most inviting roadside attraction is **Restaurant Los Reyes,** a *palapa* on the west side, open daily 7 A.M.–10 P.M. Here you can pick from a long menu of soups, seafood (cocktails, fish fillets, shrimp, snails), meat, tacos, quesadillas, guacamole, *papa del horno* (baked potato), and sandwiches (hamburger, tuna, chicken, and ham and cheese). After that, relax in the big, blue pool or stroll out into the surrounding forest.

For an extended exploration, ask the friendly family owners for a guide to the nearby *cascada* (waterfall) and curative sulfur-water lagoon. If you're lucky, they may introduce you to very knowledgeable local resident Isidro Reyes Guzmán. Along the way, he will help you spot, besides the locally abundant *ardillas, halcones,* and *aguilas* (squirrels, hawks, and eagles), some *carpinteros, tucanetas, péricos, tigrillos,* and *coatis* (woodpeckers, toucans, parrots, ocelots, and coatimundis). He can identify *plantas medicinales* (medicinal plants) in addition to the great forest trees, such as *ceiba, guanacastle, caoba,* and *macuil.*

The Restaurant Los Reyes also displays attractive for-sale furniture, crafted from big, dried *bejuco* vines by local craftsman Abel Hernand.

You may be so charmed by Chacalapa's natural delights that you want to stay overnight. If so, nearby mini-paradise **Balneario El Paraíso** can accommodate you. Get there from the Chacalapa village center, a few hundred yards north of the restaurant. At the *presidencia,* fork right, off the highway. Within a block, turn right again, at the Eco-turismo 1.5 Km sign. After exactly one mile (1.6 km) along a dirt road, turn right into the ranch gate. Here, in addition to a big 10-foot (3-meter) deep, spring-fed swimming pool, a kiddie

pool, swings, slides, and a shaded *palapa* for picnics, are two clean, tile-floored cabanas for rent for about $20 d, with hot-water shower baths.

Although impressive, Balneario Paraíso's manmade amenities are only part of the attraction. Friendly owner Octavio Ramos and his wife will provide meals and are happy to show you around their forested ranch, dotted with mango and orange trees and cinnamon and other spices. Later, explore the surrounding luxuriant stream valley and forest for rewarding views of animals and birds in their natural surroundings.

While you're at Balneario Paraíso, be sure to visit **Rancho Alegre** (on the road, just before the Balneario). Rancho Alegre, sometimes know as Tom's Garden, is the haven of German expatriate jewelry maker Tom Bachmeier and his Colombian wife Nehier. If you're lucky, one of them will show you around their tropical mini-Eden, lush with bromeliads, orchids, ginger, and a wealth of zapote, cacao, coffee, and mango trees. You may contact them by mail at P.O. Box 73, San Pedro Pochutla, Oaxaca 70900.

San José del Pacífico

This is a little mountaintop town with a tremendous view, so high that the Pacific Ocean is clearly visible far below. The climate is brisk and dry, and pine-clad mountains rise all around, an ideal setting for a few days away from the tropics. What's just as good, the village has a pair of pretty fair restaurants and an invitingly rustic hotel.

Little was spared to create the **Hotel Puesta Del Sol,** San José del Pacífico, Oaxaca 70861, tel. 951/547-4225, tel./fax 951/572-0111, sanjose@sanjosedelpacifico.com, www.sanjosedelpacifico.com, whose gardens lead downhill past the restaurant to knotty-pine cabanas. Stay in the clean, cozy mountain cabanas for $13 s or d, $20 t, with fireplace and private hot-water shower baths. Reserve directly by telephone or mail.

Food is available, either at the hotel's Restaurant Esther, with its lovely view, or the restaurant Rayito del Sol (Little Sunbeam) in the village nearby.

The main local diversions are natural, such as basking in the sun, hiking mountain trails to panoramic viewpoints, observing wildlife, watching spectacular sunsets, and resting or reading by the fireplace.

Get to San José del Pacífico by bus or car via Highway 175, either 65 miles (105 km) north of Pochutla or 81 miles (130 km) south of Oaxaca.

Bahías de Huatulco and Vicinity

The nine azure Bahías de Huatulco (wah-TOOL-koh) decorate a couple dozen miles of acacia-plumed rocky coastline east of Puerto Ángel. Between the bays, the ocean joins in battle with jutting, rocky headlands, while in their inner reaches, the ocean calms, caressing diminutive crescents of coral sand. Inland, a thick hardwood forest seems to stretch in a continuous carpet to the Sierra.

Ecologists shivered when they heard that these bays were going to be developed. Fonatur, the government tourism development agency, says it has a plan, however. Relatively few (but all upscale) hotels will occupy the beaches; other development will be confined to a few inland centers. The remaining 70 percent of the land will be kept as pristine ecological zones and study areas.

Although this story sounds sadly familiar, Fonatur, which developed Ixtapa and Cancún, seems to have learned from its experience. Up-to-date sewage treatment was installed *ahead of time;* logging and homesteading were halted, and soldiers patrol the beaches, stopping turtle poachers. If all goes according to the plan, the nine Bahías de Huatulco and their 100,000-acre forest hinterland will be both a tourist and ecological paradise, in addition to employing thousands of local people, when complete in 2020. If this Huatulco dream ends as well as it has started, Mexico should take pride while the rest of the world should take heed.

HISTORY

Long before Columbus, the Huatulco area was well-known to the Aztecs and their predecessors. The name itself, from Aztec words meaning "Land where a Tree (or Wood) Is Worshipped," reflects one of Mexico's most intriguingly persistent legends—of the **Holy Cross of Huatulco.**

When the Spanish arrived on the Huatulco coast in the 1520s, the local native people showed them a huge cross they worshipped at the edge of the sea. A contemporary chronicler, Ignacio Burgoa, conjectured the cross had been left by an ancient saint—maybe even the Apostle Thomas—some 15 centuries earlier. The cross remained as the Spanish colonized the area and established headquarters and a port, which they named San Agustín, at the westernmost of the Bahías de Huatulco.

Spanish ports and their treasure-laden galleons from the Orient attracted foreign corsairs—Francis Drake in 1579 and Thomas Cavendish in 1587. Cavendish arrived at the bay now called Bahía Santa Cruz, where he saw the cross the natives were worshipping. Believing it was the work of the devil, Cavendish and his men tried to chop, saw, and burn it down. Failing at all of these, Cavendish looped his ship's mooring ropes around the cross and with sails unfurled tried using the force of the wind to pull it down. Frustrated, he finally sailed away, leaving the cross of Huatulco still standing beside the shore.

By 1600, pilgrims were chipping pieces from the cross; so much so that in 1612, Bishop Juan de Cervantes had to rescue it. He brought the cross to Oaxaca, where he made four smaller two-foot crosses of it. He sent one specimen each to church authorities in Mexico City, Rome, and Santa María de Huatulco, head town of the Huatulco *municipio.* Cervantes kept the fourth copy in the cathedral in Oaxaca, where it has remained, venerated and visible in a side chapel, to the present day.

SIGHTS

Getting Oriented

With no road to the outside world, the Bahías de Huatulco remained virtually uninhabited and undeveloped until 1982, about the time that coastal Highway 200 was pushed through. A few years later, Huatulco's planned initial kernel of infrastructure was complete, centering on the brand-new residential service town, Crucecita (pop. 10,000), and nearby Santa Cruz de Huatulco boat harbor and hotel village on Bahía Santa Cruz.

The Bahías de Huatulco decorate the coastline both east and west of Santa Cruz. To the east, a paved road links Bahías Chahue, Tangolunda, and Conejos. To the west lie Bahías El Organo, El Maguey, and Cacaluta. Of the latter three, only Bahía Maguey is accessible by paved road. El Organo and Cacaluta are only accessible with the help of a guide; the former on foot or by horseback, the latter by truck or SUV. Isolated farther west are Bahías Chachacual and San Agustín, with no road from Santa Cruz (although a good dirt road runs to San Agustín from Highway 200 near the airport).

Besides Bahía Santa Cruz, the only other bays that have been extensively developed are Chahue, a mile (1.6 km) east, and Tangolunda, four miles (6.4 km) east. Chahue now has a marina and a sprinkling of small-to-medium-sized, medium-priced hotels. Tangolunda has a green and lovely golf course, small restaurant/shopping complex, and six resort hotels (Las Brisas, Quinta Real, Crown Pacific, Barceló, Club Gala Resort, and Zaashila) that have all been fully operational since the mid-1990s. For more details, see Exploring the Bahías de Huatulco.

Getting Around

Frequent public **minibuses** connect Crucecita and Bahías Santa Cruz, Chahue, and Tangolunda. Taxis make the same trips for about $2 by day, $3 at night. No public transportation is available to the other bays. Taxi drivers are willing to drive you for a picnic to west-side bay El Maguey, or Playa Entrega (an isolated beach on

PACIFIC RESORTS

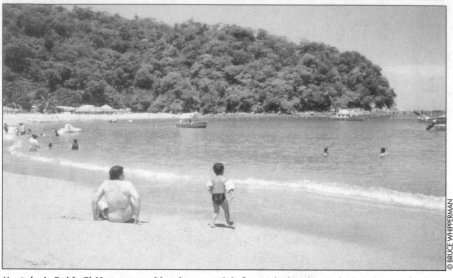

Huatulco's Bahía El Maguey provides the essentials for a relaxing day at the beach: sun, fresh seafood, soft sand, and calm, clear water.

Santa Cruz Bay), for about $5 one way, from Crucecita or Tangolunda; figure about $4 for the same to Bahía Conejos.

For an extended day trip to all road-accessible bays, figure on about $20–30 for a taxi, about $50 for a rental car. Call Alamo in Santa Cruz (at Hotel Castillo), tel. 958/587-0135 or 958/581-9074; or Budget in Crucecita at Octillo and Jazmín, tel. 958/587-0010, fax 958/587-0019.

Another option is to go by boat. The local boat cooperative (Sociedad Cooperativa Turístico Tangolunda) runs a daily excursion—around 10:30 A.M., $20 per person, kids 5–9 half price—to all nine bays, including open bar, bilingual guide, and snacks; snorkeling is $5 extra. Reserve directly through its dock office, tel. 958/587-0081, or through a travel agent, such as Paraíso Huatulco, tel. 958/581-0055, at the Hotel Barceló, tel. 958/581-0055, ext. 784; or Servicios Turísticos del Sur, at the Hotel Castillo, tel./fax 958/587-1211; or Paraíso Huatulco, at the Hotel Flamboyan in Crucecita, tel. 958/587-0181, fax 958/587-0190.

The same cooperative also rents entire boats for up to 10 people. Drop-off runs to the nearest beach are about $10 per boat roundtrip; to the more remote beaches, around $20–30.

Local travel agents offer other tour options: several hours of sunning, swimming, picnicking, and snorkeling at a couple of Bahías de Huatulco beaches runs around $20 per person. Tours to Puerto Ángel, Puerto Escondido, and wildlife-rich lagoons go for $30–50 per person. For reservations, call Paraíso Huatulco, at the Hotel Barceló, tel. 958/581-0055, ext. 784 (or in Crucecita, at tel. 958/587-0181, fax 958/587-0190); or Servicios Turísticos del Sur, at the Hotel Castillo, tel./fax 958/587-1211.

Another option is to get your own guide. An inexpensive way to do this is to hire an English-speaking taxi driver to take you wherever you want to go for several hours, up to a whole day, for $30–50, depending on the season.

Professional guides are another option. See Guide in the Information section.

Crucecita and Santa Cruz de Huatulco

Despite its newness, Crucecita (Little Cross, pop. 10,000) resembles a traditional Mexican town, with life revolving around a central plaza and market nearby. Crucecita is where the people who work in the Huatulco hotels, businesses, and government offices live. Although pleasant enough for a walk around the square and a meal in a restaurant, it's nothing special—mostly a place whose modest hotels and restaurants accommodate business travelers and weekenders who can't afford the plush hotels near the beach.

While in Crucecita, be sure to step into the church on the plaza's west side to admire the heavenly **ceiling mural** of Mexico's patron, the Virgin of Guadalupe. The mural, the largest of Guadalupe in Mexico, is the work of local artists José Ángel del Signo and Marco Antonio Contreras, whose for-sale art is on display locally. Besides the heavenly Virgin overhead, the muralists have decorated the space above the altar with the miraculous story of Don Diego and the Virgin of Guadalupe.

The several deluxe hotels and the mostly travel-oriented businesses of **Santa Cruz de Huatulco** (on Bahía Santa Cruz about two miles, 3 km from Crucecita) cluster near the boat harbor. Fishing and tour boats come and go, vacationers sun themselves on the tranquil yellow-sand Playa Santa Cruz (beyond the restaurants adjacent to the boat harbor), while T-shirt and fruit vendors and boatmen hang around the quay watching for prospective customers. After the sun goes down, not much usually happens in Santa Cruz. Tourists quit the beach for their hotels and workers return to their homes in Crucecita, leaving the harbor and streets empty and dark.

Exploring the Bahías de Huatulco

Isolation has left the Huatulco waters blue and unpolluted, the beaches white and clean. Generally, the bays are all similar: tropical deciduous (green July–January) forested rocky headlands enclosing yellow-white coral sand crescents. The water is clear and good for snorkeling, scuba diving, sailing, kayaking, and windsurfing during the often-calm weather. Beaches, however, are typically steep, causing waves to break quickly near the sand, unsuitable for bodysurfing, boogie boarding, or surfing.

Your preparations depend on which bays you plan to explore. For the five developed and

partially developed bays: Santa Cruz, Chahue, Tangolunda, Maguey, and San Agustín, you'll need nothing more than transportation, a hat, and sunscreen. Restaurants and stores can supply everything else.

By contrast, the four undeveloped Huatulco bays of El Organo, Cacaluta, Chacual, and Conejos have neither restaurants, stores, drinking water, nor lots of shade, since they're so pristine coconut palms haven't even gotten around to sprouting there. When exploring, bring food, drinks, hats, sunscreen, and mosquito repellent.

East Side

Bahía Chahue, about a mile (1.6 km) from both Crucecita and Santa Cruz, is wide and blue, with a steep yellow dune above the beach, stretching to the marina jetty at the east end. Chahue is uncrowded even on weekends and holidays and nearly empty the rest of the time.

About four miles (6.4 km) farther east is the breezy and broad **Bahía Tangolunda.** Although hotels front much of the beach, a signed Playa Pública public access road borders the western edge of the golf course (turn right just past the creek bridge). Except for its east end, the Tangolunda beach is steep and the waves break quickly right at the sand. *Palapa* restaurants at the public beach serve food and drinks; or, if you prefer, stroll a quarter mile (a half km) along the beach for refreshments at the luxurious poolside beach clubs of the Barceló and Club Gala Resort.

Over the headland about two miles (3 km) farther east, **Punta Arena** (Sand Point), a forested thumb of land, juts out into wide **Bahía Conejos.** Three separate steep beaches spread along the inner shoreline. The main entrance road arrives at high-duned Playa Punta Arena. Playa Tejoncito (Little Wild Pig) is beyond the rocks far to the right; Playa Conejos (Rabbits) is to the left on the other side of Punta Arena. A few palm-frond *ramadas* for shade and a saltwater flush toilet lavatory occupy the Playa Punta Arena dune. Trees behind the dunes provide a few shady spots for RV or tent campers. (Playa Conejos is becoming a rapidly developing residential zone. By the time you read this, most

CRUCECITA

To Mex. 200, Airport,
and Puerto Ángel

CALLE CARRIZAL

CALLE JAZMIN

OAXACA PACIFICO AND
ESTRELLA DEL VALLE

CLINIC

CALLE SIBALI

CALLE POCHOTE

POSADA PRIMAVERA

POSADA MICHELLE
CALLE
BANCO INTERNACIONAL
ESTRELLA
BLANCA
PALO VERDE
BUDGET RENT A CAR
CALLE
CRISTÓBAL COLÓN
PALMA REAL

CALLE GARDENIA
CALLE
OCOTILLO
PUBLICACIONES HUATULCO
MACUIL
REST. CENADURÍA SAFARI
AZTECA TOURS
CALLE
MACUITLE
CALLE BUGAMBILIAS
CALLE CARRIZAL
BAR LA
CREMA
CALLE
GARUMBO
HOTEL FLAMBOYAN
DISCO LA
CREMA
CALLE GUANACAXTLE
FRUTERÍA ANGELITA
TEMPLO DE
GUADALUPE
PLAZA
CALLE GUAMUCHIL
SEE DETAIL
PLAZA OAXACA/
BUCEOS SOTAVENTO
CALLE FLAMBOYAN
CALLE CHACAH
EXPLORA MEXICO
(RAFTING/RAPELLING)
PARADA DE MICROBUS
(BUS STOP)
CALLE COLORIN
HOTEL
AMAKAL
AV. OAXACA
CASCADAS MÁGICAS
(WATERFALL EXCURSIONS)
SUPER FUENTE
(GROCERIES)
HOTEL JAROJE
POST OFFICE/
TELEGRAPH/
POLICE
ADVENTURAS
PIRAGUAS
CALLE COCOTILLO
POSADA LEO
CASA DE LA
CULTURA/MUNICIPAL
TOURIST INFORMATION
CALLE CEIBA
TANGOLUNDA

0   200 yds
0   200 m

BLVD.

HOSPITAL
SEGURO SOCIAL

To Santa Cruz de Huatulco, Bahías el Organo,
Maguey, and Cacaluta

To Bahías Chahue,
Tangolunda, and Conejos

SEE DETAIL

MARKET
SCOTIABANK
INVERLAT
TACOS LOS
PORTALES
CALLE GUAMUCHIL
HOTEL
GRIFER
P L A Z A
HOTEL LAS
PALMAS
MONEY
EXCHANGE
PLAZA
CONEJO
HOTEL
POSADA DEL
PARQUE
RESTAURANT EL
SABOR DE OAXACA
CAFE
OASIS
LONG DISTANCE
TELEPHONE
HEALTH
CENTER
CALLE BUGAMBILIAS
CACTUS BAR
AND GRILL
CALLE FLAMBOYAN
CENTRA MÉDICA
PHARMACY
RESTAURANT
EL GIARDINO
DEL PAPA
LAUNDRY
ESTRELLA
CALLE CARRIZAL
SUITES
BEGONIAS
INTERNET
HOTEL POSADA JOIS
IRISH PUB

MOON

PACIFIC RESORTS

© AVALON TRAVEL PUBLISHING, INC.

of the accessible wild dunes and beach may be occupied by houses.)

Beyond **La Bocana,** near the mouth of the Río Copalita, less than a mile (1.6 km) farther on, a long, broad beach with oft-powerful surfing rollers (novices beware) stretches for at least a mile (1.6 km) east. Beach *palapas* serve drinks and very fresh seafood. A lagoon above the beach (bring your kayak) appears ripe for wildlife viewing.

After La Bocana, the road bends inland, paralleling the **Río Copalita wildlife sanctuary,** perfect for adventurous exploring. Several operators guide visitors on river eco-tours: José Aussenac, owner of Posada Michelle, tel. 958/587-0535, organizes and guides outdoor adventure-tours. Options include bird- and animal-watching walks along riverine forest trails, kayaking river rapids, rafting, and mud baths at a riverside ranch.

West Side

Bahía Santa Cruz has a pair of beaches, **Playa Entrega** and the more-visited **Playa Santa Cruz,** located past the shops and restaurants, to the right of the boat harbor. During high season and weekends, kids play and tourists improve their tans at Playa Santa Cruz.

Playa Entrega is a hidden little dab of sand slipped into the west side of Bahía Santa Cruz. It is the infamous spot where, on January 20, 1831, Vicente Guerrero, president and independence hero, was brought ashore in custody of arch-villain Francisco Picaluga and sent to be murdered in Oaxaca a few months later.

Quarter-mile-long Playa Entrega is the ideal Sunday beach, with calm, clear water and clean yellow sand. Swimming, kayaking, and often snorkeling, sailing, and windsurfing possibilities are excellent. A number of shoreline restaurants, notably, **Restaurant Arrecife,** tel. 958/587-0524, provide fresh seafood plates and drinks daily, until around 8 P.M.

Get there via the main street, Boulevard Santa Cruz, which passes the Santa Cruz boat harbor. Continue west, bearing left, at the Y intersection at the Hotel Binneguenda (mark your odometer) on the right. After .8 mile (1.3 km), the road bends left and winds uphill, past panoramic view-

points of Bahía Santa Cruz. Follow the signs and you'll soon be at Playa Entrega.

If, instead of curving left to La Entrega, you follow the highway that continues straight ahead at the same spot, you'll be headed for the Bahías El Maguey, El Organo, Cacaluta, and Chachacual. The planned roads to the latter three of these four bays have not yet been completed. Until authorities get around to finishing them, land access to the bays of El Organo, Cacaluta, and remote Chachacual will only be achievable by hikers or experienced drivers in off-road vehicles who know the myriad dirt tracks that wind through the tropical deciduous forest west of Santa Cruz. If in doubt, hire a jeep and a guide, or take a boat tour.

Bahía El Organo is closest. About 1.1 miles (1.8 km) along the highway from the hotel, look on the left side for the (one-foot-high, 30-foot-long; .3-meter-high, 9-meter-long) raised concrete curb. The unofficial foot trail to El Organo takes off through the forest from there. The beach is isolated, intimate, and enfolded by rocky shoals on both sides. Some trees behind the dune provide shade. Bring everything, including insect repellent.

Continuing straight ahead, the paved highway forks again (about 1.8 miles, 2.9 km from the hotel). Either continue straight ahead downhill to El Maguey, or fork right to Cacaluta. The sandy crescent of **Bahía El Maguey** is bordered by tidepools tucked beneath forested headlands. Facing a protected fjord-like channel, the Maguey beach is usually calm, nearly waveless and fine for swimming, snorkeling, diving, and sailing. It would be a snap to launch a kayak or a rubber boat here for fishing in the bay. Beach access is on foot, via a downhill staircase, only. A procession of permanent seafood *palapas* line the beach. Most days, especially weekends and holidays, picnickers arrive and banana towboats and *aguamotos* (mini-motorboats) buzz the beach and bay. A mile-long (1.6 km) **foot trail** (see next section) connects to Bahía Maguey.

Bahías Cacaluta, Chachuacal, and San Agustín

At this writing, the paved road that forks right toward **Bahía Cacaluta** ends at a barrier, about

SANTA CRUZ
DE HUATULCO

From Crucecita
(One Way)

To Crucecita, Bahía
Chahue, and Bahía
Tangolunda

HOTEL
CASTILLO

TAXI STAND

HOTEL
BINNEGUENDA

HOTEL
MARINA

ARTESANIAS
MARKET

BLVD.

SANTA

CRUZ

BANCOMER

BANAMEX

BOAT CHARTERS

CALLE

COYULA

BAY EXCURSIONS

Boat

DISCO
DEXKITE

ANDADOR

OTITLAN DE VALLE

CAFÉ HUATULCO
PLAZA

Harbor

MONTE ALBAN

POCHUTLA

MITLA

To Playa Entrega,
Bahías Organo,
Maguey, and Cacaluta

ANDADOR HUATULCO

CALLE

MITLA

To Bahía
Tangolunda

HUATULCO NATIONAL
PARK

MAGIC CIRCUS
DISCO

HOTEL MARLIN

HURRICANE DIVERS

COCO SOLO
GROCERIES

ANDADOR

B e a c h

ACATLAN

0   50 yds

0   50 m

Bahía Santa Cruz

© AVALON TRAVEL PUBLISHING, INC.

.7 mile (1.1 km) past the fork, at an unsigned sandy but firm jeep track. It continues past the barrier and winds and bumps ahead, past several unmarked forks (bring a guide or try to get directions from a local person) another mile (1.6 km), where you bear left to Bahía Cacaluta. There, the bay spreads along a mile-long, heart-shaped beach, beckoningly close to a cactus-studded offshore islet. Swimmers beware, for waves break powerfully, surging upward and receding with strong undertow. Many shells—limpets and purple- and brown-daubed clams—speckle the beach. Surf fishing prospects, either from the beach itself or from rocks on either end, appear excellent.

Alternatively, walkers can follow **foot trails** to both Bahía Maguey and Bahía Cacaluta. The Cacaluta trail takes off at the sign Playa Maguey y Sendero de Caminata on the right about .3 mile (.5 km) downhill east from the Maguey-Cacaluta highway fork. The Maguey trail branches east, left (at the Sendero Zanate sign) and arrives at Bahía Maguey beach after about a mile (1.6 km). The Cacaluta trail branches west, right, through the forest about two miles (3.2 km), past a lagoon on the left, to Bahía Cacaluta.

Bahía Chachacual, past the Río Cacaluta, about four miles (6.4 km) farther west from Bahía Cacaluta, is a sand-edged azure nook accessible only with a guide, via forest tracks.

Bahía San Agustín, by contrast, is well known and easily reachable by Pochutla-bound bus, then by the good dirt road just across the highway (one-way taxi from the highway runs about $10, *colectivo* van $1.30) from the fork to Santa María Huatulco (at Km 236, a mile west of the airport). After about seven miles (11 km) along a firm track, accessible by all but the bulkiest RVs, bear right to the modest village of *palapas* at the bay's sheltered west end. From there, the beach stretches eastward along a mile of forest-backed dune. Besides good swimming, sailing, windsurfing, shell-collecting, and fishing prospects, San Agustín has a number of behind-the-dune spots (follow the left fork shortly before the road's end) for possible RV and tent camping. Beachside *palapas* can, at least, supply seafood and drinks and maybe some water and basic groceries.

ACCOMMODATIONS

Huatulco accommodations have grown in both quantity and variety. In addition to many hotels,

PACIFIC RESORTS

both humble and grand, a number of bed-and-breakfasts, villas, and condominiums are now available for short or long-term rentals. Besides those described in this section, you can also find many other accommodations via websites, such as www.tomzap.com/huatulco.html or others in the Internet Resources section at the end of this book.

Furthermore, especially for villas, houses, apartments and condos, you might contact **Huatulco rental agents.** For example, try **Ideal Properties,** at Flamboyan 216, in Crucecita, tel. 958/587-0333, tel./fax 958/587-9333, sales@ huatulcoproperties.com, www.huatulcoproperties.com. Additionally, try **Holiday Rentals** agent Robert Kleman, tel. 958/581-0503 and/or his Spanish-speaking partner, Martha Campos, tel. 958/587-0763.

In Huatulco as in other resorts, hotels on the beach are the priciest. Tangolunda's are most expensive, Santa Cruz and Chahue hotels fall in between, and Crucecita's hotels are the cheapest. Virtually all Huatulco lodgings are of modern standard, with private baths with hot water. Many, but not all, have air-conditioning, a plus, especially in the warm spring.

Huatulco accommodation rates are highly seasonal; hotels in this section are arranged in ascending order of high season price for two people in one double bed.

© BRUCE WHIPPERMAN

The inner boat harbor at Santa Cruz de Huatulco is the jumping-off point for excursion boats to the outer Bays of Huatulco.

Crucecita Accommodations

Crucecita lodgings are all within a few blocks of the central plaza:

Under $50: Four budget *posada*-style hotels, two on the north side, and the other two on the south, charge about the same low rates. First, the **Posada Primavera,** a few blocks north of the plaza, at Palo Verde 5, Crucecita, Oaxaca 70980, tel./fax 958/587-1167 and 958/587-0630, offers six simply furnished but clean, light, high-ceilinged upstairs rooms with bath. Windows look out onto the palmy, bougainvillea-adorned surrounding neighborhood. Rates are about $16 s or d low season, $27 high, with fans.

At the adjacent corner, **Hotel Posada Michelle,** Gardenia 8, Crucecita, Oaxaca 70980, tel./fax 958/587-0535, run by friendly eco-tour guide José Aussenac, offers about a dozen smallish but

clean and comfortable rooms with big beds, baths, and good satellite TV. Some of the rooms are airy and light; others, although dark because of their half-mirrored windows (for privacy), do have white walls and open to a light, breezy, second-story walkway that leads to a pleasant, hammock-hung, shady porch with a view. Rooms with fans only cost $20 low season, and $35 high; rooms with a/c run about $30 d low season, $60 high.

A couple blocks south of the plaza, budget-minded visitors should check out the newish **Posada Leo,** Bugambilias 302, Crucecita, Oaxaca 70980, tel. 958/587-0372 or 958/587-2601, posadaleo-hux@hotmail.com. The six rooms, although a bit small for their two double beds, are attractively tiled and furnished with hand-woven bedspreads and modern shower baths. Rentals run $20 s, $25 d low season, $25 and $30 high, with fan and a/c. All rooms have cable TV. Furthermore, guests enjoy an airy upstairs patio for reading and relaxing.

Nearby, just a block south of the plaza, find **Posada Jois,** Chacah 209, Crucecita, Oaxaca 70980 between Carrizal and Bugambilias, tel. 958/587-0781, joishuatulco@hotmail.com. Past the welcoming female owner's storefront, are seven differing rooms on both ground and upper floors. The most attractive are upstairs. One is semi-deluxe, with king-sized bed and bath, for $25 d low season, $40 high; another room for four with two double beds goes for $30 low and $50 high. A pair of rooms with shared baths rent for $20 d low, $35 d high, all with hot water, TV, and fans. A major plus here is an inviting, shady terrace for guest use, with tropical plants and soft chairs for relaxing.

On Guamuchil, half a block east of the plaza, the **Hotel Las Palmas,** Calle Guamuchil 206, Crucecita, Oaxaca 70980, tel. 958/587-0060, fax 958/587-0057, www.hotel.baysofhuatulco.com.mx, offers small, plain but clean a/c rooms on the two floors above its good street-level restaurant. The eight rooms rent for about $25 s or d low season, $40 high; credit cards are accepted.

Two blocks south of the plaza, at the corner of Colorin, **Hotel Jaroje** (hah-RO-hay), Bugambilias 304, Crucecita, Oaxaca 70980, tel./fax 958/583-4801, jaroje@yahoo.com.mx, offers about 10 comfortable rooms. Simply but attractively decorated with color-coordinated drapes, bedspreads, and shiny-tiled baths, rooms rent for about $30 d low season, $45 high, with a/c, cable TV, and breakfast.

The **Hotel Suites Begonias,** Bugambilias 503, Crucecita, Oaxaca 70980, tel./fax 958/587-1390, at the southeast plaza corner, offers a semi-deluxe, family-run alternative. The rooms, although clean and comfortable, have motel-style walkways passing their windows, decreasing privacy. Rates for the 13 rooms run about $30 s or d low season, $35 and $45 high, with fan and TV; credit cards are accepted.

Half a block away, you might consider taking one of the attractive rooms on the very top floor of the **Hotel Posada del Parque,** Flamboyan 306, Crucecita, Oaxaca 70980, tel./fax

958/587-0219, on the south side of the plaza. Although not especially large, the top-floor rooms have high, rustic, beamed ceilings, nice views, and surround a cheery inner balcony-atrium. An airy sidewalk café downstairs serves breakfast, lunch, and dinner. All 14 rooms rent for about $20 s or d low season with fan, $25 with a/c; $45 high season with fan, $55 with a/c. All with TV; credit cards are accepted.

About three blocks east of the Crucecita plaza hubbub, the **Hotel Amakal,** Av. Oaxaca 1, Crucecita, Bahías de Huatulco, Oaxaca 70980, tel. 958/587-1500, fax 958/587-1515, www.hotelamakal.com offers, offers semi-deluxe, modern-standard rooms at reasonable prices. A stairway from the small, spartan lobby leads upstairs to about a dozen clean, light, white-tile-floored, tastefully decorated rooms with modern-standard baths. Rates are $30 s or d low season with fan, $48 high; $40 d low season with a/c, $66 high. Credit cards are accepted. Street parking only. Reserve ahead.

If, on a crowded weekend or holiday, you find Crucecita hotels full, the **Hotel Grifer,** P.O. Box 159, Crucecita, Oaxaca 70980, tel./fax 958/587-0048, at Guamuchil and Carrizal, a block east of the plaza, may still have a room. Three stories of plain, modern rooms enclose a TV-dominated atrium; a passable street-level restaurant is convenient for breakfast. The 16 rooms rent, low season, for about $30 s or d, $35 t, $40 and $50 high, with a/c and TV; no credit cards. Prices higher during Christmas and Easter holidays.

Santa Cruz Hotels
$50–100: Three blocks west of the Santa Cruz harbor, first choice goes to the **Hotel Meigas Binneguenda,** Blvd. Santa Cruz 201, Santa Cruz de Huatulco, Oaxaca 70900, tel. 958/587-0077, fax 958/587-0284, binniguenda@huatulco.net.mx. Neocolonial arches, pastel stucco walls, and copper and ceramic handicrafts decorate the interiors, while in the adjacent leafy patio, guests sun themselves around the elaborate cascade pool. In the restaurant, the customers seem as well-fed and satisfied as the waiters are well-trained and attentive. Upstairs, the neocolonial-decor rooms are spacious, comfortable, and equipped with phones,

PACIFIC RESORTS

TV, and a/c. Rates for the 75 rooms run about $60 s or d low season, $80 high, with parking, and credit cards are accepted. Ask for a discount, especially during times of low occupancy.

Over $100: Three blocks east, the **Hotel Castillo Huatulco,** Blvd. Santa Cruz 303, Santa Cruz de Huatulco 70980, tel. 958/587-0135, 958/587-0144, or toll-free Mex. tel. 800/903-4900, fax 958/587-0131, reservaciones@hotelcastillohuatulco.com, offers a recommendable alternative. Its 106 rooms, although deluxe and comfortable, are crowded into a smaller space than the Binneguenda's 75. They are nevertheless popular with families on weekends and holidays but nearly empty during quieter seasons. Low-season asking rates run about $100 s or d, $120 high. Ask for a discount, especially during times of low occupancy. Phones, TV, a/c, pool, and parking; credit cards are accepted.

Smaller, renovated **Hotel Marlin,** Paseo Mitla 107, Santa Cruz de Huatulco, Oaxaca 70989, tel. 958/587-0055, fax 958/587-0546, hmarlin@prodigy.net.mex or marlin@oaxacainfo.com, www.huatulco-hotels.com/marlin.html, is only two blocks from the beach. From street level, the small lobby leads to an appealingly intimate coral-hued inner pool patio and restaurant, enfolded by three stories of rooms. Upstairs, the three dozen rooms are thoughtfully decorated with coral bedspreads, floor-length drapes, attractive, rustic tile floors, and deluxe modern-standard bathrooms. Rates run from about $75 s or d low season, $120 high, with a/c, cable TV, phones. Ask for a discount. One possible drawback (or advantage) to all this is the hotel's popular (Thursday, Friday, and Saturday low season, nightly high season) adjoining discotheque, which the management swears cannot be heard in the rooms, even at full volume.

Another Santa Cruz hotel you can try is the 40-room **Hotel Marina,** Tehuantepec 112, Santa Cruz de Huatulco, Oaxaca 70989, tel./fax 958/587-0830 or 958/587-0963, which perches attractively on the east side of the Santa Cruz harbor-marina. Rooms are comfortable and semi-deluxe, with a/c and cable TV. The hotel features a bar, restaurant, discotheque, and pool.

Chahue Hotels

The Bahía Chahue vicinity has, in recent years, acquired a number of new hotels that dot the mostly undeveloped land a few blocks from the beach. Presently, however, underdevelopment and isolation make Chahue a less attractive beach neighborhood than either Santa Cruz or Tangolunda. Nevertheless, if you can get a low promotional rate, you might consider staying at one of the hotels recommended in this section.

$50–100: Right on the palm-decorated bayfront boulevard, find the new semi-deluxe **Hotel Real Aligheri,** Blvd. Benito Juárez, Bahía Chahue, Bahías de Huatulco, Oaxaca 70989, tel. 958/587-1242 or toll-free Mex. tel. 800/737-0783, fax 958/587-1243, hrealsigheri@prodigy.net.mx. It offers about 15 comfortable rooms with a/c, cable TV, and beach-club access for about $35 d low season, $55 high.

Nearby, off the same bayfront boulevard, check out the petite **Hotel Posada Eden,** Calle Zapoteco, Bahía Chahue, Bahías de Huatulco, Oaxaca 70989, tel./fax 958/587-2480, mambocafehuatulco@yahoo.com.mx, behind the larger Hotel Villblanca. Here the husband-wife owners, one French, the other Southeast Asian, set the international theme. The five rooms and three kitchenette suites, all with a pair of double beds are simply beautiful, with rustic-chic tiled floors and gorgeous Talavera-accented bathrooms. Rooms go for about $55 low season, $100 high; suites, $78 and $155, with cable TV, fans, attractive pool-patio and good on-site restaurant.

Larger but also recommendable is the attractive 40-room **Hotel Villablanca Huatulco,** at Blvd. Benito Juárez, corner of Zapoteco, Bahía Chahue, Bahías de Huatulco, Oaxaca 70989, tel. 958/587-1717, toll-free Mex. tel. 800/712-7757, U.S. tel. 888/844-7429, or Can. tel. 887/219-9681, fax 958/587-0606, hotelvillablanca@prodigy.net.mx. Hotel Villablanca guests, mostly upper-middle-class Mexican weekenders, enjoy simply but comfortably furnished semi-deluxe rooms and junior suites. Amenities include attractively rustic tiled floors, blue curtains and bedspreads, modern-standard baths, and private balconies overlooking a palmy pool-patio. Rates for standard rooms about $80 s or d low season, $100 high, junior suites go for about $110 s or d low, $130 high. Two kids under 12 with parents are free; third night is customarily free; all with a/c, phones, cable TV, and restaurant-bar.

Another Chahue lodging you can try is the eight-room **Huatulco Bed and Breakfast,** midway between Crucecita and the Chahue beach, tel. 958/583-4132, cell 958/589-2534, fax 958/583-4092, curt@huatulcobedandbreakfast.com, www.huatulcobedandbreakfast.com. The American-Mexican owners offer a homey-deluxe atmosphere, with lots of extras, beginning at about $45 d, low season, and figure about $60 high.

You might also take a look at the **Best Western Posada Chahue,** on the boulevard, at the west end of the Chahue bay, about two blocks from the beach, tel. 958/587-0945, toll-free Mex. tel. 800/710-7889, or U.S./Can. tel. 800/528-1234, fax 958/587-1240. This brand-new mid-sized hostelry offers about 20 rooms with a/c, cable TV, restaurant-bar, and beach club for about $75 d and up, including breakfast.

Tangolunda Luxury Resorts

Several luxury resort hotels spread along the Tangolunda shoreline. The Hotel Las Brisas dominates the sheltered western side-bay, with four stack-like towers that make the place appear, from a distance, as a big ocean liner. Moving east, next comes the elegant Hotel Quinta Real, perching atop its bayview hillside. The Hotel Barceló (formerly Sheraton) and Club Gala Resort (formerly Club Maeva) stand side by side on the bay's inner recess next to the golf course. The Camino Real Zaashila Resort spreads gracefully to its east-end cove, while in the middle, away from the beach, the gleaming white Crown Pacific stairsteps up the hillside.

The emphasis of all Tangolunda resorts is on facilities, such as multiple pools, bars, and restaurants, full wheelchair access, live music, discos, shows, and sports, such as tennis, golf, sailing, kayaking, windsurfing, snorkeling, diving, and swimming. Other amenities may include shops, baby-sitting, children's clubs, and Spanish and arts and crafts instruction.

Over $100: Of the Tangolunda luxury hotels, the **Crown Pacific,** Blvd. Benito Juárez 8, Bahía Tangolunda, Bahías de Huatulco, Oaxaca 70989, tel. 958/581-0044, fax 958/581-0221, boyce @boyce.com.mx, is both the most economical and has some of the largest rooms. Perhaps these were meant to compensate for the drawback that it's not actually on the beach: Guests must either walk or shuttle a couple of blocks to the beach club. The biggest plus of the Crown Pacific is the price, which, low season, runs only about $80 per person, double occupancy, including all meals, drinks, sports, kid's mini-club, and in-house entertainment. No fans—all rooms are air-conditioned. During high season, the same costs about $100 per person.

The **Club Gala Resort,** P.O. Box 227, Bahías de Huatulco, Oaxaca 70989, tel. 958/581-0400, U.S./Can. tel. 877/888-GALA, fax 958/581-0220, infohux@galaresorts.com.mx, www.galaresorts.com.mx, originally built and operated by the competent Mexican Club Maeva chain, is among Mexico's classier all-inclusive resorts. The beach setting is gorgeous, the tile floors in the halls and rooms shine, and bright bedspreads, immaculate bathrooms, and private ocean-view balconies grace the accommodations. All-inclusive rates run about $100 per person, low season, $140 high; kids, five years or under, go free, while kids 6–12 are half price.

The **Barceló Huatulco,** originally a Sheraton hotel, is now a worthy member of the worldwide Spanish chain, at Paseo Benito Juárez, Bahía Tangolunda, Oaxaca 70989, tel. 958/581-0055, 958/581-0005, 958/581-0039, or toll-free U.S./Can. tel. 800/346-5454, fax 958/581-0103, www.barcelo.com. Rooms are comfortable, deluxe, and decorated in soothing pastels, with private bay-view balconies, phones, cable TV, and a/c. Room-only rates for its 360 rooms and suites begin at about $110 d low season, $180 high. All-inclusive (all lodging, food, drinks, and in-house entertainment included) runs about $100 per person low season, $200 high.

The **Hotel Las Brisas Huatulco,** Bahéa Tangolunda, Oaxaca 70989, tel./fax 958/581-0355, toll-free Mex. tel. 800/227-4727, U.S./Can. tel. 866/226-3161 or 888/559-4329,

PACIFIC RESORTS

brisashotels@brisas.com.mx, www.brisas.com.mx, formerly Club Med, is now owned and operated by the Mexican Las Brisas hotel chain. Judging from the longstanding fine reputation of existing Las Brisas hotels in Acapulco, Ixtapa, and Puerto Vallarta, we should be able to expect the same excellence for the Las Brisas Huatulco.

The place is huge, spreading from its grand open-air lobby, from which carts ferry guests to hundreds of deluxe rooms, featuring fine views and equipped with all modern amenities. Hotel facilities include many sports, three pools, gym, private beaches and coves, kiddie activities, and much more. Rates run, low season, from about $130 s or d per day for standard deluxe rooms, upwards to about $250 for more posh suites with semi-private small pools. Two kids go free with parents, breakfast is included, plus a $20 lunch and dinner food/drink credit per room per day.

In contrast, the exquisite 28-room **Quinta Real Huatulco,** at Paseo Benito Juárez 2, Bahía de Tangolunda, Huatulco, Oaxaca 70989, tel. 958/581-0428, toll-free Mex. tel. 800/712-7758, or U.S./Can. tel. 888/561-2812, fax 958/581-0429, reserv-hux@quintareal.com, www.quintareal.com, offers super-luxury in an intimate setting. All guests enjoy spacious designer suites, from master to presidential, with creamy white decor, marble seemingly everywhere, hammock-equipped view balconies, and 21st-century-standard baths, all with whirlpool tub.

A few steps outside your door, find a spacious pool, a classy, domed restaurant, a similarly airy bar, shop, gym, and more. Accessible by motorized cart, the private beach club, tennis court, and a second luxurious pool are located downhill.

For all this, rates run upwards from about $250 d. Call or email for bookings or reserve through the Quinta Real's agent, the Mexico Boutique Hotels, U.S. tel. 877/278-8018, Can. tel. 866/818-8342, www.mexicoboutiquehotels.com.

If the **Camino Real Zaashila Resort,** Bahía de Tangolunda, Huatulco, Oaxaca 70989, tel. 958/581-0460 or toll-free U.S./Can. tel. 800/7CAMINO (800/722-6466), fax 958/581-0461, caminozaarsv@prodigy.net.mx,

www.caminoreal.com, hasn't yet gotten an architectural award, it should soon. Builders have succeeded in creating a modern luxury hotel that has an intimate feel. This begins right at the reception, a plush round *palapa,* where arriving guests are graciously invited to sit in soft chairs while being attended to by personable clerks, who are also seated, behind rustic, designer desks. Outside, you walk to your room through manicured tropical gardens, replete with gurgling fountains, splashing brooks, and cascading, green lawn terraces. If the Zaashila has a drawback, it's in some of the 120 rooms, which, although luxurious and comfortable, are entirely tile-floored and could use more color and warmth. However, the arrangement of separate units, nested like a giant child's building blocks, resembles a space-age Hopi native pueblo, each unit uniquely perched among the whole, affording much privacy and light, especially in upper-floor units. Outside, a few steps downhill, past the big, meandering blue pool, comes the superb beachfront: acres of luscious, billow-washed yellow sand, intimately enclosed between wave-sculpted rocks on one side and a jungly headland on the other. Low-season rentals begin at about $200, or about $230 if you must have your own little private pool. Corresponding high-season rates are around $350 and $400, with access to water sports, tennis, golf, three restaurants, and nightly live music.

Playa Conejo Bed-and-Breakfast

A personable North American couple, Richard and Brooke Gazer, have built six elegantly lovely and comfortable guestrooms into their home overlooking Playa Conejo. The luxuriously private accommodations, called **Agua Azul la Villa,** stairstep down from the main house to an airy ocean-vista garden pool-patio. Low season rates are $77, $89, and $99 s or d, including breakfast; $95, $105, and $117 high. For Christmas, add 20 percent to the high season rates; with fans, nonsmoking adults only, and a short downhill walk to a private, intimate beach. For more information, contact Richard and Brooke Gazer, Agua Azul la Villa, Playa Conejo, Oaxaca 70989, tel. 958/581-0265, gaurei@hotmail.com, www.aguaazullavilla.com.

Camping

Authorities permit camping and RV parking at some the Bahías de Huatulco: RV parking at a marina-front lot in Chahue runs about $11 per family per day; RV parking or tenting at Bahía Cacaluta costs about the same. Other Huatulco public camping areas may be available. For more information, contact the Huatulco National Park office, tel. 958/587-0849, 958/587-0808, or 958/587-0446, which issues camping permits. Find them in Santa Cruz de Huatulco, adjacent, beach side, to the boat harbor, open Mon.–Fri. 9 A.M.–5 P.M., Sat. 9 A.M.–1 P.M. Alternatively, contact the tourist information office (see the Information section).

The soldiers who guard the beaches against turtle poachers and squatters also make camping much more secure. They usually welcome a kind word and maybe a cool drink as a break from their lonely and tedious vigil.

FOOD

Aside from the Tangolunda hotels, nearly all of the good Huatulco eateries are near the Crucecita plaza.

Breakfast and Snacks

For inexpensive home-style cooking, try the *fondas* at the Crucecita *mercado* (market), between Guamuchil and Guanacastle, half a block off the plaza.

The market stalls are good for fresh fruit during daylight hours, as is the **Frutería Angelita,** open daily 7 A.M.–9 P.M., just across Guanacastle.

Also nearby, the **Panadería San Alejandro,** at the southeast plaza corner of Flamboyan and Bugambilias, tel. 958/587-0317, open 6 A.M.–10 P.M., offers mounds of scrumptious baked goodies.

The crowd of satisfied customers will lead you to Crucecita's best-bet snack shop, **Los Portales Taco and Grill,** corner of Guamuchil and Bugambilias, right on the plaza, tel. 958/587-0070. Breakfasts ($2–3), a dozen styles of tacos ($2–3), Texas chili (in Mexico, called *frijoles charros* or cowboy beans, $2), and barbecued ribs ($5) are the specialties. Beer is inexpensive, to boot. Open daily 6–2 A.M.

For a relaxing drink or a sandwich in Santa Cruz, go to the **Cafe Huatulco,** at the bandstand in the shady Santa Cruz town plaza, tel. 958/587-1228, cafeplumahua@huatulco.net.mx, a block west of the marina embarcadero. The mission of the friendly owner, Salvador López de Toledo and his wife (who operates the kitchen) is to promote the already well-deserved popularity of Huatulco's mountain-grown coffee, which they grind fresh daily for their good cappuccinos and cafe lattes. Open daily 8 A.M.–10 P.M. Furthermore, Salvador is a good source of information on Huatulco coffee and the mountain *fincas cafetaleras* (coffee farms) where it's grown.

Restaurants

The refined sidewalk atmosphere of **Cafe Oasis,** at the southeast plaza corner (Bugambilias and Flamboyan), tel. 958/587-0045, has made it Crucecita's plaza-front restaurant of choice. Beneath cooling ceiling fans, customers watch the passing plaza scene while enjoying a full bar and a professionally prepared and served menu of breakfast ($4–6), good espresso, fruit and salads ($2–5), hamburgers ($3–5), Mexican and international specialties ($5–10), and much more. Open daily 8 A.M.–midnight.

Nearly as successful is **Restaurante Sabor de Oaxaca,** on the bottom floor of the Hotel Las Palmas on Guamuchil, half a block from the plaza, tel. 958/587-0060. Wall art, folk crafts, and quiet conversation set the tone, while tasty country specialties fill the tables. Try the Oaxacan-style tamales ($6) or *botanas Oaxaqueños* (cheese, sausage, pork, beef, and guacamole snacks, $10). Open daily 8 A.M.–11 P.M.

Lovers of fine Italian cuisine can't miss enjoying a meal at Crucecita's class-act restaurant, **El Giardino del Papa** (The Pope's Garden), Flamboyan 204, tel. 958/587-4763, brainchild of owner Rossana Pandolfini, of Amalfitano, and chef Mario Saggese of Salerno. Mario, who was once the Pope's bodyguard, immigrated to Mexico to follow his passion for cooking. Rossana asked Mario to come to Huatulco because she craved pasta al dente the way it's "supposed to be" in the old country. Although Mario's suggestions include calamari *criollo* ($12), scampi al brandy

($15), *insalata* Mediterrenea ($5), and spaghetti a la Mario ($12), whatever you get will be tasty. Call for reservations, especially during the winter. Find the restaurant one block west of the plaza's southwest corner; open daily 2 P.M.–midnight.

For a treat, reserve a table at one of Huatulco's very best, the **Restaurant Las Cupolas**, at the Hotel Quinta Real in Tangolunda, tel. 958/581-0428. Here, the dishes reflect the unique creativity of the chef, who rotates his menu through dozens of yearly variations. For example, start with *ensalada de la huerta* (salad of the orchard, $5); continue with either black fettucine with clams ($10), or filet mignon, marinated in *machiote* (red sauce) with baby potatoes ($17). Finish off with *tiramisu* and coffee or tea ($6).

ENTERTAINMENT

Hangouts and Dancing

Huatulco entertainments center on the Crucecita plaza. Although the hubbub cools down weekdays and low seasons (and hot clubs seem to change as often as the Huatulco breeze), many spots heat up significantly during the high winter season.

The **Cactus Bar and Grill**, on the Flamboyan side of the plaza, tel. 958/587-0648, sometimes livens up with videos and music. On the other hand, you can get swept up nightly by the seasonal salsa and Latin rock repertoire of the band at the **Sports Bar Iguana** (or the La Selva Restaurant next door), both adjacent to Tacos Los Portales, Bugambilias side of the plaza. Open about 11 A.M.–2 A.M., in season.

You need only follow your ears to the source at **Mr. Don** bar, at the diagonally opposite plaza corner of Gardenia and Guanacastle, upstairs. Live Latin rock is featured nightly in season and on weekends the rest of the year, 8–2 A.M.

A growing platoon of visitors and expatriates go to **Café Dublin** a little bit of Ireland in Huatulco, Calle Carrizal, a block east, half a block south, of the Crucecita plaza's southeast corner. Good imported beer, Irish coffee, spaghetti and meat balls, hamburgers, satellite TV, and good fellowship keep the customers happy. In a cozy upstairs room, patrons settle in for the evening, so-

cializing, enjoying recorded music, and watching videos. Find Café Dublin open daily noon until after midnight low season, 6–2 A.M. high season.

In Santa Cruz, lights flash, fogs descend, and customers gyrate to the boom-boom at **Magic Circus** disco in the Marlin Hotel on Calle Mitla, two blocks behind Banamex off the main boulevard. Admission (from around 10 P.M.) runs about $10. Call tel. 958/587-0055 to confirm.

Nearby, continue your party at **Dexkite** disco, which offers continuous recorded reggae, salsa, and Latin rock from about 9:30 P.M. At the Marina Hotel and Resort, in Santa Cruz, Calle Tehuantepec 112; call for confirmation, tel. 958/587-0971.

Sunset Cruise, Live Music, and Tourist Shows

Lovers of quieter diversions might enjoy going on a wine and soft-music sunset cruise on the sailboat *Luna Azul,* tel. 958/587-0945.

The **Club Gala Resort** in Tangolunda is one of the most reliable sources of hotel nightlife. Live music often plays before dinner (about 6–8 P.M.) in the lobby bar, and "Gala Night" tourist buffet and shows rev up at least weekly year-round. Contact a travel agent or call the hotel directly at tel. 958/581-0400 for details and reservations (about $55 per person, including everything.) Other hotels, such as the Crown Pacific, Barceló ("Caribe Tropical" buffet and show), and Zaashila, may also offer similar entertainment in season.

SPORTS AND RECREATION

Walking, Jogging, Tennis, and Golf

Huatulco's open spaces and smooth roads and sidewalks afford plenty of walking and jogging opportunities. One of the most serene spots is along the Tangolunda Golf Course mornings or evenings. Also, an interesting sea-view forest trail takes off from Bahía Conejos.

If you're planning on playing lots of tennis, best stay at one of the Tangolunda luxury resorts. Otherwise, the Barceló, tel. 958/581-0055 or 958/581-0005, and the Tangolunda Golf Course, tel. 958/581-0037, fax 958/581-0059,

PACIFIC RESORTS

rent tennis courts for about $10/hour. Call for rental information and reservations.

The breezy green **Tangolunda Golf Course,** tel. 958/581-0037, fax 958/581-0059, designed by the site architect Mario Chegnan Danto, stretches for 6,851 yards down Tangolunda Valley to the bay. The course starts from a low building complex (watch for bridge entrance) off the Highway 200–Tangolunda Highway across from the sanitary plant. Greens fee runs about $60, cart $32, club rental $13, caddy $15. The tennis courts, maintained by the same government corporation that owns the golf course, are next to the clubhouse on the knoll at the east side of the golf course.

The luxury **Xquenda** (sh-QUEN-dah, soul in Zapotec) spa and athletic club, on the Santa Cruz–Tangolunda road in Chahue (west side), tel. 958/583-4448, 958/583-4449, xquenda @huatulcospa.com, www.huatulcospa.com, offers tennis, paddle tennis, and a lap swimming pool. Spa services include massage, facials, *temazcal* ceremonial hot room, and more. Open daily 7 A.M.–8 P.M.

Horseback Riding

Rancho Caballo del Mar, on the road (east past Tangolunda) to Copalita, about a mile (1.6 km) south of Hwy. 200, guides horseback trips along the ocean-view forest trail that stretches from its corral to the eco-preserve zone by the Río Copalita. The four-mile (6.4-km) tour, which costs about $25 per person at the ranch (more through an agent), returns via Bocana shoreline vista point for lunch. For more information and reservations (not usually necessary), taxi to the ranch or contact a travel agent; the Rancho has no phone.

Adventurers can also walk the same four-mile (6.4-km) roundtrip in a leisurely three hours. Take a hat, water, and a bathing suit, and start early (around 8 A.M.) or late (around 3 P.M.) to avoid the midday heat.

Adventure Tours

For off-road adventuring, contact **Pancho Willy's 4x4 Adventures,** at Colorín 608 in Crucecita, tel. 958/587-1930, panchowillys@hotmail.com. They offer a sturdy Mercedes truck tour along

jungle roads, through rivers, and past waterfalls. Along the way, you get a chance to hike, climb, rappel, splash in a forest waterfall, and enjoy a barbecue at a mountain coffee farm.

You might also check out **Transportadora Turistica Bahía Chahue,** Flamboyan 308, south side of the Crucecita plaza, tel. 958/587-0589, ttchahue@hotmail.com, which offers similar adventures.

By all means, please resist the urge to go on a widely advertised rip-roaring "jungle tour" by four-wheel *moto* all terrain vehicle (ATV) motor scooter. The vehicles are noisy, hazardous to the rider, polluting to the environment, tear up forest trails, and scare away animals. It would be healthier for both you and the Huatulco ecosystem to ask the provider to guide you along the same trip by much less intrusive mountain bike, or, even better, on foot.

Río Copalita Ecotouring and Rafting

José Aussenac, owner-operator of **Copalita River Tours,** tel. 958/587-0535, raftingcopalita@hotmail.com, organizes and guides outdoor adventure tours in the east-side Río Copalita wildlife sanctuary. Options include bird- and animal-watching walks along riverine forest trails, kayaking river rapids, and mud baths at a riverside ranch.

Also highly recommended are the services of whitewater rafting outfitter-guide **Aventuras Piraguas,** tel. 958/587-1333, info@piraguas.com, www.piraguas.com. Their trips combine rafting on the Río Copalita, easy family-level rappeling, a lovely jungle waterfall, and lunch at La Gloria coffee farm. They offer a *quadrimoto* (noisy, polluting four-wheeled scooters) option, which should be avoided.

Upland Jungle Ecotouring and Coffee Farms

Local tour operators guide hiking and bird-watching tours to archaeological zones, coffee farms, pilgrimage and sacred sites, springs, and waterfalls, in the jungly foothill hinterland north of Huatulco. One of the most experienced and environmentally sensitive operators is **Aventuras Huatulco** in Crucecita, at Plaza Conejo second floor, on Guamuchil, half a block east of the town plaza, tel. 958/587-1529, 958/587-0009, or 958/587-0054, erastorojas@hotmail.com. Aventuras Huatulco offers a range of options, from one-day walks along the Copalita River (ruins, bird-watching by canoe, mud bath) and jungle jeep safaris and lunch at La Gloria coffee plantation to jungle overnights (waterfalls, rock hieroglyphic paintings) to complete five-day excursions from Oaxaca city, including all of the above.

Alternatively, try other agents, such as reliable **Servicios Turísticos del Sur,** at the Hotel Castillo, tel./fax 958/587-1211, huatulco@prodigy.net.mx, for similar services. You might also contact your hotel tour desk or log on to www.tomzap.com/huatulco.html#tour for many more options.

Swimming, Snorkeling, and Scuba Diving

Swimming is ideal in the calm corners of the Bahías de Huatulco. Especially good swimming beaches are at **Playa Entrega** in Bahía Santa Cruz and **Bahía El Maguey.**

Generally clear water makes for rewarding snorkeling off the rocky shoals of all of the Bahías de Huatulco. Local currents and conditions, however, can be hazardous. Novice snorkelers should go on trips accompanied by strong, experienced swimmers or professional guides. Bring your own equipment; gear purchased locally will be expensive at best and unusable at worst.

Huatulco scuba divers enjoy the services of well-equipped and professional **Hurricane Divers** scuba shop, in the small complex between the Santa Cruz main beach and boat harbor, tel. 958/587-1107, hurricanedivers@hotmail.com. They start novices out with a pool mini-course, followed by a three-hour ($60) resort dive in a nearby bay. Snorkelers go for about $30, with good equipment furnished. Hurricane Divers' open-water certification course takes about five days and runs about $380, complete. The shorter 40-feet (12-meter) certification course runs about $220. With your certificate, you are qualified for recreational (one-tank, $43; two-tank $68) dives. After that, with additional certification, you may be ready for advanced trips, which might include local shipwrecks, night dives, and marine flora, fauna, and ecology tours. For more

information, log on to www.hurricanedivers.com. Open Mon.–Sat. 9 A.M.–7 P.M.

Alternatively, try long-time Huatulco **Buceos Sotavento,** which offers similar services. Contact them at the Plaza Oaxaca complex, on the Crucecita plaza, southwest corner (of Flamboyan and Gardenia), tel./fax 958/587-2166, tel. 958/581-0051, buceosotavento@yahoo.com.mx, www.divehuatulco.com.

Fishing and Boat Launching

The local boat cooperative **Sociedad Servicios Turísticos Bahía Tangolunda** takes visitors out for fishing excursions from the Santa Cruz boat quay. For a launch with two lines and bait, figure on paying about $40 minimum for a three-hour excursion. For big-game fishing, rent a big 40-foot (12-meter) boat, with lines for several persons, for about $400. More reasonable prices might be obtained by asking around among the fishermen at the Santa Cruz boat harbor or the village at San Agustín.

On the other hand, you can leave the negotiations up to a travel agent, who will arrange a fishing trip for you and your friends. You can stop afterward at a beachside *palapa,* which will cook up a feast with your catch. Save money by bringing your own tackle. Rates for an approximately three-hour trip for three run about $60 if you supply your own tackle, $120 if you don't. Contact the agent at your hotel travel desk, or an outside agent, such as **Paraíso Huatulco** in the Hotel Flamboyan, on the Crucecita plaza, tel. 958/587-0181, fax 958/587-0190, or **Aventuras Huatulco,** also in Crucecita, tel. 958/587-0054, 958/587-1529, or 958/587-0009.

Huatulco's best **boat-launching site** is at easily reachable Bahía Chahue marina, with about 40 slips and an excellent heavy-duty boat ramp. From the east-west beachfront boulevard, follow the sign *remolques* (trailers) to the big parking lot and ramp.

SHOPPING

Market and Handicrafts

Crucecita has a small traditional market (officially the Mercado 3 de Mayo) east of the plaza, between Guanacastle and Guamuchil. Although produce, meats, and clothing occupy most of the stalls, a few offer Oaxaca handicrafts. Items include black *barra* pottery, hand-crocheted Mixtec and Amusgo *huipiles*, wool weavings from Teotitlán del Valle, and whimsical duck-motif wooden bowls carved by an elderly, but sharp-bargaining, local gentleman.

In Santa Cruz, just west of the boat harbor, a warren of dozens of stalls offer nearly everything, from T-shirts and Taxco silver, to carved wooden fish and laquerware.

Steep rents and lack of business force many local silver, leather, art, and other handicrafts shops to hibernate until tourists arrive in December. The few healthy shops with good selections cluster either around the Crucecita plaza, the Santa Cruz boat quay, or in the Punta Tangolunda shopping complex adjacent to the Barceló (or shops in the hotel itself).

In Crucecita, one of the most reliable crafts stores is **Plata de Taxco,** next to Hotel Suites Begonias, a few doors south of the plaza's southwest corner, tel. 958/587-0818; open daily, 9 A.M.–9 P.M. Here you can select from an all-Mexican assortment—shiny *barro negro* (black pottery) from the Valley of Oaxaca, pottery moon and sun faces from Tonalá, Jalisco, *talavera* ware from Puebla, *alebrijes* (crazy wooden animals) from Arrazola, near Oaxaca, and lots of glistening silver jewelry from Taxco.

Supermarket, Laundry, and Photography

The supermarket **La Fuente,** in Crucecita on east-side Av. Oaxaca, tel. 958/587-0222offers a large stock of groceries, an ice machine, and a little bit of everything else, a block east of the Pemex station. Open daily 8 A.M.–10 P.M.

Take your washing to the **Lavandería Estrella,** on Flamboyan, corner of Carrizal, tel. 958/587-0585, open Mon.–Sat. 8 A.M.–9 P.M. Find it a block east of the Crucecita plaza.

For film and quick develop-and-print, go to **Foto Conejo,** just off the Crucecita plaza, across Guamuchil from the market, tel. 958/587-0054. Besides a photo-portfolio of the Bahías de Huatulco, the friendly owner stocks supplies,

point-and-shoot cameras, and Kodak, Fuji, and Konica slide and print film. Open daily 9 A.M.–8 P.M.

INFORMATION

Tourist Information Offices

The Huatulco office of the Oaxaca Secretary of Tourism is in the Tangolunda hotel zone, inland side, west edge of the hotel-shopping complex., tel./fax 958/581-0176, open high season, Mon.–Fri. 9 A.M.–5 P.M., Sat. 9 A.M.–2 P.M.

Alternatively, contact the Huatulco municipal tourism office, in the Casa de Cultura, in Crucecita, at the corner of Bugambilias and Ceiba, four blocks south of the plaza, tel. 958/587-1871, fax 958/587-1777, turismohuatulco@hotmail.com.

Guide

Savvy local folks recommend the services of ecologically sensitive guide **Mario Cobos,** tel. 958/587-1833. Although Mario's first love is bird-watching, he also offers fishing excursions and backcountry eco-tours. His fee begins at $50 per day, for one or two persons, with your wheels. Jeep rental (figure a minimum of about $50) is extra.

Publications

The bookshop at the Barceló in Tangolunda, tel. 958/581-0055, stocks English-language paperback novels, Mexico art and guidebooks, newspapers, such as *USA Today,* and many magazines.

In Crucecita, in season, the small **Publicaciones Huatulco** newsstand, at the corner of Gardenia and Macuil, three blocks north of the plaza, may have English-language newspapers; open daily 6 A.M.–9 P.M.

Pick up a copy of ***Huatulco Magazine,*** the handy commercial tourist booklet, at your hotel or a store or travel agent, or at the magazine office, Cerrada de Tlacolula No. 3, Santa Cruz, tel. 958/587-0342.

Ecology Association

Local ecologists and community leaders monitor Huatulco's development through their informal

Green Globe 21 association. They gather weekly at the Café Huatulco kiosk in the Santa Cruz plaza. Among the group's leaders are Ivonne Kraak, of Hurricane Divers, tel. 958/587-1107, and Federico Roth, manager of the Hotel Quinta Real, tel. 958/581-0428.

SERVICES

Money Exchange

For cash, you may either use the **ATMs** at all of Huatulco's banks, or go inside. In Crucecita, try the Banamex ATM, on Carrizal, just north of the Hotel Grifer, or **Banco Inverlat** and ATM, a few doors north. Alternatively, use the Bancomer ATM, on the Crucecita plaza, southwest corner.

Other banks are in Santa Cruz. **Banamex,** on the main street Av. Santa Cruz, corner of Pochutla, tel. 958/587-0322, exchanges both U.S. and Canadian traveler's checks Mon.–Fri. 9 A.M.–4 P.M., Sat. 10 A.M.–2 P.M. **Bancomer,** across Pochutla, tel. 958/587-0003, does about the same thing Mon.–Fri. 8:30 A.M.–4 P.M. and Sat. 10 A.M.–2 P.M. Call to check money-changing hours.

After bank hours, go to the hole-in-the-wall Money Exchange booth on Guamuchil, near the corner, at the east side of the Crucecita plaza, tel. 958/587-1309, open Mon.–Sat. 7 A.M.–9 P.M.

Communications

The Huatulco *correo* and *telecomunicaciones* stand side by side, across from the Pemex gas station on east-side Blvd. Tangolunda. The post office, tel. 958/587-0551, is open Mon.–Fri. 8 A.M.–3 P.M. only. **Telecom,** tel. 958/587-0894, is open Mon.–Fri. 8 A.M.–7 P.M. and Sat.–Sun. 9 A.M.–2 P.M.

For telephone, buy a **Ladatel** telephone card and use it at public telephones, or go to one of the *larga distancia* businesses on Carrizal, near the Hotel Grifer, such as **Caseta Telefónica Gemenis,** tel. 958/587-0735 or 958/587-0736, open daily 8 A.M.–9:30 P.M.

Internet connection is available at Cuijosnet store, at Carrizal 504, between Flamboyan and Chaca, next to the Irish Pub, tel. 958/587-1569. Find them open daily 10 A.M.–10 P.M.

Health and Emergencies

Among the better of Huatulco private clinics is **Clínica Médico,** 403 Sabali, tel. 958/587-0600 or 958/587-0687, with 24-hour emergency service. Find them at the corner of Gardenia, about eight blocks north of the Crucecita plaza.

For an English-speaking, U.S.-trained doctor, go to IAMAT (International Association for Medical Assistance to Tourists) member and general practitioner Dr. Andrés González Ayvar, tel. 958/587-0687, cell 044-958/587-6065. His regular consultation hours are Mon.–Sat. 11 A.M.–1 P.M. and 6–9 P.M.

Alternatively, go to the 24-hour government **Centro de Salud** clinic, on Carrizal, a block east of the Crucecita plaza, tel. 958/587-1421, or the big **Seguro Social** hospital, in Crucecita, on the boulevard to Tangolunda, tel. 958/587-1182, 958/587-1183, or 958/587-1185, a quarter mile south of the Pemex gas station.

For routine medications, Crucecita has many pharmacies, such as **Farmacia del Centro,** plaza corner of Flamboyan and Bugambilias, tel. 958/587-0232, open Mon.–Sat. 8 A.M.–10 P.M. Sun. 9 A.M.–2 P.M. and 5–10 P.M., at street level, below the Hotel Begonias.

For police emergencies, call the Crucecita *policía,* tel. 958/587-0210, in the Agencia Municipal behind the post office, across the Tangolunda boulevard from the Pemex *gasolinera.*

Immigration and Customs

Both Migración and the Aduana are at the Huatulco airport. If you lose your tourist permit, try to avoid trouble or a fine at departure by presenting Migración with proof of your date of arrival—stamped passport, an airline ticket, or preferably a copy of your lost tourist permit—a day (or at least three hours) before your scheduled departure.

GETTING THERE AND AWAY

By Air

The **Huatulco airport** (officially the Aeropuerto Internacional Bahías de Huatulco, code-designated HUX) is just off Highway 200, eight miles (13 km) west of Crucecita and 19 miles (31 km) east of Puerto Ángel. The terminal is small, with

PACIFIC RESORTS

only check-in booths, a few snack bars, and handicrafts and trinket shops (but, fortunately, with an ATM for arrival cash).

A few reliable carriers connect with U.S. and Mexican destinations:

American Airlines connects with Dallas, during the winter-spring high season. For reservations, call a travel agent, such as Paraíso Huatulco, tel. 958/587-0181, fax 958/587-0190.

Mexicana Airlines flights connect daily with Mexico City. For reservations, call Mexicana's office on Plaza Chahue shopping center, tel. 958/587-0223, 958/587-0243, or toll-free Mex. tel. 800/502-2000.

Aerocaribe connects with Oaxaca and Puerto Escondido. For reservations, call a travel agent.

United Airlines, American Airlines, Canada 3000, and **Canadian Air Transat** offer seasonal, mostly winter **charter-flight** connections with U.S. and Canadian destinations. For reservations, call a travel agent.

Experienced local charter airline **Aerotucan** regularly connects Huatulco with Oaxaca city. For information and reservations in Huatulco, call tel. 958/587-2427, or cell 044-958/589-0134. In Oaxaca city, call tel. 951/501-0530 or 951/501-0532. For many more details, log on to www.aerotucan.com.

Huatulco **air arrival** is usually simple. Since the terminal has no hotel booking agency or money-exchange counter (although there is an ATM), come with a hotel reservation and sufficient pesos to last until you can get to the bank in Santa Cruz or Crucecita. After the typically quick immigrations and customs checks, arrivees have a choice of efficient ground transportation to town. Agents sell tickets for collective GMC Suburbans to Crucecita or Santa Cruz or Tangolunda (about $8). A private *taxi especial* outside the airport gate only, for three, possibly four passengers, runs about $12. Prices to Puerto Ángel are double or triple these.

Mobile travelers on a budget can roll their suitcase the couple of blocks from the terminal to Highway 200 and catch one of the frequent public **minibuses** (about $1–2) headed either way to Crucecita (east, left) or the Pochutla (Puerto Ángel) junction (west, right).

Car rental agents are usually on duty for flight arrivals. If they're not, make a reservation ahead of time and they will meet your flight: **Budget** in Crucecita, tel. 958/587-0010, fax 958/587-0019, or **Alamo** in Santa Cruz, at the Hotel Castillo, tel. 958/587-0135. During the winter especially, make reservations in the United States and Canada prior to departure.

By Car or RV

Paved highways connect Huatulco east with the Isthmus of Tehuantepec, west with Puerto Ángel and Puerto Escondido, and north with Oaxaca.

Highway 200, the east-west route, runs an easy 100 miles (161 km) to Tehuantepec, where it connects with Highway 190. From there, it continues northwest to Oaxaca or east to Chiapas and the Guatemala border. In the opposite direction, the Highway 200 route is equally smooth, connecting with Pochutla (Puerto Ángel), 22 miles (35 km) west, and Puerto Escondido, 66 miles (106 km), continuing to Acapulco in a long 322 miles (519 km). Allow about three hours to Tehuantepec, 1.5 hours to Puerto Escondido, and to Acapulco, a full nine hours' driving time, either direction.

Highway 175, the cross-Sierra connection north with the city of Oaxaca, although paved, is narrow, winding, and oft-potholed, with few services in the 80-mile (128-km) high Sierra stretch between its junction with Highway 200 at Pochutla (22 miles west of Crucecita) and Miahuatlán in the Valley of Oaxaca. The road climbs to 9,000 feet (2,700 meters) into pine-tufted, winter-chilly Chatino and Zapotec country. Be prepared for emergencies. Allow eight hours northbound, seven hours southbound, for the entire 175-mile (282-km) Huatulco-Oaxaca trip.

By Bus

Four main long-distance bus lines connect Huatulco with destinations east, west, and north. They depart from three small separate terminals in Crucecita, several blocks north of the plaza.

Many daily **Cristóbal Colón** first-class buses, terminal located on Gardenia, corner of Ocotillo, four blocks north of the plaza, tel. 958/587-0261, connect west with Pochutla (Puerto Ángel) and Puerto Escondido. Buses also connect east with the Salina Cruz and Tehuantepec on the Isthmus, continuing either east to San Cristóbal las Casas and Tapachula in Chiapas, or northwest to Mexico City via Oaxaca and Puebla.

One block farther north, corner of Palma Real, a few **Estrella Blanca** buses, tel. 958/587-0103, connect west with Pinotepa Nacional and Acapulco via Pochutla and Puerto Escondido, and east with Salina Cruz.

A few second- and first-class **Estrella del Valle** and **Autobuses Oaxaca Pacífico** buses connect daily with Oaxaca via Pochutla, from Jazmin, corner Sabali, nine blocks north of the plaza, tel. 958/587-0193.

UPLAND EXCURSIONS INTO COFFEE COUNTRY

A century before the Bahías de Huatulco development even got on the drawing board, the cooler, greener Huatulco uplands were home to a community of farmers and fruit and coffee ranchers. Bypassed by the new Highway 200 and the coastal resort development, the foothill region above the Bahías de Huatulco is a treasury of traditional Oaxaca life and natural diversions—wildlife to view, springs and waterfalls to splash in, and jungle coffee ranches to visit and explore.

The foothill destinations of Santa María Xadani and La Gloria Coffee Farm make an enjoyable day trip by car or tour. By bus, allow two days, including an overnight at the coffee farm. Along the way, nature lovers will enjoy the leafy foothill country, laced with springs and cascades gurgling through leafy, vine-hung woodland, rich with birds, mammals, and fluttering butterflies.

Santa María Huatulco

Colonial-era Santa María Huatulco (pop. 9,000) is the head town of the sprawling Huatulco *municipio,* which encompasses the entire Bahías de Huatulco development. Although living at the center of a mountain, jungle, and seashore domain, Santa María Huatulco people have looked toward the emerald Sierra rising precipitously on their northern horizon. Those mountains and their foothills have traditionally been the main

source of Huatulco's wealth—the aromatic produce of a host of *fincas cafetaleras* (coffee farms).

Taste Huatulco coffee in one of the cafés, such as the inviting, family-run **Las Flores** on the town plaza, east side. While you're on the plaza, take a stroll around; inspect the unique *ollas* (jars) made into fountains, an inviting part of the plaza decoration.

Also take a look around the **historic old market,** uniquely built on pillars in the middle of the plaza. First among your purchases should be samples of the breads, for which Santa María is famous: **Pan Yemo** (egg bread), **Pan de los Muertos** (especially popular around Día de los Muertos, November 1–2), and **Pan Tarazón** (in long loaves).

Be sure to step inside the old town church, the **Templo de Nuestra Señora de la Concepción.** Inside, above the altar you'll find the Señora, and in the transept chapels a pair of mysterious, venerated objects. In the left chapel stands the **Señor de Misericordias,** an image that turned up strangely in Santa Cruz de Huatulco in the 17th century, and which people have worshipped ever since. Additionally, in the right chapel is one of the four copies of the **Santa Cruz (Holy Cross) de Huatulco,** carved from the enigmatic ancient seashore cross in 1612 and sent by the Bishop of Oaxaca, Juan de Cervantes.

Huatulco's plaza front is generally sleepy (and especially tranquil during the cool of the evening) except during fiestas and market days. The town celebrates three main fiestas. The first is on the fourth Friday of Lent (23 days after Ash Wednesday, usually in March), when folks celebrate the Señor de Misericordias. Good Friday, two days before Easter Sunday, is the Fiesta de la Santa Cruz de Huatulco. The December 8–11 fiesta honors Nuestra Señora de la Concepción. The weekly **market days** are Saturday and Sunday, when vendors' *tianguis* decorate the center of town, about three blocks south of the plaza.

If you decide to linger, a pair of basic Santa María hotels can accommodate you. Check out the **Posada del Centro,** north side of the plaza, just west of the church, tel. 958/581-4034, or the **Posada Casquito Cuatulco,** at #5 Juárez, the main ingress street into town from Hwy.

200, a block or two south of the plaza, tel. 958/58-1406. Expect to pay about $25 d, for a clean basic room, with private hot-water shower bath, fan, and TV.

The prosperity of the local folks supports a sprinkling of good down-home restaurants. Besides the previously mentioned plaza-front restaurant **Las Flores,** you can sample the excellent seafood served at **El Perro de Agua** (The River Otter), on Juárez, at the south edge of town. Furthermore, local folks also strongly recommend the relaxed river-view **Restaurant Caramba,** tel. 958/581-4094, for Huatulco country specialties.

By car, get to Santa María de Huatulco by driving several miles north of Highway 200, via the side road at Km 238, about a mile (1.6 km) west of the Huatulco airport entrance. By local minibus, get there from Crucecita (bus stop a block east of the Crucecita plaza) or the Pochutla Highway 200 crossing. If necessary, transfer to a second bus at the side road to Santa María de Huatulco, at Km 238, about a mile (1.6 km) west of the Huatulco airport or about 17 miles (27 km) east of the Pochutla crossing.

Santa María Xadani

This is a gently sloping hillside village (pop. 1,000) tucked in a luxuriantly forested valley (about 13 miles, 21 km from Highway 200). Xadani (shah-DAH-nee) is distinguished by its five separate social orders: adults, kids, dogs, pigs, and chickens. The town pride (at the village's upper end) is the **church,** dedicated to village patron the Virgen de la Concepción, whom townsfolk, joined by many outsiders, celebrate in a big fiesta climaxing on August 15.

Nearby sights include a *cascada* (waterfall) and an *ojo de agua* (spring), **Encanto,** warm on one side and cool on the other. Farther afield, one-day tours by taxi or your own car could include the **Pozo de Santa Cruz** (Well of the Holy Cross) spring and the spectacular **Cascada del Diablo** (Devil's Waterfall).

For a guide (Spanish-only), contact friendly local resident **Gregorio Cruz Cruz,** preferably at least a day or two ahead of time. Write him, Gregorio Cruz Cruz, Domocilio Conocido (address locally known), Santa María Xadani, Pochutla,

Oaxaca 70999, or better, leave a message at the town telephone, tel. 958/584-0410. (If this fails, contact kindly Celia Vasquez, who runs the long-distance telephone *caseta* in Copalita, tel. 958/587-2224, or cell 044-958/587-2224, who knows the whereabouts of nearly everyone locally.)

If you're going to stay a while, Xadani offers basic services, including a pharmacy, private doctor, and a *centro de salud* (health clinic).

If you can, time your arrival on Sunday to coincide with the town market *tianguis.*

La Gloria Coffee Farm

About five miles (8 km) past Xadani, you'll arrive at El Llano (YAH-noh), the site of La Gloria, a little German farm in the jungle. The parents of La Gloria's owner-operator Gustav Sherenberg arrived from the wreckage of World War II, seeking a new life in Mexico. The dream that they carved out remains with Gustav (now Gustavo), who, with his son Max, continues to improve on it.

The centerpiece, a Saxony-style whitewashed farmhouse and its antique furnishings—polished oak wall telephone, heirloom old-world sideboard, 1940s-vintage shortwave radio—endure for guests to admire and enjoy.

The buildup is a tour around the farm, which you should do not long after arrival. Along the path, you'll see acre after acre of green shiny-leafed coffee bushes beneath a canopy of great giants of the forest—*ceiba, caoba,* and Juan Diego trees. At the far point of the walk, the farm's sustaining source, a crystalline spring, wells up from a rocky bed. On the way back, the path winds beneath both wild and cultivated trees hung with exotic fruits—brown *mamey,* green *zapote,* and the otherworldly *piña anona.* Near the farmhouse, don't miss the **herb garden,** with familiar cilantro, *yerba buena, yerba santa,* and half a dozen others you probably have never heard of. The fun of all this climaxes at breakfast or dinner with the family around the great hardwood dinner table, big enough for a dozen.

The Sherenberg (actually Sherenberg-Noyola) family invites you to enjoy their farm with them, either for a day, including lunch, or overnight, including comfortable, cozy jungle-cabana lodging with lunch, breakfast, and dinner included. Expect to pay about $50 per person for an overnight with food, $20 for lunch and tour only.

Reserve by writing Familia Sherenberg-Noyola, Apdo. Postal 220, Bahías de Huatulco, Oaxaca 70989, or calling Max, at cell tel. 958/589-5041, or the farm number, tel. 958/587-0697, or emailing him at lagloria@hispavista.com. For more information, visit www.tomzap.com/lagloria.html.

(Another coffee farm that also welcomes visitors is Finca Montecarlo of Engineer Efren Sherenberg, Oaxaca city tel. 951/514-7038, ricaemax@hotmail.com.)

The easiest way to get to Xadani and the La Gloria coffee farm is by tour. See the Upland Jungle Eco-Touring and Coffee Farms section in the Huatulco section.

If you're going independently, Xadani is accessible via the signed side road on the north side of Highway 200, seven miles (11.4 km) miles west of **Copalita** village (store, *palapa* restaurants, basic hotel, long-distance telephone), Copalita river, and bridge (41 miles, 66 km east of Pochutla; 74 miles, 119 km west of Salina Cruz).

If by car, set your odometer as you turn off the highway. Continue immediately through a village (which has a store with unleaded gasoline) along a good gravel road, paralleling the gorgeous vine-hung, butterfly-decorated Zimatán river valley. Continue through Xadani to the church (12.7 miles, 20.4 km). Proceed, bearing left around the right rear side of the church, then straight ahead another 5.4 miles (8.7 km) to La Gloria coffee farm.

By bus, take a local minibus from Pochutla or Crucecita, which may take you at least to Copalita, or even to the Xadani Highway 200 turnoff. (See driving direction in the previous paragraph.) From there, you can catch a taxi or thumb a ride to Xadani, thence to La Gloria.

EAST TOWARD THE ISTHMUS: CHONTAL COUNTRY

The approximately 90-mile (145-km) Highway 200 stretching east from Huatulco to Salina Cruz is easy to travel, and consequently can pass swiftly without a pause. This, however, would be a pity,

for you'd miss a whole swath of interesting and beautiful country—curving, sandy beaches, wildlife-rich lagoons, and colorful Chontal villages and markets—along the way.

Santiago Astata

Astata (pop. 7,000) is near the midpoint (about 47 miles, 76 km) between Huatulco and Salina Cruz. This village is the closest thing to a metropolis along this part of the coast. The townsfolk proudly display their Chontal heritage with a big announcement *Nañoje faá loj pijeda* (Welcome to Santiago Astata) over the town entrance road.

By far the best time to arrive is during the Tuesday *tianguis*, when the townspeople are so busy buying and selling that they are less likely to notice a few camera-toting visitors.

Folks will be even less self-conscious (and so distracted that they might not mind having their pictures taken) during the big local **Fiesta del Señor de Piedad** on the second Friday of Lent (second Friday after Ash Wednesday), usually in late February or March.

Even if you don't arrive during any fiesta, you should still take a look inside the church, where you'll find both of the town patrons, Santiago (on horseback, with sword in hand) and Señor de Piedad.

Another favorite town diversion is splashing in the **community spring**, known locally as the *aguaje*. Besides all the fun, folks venerate their spring with a small chapel, *La Capilla de la Rosa Mística*. It's at the roadside a block or two west of the town entrance. Afterward, enjoy a snack at one of the several *comedores* by the town highway crossing.

For those in need of basic **services**, Astata has Doctor and Doctora Roberto and Rolanda Herrera, a pharmacy, and a public telephone, tel. 958/587-2211 or 958/587-2212, all along the main ingress road, near the church and plaza.

San Pedro Huamelula

If you missed Astata's Tuesday market, you can get in on Huamelula's market on Thursday by following the signed inland side road from Highway 200, just a fraction of a mile east of Astata. After about three miles (5 km), as you enter Huamelula town, you pass a number of new schools, including Alma Chontal (Chontal Soul) primary school, a secondary school, and Colegio de Bachilleres del Estado de Oaxaca (Oaxaca State College).

Go through town (stores, a few *comedores*, pharmacy, doctor) to the old but restored bright birthday-cake yellow-and-blue church, **Templo de San Pedro**. Inside, the same bright yellow and blue continues, right up to the altar, presided over by a very antique Saint Peter. In the right transept chapel, pay your respects to an even older Santa Lucia in the glass case.

Here, the usually serene atmosphere shifts to raucous and jubilant during the June 25–26 **Fiesta de San Pedro**. Processions, fireworks, food, carnival rides, and games climax in traditional dances, including the popular Los Turcos (The Turks).

East to Salina Cruz

The sights along the eastern stretch past Astata are mostly natural, including mangrove-tufted lagoons, palmy beaches, and breezy viewpoints. What follows is a summary of some ripe possibilities to anticipate along the way. Measure mileage east from Astata or west from the Highway 200 and Trans-Isthmus Highway intersection at the north edge of downtown Salina Cruz.

Moving east from Astata, arrive at the **Laguna Colorada** dirt side road (from Astata east seven miles or 11 km; west 41 miles or 66 km). The dirt road leads a few miles along the west edge of a glassy, wildlife-rich mangrove lagoon to a beach.

Another several miles along (east 19 miles, 31 km or west 29 miles, 47 km), another wildlife-rich mangrove lagoon, **Laguna Garrapatera,** is visible from the highway, at Km 348. A wave-washed white sandspit borders the lagoon on the ocean side. The lagoon looks fine for kayaking or rubber rafting, and the beach could be great for camping if you can get to it.

At Km 349, Highway 200 rises to a viewpoint overlooking the idyllic green **Río Bamba Valley** (east 20 miles, 32 km, or west 28 miles, 45 km). Several miles farther (east 31 miles, 50 km, or west 17 miles, 27 km) arrive at the dirt road turnoff to surfing and seafood *palapa* restaurant beach **Playa Cangrejo** (Crab Beach).

Next, pass **Morro Mazatán** town (east 36 miles, 57 km, or west 13 miles, 21 km). Finally, arrive at the signed dirt side road to **Playa Brasil,** which has a great oceanfront breeze-blown sand hill on its west end (east 41 miles, 65 km, or west eight miles, 13 km).

Puerto Escondido and Vicinity

Decorated by intimate coves, sandy beaches, and washed by jade-tinted surf, Puerto Escondido enjoys its well-deserved popularity. Despite construction of a jet airport in the 1980s, Puerto Escondido remains a place where everything is within walking distance, no high-rise blocks anyone's sunset view, and moderately priced accommodations and good food remain the rule.

Puerto Escondido (Hidden Port) got its name from the rocky Punta Escondida, which shelters its intimate half-moon cove and perhaps would have remained hidden if local farmers had not discovered that coffee thrives beneath the cool forest canopy of the lush seaward slopes of the Sierra Madre del Sur. They

began bringing their precious beans for shipment when the port of Escondido was established in 1928.

When the coast highway was pushed through during the 1970s, Puerto Escondido's then-dwindling coffee trade was replaced by a growing trickle of vacationers, attracted by splendid isolation, low prices, and high waves. With some of the best surfing breaks in North America, a permanent surfing colony soon got established. This led to more non-surfing visitors, who, by the 1990s, were arriving in droves to enjoy the comfort and food of a string of small hotels and restaurants lining Puerto Escondido's still-beautiful but no longer hidden cove.

Playa Manzanillo's light yellow crystal sand lines the inner recess of petite blue Bahía Puerto Angelito.

AROUND TOWN

Getting Oriented

Puerto Escondido (pop. 35,000) seems like two small towns separated by Highway 200, which runs along the bluff above the beach. The upper town is where most of the local folks live and go about their business, while in the town below the highway, most of the restaurants, hotels, and shops spread along a single, touristy, beachfront street mall, **Avenida Pérez Gasga.**

Avenida Pérez Gasga runs east-west, mainly as a pedestrian mall, where motor traffic is allowed only before noon. Afternoons, stop signs go up, blocking cars at either end.

Beyond the west-end stop sign, Pérez Gasga leaves the beach, winding uphill to the highway, where it enters the upper town at the *crucero,* Puerto Escondido's only signaled intersection. From there, Pérez Gasga continues into the upper town as Avenida Oaxaca, National Highway 131.

Getting Around

In town, walk or take a taxi, which should run no more than $2 to anywhere. For longer excursions, such as to Lagunas Manialtepec and Chacahua (westbound), and as far as Pochutla

(near Puerto Ángel) eastbound, ride one of the very frequent *urbano* minibuses that stop at the *crucero,* or rent a car from Budget, tel. 954/582-0312 or 954/582-0315, budget33@hotmail.com, or Alamo, tel. 954/582-3003, alamoescondido@hotmail.com.

BEACHES AND ACTIVITIES

Puerto Escondido's bayfront begins at the sheltered rocky cove beneath the wave-washed lighthouse point, Punta Escondida. The shoreline continues easterly along Playa Principal, the main beach, curving southward at Playa Marineros, and finally straightening into long, open-ocean Playa Zicatela. The sand and surf change drastically, from narrow sand and calm ripples at Playa Principal to a wide beach pounded by gigantic rollers at Zicatela.

Playa Principal

The best place to appreciate Puerto Escondido is not from the cluttered Pérez Gasga mall, but from one of the shady restaurants that front Playa Principal, the main beach. It's here that Mexican families love to frolic on Sundays and holidays and sun-starved winter vacationers

To Oaxaca

POST OFFICE/
TELEGRAPH

To Laguna Chacahua
National Park and
Acapulco

TOURIST
INFORMATION

BUDGET
RENT A CAR

MONTE

ALBAN

200

CARRETERA

COSTERA

AV. 3 PONIENTE

AV. 2 PONIENTE

AV. 1 PONIENTE

AV. OAXACA

HOTEL ALDEA
DEL BAZAR

DISCO
BACHOCO

AV. B. JUAREZ

AV. GUELETAO

LOMA BONITO

131

HOTEL
POSADA REAL

TIBURON

CLINICA
SANTA FE

CHURCH

HOTEL FIESTA
MEXICANA

AV. B. JUAREZ

SANATORIO
DEL CARMEN
(HOSPITAL)

ZÓCALO

OAXACA-
ISTMO
(BUS)

Playa Bacocho

AGENCIA
MUNICIPAL

ESTRELLA ROJA
DEL SURESTE (BUS)

ESPINAL

AV. 1 NORTE

AV. HIDALGO

PACIFIC

AV. HIDALGO

AV. 5 PONIENTE

ESTRELLA BLANCA
(BUS)

OCEAN

AV. 1 SUR

AV. 2 PONIENTE

DOCTOR/
PHARMACY

Playa
Carrizalillo

PUERTO ANGELITO

PUERTO

AV. 1 ORIENTE

HOTEL PARA SO
ESCONDIDO

HOTEL
NAYAR

ANGELITO

BANAMEX

Playa
Manzanillo

Bahía
Puerto
Angelito

HEALTH
CENTER

LIGHTHOUSE

SOLEDAD

LIBERTAD

REVOLUCIÓN

MAR Y SOL

HOTEL
HACIENDA
REVOLUCIÓN

ABARROTES
LUPITA

AVENTURA
SUBMARINA

REST. LA
GALERIA

MONEY
EXCHANGE

REST. EL
PEGASO

RESTAURANT
ALTRO MUNDO

TOURIST
POLICE

SUPER FARMAS
(PHARMACY)

HOTEL
CASA
BLANCA

STOP
SIGN

ALAMO RENT A CAR

TURISMO
RODIMAR

TOURIST
INFORMATION

AV. PEREZ GASGA (PEDESTRIAN WALKWAY)

LA
LUNA

STOP
SIGN

RUIZ
WEAVINGS

CAR RENTAL

ORO DE MONTE
ALBÁN

BITAL
ATM

REST.
CROTOS

HOTEL LAS
PALMAS

HOTEL
RINCÓN DEL
PACÍFICO

REST. PERLA
FLAMEANTE

CRAFTS
STALLS

REST. JUNTO
EL MAR

Beach

CAFE IL
CAPUCCINO

TP PALMAS DE CORTES

MARINA
NACIONAL

BAGUETTERÍA
VIVALDI

doze in their chairs and hammocks beneath
the palms. The sheltered west side is very popular with local people who arrive afternoons
with nets and haul in small troves of silvery
fish. The water is great for wading and swimming, clear enough for casual snorkeling, but
generally too calm for anything else in the cove.
However, a few hundred yards east around the
bay the waves are generally fine for bodysurfing
and boogie boarding, with a minimum of undertow. Although not a particularly windy location, windsurfers do occasionally bring their

own equipment and practice their art here.
Fishing is fine off the rocks or by small boat,
easily launched from the beach. Shells, generally
scarce on Playa Principal, are more common
on less-crowded Playa Zicatela.

Playa Marinero

As the beach curves toward the south, it increasingly faces the open ocean. Playa Marinero
begins about 100 yards from the "Marineros,"
the east-side rocky outcroppings in front of
the Hotel Santa Fe. The rocks' jutting forms

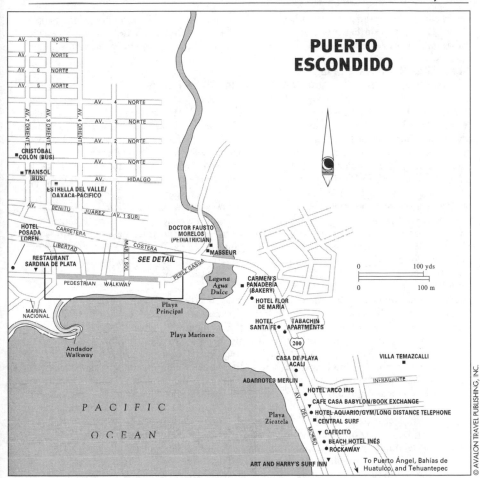

PUERTO ESCONDIDO

AV. 8 NORTE
AV. 7 NORTE
AV. 6 NORTE
AV. 5 NORTE
AV. 4 NORTE
AV. 3 NORTE
AV. 2 NORTE
AV. 1 NORTE
AV. HIDALGO
AV. 2 ORIENTE
AV. 3 ORIENTE
AV. 4 ORIENTE
CRISTÓBAL COLÓN (BUS)
TRANSOL (BUS)
ESTRELLA DEL VALLE/ OAXACA-PACIFICO
AV. BENITO JUAREZ (AV. 1 SUR)
HOTEL POSADA LOREN
CARRETERA
LIBERTAD
MAR Y SOL
COSTERA
RESTAURANT SARDINA DE PLATA
SEE DETAIL
PEDESTRIAN WALKWAY
PEREZ GASGA
DOCTOR FAUSTO MORELOS (PEDIATRICIAN)
MASSEUR
Laguna Agua Dulce
CARMEN'S PANADERIA (BAKERY)
HOTEL FLOR DE MARÍA
MARINA NACIONAL
Playa Principal
Playa Marinero
HOTEL SANTA FE
TABACHIN APARTMENTS
200
Andador Walkway
CASA DE PLAYA ACALI
VILLA TEMAZCALLI
ADAPROTES MERLIN
INFRAGANTE
HOTEL ARCO IRIS
CAFE CASA BABYLON/BOOK EXCHANGE
HOTEL AQUARIO/GYM/LONG DISTANCE TELEPHONE
PACIFIC
CENTRAL SURF
Playa Zicatela
CAFECITO
BEACH HOTEL INÉS
OCEAN
ROCKAWAY
ART AND HARRY'S SURF INN
To Puerto Ángel, Bahías de Huatulco, and Tehuantepec
AV. DEL MORRO

0 — 100 yds
0 — 100 m

are supposed to resemble visages of grizzled old sailors. Here the waves can be rough. Swimmers beware: Appearances can be deceiving. Intermediate surfers practice here, as do daring boogie boarders and bodysurfers.

Turn around and gaze inland at the giant Mexican flag, waving in the breeze on the hill above the east-side beach. At dawn every rainless day, soldiers of the 54th infantry battalion raise the colossal banner, which measures about 82 by 59 feet (18 by 25 meters) and is so heavy that it takes 25 of them to do it.

Playa Zicatela

Past the Marinero rocks you enter the hallowed ground of surfing, Playa Zicatela. The wide beach of fine golden-white sand stretches south for miles to a distant cliff and point. The powerful Pacific swells arrive unimpeded, crashing to the sand with awesome, thunderous power. Both surfers and non-surfers congregate year-round, waiting for the renowned Escondido "pipeline," where grand waves curl into whirling liquid tunnels, which expert surfers skim through like trains in a subway. At such times, the spectators on the beach outnumber the surfers by as much as 10 or 20 to one. Don't try surfing or swimming at Zicatela unless you're expert at both.

West-Side Beaches: Playas Manzanillo, Carrizalillo, and Bachoco

About a mile (1.6 km) west of town, the picture-postcard little blue bays of Bahía Puerto Angelito and Bahía Carrizalillo nestle beneath the seacliff. Their sheltered gold-and-coral sands are perfect for tranquil picnicking, sunbathing, and swimming. Here, snorkeling and scuba diving are tops, among shoals of bright fish grazing and darting among the close-in coral shelves and submerged rocky outcroppings.

Get there by launch from Playa Principal or by taxi. On foot (take a sun hat and water), follow the street that heads west from Pérez Gasga, uphill across from the Hotel Nayar. Continue to the second street on the left, Avenida 1 Poniente, turn left and go a long block to Avenida 5 Sur. Turn right and continue straight ahead for about a mile (1.6 km) to Bahía Puerto Angelito. Follow the staircase trail down the cliff (or the auto driveway on the west side) to the luscious beach, Playa Manzanillo, where a number of *palapa* restaurants offer fresh seafood, and the sand, clear blue water, and rolling waves seem perfect for a week of Sunday diversions.

Likewise picture-perfect Playa Carrizalillo, at the inner recess of Bahía Carrizalillo, is reachable by footpaths a few hundred yards farther west. Although more isolated and consequently less crowded, Playa Carrizalillo visitors nevertheless enjoy a beachfront *palapa* restaurant or two for shade and refreshment.

Playa Bachoco, another few hundred yards farther west, down the bluff from the Hotel Posada Real, is a long, scenic strip of breeze-swept sand, with thunderous waves and correspondingly menacing undertow. Swimming is much safer in the inviting pool of the adjacent Hotel Posada Real beach club.

If you're strong, experienced, and can get past the breaking waves, snorkeling is said to be good around the little surf-dashed islet 100 yards offshore.

Although Playa Bachoco's rock-sheltered nooks appear inviting for beach camping, local people don't recommend it because of occasional *rateros* (thugs and drunks) who roam Puerto Escondido beaches at night.

Trouble in Paradise

Occasional knifepoint robberies and muggings have marred the once-peaceful Puerto Escondido nighttime beach scene. Walk alone at night and you invite trouble, especially along Playa Bachoco and the unlit stretch of Playa Principal between the east end of Pérez Gasga and the Hotel Santa Fe. If you have dinner alone at the Hotel Santa Fe, avoid the beach by returning by taxi or walking along the highway to Pérez Gasga back to your hotel.

Fortunately, such problems are infrequent and seem to be confined to the beach. Visitors are quite safe on the Puerto Escondido streets themselves, often more so than on their own city streets back home.

Beach Walking

The *andador* concrete walkway, which circles the lighthouse point, provides a pleasant, breezy afternoon (or sunset) diversion. From the west stop sign, follow the street that heads toward the lighthouse. Soon, on the left, stairs head left down onto the beach cove, where, in front of the Capitania del Puerto building, the *andador* heads left along the rocks. It continues, above the spectacularly splashing surf, for about half a mile (.8 km). Return by the same route, or loop back through side streets to Pérez Gasga.

For a longer walk, you can stroll as far out of town along Playa Zicatela as you want, in outings ranging from an hour to a whole day. Best avoid the heat of midday, and bring along a sun hat, shirt, drinks, and snacks (and perhaps sunglasses) if you plan on walking more than a mile past the last restaurant down the beach. Your rewards will be the acrobatics of surfers challenging the waves, swarms of shorebirds, and occasional finds of driftwood and shells. After about three miles (5 km) you will reach a cliff and a sea arch, which you can scamper through at low tide to the beach on the other side, **Playa Barra de Colotepec.** Playa Barra de Colotepec's surf is as thunderous as Zicatela's and the beach even more pristine,

Playa Manzanillo is a prime Sunday beach for picnickers, sunbathers, and snorkelers.

being a nesting site for sea turtles. The beach continues for another mile (1.6 km) to the jungle-fringed lagoon of the Río Colotepec where, during the dry winter season, a host of birds and wildlife, both common and rare, paddle and preen in the clear, fresh water.

You could break this eight-mile (13-km) roundtrip into a pair of more leisurely options: Hike A could cover Zicatela only. On Hike B, you could explore Playa Barra de Colotepec and the Laguna de Colotepec by driving, taxiing, or busing straight to La Barra, the beach village just west of the Río Colotepec. Access is via the signed side road just before (west of) the Río Colotepec bridge.

Boat Tours

Travel agencies and the local boat cooperative, **Sociedad Cooperativa Nueva Punta Escondida,** offer trips for parties of several passengers to beautiful local bays. The minimum one-hour trip takes you to a number of sandy little coves east of town, including Bahía Puerto Angelito, with its Playa Manzanillo (Little Apple), Bahía and Playa Carrizalillo (Little Reeds), Bahía Coral,

and Bahía Puesto del Sol (Sunset). Take drinks, hats, sunscreen, and perhaps sunglasses, and don't go unless your boat has a sunroof. Trips can be extended (about $15 per additional hour) to your heart's content of beach picnicking, snoozing, and snorkeling.

ACCOMMODATIONS

With few exceptions, the successful hotels in Puerto Escondido are appropriate to the town itself: small, reasonably priced, and near the water. They dot the beachfront from Playa Zicatela around the bay and continue up Avenida Pérez Gasga to the highway. Most are either on the beach or within a stone's throw of it, which makes sense, because it seems a shame to come all the way to Puerto Escondido and not stay where you can soak up all the scenery.

Like the visitors, the hotels have separated themselves into two neighborhoods: Breezy Playa Zicatela where the surfing action is, and along Avenida Pérez Gasga, close to the palm-shadowed main town beach and most shopping and restaurants.

© BRUCE WHIPPERMAN

Picture-perfect Playa Carrizalillo offers soft sand and shady *palapa* restaurants.

Avenida Pérez Gasga Hotels

Under $50: Right on the beach amidst the tourist-mall hubbub is the longtime favorite, **Hotel Las Palmas,** Av. Pérez Gasga s/n, Puerto Escondido, Oaxaca 71980, tel. 954/582-0230, fax 954/582-0303. Its main plus is the palmy, vine-strewn patio where you can sit for breakfast every morning, enjoy the breeze, and watch the boats, the birds, and families frolicking in the billows. The big drawback, besides sleepy management and no pool, is lack of privacy. Exterior walkways pass the room windows, which anyone can see through. Closing the curtains unfortunately tends to make the (fan-only) rooms dark and warm. This doesn't seem to bother the legions of return customers, however, since they spend little time in their rooms anyway. Tariffs for the 40 smallish rooms run about $17 s, $21 d, $24 t low season, $25 s, $30 d, $35 t high, with phones and restaurant, but no parking; credit cards are accepted.

The **Hotel Rincón del Pacífico,** next door to the Hotel Las Palmas, offers about the same, at

Av. Pérez Gasga 900, Puerto Escondido, Oaxaca 71980, tel. 954/582-0056 or 954/582-0193, fax 954/582-0101, rconpaci@prodigy.net.mx. The two stories of clean, comfortable rooms enfold a shady patio that looks out onto the lively beachfront. As at the Hotel Las Palmas, a stay in one of their glass-front rooms sometimes feels like life in a fishbowl. This is nevertheless a very popular hotel. Reserve early. Rates for the 28 rooms run, year-round, about $24 s, $30 d, $36 t, with fan only; $40, $50, and $60 with a/c. Ask for a discount. Four suites with TV and a/c rent for about $70 s or d; with a restaurant, but no parking nor pool; credit cards are accepted (but not American Express).

Although it's not right on the beach like its neighbors across the street, most of the rooms of the **Hotel Casa Blanca,** Av. Pérez Gasga 905, Puerto Escondido, Oaxaca 71980, tel. 954/582-0168, fax 954/582-0737, are larger, cooler, and more private. Some rooms even have private balconies, fine for people-watching on the street below. Guests report noise is not a problem since cars and trucks are banned on Gasga noon–7 A.M. Other amenities include hot water, a shelf of used paperback books, and, beyond the graceful arches that border the lobby, a petite, inviting pool and patio. The 21 clean, comfortable rooms rent for about $26 s, $36 d, $38 t year-round, with fans; discounts are customarily available Sept. and Oct. Visa and Mastercard accepted, but no parking.

At the far west end on the uphill section of Avenida Pérez Gasga is the 1950s-genre **Hotel Nayar,** Pérez Gasga 407, Puerto Escondido, Oaxaca 71980, tel. 954/582-0319 or 954/582-0113, hotelnayar@prodigy.net.mx, www.oaxaca-mio .com. Although lacking a beachfront, the Hotel Nayar compensates with an airy view restaurant, tranquil location, parking, and an inviting pool patio. Its spacious, spartan but comfortable air-conditioned rooms have private balconies, some with sea views. The Nayar's 40 rooms run about $24 s, $27 d, $32 t, low season, $31, $36, $42 high, add $8 for a/c.

The popular **Hotel Loren,** Av. Pérez Gasga 507, Puerto Escondido, Oaxaca 71980, tel. 954/582-0057, fax 954/582-0591, next to the Hotel Nayar downhill, is as good as it first appears, from its leafy pool patio and its private balcony rooms to its rooftop sundeck. Competent clerks staff the desk while *camaristas* scrub the rooms spotless every day. The rooms spread through two three-story buildings; the front building rooms have luscious ocean views. Reserve a *cuarto con vista* if you want a room with a view. Reservations are often necessary, especially in the winter. The 24 basic but comfortable fan-only rooms rent for about $20 s or d, $30 t low season; $35 s or d, $40 t high, with parking, fans, and some a/c (add $10); credit cards are accepted.

$50–100: The **Hotel Paraíso Escondido** stands above the other hotels in both refinement and location, perched near the upper end of Pérez Gasga on a short side street, Calle Union 1, Puerto Escondido, Oaxaca 71980. tel. 954/582-0444. A tranquil colonial-chic refuge, the hotel abounds in unique artistic touches—Mixtec stone glyphs, tiny corner chapels, stained glass, and old-world antiques—blended into the lobby, corridors, and patios. The two levels of rooms

nestle around a lovely pool and restaurant patio. The rooms themselves are large, with balconies and designer tile bathrooms, wrought-iron fixtures, and handcrafted wooden furniture. Very popular with North American and German winter vacationers; get reservations in early. The 24 rooms rent for about $50 s, $58 d low season, $75 and $85 high, with a/c, pool, kiddie pool, and parking, but *no credit cards* are accepted.

Playa Zicatela Hotels

The Playa Zicatela lodgings offer similar in-house options as their Pérez Gasga counterparts; the main difference is the giant offshore (often pounding) rollers, and the surfing scene that tends to dominate the single Zicatela beachfront street during the fall high-wave season. Beach lovers, however, will most likely find the delights of the lovely golden-sand Playa Zicatela thoroughly enjoyable any time of the year.

Under $50: Surfer's haven **Rockaway,** one of the most economical recommendable hotels, is near the far south end of Playa Zicatela, at Av. del Morro, Playa Zicatela, Puerto Escondido, Oaxaca 71980, tel. 954/582-0668, fax 954/582-2420. It's a very tidy, fenced-in cluster of about 15 clean, concrete-floored, bamboo-and-thatch cabanas. Spacious and fan-equipped, they sleep about four and have private showers and toilets, mosquito nets, and shady, hammock-hung front porches. An inviting, leafy pool patio occupies the center, while the manager's cabana, offering water-sport rentals and supplies, stands to one side. Cabana rentals run, low season, about $10 s, $15 d, $25 per cabana for up to four; $20, $30, and $40 high season. Weekly or monthly discounts are negotiable, with parking and adjacent pizzeria.

A different option is available a few blocks north, at **Casas de Playa Acali,** a small colony of rustic cabanas, at Av. del Morro, P.O. Box 11, Puerto Escondido 71980, tel. 954/582-0278 or 954/582-0754, bungalowsacali@puertoconnection.com. The cabanas themselves, like a vision out of a romantic South Seas tale, are built with walls made of sticks (non-see-through) and sturdy plank floors, raised above ground level and built in a cluster around a blue pool all within a banana and mango mini-jungle. Units are clean and equipped with fans, mosquito nets, and good bathrooms. Rentals run about $18 s, $20 d, $25 t low season; $30, $32, $38 high, with fan, hot-water shower, small refrigerator, and parking. Additionally, the hotel offers a few rustic sunset-view bungalows perched on its bamboo-decorated hillside. Rentals cost about $30 low season, $40 high, for 1–4, with kitchens, and beach-view hammock-hung front porches. Credit cards are accepted. For more information, visit the Playa Acali's page on www.puertoconnection.com.

Farther south down the beach comes **Beach Hotel Inés,** Av. del Morro, P.O. Box 44, Playa Zicatela, Puerto Escondido, Oaxaca 71980, tel. 954/582-0792, fax 954/582-2344, pedrovoss@ yahoo.com, the life project of German expatriate Peter Voss and his daughter, Inés. Their 35 units occupy the palmy periphery of a lush, pool-café-garden layout, which climaxes with an attractive, stuccoed, two-story complex of rooms at the back side. At the poolside tables, longtime repeat guests linger for coffee and conversation after late-morning breakfasts, stroll the beach in the afternoon, and return for a balmy sunset happy hour. Other days, they sunbathe au naturel or relax in the petite but luxurious health club, which provides massage and hot tub. Most of the rentals are hotel-style rooms, in deluxe and super-deluxe grades, with clean, light interiors, comfortable furnishings, and well-maintained bathrooms. Additionally, they rent six downscale, second-floor (popular with surfers), shared-bath cabanas, and a pair of bungalows with outdoor kitchens, sleeping 4–6. Deluxe rooms go for about $30 s or d low season, $43 high; super-deluxe, about $50 low season, $80 high; cabanas, about $20 d; and bungalows, about $30 low, $40 high, all with discounts negotiable for long-term rentals.

Visitors hankering for a bit of class should consider **Hotel Flor de María,** Primera Entrada Playa Marinero, Colonia Marinero, Puerto Escondido, Oaxaca 71980, tel. 954/582-0536, fax 954/582-2617, pajope@hotmail.com, www.mexonline .com/flordemaria.htm, tucked on a quiet side street, off Playa Marinero, the small beach that divides the main town from Playa Zicatela. Its

rooms rise in two stories around a tranquil, leafy interior patio. At rooftop, a breezy sun-deck-bar, with a small but inviting pool and a hammock-hung *palapa* overlooks a beach-and-bay vista. The approximately dozen immaculate deluxe rooms are simply but thoughtfully decorated, each with two double beds with pretty violet covers and modern-standard, hot-water shower baths. Additionally, the hotel offers a pair of similarly inviting but more spacious second-floor ocean-view suites.

Rentals run, low season, from about $30 d standard, $45 d with ocean view, suites $50; high season $45, $50 and $55, all with fans only. Reserve ahead.

$50–100: At the south end of Playa Zicatela, hidden uphill behind the landmark Hotel Santa Fe, stands long-time **Hotel Tabachín del Puerto,** tel. 954/582-1179, info@tabachin.com.mx, www.tabachin.com.mx, managed by personable, on-site owner Paul Cleaver, one of the Santa Fe's original builders and former manager. Paul offers six large individually decorated kitchenette studios, with double beds, baths with hot-water showers, phone, internet access, use of Hotel Los Cocos beach club and pool, and breakfast in the Tabachín's airy downstairs patio. For all this, rates are reasonable: for smaller studio, $45 s, $55 d high season; for larger studio, $55 s, $65 d, and $75 for an entire three bedroom penthouse for a family. Long-term and low-season rates are negotiable. Reserve ahead.

About two blocks farther south on Avenida del Morro, which runs along Playa Zicatela, rises the three-story **Hotel Arco Iris,** Av. del Morro s/n, Colonia Marinero, Puerto Escondido, Oaxaca 71980, tel./fax 954/582-1494, fax 954/582-0432, arcoiris@hotel-arcoiris.com.mx or arcoiris@ptoescondido.com.mx, oaxaca-mio .com/arcoiris.htm. A flowery, shady green garden surrounds the hotel, leading to an attractive pool and patio. For those who love sunsets, sand, and waves (and don't mind their sometimes-insistent pounding), one of the spacious, simply furnished top-floor rooms with a view might be just the ticket. The Arco Iris's proximity to the famous Puerto Escondido "pipeline" draws both surfers and surf-watchers to the third-floor restaurant

La Galera, which seems equally ideal for wave-watching at breakfast and sky-watching at sunset. Low-season (May–June, Sept.–Nov. 15) asking rates for the 26 rooms run a reasonable $45 s or d; suites with kitchen, about $60 s or d (add about 15 percent high season); ask for a discount under any conditions.

Puerto Escondido's classiest hostelry is the newish **Hotel Santa Fe,** Av. del Morro, Playa Marinero, Puerto Escondido, P.O. Box 96, Puerto Escondido, Oaxaca 71980, tel. 954/582-0170 or 954/582-0266, fax 954/582-0260, info@hotelsantafe.com.mx, www.hotelsantafe.com.mx. Built in graceful neocolonial style, with curving staircases, two elegant pool patios, and flower-decorated walkways, the Santa Fe achieves an ambience both intimate and luxuriously private. Its restaurant is outstanding. The rooms are spacious, comfortable, and thoughtfully appointed with handpainted tile, rustic wood furniture, and regional handicrafts. The 50 rooms rent, high season, for about $75 s, $90 d, $100 t; about 10 kitchenette suites go for around $85 s, $100 d, 110 t; low season, $55 s, $60 d, suites about $75 d. All accommodations have a/c, phones, and parking; credit cards are accepted.

Apartments and Long-Term Rentals

If you're planning on a stay of two weeks or more, you may save money and yet have all the comforts of home in an apartment rental. If you're already in Puerto Escondido, first look over the classifieds in the *El Sol de la Costa* English-Spanish newspaper.

For a rental in advance of arrival, check with local realtor **Vicki Cole,** of Zicatela Properties, tel. 954/582-2495, zicatela_properties@yahoo.com, www.zicatelaproperties.com; her website lists many vacation homes for rent. Vicki also provides help—real-estate matters, immigration papers, residency—for newcomers.

Alternatively, for a vacation rental, you might contact **Nolan Van Way,** of PEP Realty, tel. 954/582-0085, nvpep@yahoo.com, www.pep-realty.com.

Other good rentals sources are general websites, especially **www.puertoconnection.com** and **www.tomzap.com,** both of which list a number of vacation rental homes, villas, apartments, and condo complexes.

Trailer Park and Camping

Occasional muggings and robberies on the beach have eliminated virtually all camping on Puerto Escondido beaches (with the possible exception of Easter week, when such large crowds flock into town that they spill onto the beaches).

Development and other uses have swallowed up Puerto Escondido's former recommendable trailer parks. A few trailer-camping parks (that I haven't recommended in the past because of on beach security problems) are still functioning, however. I looked them over and found one that appears recommendable. It's the downscale **Parque Trailer Palmas de Cortés,** right on the beach, at the east end of Pérez Gasga, tel. 954/582-3663, behind the Perla Flameante Restaurant. It's pretty enough, with about 40 smallish (up to about 20 feet or 6 meters) spaces in a palmy, fenced-in compound. Rates run about $10 for two persons, with all hookups and showers. Camping costs $4 per person.

FOOD
Breakfast and Snacks

Mornings, you can enjoy breakfast with the baked offerings of **Panadería Carmen** along Playa Marinero, on the little street that heads toward Playa Marinero from Hwy. 200, just past the bridge. It's a small homey shop with a few tables for savoring the goodies. Besides baking, co-owner Carmen Arizmendi's love is swimming. Afternoons, you might see her swimming in the bay, beyond the waves. Open Mon.–Sat. 7 A.M.–3 P.M.

Now, Carmen's devotees have a second spot to enjoy her pastries: **Cafecito Zicatela,** right on Zicatela beach (next to Bungalows Acuario). Here, you can savor a cappuccino and one of her goodies as you watch the surfers conquering the waves.

Carmen has recently acquired some competition, **Baguettería Vivaldi,** the labor of love of friendly Jenny Sinnhuber, who, besides lots of home-made bread, serves a wide selection of delicious breakfasts and sandwiches for lunch. Find her shop, in the middle of beachfront Avenida Pérez Gasga, across the street from the Hotel Casa Blanca; open daily 7:30 A.M.–10 P.M.

Nearby, right in the middle of the Avenida Pérez Gasga bustle, **Cafe Capuchino** attracts a following of tourists and local folks who enjoy good desserts and coffee with their conversation. Furthermore, the best homesickness remedy in town is their apple pie, a slice of which enables you to endure a minimum of one more hard week on the local beaches. Open daily 8 A.M.–11 P.M.

Also fun for breakfast are the shady, scenic beach-view restaurants **Junto del Mar** and **Restaurant Crotos**. (See the Restaurants section.)

Restaurants

Most of Puerto Escondido's reliable restaurants line Avenida Pérez Gasga. Just inside the west-end stop sign, on the inland side of Pérez Gasga, **Restaurant La Galería** usually has customers even when most other local eateries are empty. The reason is the excellent Italian fare—crusty, hot pizzas ($5–10), rich pastas and lasagna ($4–8), bountiful salads ($3–5), and satisfying soups ($3–5), which the European-expatriate owner puts out for her batallion of loyal customers. Open daily 8 A.M.–midnight.

Across the street, the excellent, airy **Restaurant Junto del Mar** (By the Ocean), tel./fax 954/582-1272, offers class-act breakfasts, including rich coffee, fresh fruit, hotcakes, eggs ($3–6), and many delectable lunch and dinner options ($5–15). Specialties include shrimp-stuffed fillets, octopus cooked with garlic, and lobster and shrimp brochettes. Mornings are brightened by the always-changing beach scene; evenings, the setting turns romantic, with soft candlelight and strumming guitars. Open daily 8 A.M.–11 P.M. Credit cards are accepted.

A block farther east, breakfast patrons at beachfront **Restaurant Crotos** sit at shady tables, enjoying the fascinating morning beachside scene. Later, at lunch and dinner, back beneath the luxuriously breezy, palm-fringed *palapa*, the house specialties—jumbo shrimp ($14), broiled lobster ($16), and super-fresh pompano ($12), attractively presented, competently served, and

delicious—seem like an added bonus. Open daily 8 A.M.–11 P.M.

Near the east end of the Pérez Gasga mall, the **Restaurant Perla Flameante** offers good food, incense, new-age jazz, and a beach view from beneath a big, cool *palapa*. The friendly, conscientious staff take pride that they make everything in-house, from the mayonnaise to the potato chips that come with the big fish burger ($3–4). Seafood fillets ($5–10) rule the menu. The varieties, such as sierra, tuna, yellowtail, and mahimahi, are exceeded only by the number of styles—Cajun, teriyaki, wine and herbs, pepper-mustard, butter and garlic, orange—in which they are served. Open daily 7 A.M.–11 P.M.; credit cards are accepted.

Devotees of authentic Italian food find paradise at **Restaurant Altro Mundo,** just half a block outside of the east-end stop sign. Here, white tablecloths and wine glasses set the stage. Start off, perhaps, with Crema Altro Mundo, continue with an *insalata mista* ($5), share a plate of lasagna di calamari ($10), and climax with fettuccine flameante ($8) and filete di dorado ($14). Open for dinner only, daily 6 P.M.–midnight, tel. 954/582-1455.

German owners have recently launched **El Pegaso,** east end of the Pérez Gasga mall, tel. 954/582-0800, a worthy addition to the Puerto Escondido gastronomical roster. Strictly European-international dishes fill the menu. For starters, go with French *Frite Aubergin* (stir-fried eggplant, $5), continue with Italian *Insalata Gorgonzola* ($5), and top it off with German bratwurst with potatoes, onion, and bacon ($10). Open daily, except Wed., 3 P.M.–11 P.M.

If you have dinner at the restaurant of the **Hotel Santa Fe,** on Av. del Morro, east side of the bay, tel. 954/582-0170, you may never go anywhere else. Savory food, impeccably served beneath a luxurious *palapa* and accompanied by softly strumming guitars, brings travelers from all over the world. Although everything on the menu is good, the restaurant is proudest of its Mexican favorites, such as rich tortilla soup ($5), bountiful plates of *chiles rellenos* ($7), and succulent snapper, Veracruz style ($12). Open daily 7:30 A.M.–11 P.M.

Farther south along Zicatela beach, **Restaurant Cafecito** (formerly Bruno's) is headquarters for a loyal platoon of local surfers and Canadian and American residents. Breakfasts, hamburgers, and fresh seafood plates are bountiful, tasty, and won't cost you a bundle ($3–8). Open daily, about 8 A.M.–10 P.M.

Back up on Highway 200 is **Restaurant Candiles,** at the corner of Avenida 1 Poniente, one block west of the Pérez Gasga crossing, tel. 954/582-0361, where the mission is traditional Oaxacan cuisine, professionally prepared and artfully presented. The day begins with breakfast at 8 A.M., with a long menu of goodies, such as hotcakes ($3), veggie omelette ($4), *chilaquiles Candiles* (shredded corn tortillas, baked with salsa, and cheese, $4), and *picaditas* (little corn tarts, $4). Come back for lunch or dinner and be treated to, for example, *sopesitos* (thick, small tortillas, $3), garnished with black beans, salsa, cheese, and guacamole, followed by one of very best tortilla soups (called, in this case *sopa Mixteca,* $4) made on the Mexican Pacific Coast. Open daily except Mon. 8 A.M.–11 P.M.

ENTERTAINMENT AND EVENTS
Sunsets and Happy Hours
Many bars have sunset happy hours, but not all of them have good sunset views. Since the Oaxaca coast faces south (and the sun sets in the west), bars along west-facing Zicatela Beach, such as the Hotel Santa Fe, Hotel Arco Iris, Restaurant Cafecito's, and Art and Harry's, are the only ones that can offer unobstructed sunset horizons.

If, on the other hand, you prefer solitude, stroll the bayfront *andador* walkway to near the lighthouse. Start on the Playa Principal (main beach), west side, past the Capitán del Puerto office. There, from breezy perches above the waves, you'll enjoy an equally panoramic sunset.

Strolling Pérez Gasga
Strolling the Pérez Gasga mall, known locally as the Adoquin (ah-doh-KEEN), is Puerto Escondido's prime after-dinner entertainment. By around 9 P.M., however, people get weary of walking and, since there are few benches, they

begin sitting on the curb and sipping bottles of beer near the west-end stop sign. Unfortunately, city officials frown on such apparently dissolute behavior and occasionally have a few of the curb-sitters arrested. Meanwhile, people hope that some amiable compromise will be reached.

The main attraction of curb-sitting is watching other people sitting on the curb, while listening to the music blasting nightly from the tiny open-air bars of **Bar Fly, Tubo,** and **Wipe Out,** 50 feet away. The music is so loud little can be gained except hearing impairment by actually taking a seat in the bars themselves.

Those who prefer to gyrate to the beat, go to some of the town's discos. On Pérez Gasga, try **Los Tres Diablos** (The Three Devils), across from the Hotel Las Palmas. Alternatively, try the old standby, **Disco Bachoco** on Av. Gueletao, in the west-side Bachoco suburb.

Festivals
Puerto Escondido pumps up with a series of fiestas during the low-season (but excellent for vacationing) month of November. Scheduled "Fiestas de Noviembre" events invariably include surfing and usually sportfishing, cooking, beauty contests, and notably, the dance festival, **Fiesta Costeño,** when a flock of troupes—from Pochutla, Pinotepa Nacional, Jamiltepec, Tehuántepec, and more—perform regional folk dances.

Visitors who hanker for the old-fashioned color of a traditional fiesta, make sure you arrive in Puerto Escondido by December 18, when seemingly the whole town takes part in the fiesta of the **Virgen de Soledad.** Besides being the patron saint of the state of Oaxaca, the Virgen de Soledad is also protectress of fishermen. To honor her, the whole town accompanies the Virgin by boat out to the bay's far reach, and then returns with her to the church plaza for dancing, fireworks, and bullfights.

If you can't be in Puerto Escondido in time to honor the Virgin in December, perhaps you may be able to take a day trip one hour west of Puerto Escondido to enjoy a fiesta at one of the small towns around Pinotepa Nacional, or to celebrate

Carnaval, with parades, fireworks, and lots of crazy street dancing, on the weekend before Ash Wednesday, the beginning of Lent. (See Festivals in the Pinotepa Nacional section.)

SPORTS AND RECREATION

Walking, Jogging, and Horseback Riding

Playa Zicatela is Puerto Escondido's most interesting jogging course. Early mornings, before the heat and crowds, are good for jogging along the level section of Avenida Pérez Gasga. Avenida del Morro, which parallels Playa Zicatela, is good for jogging anytime it isn't too hot. For more walking details, see Beach Walking, in this chapter.

Ease your hiking by riding horseback along Zicatela beach. Rentals are available on the beach in front of Hotel Santa Fe.

Gym and Tennis

The **Acuario Gym** on Playa Zicatela at the Hotel Acuario has a roomful of standard exercise equipment. Single visits run about $3, one-month passes $30.

One of the only night-lit tennis courts in town available for public rental ($10/hour) is at the **Hotel Posada Real.** Call the hotel at tel. 954/582-0133 for a reservation.

Surfing, Snorkeling, and Scuba Diving

Although surfing is de rigueur for the skilled in Puerto Escondido, beginners often learn by bodysurfing and boogie boarding first. Boogie boards and surfboards are for sale and rent ($7/day) at a number of shops along Pérez Gasga, such as **100 Hamacas** (next to Hotel Rincón del Pacífico) or **Central Surf** next door (and at Hotel Acuario on Playa Zicatela), open high season daily 9 A.M.–2 P.M. and 4–7 P.M. **Rockaway,** also on Playa Zicatela, rents surfboards ($7/day) and boogie boards ($7/day) and sells related supplies.

Beginners practice on the gentler billows of **Playa Principal** and adjacent **Playa Marinero,** while advanced surfers go for the powerful waves of **Playa Zicatela,** which regularly slam foolhardy inexperienced surfers onto the sand with backbreaking force.

Clear blue-green waters, coral reefs, and swarms of multicolored fish make for good local snorkeling and diving, especially in little **Puerto Angelito** and **Carrizalillo** bays just west of town. A number of Avenida Pérez Gasga stores sell serviceable amateur-grade snorkeling equipment.

A professional dive shop, **Aventura Submarina,** has recently gained a foothold in Puerto Escondido. It's run by friendly veteran PADI instructor Jorge Pérez Bravo, at Pérez Gasga 601 A, a few doors inside the west-end stop sign, tel. 954/582-2353, cell 044-954/588-1682, asubmarina@ptoescondido.com.mx. Introductory lesson, including one offshore dive, runs about $60, including equipment. For certified (bring your certificate) open-water divers, a one-tank day dive costs about $45, a two-tank day dive, about $60.

Alternately, a number of divers operate out of Huatulco, an hour and a half drive east. Contact the very professional **Hurricane Divers,** tel. 954/587-1107, hurricanedivers@hotmail.com, www.hurricanedivers.com. (For more details, see the Bahías de Huatulco section.)

Sportfishing

Puerto Escondido's offshore waters abound with fish. Launches go out mornings from Playa Principal and routinely return with an assortment including big tuna, mackerel, snapper, sea bass, and snook. The sheltered west side of the beach is calm enough to easily launch a mobile boat with the help of usually willing beach hands.

The local **Sociedad Cooperativa Nueva Punta Escondida,** which parks its boats right on Playa Principal, regularly takes fishing parties of three or four out for about $20 an hour, including bait and tackle. Check with boatmen right on the beach, or one of the organization's leaders, such as Captain Carlos Sánchez Mendes, tel. 958/582-1678. You can often find him at the Restaurant El Pescador, on Avenida Marina Nacional, the beachfront street, just west of the west-end Avenida Perez Gasga stop signs.

Additionally, travel agencies, such as Viajes Dimar, Av. Pérez Gasga 905, tel. 954/582-0734 or 954/582-0237, arrange such trips, usually for somewhat higher prices.

SHOPPING
Market and Handicrafts

As in most Mexican towns, the place to begin your Puerto Escondido shopping is the local **Mercado,** on Av. 10 Norte, one long block west of the electric transformer sub-station on upper Av. Oaxaca. Although produce occupies most of the space, a number of stalls at the south end offer authentic handicrafts. These might include Guerrero painted pottery animals; San Bártolo Coyotepec black pottery; masks from Guerrero and Oaxaca with jaguar, devil, and scary human-animal motifs; the endearing multicolored pottery animals from Iguala and Zitlala in Guerrero; and beautiful crocheted *huipiles* from San Pedro Amusgos.

Back downhill on Avenida Pérez Gasga, the prices increase along with the selection. Perhaps the most fruitful time and place for handicraft shopping is during the cooler evenings, within the illuminated cluster of crafts stalls just beyond the Gasga east stop sign.

One shop at that spot, the **Ruiz** textile stand, with genuine handmade rugs and serapes from Teotitlán del Valle near Oaxaca city, stands out. Fine-quality rugs are the most tightly woven—typically about 20 strands per centimeter (50 per inch).

Oaxaca's venerable jewelry tradition is well represented at the very professional **Oro de Monte Albán,** on Pérez Gasga, ocean side, inside the west-end stop sign. Here are authentic museum-grade replicas of the celebrated Mixtec-style trove discovered in Monte Albán's Tomb 7. Find it open Mon.–Sat. 10 A.M.–2 P.M. and 6:30–10:30 P.M., closed Sunday low season, tel. 954/582-0530.

The Uribe silversmithing family carries on the renowned Taxco silver tradition at their **Plateria Ixtlán,** a few doors east, tel. 954/582-1672, open Mon.–Sat. 10 A.M.–10 P.M. Choose from a host of fetching floral, animal, and abstract designs, in silver and turquoise, garnet, jade, and other semiprecious stones.

For unique women's resortwear, look inside **Bamboleo,** on the beach side, toward the Pérez Gasga east end, tel. 954/582-0993, a gem among the T-shirt clutter, open high season 10 A.M.–10 P.M. (low season hours shorter.) Here, find a colorful selection of skirts and tops, locally crafted from lovely Mexican cottons woven in Puebla, and plenty of fetching *huipiles* from San Pedro Amuzgos.

La Luna shop nearby, across Gasga from the Hotel Casa Blanca, tel. 954/582-0929, also displays an attractive selection, with a riot of bright silk scarves, and cool batik resort shirts, skirts, and pants made in Bali. Open daily 10 A.M.–9 P.M.

Groceries and Photography

Abarrotes Lupita, on the inland side of Gasga, outside of the east-end stop sign, a fairly well-stocked small grocery, offers meats, milk, ice, and vegetables. In addition, it may stock a few English-language publications seasonally, such as the Miami *Herald* and magazines, such as *Time, Life,* and *Newsweek.* Open daily 10 A.M.–11 P.M.

Out on Playa Zicatela, where stores are not nearly so common, the friendly **Abarrotes Merlin,** tel. 954/582-1130, offers a small grocery selection; open daily 9 A.M.–10 P.M.

Foto Express Figueroa, on Gasga next to Viajes Dimar, tel. 954/582-0526, offers fast photofinishing services, Kodak color print and slide film, and a moderate stock of accessories, including point-and-shoot cameras. Open daily 9 A.M.–9 P.M.

For a better camera selection, visit **Foto Discuento,** west end of the Pérez Gasga mall, tel. 954/582-0354, open Mon.–Sat. 9 A.M.–9 P.M., Sun. 9 A.M.–4 P.M.

INFORMATION
Tourist Information Office and Guides

Most months of the year, Oaxaca tourism staffs a small **information booth** on Pérez Gasga, just inside the west-end stop sign. Otherwise, you can

PACIFIC RESORTS

consult the friendly, well-informed *oficina de turismo* staff, tel./fax 954/582-01-75, gina@inpuerto@yahoo.com, who distribute a map of Oaxaca. It's open Mon.–Fri. 9 A.M.–3 P.M. and 6–8 P.M., just off of Hwy. 200, in the little office on the beach side of the highway, a couple of blocks east of the airport Pemex gas station.

Personable Gina Machorro, who usually staffs the Pérez Gasga information booth also gives walking tours of Puerto Escondido, including an archaeological site, and other excursions. Contact her at tel. 954/582-0076 or email ginainpuerto@yahoo.com.

Alternatively, try one of the tours led by guide **Ana Marquez.** Her itineraries cover the coast, from the renowned blowhole at Huatulco's Maguey Bay to the crocodile nursery at Chacahua National Park. Contact her at home at Futuro Mzna 7, No. 214, Fracc. Costa Chica, Puerto Escondido, Oaxaca 71984, tel. 954/582-2001, or at her Tigre Azul cyber café, beachside, near the west-end stop sign, tel. 954/582-2954 or 954/582-2855, ana@anasecotours.com, www.anasecotours.com.

Spanish Lessons

At least two teachers offer Spanish lessons: Sheila Clarke, tel. 954/582-0076, and Yolanda Park, tel. 954/582-0837.

Moreover, a small **language school** has opened up in Puerto Escondido, which invites visitors to add Spanish instruction to their sunning and surfing. The enterprising teacher-owner also offers tours and homestay arrangements. For more information, call tel. 954/588-1397, email brian@puertoschool.com, or visit www.puertoschool.com. Find the school on the east side, above Zicatela beach (and Hotel Arco Iris), across the highway from the landmark Cementos Cruz Azul concrete distributor.

Community Organizations and Projects

One of the major ongoing projects of the local ecological organization, **Eco Escondido,** is the recycling plant at the Hotel Acuario on Playa Zicatela, directed by community leaders Alejandro Villanueva and Hector Marshelli. For more

information, contact Gina Machorro, tel. 954/582-0276, ginainpuers@yahoo.com. Or, if you want to pitch in, drop by the hotel, about a quarter of a mile (a half km) south of the Pérez Gasca mall's east end.

A pair of worthwhile locally-grown eco-projects are the two reptile sanctuaries east of Puerto Escondido. For details, see Short Excursions East of Puerto Escondido, in the Excursions from Puerto Escondido section.

Another nearby eco-project is the **turtle sanctuary** at Playa Escobilla, about 20 miles (30 km) east of Puerto Escondido. There, a cadre of SEMARNAT (Secretariat of Marine Natural Resources) professionals and volunteers is rescuing, hatching, and returning tens of thousands of baby turtles to the ocean annually.

A community organization, the **International Friends of Puerto Escondido** (IFOPE), welcomes Puerto Escondido newcomers with information and assistance, a lending library, and educational and social events. One of their most helpful activities, especially for Puerto Escondido visitors, is the **Emergency Response Team,** staffed with English-, German-, Spanish-, French-, and Italian-speaking volunteers who help foreigners in trouble. For information on monthly meetings, call tel. 954/582-1900, or email ifope@hotmail.com. Alternatively, contact Vicki Cole, one of IFOPE's sparkplugs, owner of Zicatela Properties. (See Apartments and Long-Term Rentals for contact details.)

Publications

One of the few outlets of any English-language newspaper is the Abarrotes Lupita, on Pérez Gasga, just outside the east-end stop sign, tel. 954/582-0872. In season, they stock newspapers, such as the Miami **Herald,** the Los Angeles *Times* and **U.S.A. Today.** Sometimes there may be a few copies of popular magazines, such as *Time, Newsweek,* and *People.*

English-language books are available at at least two spots in Puerto Escondido: the **Book Exchange,** at the Cafe Casa Babylon, next to the Hotel Acuario on Playa Zicatela, and **Acuario Books,** on Pérez Gasga, west end, uphill, across from the Hotel Nayar, tel. 954/582-0127.

The local English-Spanish tourist newspaper, **El Sol de la Costa,** provides a load of useful information, including community events listings, emergency numbers, apartment rental listings, and many service advertisements. Pick up a free copy in one of its many advertiser-businesses along the Pérez Gasga mall. If you can't find a copy, contact Editor Warren Sharpe, tel. 954/582-2230, elsol@escondido.com.mx.

Additionally, **International Friends of Puerto Escondido** maintains a lending library. For contact details, see the Community Organizations and Projects section.

SERVICES

Money Exchange
Banamex, at Pérez Gasga 314, with ATM, uphill from the Hotel Nayar, tel. 954/582-0626, changes U.S. and Canadian cash and traveler's checks Mon.–Fri. 9 A.M.–4 P.M., Sat. 10 A.M.–2 P.M. You can also use the Banco Internacional ATM, around the mid-point of the Pérez Gasga mall, next to the Hotel Las Palmas.

After bank hours, the small *casa de cambio* (money exchange) office on Pérez Gasga, next to the Hotel Casa Blanca, tel. 954/582-1928, also exchanges cash and traveler's checks Mon.–Fri. 9 A.M.–9 P.M., Sat.–Sun. 9 A.M.–8 P.M. Another *casa de cambio* offers similar services, on Playa Zicatela, next to Hotel Acuario, tel. 954/582-0592, open daily 9 A.M.–7 P.M.

Communications
The *correo* and *telégrafo* are side by side on Av. 7 Norte, corner Av. Oaxaca, seven blocks into town from the *crucero.* The post office, tel. 954/582-0959, is open Mon.–Fri. 8 A.M.–4 P.M., Sat. 9 A.M.–1 P.M.; the *telégrafo,* tel. 954/582-0232, which has public fax, is open Mon.–Fri. 9 A.M.–7:30 P.M., Sat. 9 A.M.–noon (Mon.–Fri. 9 A.M.–1 P.M. and 3–5 P.M. for money orders).

For local and long-distance telephone, purchase a **Ladatel** public telephone card at one of many Pérez Gasga stores and use it in street telephones. Conveniently located on Pérez Gasga, west end, a *larga distancia,* across Gasga and east from Restaurant La Galería, tel./fax 954/582-

0448, offers both telephone and fax service, daily 8 A.M.–10:30 P.M. On Playa Zicatela, for a fee, you may use the public long-distance telephone at the desk of the Hotel Acuario.

Beware of certain prominently located "Call Home With Your Credit Card" telephones. Tariffs on these phones can run $10 or more per minute, with a three-minute minimum, costing $30 whether you talk three minutes or not. Ask the operator for the rate; if it's too high, take your business elsewhere.

Internet access, daily until around 9 P.M., is available at cybercafé **Tigre Azul,** beach side, about a block inside the west-end Pérez Gasga stop sign, run by guide Ana Marquez.

Alternatively, across from the Banco Internacional ATM in the middle of the Gasga mall, **Coffee Net,** tel. 954/582-0797, offers Internet connection, fax, and long-distance telephone daily; or on Playa Zicatela, Internet connection is also available at **Hotel Acuario,** daily 8 A.M.–8:30 P.M.

Health and Emergencies
For medical emergencies, go to the 24-hour **Hospital Santa Fe,** Calle 3 Poniente between Calles 2 and 3 Norte, tel. 954/582-0541, which has an internist, pediatrician, gynecologist, and a dental surgeon on call. For more routine consultations, office hours are Mon.–Fri. 9 A.M.–2 P.M. and 4–8 P.M., Sat. 9 A.M.–2 P.M. Find the hospital three blocks west of the *crucero,* uphill from the highway.

Alternatively, go next door, to the **Sanatorio del Carmen,** tel. 954/582-1876 or 954/582-0174, with a number of female doctors on call.

You could also consult with English-speaking general practitioner Dr. Francisco Serrano, above the highway, at Calle 1 Norte 205, two blocks west of the main street, across Calle 1 Norte from Bancomer.

Another option is the 24-hour government health clinic, **Centro de Salud,** on Av. Pérez Gasga, just uphill from the Hotel Loren.

Get over-the-counter remedies and prescriptions at either of the two good tourist-zone pharmacies: the 24-hour **Farmacia La Moderna,** of Dr. José Luis Esparzar, on Gasga a block below the *crucero,* tel. 954/582-0698 or 954/582-2780, or **Super Farmas,** on the Pérez Gasga mall, across from Hotel Las Palmas, tel. 954/582-0112, open 8 A.M.–2 P.M. and 5–10 P.M.

For police or fire emergencies, call the **municipal police,** tel. 954/582-0498, or go to the headquarters in the Agencia Municipal on Hwy. 200, about four blocks west of the Pérez Gasga *crucero.*

Meditation and Massage

Healing is the mission of partners Patricia Heuze and Alejandro Villanuevo, who operate **Villa Temazcalli** meditation and massage center, west end of town, on Av. Infragante, two blocks uphill from the highway, tel. 954/582-1023, masaje @temazcalli.com, www.temazcalli.com. Facilities include rustic hot baths, an indigenous-style *temazcal* hot room, and massage room in an invitingly tranquil tropical garden setting. Prices run about $20 each for massage and the hot tub, and about $15 for one, $20 for two, and $25 for three, for the *temazcal.* Contact them for information and/or appointments.

Travel Agent and Car Rental

One of the most respected travel agents in town is **Viajes Dimar,** at the middle of the tourist mall, at Av. Pérez Gasga 906, P.O. Box 22, Puerto Escondido, Oaxaca 71980, tel./fax 954/582-0734 or 954/582-0237.

Rent a car at **Budget Rent a Car** on Calle Juárez, beach side of Hwy. 200, in the Bachoco suburb, by the airport, tel. 954/582-0312.

Laundry

Get your laundry done Mon.–Sat. 8 A.M.–8 P.M., Sun. 8 A.M.–5 P.M., at the **Lavamatico del Centro,** two doors downhill from Banamex, on Pérez Gasga, about two blocks uphill from the west-end stop sign.

GETTING THERE AND AWAY

By Air

The small jetport, officially the **Aeropuerto Puerto Escondido** (code-designated PXM), is just off the highway a mile (1.6 km) west of town. The terminal, only a plain waiting room with check-in desks, has no services, save a small snack bar. Out in front, *colectivo* vans to hotels in town run $2 per person. Arrivees with a minimum of luggage, however, can walk a block to the highway and flag down one of the many eastbound local minibuses, which all stop at the main town highway crossing. Arrive with a hotel in mind (better yet a hotel reservation in hand), unless you prefer letting your taxi driver choose one, where he will probably collect a commission for depositing you there.

Although **car rental agents** may not routinely meet flights, they will meet you if you have a reservation in advance. Call **Budget,** tel. 954/582-0312 or 954/582-0315, budget33@hotmail.com, or **Alamo,** tel. 954/582-3003, alamoescondido @hotmail.com.

Be prepared to pay the $12 international **departure tax** or its Mexican peso equivalent, if your ticket doesn't already include it. If you lose your tourist card, avoid trouble or a fine by taking your passport and some proof of your arrival date (such as a stamped passport, a copy of your lost tourist card, or an air ticket) to **Migracion** at the airport, tel. 954/582-3369, for help *before* your day of departure.

A few regularly scheduled flights connect Puerto Escondido with other Mexican destinations.

Aerocaribe Airlines flights connect daily with Mexico City, Oaxaca, and Huatulco. For reservations or flight information, call tel. 954/582-2024 or 954/582-2023.

If the above flights cannot take you where you want to go, try **Aerovega,** the dependable local air-taxi service. Call tel. 954/582-0151 (or in Oaxaca city, tel. 951/515-4982) or Viajes Dimar, on Gasga, tel. 954/582-0734 or 954/582-0737, for information and reservations.

Alternatively, charter airline **Aerotucan** also runs Oaxaca–Puerto Escondido flights, depending upon passenger demand. Call the airline, at tel. 954/582-1725 or 954/582-3461, or cell tel. 044-954/588-4336. In Oaxaca city, call tel. 951/501-0530 or 951/501-0532. You can also contact travel agent Viajes Dimar, on Gasga, tel. 954/582-0734 or 954/582-0737, for information and reservations. For many more details, visit www.aerotucan.com.

Puerto Escondido is also accessible via the

Puerto Ángel–Huatulco airport, one hour away by road. See the Bahías de Huatulco section.

By Car or RV

National Highway 200, although sometimes winding, is generally smooth and uncongested between Puerto Escondido and Pinotepa Nacional (89 miles, 143 km, 2.5 hours) to the west. From there, continue another 160 miles (258 km, 4.5 hours) to Acapulco. Fill up at Puerto Escondido before you leave, although gasoline is available at several points along the routes.

Traffic sails between Puerto Escondido and Puerto Ángel, 44 miles (71 km) apart, in an easy hour. Actually, Pochutla is immediately on the highway; Puerto Ángel is six miles (9.6 km) downhill from the junction, or alternatively accessible via the very scenic paved shortcut, at San Antonio village, Km 198. The Bahías de Huatulco (actually Crucecita) are an easy 22 miles (35 km) farther east.

To or from the city of Oaxaca, all-paved but sometimes potholed National Highway 131 connects directly north, along main street, Avenida Oaxaca, via its winding but spectacular 158-mile (254-km) route over the pine-clad Sierra Madre del Sur. The route, which rises 9,000 feet (2,700 meters) through Chatino foothill and mountain country, can be chilly in the winter and has few services along the lonely 100-mile (160-km) middle stretch between San Gabriel Mixtepec and Sola de Vega. Take water and blankets, and be prepared for emergencies. Allow about nine hours at the wheel from Puerto Escondido, eight hours the other way, from Oaxaca. Fill up with gasoline at the airport Pemex stations on either end before heading out. Unleaded gasoline is consistently available only at the Sola de Vega Pemex *gasolinera* en route.

By Bus

A new bus terminal has been planned for Puerto Escondido. By the time you read this, most or all of the bus service described below may originate in the new terminal at the upper end of Avenida Oaxaca.

Several long-distance bus lines serve Puerto Escondido; some offer first-class service. **Estrella**

Blanca subsidiary lines (luxury and first-class Elite and Futura and others), from the station on Avenida Oaxaca just uphill from the *crucero,* tel. 954/582-0427, travel the Highway 200 Acapulco-Isthmus route. More than two dozen daily *salidas de paso* come through en route both ways between Acapulco and Pochutla and Huatulco (Crucecita) and Salina Cruz. Other additional buses pass through, connecting with either Ixtapa-Zihuatanejo or Mexico City via Acapulco.

Cristóbal Colón, the other major first-class bus line, maintains a station on Av. 1 Norte between Av. 2 Oriente and Av. 1 Oriente, about three blocks uphill, one block east from the Pérez Gasga highway crossing, tel. 954/582-1073. It serves the Oaxaca east coast, beginning in Puerto Escondido, connecting all the way to San Cristóbal las Casas in Chiapas and Tapachula, at the Guatemala border. Intermediate destinations include Pochutla, Huatulco (Crucecita), and Salina Cruz. At Pochutla, passengers can transfer to Cristobal Colón Oaxaca-bound buses. One of these continues, via Puebla, to Mexico City.

Cooperating lines **Autobuses Estrella del Valle** and **Autotransportes Oaxaca Pacífico** on Hidalgo, corner of 3 Oriente, tel. 954/582-0050, provide both first- and second-class connections east with Pochutla, Bahías de Huatulco (Crucecita). Also, both first- and second-class buses connect with Oaxaca, via both Highway 175 through Pochutla and Highway 131 directly from Puerto Escondido.

Other minor mostly second-class bus lines offer departures from the gravel lot at Calle 10 Norte and Highway 131 main street, Avenida Oaxaca. From there and also at a small storefront station on Hidalgo between 1 Oriente and 2 Oriente, **Autobuses Estrella Roja del Sureste** and **Transol** buses, tel. 954/582-0603 connect (via pilgimage town Juquila) along Highway 131 with Oaxaca.

EXCURSIONS FROM PUERTO ESCONDIDO

Whether you go independently or by escorted tour, outings away from the Puerto Escondido resort can reveal rewarding glimpses of flora and fauna, local cultures, and idyllic beaches seemingly half a world removed from the Pérez Gasga tourist hubbub.

Farthest afield, to the west of Puerto Escondido, are the colorful festivals, markets, and handicrafts of the indigenous Mixtec towns of **Jamiltepec** and **Pinotepa Nacional** and the crystalline beaches and wildlife-rich mangrove reaches of the **Lagunas de Chacahua National Park.** To the east lie the hidden beaches of **Mazunte, Zipolite,** and the picture-book **Bay of Puerto Ángel,** with its turtle museum, au naturel sunbathing on Playa Zipolite, and very accessible off-beach snorkeling at Puerto Ángel. A bit farther beckon the nine breezy Bahías de Huatulco, ripe for swimming, scuba diving, wildlife-viewing, biking, and river rafting. For details of all of the above out-of-town sights, refer to the corresponding sections of this chapter.

Closer at hand, especially for wildlife lovers and beachgoers, are the jungly lagoons and pristine strands of the west-side **Laguna de Manialtepec,** the nearby hot springs and Chatino sacred site of **Atotonilco,** and a duo of homegrown **animal conservation sanctuaries.**

Laguna Manialtepec

Sylvan, mangrove-fringed Laguna Manialtepec, about 10 miles (16 km) west of Puerto Escondido, is a repository for a trove of Pacific wildlife. Unlike Lagunas de Chacahua (see West to the Mixtec Coast), Laguna Manialtepec is relatively deep and fresh most of the year, except occasionally during the rainy season when its main source, the Río Manialtepec, breaks through its sandbar and the lagoon becomes a tidal estuary. Consequently lacking a continuous supply of ocean fry for sustained fishing, Laguna Manialtepec has been left to local people, a few Sunday visitors, and its wildlife.

Consequently, Laguna Manialtepec abounds with birds. Of the hundreds of species frequenting the lagoon, 40 or 50 are often spotted in a morning outing. Among the more common are the olivaceous cormorant and its relative, the *anhinga;* and herons, including the tricolored, green-backed, little blue, and the black-crowned night heron. Other common species include ibis, parrots, egrets, and ducks, such as the Muscovy and the black-bellied whistling duck. Among the most spectacular are the huge great blue herons, while the most entertaining are the northern *jacanas,* or lily

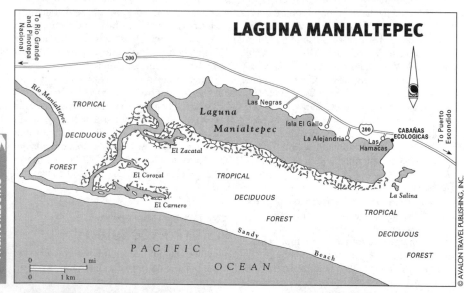

LAGUNA MANIALTEPEC

To Río Grande and Pinotepa Nacional

Río Manialtepec

200

TROPICAL

DECIDUOUS

FOREST

El Corozal

El Carnero

El Zacatal

Laguna Manialtepec

Las Negras

Isla El Gallo

La Alejandria

TROPICAL

DECIDUOUS

FOREST

Sandy

PACIFIC   OCEAN

Beach

200

CABAÑAS ECOLOGICAS

Las Hamacas

La Salina

TROPICAL

DECIDUOUS

FOREST

To Puerto Escondido

0   1 mi
0   1 km

© AVALON TRAVEL PUBLISHING, INC.

walkers, who scoot across lily pads as if they were the kitchen floor.

Manialtepec tours are conveniently arranged through travel agencies in Puerto Escondido. Although most of these advertise so-called "ecotours," a genuine one is **Hidden Voyages Ecotours,** led by Canadian ornithologist Michael Malone and arranged through the very competent travel agency Viajes Dimar, Av. Pérez Gasga 906, P.O. Box 22, Puerto Escondido, Oaxaca 71980, tel./fax 954/582-0734 or 954/582-0737. For many more tour details, see the Tours section.

If, however, you prefer to organize your own Manialtepec excursion by bus or car, you might find yourself tempted to linger—Manialtepec is ripe for kayaking, boating, and RV and tent camping along its mangrove- and palm-decorated shoreline. A handful of shady restaurant and lodging compounds along the shore offer the essentials for a week of Sundays in paradise.

The most comfortable of these lakefront mini-havens is **Las Hamacas,** at the lake's eastern end, near the Km 126 marker west of Puerto Escondido, tel. 954/588-7831. Friendly owner-manager Fernando Abascal López, of Santander, Spain (he's lived in Mexico since 1979) says he's "almost Mexican." A firm believer in ecologically appropriate land stewardship, Fernando is working to develop his environmentally friendy version of paradise. He's gotten off to a good start, with a mini-farm of ducks, goats, sheep, cattle, and rabbits; a lakeshore *palapa* restaurant; kayaks and non-gasoline sailboats; a sturdy, modern house with three comfortable rooms (about $25 d, whole house $75, with kitchen); and space for camping and RV parking for rent. A swimming pool, catamaran sailboat, and rustic cabanas are next, Fernando says.

A little more than half a mile (1 km) farther west is the sleepy little family-run pocket Eden of **La Alejandria,** which nestles along its hundred yards of lakefront, shaded by palms and great spreading trees. It's so idyllic that the *Tarzan* TV series picked La Alejandria for its setting, adding a rustic lake tree house (now totally destroyed by hurricanes) to the already gorgeous scene.

Embellishing all this is a homey restaurant/bar, screened-in from bugs, decorated with animal trophies, and reminiscent of an old-time East African safari lodge.

La Alejandria rents about six palm-shaded RV spaces with electricity and water (be prepared with your own long extension and hose) for about $10. Camping spaces also go for the same price. (Although La Alexandria also offers four shady cabanas, with private toilets, they've been allowed to become too mildewed for healthy habitation. However, it might be worth taking a look. Managers may have cleaned them up by the time you read this.)

Another half mile (1 km) west of La Alejandria is lakefront restaurant and dock **Isla El Gallo,** perfect for a day on the lagoon. Stop for lunch at the restaurant, then follow up on more local options, such as snoozing in a hammock, volleyball, swimming, bird-watching along the mangrove-decorated shoreline, launching your own canoe or boat, or hiring one of El Gallo's boatmen to take you on a lagoon excursion from the dock.

Atotonilco Hot Springs

Also on the west side, a few miles west of Laguna Manialtepec, the **Aguas Termales Atotonilco** hot springs, a Chatino sacred site, provides an interesting focus for a day's outing. The jumping-off point is the village of San José Manialtepec, about half an hour by bus or car west of Puerto Escondido.

At the village, you should hire someone to show you the way, up the semi-wild canyon of the Río Manialtepec. The trail winds along cornfields, beneath forest canopies, and past Chatino native villages. Finally, you arrive at the hot spring, where a clear bathtub-sized rock basin bubbles with very hot (bearable for the brave), clear, sulfur-smelling water.

Get there by tour, or driving or busing to the Highway 200 turnoff for San José Manialtepec, around Km 116, just east of the Río Manialtepec bridge. Village stables provide horses and guides to the hot springs. It's a very easy two-mile (3 km) walk, except in times of high water on the river, which the trail crosses several times.

Short Excursions East of Puerto Escondido

A pair of **grassroots conservation projects** on Puerto Escondido's east side are well worth a visit. First, just a few miles east of Puerto Escondido, in Barra de Navidad, just after (east of) the big Río Colotepec bridge, visit the **turtle, iguana, and crocodile sanctuary** of Galo Sánchez, which he's named Producción Ecoturístico Colotepec. Galo, his wife, family, and neighbors started with a beachfront turtle rescue effort that now includes crocodiles and iguanas. Their aim is to return all of the endangered creatures that they are nursing to the wild. They're happy to receive visitors daily, 8 A.M.–5 P.M., and ask a nominal donation of about $1 per person; if you can afford more, give it. Get there either by car or mini-bus from the Puerto Escondido highway crossing. About four miles 6.4 km) east of town, just before the big Río Colotepec bridge, turn right onto the side road to the village. Continue about a mile (1.6 km) until the road forks. Galo's house is on the left side.

A more mature, but equally laudable effort has been mounted by Marcelino López Reyes, at his **Iguana and Land Turtle Nursery** about half an hour by car or bus east of Puerto Escondido. Marcelino, a veterinarian, has been working for about 15 years at the nearby government turtle hatching station at Escobillo, helping to hatch and return about 900,000 *laut* (leatherback), *golfina* (olive ridley), and *carey* (hawksbill) turtles to the wild.

For the same number of years, friendly Marcellino has also devoted himself to his personal mission: to restore local populations of iguanas and land turtles. Although the last hurricane nearly demolished his operation, he's got it back up and running, with dozens of healthy reptilian residents in a big outside enclosure. Besides the green *iguana verde (Iguana iguana)*, and black *iguana prieta (Ctenosaura pectinata)*, he's also restoring two local species of endangered land turtles, the *tortuga del monte (Rinoclemys pulcherrima)*, and the *tortuga sabanera (Rinoclemys Ruvida)*. Don't miss visiting him (watch for the *criadero iguana* sign), at the east side of the Río Coazoaltepec bridge about 21 miles (34 km) east of Puerto

Escondido, or 23 miles (37 km) west of Puerto Ángel-Pochutla. The best time to find him there is around 5 P.M., after work on weekdays. If he's not there, one of his young assistants will probably be on hand to show you around. He appreciates a donation of about $1 or more if you have it.

Tours

Puerto Escondido agencies and guides conduct outings to all of the above and more. Besides the tour described in the Laguna Manialtepec section, the **Hidden Voyages Ecotours** of the Canadian husband-wife team of Michael Malone and Joan Walker (he's an ornithologist; she's an artist-ecologist) lead unusually informative beach, lagoon, and mountain tours seasonally, mid-December–Easter. In addition, they also offer a sunset lagoon wildlife and beach excursion and other trips, sometimes including a two-day trip to Nopala, center of Chatino native culture, including Costoche and La Perla coffee plantations in the cool Sierra Madre del Sur mountain forest. Their trips run about $40–55 per day, per person, depending on amenities. Contact them in Puerto Escondido Dec. 1–May 1 through the competent Viajes Dimar travel agency, Av. Pérez Gasga 906, P.O. Box 22, Puerto Escondido, Oaxaca 71980, tel. 954/582-0734, 954/582-1551, or 954/582-2305, fax 954/582-0737, viajesdimar@hotmail.com or michael@peleewings.ca. In the off season, contact them at Can. tel. 519/326-5193. For more information, visit www.wincom.net/~pelewing/hvecotur.html.

Other Dimar tours include a full-day jaunt east to the turtle museum at Playa Mazunte, continuing to Playa Zipolite, where you can stop for lunch and an afternoon of snorkeling around Puerto Ángel. Evenings during the dark of the moon, trips can include night snorkeling when algae coat everything underwater with an eerie bioluminiscent glow. The cost runs about $30 per person. Additionally, they offer an all-day hiking, picnic, and swimming excursion at a luxuriously cool mountain river and cascade in the sylvan Sierra Madre foothill jungle above Pochutla for about $40 per person, $80 two days, one night (minimum four persons).

Alternatively, try one of the tours guided by

PACIFIC RESORTS

Ana Marquez, aided by her daughter, also Ana, natives of Puerto Escondido. Their itineraries cover the coast, from the blowhole at Huatulco's Maguey Bay to the crocodile nursery at Chacahua National Park. Contact her at home at Futuro Mzna 7, No. 214, Fracc. Costa Chica, Puerto Escondido, Oaxaca 71984, tel. 954/582-2001, or at her Tigre Azul cyber café, beach side, near the west-end stop sign, tel. 954/582-2954 or 954/582-2855, ana@anasecotours.com, www.anasecotours.com.

Personable Gina Machorro, of Puerto Escondido *turismo,* who often staffs the booth at the west-end Pérez Gasga stop sign, also leads tours, including Puerto Escondido's newly discovered archaeological site. Contact her at tel. 954/582-0276, ginainpuerto@yahoo.com.

For more guides and tour providers, either check with your hotel desk, the local tourist newspaper, *El Sol,* or visit www.tomzap.com (and click on oaxaca, then puerto escondido, then tours).

Upland Excursion into Chatino Country

Head north from Puerto Escondido along Highway 131 and you enter the homeland of the Chatino people, who have lived quietly in their remote mountain hamlets longer than anyone can remember. Long neglected and little studied by historians and anthropologists, the Chatinos are now increasingly learning of their distinguished past and appreciating the value of their traditional language and customs.

In the old days, the only reason most outsiders ever came to Chatino country was the miraculous Virgin of Juquila, celebrated every December by adoring crowds who overflow Juquila's dozen-odd hotels and bed down in doorways, cars, buses, and the surrounding mountain forest, just to push their way to within 50 feet of the tiny, frail, beloved figurine.

Nopala people tell another story altogether. Theirs is the former domain of the great Chatino kings, whose history is just beginning to be uncovered by scholars. Nopala is also an important center of coffee production, surrounded by dozens of *fincas cafetaleras* (coffee farms), which in February and March harvest and roast a trove of fragrant beans for local, national, and international consumption.

An important consequence of the *fincas cafetaleras* is that they've sparked a renaissance of ecological awareness throughout Oaxaca's entire southern Sierra. Many growers have found markets for their produce from environmentally-aware European and North American buyers,

who prefer to buy coffee organically grown, without pesticides and herbicides, just exactly as the local growers have done since coffee was first introduced among Chatino people during the late 19th century.

Encouraged by their contacts with outside eco-activists, certain coffee farm owners and other ecologically aware local entrepreneurs have begun to offer tours, food, and lodging to visitors, who are trickling into Nopala in ever-increasing numbers.

SANTOS REYES NOPALA

Nopala (pop. 6,000, elev. 2,000 feet, 600 meters) is tucked into the upper valley of the Río Manialtepec, the heartland of Chatino country. Archaeologists reckon that the Chatino people have been living there for at least two thousand years. Stelae found at the nearby Cerro La Iglesia archaeological site resemble the famous Olmec-style *danzantes* of Monte Albán and are generally believed to date from the same period, around 500 B.C.

Nopala's townspeople nevertheless live very much in the present, enjoying a bit of the profits from their home-grown coffee. The government, moreover, has provided them with a generous sprinkling of schools: *primarias,* a *secundaria* and, for the university-bound, a *preparatoria,* unusual for such a small, out-of-the-way town. Afternoons in town, you can immediately see the positive effect of all this: hundreds of smartly dressed, bright-eyed schoolchildren trooping home after their classes are done.

Part and parcel with the increased emphasis in education, Oaxaca's unique new Usos y Costumbres law is having a significant local effect. No political parties, hubbub, or vote payoffs are necessary. A simple town-hall vote of the assembled citizenry is now sufficient to place Nopala's *presidente municipal* in office.

Sights

Nopala, Land of the Nopales in the Aztec language (which translates to La B'ya in Chatino), is a pretty little place, perched on a hill surrounded by green mountains. You can best appreciate all this by climbing the stairs (as a formality, ask the policeman on the porch if it's OK) to the top floor of the *palacio municipal*, just uphill from the main-plaza market. On the south (sunny side) rises **Cerro de Atole,** with the cross on top, where everyone climbs on February 24, the Día de la Bandera (Day of the Flag), and feasts upon the view, including the blue Pacific.

The name of the mountain, from *atole*, a nourishing Mexican drink made from corn, comes from the time when every house in town was a *jacal*, or thatched hut. In those days, building a new house was a community affair, when all the neighbors would climb the Cerro de Atole to gather the *pasto* (grass) for the new house's roof. When the work was all done, the owner would reward his friends with a party, which would include plenty of *atole.*

On the opposite side, toward the northwest, notice the apparent gash below the mountain summit, which rises perhaps three miles (5 km) beyond the town limits. That's the big waterfall **Cascada de San Juan Lachao** (about six miles, 10 km, by road), a locally popular place for cooling off on a hot day. To the right of that, approximately due north, rises **Cerro La Iglesia** (a steep, one-hour hike), named for the ruined fortified city, an important archaeological site, halfway down its flank. A bit farther to the right (east) of that, also halfway down yet another jungle-clad mountain, you can just make out some of the buildings of **Finca Costoche** (half-hour hike), a locally prominent coffee farm, named

for the jaguarundi, a wildcat and ferocious chicken-eater common in these parts.

In the northeast foreground, to the right behind the plaza-front buildings, you may be able to make out the mossy, colonial-style facade of the venerable **Templo de Los Reyes Santo Magos** (Church of the Holy Magi Kings), now replaced by the new church on its left. From here, townsfolk hold their yearly patronal festival for three days centering on El Día de Los Reyes, January 6. Invariably, townsfolk will enjoy a big party, including fireworks, a *calenda* (procession) carrying the images of their patron kings, and the town's favorite dances. These include the Guajalote (offering of the turkey) and Las Chilenas, a courtship dance not unlike the renowned Jarabe Tapatía, the so-called Mexican Hat Dance of Guadalajara.

Also in the foreground, to the east, you can see the red-brick decor of the one-of-a-kind **Hotel Palacio Chatino,** the town's most prominent hotel, labor of love of Dr. Elfego Zurita.

As you make your way down from atop the *palacio municipal,* be sure to take a close look at the several stelae embedded into the upper-floor and stairwell walls. Archaeologists, who dug them up at Cerro La Iglesia, believe them to represent Chatino high priests or kings, dating from about 500 B.C. If you look carefully around the bases, you'll see some yet-to-be deciphered name-dates, presumably of the personages represented. Notice that the upstairs figures have their arms folded over their chests, as in a burial, while the one in the middle of the stairwell is a priest in the act of human sacrifice, holding an obsidian knife in his right hand and a (gulp!) human heart in his left. (Note: Plans are afoot in Nopala to open a new museum to display their artifacts; by the time you read this, the aforementioned stelae may have been moved to the new museum, on the north side of the plaza.)

Accommodations

Nopala is ready for visitors, with a pair of good country-style hotels and at least three acceptable *comedor* restaurants. The economical lodging choice is **Hotel Palacio del Chatino,** 55 Hidalgo, Nopala, Oaxaca 71960, tel./fax

954/586-0000, whose bright red-and-white brick decor you probably already saw from atop the *palacio municipal.* The physician-owner has polished his little six-room hotel (three on top and three on the bottom, all around an interior garden) into a first-rate establishment. Rooms are clean and comfortably furnished with hot water, fans, and big double beds. The upper ones especially have plenty of air and light and look out on valley and mountain views on two sides. They're hard to beat, especially this far out in the country, for $8 s, $11 d. Reserve ahead through the owner, Dr. Elfego Zurita.

The other lodging is the **Posada Nopala,** Prolongación Calle Hidalgo s/n, Santo Reyes Nopala, Oaxaca 71960, tel. 954/586-0032, www.tabachin .com.mx/posada_nopala.htm, of American expatriate Pablo (Paul) Nunn Cleaver, also owner of Tabachín Apartments on Zicatela Beach in Puerto Escondido. Posada Nopala's hacienda garden-style layout consists of four luxuriously built rooms, complete with charming, baroque architectural details, including carved solid-hardwood doors. These rooms share one elaborately luxurious onyx and tile bathroom. Another larger house, which includes the dining room and the owner's quarters, has two similarly elaborately decorated rooms with their own baths. During high winter season, expect to pay some bucks (around $65 per day person for two, including three meals). Amenities include a big orchard in the back with all the mandarin oranges and mangos you can eat (in season). Reserve through the owner, Pablo Nunn Cleaver, in Puerto Escondido, at Apartmentos Tabachín del Puerto, Av. del Morro s/n, Colonia Marinero, Puerto Escondido, Oaxaca 71980, tel. 954/582-1179 or 954/582-1664, info@tabachin.com.mx; or in Nopala, at Posada Nopala. Ask Paul about Nopala tour arrangements, including local sights and coffee farms.

Food

Nopala can supply you with plenty of local-style food. If you want, start at the big **market,** which operates every day but is even bigger on *tianguis* days, Saturday and Sunday. The hundreds of native Chatino women flood into town in bright *traje* (native dress) with their loads of *calabazas*

(gourds), *cal* (lime or quicklime), *camote* (candied root, like sweet potato), *guajalotes* (turkeys), and much more.

If you'd rather not prepare your own dinner, pick out the goodies you want at the clean *fondas* (foodstalls) upstairs, in the building opposite the palacio municipal on plaza's east side.

Or if you'd rather, go to one of the more formal *comedores,* such as the **Sarita,** on Hidalgo, about two blocks downhill from the market; or for pizza, go to pizzería **Kore's,** on Iturbide, downhill from the plaza, next to Fredy's photo shop, tel. 954/586-0043.

Information and Services

Nopala's key service establishments are clustered right around the inviting, shady central plaza. Uphill, to the left of and facing the *presidencia municipal,* is the **correo** (post office), open Mon.–Fri. 9 A.M.–3 P.M., and the **telégrafos,** across the street adjacent to the basketball court, tel. 954/586-0079. Find it open for fax and money orders, Mon.–Fri. 9 A.M.–3 P.M.

At the end of the alley adjacent to the post office is Dr. Zurita's **Farmacia "Willey,"** open daily 6 A.M.–10 P.M. The *larga distancia* (long-distance) telephone office, is at the hotel Palacio del Chatino reception, behind the pharmacy, tel./fax 954/586-0000.

While in town, be sure to contact personable, well-informed local photographer and **guide Frédy Zárate,** who likes to show people around town. Farther afield, he can take you on excursions to local sights, such as the San Juan Lachao waterfall, the Cerro La Iglesia archaeological site, a coffee farm, and more. Expect to pay about $20 per day for his services. He speaks Spanish only, however; bring someone along to interpret. Contact him ahead of time at his house, at Esquina Zaragoza y Iturbide, Nopala, Oaxaca 71960, tel. 954/586-0043, fredyzarmen@yahoo.com.mx.

Getting There and Away

Get to Nopala from Oaxaca by second-class buses **Estrella Rojo del Sureste** or **Solteca (or Transol)** from the *camionera central segunda clase* at the Mercado Abastos (take a taxi) on Oaxaca's south side. From Puerto Escondido, go by the same bus lines from the parking lot at the upper, northern, end of town, at Calle 9 Norte and Av. Oaxaca, across from the electric station.

By car or RV from Oaxaca, drive the paved but often potholed Highway 131 south 120 miles (194 km, figure around six hours for safety) to San Gabriel Mixtepec. In the middle of town, where the road cuts sharply left, continue straight onto the paved side street to Nopala. Continue another seven miles (12 km) along a good but curvy paved road to Nopala.

In the opposite direction, from Puerto Escondido, drive 27 curving, sometimes bumpy, uphill miles (44 km) north along Highway 131 to San Gabriel Mixtepec. In the middle of town, when the road makes a sharp turn right, go left at the paved side street. Continue another seven miles (12 km) along a paved but winding road to Nopala. Allow about an hour and a half for safety.

Excursion to
Santa Magdalena Tiltepec

Santa Magdalena Tiltepec (pop. 4,000) is a very modest town perched on a hillside a few miles south of Nopala. A roadside sign a couple of miles before Nopala along the San Gabriel–Nopala road invites visitors to come see the local *artesanias alfarerias* pottery handicrafts.

The products, made by both men and women, are rustically attractive, low-fired, hand-coiled vases, jugs, and *comales* (griddles), in a handsome brown, enhanced by quizzically unique black markings. A number of potters are happy to demonstrate their wares. I stopped in at the house of Señora Ceriales Rojas, on Calle Buena Vista, a few doors uphill from the road's end town plaza. Señora Ceriales also recommended the work of others, including Jeremia Ríos, Margarita López, and her relative, prizewinning Hipolyta Rojas.

SANTA CATARINA JUQUILA: SHRINE FOR ALL SEASONS

Much of the life in the Chatino mountain town of Juquila (hoo-KEE-lah, pop. 25,000) revolves around its renowned patron, the Virgin of Juquila, the object of adoration for multitudes

who begin converging on the town around the first of December.

The reason for all the hubbub is a small, frail figurine scarcely more than a foot tall, which was donated to Juquila by a priest, Father Jordán de Santa Catalina, of the neighboring town of Amialtepec in 1713. Father Jordán feared that the image, which was already locally adored, deserved a more secure home than his rude *jacal.*

The love the faithful show for the Virgin of Juquila has grown over the centuries. Somehow, she strikes chords of sympathy in the hearts of Mexicans, perhaps partly because of her frailty and also because she's a simple figurine of a native woman, not unlike a pre-conquest goddess idol.

She was first revered by the Chatino people of Amialtepec during the 16th century when she resided in the town church. But in 1633, the entire town of Amialtepec burned down, and one of the sole remembrances left intact was the Virgin, who from that point forward became a symbol of hope for Chatino people.

TROUBLE IN CHATINO COUNTRY

Juquila's bustle appears so focused by the constant flow of faithful that you might think that the Virgin is all that Juquila is about. Beneath the busy surface, however, lies a complex network of personal relationships held together by political, business, kinship, and *compadrazgo* ties.

In the recent past, this tight social system, fueled by a communal forest property boundary dispute between Juquila and the rival town of Yaitepec, led to a local war that in some years resulted in hundreds of shootings, knifings, and machete slashings. Scores of Juquila and Yaitepec men bear scars of such violent encounters.

Fortunately, however, peace seems to have come to Chatino country, with the shaking of hands over a government-brokered pact in late 1998, fixing the boundary between Juquila and Yaitepec. For a fascinating in-depth look into Chatino social relationships and this dispute, check out James Greenberg's book, *Blood Ties: Life and Violence in Rural Mexico.* Details are contained in the Suggested Reading section.

Sights

The Juquila town plaza, half a block uphill from the terminus of Avenida Antonio Valdez, the entrance drive into town, is *the* place to appreciate Juquila. If you're driving, park your car in the lot of the Hotel del Carmen (on the right-hand side of Valdez, half a block before the plaza) and either check in at the desk or order breakfast or lunch. If busing, walk or ride a taxi from the Juquila station about a mile (1.6 km) ahead along Valdez to the plaza.

The baroque shrine-church, the **Santuario de Nuestra Señora de Juquila,** faces approximately east (unusual for Mexico, where most churches face west). If you face west, toward the church, the *palacio municipal* stands on your left, on the plaza's south side. On your right (north), sloping below the plaza level, stands the town market. Main plaza-front business street Calle Benito Juárez runs south to your immediate left, while on your immediate right, the same thoroughfare continues north as Calle Revolución, where *tianguis* awnings spread on Saturday and Sunday.

Step inside the church, where the tiny Virgin stands above the main altar, surrounded by flowers and encircled by a halo of blue fluorescent light. Multiple copies of the Virgin rest to one side of the main altar, while in a right-hand chapel, other copies, hung with *milagros* (wish medals), preside above a host of flickering candles.

Back in the nave, the faithful continuously arrive and quietly seat themselves in the pews, while others kneel before the altar, gazing at the Virgin. The diminutive figure is decorated with a pearl-garnished silk cape. Her face is of brown complexion, and upon her head rests a regal, native-style headdress. In front of the altar stand boxes for donations and personal letters to the Virgin.

Despite the supernumerary virgins in the plaza church itself, another nearby hilltop shrine, locally known as **La Capilla del Pedimento,** also draws multitudes of pilgrims. You'll find it near the clutter of roadside stalls about three miles (5 km) back, east along the highway, out of town.

At the stalls you can purchase nearly everything from food, drinks, and religious pictures

A roadside shrine to the Virgin of Juquila provides shelter and place to rest for pilgrims en route to Santa Catarina Juquila.

and reproductions of the Virgin to *milagros,* candles, and flower gifts for her. Collect your offerings and follow the human flow north of the highway about a quarter mile to the small summit chapel.

There you'll see a larger ceramic reproduction of the Virgin in a pink silken robe, heavily hung with *milagro* medals. For an appreciation of the annual mountain of adoration that the Virgin receives, stroll around behind the chapel and marvel at the pile upon pile of offerings, far too numerous to count or save, left by untold thousands of pilgrims.

Other commonly visited sights not far away from Juquila include the old Chatino center of **Amialtepec** and the spectacular 165-foot (50-meter) waterfall, **Cascada Chorro Conejos.** Ask at your hotel desk for a guide to show you the way.

Accommodations

Juquila's probable best-bet hotel is the **Hotel del Carmen,** at the town center at Antonio Valdez s/n, Juquila, Oaxaca 71900, tel./fax

954/524-0004. With an entrance driveway leading to a big rear parking lot, this is an especially convenient option for drivers in congested Juquila. The approximately 40 rooms, clean and mostly semi-deluxe, rent for about $35 s, $37 d, $39 t. Figure about double these prices during holidays and festivals, with hot-water shower baths, TV, good restaurant, and parking. Some rooms are better than others. Check the mattress before moving in.

Other cheaper options are available around the plaza half a block uphill. The best of these is probably the homey, family-run **Posada los Ángeles,** at the plaza's southeast corner, at Calle Benito Juárez 2, Barrio Grande, Juquila, Oaxaca 71900, tel. 954/524-0073. The approximately 20 rooms are clean, simply furnished, and well-maintained, with shaded (as opposed to bare-bulb) lamps. Rooms vary; if possible, get one with a balcony, plaza-front view. Rooms with one double bed rent for $20 s or d; with two double beds, $30 for three persons, $40 for four.

If the Ángel is full, try the **Hotel Juquila Plaza** on the plaza, right in front of the church at Av. Revolución 4, Juquila, Oaxaca 71900, tel. 954/524-0073. Rooms, although clean enough, aren't as thoughtfully furnished or as well-maintained as the Posada del Ángel. Some, however, have plaza-front views. They rent for about $20 s or d, $18 t. Add about 50 percent during festivals, with hot-water shower baths and parking.

If the rush of pilgrims has filled all the above accommodations, you can try others in the downtown, among them the **Hotel San Nicolas,** Calle Antonio Valdes s/n, tel. 954/524-0120, $15 s, $30 d; and the **Hotel La Conchita,** below and behind (southwest of) the church, at Calle Hidalgo s/n, tel. 954/524-0015, also $15 s, $30 d.

Food

Several sources around the plaza offer things to eat. For fruits and vegetables, go to the **market** on the plaza's north side. A convenient grocery source is **Abarrotes El Centro,** on the plaza's northeast corner, across Revolución from the market, tel. 954/524-0060. Hearty country-style food, always wholesome if hot, is available at *fondas* (permanent foodstalls) in the market.

The few good restaurants are mostly confined to the hotels. Fanciest in town is the restaurant in the **Hotel del Carmen,** on Antonio Valdez, half a block north of the church, tel. 954/524-0004, with a good standard menu of soups, sandwiches, meats, poultry, and Mexican specialties. Open daily about 7:30 A.M.–10 P.M.

For a homier option, go to the restaurant **La Angelita,** in the Hotel Posada los Ángeles, opposite the church on the plaza's northeast corner, tel. 954/524-0073. Here, the friendly female hotel owner supplies patrons with tasty local-style *desayunos, comidas,* and *cenas* (breakfasts, lunches, and suppers) daily, approximately 7 A.M.–10 P.M.

Entertainment and Events

The big Saturday and Sunday *tianguis* (spreading from the northeast corner of the plaza) is Juquila's main regular event. It swells to a 15-day marathon blowout during the December **Fiesta de la Virgen de Juquila.** The celebration begins quietly in late November with early-morning masses and religious processions; builds with a street carnival, floats, and fireworks; and climaxes around December 8 with traditional and modern dances, tapering off after the December 12 Virgin of Guadalupe festival.

Shopping

Stalls on Revolución past the plaza's northeast corner offer a variety of local handicrafts and food delicacies. Handicrafts include embroidered *huipiles, cinturones* (belts), *manteles* (tablecloths), and *servilletas* (napkins). Foods include coffee, coconut candy, and *panela* (brown sugar).

Stands near the church offer a wealth of old-time religious souvenirs. The Hotel del Carmen sells attractive replicas of the Virgin of Juquila.

Services

Juquila, the capital of the big southern Sierra Juquila governmental district, offers some basic services (but unfortunately no bank at this writing). The *correo* (post office), and the *telecomunicaciones* (public fax and money orders), are in the rebuilt *palacio municipal,* south side of the plaza, tel. 954/524-0023. A public telephone office, **Caseta Lidia,** inside, at the rear, of the market, tel. 954/524-0192, offers long-distance and public fax service from 7 A.M. to 9 P.M.

For routine medicines and drugs, try the plaza-front **Farmacia Dolores,** opposite the church. If you get sick, follow the recommendation of your hotel desk or hire a taxi to take you to the local **Hospital Civil.** Alternatively, near the plaza, consult with general practitioner **Dr. José Luis Zavaleta,** on Revolución, uphill side, at two location: either a few doors north of the plaza's northeast corner or on the second floor, above Abarrotes Zavaleta, directly across the plaza from the church.

Getting There and Away

Juquila is accessible from the coast, north via paved but sometimes potholed, Highway 131, the main north-south street through Puerto Escondido. Fill up with gasoline, then follow the winding 55-mile (88-km) route, climbing to the cool, 8,000-foot (2,400-meter) summit to El Vidrio crossing (gas station and rough, truck-stop *comedores*). There, drivers fork left and continue another 19 miles (30 km) west to Juquila.

For safety, allow about 3.5 hours for the entire curvy, uphill trip.

The same is approximately true heading south from Oaxaca city. Fill up with gasoline at the airport Pemex station south of town and continue to about two miles (3 km) south of Coyotepec, where you fork right on Highway 131. Continue, winding uphill and down, past Sola de Vega (roadside hotel, restaurant, and unleaded gasoline) to the El Vidrio summit crossing (103 miles, 166 km). Turn right at the fork and continue the remaining mostly paved, but sometimes bumpy 19 miles (30 km) west to Juquila.

A pair of long-distance second-class bus lines serve Juquila from both Oaxaca and Puerto Escondido. From the Oaxaca second-class bus terminal near the west-side Abastos market, ride either **Solteca (Transol)** or **Estrella Roja del Sureste** to Juquila. The same lines connect with Juquila from Puerto Escondido. They depart from the bus lot at the corner of Avenida 9 Norte and main street Avenida Oaxaca, across from the electric station at the north end of town. Note: Not all buses make the 19-mile (30-km) detour to Juquila. In such a case, get off the bus at El Vidrio and catch a local *colectivo* van for the remaining 19 miles.

West to the Mixtec Coast

In reality, the Costa Chica (Little Coast), which includes the Oaxacan Pacific Coast west of Puerto Escondido and the adjoining state of Guerrero coast all the way to Acapulco, isn't very little. Highway 200, heading out of Puerto Escondido, requires approximately 300 miles (480 km) to traverse it.

From Puerto Escondido, you head northwest, first passing settlements such as San José Manialtepec, on the southern fringe of Chatino-speaking country. Next, you pass the wildlife refuges of Laguna Manialtepec and Lagunas de Chacahua National Park and continue into the Mixtec coast (Mixteca de la Costa) past its main towns of Tututepec, Jamiltepec, and Pinotepa Nacional.

To many native people of Oaxaca's Costa Chica, Spanish is a foreign language. A large fraction of the *indígenas*—Chatino, Mixtec, and Amusgo—live in remote valleys and foothill villages, subsisting as they always have on corn and beans, without sewers, electricity, or paved roads. Those who live near towns often speak the Spanish they have learned by coming to market. In the Costa Chica town markets, you will brush shoulders with them—men, sometimes in pure-white cottons, and women in colorful embroidered *huipiles* over wrapped hand-woven skirts.

Besides the native Mexicans, you will often see African Mexicans—*morenos* (brown ones)—known as *costeños* because their isolated settlements are near the coast. Descendants of African slaves brought over hundreds of years ago, the *costeños* subsist on the produce from their village gardens and the fish they catch.

Costa Chica *costeños* and *indígenas* have a reputation for being unfriendly and suspicious. If true in the past (although it's certainly less so in the present), they have had good reason to be suspicious of outsiders, who in their view have been trying to take away their land, gods, and lives for 300 years.

Communication is nevertheless possible. Your arrival might be the event of the day for the residents of a little foothill or shoreline end-of-road village. People are going to wonder why you came. Smile and say hello. Buy a soda at the store or *palapa*. If kids gather around, don't be shy. Draw a picture in your notebook. If a child offers to do likewise, you've succeeded.

LAGUNAS DE CHACAHUA NATIONAL PARK AND VICINITY

The Lagunas de Chacahua National Park spreads for about 20 miles (32 km) of open-ocean beach shoreline and islet-studded mangrove lagoons midway between Pinotepa Nacional and Puerto Escondido. Tens of thousands of birds typical of a host of Mexican species fish the waters and nest in the mangroves of the two main lagoons, Laguna Pastoría on the east side and Laguna Chacahua on the west.

The fish and wildlife of the lagoons, once overfished and overhunted by local people, are now recovering. Commercial fishing is now strictly licensed. A platoon of Marines patrols access roads, shorelines, and the waters themselves, making sure catches are within legal limits. Crocodiles were hunted out during the 1970s, but the government is restoring them with a hatchery on Laguna Chacahua.

For most visitors, mainly Mexican families on Sunday outings, access is by boat, except for one upaved road. From east-side Zapotalito village, the local fishing cooperative offers full- and half-day boat excursions to the beaches, Playa Hermosa on the east side and Playa Chacahua on the west.

Exploring Lagunas de Chacahua

Zapotalito, on the eastern shore of Laguna Pastoría, is the easiest access point to the Lagunas de Chacahua. Get there from the Zapotalito turnoff at Km 82, 51 miles (82 km) from Pinotepa and 41 miles (67 km) from Puerto Escondido. (Local buses run from Río Grande all the way to Zapotalito on the lagoon, while second-class buses from Puerto Escondido and Pinotepa Nacional will drop you on the highway.)

From the Zapotalito landings, the fishing cooperative, Sociedad Cooperativa Turística Escondida, enjoys a monopoly for transporting visitors on the lagoons. The boatmen used to make their livings fishing; now they mostly ferry tourists. Having specialized in fishing, they are generally neither wildlife-sensitive nor wildlife-knowledgeable. Canopied powerboats, seating about 10, make long, full-day trips for about $70 per boat. Cheaper (about $30) half-day excursions take visitors to nearby **Playa Cerro Hermosa** at the mouth of Laguna Pastoría for a couple of hours' beach play and snorkeling—if you bring your own snorkeling gear. On the other hand, you can save yourself $30 and drive, taxi, or walk the approximately two miles (3 km) along the shoreline road from Zapotalito to Playa Cerro Hermosa. Here you'll find a lovely open-ocean beach good for surf-fishing and beach sports, camping, a wildlife-rich lagoon mangrove wetland, and several *palapa* restaurants.

The full-day destination, Playa Chacahua, about 14 miles (22 km) distant, unfortunately seems to necessitate a fast trip across the lagoon. It's difficult to get them to slow down. They roar across broad Laguna Pastoría, scattering flocks of birds ahead of them. They wind among the islands, with names such as Escorpión (Scorpion), Venados (Deer), or Pinuelas (Little Pines), sometimes slowing for viewing multitudes of nesting pelicans, herons, and cormorants. They pick up speed again in the narrow jungle channel between the lagoons, roaring past idyllic, somnolent El Corral village, and break into open water again on Laguna Chacahua.

The **crocodile hatchery** is at Chacahua village on the west side of the lagoon, home to about two dozen local *costeño* families, a shabby hotel, and a pair of lagoonside *palapa* restaurants. Past the rickety crocodile caretaker's quarters are a few enclosures housing about a hundred crocodiles segregated according to size, from hatchlings to six-foot-long (two-meter-long) toothy green adults.

The tour climaxes at the west half of Chacahua village across the estuary. Here, palms line the placid lagoon, shading the **Hotel Siete Mares** (Seven Seas) bamboo tourist cabanas. The hotel, a quiet, rustic tropical retreat, offers a small restaurant, showers and toilets, a few cabins (rent negotiable from about $12, depending upon season), and a beautiful beach a short walk away. Contact the hotel through the Chacahua village telephone *caseta*, tel. 958/582-0893.

Playa Chacahua is lovely *because* of its isolation. The unlittered golden-white sand, washed by gently rolling waves, seems perfect for all beach activities. You can snorkel off the rocks nearby, fish in the breakers, and surf the intermediate breaks that angle in on the west side. A

few *palapas* provide food and drinks, and, for beachcombers, wildlife viewers, and backpackers (who bring their own water), the breezy, jungle-backed beach spreads for 10 miles (16 km) both ways.

Río Grande

Río Grande (pop. 15,000), five miles (8 km) east of the Lagunas de Chacahua–Zapotalito access road, is a transportation, supply, and service point for the region. Right on the highway are *abarroterías* (groceries), pharmacies and doctors, and a *larga distancia* telephone in an office-booth on the right (south) side, at the west edge of town.

The downscale **Hotel Río,** Av. Puebla, Río Grande, Oaxaca 71830, tel. 954/582-6033, is the big white building off the highway's north side, at the west end of town. It offers 22 plain but clean rooms on two floors, encircling a spacious parking courtyard. The rooms rent for about $6 s, $12 d, with fans and toilets, but tepid (not hot) water.

The access to rustic south-seas hideaway Hotel Siete Mares at Playa Chacahua is by boat.

The friendly, family-run **Restaurant Río Grande,** across the street from the hotel, provides good cheer and hearty meals daily 7 A.M.–10 P.M.

On the east edge of town, the once-inviting but now somewhat-neglected **Hotel Paraíso Río Grande,** Carretera 200, Río Grande, Oaxaca 71830, tel. 954/582-6196, offers a big swimming pool (if it's in working order) and a kiddie pool in a spreading, grassy patio, plus large brick-and-tile rooms with either fans or a/c. The 20 rooms (check for mildew) rent for about $12 s, $17 d, $18 t with fan and TV, and $14 s, 23 d, $25 t with a/c and TV.

The hotel's soaring, classically vaulted ceilings and elegant brick arches flow from the expertise of its friendly and articulate architect builder. His life project has been to first build, and now extend, the hotel, using unreinforced brick and concrete only, not unlike ancient Roman buildings, but with the addition of innovative new designs. (If the Hotel's pool isn't functioning, stop instead for a swim and a picnic a few miles

west, at **Balneario Las Delicias** water park, with shaded tables, and snack bar, at Km 102.)

Roca Blanca

Travelers hankering for an afternoon or a few tranquil days on the beach, can have it at Roca Blanca (White Rock), tucked on the shoreline about six miles (10 km) east of Río Grande or 22 miles (36 km) west of Puerto Escondido. Here, a few rustic *palapa* restaurants front a long, curving beach of yellow-white sand, washed by gentle rollers. Islet Roca Blanca perches picturesquely offshore, softening the Pacific swells. On the west side, a lagoon, backed by a scenic jungle of rocky outcroppings, provides shelter for kiddie play and often some impromptu *palapas* that await restoration by new occupants.

If you want to stay, but arrive unequipped for camping, check out the adjacent **cabanas.** Here, about $10 gets you a petite, round, thatched wooden house with a bed for two, with showers and toilets in an adjacent concrete building. There are also a lot for parking self-contained RVs and a lagoon-side beach good for setting up a tent and kayaking or rubber-boating either in the ocean or the lagoon. Be prepared with bug repellent, especially around sunset. For more information, check with the owner, Andres López Solano, tel. 958/582-6328, in Río Grande.

SAN PEDRO TUTUTEPEC

Tututepec (pop. 10,000) is a locally important town that perches on the breeze-cooled heights about five miles (8 km) inland from Highway 200. Get there by turning north (right), westbound, at the signed side road at Santa Rosa de Lima, 45 miles (72 km) west of Puerto Escondido (or 44 miles, 71 km east of Pinotepa Nacional). After about two miles (3 km) from the highway, turn left at the fork, which leads a few more miles uphill to Tututepec and ends at the town plaza.

Few local residents appear aware of their town's proud tradition as the only Oaxaca kingdom that withstood the 15th-century Aztec invasion and remained independent at the time of the conquest in 1522. Today's residences are built perfunctorily on the same hilltops where Tututepec's kings raised their pyramids and temples.

Nevertheless, a few excavated remains give clues to Tututepec's past splendor. Climb the concrete stairs leading uphill from the west side of the town plaza to a hilltop mini museum-park and church. On the right side, a roof shelters a number of monoliths—of a high priest, a pair of Quetzalcoatl-like serpents, and a headless jaguar—carved in styles reminiscent of Teotihuacán and Tula (Land of the Toltecs).

While you're atop the hill, take a look inside the town church. On the altar is the image of St. Peter, the town patron (who, however, is not the object of the main local festival, which is the Fiesta de Candelaria, around February 2).

While you're in Tututepec, you can avail yourself of a number of services located in the vicinity of the town plaza. These include *abarroterías* (grocery stores), a *correo* (post office), a *telecomunicaciones* (money orders and public fax), tel. 958/581-0081, and a *centro de salud* (health center), tel. 958/581-0039. Gasoline is available at the Pemex station on Highway 200, not far east of the Tututepec turnoff.

CHARQUITO ATOTONILCO WARM SPRINGS

About 10 miles (16 km) west of the Tututepec side road, Highway 200 passes over the **Río Verde,** Oaxaca's longest river, which funnels the entire runoff from Oaxaca's central valley into the Pacific a few miles downstream. West of the river, near the Km 48 marker, just over a half mile (1 km) west of Charquito village, turn left at the Guayabo-labeled side road for Atotonilco hot springs and sacred site.

If driving, set your odometer at the turnoff. Continue through Guayabo (2.1 miles, 3.4 km), Patria Nueva (2.8 miles, 4.5 km), and a shallow river bed (about a foot and a half deep during the rainy season) to the hot spring at 4.2 miles (6.8 km).

This source of warm, sulfury, curative water has been used and revered by untold generations of local people. Folks have built a small chapel on the hill above the pair of springs: The

first is to the right, below the road, beneath an immense, spreading *guanacastle* tree, and the second is marked by a wide, waist-deep riverbank bathing pool.

A continuous stream of mostly local people bathe here, especially on Sundays and holidays. If you've got extra time, this might be an interesting place to set up a tent or park your RV for a few days (at a respectful distance from the springs themselves; as a courtesy, ask if it's OK to camp). Unless you're under three, *do not bathe nude.* Please respect local custom by wearing at least a modest bathing suit while using the springs.

On the slope above the springs, pay your respects inside the small chapel, dedicated to the **Virgen de los Remedios.** Here, at the altar, people give "thanks to the virgin for the hot waters that have been provided."

SANTIAGO JAMILTEPEC

About 68 miles (109 km) west of Puerto Escondido and 18 miles (30 km) east of Pinotepa Nacional is the hilltop town of Jamiltepec (hah-meel-teh-PAYK). Two-thirds of its 20,000 inhabitants are Mixtec, who preserve a still-vibrant indigenous culture. A grieving Mixtec king named the town in memory of his infant son, Jamily, who was carried off by an eagle from this very hilltop.

Around Town

The central plaza, about a mile (1.6 km) from the highway (follow the signed side road north—right, westbound), stands at the heart of the town. You can't miss it, because of the proud town plaza–front clock (and sundials) and market, always big, but even bigger and more colorful on Thursday, the day of the traditional native *tianguis.*

Moreover, several big festivals are instrumental in preserving local folkways. They start off on New Year's Day and resume during the weeks of Cuaresma (Lent), usually during February and March. Favorite dances, such as the Los Tejerones (Weavers), Los Chareos, Los Moros (The Moors), and Las Chilenas, act out age-old events, stories, and fables. Los Tejerones, for example, through a cast of animal-costumed characters, pokes fun at ridiculous Spanish colonial rules and customs.

Soon after, Jamiltepec people celebrate their very popular pre-Easter (week of Ramos) festival, featuring neighborhood candlelight processions accompanied by antique 18th-century music. Hundreds of the faithful bear elaborate wreaths and palm decorations to the foot of their church altars on Domingo de Ramos (Palm Sunday).

Later, merrymaking peaks again, between July 23 and 26 during the Fiesta de Santiago Apóstol (Festival of St. James the Apostle) and on September 11 with a festival honoring the Virgen de los Remedios. All this celebrating centers in the town church, the **Templo de Santiago Apóstol,** destroyed by a 1928 earthquake but brilliantly restored from 1992 to 1999. Dominican padres supervised the original construction of mortar moistened with egg yolks during the 16th century. Take a look inside, where the town patron St. James (sword in hand) and the Virgen de Los Remedios (Virgin of the Remedies) preside above the altar.

Regardless of the festivals, Jamiltepec at midday is a feast of traditional sights and sounds, accessible by simply strolling around the market and side streets. For an interesting side excursion, take a stroll to some of the local *ojos de agua* (community springwater sources). From the plaza's northeast side, head east, downhill, along Calle 20 de Noviembre. After about a block, you'll arrive at a covered *pileta* (basin) built into the hillside rocks on the left, where folks fill bottles and jars with drinking water. Continue downhill another couple of blocks to *ojo de agua* **El Aguacate,** where another covered basin, on the left, supplies drinking water, while a cluster of folks wash clothes and bathe in a natural spring beneath an adjacent shady roof.

If you're interested in a more spectacular water diversion, follow the gravel road by local minibus or car north out of town about 15 miles (25 km) to the *cascada* (waterfall) in the foothill country near San José de las Flores village.

Shopping

Jamiltepec is well worth a stop if only to visit its market handicrafts shops, such as **Yu-uku Cha-kuaa** (Hill of Darkness) of Santiago de la Cruz Velasco. Personable Santiago runs his shop at the Jamiltepec plaza market, because the government cluster of shops (Centro Artesanal de la Costa, on the highway) was closed down, victim of a dispute over control. The local Mixtec artisans wanted to manage their own handicrafts sales, while the regional branch of the INI (Instituto Nacional Indigenista) preferred to manage instead. The Mixtecs stuck together and refused to bring their handicrafts, closing the government operation.

Some of those crafts—masks, *huipiles,* carvings, hats—occupy the shelves and racks in Santiago's shop by the market's northeast entrance (ask for Santiago by name), open until about 4 P.M. His home (where he also sells handicrafts) is located on main street Av. Principal at Francisco Madero, by *seguro social,* the government health clinic (turn off at the highway sign). If you don't want to miss him, write Santiago at Av. Principal, Esquina Fco. Madero, Barrio Grande, Sec. 5, Jamiltepec, Oaxaca 71700.

Practicalities

Jamiltepec, capital of the Jamiltepec governmental district, has a number of basic hotels, restaurants, and services (but not yet a bank) near the town plaza. For an overnight, take a look at the **Hotel Díaz,** at the northeast plaza corner at Hidalgo 4, Jamiltepec, Oaxaca 71700, tel. 958/582-8050. It offers a dozen clean, basic rooms around an airy upstairs patio for about $8 s, $10 d, with fan and private bath (but room-temperature water only). If it's full, take a look at **Hotel Maris,** tel. 954/582-8042, and **Hotel Pérez,** tel. 954/582-8829 or 954/582-8249, both on Calle Josefa O. Domínguez nearby.

Additionally, out on the highway, at the west edge of town, consider Jamiltepec's deluxe new **Hotel Mirador,** perched on a hillside. Fine for an overnight, the Mirador offers about 15 comfortable (if a bit dark) rooms, for about $20 d with fans, $25 d with a/c and hot-water shower baths, and an acceptable restauraurant.

For medicines and drugs, go to **Farmacia del Perpetuo Socorro** (Pharmacy of Perpetual Relief), Hidalgo 2, tel. 954/582-9046, at the plaza's northeast corner, run by a team of friendly sisters. If you need a doctor, they recommend either **Dr. Manuel Mota,** on Hwy. 200, in town *barrio* Sección 4, or the *seguro social* **Hospital** with 24-hour emergency service, in town *barrio* Las Flores.

WEST OF JAMILTEPEC

San Andres Huaxpaltepec

For 20 miles (32 km) west of Jamiltepec, Highway 200 stretches through the coastal Mixtec heartland, intriguing to explore, especially during festival times. The population of Huaxpaltepec (oo-wash-pahl-tay-PAYK), about nine miles (14 km) west of Jamiltepec, 12 miles (20 km) east of Pinotepa Nacional, sometimes swells from 4,000 to 20,000 or more during the three or four days before the day of Jesus the Nazarene (the fourth Friday before Good Friday). The entire town becomes a spreading warren of shady stalls, offering everything from TVs to stone *metates*. Purchase of a corn-grinding *metate*, which, including stone *mano* (roller), sells for about $20, is as important to many a Mixtec family as a refrigerator is to an American. Mixtec husband and wife usually examine several of the concave stones, deliberating the pros and cons of each before deciding.

The Huaxpaltepec Nazarene fair is typical of the larger Oaxaca country expositions. Even the highway becomes a lineup of stalls; entire native clans camp under the trees, and mules, cows, and horses wait patiently around the edges of a grassy trading lot as men discuss prices. (The fun begins when a sale is made and the new owner tries to rope and harness his bargain steed.)

Even sex is for sale within a quarter of very tightly woven no-see-through grass houses, patrolled by armed guards. Walking through, you may notice that instead of the usual women, one of the houses might be offering men dressed in low-cut gowns, lipstick, and high-heeled shoes.

Santa María Huazolotitlán

At nearby Huazolotitlán (ooah-shoh-loh-teet-LAN, pop. 3,000) several resident woodcarvers

© BRUCE WHIPPERMAN

An indigenous Amusgo family displays its homemade pottery offering at the pre-Easter San Andres Huaxpaltepec fair.

craft excellent **masks.** Local favorites are jaguars, lions, rabbits, bulls, and human faces. Given a photograph (or a sitting), one of them, if asked, might even carve your likeness for a reasonable fee. (Figure perhaps $40–60.) Near the town plaza, ask for José Luna, Lázaro Gómez, or the master Idineo Gómez (who are all related and live in the town *barrio* Ñii Yucagua).

Textiles are also locally important. Look for the colorfully embroidered animal- and floral-motif *huipiles, manteles,* and *servilletas* (native smocks, tablecloths, and napkins). You might also be able to bargain for a genuine heirloom *pozahuanco* (handwoven wraparound skirt) for a reasonable price. (See the sidebar "Pozahuancos: Oaxaca's Sarongs.")

Besides all the handicrafts, Huazolotitlán people celebrate the important local **Fiesta de la Virgen de la Asunción** August 13–16. The celebrations climax on August 14 and 15, with a number of favorite traditional dances in which you can see why masks are locally important, especially in the dance of the Tiger and the Turtle on August 14. The finale comes on August 15, with the ritual dance of the Chareos, dedicated to the Virgin.

Huazolotitlán is about two miles (3 km) via the paved road that forks south uphill from Highway 200 in Huaxpaltepec. Get there by driving, hitchhiking (with caution), riding the local bus, or hiring a taxi for about $2.

PINOTEPA NACIONAL

Pinotepa Nacional (pop. about 50,000; 157 miles, 253 km, east of Acapulco; 90 miles, 145 km, west of Puerto Escondido) and its neighboring communities comprise the hub of an important coastal indigenous region. Mixtec, Amusgo, Chatino, and other peoples stream into town for markets and fiestas in their traditional dress, ready to combine business with pleasure. They sell their produce and crafts—pottery, masks, handmade clothes—at the market, then later get tipsy, flirt, and dance.

The Name

So many people asked the meaning of their city's name that the town fathers wrote the explanation on a wall next to Highway 200 on the west side of town. Pinotepa comes from the Aztec-language words *pinolli* (crumbling) and *tepetl* (mountain); thus Crumbling Mountain. The second part of the name came about because, during colonial times, the town was called Pinotepa Real (Royal). This wouldn't do after independence, so the name became Pinotepa Nacional, reflecting the national consciousness that emerged during the 1810–1821 struggle for independence.

The Mixtecs, the dominant regional group, disagree with all this, however. To them, Pinotepa has always been Ñií Yo-oko (Little Place). Only within the town limits do the Mexicans (mestizos), who own most of the town businesses, outnumber the Mixtecs. The farther from town you get, the more likely you are to hear people conversing in the Mixtec language, a complex tongue that uses a number of subtle tones to make meanings clear.

Getting Oriented

On Pinotepa's west (Acapulco) side, Highway 200 splits into the town's two major arteries, which rejoin on the east (Puerto Escondido) side. The north, west-bound branch is called Aguirre Palancares; the south, west-bound branch, the more bustling of the two branches, passes between the town-center plaza and church and is called Avenida Porfirio Díaz on the west side and Avenida Benito Juárez on the east. The main north-south street, Avenida Pérez Gasga, runs past both the church front and the *presidencia municipal* (city hall), which faces east, toward the town plaza.

Market

Highway 200 passes a block north of the main town market, by the big, fenced-in secondary school, on the west side, about a mile (1.6 km) west of the central plaza. Despite the Pinotepa market's oft-exotic goods—snakes, iguanas, wild mountain fruits, forest herbs, and spices—its people, nearly entirely Mixtec, are its main attraction, especially on the big Wednesday and Sunday market days. Men wear pure-white loose cottons, topped by woven palm-leaf hats. Women wrap themselves in their lovely striped purple, violet, red, and navy blue *pozahuanco* sarong-like, horizontally striped skirts. Many women carry a polished tan *jícara* gourd bowl atop their heads, which, although it's not supposed to, looks like a whimsical hat. Older women (and younger ones with babies at their breasts) go bare-breasted with only their white *huipil* draped over their chests as a concession to mestizo custom. Others wear an easily removable *mandil*, a light cotton apron-halter above their *pozahuanco*. A few women can ordinarily be found selling beautiful handmade *pozahuancos*. (Alternatively, Artemio López Clavel, in his market shop, local 35, sells *pozahuancos,* both machine-made and genuine hand-made.)

Festivals

Although the Pinotepa market days are big, they don't compare to the week before Easter (Semana Santa). People get ready for the finale with processions, carrying the dead Christ through town to the church each of the seven Fridays before Easter. The climax comes on Good Friday

POZAHUANCOS: OAXACA'S SARONGS

To a coastal Mixtec woman her *pozahuanco* (wraparound skirt) is a lifetime investment symbolizing her maturity and social status, something that she expects to pass on to her daughters. Heirloom *pozahuancos* are of hand-spun thread, dyed in several shades. Women dye them by hand, always including a pair of necessary colors: a light purple *(morada)* from secretions of tidepool-harvested snails, *Purpura patula pansa,*

and silk dyed scarlet red with cochineal, a dye extracted from the beetle *Dactylopius coccus,* cultivated in the Valley of Oaxaca. Increasingly, women are weaving *pozahuancos* with synthetic thread, which has a slippery feel compared to the hand-spun cotton. Consider yourself lucky if you can get a traditionally made *pozahuanco* for as little as $100. If someone offers you a look-alike for $20, you know it's an imitation.

(Viernes Santa), when a platoon of young Mixtec men paint their bodies white to portray Jews and shoot arrows skyward, simultaneously reciting traditional Mixtec prayers. On Saturday, the people mournfully take the Savior down from the cross and bury him, and on Sunday gleefully celebrate his resurrection with a riot of fireworks, food, and folk dancing.

Although not as spectacular as Semana Santa, merrymaking abounds, with plenty of food, dancing, and processions around the Pinotepa *zócalo* church on July 25, the day of Pinotepa's patron, Santiago (St. James).

Accommodations

The motel-style **Hotel Carmona,** Av. Porfirio Díaz 127, Pinotepa Nacional, Oaxaca 71600, tel. 954/543-2322, fax 954/543-2164, about three blocks west of the plaza, offers three stories of clean, not fancy but comfortable rooms and a big backyard garden with pool and sundeck. For festival dates, make advance reservations. The 50 rooms run about $16 s, $22 d, $28 t, fan only; $ $24, $33, and $40 for a/c.

If the Carmona is full, check the two high-profile newer hotels, Pepe's and Las Gaviotas, beside the highway on the west side of town. Of the two, **Pepe's,** at Carretera Pinotepa Nacional-Acapulco Km 1, Pinotepa Nacional, Oaxaca 71600, tel. 954/543-4347, fax 954/543-3602, is the much better choice. It offers 35 spacious, semi-deluxe rooms for a reasonable $12 s, $15 d fan only, $20 and $26 with a/c; with good TV, hot water, restaurant, and parking. Rooms at emergency-only Hotel Las Gaviotas, tel. 954/543-

2838, fax 954/543-2056, rent for $14 d with fan, $18 with a/c.

Third choice goes to clean **Hotel Marisa,** downtown on the highway, Av. Juárez 134, north side of street, tel. 954/543-2101, 954/543-2022, or 954/543-3190, $10 d, $13 t with fan, $16 s or d, $20 t with a/c; all with parking.

Campers enjoy a tranquil spot (best during the dry late fall-winter-spring season) on the **Río Arena** about two miles (3 km) east of Pinotepa. Eastbound, turn left just after the big river bridge. Continue a few hundred yards, past a pumphouse on the left, to a track that forks down to the riverbank. Notice the waterfall cascading down the rocky cliff across the river. You will sometimes find neighbors—in RVs or tents and sand collectors, poor but friendly—set up on the riverside beneath the abandoned Restaurant La Roca (now just a rock-wall ruin), a few hundred yards up the smooth stream, excellent for kayaking (if you have some way of returning back upstream.)

(At this writing, more space for campsites appears available on the river's west side. Get there via the access road downhill from the bridge's west side. Careful for soft sand.)

Food

For a light lunch or supper, try the very clean, family-run **Burger Bonny,** at the southeast corner of the main plaza, open daily 11 A.M.–10 P.M. Besides six varieties of good hamburgers, Burger Bonny offers *tortas,* tacos, french fries, hot dogs, microwave popcorn, fruit juices, and *refrescos,* at very reasonable prices.

Also worthy is traditional-style **Fonda Toñita,** a block north of the church-front, at the corner of Aguirre Palancares. Local folks flock here for the hearty afternoon *comida* (pick the entrée, and you get rice and tortillas thrown in free); it's also good for breakfast. Open Mon.–Sat. 7 A.M.–9 P.M.

Third restaurant choice goes to restaurant **Tacos Orientales,** with 15 styles of tacos, from fish to *carnitas,* three for $2.50. Find it on Pérez Gasga, half a block north of the churchfront, open daily 6–11 P.M.

On the other hand, consider *marisquería* **Peñitas** next door, which specializes in fresh seafood however you like it: fried, baked, breaded, *al mojo* (with garlic), and more. Open daily 8 A.M.–midnight.

For a quick and convenient on-the-road breakfast, lunch, or dinner, stop by the restaurant of high-profile **Pepe's Hotel** west of town, open daily 8 A.M.–10 P.M.

Services

Exchange money over the counter or use the ATM at all Pinotepa banks. Try **Bancomer,** corner of Díaz and Progreso, two blocks west of the plaza, tel. 954/543-3022 or 954/543-3190, open Mon.–Fri. 8:30 A.M.–4 P.M.; or **Banamex,** across the street, open Mon.–Fri. 9 A.M.–4 P.M. Alternatively, try the long-hours (open Mon.–Fri. approximately 8 A.M.–7 P.M., Sat. 8 A.M.–3 P.M.) **Banco Internacional,** also on Av. Progreso, but across Porfirio Díaz and uphill a block from Bancomer, tel. 954/543-3949 or 954/543-3969.

The *correo* (post office), by the Estrella Blanca bus station, about two blocks west and across the street from Bancomer, tel. 954/543-2264, is open Mon.–Fri. 8 A.M.–7 P.M. The *telecomunicaciones* office (money orders, public telephone, and fax) is one block north of the plaza church, on Av. Pérez Gasga, open Mon.–Fri. 8 A.M.–7:30 P.M., Sat.–Sun. 9 A.M.–noon. *Larga distancia* Lada Central telephone and fax office, on the plaza, south side, is open longer, evening hours. For film and film-processing, visit the **photo shop** next door.

For a doctor, go to the **Clínica Rodriguez** at 503 Aguirre Palancares, tel. 954/543-2330, one block north, two blocks west of the central plaza church-front. Get routine medications at one of

several town pharmacies, such as the 24-hour **Super Farmacia,** on Díaz, a block west of the central plaza church-front.

Getting There and Away

By car or RV, Highway 200 connects west to Acapulco (160 miles, 258 km) in an easy 4.5 hours driving time. The 89-mile (143-km) connection to Puerto Escondido can be done safely in about 2.5 hours. Additionally, the 239-mile (385-km) Highway 125–Highway 190 route connects Pinotepa Nacional to Oaxaca, via Putla de Guerrero and Tlaxiaco (136 miles, 219 km). Although winding most of the way and potholed at times, the road is generally uncongested. It's safely driveable in a passenger car with caution, from Pinotepa to Oaxaca (follow the toll *autopista* near Oaxaca) in about eight hours (under dry conditions), and seven hours in the reverse, downhill, direction from Oaxaca.

Several long-distance bus lines connect Pinotepa Nacional with destinations north, northwest, east, and west. **Estrella Blanca,** via subsidiaries Elite, Gacela, and Flecha Roja, tel. 954/543-3194, offers several daily first- and second-class *salidas de paso* (buses passing through) departures west to Acapulco, Zihuatanejo, Lázaro Cárdenas, and Mexico City; and east to Puerto Escondido, Pochutla (Puerto Ángel), Bahías de Huatulco, and Salina Cruz, from its station on Porfirio Díaz, about three blocks west of the *zócalo.*

Smaller, mostly second-class lines **Fletes y Pasajes, Estrella del Valle,** and **Oaxaca Pacífico** operate out of a pair of small stations one block north of the central plaza church-front, on side-street Aguirre Palancares. Fletes y Pasajes, tel. 954/543-2163, connects daily with Oaxaca via Putla, Tlaxiaco, and Nochixtlán, by Highways 125 and 190. Estrella del Valle and Oaxaca Pacífico buses, tel. 954/543-2697, also connect with Oaxaca, but in the opposite direction: first east, through Puerto Escondido to Pochutla (Puerto Ángel), then continuing north over the Sierra to Oaxaca via Highway 175.

First-class **Cristóbal Colón** also operates out of a small station on the same street, about one block farther west. A few daily departures connect, via Highways 175 and 190, northeast, via Putla and Tlaxiaco, with Oaxaca (by the fast *autopista* via Nochixtlán), and northwest, with Mexico City (via Puebla). Other departures connect east, with Puerto Escondido.

EXCURSIONS NORTH OF PINOTEPA

The local patronal festival year begins early, on January 20, at **Pinotepa Don Luis** (pop. 5,000), about 15 miles (24 km), by back roads, northeast of Pinotepa Nacional, with the uniquely Mixtec festival of San Sebastián. Village bands blare, fireworks pop and hiss, and penitents crawl, until the finale, when dancers whirl the local favorite dance, Las Chilenas.

One of the most exciting of Pinotepa Nacional seasons is during **Carnaval,** when nearby communities put on big extravaganzas. **Pinotepa Don Luis,** sometimes known as Pinotepa Chica (Little Pinotepa), is famous for the wooden masks the people make for their big Carnaval festival. The celebration usually climaxes on the Sunday before Ash Wednesday, when everyone seems to be in costume and a corps of performers gyrates in the

traditional dances: Paloma (Dove), Tigre (Jaguar), Culebra (Snake), and Tejón (Badger).

Pinotepa Don Luis bubbles over again with excitement during Semana Santa, when the faithful carry fruit- and flower-decorated trees to the church on Good Friday, explode Judas effigies on Saturday, and celebrate by dancing most of Easter Sunday.

San Juan Colorado, a few miles north of Pinotepa Don Luis, usually appears as just another dusty little town until Carnaval, when its festival rivals that of its neighbors. Subsequently, on November 29, droves of Mixtec people come into town to honor their patron, San Andres. After the serious part at the church, they celebrate with a cast of favorite dancing characters, such as Malinche, Jaguar, Turtle, and Charros (Cowboys).

Amusgo Country

Cacahuatepec (pop. about 5,000; on Hwy. 125 about 25 miles, 40 km north of Pinotepa Nacional) and its neighboring community San Pedro Amusgos are important centers of the Amusgo people. Approximately 20,000 Amusgos live in a roughly 30-mile-square (78-km-square)

© BRUCE WHIPPERMAN

The embroidered *huipiles* of San Pedro Amusgos are among Oaxaca's most treasured native garments.

PACIFIC RESORTS

region straddling the Guerrero-Oaxaca state border. Their homeland includes, besides Cacahuatepec and San Pedro Amusgos, Xochislahuaca, Zacoalpán, and Tlacoachistlahuaca on the Guerrero side.

The Amusgo language is linguistically related to Mixtec, although it's unintelligible to Mixtec speakers. Before the conquest, the Amusgos were subject to the numerically superior Mixtec kingdoms until the Amusgos were conquered by the Aztecs in 1457, and later by the Spanish.

Now, most Amusgos live as subsistence farmers, supplementing their diet with occasional fowl or small game. Amusgos are best known to the outside world for their lovely animal-, plant-, and human-motif *huipiles,* which Amusgo women always seem to be hand-embroidering on their doorsteps.

Although **Cacahuatepec** enjoys a big market each Sunday, that doesn't diminish the importance of its big Easter weekend festival, the day of Todos Santos (All Saints' Day), November 1, and Day of the Dead, November 2, when, at the cemetery, people welcome their ancestors' return to rejoin the family.

San Pedro Amusgos celebrations are among the most colorful of regional fiestas. On June 29, the day of San Pedro, hundreds of folks pay their respects in religious processions, and costumed participants dressed as Moors and Christians, bulls, jaguars, and mules dance before crowds of men in traditional whites and women in beautiful heirloom *huipiles.* Later, on the first Sunday of October, folks crowd into town to enjoy the traditional processions, dances, and sweet treats of the fiesta of the Virgen de la Rosario (Virgin of the Rosary).

Even if you miss the festivals, San Pedro Amusgos is worth a visit to buy *huipiles* alone. Three or four shops sell them along the main street through town. Look for the sign of **Trajes Regionales Elia,** the little store run by Elia Guzmán, tel. 954/582-8697. Besides dozens of beautiful embroidered garments, she stocks a few Amusgo books and offers friendly words of advice and local information.

EXCURSION SOUTH OF PINOTEPA

If you hanker for a little sea breeze and the murmur of the waves, spend a day or a week at **Playa Corralero,** about 18 miles (28 km) south by a paved but potholed, finally sandy but smooth road. Get there by car or the *camionetas* (passenger trucks) that head south on the street one block west from the Hotel Carmona. Along the way, in the beginning, you'll pass rolling tropical forest country, partially tamed to corn and cattle.

About 12 miles (19 km) from Pinotepa, the road forks. The left, paved branch continues to Laguna Corralero village, a pleasant small town (pop. about 2,000) of fisherfolk on the tidal estuary-lagoon. Hikers could probably bargain with a boatman at the village to ferry them across the lagoon to the open ocean channel and beach (say *"Ramada Guelaguetza, por el mar"*).

Otherwise, hikers should get off the truck at the fork and walk or hitchhike the right-fork road the additional six miles (9.6 km) to the beach *ramadas.* Drivers should likewise turn right at the fork. Along the way, you pass through a thick prickly pear cactus mini-forest along the beach. Finally, you arrive at the beachfront *ramada* restaurants beside a jetty and broad channel, which a dredge keeps open for fishing boats.

The beach itself is of coarse–medium yellow-white sand, rather steep, with the consequent undertow. Waves, which don't appear good for surfing, break strongly and quickly close to shore. The same conditions, however, make the beach perfect for **surf fishing.** If you prefer solitude and don't mind a few cows for company, you can set up camp along the wide, grassy dune and camp most anywhere for four miles (6.4 km) before the *ramadas.* (Caution: On the sand, use four-wheel drive with caution; if not, be very careful to avoid getting stuck, which might happen even with four-wheel drive.)

On the other hand, if you prefer company, park or tent near the road's end *ramadas.* The *ramada* **Guelaguetza,** nearest the beach, run by the friendly López Herrera family, will provide you with plenty of economical fish dinners and *refrescos,* plus shade for your vehicle and/or tent.

The Mixteca

The Mixteca, the homeland of the Mixtecs, Oaxaca's "People of the Clouds," spreads over an immense domain encompassing the state's entire northwest, stretching northward from the tropical Pacific Coast over the high, cool pine-tufted Sierra to the warm, dry "Land of the Sun" along Oaxaca's northern border. The Mixteca's vastness and diversity have led Oaxacans to visualize it as three distinct sub-regions: the Mixteca Alta, Mixteca Baja, and Mixteca de la Costa. These labels reflect the geographical realities of the Mixteca's *alta* (high) and *baja* (low) mountains and the tropical Pacific *costa* (coastal plain).

The Mixteca Alta comprises the Mixteca's highest, greenest country—all or part of the governmental districts of Nochixtlán, Teposcolula, Tlaxiaco, and Juxtlahuaca. The Mixteca Baja includes, on the other hand, the warm, dry districts of Coixtlahuaca, Huajuapan, Silacayoapan, and parts of Juxtlahuaca along Oaxaca's northern frontier. The Mixteca de la Costa lies south of all this, encompassing the tropical coastal districts of Putla and Jamiltepec on Oaxaca's southwest border.

This chapter traces a counterclockwise circle route through the Mixteca, northwest from Oaxaca city. First, we arrive in Nochixtlán, scarcely an hour from Oaxaca city, and use it as a base for exploring the hidden delights of the southern Mixteca Alta. Next, the route continues north through country renowned for its exquisite and monumental Dominican churches, then on to the warm, sunny Mixteca Baja country around Huajuapan de León. There, our journey curves through the scenic back door to the Mixteca Alta—the cool, verdant, roof of Oaxaca.

© BRUCE WHIPPERMAN

Northwest from Oaxaca City

NOCHIXTLÁN

Nochixtlán (noh-chees-TLAN, pop. 13,000), busy capital of the governmental district of Nochixtlán, is interesting for its colorful market and festivals and especially as a jumping-off point for exploring the wonders of the idyllic mountain valley of Apoala and the remains of the ancient Mixtec kingdoms of Tilantongo and Yucuita.

Sights

Nochixtlán town itself spreads out from its plaza, which is directly accessible from Highway 190, from the Oaxaca side by north-south street Calle Progreso and, from the adjacent, Tamazulapan side, by east-west Calle Porfirio Díaz. The streets intersect at the northwest corner of the central plaza. From there, you can see the 19th-century twin-towered **Templo de La Asunción** rising on the plaza's opposite side. Adjacent, to the right of the church, the *presidencia municipal* spreads for a block along Calle Hidalgo. At the plaza's northeast side is the big market, which expands into a much larger *tianguis* (Aztec word for awning) on Sunday, when native folks from all over northwest Oaxaca crowd in to peruse, haggle, and choose from a mountain of merchandise.

The major patronal **fiesta,** celebrating Santa María de La Asunción, climaxes around August 15 and includes *calendas* (religious processions), *marmotas* (giant dancing effigies), *mascaritas* (dancing men dressed as women), nearly continuous fireworks, a blaringly loud public dance, and a carnival of food, games, and rides that brightens the entire central plaza.

Accommodations and Food

Nearly everything you'll need is on or near the plaza, including one of the town's three recommendable hotels. First consider the refined downtown choice, **Hotel Botana Oaxaqueña,**

THE MIXTECA

To Cuatla, Morelos, and Mexico City

P U E B L A

Río

Mixteco

190

Huajuapan de León

San Marcos Arteaga

15

Santo Domingo Tonalá

San Agustín Atenango

Tonalá Canyon

G

Silacayoapan

Nieves Ixpantepec

San Miguel Tlacotepec

15

U

Las Huertas

San Sebastián Tecomaxtlahuaca

E

Laguna Encantada

Juxtlahuaca

R

Coicoyán de las Flores

Santa María Teposlantongo

Santa María Yucunicoco

R

San Martín Itunyoso

15

E

Chicahuaxtla

R

O

Putla de Guerrero

HOTEL BEYAFREY

0   15 mi

0   15 km

125

To Pinotepa Nacional, Puerto Escondido, and Acapulco

on a quiet side street, at Morelos 34, Nochixtlán, Oaxaca 69600, tel. 951/522-0314, tel./fax 951/522-0219. Friendly husband-wife owners offer 10 immaculate, smallish but invitingly decorated (with bedside reading lamps) rooms, for $20 s or d in one bed, $35 t or q in two beds; with hot-water shower baths, TV, fans, but no credit cards accepted. Major amenities here include an excellent Restaurant Roma downstairs and a lovely rear garden for relaxing.

On the other hand, consider the family-friendly **Hotel Santillan,** convenient for drivers and RVers, on the highway's west (Tamazulapan) side, at Porfirio Díaz 88, Nochixtlán,

Oaxaca 69600, tel./fax 951/522-0351. The motel-style rooms are arranged in an L-shaped, two-story tier around a spacious inner parking lot–pool-patio-garden. Additional amenities include a volley-basketball court and a pair of shady picnic *palapas.* Upper rooms, probably the best choice, are plainly furnished, but clean and light. Rates are $15 s, $20 d, $25 t, with hot-water shower bath, parking, and a good family-run restaurant, and proximity (half a block west of) the Cristóbal Colón-Sur bus station.

On the diagonally opposite, Oaxaca, side of town, find the newish **Hotel Juquila,** at Carretera Oaxaca Km 1, Nochixtlán, Oaxaca

69600, tel. 951/522-0581, on the highway, a few doors from the ADO bus station. The hotel's name comes from the owner's devotion to the Virgin of Juquila, for whom he keeps a candle burning in front of a picture of the Virgin on the hotel front desk. Upstairs, the rooms are sparely decorated but very clean. Many are dark, however. Ask for one with *mas luz* (more light). Rooms rent for $25 s or d, without TV, or $27 s or d with TV, all with hot-water showers and a restaurant downstairs. Find the hotel on the highway, Oaxaca side, about half a mile (1 km) from the center of town. If you're sensitive to noise, the passing trucks and buses may be a problem here.

As for **restaurants**, the **Roma**, at Morelos 34, tel. 951/522-0314, gets three stars for food and service. Genteel owner Marcela Santiago Alvarado's short but carefully prepared selection of eggs, chicken, beef, pork, and Oaxacan specialties and the refined, air-conditioned atmosphere afford a relaxing respite from Nochixtlán's street hubbub. Find the Roma one block north (along Allende) and half a block west (on Morelos, north side) from the plaza's northwest corner. (Note: The name Roma does not imply Italian food, but rather comes from the name of Marciela's husband, Romnaldo Sánchez.)

Second choice goes to **Restaurant Claudia,** one of the better family-style eateries on Díaz, along the block just west of the plaza. It's open daily 8 A.M.–8 P.M. for *desayuno* (breakfast), *comida* (lunch), and *cena* (supper), when you can stay up and watch the late-night movie with the family owners.

Services
You can get nearly anything you want on or near the Nochixtlán plaza. Moving clockwise from the northwest corner, for economical *fonda* (fixed stall) food, fruits, vegetables, and groceries, go to the **market** on the plaza's north side.

A block and a half north from the plaza's northwest corner, along Allende, you'll find the *correo* (post office), open Mon.–Fri. 9 A.M.– 3 P.M. Skip across the plaza to the south side of the church to *telecomunicaciones* (public telephone, money orders, and fax), at the corner of

Hidalgo and Reforma, tel. 951/522-0053, open Mon.–Fri. 9 A.M.–3 P.M. Next, find the **police station** *(policia municipal)* at the west end of the *presidencia municipal,* corner of Hidalgo and Progreso. For money changing, go to **Bancomer,** smack in the middle of the plaza's west side, tel. 951/522-0154, with 24-hour ATM, open Mon.–Fri. 8 A.M.–4 P.M. A few doors farther, find the big drug store, **Farmacia San Luis,** tel./fax 951/522-0484, at the plaza's northwest corner, across Díaz from the Hotel Sarita, where you can use the **long-distance telephone** and fax, tel. 951/522-0202.

A bit farther afield, you'll find a good **bakery,** on Díaz, a block and a half west of the plaza, and a travel agent, **Viajes Gran Via,** tel. 951/522-0414, four blocks west of the plaza, south side of Díaz, by the Fletes y Pasajes bus station.

For **doctors,** Marcelia at Restaurant Roma recommends Doctora Oralia Vásquez Morales, a family medicine specialist, tel. 951/522-0153. Alternatively, you can visit the Centro de Especialidades, of José Manuel Sosa Bolanos, M.D., at Melchor Ocampo 10, tel. 951/522-0494.

Getting There and Away
At least four long-distance bus lines serve Nochixtlán. First-class **Cristóbal Colón** and **Sur,** operating jointly out of their west-side station on Díaz (Hwy. 190), tel. 951/522-0387, provide broad service southeast with Oaxaca, northwest with the Mixteca Baja (Tamazulapan, Coixtlahuaca, Huajuapan), continuing to Puebla and Mexico City, and west with the Mixteca Alta and the coast (Teposcolula, Tlaxiaco, Juxtlahuaca, Putla, and Pinotepa Nacional) and intermediate points.

Fletes y Pasajes, on Díaz, one block east of the highway, tel. 951/522-0585, covers approximately the same destinations, but with both first- and second-class service. **Autobuses del Oriente** (ADO), operating out of a Oaxaca-side station, about half a mile (1 km) from the town center, at the corner of Highway 190 and Calle Progreso, provides first-class connections southeast with Oaxaca and northwest with Puebla, Veracruz, and Mexico City.

Enterprising **Transportes Turísticos de**

Nochixtlán, on the west-side highway, at Díaz 72, tel. 951/522-0503, offers some transportation options. They provide Suburban van rides to and from Oaxaca, 6 A.M.–9 P.M. daily, for $15. In Oaxaca, contact them downtown, at Galeana 222, tel. 951/514-0525. They also rent Suburban station wagons for $15 per hour; negotiate for a cheaper daily rate. This would be especially handy for a family or group visit to Apoala (see Oaxaca's Shangrila: the Vale of Apoala).

Drivers can cover the 50 miles (80 km) from Oaxaca in an easy hour via the *cuota autopista* (toll expressway). If you want to save the approximately $6 car toll (big RVs and trailers more), figure about two hours via the winding old Highway 190 *libre* route.

YUCUITA, TILANTONGO, AND MONTE NEGRO: FORGOTTEN KINGDOMS

Yucuita

Yucuita (pop. 500) was once far more important than it is today. It started as a village around 1400 B.C., then grew into a town of 3,000 inhabitants around 200 B.C., about the same time that early Monte Albán was flourishing. Later, by A.D. 200, it lost population and became a center secondary to Yucuñudahui, several miles north.

The claim to fame of drowsy, present-day Yucuita, about five miles (8 km) northwest of Nochixtlán, is that it sits atop the old Yucuita, one of the Mixteca's largest and most important archaeological zones. City officials received donations of so many artifacts that they had to organize a small **community museum** to hold them. Local volunteers offer, when possible, to open it up for any interested visitor. (Call the *presidencia municipal,* in Spanish, tel. 951/520-6868, at least a day beforehand to arrange a visit.)

Inside, your guide might point out (in Spanish) interesting aspects of the collection (mostly pottery): 2,000-year-old turkey eggs, human-effigy censers and bowls, *manos* and *metates,* just like those used today, and a platoon of small, toy-like figurines. The most intriguing piece in the museum is a carved stone relief of a seated figure, appearing Olmec-influenced, holding what

looks like a bunch of flowers. Maybe this is related to the meaning of Yucuita, which in Mixtec means Hill of Flowers.

Perhaps your guide will have time to show you around town. In any case, be sure to explore the **Yucuita archaeological zone** by climbing the reconstructed steps (fast becoming part of the ruins themselves) next to the paved through-town highway, about a mile (1.6 km) south of the town plaza. If you're slim and adventurous, you can enter the site via a dry **tunnel** that runs about 100 feet (30 meters) from the entrance steps to a big opening and then continues another hundred feet to a final opening, where you can lift yourself out. (Warning: Carry a flashlight to spot pests, such as scorpions and rattlesnakes, in time to back out. If this scares you, don't try the tunnel.)

Aboveground, what you mostly see is an expansive bean field littered with the stones from the walls and foundations of ancient Yucuita. Pottery shards are common—the colored ones es-

The adventurous can enter the Yucuita archaeological zone via a tunnel.

© BRUCE WHIPPERMAN

pecially stand out. A couple hundred feet to the south of the tunnel opening, inspect the partly reconstructed temple mound with an unfinished stairway and four belowground chambers. Archaeologists say that the entire site, elongated along a north-south axis, is riddled with buried structures, whose remains extend beyond the high hill (the original Hill of Flowers) to the north.

If possible, coordinate your Yucuita visit when the ordinarily sleepy town is at its exciting best during the **Fiesta de San Juan Bautista,** June 22–24. Many folks return home from all over Mexico and the United States for reunions and to once again enjoy country delicacies, dance the favorite old dances, honor San Juan with grand floral processions, and thrill to rockets bursting and showering stars overhead. (If you can't come in June, then come for the equally popular fiesta to honor the beloved Virgin of Guadalupe around December 18.)

Getting There: Reach Yucuita via minibus from Calle Porfirio Díaz, in front of the Nochixtlán market, or on Highway 190, northwest side of town. Drivers, head northwest on Highway 190 from Nochixtlán. Continue straight ahead along the old highway, *not* the *cuota* expressway, toward Huajuapan. Pass the gas station and continue for about two miles (3 km) until you see a signed right turnoff to Yucuita. Southbound drivers, on old Highway 190, watch for the signed left turnoff to Yucuita before Nochixtlán. If you reach the Pemex *gasolinera,* before the *cuota* toll expressway, you have gone too far. Turn around and look for the signed Yucuita right turnoff.

Tilantongo and Monte Negro Archaeological Zones

The Tilantongo archaeological zone is the town itself (pop. 4,000), which sits smack on top of storied ancient Tilantongo. In the old days, around A.D. 1050, Tilantongo was the virtual capital of the Mixteca, ruled by the ruthless but renowned Mixtec king **8-Deer of the Tiger Claws.** Carved stones built into the Tilantongo town church wall attest to Tilantongo's former glory.

The town government commissioned a mural, now on the wall inside the present *presidencia*

© BRUCE WHIPPERMAN

Walls and the remains of royal houses litter the hilltop of Monte Negro.

municipal, which dramatically portrays the legendary Mixtec Flechador del Sol (Bowman of the Sun) and copies of pages from the Codex Nuttall, a pre-conquest document in blazing color that records glorious events in Mixtec pre-conquest history. See if you can identify 8-Deer on one of the pages reproduced in the mural.

At least as important and more rewarding to explore is the much older Monte Negro archaeological zone atop the towering, oak-studded **Black Mountain** (Monte Negro) visible high above Tilantongo. A rough road, difficult for passenger cars but easier for high-clearance trucks or jeep-like vehicles, allows access to the top in about an hour. If you have no wheels, you may be able to get a taxi driver to take you up there. If not, perhaps someone with a truck might accept the job. Fit hikers should allow about three hours for the uphill climb, two hours for lunch and exploring the site, and two hours for the return.

Take plenty of water, wear a hat and strong shoes, and use a good sunscreen. You must obtain permission from authorities at the *presidencia*, who require that a local guide (whom they will furnish) accompany you.

Monte Negro flourished about the same time as early Monte Albán, from about 500 B.C. to 0 B.C. The 150-acre hilltop zone is replete with ruined columned temples, raised residences of the elite (complete with inner patios), ceremonial plazas, and a ball court, all aligned along a single avenue. Monte Negro's long, north-south orientation is reminiscent of Monte Albán, although its structures are not as grand. For reasons unknown, Monte Negro, as Monte Albán, was abandoned during the Late Urban Stage, around A.D. 800. All that remains are the old city's stone remnants, while its descendants still husband the land you see in all directions from the breezy hilltop. Some of what surrounds you is thick oak forest; other parts are fertile, terraced corn and bean fields, while much, in mute testimony to the passage of time, is tragically eroded.

Getting There: Bus passengers can go by the Tilantongo-Nochixtlán bus, which makes the trip about three times a day from Calle Porfirio Díaz, in front of the Nochixtlán market. Drivers, follow Highway 190 (old *libre* route) to the Jaltepec turnoff about eight miles (13 km) southeast (Oaxaca direction) from Nochixtlán. Mark your odometer at the turnoff. The road is paved to the Jaltepec plaza (5.8 miles, 9.3 km), where you turn right. The road is dirt and gravel, often rough, after that. Follow the signs. Turn left at a church (11 miles, 18 km) and right after a bridge (15.2 miles, 24.5 km). You'll pull up to Tilantongo plaza after 18 miles (29 km) and about an hour of steady, bumpy driving.

THE VALE OF APOALA: OAXACA'S SHANGRI-LA

It's hard to describe the valley of Apoala, tucked in the mountains north of Nochixtlán, with anything less than superlatives. A fertile, terraced, green vale nestles beneath towering cliffs far from the noise, smoke, and clutter of city life. Apoala is no less than a Oaxacan Shangri-La—a farming

community replete with charming country sights and sounds: log-cabin houses, men plowing the field with oxen, women sitting and chatting as they weave palm-leaf sombreros, dogs barking, and burros braying faintly in the warm dusk. The spring-fed river assures good crops; people, consequently, are relatively well off and content to remain on the land. They have few cars, almost no TVs, and few, if any, telephones.

What's more, the local folks are ready for visitors. I arrived at a string stretched curiously across the narrow gravel entrance road. I realized that there must be a good reason for this, so I stopped instead of just barging in. The explanation is that the local folks want to tell you about the wonders of their sylvan valley. The entrance fee is about $5 per group, including guide, who is an absolute *must*.

Exploring Apoala

The tour, which takes about two hours, begins at the **Cave of Serpent,** translated from the local Mixtec dialect, which all townsfolk speak. Just before the cave, you pass a crystalline spring welling up from the base of a towering cliff. This spring supplies a large part of the Apoala River flow, which ripples and meanders down the valley and which folks use to keep their fields green. Another major (and more constant) part of its flow wells up from beneath a huge rock across the creek, below the cave entrance.

Entering the cave, be careful not to bump your head as you descend the tight, downhill entrance hollow. Immediately, you see why your guide is so important. He carries a large battery and light to illuminate the way. In the first of the cave's two galleries, bats flutter overhead as your guide reveals various stalactites and then flashes on the subterranean river gurgling from an underground dark lagoon, unknown in extent. What *is* known, however, is that the water from the lagoon arrives at the springs at Tamazulapan, more than 30 miles (50 km) away. Someone long ago dropped some oranges into the cave lagoon in Apoala, and they bobbed to the surface later in Tamazulapan.

In the other cave gallery (careful, the access is steep and slippery), the light focuses on a towering stalagmite capped by a bishop's visage, complete with clerical miter and long beard. On the other side, you see a stalactite shaped exactly like a human leg.

After the cave, you'll probably head up-valley between a pair of cliffs that tower vertically at least 500 feet (150 meters). If you speak Spanish or have someone to interpret, be sure to ask the guide to explain the names and uses of **medicinal plants** *(plantas medicinales)* along the path. Every plant, even the notorious *mala mujer* (bad woman), which your guide can point out, seems to have some use.

Soon, above and to your left, you'll see the towering, yellowish 2,000-foot (600-meter) rampart, **La Peña Donde Murió El Aguila con Dos Cabezas** (The Rock Where the Eagle with Two Heads Died). No kidding. It seems that, once upon a time, a huge eagle that actually had two heads lived in one of the many caves in the rock face. The problem was, it was killing too many calves, so one day one of the villagers shot it. The Eagle with Two Heads, however, lives on in the imaginations of Apoalans.

Finally, after about 20 minutes of walking and wondering at the natural monuments towering around you, the climax arrives: a narrow, river-cut breach in the canyon, like some antediluvian giant had cut a thin slice through a mountain of butter. The slice remains, between a pair of vertical rock walls, called **Las Dos Peñas Colosales** (The Two Colossal Rocks).

The grand finale, down-valley about a mile (1.6 km), is the waterfall **Cola del Serpiente** (The Serpent's Tail). You walk down a steep forested trail that looks out on a gorgeous mountain and valley panorama. At the bottom, the Apoala River, having already tumbled hundreds of feet, pausing for spells in several pools, finally plummeting nearly 300 feet (90 meters) in a graceful arc to an emerald green pool surrounded by a misty, natural stone amphitheater.

Accommodations and Food

Camping, by self-contained RV or tent, would be superb here. The community has set aside a

Apoala offers accommodation, a restaurant, camping, a limestone cave, and a waterfall, La Cola del Serpiente (The Serpent's Tail).

choice, grassy riverside spot across the river from the cave at the upper end of town, heavenly for a few days of camping. The tariff, payable at the tourist Yu'u (see below) is about $15 per day per group. Clear, pristine spring water, perfect for drinking, wells up at the foot of the cliff at road's end nearby. Wilderness campers can choose among more isolated spots upstream, ripe for swimming and wildlife viewing. (Always swim with a bathing suit, however; skinny-dipping is locally disapproved.)

Non-campers shouldn't miss staying in Apoala's fine **Tourist Lodging,** where you probably first met your guide. This is a model of Oaxaca's improved second-generation government-built local tourist accommodation. Besides three very clean and comfortable modern-standard rooms with either one or two double beds, it features a light, spacious solarium–sitting room–snack café,

THE MIXTECA

© BRUCE WHIPPERMAN

© BRUCE WHIPPERMAN

The Apoala River breaches a deep gap, called Las Dos Peñas Colosales (The Two Colossal Rocks).

serving water, beer, sodas, and breakfast, lunch, and early supper. Guests can also eat their own food there. If you do, bring everything with you, as Apoala has no well-stocked stores. The lodging price, about $8 a person in the middle of paradise, is hard to beat.

Overnight reservations are strongly recommended. Reserve directly with Apoala through their satellite phone connection: in Mexico, tel. 55/5151-9154; from *lada* (area code) 951 (Oaxaca and vicinity), tel. 951/5151-9154. In Mexico City, simply dial as a local call: 5151-9154. Alternatively you can get information and lodging reservations in Oaxaca city, at the government alternative tourism office, at Murguia 206 (up the driveway, in the back), tel. 951/516-4828, sedetur5@oaxaca.gob.mx.

Guides

If you'd like a guide for more local exploring, contact very knowledgeable and personable **Leopoldo Guzman Alvarado,** who, if he can't guide you himself, will find someone who can, such as youthful **Oswaldo López Jiménez.**

Getting There

Like Shangri-La, Apoala isn't easy to get to. Bus passengers have it easiest. The Apoala community provides a white Apoala-marked minibus, which leaves from Calle 2 de Abril near the corner of Morelos (a block north of the plaza's northeast corner), three days a week (at this writing, Wednesday, Saturday, and Sunday at noon), arriving in Apoala at around 3 P.M. It departs Apoala for Nochixtlán on the same days at around 8 A.M. except 5 A.M. on Sunday. Check locally for the Apoala bus schedule with stores or bus or truck drivers parked along 2 de Abril. Otherwise, taxis and passenger trucks make the same trip hourly until about 5 P.M. from the same spot. The truck fare typically runs $3–5.

For drivers, the 26-mile (42-km) rough dirt and gravel road is a challenge, especially in an ordinary passenger car. The route heads north from downtown Nochixtlán; turn left from Calle Porfirio Díaz (the street that borders the plaza's north side) at the street just past (east) the market. Follow the road signs all the way.

Trucks, vans, and VW Beetles carry nearly all the traffic to Apoala, although a careful, experienced driver in an ordinary car can usually complete the trip with minimal damage. The ideal vehicle, of course, would be a high-clearance truck or sport-utility vehicle, such as a Jeep, with tough tires. Four-wheel drive, not necessary under dry conditions, would be mandatory in rain. Under dry conditions, lighter, maneuverable campers and RVs could make it; very large rigs would be marginal, because of the narrow, steep, rocky, and winding descent into Apoala Canyon.

Dominican Route South

Of the four missionary orders—Franciscans, Jesuits, Augustinians, and Dominicans—who established an important presence in New Spain, the Dominicans were dominant in Oaxaca. Hernán Cortés had barely begun to resurrect Mexico City from the rubble of old Tenochtitlán when a stream of Dominican padres was heading southeast to Oaxaca. For the next three centuries, until republican reforms forced many of them from Mexico during the latter 1800s, the padres earnestly pursued the spiritual thrust of Spain's two-pronged "God and Gold" mission in the New World. The Dominicans converted, educated, protected, and advocated for Oaxaca's native peoples, often in conflict with brutal and greedy Spanish soldiers and colonists.

The Dominicans' legacy remains vibrant to this day. More than 90 percent of Oaxacans consider themselves Catholics, and lovely old Dominican ex-convent/churches decorate the Oaxacan countryside. Some of these outstanding venerable monuments—notably at Yanhuitlán, Teposcolula, Tlaxiaco, and Coixtlahuaca—grace the Mixteca Alta, not far from the modern town of Tamazulapan, making it a natural base for extended exploration of what has become known as Oaxaca's Dominican route. The Dominican route's more isolated (but very intriguing) northern section—north and west of Tamazulapan—is usually explored via the *autopista* (toll expressway) that connects with Coixtlahuaca, from Nochixtlán and Oaxaca city (for details, see the Dominican Route North section).

TAMAZULAPAN AND VICINITY

Tamazulapan (tah-mah-soo-LAH-pahn, pop. about 20,000), partly by virtue of its crossroads position on the National Highway 190, has outgrown its more venerable, but isolated, neighbor towns and become the major service and business center for the Teposcolula district. You know you're in Tamazulapan immediately as you pass its town plaza, which proudly displays a semicircular columned monument right by the highway in honor of Benito Juárez, "Benemérito de las Américas." Upon reflection, nothing seems more appropriate directly on the Pan-American Highway.

Sights

As you stand on the edge of the highway (locally known as Carretera Cristóbal Colón) looking at the Benito Juárez monument, you'll be facing approximately north. The noble, portaled *presidencia municipal* will appear straight ahead, behind the square, the **Plaza Constitución.** To your right, beyond the storefronts along plaza-front Calle Independencia rise the ruddy cupolas of the 18th-century Dominican **Templo de la Natividad.** Bordering the plaza on your left are the stores and services along Calle Juárez.

Walk a block east and step into the cool calm of the venerable Dominican church which, although large and harmoniously decorated, is not architecturally comparable to the masterpieces at Coixtlahuaca, Yanhuitlán, and Teposcolula. What is unique, however, are the two images on the altar, both illuminated. The bottom figure is an unusual reclining figure of Jesus in what appears to be a transparent casket. This figure is locally paraded and celebrated, along with food, games, dancing, and a basketball tournament, in a festival culminating on May 3, **El Día de la Cruz.**

Above the figure of Jesus is the petite town patron, **La Virgen de la Natividad** (The Virgin of the Nativity), whom townsfolk celebrate in a fiesta culminating on September 8. As you retrace your steps, exiting through the church garden, you pass the old Dominican convent on the left, in a state of advanced decay.

Sights Nearby

Tamazulapan townsfolk love their **Balneario Atonaltzin.** You'll see why if you drive, taxi, or walk the 1.5 miles (2.5 km) north along the road to Tepelmeme (plaza-front Calle Independencia). Soon after a bridge, you'll see the *balneario* on the right. This spot would be a merely typical Sunday family bathing resort if it were not for its crystalline, naturally disinfected sulfurous springs.

The waters gurgle up, cool and clear, from a pair of sources in the rocky cliff behind the Olympic double-size pool—a lap swimmer's delight (except on Sundays and holidays, when it's filled with frolicking families). It's open daily 9 A.M.–6 P.M., admission about $3 for adults, $2 for kids. Besides the big main pool, there are a pair of kiddie pools, a local-style restaurant, volleyball, dressing areas, and a few picnic tables.

Two lesser-known but nevertheless interesting spots are the nearby *ojo de agua* swimming hole and the **Xatachio** (shah-TAH-cheeoh) archaeological zone. The *ojo de agua* (literally, eye of water), a general term for a natural spring or source of water, is about 300 feet (90 meters) back from the *balneario* toward town, on the right, below the creek bridge. Step toward the ruined building on the right, and you'll see the creek cascading into a big blue pool. Before the Balneario Atonaltzin was built, this was a popular swimming hole. Today, the water, although invitingly blue, is probably much less than pure, since it's mostly used by women for washing clothes. Although the tall, steep riverbank near the bridge is nonnegotiable, you can get down to the water via a path to the right around the

ruined building, through the brush, up some stone steps, and down again to the creek.

The unexcavated Xatachio archaeological zone is accessible via the dirt side road on the left just past the Balneario Atonaltzin. You'll first spot the zone as a brush-covered hill (actually a former sacred pyramid), about half a mile (1 km) away on the left. *Note:* Do not try to explore the site on your own, however. The site lies on communal land, and people are rightly suspicious of possible artifact looters. Go to the *presidencia municipal* on the plaza and ask for permission (preferably through a local spokesperson, such as the owner or manager of your hotel); offer to pay someone (approximately $10) to act as a guide for a couple of hours. Any artifacts you might stumble upon are legally the joint property of the INAH (National Institute of Archaeology and History) and the local community.

Tejupan

If you have time, stop for a few minutes for a look inside the relatively humble, but nevertheless worthy, Dominican church and ex-convent at Tejupan (Tay-HOO-pahn) in the Tamazulapan valley, a 15-minute drive east of Tamazulapan.

Tejupan is a sleepy farming town, basking in its past glory, visibly represented by its noble, multiportaled *palacio municipal* and the distinguished 17th-century Dominican **Templo y Exconvento de Santiago Apóstol,** across the street. Memorable inside the church is the pretty, pink transept chapel, left side, dedicated to the Virgin of Guadalupe. The ex-convent section, in severe need of repair, stands to the right of the church front entrance.

Get to Tejupan by bus or car via the signed side road off Highway 190 about seven miles (11 km) southeast of Tamazulapan, or about eight miles (13 km) northwest of the Highway 190– Highway 125 junction northwest of Yanhuitlán.

Accommodations

Of Tamazulapan's three basic but acceptable hotels, most prominent is the four-story **Hotel Dom Pedro,** a few doors north of the plaza at Cristóbal Colón 24, Tamazulapan, Oaxaca 70280, tel./fax 953/533-0019. The 25 plain but clean upstairs rooms (no elevator) run about $14 s or d (in one bed), $16 d (in two beds), $18 t, with toilets and hot-water showers, a basic restaurant downstairs, and parking, but no TV or phones. Credit cards are not accepted.

Although **Hotel Puerto Mexico** a few doors farther north at Cristóbal Colón 12, Tamazulapan, Oaxaca 70280, tel. 953/533-0044, appears humdrum from the outside, guests enjoy an inviting tropical patio blooming with leafy banana trees. Rooms are clean and carpeted but have the almost universal Mexican small-town bare bulb hanging from the middle of the ceiling. Bring your own clip-on lampshade. Rates are about $13 s, $16 d, $21 t, with hot-water showers, parking, and TV, a pretty fair restaurant downstairs, but no phones. Credit cards not accepted.

With approximately the same room price and basic amenities as the Dom Pedro is the highrise **Hotel Gilda** (HEEL-dah), 16 Madero, Tamazulapan, Oaxaca 70280, tel. 953/533-0153. Find it about two blocks along the street running uphill across the highway from the north end of the plaza. (Hotel Gilda was closed at this writing and perhaps will have reopened by the time you read this.)

The only hotel in town with any old-Mexico charm is the downscale **Hotel Hidalgo,** Hidalgo 7, Tamazulapan, Oaxaca 70280, tel. 953/533-0091 (phone not working at this writing). It offers a quiet, off-highway location one block east along the street that runs in front of the *presidencia municipal.* The 12 basic but clean rooms around a parking patio rent for about $5 s, $9 d, with bath.

Food

For inexpensive prepared food, try the *fondas* (permanent food stalls) inside the market and the nighttime taco stands or one of the several sit-down snack bars along the highway by the plaza.

As for restaurants, although the Hotels Dom Pedro and Puerto Mexico offer breakfast, lunch, and dinner, you might do better by walking a few steps to **Restaurant Noemi,** Cristóbal Colón 12, tel. 953/533-0047, between the two hotels. The grandmotherly owners puts out Mexican home-style breakfasts, lunches, and suppers, including savory *café de la olla* (pot-brewed coffee, with cinnamon), at very reasonable prices.

You'll probably do just as well at the clean, highway-front **Restaurant Coqui** (KOH-kee), Cristóbal Colón 57, tel. 953/533-0109, open daily 7 A.M.–10 P.M., is a block and a half east from the plaza. Although she'll cook nearly anything you want, the friendly owner is best at Oaxacan country delicacies, such as *chiles rellenos, enchiladas tasajos* (beef enchiladas), and Oaxacan tamales, all covered with plenty of *mole negro.*

Shopping

You can buy groceries and fruits and vegetables at either the town market (biggest on Wednesday), behind the *presidencia,* or at one of the plaza-front *abarroterías,* such as **Proveedora** (Supplier) de Abarrotes, tel. 953/533-0089, Juárez 4, west side.

Especially during the big Wednesday *tianguis,* the market can be a good spot for local indigenous **handicrafts** shopping. Items might include palm-leaf woven goods, such as *tenates* (tump-line baskets), *petates* (mats), soft woven Panama hatlike sombreros, and pottery.

Services

Tamazulapan provides a number of basic services along the blocks near the plaza. The town **bank,** Bital, with ATM, beneath the *presidencia municipal* portal is open Mon.–Fri. 8 A.M.–7 P.M., Sat. 8 A.M.–3 P.M., near the plaza's northwest corner.

The *correo* (post office) is a block north, behind the *presidencia* and the market, on Obregón, a few doors west of the corner of Independencia. Find it open Mon.–Fri. 8 A.M.–noon. A few doors east of the post office, at the corner of Independencia and Obregón, **Telecom** offers public telephone, money order, and fax, tel. 953/533-0113; hours are Mon.–Fri. 9 A.M.–3:30 P.M. For after-hour long-distance calls, go to the *larga distancia* across the highway from the plaza.

Two doctors offer consultations and medicines at their highway-front pharmacies. Choose either **Dr. Josefina Clemente,** at her Farmacia Ideal, on the highway directly opposite the plaza, tel. 953/533-0224, hours Mon.–Fri. 8 A.M.–2 P.M. and 4 P.M.–8 P.M.; or **Dr. Aguilar Aguas,** a block and a half east at Cristóbal Colón 43, tel. 953/533-0084, consultation hours Mon.–Fri. 2–8 P.M., Sat. 8 A.M.–2 P.M. and 4–8 P.M.

For a **police** emergency, go to the Delegación de Transito highway police, on duty 24 hours, half a block east and across the highway from the plaza, or call tel. 953/533-0213.

Get your **laundry** done at the corner launderette, on Hidalgo, a block east from the plaza's northeast corner.

Getting There and Away

Bus lines **Cristóbal Colón** and **Sur** operate jointly out of their highway-front station, across from the plaza, tel. 953/533-0699. Their buses connect southeast with Oaxaca via Nochixtlán, west with Coixtlahuaca, northwest via Huajuapan with Puebla, Cuatla (Morelos), and Mexico City, and southwest with Teposcolula and Tlaxiaco, where you can transfer to a bus headed for Pinotepa Nacional on the Pacific Coast.

For drivers, via Highway 190, Tamazulapan is approximately 84 miles (133 km) or two hours northwest of Oaxaca, and 25 miles (41 km) or 45 minutes southeast of Huajuapan. By paved

secondary road via Tejupan, Tamazulapan is 22 miles (34 km) or 45 minutes west of Coixtlahuaca; via paved Highway 190–Highway 125, it is 22 miles (36 km) or 45 minutes north of Teposcolula.

TEPOSCOLULA

Although smaller in population than Tamazulapan, Teposcolula (pop. 5,000) continues to outrank it as district capital, a distinction it gained back in 1740. Its history, however, reaches back much farther. When the Spanish arrived in the 1520s, they found well-established Mixtec towns on the hillsides above a beautiful lake-filled valley. They drained the lake for farmland and moved the population down to Teposcolula's present location. Abiding by common practice, the Span-

The cupola of the celebrated Capilla Abierta (Open Chapel) at Teposcolula underwent successful restoration thanks to this architect (shown here with his wife).

© BRUCE WHIPPERMAN

ish kept the Mixtec name, Teposcolula (Place Surrounded by Springs), tacking on the Catholic patronal title San Pedro y San Pablo. This produced a name so long that practically no one refers to the official San Pedro y San Pablo Teposcolula. People, however, still remember the old pre-conquest settlements on the hillsides. The old palace and temple foundations still stand, as El Fortín (The Fort) on the uphill slope behind the town and Pueblo Viejo (Old Town) on the pine-clad hilltop across the valley.

Orient yourself by standing (or imagining you're standing) on the sidewalk on the through-town highway, facing the tree-shaded town plaza. North will be straight ahead, toward the cartoon-bright, repainted *presidencia municipal* on the far side of the plaza. The main streets are 20 de Noviembre (the highway), Madero (along the plaza's left, west side), and Iturbide (along the plaza's right, east side). Diagonally on your left stands the renowned church and ex-convent Templo y Exconvento de San Pedro y San Pablo.

Templo y Exconvento de San Pedro y San Pablo

Most visitors head right over to the venerable 1538 Dominican church and ex-convent, one of Oaxaca's most important, not only for its historical significance, but also for its monumental architecture, much of which you can view from the exterior by walking around to the church's back (west) side. Here rises the famous recently restored **Capilla Abierta** (Open Chapel), with massive, soaring arches and gigantic buttresses. Visitors often wonder why such a huge outdoor chapel was needed right next to an equally massive indoor church. The adjacent grassy expanse provides the reason. It's the **atrium,** the extension of the outdoor chapel, the largest in Mexico, where the Dominican builders imagined 10,000 native faithful (so numerous that they were not allowed inside) gathering for mass. Although their vision was fulfilled for a span of perhaps a generation after the conquest, European diseases had decimated the Mixtec population by 1600, leaving the huge expanse, equal to three football fields, forever empty.

Walk inside the church and you'll see the original towering gilded *retablo,* which was removed from behind the altar and placed on the left side of the nave. Straight ahead, replacing it in the apse, behind the altar, rises a cheerier, simpler collection of saints and angels, surrounding Teposcolula's diminutive god-hero, the **Señor de Vidrieras** (Lord of Glass), above the altar. Local people celebrate him in a big eight-day festival climaxing on the first Friday of Lent. Events include traffic-stopping processions, pilgrimages, a flower parade, plenty of fireworks, crowning of a queen, floats, bull roping and riding, and a big community dance. (Note: The Teposcolula church was seriously damaged by the 1999 earthquake; by the time you read this, it may have been restored to its former glory.)

Find the side door to the **ex-convent** (open daily 9 A.M.–6 P.M.) on the right of the nave (or go outside to the atrium and enter the ex-convent at the atrium's southeast corner). The ex-convent serves mostly as a museum of paintings by noted 16th-century artists Andrés de la Concha and Simón Pereyns. As you walk, see if you can recognize the functions—refectory (dining), kitchen, chapel, cloister, monks' cells (upstairs)— of the various rooms that you pass by or through. (See the sidebar "Building Churches" in the Around the Valley of Oaxaca chapter.)

During your visit, be sure to notice one fresh, very recognizable modern or restored painting of Jesus with wounds, at the right hand of a very youthful God the Father, with the Holy Spirit (in the form of a radiant dove) above them. In the middle of the dining hall (refectory), notice the interesting painting of St. Michael the Arcangel, dangling a fish. Also, around the cloister, note the paintings that depict the baptism, school days, mission, and dreams of Santo Domingo.

Archaeological Sites and the House of the Chiefess

If you're interested, you might inquire at the *presidencia municipal* for a volunteer to take you to the **El Fortín** and **Pueblo Viejo** archaeological sites. (Note: Don't try to go to these sites without permission, since local folks are rightly suspicious of strangers poking around their archaeological zones.)

A close-in site that you can visit without permission is the **Casa de la Cacica** (kah-SEE-kah, House of the Chiefess). Walk west about three blocks, along the street heading due west from the middle of the church's huge grassy atrium. The street ends at a school, and on the right is the Casa de la Cacica.

The building is unique, for it is one of the few remaining stone structures built by the Spanish specifically for indigenous nobles. The Spaniards' motivation was probably to concentrate and thus more easily control the local Mixtec population, who were living in dispersed hillside settlements when the Spanish arrived. They built a house and evidently persuaded the local *cacica* to live there, hoping that her people would follow her.

Step inside, and on the right notice the upper-level *tapanco* (grain-storage room) floored with ancient wooden beams. In an opposite, left-side corner, see the small "escape" door. (The House of the Chiefess was in the process of being restored at this writing.)

Accommodation and Food

Teposcolula's first hotel (at least in recent times), the **Hotel Juvi**, Teposcolula, Oaxaca 69500, tel. 953/518-2064, now makes an overnight stay possible. The hotel's layout remains unique— 12 rooms around a parking courtyard containing the ancient, crumbling family homestead.

Anyway, children of the original ancestors have built a brand-new, sparely furnished (but clean) lodging, with bare, correctly country Mexican fluorescent bulbs to go with the shiny new bathroom fixtures. Rates run about $12 s, $14 d (in one bed), $16 d (in two beds), $16 t, $18 q.

You can buy basic food supplies at plaza-front groceries or treat yourself to a hearty afternoon *comida* at the town's good **Restaurant Eunice**, a block behind the east side of the *presidencia municipal,* open daily 8 A.M.–8 P.M.

Services

If you're sick, consult the **doctor** in his **Farmacia Nelly** on the plaza-front east side, by the highway. Alternatively, go to the **Centro de Salud** (follow

Calle Madero, to the left of the *presidencia* two blocks, turn left and go four blocks). To mail a letter, make a phone call, or use a fax, go to the *correo* or *telégrafo,* side by side on Madero, upstairs, half a block north of the plaza's northwest corner, tel. 953/512-0057, both open Mon.–Fri. 9 A.M.–3 P.M. After-hours, go to the *larga distancia* (long-distance telephone) office, at the plaza's northeast corner, tel. 953/518-2057 or 953/518-2018, open daily 9 A.M.–2 P.M. and 4–8 P.M.

Getting There and Away

Bus transportation to and from Teposcolula is easy and frequent. Bus passengers arrive at and depart from the bus station (Autobuses Sur, Cristóbal Colón, and Fletes y Pasajes) on Hwy. 125, half a block east from the plaza, tel. 953/518-2000. Buses connect southeast with Oaxaca, north with Tamazulapan, Huajuapan, and Mexico City, and south with Tlaxiaco, Putla, and Pinotepa Nacional on the Pacific Coast.

For drivers, Highway 125 runs right past Teposcolula's town plaza, about eight miles (13 km) southwest of its junction with the Oaxaca–Mexico City Highway 190. Using the Nochixtlán *cuota* (toll) expressway, drivers should allow around two hours to safely cover the approximately 78-mile (125-km) Oaxaca-Teposcolula distance; add at least another hour if going by the old *libre* route. From Tamazulapan in the north, allow about 45 minutes for the 22 miles (36 km) via Highway 190–Highway 125 and about an hour for the 29 miles (47 km) along Highway 125 to or from Tlaxiaco in the south.

YUCUNAMA

Teposcolula's petite neighbor, Yucunama (pop. 600), is attractive partly *because* of its small size. Imagine taking a seat on a stone bench one bright, blue summer morning in Yucunama's flower-decorated town plaza. Birds flit in the bushes and perch, singing, in the trees. Now and then, someone crosses the square and returns your *"Buenos días."* You admire the proud, whitewashed bandstand at the plaza center; behind it rises the old church facade, patriotically decorated like a birthday cake in red, white, and green. From the plaza, cobbled streets pass rustic stone houses and continue downhill to verdant fields, which, in the distance, give way to lush oak and pine tufted woodlands.

Although it sounds too good to be true, it isn't. Yucunama's beauty is probably one reason that Mixtec people have been living there for at least 4,000 years. Its name, which means Hill of Soap, perhaps reflects the town's spic-and-span plaza, clean-swept streets, and newly painted public buildings. It's a pure Mixtec town, for although Yucunama is part of the Teposcolula district, Spanish settlers never lived here. In fact, in 1585 the all-Mixtec townsfolk declared themselves an independent republic. Nothing came of that, but Yucunama's people nevertheless retain their independent spirit.

Sights

Make the community museum, **Bee Nu'u** (House of the People), on the plaza opposite the dignified, porticoed *presidencia municipal,* your first stop. If it's not open, walk across to the *presidencia municipal* and ask if someone might open it. Say (or show them) this: *"¿Puede alguién mostrar el museo para nosotros?"* ("Can someone show us the museum?") If you're lucky, you'll get introduced to Maestro Antonio Martínez Sánchez, the museum's guiding light.

He articulately explains (in Spanish) the museum's several very interesting exhibits. These include the original of the *Lienzo Yucunama,* an *amate* (wild fig bark paper) document from the 1300s that details the 35 tribute payments of a Yucunama Mixtec noblewoman with the name-date 5-Eagle, and her first and second husbands, 12-Flower and 10-Eagle, to her father, who lived in a nearby town. In the cabinet below the *lienzo* stands a copy of the famous **Codex Nuttall** (folded like an accordion), which details, in full color, the exploits of the renowned Mixtec lord 8-Deer. Maestro Antonio will provide some details (including odysseys to Coatzacoalcos on the Gulf Coast, and perhaps as far as Panama) of 8-Deer's adventures. If you don't understand Spanish, Maestro Antonio (whose many talents include teaching and leading local

dance groups) is worth your bringing a friend to translate for you.

Another fascinating exhibit displays the complete remains of a robust 70-year-old noblewoman (notice her very husky leg bones) and the trove of goods recovered from her grave, one of a score of burials retrieved by archaeologists locally.

Yucunama's richness as an archaeological zone is further evidenced by the two 1996 INAH (National Institute of Archaeology and History) survey maps of the buried remains of a pair of Classic-period (300 B.C.–A.D. 300) towns nearby. If you're strongly interested, ask Maestro Antonio or at the and you may be able to get permission and a guide. Expect to pay $20 for a full-day guided trip; transportation is extra.

On the other hand, you can step outside the museum and guide yourself on a short stroll to a pair of nearby local sights. Walk down Calle Independencia (from the museum, follow the left side of the plaza, past the *presidencia*) about three long blocks east to the picture-perfect **town fountain,** fed by the old town aqueduct. You may see women doing the day's laundry in the adjacent arched, public washhouse basins. A block south and a couple more blocks downhill east, at the end of Calle Libertad, you can marvel at Yucunama's oldest resident, the gigantic 1,000-year-old (at least that old, Maestro Antonio says) **El Tule,** or *ahuehuete* cypress tree *(Taxodium mucronatum),* a distant cousin of the California redwood. If you get lost, you can identify El Tule by its tall, bushy green silhouette, or mention El Tule (TOO-lay) to anyone.

Accommodation and Food

Maestro Antonio invites visitors to his **Cafe and Posada El Danzante,** across the street from the north portal of the *presidencia municipal,* open daily 8 A.M.–10 P.M. He and his wife take pride in their home-cooked Oaxaca *moles,* mild *chiles rellenos,* giant *tlayudas* (flour tortillas), and their pre-Columbian specialties.

Antonio and his welcoming wife also invite visitors to stay with them, in several of the rooms they've prepared in their refined, art-decorated house. Rates run about $15 per person. Reserve by writing Maestro Antonio Martínez Sánchez, Hotel

Posada El Danzante, Yucunama, Oaxaca 69556, or calling them, in Spanish, tel. 953/545-5058.

Festivals

You'll have even more fun if you arrive during one of Yucunama's festivals. The biggest is the patronal **Fiesta de San Pedro Mártir de Verona**, which culminates on April 29. Festivities begin on April 26 with a *calenda* (procession) and plenty of *mescal, aguardiente,* and *pulque* for those so inclined. Sometimes town men dress up like women and perform the dance of the *mascaritas* (little masks). The fun continues with more processions, plenty of flowers, food, fireworks, masses, and a dance on April 29.

Other especially festive times in Yucunama include the fiesta of the Virgen del Rosario (first Sunday in October), the Day of the Dead (November 1 and 2), and the Christmas Eve procession, where everyone in town accompanies the infant Jesus to the church, then watches (or does) the traditional dance of the Pastor y Pastorela (Shepherd and Shepherdess).

Getting There and Away

Yucunama is about six miles (9 km) northwest of the Highway 125–Highway 190 intersection. Drivers, follow the signed graded gravel road that takes off from the north corner of the intersection. By bus, ride a Cristóbal Colón, Sur, or Fletes y Pasajes bus to the Highway 125–Highway 190 intersection, then hike the six miles (9 km) or take a *colectivo* (collective taxi) from there. A number of snack stands and small stores at the intersection can provide water and food. Unless prepared to camp, visitors should arrive early and have called ahead for reservations at Posada El Danzante.

YANHUITLÁN

It sometimes seems a miracle that the Dominican padres, against heavy odds and isolated as they were in the far province of Oaxaca, were able to build such masterpieces as their convent and church in Yanhuitlán. Upon reflection, however, their accomplishments seem less miraculous when you realize the mountain of help the padres re-

ceived. When Father Domingo de la Cruz began the present church, in 1541, Yanhuitlán retained the prosperity and the large skilled population that it had when it was a reigning the Mixtec kingdom prior to the arrival of the Spanish. For a workforce, de la Cruz used the labor of thousands of Mixtec workers and artisans, who deserve much of the credit for the masterfully refined monuments that they erected.

And monuments, indeed, they still are. Approaching Yanhuitlán from the northwest, the road reaches a point where the entire Yanhuitlán Valley spreads far below. In the bright afternoon sun, the white-shining, massively buttressed Yanhuitlán church and adjacent atrium (now soccer field), big enough for 15,000 indigenous faithful, dwarfs everything else in sight.

The Dominican church of Yanhuitlán has withstood many earthquakes since it was begun in 1541, a tribute to the skill of its native builders.

Up close, you see why. The building's exquisitely sculptured Renaissance facade towers overhead, making those standing on the front steps appear like ants. A graceful semicircular arch frames the entrance, while in the niche to the left stands the robed St. Francis of Assisi. In the right niche, Santa Margarita de Alacoque occupies the position customarily reserved in Dominican church facades for Santo Domingo de Guzmán, the Dominican order's revered founder. Santo Domingo is nevertheless present. Directly above the front portal, a masterful relief of Holy Mother Mary shelters a diminutive Santo Domingo and Santa Catarina de Siena, like small children, beneath her cape.

The church, officially the **Templo y Exconvento de Santo Domingo de Guzmán**, is as much a museum of national treasures as it is a place of worship. In fact, it is divided so: The ex-convent, which you enter on the right, has been converted to a museum, open daily 9 A.M.–3 P.M. Inside, you begin to appreciate the gigantic proportions of the place as you circle the cloister, passing beneath ponderous but delicately designed arches that appear to sprout and spread from stone cloister columns like branches from giant trees. On the stairway leading upstairs at the cloister's corner, don't miss the mural of Jesus dressed like a 16th-century dandy except for his bare feet and the little angel perched on his shoulder.

The nave (which will probably be beautifully restored by the time you read this) glows with golden decorations. Overhead, stone rib arches support the ceiling completely, without the need of columns, creating a single soaring, heavenly space. Up front, above the altar, Santo Domingo presides, gazing piously toward heaven, his forehead decorated by a medallion that appears remarkably like a Hindu *thika*. Before you exit, take a look by the front door for the dramatic painting of Jesus, whip in hand, driving the money changers from the temple.

Get to Yanhuitlán, on Highway 190, by Sur, Fletes y Pasajes, or Cristóbal Colón bus. By car, head 12 miles (19 km) north along Highway 190 from Nochixtlán (62 miles from Oaxaca via the toll expressway, allow an hour and a half), or 23 miles (37 km) south from Tamazulapan.

Dominican Route North

This corner of the Mixteca hides a treasury of undiscovered gems, just right for adventurers hankering to get off the beaten path. First, make sure you spend some time at the grand old Dominican church at Coixtlahuaca, the Templo y Exconvento de San Juan Bautista. Then continue north to the hamlet of San Miguel Tequixtepec, to contemplate the ancient (1590) stone bridge, the community museum's mammoth fossils, and the restored 16th-century Dominican rest house; continue on a prehistoric rock painting excursion, and finally enjoy an overnight in Tequixtepec's cozy community-built cabana. Carry on north to Tepelmeme de Morelos and climax your adventure by boulder-hopping down into a tropical canyon to the astonishingly grand Puente Colosal, probably the world's tallest natural bridge.

COIXTLAHUACA

Coixtlahuaca (pop. about 3,000), although the capital of an entire governmental district encompassing a significant fraction of the Mixteca Baja's *municipios*, is a modest town even by Oaxaca standards. Before the conquest, it was a powerful Chocho-speaking (Chocholteco) chiefdom, so strong that in the 1400s the Coixtlahuaca warriors stopped the invading Aztecs, forcing them to detour through Tlaxiaco. During colonial times and through the 19th century, Coixtlahuaca (koh-eeks-tlah-OOAH-kah) continued to be an important Chocholteco market center. But depopulation by emigration and increased education and literacy in Spanish have reduced the number of Chocho speakers to a handful of elderly folks in the surrounding countryside.

© BRUCE WHIPPERMAN

It seems remarkable that, so long ago in 1546, a handful of isolated Dominican padres were able to inspire their faithful (whose influence is clear in the designs above this side door) to build the massive yet lovely church at Coixtlahuaca.

Most visitors enter Coixtlahuaca by the toll *autopista* from Oaxaca. Just inside the edge of town, a big sign on the left marks the road north to San Miguel Tequixtepec. Straight ahead a couple of more blocks, most drivers turn right on Independencia, the main town street. Nearly all stores and services are spread along Independencia, which continues several blocks past the plaza and then the church, both above and to the left of the street. Bus passengers will arrive at the Autobuses Sur bus station, one block along Independencia.

Sights

Coixtlahuaca's past importance is reflected in its grand church, the **Templo y Exconvento de San Juan Bautista,** one of Oaxaca's largest. Inside, its nave stretches to the proportions of a grand Eu-

ropean cathedral, its vault soaring overhead, supported by a delicate network of brilliantly painted, colored stone arches. Dominican friar Francisco Marín, Coixtlahuaca's first vicar, was the moving force behind all this grandeur, initiating construction in 1546. Although the Reforms forced closure of the convent in 1856, the Dominicans continued to run it as a church until 1906, when locally based "secular" clergy took over.

In addition to its grand proportions, the church has much of interest. As you enter, notice the dark-complexioned image of African padre San Martín de Porres, in a friar's robe, on the right. Farther into the nave, gaze overhead and admire the whirling, rainbow-hued floral designs, lovingly executed by long-dead native artists. All are original, although time and recent replastering have erased much that you don't see. On the right, take a look at the unusually large side altar to the Virgin of Guadalupe and continue to the main altar, where St. John the Baptist, Coixtlahuaca's patron saint, presides at the foot of the towering, gilded *retablo* (altarpiece).

The town is mostly quiet, except for fiestas, which include the patronal festival of San Juan Bautista, around June 24, and the festival of the Señor del Calvario (Lord of Calvary), during the last half of May. The fiestas include processions, carnival games, traditional food, the hazardous *jaripeo* bull roping and riding, and the Jarabe Chocholteco traditional Coixtlahuaca courtship dance.

Practicalities

One of the few hotels, if not the only one, along the expressway between Nochixtlán and Tehuacán, Puebla, is the local **Hotel Marina Sol,** Calle Independencia s/n, Coixtlahuaca, Oaxaca, no telephone. Although the rooms are of the basic bare-bulb variety, they're clean and spacious, with shower bath and hot water. Summer humidity, however, might cause rooms to accumulate mildew. Beds may need fresh linens; don't hesitate to request them before moving in. Guests additionally enjoy a tranquil garden setting, decorated with statuesque, green Roman cypresses, and a countryside-view deck behind the reception. Prices run an economical $10 d. Reservations are rarely necessary. (Although you may have to ask around for the caretaker, who only seems to be present when guests are expected.)

Coixtlahuaca has two or three restaurants and taco shops on Independencia, the main street, plus a pharmacy–*larga distancia,* La Lupita, and a couple of stores where you can buy the renowned Coixtlahuaca rolls—big, brown, and not too sweet, sprinkled with a bit of sesame— perfect with coffee or tea.

Around the town plaza, other services include *telégrafos* (fax, money orders), next to the *presidencia municipal,* and a post office, both open Mon.–Fri, 9 A.M.–3:30 P.M., above and to the right of the *presidencia municipal,* and a pharmacy.

Bus passengers can get to Coixtlahuaca via Nochixtlán. From the Oaxaca first-class terminal, take a **Sur** or **Cristóbal Colón** bus to Nochixtlán. Continue via Sur to Coixtlahuaca. From Tamazulapan, get to Coixtlahuaca by the Sur bus line via the paved road through Tejupan.

Drivers from Oaxaca simply follow the *cuota* (toll) *autopista* north approximately 70 miles (113 km), 80 minutes, to Coixtlahuaca. From Tamazulapan, Yanhuitlán, or Teposcolula, drivers get to Coixtlahuaca via the paved road east from the

Highway 190 junction at Tejupan, south of Tamazulapan, continuing an easy 15 miles (24 km) to Coixtlahuaca.

SAN MIGUEL TEQUIXTEPEC

Tequixtepec (Hill of the Conch) is the Aztec translation of the town's original Chocho name, Jna Niingui. Local legend says that Tequixtepec was the site of a now-lost temple dedicated to the god of the conch.

The local region comprises the *municipio* of San Miguel Tequixtepec; once rich, fertile, and thickly populated, it has fallen on hard times. Overgrazing, tree cutting, and selling the stones from the old irrigation terraces have degraded the Tequixtepec region into a semi-desert. Many hills are half-eroded, bare stone. Some good land exists at the stream bottoms, but many people are discouraged by such hardscrabble farming. Most residents leave to work for a year in Oaxaca, Mexico City, or the United States, then come back and live for three or four years on their earnings. The population has dwindled from 3,000 around 1900 to perhaps 400 now.

© BRUCE WHIPPERMAN

The antique bridge just south of San Miguel Tequixtepec, still standing after more than 400 years, is nevertheless in need of repair.

It turns out, however, that San Miguel Tequixtepec is a village with grit. It shows in the people and their efforts to reverse their fortunes. A major moving force behind the local folks' determination is personable community leader Juan Cruz Reyes, who spearheaded the remodeling of a ruined schoolhouse into a working museum, now a focus for showing off Tequixtepec's valuable touristic assets: a graceful 1909 *presidencia municipal,* a dignified 18th-century church, woven-palm handicrafts, and, in the vicinity, a colonial-era fossil bridge and prehistoric rock paintings. Works in progress include restoration of the 16th-century **rest house** (next to the church), used by traveling padres and pilgrims and a *comedor* (dining room restaurant), and cozy cabanas for overnight visitors. (See Practicalities.)

Sights

If you arrive heading north along the road from Coixtlahuaca, after about five miles (8 km) you cross a creek bridge, where you can gaze upon an adjacent crumbling early colonial-era **stone-arched bridge.** It's a remnant of Tequixtepec's glory days, when merchants marketed small fortunes of locally grown silk and red cochineal dye. Tequixtepec tradition says that one such merchant, Don Diego de San Miguel, built the bridge around 1590 to easily transport his valuable silk and cochineal to the formerly big market in Coixtlahuaca. (Although still crossable on foot at this writing, the old bridge, hopefully will be restored before it falls victim to one of Oaxaca's frequent earthquakes.)

At the town plaza two miles (3 km) farther north, make your first stop at the **community museum.** If available, a volunteer will show you the exhibits of local historical lore, fossils (notably, a huge mammoth tusk), local archaeological finds, and handicrafts. (If the museum is closed, ask around to see if someone, such as Juan Cruz Reyes, might be available to open it up for you.)

If you've made a prior appointment (see the Guides section), volunteers will be available to show you around the town, probably starting at the town church, the **Parroquia de San Miguel Arcángel,** built of locally quarried rose *cantera* stone and finished in 1766. The vases you see

topping the churchyard fence are from Atzompa, near Oaxaca, and are always ready to be filled with flowers during the town's festivals. Foremost is the big September 27–29 town patronal fiesta in honor of San Miguel. Highlights include traditional dances, such as the Cristianos y Moros (Christians and Moors), each of the festival days. Other important fiestas are celebrated on Palm Sunday (Domingo de Ramos) and Sábado de Gloria (the Saturday before Easter Sunday), when people, for the occasion called *mecos,* don masks and do a kind of adult trick or treat. They go from store to store, asking for something to drink and dancing with whomever is present. Yet another important day in Tequixtepec is Sunday, when, before 3 and 4 P.M., teams face off for a game of *pelota mixteca,* the local version of the ancient Mesoamerican ball game.

As you walk around town, be sure to ask your guide to take you to someone who is weaving palm leaves. This won't be difficult, since everyone appears to be doing it during most of their waking hours. Townsfolk gather and sun-dry the leaves of the little local wild palms, which they craft into a number of useful items, notably mats, grain bags, rope, and sombreros. Although their reward (about \$.25 for a sombrero) is pathetically small, at least the raw materials are free and everyone seems to have plenty of time on their hands. This is especially true during the hot (February–June) dry season, when people do their weaving in cool, backyard *cuevas* (caves), most often in the company of others, when work becomes a party.

Something else you shouldn't miss during your around-town walk is a traditional *temazcal* ritual hot room. Many local traditional curers have built *temazcales* of stone in their backyards for healing, especially for women after childbirth.

Finally, if the season is right, don't miss sampling a tuna (cactus apple). Simply pluck one from the leaf-tip of the many neighborhood nopal (prickly pear) cactuses. If it's red and ripe, you'll be in for a sweet, delicious treat.

Hieroglyphic Rock Painting Excursion

Farther afield, but well worth a day's time for travelers interested in antiquities and the great outdoors, are the local *pinturas rupestres* (rock

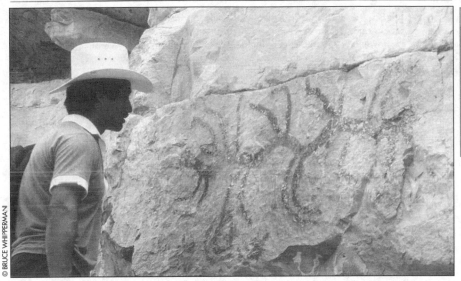

© BRUCE WHIPPERMAN

Petroglyphic rock paintings are one of the highlights of a San Miguel Tequixtepec tour.

paintings), which adorn the walls of a nearby river canyon. The jumping-off point, for which you certainly will need a guide, is Rancho La Barrete, a few miles from town, where a rocky but easy trail heads down into a shallow canyon, the Arroyo Palo Solo Arroyo, of the local Río Grande.

As you descend, keep quiet and keep your eyes peeled for armadillo, coyote, deer, fox, skunk, wild turkeys, or any of a host of bird species. Your immediate destination is the **Cueva de la Iglesia**—a sacred site where children used to be baptized on a large flat rock below the cave. In the cave above, you can see an eagle's nest; nearby is a prehistoric painting dubbed the "alligator man."

Farther down the canyon, climb over a low ridge and cross an often-dry tributary, the Río Seca. Soon you pass Peña Pirul and Peña Amarillo, a pair of painting-decorated cliff faces pocked with caves, and, above, ancient walls and irrigation terraces. Finally, after passing through a forest of moss-draped trees, comes the climax, the **Peña de los Guerreros** (Rock of the Warriors), adorned with plumed figures carrying shields and feathered lances.

Guides

It is best to have made an appointment before arriving at the Tequixtepec museum. Call Tequixtepec, tel. 953/533-0193 (in Spanish), directly. If your Spanish is rusty, ask a friend or your hotel desk clerk to do it. Leave a message (or a fax—ask for *"tono fax, por favor"*) telling your arrival time. Either Juan Cruz Reyes or another of the museum committee members should reply. You can also contact them weeks ahead of time, by writing to the Museo Comunitario, Juan Cruz Reyes, Presidente, Domocilio Conocido, San Miguel Tequixtepec, Oaxaca 79360.

Even if you arrive unannounced (but by noon) you still might be able to hire a guide (Spanish-speaking only) to lead you to the rock paintings for a modest fee, perhaps $10. If not Juan Cruz himself, Nazario Zacarias Zacarias, Jacobo Cruz Gúzman, and Joventino Cruz Cruz are all capable and competent.

Practicalities

Townsfolk, with government help, have built a pair of cozy **rustic cabanas** with hot-water showers and bunk beds for overnight visitors, for about

$6 per person. Bring your own towel and soap. Moreover, you can **camp** by tent or self-contained RV, for which it would be no problem to obtain permission from the generally hospitable townsfolk. Ask Juan Cruz Reyes or one of the other museum volunteers. Call the Tequixtepec number, tel. 953/533-0193, for reservations (although they will not generally be necessary). If this fails, you might contact the Oaxaca Alternative Tourism department for information and reservations, in downtown Oaxaca, at Murguia 206, tel. 951/516-4828, sedetur5@oaxaca.gob.mx. (For more details, see Tourist Yu'u Community Lodging in the Around the Valley of Oaxaca chapter.)

You may arrange a guided tour through Oaxaca Tours, in Oaxaca city, at 417 Alcalá, second floor, tel. 951/516-1005, toll-free U.S. tel. 800/446-2922, fax 951/514-6699, oaxacatours@oaxaca-tours.com.

Basic groceries are available at a pair of **grocery stores,** one of which also runs the long-distance telephone. It's on the corner across the main street, half a block south from the museum. The other, a block north, is run by the friendly sisters Elvia and Cari Córdoba Reyes. Given half a day's notice, the sisters will also cook hearty, wholesome, reasonably priced meals for you.

By the time you read this, you may also have the option of meals at the town *comedor* (dining room), which Juan Cruz Reyes told me during my most recent visit would be built soon.

From Oaxaca, **get to Tequixtepec** by bus via Nochixtlán and Coixtlahuaca. From the Oaxaca first-class terminal, ride a bus, such as **Sur** or **Cristóbal Colón,** to Nochixtlán. Continue via Sur, to Coixtlahuaca, where you can catch a *colectivo* (collective taxi) north the seven miles (11 km) to Tequixtepec.

Bus passengers can also get to Coixtlahuaca, thence Tequixtepec, from Tamazulapan, by the Sur bus line, via the paved road through Tejupan.

For drivers, access to Tequixtepec is also best through Coixtlahuaca. From Oaxaca, simply follow the *cuota autopista* north approximately 70 miles (113 km), 80 minutes, to Coixtlahuaca, and continue another seven miles (11 km) north via the signed gravel road (that forks left as you enter Coixtlahuaca) to Tequixtepec.

From Tamazulapan, Teposcolula, or Yanhuitlán, access is best via the paved road that intersects Highway 190 at Tejupan, from which Coixtlahuaca is an easy, scenic 15-mile (24-km) half-hour drive.

TEPELMEME DE MORELOS

Tepelmeme de Morelos (pop. 1,600), eight miles (13 km) north of Tequixtepec, welcomes visitors with a **community museum,** inviting everyone to share in the town's rich history. Before the conquest, it was a semi-independent chiefdom, a tributary of Nochixtlán, at times allied with neighboring Mixtec and Ixcatec chiefdoms. The Mixtec connection was so strong that anthropologists sometimes speak of pre-conquest Tepelmeme as a fused Mixtec-Chochotec culture. Tepelmeme's earliest Christian church, founded by the Dominican missionaries not long after the conquest, was built over an earlier Mixtec-style temple at the same spot where the present church stands on the town plaza.

Despite Spanish dominance, Tepelmeme's Chocho-speaking rulers retained influence over their people into the 18th century. At that time, during the 80 years until 1743, their dynasty was united with the Ixcatec kingdom of Ixcatlán, to the northwest. The great majority of Tepelmeme people continued to speak Chocho until around 1900, when improved education and Spanish literacy began to reduce the number of Chocho speakers to the small group of elderly folks who still speak it.

The present town appears to be the rival metropolis of the Coixtlahuaca district, sometimes overshadowing the district capital in hustle and bustle. One sign of Tepelmeme's vitality is its market, which sometimes sprawls over the center of town during the big indigenous **Monday *tianguis.*** The source of Tepelmeme's prosperity is its relatively fertile valley soil, not nearly as eroded as many other Mixteca communities. Some farmers, consequently, have money for wells, pumps, and electricity for irrigation. A number are prosperous enough to even own tractors.

Sights

Tepelmeme, laid out along a north-south axis, has two town plazas. The more formal of the two, a *jardín* with grass and a promenade-encircled bandstand, borders the church on its east side and the *presidencia municipal* on the south. Farther south, behind the *presidencia*, is the town's real heart—the scruffy but busy **market plaza.**

Your first stop should be at the community museum, **Niace** (nee-AH-say), which in Chocho means Mountain of Honey. The museum is behind the *presidencia* at the market plaza's northeast corner. It's best to arrive by appointment; leave a message, specifically for the *museo comunitario*, at the Tepelmeme long-distance *caseta*, tel. 953/533-0198, stating your arrival time. Otherwise, the museum will probably be closed.

The museum's collection, mainly artifacts, includes a huge ceremonial conch shell uncovered from one of the region's several excavated archaeological sites. Most prominent are the copies of the ancient but sophisticated glyphs painted on the cliff face at the awesome Puente Colosal natural bridge.

Townsfolk built the *jardín*-front church, the newly restored **Templo de Santo Domingo de Gúzman,** in 1769 to replace an earlier, conquest-era church. Community adoration climaxes here during the major August 1–4 festival in celebration of Santo Domingo. Folks mark his memory with pilgrimages, processions, baptisms, confirmations, fireworks, and a big carnival.

Inside, don't miss the right transept chapel, dedicated to the Sacred Heart of Jesus. Here, you'll find several intriguing banners, one for each of the town's *mayordomías*, the community organizations separately responsible for Tepelmeme's 10 yearly religious festivals. The pervasive influence of the *mayordomías* is visible, both separately during the individual festivals that they each organize, and collectively, on the first Friday morning of each month, when their dozens of members, representing virtually all the town's families, gather to parade their five respective banners around the *jardín.*

Practicalities

For accommodation, Tepelmeme offers **cabanas** near the road's end on the way to Puente Colosal.

Reserve by leaving a message for the *museo comunitario* at the Tepelmeme town *caseta*, tel. 953/533-0198, specifying how many in your party and when you'll be arriving. If this fails, contact the Oaxaca Alternative Tourism department, in downtown Oaxaca, at Murguia 206, tel. 951/516-4828, sedetur5@oaxaca.gob.mx, or Chicago-based **Zapotec Tours,** tel. 773/506-2444 or 800/44-OAXAC (800/446-2922), fax 773/506-2445. (For more details, see Tourist Yu'u Community Lodging in the Around the Valley of Oaxaca chapter.)

You may also be able to arrange a guided tour through Oaxaca Tours, in Oaxaca city, at 417 Alcalá, second floor, tel. 951/516-1005, toll-free U.S. tel. 800/446-2922, fax 951/514-6699, oaxacatours@oaxaca-tours.com.

Around the market plaza, you'll find sources of both **food and basic services.** Get groceries, fruits, and vegetables at market stalls. Wholesome cooked food—chicken, soups, stews, tacos, and tamales—is available from market-front *fondas.* Alternatively, for cooked food, go to dining room **Cocina Economica Mary,** five blocks north of the plaza, two blocks past the SUR bus station.

For stamps and letter-mailing, go to the *correo* (post office), by the museum on the market plaza's north side, open Mon., Wed. and Fri. 4–8 P.M. If you're ill, go to the **Centro de Salud** health clinic, at the *jardín* southeast corner, between the *presidencia* and the church. You can also make long-distance phone calls at the little *larga distancia* at Lupita grocery, open daily 8 A.M.–9 P.M., three blocks north of the jardín, past the bridge, before the SUR bus station.

Bus passengers, from Oaxaca, **get to Tepelmeme** via Coixtlahuaca and Tequixtepec, where you should continue via *colectivo* (collective taxi) the eight more miles (13 km) north to Tepelmeme. From Tamazulapan, ride a SUR bus or *colectivo* to Tepelmeme, via Teotongo and Ihuitlán.

Drivers, from Oaxaca drive north two hours, approximately 85 miles (137 km), via the *cuota* (toll) expressway to the Tepelmeme exit. From Tamazulapan, drivers head along Calle Independencia, which becomes the gravel road leading directly to Tepelmeme (via Teotongo and Ihuitlán). Figure about an hour and a half of relatively easy, but sometimes bumpy driving for the 27-mile (43-km) trip.

Excursions: Puente Colosal and Huerta de Juquila

With a prior appointment, a museum guide will be available to escort you (13 miles, 21 km) to the point of departure for the two-mile (three-km), two-hour round-trip hike down a forested boulder-strewn creek bottom to Puente Colosal. Here it appears as if a glacier-era lake once filled a deep limestone box canyon. Over eons, the water gradually dissolved the limestone, finally scooping out a yawning, 200-foot-high (60-meter-high) tunnel through a towering mountain ridge. The result is spectacular Puente Colosal, probably the world's tallest natural stone bridge.

Puente Colosal has most certainly inspired awe in human visitors for thousands of years. Some inscribed their presence, in both primitive rock paintings and refined (probably city-state stage A.D. 1000–1500) Mixtec glyphs, graphically painted on Puente Colosal's stone face. Someday, when archaeologists finally crack the ancient Mixtec code, humanity will know what Puente Colosal inspired them to record for posterity on its stark bedrock walls.

Get there, by permission only through the Tepelmeme museum or municipal authorities, accompanied by a local guide. A rugged, high-clearance vehicle is necessary for the last few miles of this route: mark your odometer at the Tepelmeme town center. Head north through town to the expressway entrance (1.2 miles, 2 km). Continue north to the expressway bridge, Puente La Unión (six miles, 9.6 km). With caution, just before the bridge, exit left at the unofficial dirt driveway. Cross back over the expressway via the bridge, then, after a fraction of a mile, turn right (6.3 miles, 10 km) at the T at Ranchería La Unión. At mile 8.3 (13.4 km), turn left at another T, at Ranchería Puerto Mixteco. Continue down a mountain-rimmed farm valley past a hillside spring and small dam at Rosario (10.4 miles, 16.7 km). Continue down-canyon via the increasingly rough track to road's end (13.5 miles, 21.7 km). Puente Colosal is at the downstream end of the canyon. Scramble downhill via a steep trail to the shady stream bottom, then boulder-hop the remaining mile and a half (2.4 km). Although the stream bottom is usually dry, *beware of possible flash flooding* from upstream thunderstorms. Take a hat, binoculars, camera, strong shoes, and drinking water.

Well-equipped wilderness backpackers might enjoy spending an overnight or two beneath Puente Colosal's grand, sheltering rock ceiling. The environs are ripe for wildlife viewing, expert-grade vertical rock climbing, and exploring past Puente Colosal's downstream portal, where the stream bottom continues into a lush, semitropical, mountain-walled wild valley.

Even more remote is the locally famous and idyllic **Huerta de Juquila** grove and waterfall. Access, strictly by museum or municipally approved guide only, is also north of Tepelmeme via the expressway to Puente La Unión. In this case, however, you turn left at the T (see Puente Colosal directions) at Ranchería La Unión. The route continues another 18 miles (29 km) into the mountainous backcountry on foot or by horseback. The key intermediate destination is Mahusipan village (jeep-accessible, at 13 miles, 21 km), where you continue on foot or by horse approximately another five miles (8 km) to Huerta de Juquila.

The Mixteca Baja: Land of the Sun

HUAJUAPAN DE LEÓN AND VICINITY

Huajuapan de León (pop. 50,000), with good hotels, restaurants, and many services, makes a comfortable base for enjoying the intriguing corners of the northern Mixteca Baja. Day trips north, via the Tehuacán road, open the fertile, green vale of the Río Mixteco with its colorful hamlets, venerable churches, and ancient archaeological sites. Similarly, excursions south, along the high road to the Mixteca Alta, reveal a wealth of hiking, camping, boating, and fishing opportunities.

What's even better is that the town itself has much to offer. For first-time arrivals, untouristed Huajuapan de León is a pleasant surprise. The town center—plaza, church, and *presidencia municipal*—is removed a few blocks south of the Highway 190 clutter and bustle. Although the present town dates only from colonial times, the surrounding region, which city hall boosters call Tierra del Sol (Land of the Sun), has been inhabited for many millennia. The extensive Cerro de Las Minas (Hill of the Mines) archaeological zone, just a mile (1.6 km) north of the present town, was a ceremonial, market, and governmental center for thousands of inhabitants during its apex, around A.D. 500. It was excavated and partially restored during the late 1980s.

Huajuapan (a tongue twister; say ooah-WAH-pahn) put itself on the map during Mexico's War of Independence. After two years of seesaw rebellion, national attention focused on Huajuapan, where *insurgente* Valerio Trujano was leading local forces in blocking the advance of a well-disciplined royalist force. Inspired by faith in their patron saint, **El Señor de los Corazones** (The Lord of the Hearts), the Huajuapan fighters resisted a royalist siege of 111 days, until relieved by Independence hero General José María Morelos on June 23, 1812.

Later, in the early 1820s, Huajuapan's favorite son, Antonio de León (thus, Huajuapan de León) played a crucial role in securing Mexican Independence. He was among the first leaders in con-servative Oaxaca to support Agustín de Iturbide's Plan de Iguala, which finally freed Mexico from Spain. Later, León headed the fight against Iturbide when he proclaimed himself emperor and dissolved Congress. León (by then a general at the age of 29) and Nicolas Bravo captured Oaxaca city for republican forces on June 9, 1823.

Sights Around the Plaza

The town's choice people-watching spot is the tranquil, old-fashioned town plaza, **Plaza Central**

The gate to the town cathedral, dedicated to Virgen de Guadalupe, provides a bit of shade on a warm day.

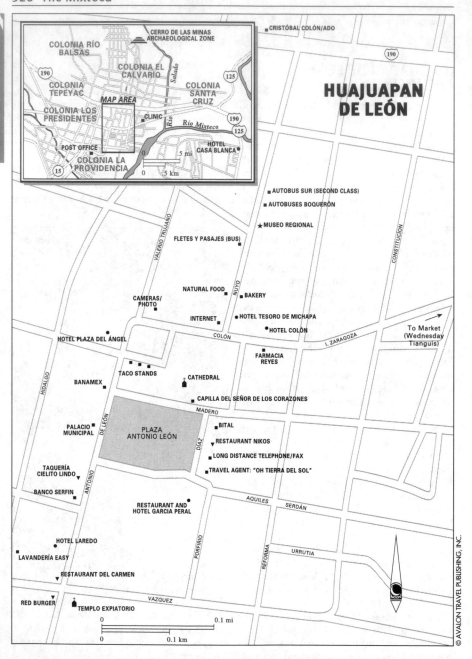

HUAJUAPAN DE LEÓN

CRISTÓBAL COLÓN/ADO

190

CERRO DE LAS MINAS
ARCHAEOLOGICAL ZONE

COLONIA RÍO
BALSAS

COLONIA EL
CALVARIO

190

125

COLONIA
TEPEYAC

COLONIA
SANTA
CRUZ

MAP AREA

COLONIA LOS
PRESIDENTES

CLINIC

190

Río Mixteco

125

POST OFFICE

HOTEL
CASA BLANCA

5 mi

COLONIA LA
PROVIDENCIA

15

0   5 km

AUTOBUS SUR (SECOND CLASS)

AUTOBUSES BOQUERÓN

★ MUSEO REGIONAL

FLETES Y PASAJES (BUS)

NATURAL FOOD

BAKERY

CAMERAS/
PHOTO

INTERNET

HOTEL TESORO DE MICHAPA

HOTEL COLÓN

HOTEL PLAZA DEL ÁNGEL

COLÓN

I. ZARAGOZA

To Market
(Wednesday
Tianguis)

FARMACIA
REYES

TACO STANDS

CATHEDRAL

BANAMEX

CAPILLA DEL SEÑOR DE LOS CORAZONES

MADERO

PALACIO
MUNICIPAL

PLAZA
ANTONIO LEÓN

BITAL

RESTAURANT NIKOS

LONG DISTANCE TELEPHONE/FAX

TAQUERÍA
CIELITO LINDO

TRAVEL AGENT: "OH TIERRA DEL SOL"

BANCO SERFIN

RESTAURANT AND
HOTEL GARCIA PERAL

AQUILES

SERDÁN

HOTEL LAREDO

LAVANDERÍA EASY

PORFIRIO

URRUTIA

RESTAURANT DEL CARMEN

VAZQUEZ

RED BURGER

TEMPLO EXPIATORIO

0   0.1 mi

0   0.1 km

© AVALON TRAVEL PUBLISHING, INC.

Antonio de León, bordered by the *presidencia municipal* on its west side. On the plaza's north side stands a distinguished bronze statue of General Antonio de León (1794–1847). Also on the north side, across the street from the plaza, rise the twin spires of the late-19th-century **Catedral de la Virgen de Guadalupe.** A major plaza-front thoroughfare is Antonio de León, on the west side, which becomes Valerio Trujano as it continues north to its highway crossing. On the plaza's east side runs Avenida Porfirio Díaz, which jogs around the back side of the cathedral, becoming Avenida Nuyoo (noo-YOH-oh) as it heads north to the highway.

The plaza's major source of early-evening entertainment is the army of birds, mostly black grackles, who around sunset head from all directions straight for the big, bushy plaza trees. For about an hour, they flutter, cackle, and squabble for perches until they finally settle down for the night.

Stroll over for a look inside the cathedral. For Mexico, this is a new church. Earthquakes repeatedly damaged the previous structures occupying the site since colonial times. The present church, built in the late 1800s, was so severely damaged by earthquakes that it had to be extensively rebuilt and earthquake-proofed in the 1960s. But for the people of Huajuapan, it's not the building but what it contains that counts.

Inside, a brilliantly illuminated Virgin of Guadalupe occupies the main front altar, while in the right-side chapel, the **Capilla del Sagrario del Señor de los Corazones,** a painted celebration of baroque glitter climaxes in the beloved, dark-complexioned Señor hanging limply above the altar. On auspicious days, the faithful arrive in a near-continuous stream to pay their respects. As you leave, on the wall in the small sub-chapel on the left, just outside the door, look for the heart festooned with little metal *milagros* (wish offerings), which beseeching pilgrims have left for the Señor.

Huajuapan Market

If it's Wednesday, the day of Huajuapan's big *tianguis* market, walk to Colón, which borders the church's north side. Continue east for a block

and follow Zaragoza, the street that heads diagonally northeast, two long blocks to the market on the right. Besides doing your grocery shopping from stalls in the covered section, wander beneath the shady *tianguis* (awnings) for your pick of the best, from mounds of luscious bananas, tomatoes, cucumbers, and squashes. During the summer and fall, you'll also see plenty of pears, peaches, guavas, and grapes. Also admire the piles of deep-red chilies and bright-yellow *flor de calabaza* (squash flower) used for flavoring soups and stews. Here and there, you'll glimpse piles of old-fashioned items, such as corn husks (for wrapping tamales), *cal* (lime or quicklime) for soaking corn, red *jamaica* (hah-MAHEE-kah) petals for delicious drinks, nopal cactus leaves, *tamarindo* and *guaje* pods, yellow *manzanilla* (chamomile) flowers, and hunks of *panela* (brown sugar). Throughout your walk, take note that the women vendors are definitely in charge, although few wear *traje* (native dress).

You'll also find some **handicrafts.** Locally made items include red- and black-streaked **pottery,** in practical shapes, such as *ollas* (pots), bowls, and *comales* (griddles); and **stone,** carved into *manos, metates,* and *molcajetes* for grinding corn and chilies. Local folks also sell plenty of items woven from **palm.** These include *sombreros, bolsas* (purses), *petates* (mats), and *cestas* (baskets).

Although few if any local people make textiles, they do import and sell, mostly *huipiles,* from other parts of Oaxaca. You'll probably find some on Wednesday, if you look around the covered section.

Another fruitful source of woven-palm handicrafts is the precious little **Artesanías de Palma** store downtown at Nuyoo 13, half a block uphill from the cathedral. Stop by and pick a few items from their selection of old-fashioned dress-up costumes, cowboy hats, and *calabazas* for carrying water.

Municipal Museum and Cerro de las Minas Archaeological Zone

Be sure to spend at least an hour investigating the remains of Cerro de las Minas, a major urban stage (A.D. 300–800) Mixtec town. Artifacts uncovered on this hill just north of town during the 1980s demonstrate characteristics of so-called Ñuiñe glyphs, which archaeologists recognize as one of the five unique writing systems of ancient Mesoamerica.

Similar finds unearthed at contemporaneous Mixteca Baja ruined cities, such as Tequixtepec, Chazumba, Miltepec, Suchitepec, Lunatitlán, and Mixtlahuaca, led archaeologists to name the style by the Mixtec label, Ñuiñe (nyoo-EE-nyay), for the "Hot Country," the Mixteca Baja, where they have been found.

Before charging up the hill, however, first visit the **municipal museum,** at Nuyoo 15, half a block uphill from the church; open daily except Monday, 9 A.M.–2 P.M. and 4–8 P.M. Professionally prepared exhibits on the bottom floor give an overview and explanations of the exquisite finds at Cerro de las Minas. Upstairs is a library and beautifully displayed life-sized mock-ups—community, costumes, economics, fiestas, religion, and work—of present Mixteca Baja people. Another room exhibits local colonial–modern history.

Exploring the Site: After the museum, get to the ruins by driving, hiking, or hailing a taxi. Wear sturdy walking shoes, a hat, and take water. From the town center, follow Nuyoo north across the highway and three blocks past the uphill church. Continue straight ahead, up a steep, rocky track and turn right to the parking lot, marked by a Zona Arqueología sign. From there, on foot, scramble uphill past the retaining wall to the highest point, **Mound 1,** on the east side.

From the top, the entire Huajuapan Valley spreads in all directions. On the south side, in the distance, rise the downtown cathedral's ruddy twin towers. Far behind them stand the cloud-draped heights of the Mixteca Alta. On the opposite, north side, flat-topped Cerro Yucunitza, the site of another hilltop ruined city, towers over the valley. Below Yucunitza's right shoulder, the Río Mixteco meanders below the high brushy hills of the Mixteca Baja.

Unrestored Mound 1, most certainly a former pyramid, slopes downhill past some reconstructed walls and stairs to a wide ceremonial courtyard. Descend Mound 1 to the courtyard. On its north side are the previously excavated Tombs 4 and 5. On the south side, a staircase

descends to a smaller courtyard complex of what appear to be residential walls and patios. Continue west to **Mound 2,** a partly reconstructed ceremonial pyramid. Looking south toward town from its summit, you can view the clear outlines of a partially excavated **ball court** about a hundred yards down the slope.

Continue west, descending the regal, restored ritual staircase, down the west side of Mound 2 to a grand 100-yard-square courtyard. Ahead rises **Mound 3,** a brushy hill that probably conceals yet another staircase and pyramid summit.

The visible hilltop remains of Cerro de las Minas around you were the ceremonial hub of a small city that, at its apex around A.D. 500, was home to perhaps 4,000 people whose hundreds of homes extended over scores of surrounding hillside acres. Like many of Oaxaca's forgotten cities, the city's original name has been lost over time. What archeologists do know, however, is that, like Monte Albán and several other of Oaxaca's ancient cities, the inhabitants of Cerro de las Minas mysteriously abandoned it around A.D. 800.

Las Campanas

Las Campanas park, a lovely streamside stroll on Huajuapan's northwest outskirts, is worth at least an hour's visit. At Las Campanas, community efforts have preserved a unique natural desert-like spring and habitat, decorated with rock outcroppings and ferny, shaded nooks. Tables beneath streamside willows make for restful picnicking.

The name Las Campanas (The Bells) derives from the stalactites hanging from the ceilings of shallow, streamside caves. If struck just right, a stalactite will vibrate and ring with a soft, bell-like monotone.

(Note: Experienced cavers might enjoy exploring the cave complex upstream from Las Campanas. A large tree, locally known as Palo Blanco, marks the entrance. The cave extends a mile or two uphill to around Agua Dulce village. *Ordinary travelers should only attempt this led by an experienced guide.* For information and guide recommendations, check with the municipal museum director and/or the tourism office at the *presidencia municipal.*)

Las Campanas, although readily accessible, is not well marked and is easy to miss. Follow the road to Mexico City about a mile (1.6 km) west of Huajuapan town center. Las Campanas nestles in a shallow arroyo on the left, marked by an old Hotel Crystal sign about a block or two after the entrance driveway to the Universidad Tecnología de la Mixteca. If you pass a government *vivero* (nursery) on the left, you've gone too far; turn around and return one block to Las Campanas.

Accommodations

Of Huajuapan's several acceptable hotels, two stand out. Visitors who enjoy soaking up Mexico should choose the immaculate **Hotel García Peral,** by the central plaza at Porfirio Díaz 1, Huajuapan de León, Oaxaca 69000, tel. 953/532-0777 or 953/532-0742, fax 953/532-2000, garcia_peral@hotmail.com or garcia.peral@yahoo.com. The 37 rooms in three levels surround an inviting pool patio blooming with tropical plants and birdsong. Rooms are comfortably furnished with beige bed covers, reading lamps, attractively rustic tile floors and modern-standard bathrooms. Rates run about $39 s, $49 d, with fans, a good restaurant-bar, pool, and sauna; credit cards accepted.

Second choice goes to suburban **Hotel Casa Blanca,** on Hwy. 190, Oaxaca side, about a mile (1.6 km) from town at Amatista 1, Colonia Sta. Teresa, Huajuapan de León, Oaxaca 69000, tel./fax 953/532-0779 or 953/532-0979. This is a good option for drivers anxious to avoid downtown traffic. The Casa Blanca's 80 semi-deluxe rooms, in two-story tiers scattered through a spacious garden complex, are carpeted and comfortable. Make sure, however, that everything is working before moving in. Tariffs are about $27 s, $35 d, $43 t, with baths, TV, fans, pool patio, a good restaurant, and parking; no phones, but credit cards are accepted.

Back downtown, you'll find some downscale, but acceptable, choices. Take a look at **Hotel Laredo,** just a block south of the plaza, at Antonio de León 13, Colonia Centro, Huajuapan de León, Oaxaca 69000, tel. 953/532-0402. The 26 rooms, stacked in three levels around a parking courtyard, are plain and less than immaculate.

If not acceptable, ask them to clean up what's wrong before paying. Rates, however, are right, at about $16 s, $19 d, $21 t, with bath, fan, parking, and a restaurant; credit cards not accepted.

On the opposite, north side of the plaza, you might also consider **Hotel Plaza del Ángel,** Valerio Trujano 22, Huajuapan de León, Oaxaca 69000, tel. 953/532-0851. Although not much to look at from the outside, the Ángel has carpeted, and therefore quiet, hallways. Rooms, plain but clean, have baths. Rates run about $23 s, $30 d, $33 t, with TV, fans, parking, but no phones; credit cards not accepted.

Other cheaper hotel choices dot Nuyoo and Colón near the second-class bus stations. **Hotel Colón,** at Colón 10, at Colón 10, tel. 953/532-0817 or 953/532-1860, is probably the best of these. It offers about 20 clean but smallish dark rooms with hot-water shower baths, around a parking patio, with *gratis* songs from the owner's many birds. Rates run $14 s or d, $22 t.

Another worth consideration is the **Hotel and Restaurant El Tesoro,** at Nuyoo 7, tel. 953/530-0895. Choose from around 20 basic rooms with bath around an inviting plant-decorated restaurant patio, also embellished by birdsong. Here, clean but small rooms, which rent for about $14 s, $16 d, are set back from the busy street and consequently insulated from traffic noise.

Food

Huajuapan's best grocery, vegetable, and fruit source is the town **market,** about four blocks west of the plaza. On the other hand, **health food** fanciers can get plenty of honey, grains, juices, soya, vitamins, supplements, granola, and yogurt, at **Natura,** Nuyoo 18, a block uphill from the cathedral, open Mon.–Sat. 9 A.M.–9 P.M. Satisfy your hankering for cake, pie, and cookies, at the **bakery,** the Espiga de Oro, nearby at Nuyoo 9, half a block uphill from the cathedral.

The town-center blocks abound with wholesome cooked food. For inexpensive snacks, try the **taco stands,** on the corner, northwest of the church. On the other hand, cross Colón and walk up Nuyoo a few doors and step into the sheltered patio of the **Restaurant El Tesoro de Michapa,** Nuyoo 7, tel. 953/532-0895. Here, you can enjoy a good home-cooked meal ($4–8) accompanied by the melodies of the owner-chef's pet tropical birds. Alternatively, across the street, you can do plenty of wholesome local-style eating at the **Restaurant El Dorado,** a few steps uphill from the corner of Colón ($3–6).

For refined plaza-front dining, try the open-air restaurant at the **Hotel Garcia Peral,** tel. 953/532-1532. Pick from the long menu of a little bit of everything, from cream of asparagus soup ($4) and hamburgers ($3–5) to shrimp salad ($6), filet mignon ($10), or *cabrito al pastor* (baby goat shepherd style, $8). Open daily 8 A.M.–10:30 P.M.

Relaxing courtyard ambience, quiet music, and genteel conversation draw a steady stream of middle- and upper-class patrons to **Restaurant Nikos,** on the plaza's east side, on Díaz next to Banco Internacional, tel. 953/532-1871. Here, diners choose from a list of tasty American-style hamburgers and hearty Oaxacan-style specialties ($4–8). Also open for good breakfasts ($3–6), daily except Monday, 8 A.M.–10:30 P.M.

Information and Services

A number of **banks** around the plaza, all with ATMs, change money. Best for its long hours is **Banco Internacional** (Bital) on Díaz, at the plaza's northeast corner, tel. 953/532-0169; open Mon.–Sat. 8:30 A.M.–6:30 P.M.

If somehow Bital isn't satisfactory, walk a block to **Banco Nacional de Mexico** (Banamex), at the plaza's northwest corner, tel. 953/532-1282, open Mon.–Fri. 9 A.M.–4 P.M.; or **Banco Serfin, a long block south of Banamex, at the corner of de León and Galindo,** tel. 953/532-0424, open Mon.–Fri. 9 A.M.–4 P.M., Sat. 10 A.M.–2 P.M.

Find the *correo* (post office), open Mon.–Fri. 8 A.M.–6 P.M., Sat. 9 A.M.–1 P.M., tel. 953/532-0692, at 5 de Febrero 16, on the south side. (From the plaza's southwest corner, walk south on de León three blocks to 5 de Febrero; turn right and continue another two blocks to the post office on the left side of the street.)

Long-distance telephone and fax are readily available at **Caseta del Centro,** on Díaz, east side of the plazatel, tel. 953/532-1915, fax 953/532-0350. It's open Mon.–Sat. 8 A.M.–9 P.M.

Internet connection is available daily, 9 A.M.–10 P.M., at **Internet Satelital,** at Nuyoo 12A, tel. 953/532-2724.

If you get sick, one of the best places to go for a doctor is the **Centro de Especialidades de la Mixteca,** Zaragoza 24, tel. 953/532-1355, across from the town market three blocks west of the plaza. It has about 15 specialists on call, from gynecologists and pediatricians to internists and a cardiologist.

For routine remedies and prescriptions, go to one of the several pharmacies near the plaza, such as **Farmacia Reyes,** on Colón, behind the church, or **Farmacia La Providencia,** at Nuyoo 18, half a block north from the church.

Although Huajuapan has a city *turismo* office on the upper floor of the *presidencia municipal* at the west side of the plaza, you might get more good information by consulting friendly José Flores Cubas, owner of the **Turismo "Oh Tierra del Sol,"** at the plaza's southeast corner, tel. 953/532-4555, fax 953/532-2656. He's open Mon.–Sat. approximately 9 A.M.–2 P.M. and 4–7 P.M.

Get your wash done at **Lavandería Easy,** on Hidalgo, one block west, one block south from the plaza's southwest corner

Getting There and Away

Several first- and second-class bus lines operate out of various terminals, providing direct connections with many Oaxacan and national destinations. The busy all-first-class terminal, six blocks north of the plaza at the Hwy. 190 intersection with Nuyoo, tel. 953/532-9309, is the center for **Cristóbal Colón, Autobuses del Oriente (ADO), Sur, and Autobuses Unidos (AU)** ticket sales, arrivals, and departures. Principal connections, including many intermediate destinations, are southeast with Nochixtlán and Oaxaca; south via Highway 15 and Tonalá with Juxtlahuaca, where you can transfer on to Tlaxiaco, Putla, and Pinotepa Nacional; and northwest with Puebla and Mexico City.

The several second-class bus stations are scattered along Nuyoo, on the block north of the cathedral. **Sur,** at the corner of Bravo and Nuyoo, tel. 953/532-5631, offers connections southeast, including a swarm of intermediate destinations, with Tamazulapan, Nochixtlán, and Oaxaca; south with Juxtlahuaca, Putla, and Tlaxiaco; north with Puebla; and northwest with Cuautla, Morelos, and Mexico City.

Fletes y Pasajes, at Nuyoo 14, ticket office in the video parlor across from the museum, a block uphill from the cathedral, offers a broad range of connections in Oaxaca, approximately the same as Sur.

A third, smaller line, **Boqueron,** formerly Tonalteca, at Nuyoo 21, tel. 953/532-9451, offers connections along the north-south Tonalá-Juxtlahuaca-Putla route all the way to Pinotepa Nacional, on Oaxaca's Pacific Coast.

Furthermore, **Autobuses Erco** (Linea Oro), at Nuyoo 19, tel. 953/532-1513, offers first-class expressway connections with northern destinations of Tehuacán and Puebla.

In addition, long-distance **collective van transportation** is available via **Servicios Turísticos Lázaro Cárdenas,** on Nuyoo, east side, about half a block north of the church, tel. 953/532-0007. Service includes south and southeast destinations of Oaxaca, Tonalá, Juxtlahuaca, and Tlaxiaco.

Drivers have their pick of four major paved highways radiating from Huajuapan. Northwest, Highway 190 connects—196 miles (316 km) via Cuautla, Morelos—with Mexico City. Two winding lanes and numerous big trucks along the way usually slow traffic along this route. Figure about seven hours under good conditions, either way. A quicker alternative is to first head northeast via Highway 125, 74 miles (118 km), two hours, to Tehuacán, Puebla. There, connect with the *cuota* (toll) expressway, which will whisk you in another three hours, via Puebla, to Mexico City.

For Oaxaca city, follow Highway 190 for 70 miles (113 km), two hours, southeast to Asunción Nochixtlán. Continue via the toll expressway to Oaxaca, another 50 miles (80 km), about one additional hour.

Drivers can also head south, via Tonalá, along the paved, lightly trafficked secondary road, which takes about two hours to Juxtlahuaca (62 miles, 100 km). South of Juxtlahuaca 25 miles (40 km, one hour), at the Highway 125 junction, either head left (east) along Highway 125 another 21 miles (34 km) and one hour to Tlaxiaco,

or go right, south along Highway 125 via Putla to Pinotepa Nacional on the Pacific Coast (a total, from Huajuapan, of 206 miles or 332 km). Allow six hours' driving time south to the coast, four hours east to Tlaxiaco.

NORTH OF HUAJUAPAN: INTO THE ÑUIÑE REGION

National Highway 125 winds north along the rural, tree-shaded valley of the Río Mixteco, passing a sprinkling of little towns, sleepy except during fiestas, when they liven up with days of processions, barbecues, and carnivals. Along this route, interest climaxes at San Pedro y San Pablo Tequixtepec, where townsfolk welcome visitors to explore their community museum. There, you can view the *Ñuiñe* engraved monoliths, whose cryptic inscriptions have convinced archaeologists that they represent a unique written language.

By car, starting early, you could enjoy this 75-mile (121-km) round-trip excursion in a day, allowing time for a picnic in Tequixtepec (22 miles, 35 km from Huajuapan) around the midpoint. Bus travelers, head out by ADO, Sur, or AU bus straight from Huajuapan, for Tequixtepec. At the entrance road, catch the town *colectivo* van and ride the three miles (5 km) to town. Afterward, either continue north or return to Huajuapan stopping along the way, if time allows.

Santiago Huajolotitlán

This small town four miles (6.4 km) north of Huajuapan is well known, both for its annual patronal festival and as the place where the Virgin of Guadalupe appeared in 1978. First, stop at the town church, the **Templo de Santiago Apóstol,** built between 1835 and 1840. Inside, to the right as you enter, notice the popular San Isidro Labrador, the patron of farmers, animals, and children, with his customary *yunta* (yoked pair) of oxen and a child. Folks celebrate his memory on May 15, when children bring their animals to church to be blessed.

Also, don't miss the uniquely quaint town patron, **Santiago Caballerito** (Little Saint James), mounted on a small horse, waving a big sword. His festival, celebrated July 26–29, usually includes

COHETES: BANGS, FLASHES, AND HISSES IN THE NIGHT

Like everyone, Mexicans love celebrations, and every one of them, humble or grand, must be accompanied by *cohetes*. Although *cohetes* literally means "rockets," folks always associate them with the myriad of other booming, flaring, whooshing, banging, and whirling incendiary devices that traditionally go along with *cohetes*. And while in most of the United States bland "Safe and Sane" fireworks are all that ordinary folks set off on the Fourth of July, and maybe New Year's, the sky seems to be the limit during the dozens of fiestas that Mexicans celebrate, even in the small country villages.

One big climax of celebrating peaks during the several weeks before Easter Sunday, when folks start out with a rip-roaring Carnaval (Mardi Gras) and parade the six succeeding Friday afternoons to the cannonades of *cohetes de*

trueno (thunder rockets) overhead and end up with a grand explosive bash on Easter Sunday.

Whatever the occasion, the *coheteros* (rocketeers) have plenty of tricks up their sleeves, from the familiar, colorfully brilliant *cohetes de luces* (rockets of lights) to a dozen other strictly Mexican varieties. These include *toritos*, a bull-shaped frame, decorated with papier mâché and loaded with flares and firecrackers that some daredevil wheels or carries on his back, through the crowds of merrymakers.

Sometime after that, someone usually scatters some *buscapies* (heel-chasers) that go whizzing, whirling, and shrieking under the feet of the crowd.

Finally, the *cohetero* lights up the *castillo*, a grand framework laced with pinwheels, flares, and smoke bombs, from which a spinning *corona* finally swishes skyward, scattering a trail of stars in the inky firmament overhead.

plenty of fireworks, flowers, music, marches, and *mañanitas* (early morning masses).

Also, on the slope of Cerro del Chilar, northwest of town, is the **Capilla de la Virgen de Guadalupe,** built over the spot where a shepherd saw the Virgin in December 1978. Thousands of believers subsequently flocked to the site, now relatively unfrequented, where this chapel stands.

Río Mixteco Valley and Asunción Cuyotepeji

North of Huajolotitlán is the river valley, especially lush during the cooler summer rainy season when it's abloom with fields of vegetables, tall green corn, and waving wheat. The natural charm climaxes at the riverbank itself, decorated by groves of stately *ahuehuetes* or *sabinos* (Mexican cypresses). Here and there, where the highway nears or crosses the river, pause for a stroll along the river and enjoy a spell in the company of the old shady giants.

During mid-August, you also might enjoy getting in on the fun of the **Fiesta de Santa María de la Asunción,** at Cuyotepeji, about 12 miles (19 km) north of Huajuapan. At least take

a look inside the church, known for its gilded baroque main *retablo* (altarpiece), which is adorned by the Holy Mother ascending to heaven guided by a choir of adoring cherubs.

San Pedro y San Pablo Tequixtepec

You could easily spend your entire day at Tequixtepec (formally, San Pedro y San Pablo Tequixtepec), pop. 1,400, the head town of the *municipio* of the same name. Make your first stop at the community museum, **Memorias de Yucundaayee** (yoo-koon-dah-ah-YAY-ay), named with the town's original Mixtec label (Hill of the Standing Conch), which the Aztecs translated to Tequixtepec.

The museum, adjacent to the town *presidencia municipal,* is regularly open Mon.–Thurs., about 10 A.M.–2 P.M. and 4–7 P.M. The professionally prepared exhibits display the intriguing, glyph-carved monoliths, with Spanish-language explanations of their Ñuiñe writing style. Despite a generation of study and excavations, archaeologists still can say little about the people depicted. Although their feathered visages remain mute to us, maybe someday experts will decipher the Ñuiñe glyphs and understand their messages.

If you have arranged a tour appointment, a museum volunteer will be available to take you on an extensive exploration, including a three-hour round-trip hike to **Cerro de La Caja** (Mountain of the Box), a regal hilltop ruined town. There, among other things, you'll be able to inspect a ponderous box-like monolith, inscribed with a number of graphic Ñuiñe reliefs, one of which includes a personage devouring a captive. Make an appointment by leaving a message, specifically for the *museo comunitario* (Abigail Moran Morales in charge at this writing), with the town long-distance *caseta*. Contact them at tel. 753/522-0709, or long-distance within Mexico tel. 200/123-7044, 200/123-7045, or 200/123-7046. (More conveniently, you can arrange a guided tour through Oaxaca Tours, in Oaxaca city, at 417 Alcalá, second floor, tel. 951/516-1005, toll-free U.S. tel. 800/446-2922, fax 951/514-6699, oaxacatours@oaxaca-tours.com.)

Back in town, be sure to visit the church, dedicated to the **Señor del Perdón** (Lord of Forgiveness), who is celebrated in a big regional fiesta and pilgrimage climaxing on the second Friday of Lent. At that time, 20,000 people crowd into little Tequixtepec, sleeping in the plaza, the town pilgrimage shelter, and in scores of buses parked along the road into town. The object of all is to ask forgiveness from the Señor del Perdón, who presides above the church's front altar.

Before you leave, ask your guide for a demonstration of **palm weaving,** which many townsfolk do during their spare moments. Both individual weavers and the museum sell examples of woven sombreros, *petates* (mats), *tenates* (tumpline baskets), and more. Additionally, be sure to step 100 years into the past into the Porfirian-era store of grandfatherly **Faustino "Tino" Moran Castillo.** Here you might say a good word, make a small purchase, and enjoy a sip of his zingy homemade brandy, which Faustino claims is "very good for your health."

Santiago Chazumba

The main yearly attractions here, at dusty Chazumba, about 37 miles (60 km) north from Huajuapan, are its two major festivals, in honor of **Santiago** (July 24–26) and the **Señor de**

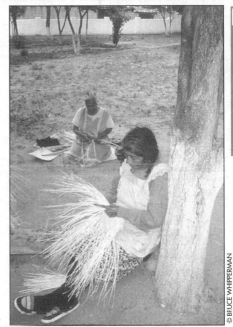

Everyone in San Pedro y San Pablo Tequixtepec seems to weave palm baskets, mats, and sombreros.

Esperanza (Lord of Hope—the 15 days beginning Good Friday).

The town's permanent jewel is its church, dedicated to Santiago Apóstol (St. James the Apostle). Although it seems a small miracle that such a monumental building and refined works of art can be found in such an isolated little place, it is the Chazumba townsfolk's intense devotion, rather than divine intervention, that has produced the monumentally resplendent results over centuries of effort. While inside, among all the glitter, don't miss the baptismal chapel to the right of the front door, the Señor de Esperanza in the transept chapel, and Santiago above the front altar.

The Chazumba bus station supports a few highway-side eateries. Best seems to be the **Restaurant Los Arcos,** where you can enjoy house specialties, such as *mole de guajalote* (turkey with mole sauce), *tamales de frijol* (bean tamales), and *barbacoa* (barbecued beef, pork, or chicken).

Besides food, Restaurant Los Arcos also provides a **long-distance telephone and fax**, tel. 953/525-0083. Moreover, in town, across the highway, you'll find a *correo* (post office) open Mon.–Fri. 9 A.M.–1 P.M. and 3–6 P.M., and a *telégrafos* for money orders and fax, open Mon.–Fri. 9 A.M.–3 P.M.

ADO and Sur buses, which depart from the Restaurant Los Arcos, connect several times a day north with Tehuacán, Puebla, and Mexico City, and south with Huajuapan, Nochixtlán, Oaxaca, and intermediate points.

SOUTH OF HUAJUAPAN: ALONG THE HIGH ROAD TO THE MIXTECA ALTA

This lightly traveled but all-paved route, Oaxaca State Highway 15, branches south from Huajuapan, opening a scenic back door to Oaxaca's cool, green, and culturally rich Mixteca Alta. Along the way, you'll cross rushing mountain rivers, wind through fertile, mountain farm valleys, and climb to high ridges where you can gaze back down upon it all.

Pleasant surprises along the way include boating, fishing, camping, and lakeside cabins at **Yosocuta Reservoir** and riverside hiking and wilderness camping in spectacular **Tonalá Canyon**. A few miles farther, at colonial-era Tonalá town, you can enjoy a cool, shady walk, and a picnic in the town's grand old *sabino* cypress grove. Finally, at the route's end, at Juxtlahuaca, enjoy the color of the grand indigenous Thursday–Friday **tianguis**, a relaxing stroll, and restful overnight camping in the pine grove beside the crystalline, emerald-green **Laguna Encantada**.

Yosocuta Reservoir

This big artificial lake, eight miles (13 km) south of Huajuapan, confined by the government-built Yosocuta dam on the Río Mixteco, rises and falls

The precipitous gap of the Río Mixteca, called El Boquerón (Big Mouth), provides entrance to a backpacker's paradise of riverside tenting, wildlife-viewing, and backcountry hiking.

with the seasons. From February through July, the reservoir drains, nourishing irrigated crops. Its level consequently falls, leaving an ugly bathtub-like lakeshore ring. However, by October, the lake usually refills, rising to its brim, gently lapping the shoreline at **Parador Yosocuta,** the major lakeside access point.

Here, you have several choices. Lake-view restaurants offer snacks, drinks, and fresh black bass dinners. A concession, owned by the Yosocuta town fishing cooperative and managed by friendly English-speaking Samuel Martínez, offers lake tours by boat ($7–12 per party), fishing excursions ($20 an hour), boat rentals, bait, and fishing poles (from about $40); launching fee for your own motorboat runs about $5.

If you decide to stay overnight, Samuel will let you set up your tent on the lakeshore or park your self-contained RV overnight in the parking lot free. He also rents out a few attractive lakeshore four-person cabanas, with their own hot-water baths and porch-front hammock hooks, for about $10 nightly. Reserve cabanas by leaving a reservation message for Samuel Martínez at the Yosocuta long-distance *caseta,* tel. 953/532-2842.

(Alternatively, you can reserve a Yosocuta cabana through the government alternative tourism office, at Murguia 206, tel. 951/516-4828, in downtown Oaxaca. For more details, see Tourist Yu'u Community Lodging in the Around the Valley of Oaxaca chapter.)

Tonalá Canyon

South, past a high, pine-studded ridge and pass, Oaxaca Highway 15 winds down to the Tonalá valley. There, 27 miles (43 km) south of Huajuapan, beneath the foot of **Puente Morelos,** a steel-arch highway bridge, the Río Mixteco issues through the deep defile of Cañon de Tonalá (known locally as El Boquerón, Big Mouth).

A trail cut into the canyon wall leads to a diversion dam about a mile (1.6 km) upstream. The trail begins at some stairs not far from the bridge's north footing. It continues spectacularly, above the river along the diversion canal, winding beneath towering 1,000-foot (300-meter) moss-mottled cliffs, green-tufted like a classical Chi-

nese painting. At one point, a great boulder overhangs the trail; at another, a mass of ferns appears to cascade from the vertical rock wall.

At the dam, the trail ends at a small park and commemorative plaque that records that President Gustavo Díaz Ordaz came here during the late 1960s to dedicate the dam, a part of the federal Río Balsas Basin Development Project. A rough, informal trail continues past the dam. After 50 downhill yards it leads to a flat spot on the right, with a bit of shade, safely above the river for camping.

For equipped and prepared wilderness adventurers, the river farther upstream, which runs about 10 miles (16 km) through a wild, deep gorge, might be heaven. Overhead, vultures and eagles soar; coyotes, foxes, and wildcats hunt along the shore; and butterflies flutter among streamside trees and wildflowers. The river, rushing and often muddy during the summer rainy season, slows to a clear, tranquil creek during the dry winter and spring. *Warning:* Although the Yosocuta Dam upstream probably minimizes the hazard, hikers should be aware of possible flash flooding from upstream thunderstorms.

Santo Domingo Tonalá

The sleepy little farm community of Santo Domingo Tonalá (pop. 3,000) owns a pair of gems: its 16th-century Dominican-founded church and ex-convent, the **Templo de Santo Domingo,** and the lovely sylvan *sabinera* (cypress grove) behind the church. First, take a look inside the church, behind its front garden, a block north of the town plaza. Just past the entrance hangs an intriguing portrait of Angel Gabriel holding the scales of justice, deciding which of a cluster of beseeching souls will be admitted to Paradise. Farther on stands an image of the beloved African Dominican padre San Martín de Porres. The treasures climax in the right-side chapel, in a glittering, gorgeous small *retablo,* appearing as intricate as filigree and dedicated to the Holy Sacrament. Continue outside to the church's right, east side and enjoy a turn through the garden within the old convent cloister.

If you arrive on Sunday, you might be able to see a *pelota mixteca* ball game in the field across

© BRUCE WHIPPERMAN

Temazcales, traditional hot rooms for healing, are common throughout the Mixteca.

the highway at the town entrance road. A direct descendant of the ancient Mesoamerican tradition, the modern game has players batting a big rubber ball back and forth, not unlike tennis (except without a net).

Farther afield, you might investigate a trove of local archaeological sites. These include a cave with *pinturas rupestres* (prehistoric hieroglyphic rock paintings), walls of ancient crumbling temples (from a time long ago, when the local population is said to have migrated from present Chiapas state). For information, and possibly a guide, check with the Semarnat (Secretary of the Environment and Natural Resources) people in the Tonalá *presidencia municipal.*

Tonalá's annual **festivals** revolve around the church. Arrive between May 1 and May 4 and get in on the fun (dancing, cockfights, and bull roping and riding) of the **Fiesta de la Santa Cruz.** A few months later, around August 4, Tonalá folk rev up again for more of the same during the **Fiesta de Santo Domingo.**

You'll find the *sabinera* two blocks behind the church. Stroll around and soak in the cathedral-like loveliness beneath the old trees. Perhaps you will agree that the magnificent, gnarled old veteran *sabinos,* or *ahuehuetes,* are in their own way as magnificent as the stately old-growth groves of their cousins, the California redwoods. They certainly approach the size of redwoods. At the grove's far west (left as you enter) end, find the gnarled old grandparent of them all, 15 feet (4.5 meters) in diameter and 50 feet (15 meters) around. During your walk, you probably will notice the several small, clear rivulets running through the grove. This is no coincidence; local folks believe *sabinos* to be the most intelligent of trees; they always grow where the water flows.

Accommodations and Food: Consider Tonalá's one hotel, the homey **Los Mangos,** Lázaro Cárdenas 27, Santo Domingo Tonalá, Oaxaca, tel. 953/531-0023, marked by a tall mango tree, on the entrance road from the highway. The grandmotherly owner offers 10 rooms beside a flowery garden and the loveliest of crimson-blossomed *tabachín* (flame tree). Check the rooms before moving in; mildew can be a problem here, especially in the rainy summer. Ask for fresh linens if necessary. All rooms have baths, with 24-hour hot water. Rentals run about $8 s, $15 d, with all the mangos you can eat, in season.

For cooked food, the Los Mangos' owner runs an inviting restaurant on the premises. Alternatively, for some tacos, *tortas,* or a hamburger, you can try the *lonchería* across the street from her restaurant. A store or two on or near the plaza can supply basic groceries. The plaza-front **market,** biggest on Friday, is the best local source of fruits and vegetables.

Services

If you're sick, go to the **centro de salud,** on Lázaro Cárdenas, the main entrance thoroughfare, downhill past the church. For routine medications and drugs, try the **Farmacia Santa Cruz** a block uphill from the hotel. For **long-distance telephone and fax** go to the *larga distancia* across the street from the Hotel Los Mangos.

Getting There

Bus passengers can reach Yosocuta, Tonalá Canyon, and Tonalá town by second-class **Fletes y Pasajes, Boquerón,** or **Sur** buses, either south from Huajuapan or north from Juxtlahuaca.

From Huajuapan, drivers should first head west along Highway 190 to a signed Juxtlahuaca or Tonalá left turnoff, about a mile (1.6 km) west of the city center. After another mile (1.6 km) turn right at the main street, Avenida Mina; continue another eight miles (13 km) to Yosocuta. Continue a total of 27 miles (43 km) to Tonalá Canyon, 30 miles (50 km) to Tonalá town, and 62 miles (100 km) to Juxtlahuaca. North from Juxtlahuaca, the distances are approximately 32 miles (51 km) to Tonalá, 35 miles (56 km) to Tonalá Canyon, and 54 miles (87 km) to Yosocuta. Figure about an hour and a half at the wheel, either direction.

SANTIAGO JUXTLAHUACA AND VICINITY

Santiago Juxtlahuaca (pop. about 30,000) is the largest town and major service and governmental center for the Juxtlahuaca district. It's clear why the town has prospered. It nestles in a deep, fertile valley between a pair of towering oak- and pine-studded mountain ranges. Main roads branch south, west, and north, connecting Juxtlahuaca with the outside world.

A second glance at the surrounding mountains reveals sinuous trails so steep that it's a wonder how anyone could climb them. But people do—the indigenous Mixtec- and Trique-speaking mountain people, for whom Juxtlahuaca's big *tianguis* is the focus of their week. They rise long before dawn and bundle up their merchandise—perhaps a basket packed with flowers, potatoes, or carrots; maybe they pile on a few hand-loomed bright red-striped *huipiles.* Husband and wife sling the loads on their backs, adjust the tumplines on their foreheads, and begin the steep trek downhill, with hope that this will be a good *tianguis,* and they won't have to haul everything back uphill tomorrow night.

Orientation and Sights

Orient yourself by the tall, straight-laced bell tower of the town church, the **Templo de Santiago Apóstol,** visible from all over town. The church faces the customary west, downhill. If you stand looking at the church-front, south will be on your right, north on your left. The uphill direction, toward the rear of the church, is east. Main east-west streets are Libertad, which runs along the church's north side; Porfirio Díaz, along the church's south side by the plaza; and Benito Juárez, along the plaza's south side. Important north-south streets are Lázaro Cárdenas, a block behind the church, and Independencia, a block farther east, uphill.

If at all possible, schedule your Juxtlahuaca visit to coincide with its two-day *tianguis,* big on Thursday but among Oaxaca's biggest on Friday. Vendors' awnings (known in the Aztec language as *tianguis*) stretch from curb to curb, beginning at the town plaza just downhill from the church, and overflow, filling half of Juxtlahuaca's south-side streets.

The star actors of the *tianguis* are the **Trique women,** who proudly wear their horizontally striped bright-red wool *huipiles* over their black

THE MIXTECA

© BRUCE WHIPPERMAN

The straight-laced bell tower of Juxtlahuaca's Templo de Santiago Apóstol presides over the town.

woolen skirts. (If you wonder why in sunny Mexico they wear wool, it's because afternoons are often cloudy and cool in Juxtlahuaca, especially during the summer and fall rainy season, and doubly so in the Triques' mountaintop villages.)

A number of Trique women congregate in the town plaza's center, selling their home-spun textiles: *huipiles,* black *enredos* (skirts), and blouses. They don't like having their pictures taken, but several remedies exist for curing camera shyness. (See the sidebar "Taking People Pictures" in the Introduction.)

From the plaza, plunge into the hubbub of stalls on the south-side street, Benito Juárez. Along your meandering path you'll find loads of lovely fruit—many exotic tropical varieties—*anonas, guanabanas, pitahayas, zapotes*—but also apples, grapes, peaches, pears, and plums in the summer.

You'll also see a fair amount of pottery, especially along Calle Lázaro Cárdenas, the north-south street that runs behind the church. Varieties include flower-painted, hard-glazed bowls, cups, and plates from Santa Rosa in the Valley of Oa-

xaca; green ware from Atzompa, also in the Valley of Oaxaca; and red and black jugs, plates, and bowls from Puebla. A few stalls also sell soft woven palm *tenates* and *petates* (tumpline baskets and mats), and sombreros from around Huajuapan de León.

If you're in the market for **masks,** go to the shop of master craftsman Alejandro Jesús Vera Guzmán, at Lázaro Cárdenas 301 Sur, corner of Melchor Ocampo, tel. 953/554-0060, two blocks west of the uphill side of the church. His store is in the left-hand side of the southwest corner grocery. He got started creating masks (devils seem to be his specialty) for local fiesta dances; now he sells to the public. His prices aren't cheap; expect to pay $40 and up. From him, however, you're getting the genuine article. If you lend him your photo, he'll even create a mask of you, for around $150. For more information, email him at alexvera@juxtlahuaca.com.

While you're wandering around, you might take a look inside the **church.** Just as you enter the door, look into the small alcove on the right and you'll see the town patron, **Santiago** (St. James), sword in hand, on his usual white horse, but this time with a cowboy hat atop his head. Up front, above the altar, you'll see Santiago in more traditional dress. Step left, into the left transept chapel, and see the **Virgen de Soledad** presiding above the altar.

Laguna Encantada

Yet another good reason for coming to Juxtlahuaca is Laguna Encantada (Enchanted Lagoon), a deep crystalline emerald-green lake beside the Huajuapan highway about two miles (3 km) north of town. Laguna Encantada, set like a jewel at the foot of a towering mountain, is a precious asset that, besides supplying irrigation water, supplies the adjacent communal swimming pool and picnic and camping ground. Even if you don't camp there, you should at least go for a stroll around its shoreline, made picture-perfect by the family of gnarled old *ahuehuete* cypresses inhabiting its banks.

Both tent and RV **camping** prospects at Laguna Encantada could hardly be better. A broad cypress-shaded campground on the lake's north side provides plenty of grassy space to spread out. As a courtesy, ask the caretaker, friendly Natalia Ramos de Morales, who runs the snack stand, if camping is OK. It always will be both allowed and free, especially if you buy a few tacos and drinks from her.

She recommends that visitors hike up to the top of the hill, Mogote de la Tialeja, just north of the campground. Natalia (a definite local booster) says that the Mogote, a former Mixtec settlement, is full of artifacts (which must remain in place; Mexican law forbids their removal). Artifacts or not, your reward for the 750-foot (250-meter) summit climb will be an airy, panoramic valley and mountain view.

San Miguel de la Cueva

Townsfolk of San Miguel de la Cueva town, south of Juxtlahuaca, invite visitors to explore their big limestone cave. An adventurer's delight, the cave has plenty of dripping stalagmites, fluttering bats, and a river that flows down from a hidden subterranean lake. Bring a strong flashlight and a hard plastic hat. First get permission and a guide (offer to pay) at the *presidencia municipal*. Get there at the signed side road from Highway 15, two miles (3 km) south of Juxtlahuaca. Continue about eight miles (13 km) to the town plaza.

Accommodations and Food

Juxtlahuaca has a few hotels, at least two of which are recommendable. Most inviting is the family-run **Hotel Mixteco,** Independencia 200, Juxtlahuaca, Oaxaca 69700, tel. 953/554-0025, near the corner of Libertad, two blocks behind the church. The 13 plainly furnished but clean rooms encircle a homey mango and lemon tree decorated patio. Rooms rent for about $8 s, $ 14 d, and $22 t, with hot-water shower baths and parking; credit cards not accepted.

Alternatively, try the **Hotel Diana,** at Porfirio Díaz 300, Juxtlahuaca, Oaxaca 69700, tel. 953/554-0076, a block downhill from the plaza. The 30 basic but clean rooms with hot-water baths begin at about $11 s, $15 d, and $30 t, with TV, hot-water showers and parking; credit cards not accepted. Larger-size rooms with two beds run about $22 d.

Plaza-front taco stands and market *fondas* (permanent stalls) provide plenty of very inexpensive local-style food. Remember: If it's hot, it's

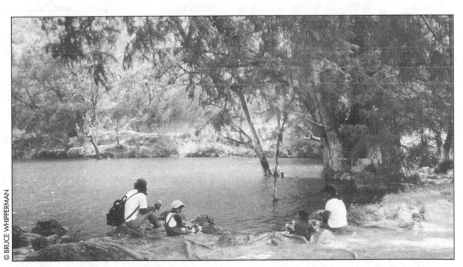

The Laguna Encantada, with its crystalline green waters, tree-shaded banks, and adjacent camping-picnic ground, lives up to its name, Enchanted Lagoon.

© BRUCE WHIPPERMAN

wholesome. For dessert, go to the *panadería* (bakery) on Juárez, a block uphill from the plaza's southeast corner.

Market vegetable and fruit selection is super, especially during the summer. To be on the safe side, peel, cook, or scrub with soap and water any fruit or vegetable you eat. Stores, such as **Estrada Fería,** on Lázaro Cárdenas, half a block south of Díaz and a block uphill from the plaza, opposite BITAL, supply basic groceries.

Juxtlahuaca people are prosperous enough to support a few restaurants. Always busy is the **Comedor Tere,** behind the church on Lázaro Cárdenas, a block uphill from the plaza, by BITAL, open Mon.–Sat. 7 A.M.–11 P.M. The specialty here is a hearty afternoon four-course *comida,* typically, soup, rice, stew, and dessert, for about $3.

Another good restaurant choice is the family-run **López Pizza** (pizza, spaghetti, calzone, hamburgers, and lettuce and tomato salad if you ask for it, $2–7) Find them both near the corner of Lázaro Cárdenas and Libertad.

Festivals and Events

Local townsfolk celebrate both Santiago and the Virgen de Soledad in big festivals. Santiago's culminates around July 25, with a number of traditional dances: the Christians and Moors (a variation of the Dance of the Conquest; the Moors are the bad guys); the Chilolos (masked men, posing as women, in bells and skirts); and the town favorite, the Diablos (Devils). Much the same thing goes on during the December 8 Virgen de Soledad festival. In addition, **Carnaval** is big in Juxtlahuaca. On the four days before Ash Wednesday, the beginning of Lent, townsfolk whoop it up with the masked dance Rubios (Blondes), a parody of the Spanish conquistadores, and the Machos dance.

Juxtlahuaca, moreover, is a center of *pelota mixteca,* the Mixtec version of the ancient Mesoamerican ball game. Although commonly played with a *hule* (natural rubber) ball, the local variation is to use a leather ball. Players wrap their hands in thick cloth and bat the ball in a court, not unlike tennis. Local teams get ready

EASTER CALENDAR

Although Christian religious denominations' Easter calendars vary, virtually all Western Christian churches follow the same calendar as the Roman Catholic version, universally used in Mexico. This calendar originated with the Council of Nicaea, which in A.D. 325, set Easter as the first Sunday after the first full moon of Spring (or, more precisely, the first full moon after the Vernal Equinox, which the church authorities fixed as March 21).

The Easter season customarily kicks off with **Carnaval,** a rip-roaring party that runs the few days preceding **Ash Wednesday** (Miercoles de Ceniza), when all merriment ceases. Ash Wednesday, in turn fixed as the 46th day before Easter Sunday, occurs most often in February, and marks the beginning of **Lent,** a period of penitence and fasting. The gravity of Lent is literally rubbed in via ashes that the faithful get smeared on to their foreheads during solemn Ash Wednesday Christian church ceremonies worldwide.

In Mexico, religious processions and sober observances continue on each of the subsequent six Fridays. **Palm Sunday** (Domingo de Ramos), immediately follows the fifth Friday, and finally, after the sixth, or **Good Friday, Easter Sunday** (Domingo Gloria) breaks the fast of Lent as folks celebrate the risen Christ, with joy and feasting.

The U.S. Naval Observatory explains the Easter calendar's historically interesting origin in concise detail on its website (see http://aa.usno .navy.mil/faq/docs/easter.html). They also furnish a number of past and future dates for Easter Sunday.

for the yearly November 20 and February 5 tournaments nearly every afternoon in the long sandy court marked out just below the church.

Services

Change money at the air-conditioned **Banco Internacional** (Bital), on Lázaro Cárdenas behind and a block south of the church, tel. 953/554-0427 or 953/554-0428. Its long money-changing hours are Mon.–Fri. 8 A.M.–7 P.M., Sat. 8 A.M.–3 P.M. If they're closed, use their ATM. If

Bital doesn't suit you, go to Juxtlahuaca's **Banorte,** one block directly south of the plaza, tel. 953/554-0417 or 953/554-0418, also with an ATM, open Mon.–Fri. 9 A.M.–5 P.M., Sat. 9 A.M.–2 P.M.

Juxtlahuaca's *correo* (post office) is on Juárez, at the southwest plaza corner, open Mon.–Fri. 9 A.M.–1 P.M. and 3–6 P.M., Sat. 9 A.M.–noon. **Telecom,** on Díaz, half a block downhill from the plaza, providing public fax 953/554-0044, and money orders, is open Mon.–Fri. 9 A.M.–3 P.M. and Sat. 9 A.M.–noon. For after-hours long-distance phone and fax, go to either of the two private *larga distancias* on the plaza's south side.

Answer your email at **Bin@ry Internet,** on Lázaro Cárdenas, south side, corner of Libertad, open daily 9 A.M.–11 P.M.

For travel services, go to **Micsa Agencia de Viajes,** 300 Lázaro Cárdenas Sur, corner of Melchor Ocampo, three blocks south of the church, tel. 953/554-0446 or 953/554-0232, open daily 9 A.M.–9 P.M.

A few doctor-owned pharmacies on Lázaro Cárdenas, such as the **Farmacia Diana Luz** of Doctor Amadeo T. Chaves, tel. 953/554-0014, are open until 9 A.M.–9 P.M. for consultation, prescriptions and sales right on the spot. For hospital or emergency medical service, Juxtlahuaca has a **general hospital** about a mile (1.6 km) north of town on the Huajuapan highway, tel. 953/554-0307, 953/554-0308, or 953/554-0309.

For gynecological consultation, see **Doctora Iralda Budar Villavicenzio,** at her house at 104 Independencia Norte, or her office, on Lázaro Cárdenas, a block and a half south of Díaz, tel. 953/554-0184. Her hours are Mon.–Fri. 8 A.M.–2 P.M. and 4–8 P.M., on call 24 hours in emergency.

Getting There and Away

Several long-distance bus lines connect Juxtlahuaca with various Oaxaca and national destinations. Most terminals are on the highway. First-class **Sur** and **Cristóbal Colón** buses, tel. 953/554-0181, connect north with Huajuapan, Puebla, and Mexico City; northeast with Tlaxiaco, Teposcolula, and Tamazulapan; southeast with Nochixtlán and Oaxaca; and south with Putla and Pinotepa Nacional.

Second-class service includes **Fletes y Pasajes** buses that connect north with Tonalá, Huajuapan, Cuautla (Morelos), and Mexico City, and east and southeast with Tlaxiaco, Teposcolula, Nochixtlán, and Oaxaca. **Boquerón** second-class buses connect south with Putla and Pinotepa Nacional and north with Tonalá and Huajuapan.

Sur offers a broad range of second-class connections, similar to Fletes and Pasajes above, out of a **downtown station,** on the north end of Lázaro Cárdenas, corner of Progreso, tel. 953/554-0033.

For drivers, paved (but sometimes potholed) mountain roads connect Juxtlahuaca with Oaxaca destinations: north with Huajuapan de León, 62 miles (100 km), two and a half hours; south with Putla de Guerrro, via Oaxaca Highway 15 (20 miles, 32 km), thence via National Highway 125 (17 miles, 28 km), a total of 37 miles (60 km), in about an hour; or east, with Tlaxiaco, via Oaxaca Highway 15 (20 miles, 32 km), then via National Highway 125 (30 miles, 48 km), a total of 50 miles (80 km), in about two hours.

The Mixteca Alta: Roof of Oaxaca

The Mixteca Alta, Oaxaca's temperate Mixtec highland, is a land poor in gold but rich in scenic and cultural assets: airy mountain vistas, colorful village markets, pine-scented breezes, beloved old churches, tumbling waterfalls, ancient ruins, and crystalline springs await the traveler who ventures into the Mixteca Alta.

Moreover, travel within the Mixteca Alta is not difficult. Tlaxiaco, with its hotels, restaurants, bus connections, and services, is a good base for exploring the Mixteca Alta. From Tlaxiaco, roads lead out east past cool, green mountain vistas to the enigmatic ruins at Huamelulpan and Achiutla, south over the airy Chalcatongo plateau to the Cascada Esmeralda waterfall at Yosundua, and west to the friendly little Mixtec-speaking museum towns of Cuquila and San Miguel Progreso.

TLAXIACO

Asunción Tlaxiaco (tlah-shee-AH-koh) is far more important than its population of about 20,000 would imply. It's the economic capital of the entire Mixteca Alta, a magnet for many hundreds of vendors from all over central and southern Mexico and thousands more native folks who swarm into town for the **Saturday** *tianguis* (native market), second only to the big Saturday market in Oaxaca city.

The town, also capital of the Tlaxiaco governmental district, was even more important in times past. During the "Order and Progress" of President Porfirio Díaz (1876–1910), Tlaxiaco's significance perhaps eclipsed even Oaxaca city. Its key position on the trade route between Puebla and Veracruz and the southern Pacific Coast, as well as its large hinterland population, made Tlaxiaco the trading and supply center for much of southwest Mexico. Rich merchants and entrepreneurs, both Mexican and foreign, together with wealthy *hacendados* (landed gentry), constituted a local upper crust who, for a generation, earned Tlaxiaco the unofficial title of "Little Paris."

The Dominican friars certainly understood Tlaxiaco's importance as early as 1550, when Friar Francisco Marín began building the monumental town church, the Templo de la Asunción. Scholars have identified details in the church's decorations that resemble those of the main church in the city of Caceres, Spain. This link has added a piece to one of the puzzles of Oaxaca's great Dominican churches: where did the Dominican clerics, presumably isolated in the Oaxaca hinterlands, acquire the skill to create the masterpiece churches of Yanhuitlán, Teposcolula, Coixtlahuaca, and Tlaxiaco? The answer may lie in a previously unknown connection between the Dominican friars and the noted Rodrigo Gil de Montañon, master of Spanish Gothic-Plateresque architecture and builder of the Caceres church. (See the sidebar "Building Churches" in the Around the Valley of Oaxaca chapter.)

Sights

Let **Plaza Constitución,** the hub of the Tlaxiaco market, a few blocks uphill from the cluttered and bumpy through-town highway, be your key to finding your way around town. Main east-west streets Colón and 5 de Mayo run along the north and south sides, respectively, of Plaza Constitución. East of the plaza, they intersect the other main town streets, Independencia and Hidalgo, which both run north, uphill from the highway. The perfect spot to view all of this is the front porch of the **Hotel del Portal,** which perches on the uphill (north) side of the plaza. From there, you'll see the town **clock** in the plaza foreground; and in the background, bell tower of the town church, Templo de la Asunción, a few hundred yards to the southwest. To the right of the church, behind some trees on the west side of a shady *jardín,* stands the town *presidencia municipal.*

Make sure to arrive in Tlaxiaco by noon, Saturday, in time to soak in its spreading, colorful, Saturday *tianguis.* It's fun to just wander around beneath the rainbow of awnings shading a galaxy

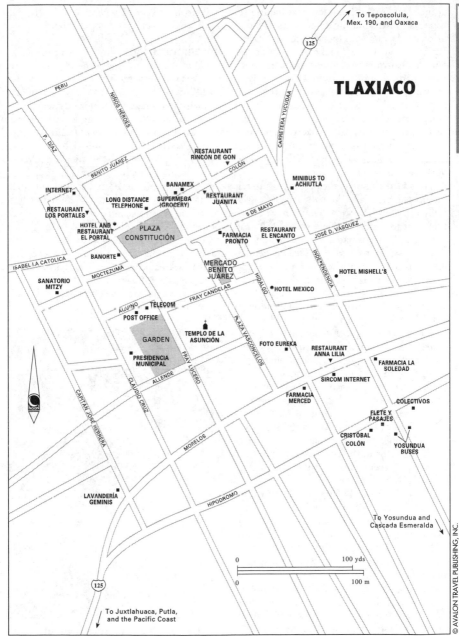

To Teposcolula,
Mex. 190, and Oaxaca

125

PERU

NIÑOS HÉROES

CARRETERA YUCUDAA

TLAXIACO

P. DÍAZ

BENITO JUÁREZ

RESTAURANT
RINCÓN DE GON

COLÓN

INTERNET

LONG DISTANCE
TELEPHONE

BANAMEX

SUPERMEGA
(GROCERY)

RESTAURANT
JUANITA

MINIBUS TO
ACHIUTLA

RESTAURANT
LOS PORTALES

5 DE MAYO

HOTEL AND
RESTAURANT
EL PORTAL

PLAZA
CONSTITUCIÓN

FARMACIA
PRONTO

RESTAURANT
EL ENCANTO

JOSE D. VÁSQUEZ

ISADEL LA CATOLICA

BANORTE

MOCTEZUMA

MERCADO
BENITO
JUÁREZ

INDEPENDENCIA

HOTEL MISHELL'S

SANATORIO
MITZY

FRAY CANDELAS

HIDALGO

HOTEL MEXICO

ALVINO

TELECOM

POST OFFICE

PLAZA VASCONCELOS

GARDEN

TEMPLO DE LA
ASUNCIÓN

FOTO EUREKA

RESTAURANT
ANNA LILIA

PRESIDENCIA
MUNICIPAL

ALLENDE

FRAY LUCERO

FARMACIA LA
SOLEDAD

SIRCOM INTERNET

CLAUDIO CRUZ

FARMACIA
MERCED

COLECTIVOS

FLETE Y
PASAJES

CRISTÓBAL
COLÓN

YOSUNDUA
BUSES

CAPITÁN JOSÉ HERRERA

MORELOS

LAVANDERÍA
GEMINIS

HIPODROMO

To Yosundua and
Cascada Esmeralda

Moon

0   100 yds

0   100 m

125

To Juxtlahuaca, Putla,
and the Pacific Coast

THE MIXTECA

of merchandise, both modern and traditional. Especially interesting are the time-tested hand-made goods: *calabazas* (gourds) cut and carved into bowls, utensils, and musical instruments; extensive assortments of forest-gathered roots, seeds, bark, dried flowers, and nuts, ready to brew into teas to cure dozens of illnesses; traditional clothes—hand-embroidered *huipiles* and *blusas* from all over Oaxaca—*canastas, tenates, petates* (reed baskets, palm baskets and mats)—and soft sombreros woven from palm; and leather *cinturones, bolsas,* and *billeteras* (belts, purses, and billfolds).

The added plus of all the bustle, of course, is the people, especially the native women, who really run the whole show. The men, who help transport the goods, usually stand back (and sometimes, unfortunately, get drunk) and let their spouses do the buying and selling. Perhaps the best two spots for native action are the narrow **Plaza Vasconcelos,** which heads downhill for a block from the southeast corner of Plaza Constitución, and the front steps of the church, a hubbub of native fruit and vegetable sellers.

While you're people-watching in front of the church, the **Templo de la Asunción,** take a break and step into its cool, calm interior. Although begun in 1550, the church, once a Dominican convent, has been continually modified and strengthened since that time. Towering overhead, a network of unreinforced (no steel: all stone) Gothic arches have, amazingly, supported the entire ceiling for more than 400 years, freeing the nave from the clutter of columns and creating a heavenly, soaring space for worship, rest, and contemplation.

Tlaxiaco's patron, the **Virgen de la Asunción,** presides from above the altar. High above her, note the all-seeing eye (which looks every bit like its counterparts painted on many Buddhist and Hindu stupas in India and Nepal).

Townsfolk celebrate their beloved patron in a pair of annual **fiestas.** The first, the official patronal religious festival, kicks off on August 14 and continues for two more days with processions, food, and fireworks. The second, the secular town **Fiesta de Octubre,** occurs around the third Sunday of October and includes fireworks,

basketball and *pelota mixteca* (traditional ball game) tournaments, and popular dances.

Accommodations

Of Tlaxiaco's sprinkling of hotels, the **Hotel del Portal,** Constitución 2, Tlaxiaco, Oaxaca 69800, tel. 953/552-0154, affords a superb plaza-front vantage for exploring the colorful town center. Inside past the reception, you enter an elegantly restored grand patio, softly illuminated by an overhead skylight. The three stories of approximately 50 rooms encircle a back parking courtyard. The rooms are spartan, but clean, comfortable, and well maintained. Rentals run from about $20 s, $23 d, with hot-water shower baths and parking; credit cards not accepted.

Although less favorably located a few blocks southeast of the town center, the **Hotel San Mishell's,** Independencia 11, Tlaxiaco, Oaxaca 69800, tel. 953/552-0064, offers attentive on-site family management. The dozen superior-grade rooms in a two-story tier surround an inviting

The Tlaxiaco Saturday market is one of Oaxaca's most lively and colorful.

© BRUCE WHIPPERMAN

inner garden patio. Inside, rooms are clean, carpeted, and thoughtfully decorated. Outside the rooms, on a shady garden-view porch, guests enjoy soft chairs for reading and relaxing. Standard-grade rooms, although clean and comfortable occupy a two-story tier beside an adjacent parking patio. Standard-grade run about $13 s, $18 d, without TV. Superior-grade rooms rent for about $20 s, $26 d, with TV. All rooms have hot-water shower baths and parking; credit cards not accepted.

Nearby, a block and a half west of Plaza Constitución, stands the downscale old standby, the family-run **Hotel Mexico**, at Hidalgo 13, Tlaxiaco, Oaxaca 69800, tel. 953/552-0086. Rooms, in "new" (private bath) and "old" (shared bath) sections, surround a rambling inside patio. All of the 20-odd rooms are clean; the "old" rooms are plainly furnished, while the "new" are thoughtfully decorated with wood furnishings, attractive bedspreads, and drapes. Rates for "old" rooms run about $8 s, $9 d, $14 t; the "new," $18 s or d, $26 t, all with hot water available only in the morning until 11 A.M.; credit cards not accepted.

Food

Taco stands and *fondas* (food stalls) at the covered **Mercado Benito Juárez** (one block south of the Plaza Constitución's southeast corner) are your best source of economical meals and snacks. Basic groceries are available at plaza-front *abarroterías*, notably at **Super Mega**, at the plaza's northeast side, a block east of Hotel del Portal, next to Banamex. Baked goods are also sold at several stalls at the Mercado Benito Juárez and the **Panificadora Evelyn**, corner of Díaz and Juárez, a block north of Plaza Consitución.

A few **restaurants** cater to the trickle of visitors and handful of Tlaxiaco residents who can afford to eat out. Tlaxiaco's fanciest is the **Restaurant El Patio** in the airy inner courtyard of the Hotel del Portal, tel. 953/552-0154, open daily 8 A.M.–9 P.M. Fine Oaxacan cuisine is the main event here; pick from a long list of appetizers, such as roasted onions with leaves of nopal ($2) or tortilla soup ($3); for a main dish, you might choose leg of pork smothered in rich black *mole* ($5) or Tlaxiaco-style tacos ($3).

Also excellent is another of the Mixteca Alta's best restaurants, the old-Mexico rustic-style **Restaurant Los Portales**, on Porfirio Díaz (the north-south street just west of the Hotel del Portal), a block north of the plaza. Here, you can choose from a long menu of professionally prepared and served soups and salads ($3–4), and meats, seafood and poultry ($4–8). Although they suggest several house specialties, no matter; everything they serve is good. Open daily 7 A.M.–10 P.M.

Also very popular is the refined **Rincón de Goti** at Colón 11, tel. 953/552-0804, a block east of the plaza. You can start with a choice of breakfasts, including *huevos con jamón* (ham and eggs), omelettes, fruit, granola, and hotcakes. For lunch or supper, choose from several salads, and among entrées of fish, meat, poultry, and Mexican specialties. Some evenings, beginning around 9, patrons enjoy relaxing guitar music. Open daily 7 A.M.–11 P.M. (Unfortunately, they've acquired a TV. If it bothers you, don't hesitate to ask them to turn it off or at least lower the volume.)

Across the street and half a block west, at Colón 6, find country-style **Restaurant Juanita.** Here, the menu is long on local fare, including eggs *al gusto* (any style, $2–3), *pollo frito* (fried chicken, $3), *chuleta de puerco* (pork chop, $4), and *enchiladas de mole* ($4), accompanied by all the tortillas you can eat and all the TV you can watch. For dessert, you can have *duraznos* (canned peaches, $1) or *platanos fritos con miel* (fried bananas with honey, $1). Open daily except Sun. 8 A.M.–9 P.M.

For a leisurely *comida corrida* (set lunch, $4) on a warm afternoon, go to airy, family-run, patio restaurant **El Encanto**, at Vásquez 6, a block south and a block and a half east of the main plaza's southeast corner, tel. 953/552-0990. Find them open also for à la carte breakfast ($2–4) and *cena* (supper, $2–4) Mon.–Sat. 8 A.M.–9 P.M.

Information and Services

Change money at Tlaxiaco's plaza-front **Banamex,** at Colón 1, tel. 953/552-0166 or 953/552-0098, open Mon.–Fri. 9 A.M.–3 P.M., Sat. 9 A.M.–1 P.M. After hours, use its up-front **ATM** for cash.

MEXICAN NAMES

Nearly every Mexican, from native country folks to pure Spanish-origin bluebloods go by their Spanish-origin Mexican names. Outsiders, confounded by long handles, such as Doña Juana María López de Díaz, wonder how Mexican names got so complicated.

The preceding "Doña Juana" example is especially complicated, because it's a typical woman's name, which is generally more complex than that of a typical man.

So, let's explain a man's name first. Take the national hero, Vicente Ramón Guerrero Saldaña. Vicente is his first given name; Ramón, the second given name, corresponds to the "middle" name in the United States. The third, Guerrero, is customarily the father's first surname, and the last, Saldaña, his mother's first surname. Only on formal occasions are men referred to with all four of their names. Simply, "Vicente Guerrero" would do most of the time.

Now, back to "Doña Juana." I threw a curve at you by introducing "Doña." It's an honorific, used as "Dame," for a distinguished woman.

("Don" is the corresponding honorific for Spanish men.)

So, skipping the honorific, women's names start out like men's: First given name, Juana; second given name María, and father's first surname López.

Now, things get more complicated. For unmarried women, the naming is the same as for men. But when a woman gets married, she customarily replaces her second surname with her husband's first surname, preceded by "de," meaning "of." So, in the example, Juana is evidently a married woman, who has substituted "de Díaz" (her husband's first surname being Díaz) for her second surname, all adding up to "Juana María López de Díaz."

Thankfully, however, informal names for women also are simplfied. Juana, above, would ordinary shorten her name down to her first given name, followed by her husband's first surname: simply Juana Díaz.

All the above notwithstanding, many Mexican women do not go along with this male-dominated system at all and simply use their maiden names as they were known before they were married.

Alternatively, go to **Banorte,** at the plaza's southwest corner, tel. 953/552-0662, for similar services and ATM. Find them open Mon.–Fri. 9 A.M.–4 P.M.

Buy stamps or send letters at the *correo* (post office) on the north side of the *jardín* in front of the church, open Mon.–Fri. 8 A.M.–3 P.M., Sat. 10 A.M.–noon. Next door, at *telecomunicaciones,* tel. 953/552-0465 or 953/552-0190, you can send or receive a fax or money order; open Mon.–Fri. 8 A.M.–7 P.M., Sat. 9 A.M.–noon.

Telephone long distance or send a fax at the *caseta larga distancia,* at the northeast plaza corner next to the Hotel del Portal, tel. 953/552-0313, 953/552-0314, or 953/552-0147, open daily 7 A.M.–11 P.M.

Answer your email and access the **Internet** at the hole-in-the-wall store, on Juárez, corner of Díaz (a block north of the plaza's northwest corner). Alternatively, go to **Sircom Internet,** on Morelos, three blocks south of the plaza,

between Hidalgo and Independencia, tel. 953/552-0063; open daily 11 A.M.–11 P.M.

If you need a **doctor,** ask at your hotel desk for a recommendation or contact one of Tlaxiaco's highly recommended physicians: either **Dr. Javier Noé Alavez Cervantes,** at **Sanatorio Mitzy,** Moctezuma 4, a block and a half west from the plaza, tel./fax 953/552-0028; or general practitioner **Doctor Manuel López Hernádez,** at the ISSTE (Seguro Social) clinic, on Hwy. 125, Oaxaca direction, about a mile east of town, tel. 953/552-0750; or surgeon **Dr. Geraldo Cruz Vela,** tel. 953/552-0210.

For nonprescription medicines and drugs, try either **Farmacia La Soledad,** at Morelos 5, corner of Independencia, tel. 953/552-0159, open daily 9 A.M.–11 P.M.; or **Farmacia La Merced,** one block west at the corner of Morelos and Hidalgo, tel. 953/552-0483, open Mon.–Sat. 8 A.M.–9 P.M., Sun. 10 A.M.–2 P.M.; or **Farmacia Pronto,** half a block east of the plaza's southeast corner, open Mon.–Sat. 9 A.M.–9 P.M.

For film, development, and some point-and-shoot cameras and photographic supplies, go to Tlaxiaco's Fuji film dealer, **Foto Eureka,** on Hidalgo, two blocks south, one block east of the plaza, tel. 953/552-0249, open Mon.–Sat. 8 A.M.–9 P.M., closed Sunday.

Tlaxiaco's friendly, family-owned laundry, **Lavandería Geminis,** Capitán José Herrera 20, tel. 953/552-0708, is open Mon.–Sat. 8 A.M.–4 P.M. and 5–8 P.M. Find it two blocks west, three blocks south of the plaza.

Getting There and Away

A welter of taxis, local buses and minivans, and long-distance buses deposit and pick up a small army of passengers daily downhill on Highway 125, locally called Avenida Hipodromo.

Long-distance service includes **Sur** and **Cristóbal Colón,** from their station at Hipodromo 24 B, tel. 953/552-0182, between Independencia and Hidalgo. Buses connect east and southeast, with Teposcolula, Yanhuitlán, Nochixtlán, and Oaxaca; north with Tamazulapan, Huajuapan, Puebla, Cuautla (Morelos), and Mexico City; and south with Putla and Pinotepa Nacional on the Pacific Coast.

Also, second-class **Fletes y Pasajes** long-distance buses, tel. 953/552-0432, connect east and southeast with Teposcolula, Yanhuitlán, Nochixtlán, and Oaxaca, and south with Putla.

Drivers can connect southerly, to or from Tlaxiaco, with Putla, via Highway 125 in about 47 miles (75 km) or two hours; westerly, with Juxtlahuaca (50 miles, 80 km) also in about two hours; and easterly with Teposcolula (26 miles, 42 km) in about an hour, thence another three hours, to or from Oaxaca.

SOUTH OF TLAXIACO

Although the glorious Cascada Esmeralda (Emerald Waterfall) at the end of the road is reason enough to venture out on this 106-mile (171-km) round-trip excursion, the sights along the way make the journey doubly enjoyable. You'll gaze at a succession of mighty pine- and oak-studded mountains mile upon mile of green, terraced fields, and, oddly in contrast, one of the

most spectacularly eroded landscapes in Oaxaca. Moreover, you'll pass more log cabins here than on a trip through all of Montana and Wyoming. And if you go on Sunday, you'll get a chance to visit a pair of busy country markets. Finally, self-contained RV or tent campers can enjoy a superbly scenic natural camping site at the dramatic top of Cascada Esmeralda. The all-paved route climbs to the top of the Mixteca Alta—the 9,000-foot (2,700-meter) cool, fertile, Chalcatongo plateau—before descending to Yosundua and the subtropical Esmeralda valley, where on a clear day, folks say, you can glimpse the blue Pacific.

The Road to Chalcatongo

Drivers, start out by at least 10 A.M., because in the Mixteca (Land of the Clouds), especially in the summer-fall rainy season, sunny mornings often turn gray, drizzly, and cool by the midafternoon. By bus, go earlier, just south of the corner of Highway 125 (Tlaxiaco's Calle Hipodromo) and Independencia. Look for either the yellow, orange, and white **Unión de Transportistas Ñundeya,** minibuses, or the orange, yellow, blue, and white **Auto Transportes Yosundua** buses, which head south about every half hour, 6 A.M.–6 P.M. Drivers, take the same route and mark your odometer at the Highway 125 crossing as you start south. Best fill up with gasoline in town (gas on east, Oaxaca, side only) beforehand. There is only one gas station en route, at Chalcatongo (although stores along the way do sell Magna). If you want to eat well along the way, best take your own picnic, especially during the winter, when upcountry fresh fruit and veggie supplies are at low ebb.

At mile 10 (km 16), the road reaches an overlook where you can gaze down upon the **Magdalena Peñasco** valley, with erosion so dramatic that, like the scenic Badlands of Dakota, it's a sight in itself. The reason isn't so difficult to figure. Long ago, the people cut the trees for fuel and houses, then farmed the hills without contour terracing. They let sheep and goats overgraze the meadows, and when downpours began forming gullies, it was too late. Today the entire valley looks like a red, rutted devil's playground.

As you continue downhill, you'll see folks along the road weaving palm leaves, especially on Sunday, as they walk toward the weekly Magdalena Peñasco *tianguis* (country market). Passing the town square and market, at around mile 12 (km 19), notice one of Magdalena's major public buildings—a turquoise-blue log house—on the right.

Around mile 21 (km 34), continuing through San Mateo Peñasco, it's difficult not to be awed by the towering, stone-faced mountain on the right. In times past (or maybe even in times present) this awesomely rugged rampart, which local people call simply La Peña (The Rock), must have been a sacred mountain, with its own *Señor del Monte* (Lord of the Mountain).

Today, a cross stands partway up the slope, where the villagers climb on May 3, the Día de la Santa Cruz (Day of the Holy Cross). Although arduous, the climb to the summit appears doable with effort by fit people wearing hats and sturdy shoes and carrying drinking water. Don't attempt it, however, without permission from the San Mateo Peñasco municipal authorities, who can probably suggest a guide whom you can hire to show the way.

In contrast to the eroded Magdalena valley, the surroundings of San Pedro Molinos, at mile 28 (km 45), appear the model of progressive farming practice. Lush valley-bottom fields give way to terraced, mid-slope gardens, which lead to a crown of thick, summit forests. Molinos town is marked by its spiffy, portaled *presidencia municipal*.

Farther on, at Santa Catarina Ticúa at around mile 31 (km 50), note the uniquely picturesque three-story log house, on the right just as you arrive at the town plaza and church. Next, step across the plaza and take a look inside the brilliantly painted 18th-century church, dedicated to martyr Saint Catherine. If you're lucky, you'll arrive on November 24 or 25, when local people are celebrating Santa Catarina with processions, fireworks, sports contests, and dances. If not, at least, you can admire the Mixtec pre-Columbian floral designs on the church's walls and ceiling, and maybe afterwards, if its a warm day, you might pause for a dip in the community swimming pool outside next to the church. Finally,

after working up an appetite, stop for a break at the local restaurant, La Mixteca, on the left of the highway (southbound) behind the water tower–clock on the way out of town.

Chalcatongo

At around mile 37 (km 60), you reach high and cool, sometimes even chilly, Chalcatongo (pop. 2,000). Chalcatongo has two plazas, the first one bordered by the distinguished church, the Templo de la Natividad, whose patron is the Virgen de la Natividad. Townsfolk celebrate her with a fiesta on September 8. Chalcatongo is quiet except for Thursday, when thousands of local folks and dozens of vendors from as far as Mexico City crowd in for a big country *tianguis* market.

At the second plaza, one block ahead, one block left, stands the *presidencia municipal*. Although both plazas have a sprinkling of taco shops, only a couple places in town appear to qualify as restaurants. One is the Restaurant Tres Coronas (at the hotel, below) and Restaurant El Calvario, which you'll see at the corner of Guerrero and Insurgentes, second floor, as you continue south out of town. Both of these places have no menu and customarily offer only one entrée—usually a tasty beef or chicken stew, usually served with rice and tortillas. If you order à la carte, you'll probably have to settle for something basic, such as eggs *rancheros* or *a la Mexicana* chicken tacos, or maybe a hamburger. For salad, you usually can count on *jitomate* (Roma tomatoes) and avocado.

Chalcatongo also has the Hotel Cliserio, owned and operated by friendly English-speaking Señor Eliseo Cliserio Nicolas Valdez. His hotel stands across the plaza from the church. Unfortunately, the rooms, which rent for about $7 s, $13 d, with bath and hot water (when the heater's working), are plain to the point of drabness and could use a good scrubbing. But they'll provide a roof over your head and a blanket or two, if you need them. Look at several rooms and choose the best.

Yosundua and Cascada Esmeralda

Drivers lucky enough to arrive in Yosundua (at mile 51, km 82) on Sunday will probably find the way to the waterfall blocked by the big, colorful *tianguis*. Stroll around for a while, then detour downhill, then ahead, via the street that runs in front of the big church, **Templo Santiago Após-tol.** The church is dedicated to Saint James the Apostle, whom townsfolk celebrate July 23–26. Bus passengers should either hire a taxi or hike straight ahead from the Yosundua bus stop about 2.5 miles (4 km) and 1,000 feet (300 meters) downhill to the Cascada Esmeralda.

If you're hungry, stop by the clean, family run, home-style **Restaurant Manantial** (Restaurant Spring), named for the town's crystal-clear water source, nearby. It's open daily 8 A.M.–9 P.M., at the far, southeast edge of town, where the gravel road heads south to the Cascada Esmeralda.

If you miss the last bus back, you can stay at very rough and ready **Hotel California**, whose owner returned from California with a wad of cash and decided to build himself a hotel. He now has 31 mostly empty, extremely basic concrete-floored rooms that he rents for $8 s, $12 d, with bath and (maybe) hot water. You can't miss the place, because it's purple and green, and, except for the church, is the biggest building in town.

A better overnight option, for people who are equipped, is to set up their tent or park their self-contained RV in the informal meadow **campground** at the top of the Cascada Esmeralda, at mile 53 (km 85). There, the blue-green (a bit murky during the summer rains, however) Río Esmeralda (Emerald River) pauses a while in an inviting pool (safe only at low water) before it plunges over the cliff. The road winds another few hundred yards down a steep grade; continue on foot down a steep, short path to the foot of the falls, where you're surrounded by natural beauty. On one side, the waterfall, split into a lacy network of petite cascades, cools you with gentle spray, while on the other, far below, a grand, sun-dappled verdant valley of field and forest nestles beneath a host of sharp, soaring peaks.

EAST OF TLAXIACO

The country east of Tlaxiaco undulates over small, fertile vales and green, pine-forested hill-tops, many crowned with the ruins of ancient buried towns and cities. Two of the largest and most interesting of those ruins are at Achiutla and Huamelulpan, not far from Tlaxiaco.

San Miguel Achiutla

The archaeological site at Achiutla (ah-shee-YOO-tlah, pop. 1,000) is among Oaxaca's historically most intriguing, partly because it contains both pre- and post-conquest ruins. These include the remains of the earthquake-collapsed original Dominican church and a grand pre-conquest ruined complex, once the site of a renowned Mixtec oracle.

Getting There: The gorgeous pine-forested mountains and lush (summer-fall rainy season)

The 17th-century town church, dedicated to St. Michael, perches atop a background hill; in front of that are the ruins of the original 1558 church built atop the pre-conquest oracle temple, El Corazón del Pueblo; and in front of that is the Achiutla cemetery, honeycombed with pre-Columbian remains.

valleys you pass along the way are part of the fun of Achiutla. Bus travelers go most conveniently by the minibuses that leave for Achiutla (via Santa Caterina Tayata), from the corner of Calle Cinco de Mayo and Highway 125 (Avenida Independencia) at the northeast corner of downtown Tlaxiaco. Alternatively, bargain for a taxi to take you to the Achiutla turnoff (signed Santa Catarina Tayata) about nine miles (14 km) east of town, then catch a truck from there. If so, find out the price—ask, *"¿Cuanto cuesta a Achiutla?"* ("How much to Achiutla?")—before getting on.

The road, although gravel, is easily passable by experienced drivers in ordinary cars. From Tlaxiaco, along Highway 125, drive east about nine miles (14 km) (or west from Teposcolula about 17 miles, 27 km). Set your odometer at the signed Santa Catarina Tayata turnoff. After 1.2 miles (1.9 km), turn left at the fork. Continue through Santa Catarina Tayata (5.2 miles, 8.4 km) and follow the left fork (5.4 miles, 8.7 km). At 6.4 miles (10.3 km) pass over Río Tayata bridge and by the lovely creekside grove of ancient *ahuehuete* trees. Some of the gnarled giants, 10 feet (16 meters) in diameter, must be at least a thousand years old. The adjacent creekside meadows provide good **camping** spots. (Bring water.) First, however, get permission (usually no problem) from the municipal authorities at Santa Catarina Tayata.

At mile 10.5 (km 17) you get the first glimpse of the old San Miguel Achiutla church on the hill straight ahead. Take a left at the T (10.8 miles, 17.4 km), then right (11.2 miles, 18 km) and continue straight ahead for the old church on the right, ruins on left (12.6 miles, 20.3 km), and San Miguel Achiutla town at 14 miles (22.5 km).

Exploring the Site: The area of historical and archaeological interest lies on an airy, scenic hilltop, west of the modern town. The present church, the antique **Templo y Exconvento de San Miguel Achiutla,** stands on the rise to the south of the road. It supplanted an even older church, now in ruins, on the other side of the road, probably built atop the pre-conquest oracle temple. Beyond that rises a cemetery occupying what appear to be three pre-conquest ceremonial courtyards cut, like grand stair steps, into a

mountainside that rises another mile (1.6 km) to a high, breezy summit.

First, however, walk south across the broad atrium that leads to the present church. On your way, take a look at the pair of ponderous bronze bells, dated 1848, hanging from a rustic, ground-level *campanario.* The Dominicans built the church probably during the 1600s, several decades after the original building was begun in 1558 across the road. The new church, dedicated to Archangel St. Michael, grew into a prosperous vicarage, surrounded by a cluster of dependent congregations. Times changed, however. The once-new church is now crumbling and nearly abandoned. Its doors open regularly only for Sunday mass at 10 A.M., after which folks lock up and return downhill for an 11 A.M. mass at the church in town.

A major exception occurs during festivals, celebrating the Sacred Heart of Jesus (June 19), **Carnaval** (Sunday, Monday, and Tuesday before Ash Wednesday), and especially the **Fiesta de San Miguel** (September 21–29), when masses fill the old church every day.

The old place is well worth a look around inside. Try finding the *sacristan* (church-keeper), who's often nearby. If you're sufficiently persuasive, he might open the door for you.

You'll find the inside completely unrestored except for the gilded, baroque main altarpiece, recently refurbished after it collapsed under its own weight. In addition to the native artists' colorful floral designs, the nave walls hold a gallery of precious 16th-century paintings. Don't miss the one showing the angel St. Michael enticing a mortal into heaven. Up front, bats flit and flutter out of the baptismal chapel on the left. On the opposite side, note the unusual screened platform high on the south wall, said to have accommodated cloistered nuns who nevertheless wanted to view mass in the nave. The door on the nave's right front leads to an open courtyard, which in turn leads to the ex-convent's former working and living quarters.

Outside, across the road, the ruin of the original church probably stands atop the renowned Achiutla oracle temple. This spot abounds with legends. A Mixtec codex records that one Tilantongo queen was born from a tree in Achiutla. So powerful was Achiutla's magic that people came, believing it to be the home of an all-seeing spirit, an oracle, known then as the **Corazón del Pueblo** (Heart of the People), who, acting through the local priests, could portend future events. No less than the Emperor Moctezuma, when Cortés threatened his capital, sent emissaries to Achiutla. They asked that proper sacrifices be made to the oracle in return for a divination of the result of Cortés's threat. The answer was that Moctezuma's grand empire would be destroyed.

Past the ruined church, climb along paths through the ancient retaining walls, built by long-dead Mixtec masons, to the cemetery's upper levels. Gaze out toward the fertile Achiutla valley far below, encircled by a verdant crown of pine-capped mountains.

Nearby, scattered around you, the cemetery's oldest legible tombstones date from around 1900; many others, unreadably weathered and crumbling, appear much older. Buried beneath those—no one yet knows how deep or old—lie the relics of Achiutla's past.

Achiutla Services: Drowsy little Achiutla town downhill has a basic grocery store, a *centro de salud* (health clinic), police (at the *presidencia municipal*), and gasoline, at a store at the west edge of town.

San Martín Huamelulpan

The community museum at Huamelulpan (oo-wah-may-LOOL-pahn), about a mile (2 km) off Highway 125, three miles (5 km) east of the Achiutla turnoff, was built partly to display the artifacts uncovered at the town's important archaeological zone. The National Archaeology and History Institute (INAH) installed the museum's archaeological exhibits in 1978. Later, the local community took over and did its own oral history project during the late 1980s, which resulted in the museum's traditional medicine displays.

Note the sign on the post on the right as you reach the town plaza. It reads, roughly: "Please stop and register at the community museum and get a guide to show you the ruins." If you arrive

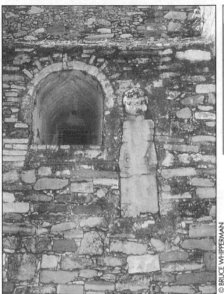

© BRUCE WHIPPERMAN

This stone skeleton, a grinning pre-Columbian god of death, is built into the church wall at Huamelulpan.

when the museum is closed, ask around for someone to guide you.

The museum, officially the **Museo Comunitario Ihitalulu** (ee-ee-tah-LOO-loo), is open regularly Wed.–Sun. 10 A.M.–5 P.M. Inside, on the left after you enter, you'll see the archaeological section first, with its especially notable monolith of Dzahui, the Mixtec god of rain, lightning, and thunder (akin to the Zapotec god Cocijo). Also fascinating are burial remains, including a complete skeleton and bowls for portions of water, food, and pulque for the afterlife. On the museum's opposite side, find the equally intriguing **traditional medicine** exhibit, detailing methods that *curanderos* (curers), *yerberas* (herbal healers), and *parteras* (midwives) use to treat their clients. Conditions commonly treated include *el parto* (childbirth), *el empacho* (stomach infections), *mal de aire* (shivering, and head and body aches; compare: malaria), and *el espanto* (soul loss, accompanied by severe anxiety). Displays illustrate many remedies, from herbal teas and *temazcal* hot baths

DUENDES: SPIRITS OF MEXICO

Once upon a time, most everyone believed that the world was full of spirits that inhabited every object in creation: trees, rocks, animals, mountains, even the wind and the stars. World mythology is replete with examples, from the leprechauns of Ireland and the fairies of Mount Tirich Mir in Pakistan, to the spirits who haunt old Hawaiian *heiaus* (temples) and the *duendes* of Mexico.

Such beliefs persist, especially in the Mixteca countryside. Eventually, many a campesino will take his children to his mountainside cornfield to introduce them to the *duendes,* the elfin beings who folks sometimes glimpse in the shadowed thickets where they hide from mortals.

At the upper end of his field, the campesino father addresses the *duendes:* "With your permission we clear your brush and use your water because it is necessary to nourish our corn and beans. Please allow us, for otherwise, we would starve."

Modernized city Mexicans, generations removed from country village life, often scoff at such antique beliefs. That is, until the family doctor fails to cure their weakened spouse or sick child. Then they often run to a *curandero* or *curandera* folk healer.

"Enduendado," affliction by an angry *duende,* the curandero sometimes diagnoses. Often, the cure is simple and savvy: teas and poultices of forest-gathered herbs; other times, it is mystical, such as "purifying," by passing an egg all over the afflicted one's body to draw out the illness, and then breaking the egg into a bowl. The shape the broken yolk takes, maybe of a snake, might determine the treatment, which may be long and intricate: massage with lotions of herbs and oils, followed by a *temazcal* (sweat bath) rubdown with rough maguey fibers, all consummated by intense prayers to the Virgin of Guadalupe to force the *duende* to cease the affliction.

Many times, the folk cure fails; other times, however, it succeeds; and with enough frequency to convince millions of Mexicans of the power of the village folk healer to purge a *duende*'s poisonous spell.

to doses of chicken blood and incantations beseeching forgiveness from earth spirits.

Exploring the Archaeological Zone: Leave time for a stroll around the archaeological zone. It was first visited in 1933 by Alfonso Caso of Monte Albán fame, and it has been intensively excavated and partly reconstructed by several others since the 1950s. Finds reveal that Huamelulpan was a small city occupied between 400 B.C. and A.D. 600, approximately the same epoch as Monte Albán.

The zone rambles extensively over many hundreds of acres, running north of town along an approximate east-west line. The most westerly discovered (but unreconstructed) remains lie on the high west-side **Cerro Volado** hilltop. The most intensively reconstructed portion is the so-called Church Group, near the church, a few hundred yards east beyond the town plaza and museum.

Start at the church itself, which has what appears to be a grinning pre-conquest god of death skeleton-monolith built into its right (south) wall. If you continue walking south along the road in front of the church, you will be passing the partly reconstructed **ball court,** reachable by ascending the rise to the left (east) of the road. Note, at the ball court's south end, the reconstructed half of its I-shaped layout. Continue east, up the second embankment, to a regal **ceremonial courtyard** climaxed on its east side with an elegant staircase and retaining walls. Climb those stairs to another level and yet another courtyard crowned by an equally elegant but smaller **ceremonial platform.**

Huamelulpan community museum volunteers lead visitors on tours of their archaeological zone, including Cerro Volado, for a fee of about $20. Arrive early and you may be able to arrange such a tour on the spot. Guides and **lodging** at Huamelulpan's tourist house dormitory can also be reserved ahead of time by leaving a message, including time of arrival and number in your party, at the Huamelulpan long-distance telephone *caseta* office, tel. 555/329-0982. Alternatively, you can reserve at the lodging through the Oaxaca government alternative tourism office, in downtown Oaxaca, at Murguia 206 (up the driveway, in the back), tel. 951/516-4828, sedetur5@oaxaca.gob.mx. (See the Tourist Yu'u Community Lodging in the Around the Valley of Oaxaca chapter for more details.) For a guided tour, contact Oaxaca Tours, in Oaxaca city, at 417 Alcalá, second floor, tel. 951/516-1005, toll-free U.S. tel. 800/446-2922, fax 951/514-6699, oaxacatours@oaxaca-tours.com.

Get to Huamelulpan by car or Tlaxiaco-bound second-class Fletes y Pasajes bus from either Oaxaca, Nochixtlán, Tamazulapan, or Teposcolula. Get off at the Huamelulpan turnoff on Highway 125, about half an hour (13 miles, 21 km) past Teposcolula. In the reverse direction, drive or ride a Fletes y Pasajes bus east from Tlaxiaco a similar 13 miles (21 km), half an hour, and get off at the Huamelulpan side-road turnoff. Continue about a mile (2 km) to the museum on the town plaza.

WEST OF TLAXIACO

This is high, cool country of pine-brushed mountains, villages, and cornfields. The people are reserved but quick to return your wave and smile. They see so few outsiders, that although they try to avoid it, they can't help staring as you pass, wondering why you've come. For at least two of these communities, Santa María Cuquila and San Miguel Progreso, visitors have an immediate reason for coming: to see the community museums.

Santa María Cuquila

The Aztecs, to whom the Cuquila (koo-KEE-lah) people were tributaries at the time of the conquest, coined the name Cuquila, which roughly translates to Snakes in the Brush. The Mixtec-speaking local people, however, previously called their village Ñu Kuiñe, which means Town of the Tiger in the local tongue.

Now, Cuquila (pop. 1,000) is organizing a museum with a number of rare artifacts, including hieroglyph-inscribed stones found in the big archaeological zone nearby, and documents from the 1580s, such as a map of the town and several yellowed pages recording a plethora of information—town borders, officials' names, events, and perhaps even a little gossip—of early colonial days in Cuquila.

The museum also displays examples of locally made present-day pottery and hand-woven *huipiles.* If you ask to see the *artesanos*—potters and weavers—at work, they would be happy to oblige if at all possible.

The museum committee is currently headed by its president, Emiliano Melchor Ayala; other current or former committee members are former president Severino Ayala, local *primaria* school teacher Nicolas Ayala, his nephew, Eduardo Escobar, and Maximiliano Ilario Santiago. All are qualified to take you on a tour (about two miles, 3 km, and two hours round-trip) to their "old town" archaeological site on a hill nearby.

Archaeologists estimate that the site was occupied for about 1,300 years, from 400 B.C. to A.D. 900. The ceremonial area, consisting of the remains of a pair of royal residences, a main plaza, two tombs, and a ball court, spreads over about two and a half acres. Expect to pay about $20 for a two-hour guided tour on foot. The Cuquila museum is open by appointment, which you can make, or better yet, ask your hotel desk clerk to make by calling the town long-distance telephone, tel. 953/554-0716.

Get to Cuquila by local minivan, or Fletes y Pasajes or Cristóbal Colón bus from Juxtlahuaca, Tlaxiaco, or Putla. By car, Cuquila is right on Highway 125, 12 miles (19 km) west of Tlaxiaco, 35 miles (56 km) east of Juxtlahuaca, or 32 miles (51 km) northeast of Putla.

San Miguel Progreso

Two miles (3 km) from the signed turnoff from Highway 125, San Miguel Progreso (pop. 3,000) welcomes visitors to its museum. The museum committee has arranged the museum displays in four different sections. First are the historic papers, such as a 1780 document defining the town limits and a copy of a 1580 *lienzo* that maps the location of buildings, roads, rivers, and town boundaries. Next comes an excellent exposition of the local wool-weaving craft, then a mock-up of a typical indigenous dwelling. An archaeological section demonstrates finds, such as stone ax blades, ceramic vases, lance points, and human burial remains, including grave offerings. A final display models the preconquest method of terraced agriculture.

The local area contains a number of interesting sites, enough for a whole day of exploring. These include three unexcavated archaeological zones: Lomatutaya (Where the People Rest), Tuxau (Fifteen Words), and Panteón de los Angelitos (Cemetery of the Little Angels). Also nearby are two sacred caves, where masses are celebrated on May 3, El Día de la Santa Cruz (The Day of the Holy Cross).

Time your arrival on the locally important festival dates, September 29 (Fiesta de San Miguel) or the fifth Friday of Lent (Fiesta de las Tres Caidas de Jesús), when you can get in on the fun of fireworks, food, dancing, processions, music, flowers, and carnival diversions.

To make sure that one of the museum committee members is available to show you the museum and perhaps lead you on a tour, make an appointment or ask your hotel desk clerk to make one by calling the town long-distance telephone operator, tel. 953/532-2656. More conveniently, you can arrange a guided tour through Oaxaca Tours, in Oaxaca city, at 417 Alcalá, second floor, tel. 951/516-1005, toll-free U.S. tel. 800/446-2922, fax 951/514-6699, oaxaca-tours@oaxaca-tours.com.

Get to San Miguel Progreso by bus or car as described for Cuquila above, except that the signed side road (off of Highway 125) to San Miguel is about four miles (6 km) past Cuquila (from Tlaxiaco) and a corresponding distance closer to Juxtlahuaca and Putla. Continue about two miles (3 km) along the side road to San Miguel.

PUTLA DE GUERRERO: LAND OF WATER

After a week traveling in the cool high, Mixteca Alta, the rush of balmy moist tropical air you enjoy when entering the upland valley of Putla de Guerrero (pop. 15,000) feels like another country. Banana trees overhang the road; mangos, in season, sell for a dime apiece; the aroma of roasting coffee scents the air; and people fill their afternoons by splashing in their favorite local swimming holes.

You might want to linger a day or two and bask in the warmth. If so, Putla's colorful market and its modicum of hotels, restaurants, and services can help make your visit interesting and comfortable.

Orientation and Sights

The town centers on a leafy *jardín,* about four blocks west, downhill from Highway 125. The *jardín,* bordered by the *presidencia municipal* on the south, a line of shops on the north, and the church, at its northwest corner, focuses community activity.

The colorful, bustling market, busiest on Sunday, is a block behind the *presidencia.* Here you'll find stalls offering the handmade textiles—*huipiles, rebozos* (shawls), *blusas,* and *enredos* (wraparound skirts)—for which Putla is well known. Materials vary from wool, homespun and woven by highland Trique women, to cottons, hand-embroidered by coastal Mixtecs.

Accommodations

Putla's best hotel is the comfortable **Hotel Beyafrey,** about three blocks south and two blocks west of the plaza, at Guerrero 9, Putla de Guerrero, Oaxaca 71000, tel. 953/553-0294. The approximately 30 high-ceilinged, clean rooms rent for about $13 s, $18 d, and $22 t, with toilets and hot-water showers, fan, TV, a restaurant, big pool and patio around in back, and parking.

Nearby, but not nearly so inviting, is the **Hotel Nieto,** corner Sonora and Guerrero, Putla de Guerrero, Oaxaca 71000, tel. 953/553-0331, about three blocks south and one block west of the plaza. The 20 rooms are stacked in three stories. Plain but clean, they rent for about $9 s or d, and $15 t, with bath, hot water, TV, and parking. Get an upper room for more light and privacy; look at more than one before moving in.

Food

You can find plenty of luscious fruits and vegetables and many inexpensive, local-variety meals in *fondas* in and around the market. For basic groceries, try the **Abarrotería Mary Carmen,** at the southwest plaza corner across the street from the *presidencia municipal.*

For a tasty pastry or pizza snack, go to the TV-free coffee nook **C and S Café** on Guerrero, across the street from the Hotel Beyafrey. Friendly owners Cristina and Silvio, who make all their pastries and roast their own coffee, say that they prefer the soft music that emanates from their speakers to television.

As for restaurants, the most visible town-center eatery seems to be the family-style **Comedor Familiar Gonzales,** on the corner at the north side of the basketball court, a block north of the jardí, open daily 8 A.M.–8 P.M. If you want something fancier, go a few doors farther uphill, to **Restaurant Don Memo** open Mon.–Sat. noon–8 P.M.

More restaurant choices are on the highway. Try **Restaurant Tito's,** decorated with a gallery of paintings, showing sentimental old-time Putla scenes. You also might say a good word to the friendly travel agent–owner, Tito Chaves, who's proud of his eclectic menu of soups, salads, and seafood, beef, chicken, and pork entrées ($3–10). Find it next to the Cristóbal Colón bus station, open daily 10:30 A.M.–10 P.M.

Also, on the highway, next door, downhill from Tito's, you can choose the clean, airy **Abarrotes-Restaurant Velasco,** tel. 953/553-0047. Find them open daily for breakfast, lunch and supper ($2–8), 8 A.M.–9 P.M.

Entertainment and Events

Ordinarily quiet Putla livens up during its regionally important fiestas. **Carnaval Putleco,** celebrated the Sunday, Monday, and Tuesday before *miércoles ceniza* (Ash Wednesday), is rich in traditional dances. Local favorites, nearly always performed, are Los Viejos (The Old Ones), El Macho, and Los Copala.

Later in the year, folks crowd the church-front atrium for the **Fiesta de la Natividad,** which kicks off on September 6 with a grand *calenda*

(procession) and flower-decorated floats, continues with a feast of fireworks on September 7, and climaxes on the following day with *peleas de gallo* (cockfights), *jaripeo* (bull roping and riding), and a big community dance.

Other times, Putla people cool off from the heat, frolicking in the mountain streams that flow past the town. You can join the fun on a hot afternoon by asking a taxi driver to take you to a *balneario* (bathing spot); one of the best is about two miles (3 km) along the highway uphill from town.

Services

You'll find nearly all of Putla's basic services near the town *jardín.* Change money or use the ATM at **Bancomer,** a block north from the *jardín's* west side, across from the basketball court, tel. 953/553-0028, open for money changing Mon.–Fri. 9 A.M.–4 P.M., Sat. 9 A.M.–2 P.M. Alternatively, go to **Banamex,** on Calle Oaxaca nearby.

The Putla *correo* (post office), is just west, next to the *presidencia municipal,* south side of the plaza, open Mon.–Fri. 8 A.M.–3 P.M. **Long-distance phone** and fax are available at the *caseta* on the *jardín's* north side, tel./fax 953/553-0030.

For routine nonprescription medicines and drugs, go to the **Pastillería de Descuento,** on the *jardín's* west side, open daily 7 A.M.–10 P.M. If you're ill, however, ask at your hotel desk for a doctor or go to see **Doctora Silvia Zarate** at her *Farmacia Popular,* at the *jardín's* northeast corner, tel. 953/553-0252, open daily 7 A.M.–2 P.M. and 4–8 P.M. Medical consultations are also available at the **General Hospital,** a block north of the *jardín's* east side, across the street from the basketball court.

Getting There and Away

Five long-distance bus lines operating from stations on or near the highway connect Putla with many Oaxaca destinations. First-class **Cristóbal Colón,** on the highway, tel. 953/553-0163, connects south with Pinotepa Nacional, northeast with Oaxaca via Tlaxiaco and Nochixtlán, and north with Mexico City via Juxtlahuaca, Huajuapan, and Puebla. First- and second-class **Sur,** at Sonora 34A, tel. 953/553-0350, downtown by the Hotel Nieto, offers approximately the same connections as Cristóbal Colón. **Fletes y Pasajes** second-class buses, on the highway next to Cristóbal Colón, tel. 953/553-0047, connect northeast with Oaxaca via Tlaxiaco and Nochixtlán; and north with Mexico City via Juxtlahuaca, Huajuapan, and Cuautla (Morelos). Additionally, second-class **Boquerón** buses (which simply stop on the highway near Cristóbal Colón) and **GMC Suburban vans,** uphill a block from Cristóbal Colón, connect south with Pinotepa Nacional and north with Juxtlahuaca, Tonalá, and Huajuapan.

For drivers, paved Highway 125 connects Putla south with Pinotepa Nacional, on the Pacific Coast via 80 miles (128 km) of winding, sometimes potholed, mountain road. Allow three hours for safety. In the opposite direction, Highway 125 and Oaxaca Highway 15 connect Putla north with Juxtlahuaca in about 37 miles (59 km). Winding and sometimes steep grades require slow going. Allow an hour and a half uphill, an hour downhill. About the same is true for the 48-mile (77-km) connection northeast, along Highway 125, with Tlaxiaco, which, for safety, requires about two hours uphill, an hour and a half down.

Northern Oaxaca

The vast, extravagantly diverse northern Oaxaca landscape encompasses three of Oaxaca's traditional geo-cultural regions: the pine-tufted northern Sierra, the fertile, tropical Papaloapan basin, and the oases of the desert-like Cañada canyon land. Here travelers ready to venture north of the Valley of Oaxaca can find their heart's content of high mountains for camping, hiking, and climbing; tropical rivers and grand, glassy lakes for fishing, swimming, and boating; crystalline springs welling from the base of emerald mountains; and country markets where people wear colorful age-old village costumes and speak ancient traditional dialects.

This chapter is organized as a grand circle tour, initially exploring the cool mountain country villages of Benito Juárez and Cuajimoloyas, as well as other villages that perch at the first high crest north of Oaxaca city. Continuing north, deeper into the mountains, visitors will find the lushly forested, wildlife-rich country around the beloved president Juárez's northern Sierra birthplace. The route continues north again, down into the luxuriantly fertile Papaloapan basin. Using the tropical river town Tuxtepec as a base, we explore the cultural and natural riches of the Chinantec and Mazatec ancestral homelands. The road heads west, into the high Mazateca, to Huautla de Jiménez, a mountain town made internationally famous by the hallucinogenic mushrooms of renowned *curandera* (indigenous medicine woman) María Sabina. Finally, while returning south toward Oaxaca city, travelers experience the warm, irrigated grove and orchard country of Teotitlán del Camino and Cuicatlán.

Northern Sierra

NORTHERN OAXACA

UP FROM THE VALLEY: BENITO JUÁREZ AND CUAJIMOLOYAS

This pair of little mountain towns perch nearly a mile (1.6 km) above the Valley of Oaxaca at the first towering crest of the cool, pine-tufted Sierra Juárez. The attraction here is not the towns themselves, but their gorgeous mountain environs and all that implies: great billowing clouds, summer wildflowers, cool crystalline spring water, and the scent of spruce and pine.

Furthermore, the communities and the Oaxaca government, in their effort to develop the outdoor touristic resources of the northern Sierra, offer a number of food and lodging options in Benito Juárez, Cuajimoloyas and, lately, in nearby Llano Grande village.

Sights

The modest houses and farms of Benito Juárez village (pop. approx. 1,000) are sprinkled along a single east-west ridge-crest road. The tourist Yu'u and the community center, **Casa del Pueblo,** with the *comedor* (dining room restaurant) and a cozy fireplace, are at the east end, uphill. At that point, signs direct you toward a number of possible diversions: You can stroll among the springs trickling downhill through the adjacent pine-shaded **Parque Recreational** or follow the sign marked Mirador, walking along the road (follow each uphill fork) about 1.5 miles (2.5 km) north to the *mirador* (viewpoint) tower atop a craggy 10,300-foot (3,100-meter) high perch. Here the view seems limitless. On clear days, early risers can even recognize the sunrise silhouette of Mt. Orizaba (elev. 18,856 feet, 5,747 meters) Mexico's tallest mountain, hundred of miles to the east. On the south side, steeply beneath you, spreads the central valley's verdant checkerboard of meadow, field, and pasture. On the north side, a succession of dark green mountain ridges stretch northward until they merge and become a deep purple silhouette on the horizon. On another day, walk or get a ride about eight miles (12 km) east, past the little settlement of

Los Llanos, to another viewpoint, the famous **Peña Larga,** a gigantic, 50-foot (15-meter) rock where you can perch to your heart's content.

Another possibility is to follow the six-mile (10-km) *sendero peaton* (pedestrian trail) by mountain bike or on foot. The tourist Yu'u manager rents the bikes ($10) and furnishes you with a guide ($12). For more information and cabana reservations, you may contact the Benito Juárez tourism manager directly, at tel. 951/545-9994. For more details and more extensive trips, see the Mountain Guides section.

Alternatively, you can simply wander around and enjoy yourself. Plenty of folks, Zapotec people (most of whom speak Spanish), are out tending their terraced cornfields, watching their cattle, and doing household chores.

Cuajimoloyas (kooah-hee-moh-LOY-ahs, pop. 1,000), four miles (6 km) east along the ridge road from Benito Juárez, is the metropolis of this part of the mountains. Besides lodging and restaurants (see Accommodations and Food), it has a pharmacy, health center, small grocery stores, and a telephone.

Your first stop should be the tourism headquarters, in the small hotel **Yacautzi** (Place of the Maguey) on the road, left side as you enter town. The manager can rent accommodation and set you up with bicycles, a guide, or both to help you explore the local **sights.** These include **El Calvario,** a sacred spring; **Cuevas del Coyote,** caves; a climb to the top of **Piedra Colorada,** a gargantuan red monolith; and a hike to **Llano de las Tarajeas,** a sylvan, wildflower-rich camping area, bisected by a trout stream, and much more.

A little farther off the beaten track, **Llano Grande** village along the same paved mountain-crest road six miles (10 km) farther east, also welcomes lovers of the outdoors. Village offerings include rustic cabanas, meals, camping, bicycles, guides, and a menu of activities. These include wildlife viewing, panoramic vistas, rappeling, and the highest local viewpoint, sacred **Yaa Tini** peak (elev. 10,600 feet, 3200 meters), where pilgrims

NORTHERN OAXACA

To Tehuacán, Puebla, and Mexico City

To Córdoba and Veracruz

Tierra Blanca

VERACRUZ

To Loma Bonita and Minatitlán

PUEBLA

Naranja Titla

Temascal Reservoir

Parque Natural Laguna de Temascal

Cerro Palma

Santa Elena

Río Lodo

Santa María Chilchotla

Sierra Mazateca

Buenos Aires

Temascal

145

Río Papaloapa

San Francisco Huehuetlán

Limestone Cave

Isla Soyaltepec

MIGUEL ALEMÁN DAM

182

Tonto

San Antonio Nanahuatipan

Eloxochitlan

San José de Tenango

San Pedro Ixcatlán

San Francisco Salsipuedes

Teotitlán del Camino

Plan de Guadalupe

Huautla de Jiménez

HOTEL VILLA DEL LAGO

Tuxtepec

182

Zoquiapan

Santa María Ascunción

Cerro Rabón (2,350 m)

Jalápa de Díaz

San Juan de los Cues

San Juan Cuatzospan

182

San Lucas Ojitlán

Mazatlán de Flores

Santo Domingo

Santo Domingo

Paso Canoa

MIGUEL DE LA MADRID DAM

Cuyamecalco

Chiquihuitlán

Flor Batavia

Cerro de Oro Reservoir

San José Chiltepec

HOTEL POSADA CHINANTECO

147

Santa María Tecomavaca

Santa María Tlalixtac

San Felipe Usila

Santa María Jacatepec

Río Valle Nacional

Río El Obispo

To Juchitán, Tehuantepec, and Salina Cruz

Santiago Quiotepec

San Miguel Santa Flor

Río Piedras

Cuicatlán

Cerro Cheve (3,255 m)

Santa María Pápalo

Valle Nacional

Zuzul

Flor de Monte

San Juan Tepeuxila

To Nochixtlán, Huajuapan, and Mexico City

San José del Chilar

Santiago Dominguillo

Las Vueltas

135

San Juan Quiotepec

San Pedro Yolóx

175

Santiago Comaltepec

Cerro Analco (3,100 m)

Río Oaxaca

Santiago Nacaltepec

San Pablo Macuiltianguis

Santa María Zoogocho

Lachichina

Camotlán

Cerro Zempoaltepetl (2,750 m)

San Juan Yaé

Yuquila Vijanos

Villa Alta

La Carbonera

Ixtlán de Juárez

Limestone Cave

CABAÑAS

Calpulalpan

Las Delicias

San Francisco Telixtlahuaca

Güelatao

Amatlán

Santa María Yalina

San Pablo Huitzo

190

Santa Catarina Ixtepeji

CABAÑAS

Lachatao

La Cumbre

Santa María Yavesia

Zoogocho

Cerro San Felipe (3,250 m)

CAMPAMENTO DEL MONTE

175

Latuvi

Las Vigas

San Miguel Cajonos

Yalalag (Saturday Market)

San Pablo Yaganiza

TOLL (CUOTA)

190

135D

San Andrés Huayapan

Cuajimoloyas

Llano Grande

Benito Juárez National Park

Benito Juárez

CABAÑAS

PUEBLOS MANCOMUNICADOS

OAXACA

Teotitlán del Valle

175

135

Tlacolula

Díaz Ordaz

190

0   20 mi

0   20 km

NORTHERN OAXACA

© AVALON TRAVEL PUBLISHING, INC.

still arrive on Easter Sunday to pay their respects to the Lord of the Mountain.

Accommodations and Food

Probably the best local accommodations are in Benito Juárez. They offer an assortment of rustic lodgings. The most economical is the large original tourist Yu'u for about 20 persons ($9 per person), with shared toilet and hot-water showers. The facility has several guest rooms, without bath, that open to a large common hall. Although a bit run-down, the Benito Juárez Yu'u is still a relatively cozy place, with a big fireplace, plenty of wool blankets, and a basic kitchen with refrigerator available for guest use. Bring your own soap and towel, and if you plan to cook, most of your own food, especially fresh fruits and vegetables. The local water is crystal pure on this mountaintop.

Besides the Yu'u, Benito Juárez also offers comfortable rustic private cabanas, with hot-water baths. The biggest is comfy and sleeps four, with fireplace, for $30. Another also sleeps four, has a kitchenette, but no fireplace, and also costs $30. Four more cozy smaller cabanas for two, with bath, rent for $9 per person. For more information and reservations, call the manager, tel. 951/545-9994, or (in Spanish) the town long-distance *caseta,* tel. 951/514-1871. You can also reserve through the government alternative tourism office in Oaxaca, Murguia 206 (up the driveway, in the back), tel. 951/516-4828, sedetur5@oaxaca.gob.mx. (If somehow you are not able to make contact with the alternative tourism office, check with the Oaxaca government tourism office, tel./fax 951/516-0123, info@oaxaca.gob.mx.)

Cuajimoloyas has a pair of tourist cabanas and a downscale hotel, the **Yacautzi,** on the road, left side, as you enter town from Benito Juárez. The hotel offers three clean, but unheated basic bare-bulb rooms with double bed, toilet, and hot-water shower, for $10.

More comfortable is the big Cuajimoloyas double **cabana,** up the hill, with two large units, sleeping four, with fireplace. Toilet and hot-water shower is shared between the two units. Figure about $30 for four. Reserve, through the town *caseta,* tel. 951/514-0601, or the government

alternative tourism office in Oaxaca, Murguia 206 (up the driveway, in the back), tel. 951/516-4828, sedetur5@oaxaca.gob.mx.

The four Llano Grande cabanas consist of two larger cabins, with bunk beds for up to four, and two smaller, with double beds, for two. Hot-water showers and toilets are shared between all cabanas. The community offers packages, including accommodation, meals, and a guide, for about $25 per day per person. Reserve through the village telephone, tel. 951/562-0419.

Alternatively, the whole mountaintop area is ripe for tent and some self-contained RV **camping.** The communities have designated at least four spots. Two walk-in-only campgrounds are close to and administered in Benito Juárez. Closest is in the **Parque Recreativo,** near the village center; and another **camping site**—with a view—about half a mile (one a km) away on foot.

Farther afield, campers may enjoy a pair of sylvan meadow campsites, with good spring water. The closest is called **Llano de las Tarajeas,** a total of about eight miles (13 km) east of Benito Juárez, past Cuajimoloyas. During the summer and fall, this meandering pine-bordered meadow is decorated with a galaxy of wildflowers—lavender buttercups, red lilies, baby blue eyes, white and yellow daisies, and many more. Water comes from a pristine brook, home to some little darting fish. (Foresters have set up a small fish hatchery here, evidently in an attempt to breed more of the little critters, some of whom become healthy adult rainbow trout.) **Las Vigas** (The Timbers), a similar meadow, also good for camping, is about four miles (6 km) farther east.

To camp at either Llano de las Tarajeas or Las Vigas, reserve ($3 per person per night) with the Benito Juárez tourism manager, tel. 951/545-9994 (or the corresponding Cuajimoloyas or Llano Grande managers). Get there by car, taxi, or hike four miles (6.4 km) east along the ridgeline through Cuajimoloyas. Continue another three miles (five km) to a Las Tarajeas sign on the left. Follow similar signs another 1.8 miles (3 km) to Llano de las Tarajeas. (The road is narrow, rough, and only marginally negotiable by passenger cars. Big RVs won't make it; smaller campers could.) For Las Vigas, back on the road, continue another mile or two past the Las Tara-jeas sign; turn left (north) at the road to Lavasia and Lachatao. Continue a few more miles to the Las Vigas turnoff on the right.

The late ecotourist influx supports a few modest restaurants in Benito Juárez and Cuajimoloyas. Best choices are **La Montaña,** run by friendly Gilda and Sergio Hilser in Cuajimoloyas, and the **Casa del Pueblo** community *comedor* in Benito Juárez.

Campers should probably arrive with all food supplies in hand. Local stores may have only minimal supplies, especially fresh fruits and vegetables.

Getting There and Away

From Oaxaca, for Benito Juárez, the best option is to ride the "Expediciones Sierra Norte" green bus that leaves Calle Ribera (the street that parallels the river) behind the *camionera central segunda clase* (second-class bus terminal) on the prolongation of Calle Las Casas on the west side of Oaxaca city. Check departure times with the Expeditions Sierra Norte, tel. 951/514-8271.

Alternatively, from Oaxaca, ride the **Sociedad Cooperativa Flecha de Zempoatepetl** bus from the same Oaxaca second-class bus terminal, headed for Cuajimoloyas (and also Llano Grande). They leave approximately six times a day for Cuajimoloyas, via Tlacolula. (They go several places, so say "*¿A Cuajimoloyas?*" before getting on.) For Benito Juárez, get off at the mountain crest, at the junction where the Benito Juárez road splits left (west). Walk or catch a ride the four miles (6 km) to the Benito Juárez Tourist Yu'u and Casa del Pueblo. *Note:* Super-fit backpackers could, alternatively, hike or thumb a ride up the car-RV route, described below, via Teotitlán del Valle.

If, however, you're in Tlacolula already, wait for the same Flecha de Zempoateptl bus, on the highway, at the corner across from the Tlacolula Pemex gas station and proceed as described above.

By car or RV, for fearless drivers only, it's quickest to drive to Benito Juárez via the spectacularly scenic Teotitlán del Valle. Turn left at the signed Teotitlán del Valle Highway 190 turnoff about 18 miles (30 km) east of Oaxaca city. Continue straight through town, uphill on an initially bumpy road. A mile or two later,

past the Teotitlán dam, the graded gravel road gets better. Ordinary cars and most RVs could negotiate it readily under dry conditions, although it would be marginal when wet. Four-wheel-drive vehicles could do it anytime. At Benito Juárez, at mountain-top, follow the Cabañas signs right (east) about half a mile (1 km) to the tourist Yu'u and the town community center, Casa del Pueblo (turn left half a block uphill past the Yu'u).

Alternatively, drivers can follow the safer but longer paved route that the bus Flecha de Zempoateptl takes: At the Tlacolula Pemex station, turn left and continue about four miles (6 km) to Díaz Ordaz village, where you turn left again. Continue winding uphill about 14 miles (22 km) to the mountain-top and a big road fork. Turn left for Benito Juárez (four miles, 6 km); continue straight ahead for Cuajimoloyas (two miles, 3 km) and Llano Grande (8 miles, 13 km).

Mountain Guide

A more convenient option is to go with well-equipped **Empresa Ecoturística Comunitaria** (Community Ecotouristic Enterprise) (sometimes known as Expediciones Sierra Norte), 201 M. Bravo, Oaxaca, Oaxaca 68000, tel. 951/514-8271, fax 951/516-7745, sierranorte@oaxaca.com, run by friendly, English-speaking Adriana Guzmán. She and her staff work in cooperation with a network of about a dozen Sierra Norte communities, called **Pueblos Mancomunados,** that include, besides the Benito Juárez–Cuajimoloyas–Llano Grande trio, Yavesia, Latuvi, Amatlán, and Lachatao. Jointly, they have established a 60-mile (100-km) signposted hiking and mountain-biking trail network and offer accommodation in rustic village cabins and tourist Yu'u.

Adriana and her staff make reservations for the cabins and help obtain access and camping permits. They also outfit and guide parties for camping, hiking, and biking outings into the mountains north of Oaxaca city, beginning in the area around Benito Juárez and Cuajimoloyas and extending north toward the other villages. They can furnish camping gear, mountain bikes, transportation, and more.

ALONG THE ROAD TO IXTLÁN

The high road to northern Oaxaca winds far uphill, climbing over lush, pine-clad crests and descending into deep river canyons to the Sierra Juárez, the mountainous birth-land of Benito Juárez, Oaxaca's beloved favorite son. Besides its historical and sentimental significance, the Sierra Juárez's pristine, thickly forested ridges and shadowed stream valleys are a natural garden of springs, meadows, caves, and waterfalls—a de facto wilderness refuge for dozens of endangered species, including all of Mexico's wild cats.

The best hub for exploring the Sierra Juárez is the small town of Ixtlán de Juárez, easily reachable by bus or car, about 37 miles (60 km) north from Oaxaca city via Highway 175.

Although Ixtlán de Juárez is a worthy destination, journeys are sometimes equally memorable for the bright moments en route. The road to Ixtlán is no exception. You might uncover some pleasant surprises while lingering along the way, such as the invitingly rustic mountain restaurant and refuge Campamento del Monte, or San Andrés Huayapan and Ixtepeji, a pair of little towns with nevertheless big gems of churches.

By bus, ride a Cuenca (koo-AYN-kah) bus bound for Ixtlán (or Valle Nacional or Tuxtepec) from Oaxaca's ADO–Cristóbal Colón first-class station, on Hwy. 190 at the north side of town. Drivers, set your odometer and head out from the junction where Highway 175 splits north from Highway 190, about three miles (five km) east of the Oaxaca city center.

San Andrés Huayapan Church and Reservoir

If you have time, detour into San Andrés Huayapan (left turnoff from Highway 175), approximately 2.5 miles (4 km) uphill from Highway 190. First of all, take a look inside the town's jewel—the distinguished, double-towered 17th-century **Templo de San Andrés.** Past the front door, admire the mural of the Last Supper in the nave and the colorful sculpture of San Andrés in the main altarpiece's central niche.

Afterward, taxi or drive to the **Presas de Huayapan** (Dams of Huayapan) a mile or two southeast of town. The pair of dams, although built for irrigation, have created a popular, scenic recreation reservoir (prettiest during late-summer high water, when no ugly bathtub-like ring scars the lakeshore), forming petite bays in the folds of the surrounding forested hillsides. Restaurants serve food, and concessionaires rent boats. Swimming, however, is not recommended, due to the lakeshore's steep incline.

Campamento del Monte

About 17 miles (27 km) north, you arrive at an attractive restaurant perched on the right, or east, side of Highway 175. Although the restaurant is worth a stop all by itself, the Campamento del Monte, Km 27, Carretera Oaxaca-Guelatao, Oaxaca, tel. 951/513-2651 (Mon.–Fri. 3–9 P.M.), a small resort of a few rustic cabins sprinkled in the pine-oak forest above the highway, offers even more. The family Pérez Chaves, who first built the restaurant, then the cabins, has named them individually: Toro de Silviero, Laguna Azul, Colmilla Blanco, and Luna de Octubre. Like their names, each is uniquely inviting, built with rustic wood, tile, and brick, with plenty of light, tree-framed mountain and forest vistas, a fireplace with lots of wood, an outdoor grill, hot-water shower bath, stove, and refrigerator (although you have to furnish your own towels, bedding, and pots, pans, dishes, and utensils). All this for about $15 per night.

Rentals are popular, so be sure to reserve, including a 50 percent deposit, at least 10 days ahead. Although their literature insists on prior reservations, they do rent to drop-ins between 3 and 9 P.M. if they have a cabin available, which is likely Sunday–Thursday. Bring mosquito repellent, especially necessary early evenings during the summer wet season.

In addition to cabin rentals, the managers also welcome day visitors for about $7 per car. Diversions include picnicking, bird- and animal-viewing, and rambling through the gorgeous pine- and oak-studded hillside to local view summits.

Santa Catarina Ixtepeji

This formerly sleepy little canyon community, at the headwaters of the Río Grande, is waking up.

Now, folks are welcoming nature lovers to enjoy their great outdoors. They've even established an easily accessible visitor's center on Highway 175 at La Cumbre, about 21 miles (34 km) from Highway 190, tel. 951/516-7898.

At the visitor's center, find out about the 4,000-acre (six-square-mile) Ixtepeji (eeks-tay-PAY-hee) nature preserve, with hiking and biking trails through shadowed spruce, pine, and oak forests past ferny dells and cold crystal-clear springs, a cascading waterfall, and spectacularly panoramic viewpoints. All this for a $4 entrance fee.

Furthermore, the Ixtepeji community invites you, after a day of such exhilarating exploring, to set up your tent in their **campamento** (campground) or stay overnight in one of their six **mountain cabanas.** Each cabaña has three bunk beds. Hot-water shower baths and toilets are shared. Expect to pay about $10 per person for a cabana, $4 for camping. Meals are also available. For more information, log on to the Ixtepeji page on Ron Mader's super website, www.planeta.com/ecotravel/mexico/oaxaca/ixtepeji.html.

Reserve Ixtepeji accommodations through the Ixtepeji visitor center, tel. 951/516-7898, or the government alternative tourism office in Oaxaca, Murguia 206, tel. 951/516-4828, sedetur5@oaxaca.gob.mx.

Bus riders, either take the Cuenca bus as described under the Along the Road to Ixtlán section, or hire a taxi to the intersection, three miles (five km) along Highway 190, east of downtown Oaxaca, where Highway 175 forks north. From there, ride the Transportes Ixtlecos bus, hourly 8 A.M.–7 P.M.; or the *colectivo* taxi Laa Yetzi 200 yards north of the Benito Juárez statue.

Drivers, at La Cumbre, 21 miles (34 km) from the Highway 190 intersection, follow the signed turnoff and simply continue for about four miles (6 km) down-mountain to the town.

While you're there, be sure to see the beloved old **Templo de Santa Catarina,** by far the biggest building in Ixtepeji. The church's main attraction (unless you plan your visit to coincide with three days of the Fiesta of Santa Catarina, around November 25) is the towering, superb Renaissance facade. Prominent are the eight exquisitely spiraled Solomonic columns, four above and four below. Notice also the facade's empty niches, which once sheltered St. John the Evangelist, St. Nicolas, and St. Michael, until they were probably toppled by an earthquake. Nevertheless, St. Peter remains, with Bible, flag, and staff, on the left, as does St. Catherine, high above, with flowing robe and sword.

AT THE SUMMIT: IXTLÁN DE JUÁREZ AND VICINITY

If a Mexican person told you that he lived in Ixtlán, you still wouldn't know where that is, for there are many Ixtláns in Mexico. The reason is twofold. The maguey plant is widespread in Mexico, and the Aztecs were so dominant at the time of the conquest that their names for local towns are still used today. The prefix *ix* refers to *ixtle,* the Aztec word for the fibers of the maguey plant. The suffix *-tlan* means land, or place of. So the many Ixtláns are all places the Aztecs named Land of the Maguey. Oaxaca Ixtlán people gave their town a unique name, honoring President Benito Juárez, by calling their town Ixtlán de Juárez.

People don't grow much maguey around Ixtlán de Juárez anymore, nor do they grow any cochineal, cultivation of which created a number of millionaires in the vicinity. Their money built the ornate old Churrigueresque churches in Ixtlán and the neighboring town of Calpulalpan.

What Ixtlán people do grow a lot of is wood, in the thick forests coating this part of the northern Sierra. Wisely, they don't cut too much of it, so their forests remain rich habitats for many wild creatures, notably, all species of Mexican native cats (notably the jaguar and mountain lion), spider monkeys, and tapirs, many of which have disappeared in other parts of southern Mexico. The diversity of species is so rich in Ixtlán's woodlands that a panel of experts convened by the World Wildlife Fund has rated the local forest as one of the world's 17 outstandingly biodiverse ecosystems. What's great for visitors is that the Ixtlán de Juárez community invites them to come see and appreciate their wild treasures through a special community-run ecotourism company.

BENITO JUÁREZ: MEXICO'S PRESIDENT FOR ALL SEASONS

Mexico's memory of Benito Juárez, its most revered president, is draped in legend. What's certain is that he was born on March 21, 1806, in the northern Oaxacan *municipio* of San Pablo Guelatao, at the hamlet of Santo Tomás Ixtlán. When his parents of pure Zapotec origin, Marcelino Juárez and Brigida Garcia, died tragically when Benito was three, his uncle took him in. After a quiet childhood, mostly spent shepherding his uncle's flocks in the surrounding hills, Benito left for Oaxaca city in December 1818 to live with his sister, María Josefa.

For Benito, this was a lucky stroke. He became part of the Maza household, where María Josefa lived and worked as a cook. In the genteel, well-to-do Maza family surroundings, young Benito gained exposure to music, books, politics, and people—not possible for a poor boy in the country. Moreover, he met Margarita Maza, who, with the blessing of her parents, later became his wife.

While living with the Mazas, Benito immediately gained the attention of priest and bookbinder Antonio Salanueva, who, recognizing his exceptional qualities, took Benito under his wing and sent him to school in town in January 1819. With Salanueva as his patron, Benito made rapid progress. He entered Oaxaca's new Scientific and Literary Institute in August 1828 to study law. Four years later,

he was a practicing attorney. He entered politics, rapidly rose from state to federal legislator, then Supreme Court judge, finally being unanimously elected governor by Oaxaca's legislature on August 12, 1849.

Guelatao, birthplace of President Benito Juárez, honors him with a bronze statue beside the "Enchanted Lagoon," depicting the time when as a poor shepherd boy Benito wandered the local hills tending his flock.

© BRUCE WHIPPERMAN

From a successful term as governor, Juárez returned to national prominence. He was elected Mexico's president for two separate terms, both interrupted, first by civil war during the latter 1850s and then by the French Intervention from 1862 to 1867. Victory over the French finally brought peace, and Juárez was elected president for the third time, in October 1871. He toiled day and night to realize his dreams for Mexico, but he died from exhaustion on July 18, 1872.

Sights

Ixtlán de Juárez (pop. 8,000), despite being the capital of its own sprawling governmental district, feels like a village, where the main evening activity is to either watch or join the kids playing basketball on the courts in the central plaza, then get *cena* (supper) before the mom-and-pop *comedores* close around 8:30 P.M. Walk three blocks in any direction and you're in the woods. But don't worry, you won't get lost. Just let the faithful chime of the plaza-tower clock lead you back.

Likewise, the landmark plaza-front *presidencia municipal,* on the plaza's north side, can help get you oriented. Main north-south streets are Sidencio Hernández on the plaza's west side, and 16 Septiembre on the east side. Crossing those is Revolución, which runs east-west, behind the *presidencia municipal.*

Ixtlán's main in-town sight is its treasured 17th-century **Templo de Santo Tomás Após-tol,** just northwest of the town plaza, behind the faithful, very proper plaza clock. The present *templo,* started by Dominican fathers around 1640, replaced an earlier all-adobe church. Construction was completed about a century later, in 1734. The first thing to notice about old Santo Tomás is that it's made of the same light green *cantera* that you see so much of in Oaxaca city's public buildings. Ixtlán's source, however, is local.

Decorating the baroque facade's summit is a bas-relief showing the dramatic confrontation of doubting Thomas with the risen Jesus. Inside, instead of the usual one golden *retablo* (altarpiece) behind the altar, several more decorate the nave walls, with gilded saints, angels, and masterfully pious 16th- and 17th-century oil paintings. The main *retablo,* behind the altar, shows the kneeling St. Thomas touching the chest of the risen Jesus, the act that, according to the Gospels, removed all doubt of the resurrection's reality. Finally, before you leave, glimpse inside the baptistery, on the right side of the nave, where Benito Juárez was baptized in 1806.

If you're lucky enough to arrive between December 19 and 22, you can join the local folks in the patronal **Fiesta de Santo Tomás Apóstol.** Festivities include tying up traffic on the highway with *calendas* (processions) while bombs blast overhead, *mañanitas* (5 A.M. masses), *jaripeo* (bull roping and riding), and the Betaza traditional courtship dance.

Ecotours

Most of the natural sights around Ixtlán are on communal land, so you must make arrangements for a guide from the community-run Ixtlán ecotour agency, **Viajes Ecoturísticos Schiaa Rua Via** (Mountain Where the Clouds Are Born), Calle 16 de Septiembre, Ixtlán de Juárez, Oaxaca 68725, tel./fax 951/553-6075, ecoturismo_ixtlan@msn.com, www.oaxacamcx.info/ixtlan, to accompany you. Tours range widely over Ixtlán's spreading 48,000-acre preserve. They include bird- and animal-watching, cloud forest hikes, mountain biking, sportfishing, cave exploring, wilderness camping, and more.

Spreading ferns and moss-hung trees are signs that you've entered the cloud forest vegetation zone around Ixtlán.

© BRUCE WHIPPERMAN

NORTHERN OAXACA

All tours leave from the agency's headquarters at the northeast corner of the town plaza. Guides are competent and well trained by the agency's guiding lights and founders, biologists Norma Angélica Montes Rodríguez and Gustavo Ramírez Santiago. Expect to pay about $25 per person per day, excluding transportation. Their office is open daily, Mon.–Sat. 9 A.M.–2 P.M. and 4–7 P.M. They also rent mountain cabanas (see Accommodations and Food).

With a guide, you can reach the natural sights by bus or by passenger car via Highway 175 north and the road southeast to Calpulalpan. What follows is a summary of the guided ecotour that, in the capable hands of Viajes Ecoturísticos, I enjoyed in a single day, driving my car. (Using local bus transportation, together with about 15 miles of hiking, fit travelers, accompanied by a guide, could cover the same ground in two days.)

First, follow Highway 175 north 18.6 miles (30 km) and turn right onto a gravel road at the red cross, labeled Zoogochi. Set your odometer. On the gravel road, follow the right fork at 1.5 miles (2.4 km); continue a total of 4.2 miles (6.7 km) from the highway to a summer wild-flower–carpeted grassy meadow on the left, known locally as **Latziruetze** (Meadow of the Thistles), with good spring water and possible wilderness tenting spots.

Continue along the same route (bear right at the first fork and left at the next two) another 2.2 miles (3.5 km) from the highway, a total of 6.4 miles (10.3 km) to **Los Pozuelos** shelter, cozy for camping (no tent needed; the sturdy roof shelters against rain). From there, you can walk the rough jeep track a quarter mile (.4 km) uphill to the *mirador* tower, where on a clear day you can see 18,700-foot (5,700-meter) Volcán de Orizaba, Mexico's highest mountain, jutting above the northern horizon.

Also from the Los Pozuelos shelter, walk the trail signed **Camino Real,** and you will be following the route of long-vanished Aztec, Zapotec, and Mixtec traders, who trekked between the Gulf Coast and the Valley of Oaxaca. A few hundred yards along the trail downhill (actually about 320 paces from the shelter) you'll see a big, standing tree trunk on the left; at the end of a rough path about 200 feet (60 meters) downhill is a permanent spring, fine for drinking.

Around the spring, you can't help but notice the long clumps of moss hanging eerily from the trees. This is a sure sign that you're in the **cloud forest,** a remnant island of Ice Age flora, with many species, such as wild begonias (look for clusters of their small-blossomed magenta flowers), ferns, dwarf bamboo, liquid amber, and many others in common with the mountains of the southeastern United States. Here in the Sierra Norte of Oaxaca, the cloud forest covers the humid Gulf-facing northern slopes at altitudes between 6,500 and 10,000 feet (2,000 and 3,000 meters).

Next, return to Ixtlán and head out to explore a hidden cave, spring, and waterfall all in one. Go by the road to Calpulalpan from the southeast edge of Ixtlán. About four blocks east of Highway 175, follow the paved road past the lumber mill for 3.2 miles (5.1 km), where you turn left onto a gravel road. Follow about a mile (1.6 km), or as far as you can, by car. Park and continue on foot downhill. Before the creek, go left at the rough trail, uphill into the woods. After about 300 feet (90 meters), you'll be at **Arco de Yagela,** a cave that you approach via a yawning, stalactite-walled rock amphitheater (thus *arco,* or arc). Just inside the cave's mouth, a waterfall splashes into springs welling up from beneath the rocks. The cave itself, whose dark cavity beckons a few feet behind the waterfall, can be accessed only with an expert guide and equipment. It has not been completely explored. A small party could camp on the small, level dry space in the arc to the left of the cave mouth, or a larger party could spread out in the big open spot across the creek.

Calpulalpan

Little Calpulalpan (pop. 3,000) perches on its hillside about six miles (9.6 km) east along the road from Ixtlán. The town's pride is its church, the **Templo de San Mateo,** completed by the Dominicans in 1718. Ordinarily serene, the church grounds overflow with merrymakers during the **Fiesta de San Mateo,** which climaxes yearly on September 21.

The church's renovated interior soars to a magnificent wooden ceiling. Charmingly naive designs painted by early native artisans decorate the front, below the choir, while a pair of angels, following Jesus' exhortation to become "fishers of men," dangle fish from opposite sides of the front altar. Lining both side walls, several elaborate baroque *retablos* display a gallery of colorful saints and pious 18th-century oil paintings.

Uphill a few blocks from the church, the town *centro de salud* (government health clinic) has a unique twin, the **Centro de Medicinas Tradicionales** (Center of Traditional Medicine), across a connecting patio. An herb-drying apparatus out front gives hints of the treatments practiced by the traditional healers (hours Mon.–Fri. 9 A.M.–2 P.M. and 4–7 P.M.) inside the conventional-appearing modern white stucco building.

Guelatao

A government-constructed monumental **Plaza Cívica** has converted this modest mountain town on Highway 175 two miles (3 km) south of Ixtlán into a shrine for beloved President Benito Juárez, who was born nearby on March 21, 1806.

Juárez's timeless credo, *"El respecto al derechos ajenos es la paz"* ("Respect for the rights of all is peace"), marks the museum, on the plaza, two blocks uphill from the town highway crossing. Inside, glass cases preserve a few precious mementos: a photograph, Juárez's death mask, a letter, a diary, a graduation certificate from the seminary in Oaxaca, and a model of the renowned black carriage in which Juárez for years fulfilled his duties of office, one jump ahead of his enemies.

Also on the plaza is a bronze of Juárez's mother, Brigida Garcia, and, at the *presidencia municipal*, a bust of Juárez, together with the historic letter that Juárez wrote to his ambassador in the United States, opposing the meddling of the United States in Mexican affairs.

Just north of the plaza, a shady path borders the petite spring-fed lake from which the town derives its name, in Zapotec, Guelatao (gooaylah-TAH-oh), which translates as Enchanted Lagoon. On the lakeshore, see the famous sentimental bronze sculpture of young Benito, the humble shepherd boy, tending his flock.

The local community joins with the entire country in celebrating the memory of Benito Juárez, "Benemérito de las Américas" ("Hero of the Americas"). Yearly, on March 21, Mexico's president and Oaxaca's governor kick off a six-day fiesta of tournaments, fireworks, and a whirl of traditional dances by performing groups from a host of Zapotec communities.

Accommodations and Food

Viajes Ecoturísticos recommends the competently managed local **Casa de Huéspedes La Soledad,** Calle Francisco Javier Mina, Barrio de la Soledad, Ixtlán de Juárez, Oaxaca 68725, tel. 951/553-6171, with about 12 clean basic rooms (two with private baths, the rest with shared bath) $7 s, $9 d, and $12 t. Reserve ahead.

Also recommendable is the **Hotel Casa del Cielo,** on Sidencio Hernández, across from the Jiménez grocery, just downhill from the plaza's southwest corner, tel. 951/553-6119, with four rooms, with hot water, above the back patio. Rates run about $18 s or d, $20 t. Call for reservations.

Furthermore, Viajes Ecoturísticos invites visitors to stay in their forest **cabanas** near Arco de Yagela (see Ecotours) a few miles out of town. Facilities include four rooms with five bunks each, shared toilet and hot-water showers, fireplace, and dining room, for about $9 per person. Reserve through them, tel./fax 951/553-6075, ecoturismo_ixtlan@msn.com, or through the government alternative tourism office in Oaxaca, Murguia 206, tel. 951/516-4828, sedetur5@oaxaca.gob.mx.

Ixtlán offers several **food** possibilities. Stock up on fruits and vegetables during the Monday **market,** on the town plaza. Otherwise, for some fresh items and a pretty fair grocery selection, go to **Abarrotes Jiménez,** on Servidio, just downhill from the plaza's southwest corner.

Ixtlán supports a few restaurants around the plaza. Best is **Restaurant Jiménez** (open daily 8 A.M.–8:30 P.M.). Guelatao, two miles downhill, also has some restaurants, such as **El Tío,** across the street from the plaza and museum.

After hours, in Ixtlán, eat at the taco stands around the plaza.

Services

Nearly all of Ixtlán's services are available near the plaza. The bank, **Banorte,** at the corner of Revolución and 16 de Septiembre, a block uphill from the plaza, changes money Mon.–Thurs. 9 A.M.–3 P.M., Fri. 9 A.M.–5 P.M. You can also visit the town *biblioteca* (library) next door to the bank.

The *correo,* also next to the bank, is open 9 A.M.–1 P.M., 3–6 P.M. For public fax and money orders, go to *telégrafos,* at the plaza's northeast corner, open Mon.–Fri. 9 A.M.–3 P.M. After hours, you can also send a fax at the Jiménez long-distance telephone and fax, next to the Jiménez grocery, tel./fax 951/553-6097 or 951/553-6098.

If you get sick, go to the *centro de salud* (government health clinic) on Revolución behind the *presidencia municipal,* open 24 hours. Alternatively, consult one of the towns **private doctors.** Your choices are Dr. Javier Salazar Ventura, across Revolución from the *centro de salud,* with hours Mon.–Thurs. 4–8 P.M., or Doctora Ofelia Maldonado Ruiz, at her **Farmacia La Soledad,** 16 de Septiembre 17A, two blocks uphill from the plaza, tel. 951/553-6003, open 8 A.M.–3 P.M. and 5–9 P.M.

Both the *gasolinera* (gas station) and the **bus station** are on Highway 175, about three blocks west of the plaza. The second-class line **Cuenca de Papaloapan** provides several daily connections south with Oaxaca city and north with Valle Nacional, Tuxtepec, and intermediate destinations.

Into the Papaloapan

Humid, tropical air, moving gently westward from the Gulf of Mexico, cools, clouds, and drops a deluge of rain on the northern slope of the Sierra Madre de Oaxaca. The water collects and cascades down the mountains, gathering into great, rushing rivers that finally deepen and wind slowly through a grand tropical lowland plain called the Papaloapan (pah-pah-loh-AH-pahn), after the river system that drains it. The Tonto, the Santo Domingo, and the Valle Nacional join near the town of Tuxtepec to form the Río Papaloapan. The rivers are the region's prime asset—at high elevations on the Sierra's northern slope, the waters nourish vast, thick forests: pine-oak at the higher elevations and a fantastically lush, tropical hardwood rain forest that spreads downhill into the valleys. There, farmers have replaced the forest with rich fields of corn and tobacco, great thickets of rubber trees, and, in the shady underlay, plantations of shiny-leafed coffee bushes. The government, moreover, has tamed and harnessed the rivers, gathering them into a pair of immense reservoirs—Temascal and Cerro de Oro—for irrigation, recreation, and electric power.

VALLE NACIONAL: LAND OF SPRINGS

As the rainwater makes its way to the valleys, it sometimes wells up as crystalline, mountain-foot springs before gathering into rushing rivers. One of the loveliest of these spring-fed rivers collects at the foot of the Sierra Chinantla, a spur of the Sierra Madre de Oaxaca. It rushes downhill past the town of Valle Nacional, where it's called the Río Valle Nacional.

Valle Nacional (pop. 10,000) is interesting mostly as a springboard to the lush valley and water country that winds north 20 miles (32 km) from its outskirts. The town itself is a commercial service center for the local *ranchos* (ranches) and *fincas* (farms). Although Valle Nacional is an important coffee-producing center, it would be much easier to get an irrigation pump here than a cappuccino. Lunch-table talk centers mostly around crop prices and government plans for repairing the Oaxaca highway. Although nearly everyone in town has abandoned the original Chinantec tongue for Spanish, things change on Sunday during the big weekly *tianguis* (native market). Then, you'll most likely

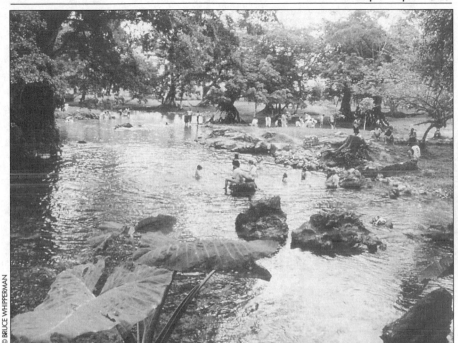

© BRUCE WHIPPERMAN

A swim in the crystal waters of Balneario Monte Flor and a picnic under a spreading tree nearby make for the perfect way to spend a relaxing afternoon.

rub shoulders with plenty of Chinantec-speaking people, including women in colorful, striped, local *huipiles*.

Besides Sunday, other good times to arrive in Valle Nacional (officially San Juan Bautista Valle Nacional) are during the local fiestas, in memory of Saint John the Baptist around June 24, and, even bigger, the **Fiesta de San José,** celebrated for three days beginning March 18. During these times, *calendas* (processions) and floats block the street, fireworks boom overhead, masses fill the church, and merrymakers dance in the plaza.

Valle Nacional Springs

A pair of nearby *balnearios* (developed springs) are perfect for a relaxing afternoon picnic or a pleasant camping overnight. **Balneario Monte Flor,** at what seems the loveliest of the valley springs, is at Cerro de Marín village, Km 43,

about three and a half miles (6 km) north of Valle Nacional and about 17 miles (27 km) south of Tuxtepec. On the river side of Highway 175 northbound, watch for the small *museo comunitario* sign and rough entrance driveway on the right, at the last village *tope* (speed bump).

Downhill, below the village, under grand, spreading trees, cool, crystalline water wells up beneath a great hillside monolith into an idyllic natural bathing pool. Kids run around, families splash in the water, chickens scratch in the grass, while downstream, women do their weekly wash. Especially on weekends and holidays, vendors set up tarps and offer barbecued beef, pork, and chicken and soft drinks.

Back uphill, in the broad grassy village commons, ask and someone may be available to open the community museum for you. (Although the keeper was out of town when I was there, folks told me that the museum displays

© BRUCE WHIPPERMAN

The clear blue waters of Zuzul natural spring make it everybody's favorite on a warm day.

include a collection of locally discovered archaeological artifacts.)

Good **camping** is available (walk downstream from the spring source a couple hundred yards) at the private paradise of friendly Diego Alonzo Francisco and his family. They offer a several grassy acres shaded by big old trees, with a few chickens and turkeys pecking around, dogs, and lots of *toronjas* (grapefruit) and mangos in season.

On holidays, folks crowd in, but on any other day you'd have the place nearly to yourself for $1 per person. You may put up your tent, or pull in your self-contained RV, for about $4 a day. Señora Alonzo furnishes all of the drinks and home-cooked food you can eat in the adjacent restaurant. If you prefer, try your luck at fishing for *mojarra* or *pepesca* in the spring for your dinner. The family (or a neighbor) might have a spare room for the night if you have no RV or tent.

Queen of the valley's bathing springs is the local favorite, **Balneario El Zuzul,** a name every-

one from Valle Nacional to Tuxtepec knows fondly. Part of the fun is getting there, because you have to cross the bridge over scenic, swift-flowing Río Valle Nacional. Once across, you see what the fuss is all about: a big, round, stone-edged blue pool of clear, cool spring water, which wells up from the depths for everyone's enjoyment, a perfect antidote for a hot afternoon.

Surrounding the pool is a shady, grassy park, great for **tent camping.** If no one seems to be in charge, you might still ask if it's OK to camp. Ask *"¿Es bueno campar?"* You might have to look around for a while before someone understands you, because the standard dialect at Zuzul is Chinantec. Bring your food and drinking water (although on weekends, folks will probably be around, selling most of what you need).

Get there via a turnoff road (signed in the southerly direction) between Km 36 and Km 37, about seven miles (11 km) north of Valle Nacional, or 15 miles (24 km) south of Tuxtepec. Follow the turnoff and continue to the riverbank and over the bridge for a total of about .4 mile (.6 km) until you reach the Zuzul parking lot and spring.

Practicalities

Valle Nacional has one main business street, Highway 175, locally called Avenida Benito Juárez, where you'll find most basic services, except for a bank. The town plaza (which accommodates few businesses) is on the right side, northbound, approximately at the center of town.

Of the town's three hotels, the best appears to be the downscale **Hotel Valle,** at Calle 2 Poniente 3, Valle Nacional, Oaxaca 68480, on a side street a few blocks south of the plaza, three doors from the highway. It offers 16 bare-bulb but acceptably clean rooms in a two-story building, with tepid-water baths. Rates are $8 s, $10 d.

Stores along the main street, notably **Frutería Las Mexicanas,** sell plenty of luscious fruits, while *abarroterías* (grocery stores) such as **Las Triunfada,** sell lots of groceries, and a parade of *taquerías, loncherías* and *refresquerías* supply plenty more.

One of the town's best restaurants is the very clean, refined **Desgarenes,** Juárez 29, tel. 287/877-4005, beneath the luxurious big *palapa* on the left side of the street a few blocks north of the plaza. Open daily for breakfast, lunch, and early supper, 10 A.M.–6 P.M.

Find the *correo* (post office) and *telégrafos* (money orders and fax), open Mon.–Fri. 9 A.M.–3 P.M., at the *presidencia municipal* on the plaza. Do your telephoning at a pair of Ladatel card–operated street telephones, on the town plaza's east side.

For a doctor, go to the town *centro de salud* (government health clinic), tel. 287/877-4126; turn east at the sign at the north (Tuxtepec) end of town; continue a block, off the highway.

Gasoline is available at the Pemex station, at the north end of town.

Getting There and Away

The best way to reach Valle Nacional is on a Cuenca de Papaloapan second-class bus. From the bus station in the middle of town, buses connect north with Tuxtepec and south with Oaxaca, including many intermediate destinations.

From Oaxaca, drivers should follow federal Highway 175 about 110 miles (177 km) north, via Ixtlán, to Valle Nacional. The route, although well-maintained much of the way, winds nearly continuously, with a number of steep grades along most of its length. Furthermore, at this writing, severe ruts and worn pavement slow traffic significantly for about 30 miles (48 km) around the summit between Ixtlán and Valle Nacional. Allow about five hours, either direction, for the entire trip from Oaxaca.

SANTA MARÍA JACATEPEC

In between Valle Nacional and Tuxtepec, Jacatepec (pop. 3,000) is a village of friendly, frankly curious, Chinantec-speaking folks. Well worth a stop, it's tucked on the far side of the river, once accessible only by boat or a *puente colgante* (pedestrian suspension bridge). Now, a new automobile bridge connects Jacatepec to the main road, but it's still a quiet little place, fine for a *refresco* (refreshment) and a stroll around town. Also, be sure to walk across the hanging bridge. You'll see it about 300 feet (90 meters) upstream from the highway bridge. If you like the place, ask around for a room for the night. Say *"¿Hay cuarto para la noche?"* and someone may be able to oblige. Like most of the houses, it will probably be a clean abode with a cement floor, surrounded by a yard full of leafy plants; it might even have a sturdy, thatched palm-leaf roof.

While you're there, take a look inside the church at the far end of the town's main street. You'll see a rare surrealistic Catholic altar, set with Jesus on the cross amid an apocalyptic landscape, with the town's patron, the Virgen de la Concepción, the only apparent ray of hope, floating above. Jacatepec is about 11 miles (18 km) north of Valle Nacional, or the same distance south of Tuxtepec.

Enliven your Jacatepec visit by arriving during the community's two major festivals, on August 15, celebrating their Virgen de la Concepción, and on April 23, honoring San Jorge (St. George). Folks flood into town from all over Mexico, the United States, and Canada for tearful reunions. They honor their holy

Despite the existing automobile bridge to town, the people of Santa María Jacatepec prefer the leisurely stroll over the Río Valle Nacional via the *puente colgante* (hanging bridge).

patrons with processions and *mañanitas* (early masses), then let loose, with carnival rides and games, plenty of old-fashioned country food, favorite old dances, and climax the whole thing by enjoying rainbows of fireworks that paint the night sky.

SAN JOSÉ CHILTEPEC

Chiltepec (pop. 3000) is a friendly little Chinantec town with lots of thatched houses surrounded by yards abloom with bananas, red and yellow hibiscus, and crimson torch ginger. Chiltepec is a ripe prospect for an overnight, mainly because of its inviting hotel and pair of riverside *balnearios* (springs). Visitors also enjoy a sprinkling of *comedores* (dining room restaurants) and a modicum of services, including post office, long-distance telephone, health center, doctor, and pharmacy.

The **Balnearios Mingo** and **Cocos** are relaxed local-style places on the winding Río Valle Nacional, with food *palapas* and plenty of shoreline for sunning, frolicking, and splashing. They're best during the warm winter-spring season, when the water is clear and inviting. During the summer rains, the high, sometimes muddy river water sends most bathers to Balnearios El Zuzul or Monte Flor. Get to the Mingo from the highway by following the signed side road at the south end of town. Cocos is just off the highway; turn at the sign about a mile (1.6 km) north of town. It has plenty of grassy space beneath a palm grove, perhaps just right for tenting or parking your RV.

The hotel **Posada la Chinantla,** right in the middle of town at Benito Juárez 17, San José Chiltepec, Oaxaca 68456, tel. 287/874-7031, would be fine for an overnight. Guests enjoy a shady *palapa,* with comfortable chairs for sitting, set in a flowery garden patio. Six clean, thoughtfully decorated rooms, with hot-water baths and fans, rent for about $8 s, $9 d.

TUXTEPEC: RIVER COUNTRY

Tuxtepec (pop. 140,000), Oaxaca's second-largest city, is the administrative and commercial center of the rich governmental district of the same name. For at least a millennium, the town, at its strategic river-junction location, has been an important trading center. Archaeologists believe that the Popoluca people, direct inheritors of the ancient Gulf Coast Olmec mother culture, first settled Tuxtepec perhaps 2,000 years ago.

History

The name Tuxtepec is the Spanish version of the town's Aztec label, Tochtepec, or Hill of the Rabbits, which probably describes the town's original site, atop some low hills about a mile and a half (two and a half km) west of present downtown Tuxtepec.

At that vital spot, Tuxtepec's early Popoluca people became traders and transporters for the valuable goods—cacao, copper, cotton, feathers, gold—of upstream producers, notably the Mazatecs and Chinantecs. Both still occupy their ancestral homelands: the Mazatecs (People of Mazatlán, Land of the Deer) between the rivers Santo Domingo and Tonto, west of Tuxtepec, and the Chinantecs (People Atop the Mountains) in the basin of the Río Valle Nacional, to the southwest.

The ambitious Aztec emperors, expanding their domain in the 1400s, saw strategic Tuxtepec as a key to realizing their dreams of grandeur. Aztec forces under Moctezuma I subdued Tuxtepec in the 1460s. They built a ceremonial pyramid, known locally as the Castillo de Moctezuma, which still stands in a west-side residential neighborhood.

Aztec governor-generals commanded a Tuxtepec garrison of several thousand warriors for two generations, putting down rebellions and enforcing tribute from Tuxtepec's many subject towns. The codex Mendocino recorded the yearly spoils, including: "eight hundred loads of . . . red and white blankets . . . eighty bundles of quetzal feathers . . . twenty loads of clear amber, set in gold . . . twenty loads of quartz, enameled

and finished with gold . . . 200 loads of cacao . . . twenty thousand rubber balls. . . ."

Hernán Cortés, almost immediately upon marching into the Aztec capital in 1519, asked Moctezuma II of his empire's source of gold. Moctezuma told him, "In Tochtepec the people wash the soil in bowls with water, and afterward, small grains of gold remain." He went on to say, "Not far from Tochtepec are some mines, said to be worked by Zapotecs and Chinantecs, who are not our subjects. If you desire to send soldiers to investigate, I will furnish emissaries to accompany them."

Cortés immediately dispatched his first gold-searching expedition outside of the Valley of Mexico, to Tuxtepec. They eventually brought back what was estimated to be 1,000 pesos' worth—perhaps a small sackful—of gold dust and small nuggets.

In late 1521, Gonzalo de Sandoval, after passing through the Valley of Oaxaca, took possession of Tuxtepec for Spain. Cortés instructed him to found a new town at Tuxtepec and name it Medellín, after the town in Spain where Cortés was born. Although the name Medellín didn't stick, Cortés persuaded the Spanish king to award him Tuxtepec as part of his Marquesate.

Tuxtepec was only a minor player in Mexican colonial and Independence history until it jumped onto the national stage in 1876 when Porfirio Díaz "pronounced" against the reelection of President Lerdo de Tejada. Díaz, a war hero and liberal ally of the revered late President Benito Juárez, threatened civil war. A group of his supporters organized in Tuxtepec, where they formulated the **Plan de Tuxtepec,** which reasserted the principles of the Reform Constitution of 1857 and invented the slogan "¡No Reelección!" opposing reelection of the president, a principle that remains as Mexico's law of the land to the present day.

Lerdo de Tejada, nevertheless, refused to step down. So, with the entire state of Oaxaca behind him, Díaz marched on Mexico City. Soon, Tejada fled the country and Díaz took brief de facto control of the government on November 28, 1876. Shortly thereafter, Congress endorsed his action. Díaz served as legal president until

1880, as governor of Oaxaca from 1880 to 1884, then resumed the presidency, ignoring *¡No Reelección!* until revolution forced him into exile in 1911.

Orientation

Tuxtepec is a modern town that spreads for two or three miles along the steep bank of the broad Río Papaloapan, which flows nearly due east past Tuxtepec's busy downtown. The main business streets begin at the Highway 175 bridge at the west end and continue for about a mile (one and half km) east to the town plaza. Moving away from the river, the main streets are Independencia, 20 de Noviembre, 5 de Mayo, and Libertad. A fifth street, quieter, river-view boulevard El Muro also runs parallel to the river, beginning at the east end of Independencia and gradually curving northerly, then westerly, until its course is completely reversed as it runs west along the north side of town.

Unlike most Mexican towns, Tuxtepec's main plaza, the **Parque Benito Juárez,** is not at the center of Tuxtepec, but rather at the east end, where the *presidencia municipal* and the town church, **Templo de San Juan Bautista,** face adjacent sides of the plaza.

A Walk Along the River

Although Tuxtepec owes its existence to the Río Papaloapan, the town has pretty much turned its back on the river ever since trucks and trains have replaced the rafts, canoes, and barges that used to carry small mountains of cotton, rubber, coffee, and lumber from the upstream hinterlands. Nevertheless, a walk along the river is an entertaining route to enjoying Tuxtepec. Avoid the heat by starting out in the morning or late afternoon from the de facto town center—judging by the hustle and bustle—at the corner of Libertad and Matamoros, three short blocks from the river, about halfway between the highway and the plaza. Here, buses arrive and depart with loads of passengers. While people wait, a host of vendors hawk a varied assortment of goods, from CDs and socks to mangos and machine screws. A number of street-front *comedores* and *loncherías* provide hearty meals and snacks.

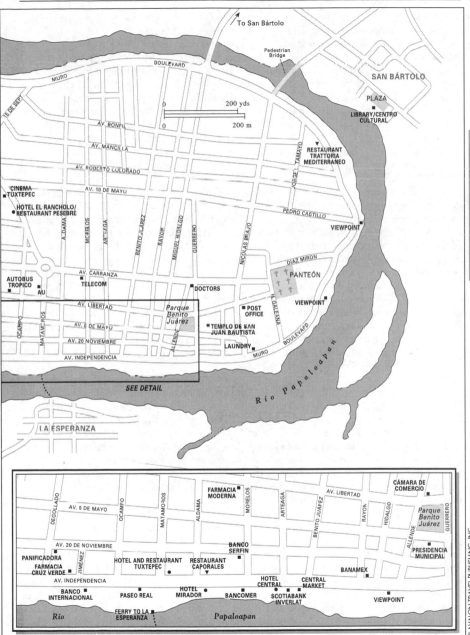

From there, head along Matamoros toward the river. At the end, Independencia, turn left to the small riverfront square, **Paso Real,** nearly immediately on the right. Here you can enjoy the river view, the breeze, and, if it's evening, perhaps a radiant sunset mirrored from the river's glassy surface. Descend the stairs to the dock, and, for fun, ride the **riverboat** that ferries folks across to **La Esperanza** village on the opposite bank.

Continue east along Independencia two more blocks to the **market** (biggest on Sunday). Find the stairs (inside, on the left) and climb to the second level. Here, take a table at one of the *fondas* (small restaurants) and enjoy a refreshment while feasting on the river view.

While at the market, be sure to visit **Artesanías Mitla** handicrafts shop, just inside the market's street-front central doorway entrance. Friendly proprietor Señora Anita Morales, who is actually from Mitla, in the Valley of Oaxaca, offers many fetching local woodcrafts, plus black pottery from Coyotepec. Find her open Mon.–Sat. 9 A.M.–8 P.M., Sun. 9 A.M.–2 P.M.

Other stores in the market you might check out are the **piñata and party goods** store (stall 42), and the **huipiles** of Señora Eva Cruz (stall 24).

Hanging Bridge to San Bártolo

Enjoy a scenic diversion by continuing east, to the end of the downtown at Independencia. Either on foot, or by taxi, continue straight ahead along airy river-view boulevard El Muro, following (a total of about half a mile, 1 km) along as the river bends northerly to the *puente colgante* (hanging bridge). Cross over to **San Bártolo Tuxtepec,** a sleepy village of yesteryear. Turn right at the first street and stroll up to the town *jardín* (garden) and library, where spreading, shady trees frame the view back across the river. One of the few times that San Bartolo wakes up is during its **fiesta** on August 23 and 24, when, besides the feasts, fireworks, processions, and masses, the town sponsors musical performances, often including marimba and local-style *música cuenqueuña.* If drowsy San Bártolo tempts you to linger, a few taco stands in the park and a sprinkling of restaurants along the main street can supply refreshments.

El Castillo de Moctezuma

This is a 15th-century unreconstructed ceremonial pyramid uncovered around 1916, now the centerpiece of a small neighborhood park in a Tuxtepec west-end suburb. Archaeologists believe that despite its *castillo* label, it was not built as a castle or fortress, but probably served as both a signal post and a ceremonial site for the populous Tuxtepec Aztec colony from around 1460 to 1520.

El Castillo rises gradually from the west side in three steps, to a height of about 25 feet (eight meters), and drops precipitously on the east side. Its surface is littered with crumbling masonry walls, which, on the north side, appear to open to a niche or tunnel.

Get there via Calle Reforma, the last street, Tuxtepec side, before the Highway 175 bridge. Turn right and continue three blocks; turn left at the T. Continue four more blocks to a store with a big blue Pepsi sign. That's Calle Ruinas; turn right and continue one block to the park and ruins at the corner of Calles Ruinas and Tabasco.

Accommodations

Tuxtepec accommodates its many business visitors with a number of good hotels. With few, if any, exceptions, the fancier establishments lie along west-side Boulevard Benito Juárez, the northern prolongation of Highway 175, or in the quieter neighborhoods away from the downtown. The cheaper, more workaday accommodations are in the busy downtown either on, or near the river.

Of the downtown good choices, the best is probably the **Hotel Central,** which occupies a choice riverfront perch at Independencia 565, Tuxtepec, Oaxaca 68300, tel. 287/875-0966 or 287/875-0913, fax 287/875-0801. Of the hotel's 23 rooms, reserve one of the three best, either numbers 122, 119, or 107 along the airy upper view walkway, overlooking the river. Rooms themselves are clean and simply but invitingly decorated. Rates are about $16 s, $19 d, with fan, $18 and $20 with a/c. All come with private hot-water baths, TV, phone, parking, and a good restaurant downstairs. Credit cards are not accepted.

A few doors west and attractively renovated is the **Hotel Mirador,** also overlooking the river, next to the Paso Real ferry dock, at Independencia 531, Tuxtepec, Oaxaca 68300, tel./fax 287/875-0652, 287/875-0500 or 287/875-0797. Of the 51 attractively decorated rooms, reserve one of the second-floor ones, numbers 219–223, along the quieter, upper river-view corridor. Rentals run about $18 s or d with a/c, $16 with fan only; all with TV, phone, hot-water bath, and parking. Credit cards are not accepted.

Half a block west is the **Hotel Tuxtepec,** Matamoros 2, Tuxtepec, Oaxaca 68300, tel. 287/875-0934, a few steps off Independencia in the middle of downtown. Lacking a river-view location, the Hotel Tuxtepec management makes up for it by trying harder. Past the reception and appealingly airy streetfront restaurant, the small but attractive lobby, set around a bubbling fountain, leads upstairs to 40 immaculate, comfortably furnished rooms. Rentals run a reasonable $16 s, $19 d fan only; $20 and $23 with a/c, all with baths, hot water, and parking, but credit cards are not accepted.

Moving west half a mile (1 km), three blocks from the highway and somewhat up the economic scale, try the renovated four-star **Hotel Playa Bruja,** at Independencia 1531, Tuxtepec, Oaxaca 68300, tel./fax 287/875-0325. The hotel's 40 clean, comfortably furnished rooms rise in three stories around a small inner pool patio. Rates are about $26 s, $30 d, $34 t with a/c, TV, phone, parking, and a restaurant-bar. Credit cards are not accepted.

On the highway, a block from the bridge, stands Tuxtepec's best value hotel, the spacious four-star **Hotel Hacienda** at Blvd. Benito Juárez 409, Tuxtepec, Oaxaca 68300, tel./fax 287/875-1500, 287/875-1621, 287/875-1732, or 287/875-1998, haciend@tuxcom.net.mx. Past the entrance and parking, relegated thoughtfully to the outer periphery, the reception leads to a cool, air-conditioned restaurant bordering a relaxing pool patio and shady tropical garden. The 60 semi-deluxe rooms in three-story tiers are secluded, clean, and comfortable. The most attractive rooms have small

balconies overlooking the garden (ask for *"balcón con vista del jardín, por favor."*) For such amenities, rooms rent from a reasonable $30 s or d, with a/c, hot-water bathrooms, cable TV, phone, parking, and credit cards accepted.

For not many more pesos, stay in Tuxtepec's newest and fanciest lodging, the garden-style **Hotel Villa Esmeralda,** at Articulo 123 No. 74, Tuxtepec, Oaxaca 68300, tel./fax 287/875-5111, 287/875-5112, or 287/875-5113. The Villa Esmeralda, tucked into a quiet residential neighborhood, convenient to the first-class ADO bus station offers immaculate, semi-deluxe rooms, furnished with color-coordinated bedspreads, drapes, tiled floors, and shiny modern-standard baths. An additional trio of pluses are a good restaurant, parking thoughtfully removed to the periphery, and an invitingly tranquil inner patio-garden with large lap pool and adjacent kiddie pool. Get all this for $35 s, $40 d, and $46 t, with a/c, phone, cable TV, parking, and credit cards accepted.

If the Villa Esmeralda is full, consider the nearby refined, 1960s motel-style **Hotel El Rancho,** 435 Blvd. Avila Camacho, Tuxtepec, Oaxaca 68300, tel./fax 287/875-0722, 287/875-0469, or 287/875-0704, elrancho@prodigy.net.mx. The El Rancho, in a mixed residential-business neighborhood, just a block west of the ADO first-class bus station, surrounds a pleasant tropical pool and parking patio. The hotel's drawback appears to be the room arrangement on exterior corridors, where guests must unfortunately draw blinds for privacy. Inside, the 49 semi-deluxe rooms are immaculate and thoughtfully and comfortably furnished. Rates are $33 s, $39 d, $47 t, with a/c, bath, TV, parking, a good restaurant-bar (see Food), and limited wheelchair access. Credit cards accepted.

Also recommendable among Tuxtepec's semi-deluxe choices is **Hotel Mesón,** on the highway about a mile (1.6 km) from the river, at Blvd. Benito Juárez 1684, Tuxtepec, Oaxaca 68300, tel. 287/875-1200, 287/875-1359, or 287/875-1292, hotelmeson@prodigy.net.mx. Here, the builder ingeniously packed three stories of 65 rooms into a small space. The little pool, unfortunately relegated to a cramped upstairs patio, seems like an afterthought. The rooms inside, however, are clean, private, spacious, tiled, and furnished with comfortable 1980s-standard amenities. Rentals cost about $33 s, $40 d, $47 t, with a/c, bath, TV, phone, restaurant-bar, and parking. Credit cards are accepted.

Food

Tuxtepec visitors enjoy plenty of good food. The two town markets, the Mercado Flores Magón, on 20 de Noviembre, west side, two blocks from the river bridge, and the central market, on Independencia in the town center, by the river, are the best sources of groceries, fruits, and vegetables. At the central market, *fondas* (food stalls) upstairs serve economical, wholesome *comidas* at luxuriously airy river-view tables.

For good baked offerings, go to the **Panificadora Principal,** 20 de Noviembre, tel. 287/875-0755, open Mon.–Sat. 7 A.M.–9 P.M., Sun. 7 A.M.–1 P.M., on the corner of Degollado, about five blocks from the highway; or **Petit Cafetería y Pastelería,** 689 5 de Mayo, tel. 287/875-4742, open Mon.–Sat. 9 A.M.–8:30 P.M., Sun. 10 A.M.–4 P.M., nearer the center of town.

A longtime favorite downtown restaurant, famous for its local-style food and relaxed atmosphere, is town center **Caporales,** Independencia 560, upper floor, tel. 287/875-4405, open Mon.–Sat. 8 A.M.–8 P.M., Sun. 9 A.M.–6 P.M. Find it at across the street from the Hotel Mirador. Entrées run a moderate $3–4 for breakfast, $4–8 for lunch and dinner.

Second choice downtown, half a block west, goes to the immaculate restaurant of the **Hotel Tuxtepec,** tel. 287/875-0934. Enjoy a good breakfast, lunch, or supper ($3–7) every day 7 A.M.–11 P.M.

Three stars for refined ambience and attentive service go to the restaurant **El Pesebre,** 435 Blvd. Manuel Avila Camacho, tel. 287/875-0722 or 287/875-0469, at the Hotel El Rancho, about a mile (1.6 km) diagonally northwest of downtown, two blocks from throughway Boulevard Benito Juárez. Here, you can escape from the heat and the hubbub into a cool, air-conditioned TV-free atmosphere and select from a professionally prepared international-style menu of soups and salads ($3–5),

sandwiches and pasta ($4–6), eggs ($2–5), and fish, fowl, and meat entrées ($4–10).

The immaculate, cheery **Restaurant Mogala** at the Hotel Villa Esmeralda (see Accommodations), tel. 287/875-5113, is a fine place to both start and end your day. Tasty, professionally prepared and served breakfasts (eggs, hot cakes, ham, bacon, fruit, $2–5), soup, sandwich, and salad lunches ($3–4), and seafood, meat, and fowl dinners ($4–7) are prepared to please even demanding palates. Open daily 8 A.M.–10 P.M.

A pair of **special restaurants** have racheted up culinary standards in Tuxtepec. Authentically prepared Italian-style specialties are the main attraction to the refined dining room of **Trattoria Mediterraneo,** on the river, east side of town, at Blv. Muro 1759, tel. 287/875-8488. The menu lists many excellent choices. For example, start off with *prosciutto e melone* ($4.50), followed by salad, *insalate caprese* ($3), and soup, *minestrone di verdure* (vegetable minestrone, $3). Continue with the first plate, *linguini frutti di mare* (seafood linguini, $6); and finish with the second, *costolette di maile* (barbecued pork ribs, $8). Best skip dessert. Find them open daily noon–midnight; weekend reservations recommended.

Patrons at Tuxtepec's upscale restaurant–night club, **La Carreta,** on Blv. Benito Juárez, west of downtown, tel. 287/875-3880 or 287/875-3772, seem to do fine, especially with the chef's recommendations. For example, make up a party and share all three: *pompano enpapelada* (pompano in paper, $7), *fillete de robalo* (snook filet, stuffed with shrimp, $7); and *fillete tampiquena* (beef filet, tampico-style, $8). If possible, go Thursday, Friday, or Saturday early evening to enjoy the elegant *palapa* river-view ambience and linger over after-dinner wine or margaritas until live oldies-but-goodies dance music begins at 9 P.M. Open daily, noon–midnight. Find it beyond the second traffic circle, northbound, on the east (right) side of Boulevard Benito Juárez.

Entertainment and Events

Tuxtepec's biggest party is the **Feria Tuxtepec,** which runs for about a week during late May or early June, when local people pull all of the rabbits out of their collective hat: election of a queen,

© BRUCE WHIPPERMAN

A local favorite, the pineapple dance is *de rigueur* at Tuxtepec fiestas.

grand parade of floats, horse and cowboy parade, cockfights, fireworks, a big commercial exposition, and a folkloric dance festival, including Tuxtepec's own charming **Danza de la Flor de Piña** (Dance of the Pineapple Flower).

If you're in town on July 23 and 24, during the **Fiesta de San Juan Bautista,** be sure to get in on some of the fun around the plaza, including processions, *marmotas* (dancing giants), fireworks, and a community dance.

Tuxtepec folks also make a big celebration of the **Día de los Muertos** (Day of the Dead) on November 1 and 2. At the *panteón* (cemetery) three blocks east of the plaza's northeast corner, whole families arrive in the early evening to clean up and decorate the graves with flowers, candy, candles, and the favorite foods of the deceased, then settle down for an all-night vigil.

Tropical Tuxtepec is warm all year-round, and especially so during the warm spring dry season, when folks enjoy the many local *balnearios* (river swimming beaches and natural springs). Some of

the best are scattered along Highway 175 south of town. (See the Valle Nacional and San José Chiltepec sections.)

Information and Services

Tuxtepec has several banks, all with ATMs. The long hours (Mon.–Sat. 8 A.M.–7 P.M.) of **Banco Internacional** (Bital) make it a good choice, at 805 Independencia, tel. 287/875-2111, between Degollado and Jiménez, about three blocks west of the town center. Alternatively, moving east, try **Bancomer,** at Independencia 647, next to the market; or **Banamex,** farther east, at Independencia and Rayón, tel. 287/875-1974, open Mon.–Fri. 9 A.M.–4 P.M.

Find the **post office** at the corner of Libertad and Nicolas Bravo, a block behind the town plaza church, open Mon.–Fri. 8 A.M.–7 P.M., Sat. 9 A.M.–1 P.M. *Telecomunicaciones,* at the corner of Carranza and Morelos, tel./fax 287/875-3577, provides public fax and money orders, Mon.–Fri. 8 A.M.–6 P.M., Sat. and Sun. 9 A.M.–noon. From the downtown market, walk four blocks from the river, inland, along Morelos. A number of **Internet** stores downtown provide email and computer services.

Doctors are plentiful in Tuxtepec. Ask at your hotel desk for a recommendation or go to the **Consultorio Médico** of Dr. Olegario Completo, at the corner of Av. Jesús Carranza and Allende, a block north of the plaza, tel. 287/875-2425. After hours in emergency, have a taxi take you to the **Hospital Regional Civil,** at Sebastián Ortiz 310, tel. 287/875-0023; or the **Hospital Seguro Social,** on Blv. Benito Juárez on the town side of the river.

For nonprescription medicines and drugs, go to a *farmacia,* such as (moving easterly from the downtown west side): **Farmacia Cruz Verde,** 908 Independencia, across from Banco Internacional; or 24-hour **Farmacia Albatros,** 20 de Noviembre 881, tel. 287/875-2582, fax 287/875-3219.

For police or fire emergencies, contact the municipal police, at the *presidencia municipal,* tel. 287/875-3166.

The local **Cámara Nacional de Comercio** (National Chamber of Commerce), at the plaza's northeast corner (of Libertad and Allende), tel. 287/875-0886, open Mon.–Fri. 9 A.M.–2 P.M. and

NORTHERN OAXACA

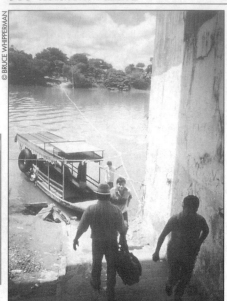

The quickest way from downtown Tuxtepec to cross-river La Esperanza village is via the ferry boat.

5–8 P.M., Sat. 9 A.M.–1 P.M., will try to answer your questions. Alternatively, travel agents, such as **Viajes Sotelo,** at Morelos 118, tel./fax 287/875-2656, at the center of town, a block from Independencia and a block west of the market, open Mon.–Fri. 9 A.M.–2 P.M. and 4–8 P.M., Sat. 9 A.M.–2 P.M., are usually willing to answer travel-related queries.

Getting There and Away

Bus lines at a number of different stations provide many connections with both Oaxaca and national destinations.

The terminal for first-class **Autobuses del Oriente (ADO)** and associated lines, at the corner of Sebastián Ortiz and 1 de Mayo, tel. 287/875-0473, can be found one block south, one block behind highway-front Hotel del Mesón. They connect south with Oaxaca via Valle Nacional and Ixtlán de Juárez, and northwest with Orizaba, Puebla, and Veracruz, and northeast with Minatitlán and Coatzacoalcos.

Mixed first- and second-class **Autobuses Unidos (AU) and Cuenca de Papaloapan,** buses, on Matamoros between Libertad and Carranza, tel. 287/875-0237, operate cooperatively at the same station. They connect south with Oaxaca via Valle Nacional and Ixtlán; southeast with Isthmus destinations of Matías Romero, Juchitán, Tehuantepec, and Salina Cruz; and northwest with Temascal, Orizaba, Córdoba, Veracruz, Puebla, and Mexico City.

Additionally, **Autobuses Unidos** (AU) second-class buses, operate out of a second terminal at the Flores Magón market on 20 de Noviembre, just east (town side) of the Highway 175 ingress boulevard. They connect west several times daily with Mazateca destinations of Jalapa de Díaz and Huautla de Jiménez.

Small, second-class line **Autobuses Trópico,** Libertad 1215, tel. 287/875-2895, from its terminal a block and a half west of Matamoros, connects six times daily with Oaxaca via Valle Nacional and Ixtlán.

For drivers, mostly good paved roads connect Tuxtepec with both Oaxaca and national destinations. Highway 175 connects south with Oaxaca via Valle Nacional and Ixtlán, over the Sierra Madre, in about 132 miles (213 km). However, steep, winding grades and a seriously rutted (unrepaired at this writing) 30-mile (48-km) section near the Sierra summit can slow traffic to a crawl. Allow about five hours for safety in either direction.

Combined National Highways 147 and 185 connect Tuxtepec southeast with Tehuantepec, via Matías Romero and Juchitán. The nighttime robberies and hijackings that used to plague the lonely, northern Highway 147 leg of this route have fortunately abated. To be sure, stop at the Highway 175–Highway 147 intersection gas station to check if the highway remains secure. Allow about five hours of road time, either direction, for this 189-mile (304-km) trip.

A good paved route, Highway 182, connects Tuxtepec with Huautla de Jiménez in the high Mazateca, via Jalapa de Díaz. Allow about three and a half daylight hours westerly, three hours easterly, for this exhilaratingly scenic 74-mile (119-km) top-of-the-world trip.

TEMASCAL AND MIGUEL ALEMÁN DAM AND RESERVOIR

Temascal (pop. about 5,000) is the town where the Mexican government, under the leadership of President Miguel Alemán (1946–1952) began building a huge dam to control and harness the waters of the Río Tonto in 1946. The project, officially the Miguel Alemán Dam, was complete in 1955. A subsequent project, the Cerro de Oro Dam and Reservoir, was completed a generation later. The entire Papaloapan basin benefits from the two reservoirs, now connected, which provide irrigation water, low-cost electric power, and relief from flood devastation.

On the negative side, the dam's social cost was high. Many thousands of Mazatec, Chinantec, and Mixe indigenous campesino families suffered. Thousands had to be moved, some forcibly, from their land and relocated to new, unfamiliar locations.

Today, the Miguel Alemán Dam, towering hundreds of feet, just upstream from the town of Temascal, is the project's most visible reminder. It compares in magnitude with the great hydroelectric projects of the American West. Its reservoir stretches about 20 miles long and 15 miles wide (32 by 24 km) and totals about two cubic miles (eight cubic kilometers) of water, with an average depth of around 40 feet (12 meters). The reservoir's maximum flow can generate about 500 megawatts of electric power, more than enough for the entire state of Oaxaca and nearly enough for a U.S. city the size of San Francisco.

Sights and Activities

Follow the road through Temascal town and continue another half mile (1 km) uphill to a road fork. Bear right for the Temascal *embarcadero* (wharf), where *palapas* serve fresh fish *comidas* and motorboats on the shoreline wait for passengers. The lake is especially lovely considering that it's artificial. Fortunately, adequate water flows ordinarily keep the level constant and thus avoid the appearance of an ugly bathtub-like

© BRUCE WHIPPERMAN

The Temascal Reservoir *embarcadero* near the Miguel Alemán Dam offers shoreline camping, boating, fishing, and fresh bass dinners at lakefront *palapa* restaurants.

NORTHERN OAXACA

ring. From the *embarcadero,* the lake appears to stretch endlessly, invitingly blue and smooth, among green hills and small islands. The **shoreline restaurants** specialize in *mojarra* (bass) and *camarón* (shrimp) dinners. Boatmen offer to take you on a two-hour *recorrido* (tour) around the lake for around $25 per boat, for up to about eight persons. Save money by doubling up with others. The prime destination, besides a number of shoreline hamlets, is Soyaltepec, one of the few villages, along with Ixcatlán, that didn't get swallowed up by the reservoir. (See Ixcatlán.) Ask for young boatman **Alex Vasquez Ramírez,** or kindly **Juan Palma Mina** (who's old enough to tell you how things were here before the dam).

Besides boat rides and swimming, **fishing** for bass is a major local diversion. Boatmen say that the typical fish amounts to about a quarter pound, and typical catches add up to around 20 fish in a couple of hours. You can launch your own boat for free if you check with the *capitán del puerto,* at the *presidencia municipal* in Temascal; watch for the sign on the main ingress-egress street.

Parking a self-contained RV or setting up a tent is welcomed anywhere around the *embarcadero* (although level spots appear to be scarce). A small store at the road, just above the *embarcadero,* could supply water and basic food items. Better-stocked stores in Temascal could supply even more.

Before you leave, reverse your path and instead of turning left for the town, head straight along the upper level road and take a look at the **Monument to President Miguel Alemán,** on the right before the dam. The main attraction, besides the heroic statue of Alemán, is the big mural in the open building atop the staircase. Here, government artists have tried their best to dramatize the planned benefits of the dam project. A big mural shows two contrasting worlds: before the dam, a forbidding landscape of disease, superstition, poverty, and starvation, and the bright busy modern world—natives reading, surgeons operating, scientists experimenting, engineers building, teachers teaching, farmers harvesting—after the dam.

Temascal town back below the dam bustles with plenty of *taquerias* for cooked eats, fruits, vegetables, and groceries, a *centro de salud,* post office, and telecom near the *presidencia muncipal,* and Ladatel card–operated street telephones.

Getting There and Away

Second-class AU buses connect Temascal east, with Tuxtepec (west-side Flores Magón market), and north, with Tierra Blanca and Veracruz.

Drivers, from Tuxtepec follow Avenida Benito Juárez (the northern prolongation of Highway 175). After about eight miles (13 km), turn left at the Ciudad Alemán sign. Continue approximately another half hour, or 16 miles (26 km), and turn left at the Temascal sign. After another 13 miles (21 km), continue through Temascal town to the dam, a total of 37 miles (60 km) from Tuxtepec.

SAN PEDRO IXCATLÁN AND THE ISLANDS

An alternate gateway to the Miguel Alemán reservoir shoreline is through Ixcatlán, a prime spot for a country stay. The town stands at the eastern boundary of the Mazateca, where many townspeople and virtually everyone in the surrounding countryside speak Mazatec, and women wear the bright blue-and-white horizontally striped local *huipil.*

Along the Road

A major sight along Highway 182, about half an hour west of Tuxtepec, is the **Puente Pescadito,** which bridges the channel connecting the Temescal and Cerro de Oro reservoirs. *Palapa* restaurants at both ends of the bridge supply refreshments and bass dinners. Below, the riverbanks, accessible on foot or by negotiable dirt roads, are level and invite fishing for *mojarra* (bass) and RV or tent camping.

The grand lake vista spreads for miles south and north. The southern arm, Reservoir Cerro de Oro, began to fill when the **Miguel de la Madrid** dam was built downstream during the 1970s. The reservoir level rose until it finally connected with the Temescal reservoir during the mid-1990s. In joining the two reservoirs, the channel consequently also connects the drainage basins of the Río Tonto, in the north, and the Río Santo Domingo, in the south. Although the Cerro de Oro reservoir is large, with about 100 square miles (256 sq. km) of surface area, this is only a fraction of the size of the Temascal reservoir.

Past the bridge, Highway 182 leads through gently rolling, pastoral country—once dense rain forest, now undulating, parklike green pasture, sprinkled with palms and leafy trees. Thatched, whitewashed country houses appear atop the hills and around the bends. This is country where an unknown vehicle is an event. If you're driving, wave as you go by and the people will wave back.

Ixcatlán perches atop a long hill, surrounded by picture-perfect vistas of the verdant countryside, the deeply indented, island-dotted reservoir, and in the background, the precipitous silhouette of Cerro Rabón, the Mazatecs' holy mountain. Besides all this, Ixcatlán has an inviting small hotel, a sprinkling of country *comedores*, services, and excursions to even more remote, even uninhabited, islands.

Isla Soyaltepec

If it's no later than 3 P.M., you're early enough for the trip to Isla Soyaltepec. Once a small isolated town, Soyaltepec (pop. 500) is even more isolated since the reservoir has confined it to an island where most of its friendly, frankly curious inhabitants speak only Mazatec. The only way to go is by boat, for which you can bargain (figure $15–20 for a two-hour round trip for up to about six people) at the *embarcadero* on Ixcatlán's west lakeshore (below the Ixcatlán church). Beforehand, ask for boatman Fidel Alto Hermengildo or his brother Eloy. Fidel is the Soyaltepec elementary schoolteacher and will help you find lodging if you decide to stay overnight on his island.

The six-mile (9.6 km) trip takes about half an hour. Along the way, butterflies flutter, herons stalk their prey, and clouds billow above the mirror-smooth lake surface. On the western

© BRUCE WHIPPERMAN

On Isla Soyaltepec, it's a must to climb to the top of the hill (with several young guides leading the way, of course) and enjoy the breeze and the view of the many islands of Temascal Reservoir below the cloud-capped shadow of Cerro Rabón.

horizon rises the towering massif of **Cerro Rabón,** often cloaked in a blanket of clouds. You'll pass through a fleet of little islands, some with small wooded crowns, perfect for an afternoon or overnight soaking in the scenery and solitude. If you do opt for an overnight, be prepared with a tent and mosquito repellent. Have your boatman return to pick you up at an appointed time.

At Soyaltepec, climb (one hour, round-trip) to the old village and church on the island hilltop. Half a dozen kids will probably accompany you. Halfway up, you scale a pre-conquest–appearing, ponderous stone staircase. At the top, take a look inside the venerable (1744) church, gaze westerly over the many-island lake vista, and get a *refresco* at the hilltop store.

Accommodations and Food

Villa del Lago would be a pleasant surprise anywhere, but here in little, out-of-the-way Ixcatlán, it seems even more so. The hotel is the labor of love of its friendly owner, Patricia Sarmiento Castillo, who rents six immaculate, thoughtfully furnished rooms for $8 s or d, $12 t, with fans and hot-water shower baths. She has made the hotel even more inviting with a top-level porch from which guests can enjoy Ixcatlán's dramatic lake-view panorama. Write for a reservation: Hotel Nanguina, Calle Benito Juárez s/n, Ixcatlán, Oaxaca 68450, or leave a message with the town operator, tel. 287/877-2088, 287/877-2089, or 287/877-2093.

The reservoir, whose waters Ixcatlán escaped because of its hilltop perch, has brought fresh fish to Ixcatlán. A scattering of country *comedores* serve good lake bass dinners, notably the homey, clean **El Vaquero** *palapa,* in mid-town, on main street Benito Juárez, next to the *larga distancia* (long-distance telephone) sign. Best for breakfast is **El Paraíso** *palapa,* downhill, overlooking the lake, where, besides the good food, you can feast on the luscious lake view.

Other Practicalities

Plan your visit to coincide with Ixcatlán's main festival, honoring **San Isidro Labrador** (Saint Isador the Farmer) May 13–15. The fiesta's highlight is the traditional dance La Puta Chichi (Chichi the Prostitute).

A number of Ixcatlán women embroider **blouses and huipiles.** Check at the hotel for names of whom to visit. Moreover, Señora Castillo makes **art-to-wear cottons** that she displays at Hotel Villa del Lago.

Visitors to Ixcatlán can count on a number of basic services, including a doctor, a *centro de salud* (health center) at the town entrance, pharmacies, grocery stores, post office, and long-distance telephone.

Get to Ixcatlán by the **Autobuses Unidos** (AU) bus bound for Huautla de Jiménez or Jalapa de Díaz from Tuxtepec's west-side Flores Magón market. Ride to the Ixcatlán side road, then taxi, catch a ride, or walk the four miles (6.4 km) to town.

Drivers, from Tuxtepec, turn left (west) from Highway 175 onto Highway 182 at the Jalapa de Díaz sign at the traffic circle, just three blocks north of the Río Papaloapan bridge. Continue along Highway 182 west 34 miles (about 55 km) to the signed Ixcatlán right turnoff. Continue four miles (6 km) to town.

SAN LUCAS OJITLÁN

While on your way to or from Ixcatlán, you might detour to San Lucas Ojitlán at the signed junction, 27 miles (43 km) west of Tuxtepec and six miles (10 km) east of the Ixcatlán turnoff. Ojitlán is the *cabercera* (head town) of a medium-size Chinantec-speaking *municipio.* Its main street bustles so continuously that few stores take the customary afternoon siesta.

Ojitlán's main establishments front the town's single main street, Independencia. They include a private doctor; *correo* (post office); *telecomunicaciones* (money orders and public fax); long-distance telephone; *centro de salud* (health clinic), and a number of grocery stores, notably the friendly general store **Centro Comercial del Sureste,** known locally as Tienda de Tinito, right in the middle of town.

Textiles make up the principal local handicraft, mostly colorful *huipiles,* which some women weave and embroider. One of them is

Juana Muñoz; many people, especially the proprietor of Tienda de Tinito, know her and can direct you to her house. If she's not home, people will most likely be able to direct you to someone else.

Ojitlán's hubbub overflows on Wednesday, the regular day of *tianguis* (native street market), when hosts of country folk, including Chinantec- and Mazatec-speaking women in their brilliant *huipiles*, flock into town.

Local excitement peaks during the big fiesta in honor of Santa Rosa, on August 28–30. Santa Rosa's popularity is a curiosity, since San Lucas, rather than Santa Rosa, is the official town patron. Community frustration over the local liturgy seems to have led to the preference for Santa Rosa. It turns out that a majority of faithful prefer the service to be in Spanish, but the local priest and the bishop in Tuxtepec insist on Latin, which no one understands.

Townsfolk do celebrate San Lucas, but with only a token fiesta. You can see evidence of the community preference inside the old church atop the hill, at the end of the main street. Behind the altar, notice the all-female cast of saints, with Santa Rosa in the middle, and San Lucas conspicuous by his absence.

The Mazateca

JALAPA DE DÍAZ AND VICINITY: THE LOW MAZATECA

By the time you arrive at Jalapa de Díaz, you're well into Mazatec country; walk a quarter mile (a half km) from town in any direction and you'll hear little, if any, Spanish spoken. For women here, wearing the *huipil* is the rule rather than the exception. Local women distinguish three grades of *huipil*: everyday, fancy, and super-fancy. The latter are beautifully crocheted all by hand, often displaying a glittering throng of birds and animals, fit for a bride.

You'd have little trouble finding Jalapa even if you had no Highway 182 to guide you. Jalapa de Díaz stands at the foot of the vertical wall of whale-shaped **Cerro Rabón** (elev. about 7,700 feet, 2,350 meters), arguably Oaxaca's most uniquely prominent landmass.

Sights

The most colorful times to arrive at Jalapa are Thursday and Sunday, for the big country *tianguis*, when sellers' awnings cover half the town, thronging with native folks. Another good time to arrive is during either of the two patronal fiestas, in honor of San Sebastián (January 19–20) and San Antonio de Padua (June 12–13).

The **Cañon del Río Santo Domingo,** which you can begin to appreciate about five miles (8 km) up the highway from Jalapa, is one of Mexico's little-known wonders. The road climbs, rounding the foot of Cerro Rabón, and enters a vast cirque of verdant, jungle-clad ramparts on one side and the deep, plunging canyon on the other. At about 10 miles (16 km) uphill from Jalapa, you begin to cross rushing creeks, first Arroyo Blanco, then Arroyo Caballo, then finally the blue, boiling **Río Uluapa.** Walk the (sometimes steep and slippery) path to the right of the river; after about 900 feet (270 meters), follow the left fork steeply uphill. Continue about 45 minutes over rocks and beneath great, vine-hung trees to a boulder-decorated pool, perfect for bathing. Above, see the river flow from a cave, as a pristine spring, then drop and tumble as a foaming waterfall and cascade.

Climbing Cerro Rabón

At first glance, Cerro Rabón appears tempting to climb. In fact, many local people do it every day. They tend fields on the mountainside and walk down to town afterward. The net rise amounts to about 6,500 feet (2,000 meters) and should be attempted only by fit hikers, with a guide, who start at the crack of dawn with good shoes, hat, food, and a jacket against cold. If the weather turns sour, go back or get shelter in someone's house. Lightning and cloudbursts up there could spell disaster. Clouds without rain are OK; they cap Cerro Rabón most of the time. This has resulted in the **cloud**

© BRUCE WHIPPERMAN

The Río Uluapa issues as a pristine spring from a cave, about a quarter mile uphill from the popular bathing spot a short walk from Highway 182.

forest coating the mountaintop—a Pleistocene remnant ecosystem of tree ferns, hanging moss, bright liquid amber maples, spiny bromeliads, and orchids.

Pack something to drink, although springs along the way should suffice for most of the water. You must get formal permission from the authorities at the *presidencia municipal,* who can probably suggest a guide, such as the experienced Antonio Bravo or his son Ángel (bee-keepers who produce honey at their nearby *rancho*).

Accommodations and Food

Most of Jalapa's business establishments line the main street, Benito Juárez, which leads about a quarter mile (a half km) from the highway to the town plaza, bordered by the *presidencia municipal* on one side and the church, the Templo de San Sebastián, on the other.

Right in the middle of everything is the town's one lodging house, the family-run **Casa de Huéspedes Robertina,** at Calle Benito Juárez s/n, Jalapa de Díaz, Oaxaca 68460, tel. 287/877-2009. The grandmotherly owner rents plain but

clean rooms for about $8 per person, with bath down the hall.

Buy fruits and vegetables at the several curbside market stalls (which multiply into a big native *tianguis* Thursday and Sunday). Groceries are available at street-front *abarroterías,* such as Abarrotes del Centro, open Mon.–Sat. 7 A.M.–8 P.M. and Sun. 7 A.M.–3 P.M. A sprinkling of *comedores* along Juárez supply wholesome, local-style *comidas.*

For good restaurant food, try the locally recommended **Comedor Abi,** at the first *tope* (speed bump) on the Tuxtepec end of Highway 182 through town; or **Comedor Las Brisas** a couple of blocks farther.

Shopping

Stop at the store of **Fausto** (real name Roberto Osorio), on the highway about a block (Tuxtepec direction) before the town ingress road. He'll be happy to show and sell you examples of the lovely *manteles* (tablecloths), *rebozos* (shawls), *camisas* (shirts), and *huipiles* that he, his wife, and his friends craft.

Services

If you get ill, go to the friendly town doctor, Abelardo Cruz Abejo, near the highway. For non-prescription drugs, try one of the basic *farmacias* on the main street.

Find the town *correo* (post office) and *telecomunicaciones* (money orders and public fax) next to the downtown *presidencia municipal.*

Getting There

Bus passengers get to Jalapa just as from Ixcatlán and Ojitlán. Ride second-class **Autobuses Unidos** (AU) east from Huautla de Jiménez or west from Tuxtepec's market Flores Magón bus terminal. From Tuxtepec, drivers proceed exactly as for Ixcatlán but continue 11.5 miles (18.5 km) past the Ixcatlán turnoff to Jalapa de Díaz, a total of 44 miles (71 km) west of Tuxtepec or 32 miles (53 km) east of Huautla de Jiménez. Turn left, at the town ingress road and continue about a quarter mile (a half km) uphill to the plaza and church.

Local folks gather for a protest meeting in the town plaza–basketball court in Huautla de Jiménez.

HUAUTLA DE JIMÉNEZ AND VICINITY: THE HIGH MAZATECA

Huautla de Jiménez (pop. 20,000), tucked on a high Mazateca mountainside, was put on the world map during the 1960s by María Sabina, a local Mazatec-speaking *curandera* (indigenous medicine woman) who, like many others, used hallucinogenic mushrooms as part of her bag of remedies. The word somehow got out, and a small army of Love Generation devotees of hallucinogens from the United States and Europe, known locally as *gippis* (HEE-pees), quickly descended on Huautla. With them soon came a continuous stream of doctors, journalists, and anthropologists.

María Sabina seemed to enjoy her renown. She was invited far and wide to testify to the efficacy of her remedies at learned international medical conferences. But after a generation of fame, she passed away in 1985 at the age of 90, leaving Huautla to slumber again.

Her legacy, however, remains plainly visible in Huautla today, in the several businesses and institutions that carry her name, such as the María Sabina Cultural Center, the Comedor María Sabina, and the Farmacia María Sabina.

Besides such obvious reminders, many new-generation *curanderos* carry on María Sabina's mission. Notable among them are two of her grandsons, Filongonia Garcia and Eduardo Valladares, now both middle-aged. Eduardo, who was a constant companion of his grandmother during her heyday, was asked by author Juan Garcia Carrera of his thoughts concerning death. He replied, "By offering you enlightenment, my mushrooms also resign you to the reality of death."

Orientation

Although the town itself spreads over a broad mountainside, the business and service center is concentrated mainly along a few downtown streets. Most important is the east-west street Calle Benito Juárez. Addresses start at number one on Juárez and increase to the east. Just downhill from the west end of Juárez are the

HUAUTLA DE JIMÉNEZ

GONZALES

GARCIA

To Mex. 182

PANIFICADORA LA SEÑORA DE OJATITLÁN

NATURAL FOODS

RESTAURANT FAMILIAR SAN ANGEL

CASO

FLETES Y PASAJES (SECOND-CLASS BUS)

POSADA SAN ANTONIO/GROCERIES

PANADERÍA GIRALDA

MAGDANI

DR. SAUL MARTINEZ/ PHARMACY

ANTONIO

ABARROTES EL SURTIDOR (GROCERIES)

HOTEL 1 DE MAYO

HUIPLES VICTORIA ENRIQUEZ

FARMACIA FENIX

FARMACIA DE JESÚS

INTERNET

AUTOBUSES UNIDOS (SECOND-CLASS BUS)

DR. LÁZARO P. GARCIA

5 DE MAYO

LAUNDRY

BANCO INTERNACIONAL

POST BOX

HOTEL AND RESTAURANT RINCONCITO

JUÁREZ

HOTEL OLÍMPICO

MERCADO

BENITO

TEMPLO DE LA NAVIDAD

CUAUHTÉMOC

HOTEL AND RESTAURANT SANTA JULIA

PROVEEDORA DEL HOGAR (HARDWARE)

PRESIDENCIA MUNICIPAL

PLAZA (BASKETBALL COURT)

RESTAURANT GEMENIS

RESTAURANT ROSITA

POST OFFICE

ARTESANIAS JULIETA (HANDICRAFTS)

TELECOM

SCHOOL

0   50 yds

0   50 m

© AVALON TRAVEL PUBLISHING, INC.

town market, *presidencia municipal,* and the church, dedicated to the Virgin of the Nativity—all situated around the town plaza–basketball court *(cancha).* A second street, Cuauhtémoc, downhill from the plaza, runs parallel to Benito Juárez to its intersection with a third street, Antonio Caso, which angles diagonally west, downhill from its intersection, at the east end of Benito Juárez. Highway 182 contours along the mountainside three or four blocks downhill from the town plaza.

Casa María Sabina and Cerro de Adoración

El Fortín, the east-end ridgetop *barrio* where María Sabina lived, is revered by many Huautlecos. Her house, a simple rust-roofed white dwelling, has been unoccupied for years. It's in the neighborhood just beyond the government hospital not far from the highway. Ask for Casa María Sabina, and most likely a child will lead you there.

From there, continue to sacred site Cerro de Adoración along the path heading gradually upward along the right-hand (western) slope of the ridgetop. Your destination is just beyond the highest hill along the ridgetop, where, after a half-hour climb, you'll reach the pinnacle called

© BRUCE WHIPPERMAN

Cerro de Adoración, a local May 3 (Día de la Santa Cruz) pilgrimage spot, occupies the highest point in Huautla.

Cerro de Adoración. Here, you'll find a monument with four crosses where local folks carry offerings, especially around May 3, La Día de la Santa Cruz (The Day of the Holy Cross). Besides meeting folks along the trail carrying wood or herding goats, your reward will most likely be a cool breeze and a breathtaking panoramic vista of billowing clouds and rugged peaks, sprinkled with a dozen seemingly Lilliputian villages on their slopes.

Accommodations

New **Hotel Santa Julio,** at Calle Cuauhtemoc 12, Huautla de Jimémez 68500, tel. 236/378-0586, is a welcome addition to Huautla. Twenty-one spacious, clean, and comfortably furnished rooms, with hot-water shower baths provide the basics, with TV, parking, and restaurant. They rent for $15 s, $17 d, and $23 t. Find it on the south, downhill side of the plaza.

Second choice goes to **Hotel Rinconcito,** Juárez 8, Huautla de Jiménez, Oaxaca 68500, tel. 236/378-0136, 236/378-0243, or 236/378-0005, across Juárez from the market. Friendly husband-wife owners Leonardo Altamirano and Catalina Casamiro rent eight plain but clean rooms for $17 s, $20 d (in one bed), $22 d (in two beds), and $27 t, with hot-water baths. The best are in front, with views of the market below and the mountains in the distance.

Running a distant third, two blocks west, is the rough but clean **Hotel 1 de Mayo,** at Juárez 30, Huautla de Jiménez, Oaxaca 68500, tel. 236/378-0076. The three stories of approximately 20 small bare-bones rooms rent for about $15 s, $17 d, with hot-water baths.

Fourth choice goes to the extremely basic, emergency-only **Hotel Olímpico,** next door to the Hotel Rinconcito; tel. 236/378-0107, $12 s, $16 d.

Food

Go to the **market** for the freshest fruits and vegetables. Get groceries at **Abarrotes El Surtidor** at Juárez 27, one block east, corner of Juárez and Garcia González. Find it open daily 9 A.M.–10 P.M.

NORTHERN OAXACA

For fresh-baked goods, try **Panadería Giralda,** at 2 E. Garcia González, the street that angles uphill two blocks east of the Hotel Rinconcito. Alternatively, go to **Panadería La Señora de Ojatitlán,** a long block farther east, at the corner of Caso and Juárez. Find snacks, such as hamburgers, hot dogs, and *tortas,* at the stand in front of the Hotel Rinconcito, across Juárez from the market.

All of Huautla's restaurant are strictly local country-style. You can expect cleanliness and at least a choice of avocado, beans, *bolillos* (crunchy bread rolls), bottled water, cheese, chicken, cucumber, eggs, fruit juice, milk, pork, salsa, spaghetti, steak, tomatoes, and tortillas. A trio of acceptable eateries is on or near Avenida Cuauhtémoc. Highly recommended is family **Restaurant Rosita,** below the plaza's southwest corner, a few doors down the lane that angles off of Cuauhtémoc. Its airy porch dining room is an extra plus, especially for breakfast and lunch.

Nearby, at Cuauhtémoc 11, is **Restaurant Gemenis,** open about the same hours, and the dining room of the **Hotel Santa Julia,** half a block east. Alternatively, back uphill, on the east end of Juárez, try the family-run **Restaurant Familiar San Ángel,** open daily 8:30 A.M.–8 P.M.

© BRUCE WHIPPERMAN

Huautla embroidery is among the most prized in Oaxaca.

Festivals and Events

The most colorful times to arrive in town are during the patronal celebration **Fiesta de la Virgen de La Natividad** (September 7–8), the Día de los Muertos (Day of the Dead, November 1–2), and the **Feria Comercial** (climaxing on the third Friday of Lent, 22 days before Easter Sunday). The Feria Comercial is attended by a host of villagers who crowd in from the surrounding mountains to watch their favorite traditional dances, including the Flor de Naranjo (Orange Tree Flower), Flor de Piña (Pineapple), Flor de Lis (Heaven), and Anillo de Oro (Ring of Gold). If you miss these, at least try to be present on Sunday for the big *tianguis,* when vendors' awnings fill the entire center of town.

Shopping

Huautla offers some opportunities to shop for its well-known **textiles.** Around the market espe-

cially, you'll see women in handmade *huipiles,* adorned with bright embroidered birds, fruits, flowers, and rainbows of pink-, yellow-, and blue-striped satin. **Victoria Enriquez,** at her shop (on Juárez, just east of the Hotel 1 de Mayo), crafts and sells *huipiles* daily except Sun. 8 A.M.–4 P.M. and 6–9 P.M. Also, for additional choices, across the street, step into **Magdani,** at Juárez 37.

In addition to the *huipiles,* local women craft and decorate blouses, napkins, shirts, skirts, and tablecloths in floral and animal designs. Buy them at either market stalls or the small handicrafts shop, **Artesanías Julieta,** on the plaza, west side, lower level. You might be able to see more examples at the homes of individual craftswomen; ask Catalina Casamiro, at the Hotel Rinconcito.

Services

For money, go to the **Banco Internacional** (Bital), across Juárez from the market, tel. 236/378-0029, open Mon.–Sat. 8 A.M.–6 P.M. After hours, use its ATM.

9 P.M. at the small shop, at Juárez 14A, tel. 236/378-0054.

Photographic services, such as develop-and-print, cameras, supplies, film, and black-and-white development, have come to Huautla, at Foto Isis, at 19 Juárez, open daily 9 A.M.–9 P.M.

Getting There and Away

Buses operate out of terminals on Calle Antonio Caso, which runs diagonally downhill from Calle Juárez. Second-class **Fletes y Pasajes** buses, tel. 236/378-0406, connect west with Teotitlán del Camino, thence south with Oaxaca via Cuicatlán; northwest with Mexico City via Tehuacán and Puebla. Second-class **Autobuses Unidos** (AU), no phone, buses connect east with Tuxtepec via Jalapa de Díaz; and northwest with Mexico City via Teotitlán, Tehuacán, and Puebla. Local-class white **Transportes Regionales Sierra-Cañada-Teotitlán-Oaxaca** minibuses connect south with Oaxaca, via Teotitlán and Cuicatlán.

For drivers, paved Highway 182 connects Huautla east with Tuxtepec via Jalapa de Díaz, along 76 miles (122 km) of winding but breathtakingly scenic mountain road. For safety, allow three hours eastbound, downhill, or three and a half hours westbound, uphill. In a westerly direction, Highway 182 connects Huautla east with Teotitlán del Camino in 41 miles (66 km) of paved, downhill-winding, scenic mountain road. (From Teotitlán, Highway 135 connects south an additional 100 miles, 161 km, about 3.5 hours, with Oaxaca.) Allow two hours downhill (westerly), 2.5 hours uphill (easterly).

Unleaded gasoline is available at the Pemex gas station on the highway a few blocks south, downhill from the town center.

Excursions: Las Regaderas, Nindo-Da-Gé, and Sotano de San Agustín

The area around Huautla, a dramatically folded green landscape of mountains and deep valleys, hides a number of natural wonders, the best known of which include two limestone caves and a twin waterfall.

Easiest to get to and see is **Las Regaderas,** a pair of waterfalls not far west along Highway 182

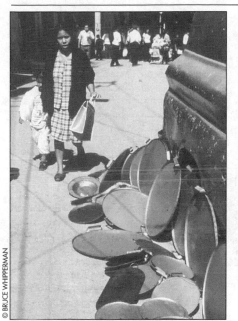

The traditional clay *comal* griddle is giving way to factory-made steel among those folks with the cash to buy one.

A pair of **doctors** maintain offices on Juárez. Moving east, first comes **Dr. Lázaro Pérez Garcia,** open Mon.–Sat. 8:30 A.M.–3 P.M. and 5–9 P.M. and also available on call at Juárez 12, upstairs. A block farther east, you'll find **Dr. Saul Martínez,** at his pharmacy, tel. 236/378-0257, and on call 24 hours.

Nonprescription medicines and drugs are available at additional **pharmacies** on Juárez, such as **Farmacia Fenix,** at Juárez 21D, open Mon.–Sat. 9 A.M.–9 P.M., Sun. 9 A.M.–4 P.M., and **Farmacia de Jesús,** at Juárez 16.

The *correo* (post office) and *telecomunicaciones* (public fax and money orders) stand side by side on the plaza's west side, above the shops, across the street (west) from the *presidencia municipal.*

Long-distance telephone is available at the Hotel Rinconcito, daily 8 A.M.–9 P.M., and three doors east, at the *larga distancia* by the bank.

Internet connection is available daily 9 A.M.–

©BRUCE WHIPPERMAN

NORTHERN OAXACA

The biggest day of the Huautla market is Sunday, when campesinos come from all over the high Mazateca to buy and sell.

from Huautla. Get there by car or white local minibus at Puente de Fierro bridge, about four miles (6.6 km) west, Teotitlán direction, from Huautla. Just before the bridge, turn right on to a side road and continue .6 mile (1 km) to the falls.

Las Regaderas (The Showers) plummet 100 feet (30 meters) out of a jungle cliff into a wild, tumbling river. Great trees resembling California sycamores shade both banks. An aging steel-cable suspension walkway crosses the river next to a rustic riverside cabin. Access to the rocky foot of the falls is steep and slippery, however. Bring a rope to steady your steps and avoid a nasty fall. Some informal riverbank camping sites may be usable during low water, February–May. Security may be a problem, however. Drunkenness seems to be a major local pastime. Ask at the stores past the bridge on the highway.

Even more spectacular is **Nindo-Da-Gé** (Broad Spring Mountain) cave, first explored completely in 1905, near the little town of San Antonio Eloxochitlán (ay-loh-shoh-CHEET-lahn). You probably can explore a majority of its 19 galleries—some gigantic, some petite—in a

few hours. The seemingly endless procession of dripping limestone formations, which have names such as The Infernal Hill, The Fort, The Snail, and Marimba, are even more fun if you dream up your own names.

The town invites visitors to both camp locally (town stores can supply food and water) and explore their cave. Recently, authorities have partially completed a road most of the way to the cave, which can be reached from town in about one mile (2 km) by road, and only another half mile (1 km) by foot trail.

The only obstacle to exploring the cave is the reasonable one that for safety reasons you must have a guide recommended by civic authorities. (The guide receives no money; he serves as part of his community service obligation. However, do offer a donation, perhaps about $20, in a sealed envelope, to the *ayuntamiento,* city government.)

A town committee, at this writing consisting of Isidro Beseril, Octavio Nieto, and Alonzo Nieto, are in charge. Another good person to contact for information is former cave committee member and friendly schoolteacher Profesor Froilan Ríos, whose house stands on the left side of the paved road as you enter town. He recommends Alonzo Nieto as the best guide. If you're really serious about exploring the cave, notify Alonzo by leaving a message with the Elochotitlán long-distance telephone operator, tel. 236/378-0126 or 236/378-0027, detailing when you're planning to arrive. Do not fail to keep the appointment. Bring at least two strong (four-celled or more) flashlights, good traction shoes, and enough hard hats (hard plastic construction type) for everyone.

Get to San Antonio Eloxochitlán by bus or car seven miles (11 km) along the Teotitlán (west) direction on Highway 182, to the San Antonio turnoff gravel road on the right (north). Continue 4.8 miles (7.7 km) to the town church and plaza.

Cave enthusiasts might also enjoy hiking to the **Sotano de San Agustín** (Pit of San Agustín), near the village of San Agustín, on Highway 182 a few miles northeast of Huautla. The cave was only discovered during the 1990s. With a total depth of about a mile (4,800 feet, 1,440 meters) and a number of long single drops (the longest at around 350 feet, 105 meters) the San Agustín cave is considered among the deepest in the world. You can reach the cave entrance accompanied by a local guide (inquire at the San Agustín *presidencia municipal)* via the steep downhill trail from near the town church. As for exploring the cave itself, only super-equipped and experienced speleologists should apply to local authorities for permission to enter.

The Cañada: Canyon Country

Shadowed from rain by mountains on all sides, the dry, tropical Cañada canyonland comprises one of Oaxaca's major geo-cultural regions. It encompasses the Cuicateca—the land of the Cuicatecs—a Mixtec-related people who, for longer than anyone can remember, have scratched out a living from their homeland's warm, desert canyon bottoms and steep mountain slopes. Reclusive and traditional, Cuicatec people generally venture out from their home villages only infrequently, mostly to trade at the market towns—sometimes Teotitlán del Camino, more often at Cuicatlán.

TEOTITLÁN DEL CAMINO

Just shy of Oaxaca's border with the state of Puebla stands Teotitlán del Camino (pop. 5,000), the jumping-off point for the Mazateca highlands to the east and the Cañada to the south. Teotitlán's elevation, 3,600 feet (1,100 meters), places it about a mile (1.6 km) lower and many degrees warmer than sometimes-chilly Huautla de Jiménez, in the Mazateca highlands. Teotitlán's fortunate combination of warmth, sunshine, and abundant spring water nourishes a local oasis of mangos, bananas, lemons, oranges, and avocados.

Sights

Despite Teotitlán's significance as the capital of the sprawling governmental district of the same name, it nevertheless feels much like a small town, with a modicum of stores and services within a block or two of the central plaza. Streets run approximately east-west (uphill-downhill) and north-south. The three main east-west streets are Hidalgo, the Highway 135 ingress street that runs along the plaza's north side; José Silones,

between the plaza and the church; and 5 de Mayo, a block south of the plaza along the church's south side. The main north-south streets are Josefina Ortiz de Domínguez, which runs along the west side of the plaza; Juárez, behind and east of the church; and Independencia, the Highway 182 ingress from Huautla, one block farther east uphill.

The town's pride is its church, the **Templo de San Miguel Arcángel,** built by Franciscan padres during the 17th century. Outside, an image of angel San Miguel decorates the pinnacle of its Roman Doric–columned facade. Inside, the ceiling is a cheery sky blue, with bright paintings of Saints John (Juan), Matthew (Mateo), Luke (Lucas), and Mark (Marcos) around the central cupola overhead. The broad church atrium is usually very quiet, except around September 29, when local folks honor San Miguel with processions, fireworks, and floats ridden by children dressed as angels.

Take a stroll around the adjacent town plaza, where big, shady trees provide a welcome refuge from the warm afternoon sun. At night, the plaza becomes the town's central meeting ground, where couples stroll and people relax on benches attractively decorated with bright Puebla tile.

If it's Wednesday or Sunday, another focus of activity is the **market** on Independencia, about two blocks south of the plaza. The big Teotitlán market structure was obviously built for better times. It's presently empty as a tomb five days a week.

Accommodations and Food

The town has three acceptable hotels, a *casa de huéspedes* (guesthouse), and a sprinkling of restaurants, one highly recommended. The best hotel is **Hotel Doña Ofelia,** three blocks west (downhill) and north from the plaza, at Calle Ricardo Flores

Magón 39, Teotitlán del Camino, Oaxaca 68540, tel./fax 363/372-0220. (From the plaza corner of Hidalgo and Josefina Ortiz de Domínguez, walk two blocks downhill past the secondary school to Pino Suárez, then turn right and continue one block north to Flores Magón and the hotel). Its six rooms in two stories are clean and comfortably furnished. Best of all, they open onto a shady, homey garden, with chairs and tables for relaxing. In the morning especially, birds sing, and rarely does anything disturb the tranquility. Rentals run $10 s, $15 d, $20 t, with fan and hot-water shower bath. The hotel, the best along Highway 135 between Oaxaca and Tehuacán, is often full; be sure to call ahead for a reservation.

The town's second-best but newer hotel has both the same name and the same kindly owner, Ofelia Mesa Muñoz. The newer hotel occupies the corner of Independencia and José Silones, a block and a half uphill east of the plaza. It's not as tightly managed, since Ofelia stays at her favorite, original hotel. The rooms, however, are just as clean and are attractively painted and highlighted with fine Puebla tile. Rooms open to an inviting shaded garden patio. And it's the only hotel in Oaxaca with an irrigation aqueduct (albeit a small one that gurgles quaintly past the

edge of the patio). Unfortunately, the location suffers from noisy trucks and buses, which seem to run past the front door every few minutes during the morning. Despite the noise, this is a good second choice. Prices are the same, $10 s, $15 d, $20 t, with fan and shower bath with hot water. Reserve through the address and telephone number for the Hotel Doña Ofelia.

Third choice goes to **Hotel Isabel,** at Colonia 7, Teotitlán del Camino, Oaxaca 68540, tel. 363/372-0097, two blocks north of the plaza. The rooms, in an apartment-style block on the quiet edge of town, which rent for about $9 d, are plainer and not as clean, with none of the garden amenities as Ofelia's hotels. Find it by walking two blocks downhill west, to Colonia (at the secondary school), then two blocks north of the plaza.

On the other hand, budget travelers may prefer the plain but homey **Casa de Huéspedes Mary,** $4 s, $8 d, tel. 363/372-0242, diagonally across the street from the plaza's southwest corner.

Stop to cool off from the Teotitlán heat beneath the shady plaza-front portal of **Paleteria La Michoacana.** Take your pick from a host of flavors of juices, ices, and ice cream. For more light fare, try the **Taquería and Cafetería,** at the corner of 5 de Mayo and Juárez.

On the other hand, you might as well go to Teotitlán's best, the inviting, family-run **Restaurant Silvia** on Juárez, a block east and around the corner from the plaza, which lives up to its high local reputation. Although busily patronized by *rancheros*, businesspersons, and occasional tourists, you can usually retreat to the relaxing, airy patio section in the rear. Open daily for *desayuno*, *comida*, and *cena* (breakfast, lunch, and dinner), 7:30 A.M.–10 P.M.

Another good choice is the highly recommended **Restaurant Blanca Flor**, on Hwy. 135, just south of the big obelisk.

Services

Teotitlán plaza-front establishments can supply most emergency needs. Start with the *correo* (post office), open Mon.–Fri. 9 A.M.–noon, at the northeast corner of the plaza. Diagonally opposite, at the southeast plaza corner, is the small grocery, **Abarrotes Santa Lucia.** One block south, you'll find the *telégrafos*, J. Ortiz 12, tel. 363/372-0171, open Mon.–Fri. 9 A.M.–3 P.M., offering money orders, telex, and telegraph, but no fax. Try the *larga distancia* on Hidalgo by the bus station, half a block downhill from the plaza, for fax.

For medicines, go to the **Farmacia Rex,** behind the church at the corner of Juárez and 5 de Mayo, tel. 363/372-0374, open daily 7 A.M.–11 P.M. If the Rex doesn't have what you need, continue uphill along 5 de Mayo half a block to Farmacia El Fénix.

As for doctors, visit either **Dr. Sergio Mendoza,** general practitioner, or **Doctora María Teresa Noriega,** family medicine, tel. 363/372-0154, who at this writing were maintaining joint offices in their home at Juárez 50, next to the state water office, about three blocks south of the center of town. Alternatively, go to the **Seguro Social** clinic, several blocks north of the town center, on Hwy. 182, uphill from the Hwy. 185 obelisk, tel. 363/372-0139.

Getting There and Away

Second-class buses operate out of a pair of terminals on Hidalgo, a block downhill from the plaza. **Fletes y Pasajes** buses connect south with Oaxaca via Cuicatlán, northwest with Mexico City via

Tehuacán and Puebla, and east with Huatla. Second-class **Autobuses Unidos** (AU) buses, tel. 363/372-0061, connect south with Oaxaca via Cuicatlán, northwest with Mexico City via Tehuacán and Puebla, and east with Huautla. Additionally, local-class white minibus **Transportes Regionales Sierra-Cañada-Teotitlán-Oaxaca** buses connect south with Oaxaca, via Cuicatlán, and east with Huautla.

For drivers, paved Highway 182 connects Teotitlán east with Huautla in 41 miles (66 km) of scenic but winding uphill mountain road. For safety, allow 2.5 hours (or two hours in the opposite, downhill, direction). In a southerly direction, Highway 135 connects with Oaxaca in a winding but easy (with caution) 100 miles (161 km). Allow about 3.5 hours of driving time, either direction. In a northerly direction, Highway 135 connects with Tehuacán (39 miles, 63 km, one hour). From there, you can continue northwest to Puebla via Highway 150 in an additional three-hour, 70-mile (93-km) trip.

Unleaded gasoline is available at the Pemex *gasolinera* on the highway, about a mile (2 km) northwest of the town plaza.

CUICATLÁN

Cuicatlán (pop. 10,000) is the commercial capital of the Cañada, the emporium for the entire high Sierra hinterland that rises immediately east of town. Cuicatlán, like Teotitlán, owes its wealth to abundant sunshine and water. In Cuicatlán, water is synonymous with the Río Grande, the river that passes just west of the highway and west of town. After nourishing a local oasis of fruit, vegetables, and grain, the Río Grande continues its good work downstream. It joins with the swarm of tributaries draining the entire Cañada basin, becoming the Río Santo Domingo, the major electrical power source at the Miguel de la Madrid dam. The river unites with the Río Papaloapan past Tuxtepec, finally feeding thirsty crops and people all the way to the Gulf of Mexico.

Sights

Cuicatlán (Place of Song) is home to a busy market, often packed with Cuicatec-speaking people, especially women, wearing their handmade *huip-iles.* Head there via the turnoff road from Highway 135, which, as it becomes Avenida Hidalgo, Cuicatlan's main business street, leads a mile (1.6 km) north to the plaza at the town center. There stands the church, the **Templo de San Juan Bautista,** on the plaza's east side. A block farther east is the *presidencia municipal.* Across the street from the *presidencia* is the **market.** Although it's lively enough most days, the market is especially big on Sundays and overflowing around June 24, when merrymakers crowd the streets and celebrate the **Fiesta de San Juan Bautista** with costumes, parades and floats, community feasts, fireworks, and traditional dances.

Accommodations and Food

Cuicatlán offers a pair of marginally acceptable hotels, a good restaurant, and a number of essential services. The best hotel, in a parklike setting by the Río Grande, is named, appropriately, the **Hotel Oasis,** Carretera Federal, San Juan Bautista Cuicatlán, Oaxaca 68600, tel. 236/374-0266, right on the highway. (Unfortunately, at this writing, the once-beautiful Hotel Oasis has been allowed to run down.) The approximately 20 plainly furnished rooms rent for about $10 s or d ($17 for two beds), with hot-water shower baths, fans, restaurant, and parking. Credit cards are not accepted. (A splash in the hotel pool in the adjacent garden—if it's working—or in the river nearby, might provide a cooling diversion during a hot Cañada afternoon.)

In town, a couple of blocks from the bus station, bus travelers might find the **Casa de Huéspedes Dani,** Calle Hidalgo, San Juan Bautista Cuicatlán, Oaxaca 68600, tel. 236/374-0091, too convenient to pass up. It offers about 10 plain rooms around a parking patio for about $7 s, $9 d, with fans and hot-water showers and toilets. Credit cards not accepted.

As for food, you'll find the freshest fruit and vegetables in the market and the best grocery selection at the **Super El Molino** grocery, open daily 7 A.M.–10 P.M., at the plaza's southeast corner, across the street from the church.

Cuicatlán's best place to eat by far is the airy *palapa* of the clean, seafood-specialty

Restaurant Boringuen, two blocks east of the plaza, across the street from the *presidencia municipal,* tel. 236/374-0222. Enjoy the relaxing open-air atmosphere and fresh fish fillet or shrimp for lunch or dinner. Open daily 8 A.M.–9 P.M.

Services

Most of Cuicatlán's service establishments are either on the town plaza or along Calle Hidalgo, the north-south Highway 135 ingress street. Although at this writing Cuicatlán still had no bank, you might be able to cash a small traveler's check (or at least a $20 bill) at the grocery store **Super El Molino,** at the town plaza's southeast corner. A long-distance telephone is available at the small *caseta larga distancia,* on the plaza at the east corner of Hidalgo, open daily 7:30 A.M.–10:30 P.M.

For nonprescription medicines and drugs, cross to the west, plaza-front side, of Hidalgo to **Farmacia San Juan,** tel. 236/374-0098. If, however, you need a doctor, see **Dr. Rudolfo Reyes Escalante,** at Calle Centenario 30, tel. 236/374-0033. (From the plaza, walk two blocks down Hidalgo to Centenario, then turn right half a block.) Alternatively, go to the public *centro de salud* clinic and hospital on Hidalgo, three blocks downhill from the plaza.

Buy stamps or mail a letter at the *correo* (post office), diagonally across the street from the plaza's southwest corner, second floor.

Getting There and Away

Fletes y Pasajes and **Autobuses Unidos** (AU) long-distance buses operate out of separate stations on Hidalgo, about four blocks downhill from the plaza. They both offer departures connecting north with Mexico City via Teotitlán, Tehuacán, and Puebla, and south with Oaxaca.

For drivers, Highway 135 connects south with Highway 190 at Telixtlahuaca, thence with Oaxaca, a total of 63 miles (101 km). The route, paved and in good condition but winding, requires about two hours for safety.

In the northerly direction, Highway 135 connects with Teotitlán del Camino in about 37 miles (60 km). Allow about an hour and a quarter for this winding but easy (with caution) trip.

The Isthmus: Land of Plenty

A trip to the Isthmus from the Oaxaca central highlands sometimes seems like a journey to another country. At the Isthmus, the North American continent narrows to a scarce 100 miles (160 km) in width; the mighty Sierras shrink to mere foothills. The climate is tropical; the land is fertile and well-watered. Luxuriant groves hang heavy with almonds, avocados, coconuts, mangos, and oranges. Rivers wind downhill to the sea, springs well up at the foot of mountains, and swarms of fish swim offshore. The Isthmus is a land of abundance, and it shows in the people. Women are world-famous for their beauty, spirit, and their incomparably lovely flowered skirts and blouses, which young and old seem to wear at any excuse.

And they have excuses aplenty, for the Isthmus is the place of the *velas,* called fiestas in other parts of Mexico. But in the Isthmus, especially in the towns of Tehuantepec and Juchitán, where *istmeño* hearts beat fastest, *velas* are something

© BRUCE WHIPPERMAN

398 The Isthmus: Land of Plenty

more special. Most every *barrio* (neighborhood) must celebrate one in honor of its patron saint. A short list names 20 major yearly *velas* in Juchitán alone. The long list, including all the towns in the Isthmus, numbers more than 100.

This all climaxes in the town of Tehuantepec on December 26, in a grand one-day celebration, the **Vela Tehuantepec,** when everyone dresses up, women in their spectacular flowered *trajes* and men with their diminutive Tehuantepec sombreros, red kerchiefs, sashes, and machetes. The entire town celebrates all night, dancing to the beautiful melody of the *Sandunga,* which, once you've been captured by its lovely, lilting strains, will always bring back your most cherished Isthmus memories.

Tehuantepec and Vicinity

HISTORY

Although strictly connected only with a single location, the name Tehuantepec (Hill of the Jaguar) is, in many minds, synonymous with the entire Isthmus region: thus the label the "Isthmus of Tehuantepec." The connection is historical, for Tehuantepec's dominance was born in events of long ago.

The earliest known settlers in the Isthmus left Olmec-style remains, which archaeologists date from as early as 4000 B.C. Much later, around 500 B.C., the Olmecs' inheritors, probably the ancestors of present-day Mixe- and Huave-speaking people, occupied the Isthmus lands. But times changed, and by A.D. 500 the Isthmus had become a strategic funnel: a trade gateway between the great civilizations, such as Teotihuacán and Monte Albán, of the Mexican central highlands, and the rich Mayan cultures of Chiapas, Yucatán, and Guatemala.

Eventually, the more populous Zapotec-speaking people displaced the Mixe and Huave in the Isthmus. By A.D. 1400, the Zapotec kings of Zaachila in Oaxaca's central valley controlled the Isthmus gateway with a mountaintop fort at Guiengola, which guarded their Isthmus capital at the present-day town of Tehuantepec.

The ambitious Aztec emperors also coveted the Isthmus gateway. In the 1440s, they sent armies to Oaxaca to pressure the Mixtec and Zapotec kingdoms, who allied themselves against the Aztecs. But forced by Aztec victories in 1486, many Zapotec people, including their king Cosijoeza, retreated from Zaachila and took refuge in Tehuantepec.

There, together with the Mixtecs under King Dzahuindanda, the Zapotecs, attacking from their stronghold at Guiengola, held off the Aztecs, who offered Emperor Moctezuma's daughter in marriage to King Cosijoeza as part of a peace pact.

With tranquillity established, Cosijoeza returned to reign once again over Zaachila, leaving his son, Cosijopí, as king of the Isthmus, with his court at Tehuantepec. Later, when the Spanish arrived, King Cosijopí joined with Cortés against the Aztecs. After Aztec power was erased, Cosijopí, along with thousands of his subject-inhabitants of Tehuantepec, converted to Christianity.

SIGHTS

Orientation

Although the Río Tehuantepec splits the Santo Domingo Tehuantepec town (pop. 52,000) along a roughly north-south line, the west-side portion, across the river via the Puente Metalico (Metal Bridge), first built for locomotives around 1900, seems like a mere suburb of the town center, east of the river. On the central plaza itself, the *presidencia municipal* (city hall) occupies the south side, along Calle 5 de Mayo; the main market, **Mercado Jesús Carranza,** lies on the plaza's west, river side, along Calle Juana C. Romero; and to the northeast, past the end of main north-south street Benito Juárez, about a block and a half northeast of the plaza, stands Tehuantepec's most venerable monument, the **Church and Ex-convent of Santo Domingo.**

Around the Plaza

First, take a stroll around the plaza, where you'll find some interesting sculptures, including noble likenesses of Miguel Hidalgo (the Father of Mexican Independence) and a pair of Tehuantepec heroes. On the north side, look for the bronze of a seated **Doña Juana Catalina Romero** (1855–1915), a Tehuantepec legend. She is famous partly for her good works, establishing schools for Tehuantepec children during the days when public education was a rarity in Mexico.

On the plaza's west (market) side, you'll find the bronze bust of **A. Maximino Ramón Ortiz**, the first and only governor of the Isthmus, when it was separated from Oaxaca as the territory of Tehuantepec for a few years during the 1850s. Politics, however, were not Ortiz's first love. He is best remembered as the composer of the *Sandunga,* Tehuantepec's beloved theme. His ageless melody seems to perfectly capture the essence of the Isthmus in a gracefully drowsy rhythm that swings slowly, yet deliberately, like the relaxed sway of lovers in a hammock beneath the deep shade of a Tehuantepec grove.

Templo y Exconvento de Santo Domingo

From the plaza's northeast corner, walk north along Calle Hidalgo one block to the venerable Santo Domingo church, behind its broad fenced atrium, on the right. The aging landmark (to the left of the new church) is interesting, partly because it was one of the few, if not the only, Christian churches in Mexico financed by a native ruler. Cosijopí, the last king of the Zapotecs, who was baptized as Juan Cortés de Cosijopí after his friend and ally Hernán Cortés, paid for the construction with both cash and the labor of thousands of his subjects. The building was erected under the supervision of Fray Fernando de Albequerque, vicar of Tehuantepec, between 1544 and 1550.

Given the warm relations between King Cosijopí and the Spanish, it is ironic that the Inquisition authorities burned Cosijopí at the stake a generation later for continuing (and for encouraging his people) to worship the old gods.

Enter through an interior side door, off the left-aisle of the very attractive new church. Inside, old Santo Domingo's most remarkable

The gilded statue of Doña Juana Catalina Romero graces the Tehuantepec town plaza.

THE ISTHMUS

THE ISTHMUS: LAND OF PLENTY

THE ISTHMUS

To Tuxtepec

To Minatitlán

Gustavo Díaz Ordaz

Río Coatzacoalcos

Río Chalchijapan

La Mixtequita

San Carlos

La Esmeralda

Santiago Tutla

Palomares

Cuauhtémoc

Río Escondido

Boca del Monte

Río Verde

San Juán Mazatlán

Río Sarabia

San Juan Guichicovi

Santiago Ixcuintepec

El Zacatal

Santa María Chimalapa

San José El Progreso

Matias Romero

Santa María Petapa

Petapa

El Barrio

Río Chichihua

Guevea de Humboldt

Loma Esperanza

Lachidola

Limestone Cave

Lagunas

Lázaro Cárdenas

San Miguel Chimalapa

Cofradia

Santa María Guienagati

Río Tehuantepec

Santiago Lachiguiri

Lachivixa

El Mezquite

Santiago

El Porvenir

Cuauhtémoc

Río Espíritu Santo

Santa María Totolapilla

Río Los Perros

Spring

Santo Domingo Chihuitán

La Venta

Santo Domingo

190

Niltepec

Reservoir Benito Juárez

Santiago Laollaga

Ixtepec

La Ventosa

HOTEL NILTEPEC

To Oaxaca

Llano Vena

Piedra de Cal

Spring

Magdalena Tlacotepec

Ixtaltepec

El Espinal

Unión Hidalgo

Cerro Iguana

Chicapa de Castro

Río Niltepec

BENITO JUÁREZ DAM

Jalapa del Marqués

GUIENGOLA ARCHAEOLOGICAL ZONE

Juchitán

Isla Cerro Prieto

Isla Cerro Venado

Playa Copalito

Magdalena Tequisistlán

Hot Spring

Yerba Santa

Mixtequilla

San Blas de Atempa

Santa Rosa de Lima

Laguna Superior

Embarcadero

San Dionisio del Mar

Laguna Inferior

Tequisistlán

Asunción Tlacolulita

San Miguel Ecatepec

San Miguel Tenango

Tehuantepec

San Pedro Huilotepec

Álvaro Obregón

Laguna Inferior

Puerto Estero

San Francisco del Mar

Cerro Conejo (1,560 m)

Loma Atravesada

Río Tenango

Salina Cruz

Playa La Ventosa

San Mateo del Mar

Santa María del Mar

POSADA RÚSTRIAN

To Bays of Huatulco and Puerto Ángel

Punta Conejo

Punta Chivo

Morro Mazatán

San Pedro Huamelula

Laguna Garrapatera

Punta Embarcadero

Santiago Astata

Lushu

Laguna Colorada

La Colorada

Laguna Grande

0   20 mi

0   20 km

THE ISTHMUS

feature is its lovely wooden *tabla* (altarpiece), with an unusual ebony Lord of Creation perched on its crest, with a dog, turtle, and deer in tow. (At this writing, the ebony statue had been removed, but a local priest told me that it would probably be returned after the present church remodeling work is finished.)

The ex-convent section, on the old church's north side, was abandoned not long after the Reforms of the late 1850s forced the Dominicans from Mexico. It had crumbled into a virtual ruin by the mid-20th century, when local people rolled up their sleeves and began restoring it in 1953. In 1982, with the restoration complete, the townsfolk christened their ex-convent as the **Casa de la Cultura.** Now, in the evenings it resounds with the noises of young musicians and dancers at practice.

To take a look inside the restored ex-convent (open Mon.–Fri. 10 A.M.–2 P.M. and 5–8 P.M., Sat. 10 A.M.–2 P.M.), retrace your steps out across the atrium, turn right at Calle Hidalgo, and walk north. After two short blocks, turn right at Guerrero. Walk one long block. Just after the *centro de salud* turn right into an alley, which leads south to the Casa de la Cultura and the old convent.

Inside the Casa de la Cultura, look for the faded but still-visible flower and animal motifs that Cosijopí's long-gone artists painted on the walls three and a half centuries ago. Head upstairs where the ancient wall decorations appear as fresh as if they were painted only a generation ago. In other upstairs rooms you'll see a host of historical mementos, from ancient Olmec-style figurines to a lovely jade necklace, once scattered, but excavated piece by piece and finally reassembled here. (Sometimes the upstairs is closed. If so, it's worth seeking permission from the administrative secretary on the ground floor, in the cloister, to let you go upstairs.)

TEHUANTEPEC

To Juchitán, Tuxtepec, and Chiapas

CALLE ABASOLO

PIPILA

WEDNESDAY MARKET (TIANGUIS)

HÉROES

200 190

GUERRERO

HEALTH CENTER

HIDALGO

CASA DE CULTURA (EX-CONVENT AND TEMPLO DE SANTO DOMINGO)

CATHEDRAL

VASCONCELOS

PLAZA JUÁREZ

FARMACIA SANTO DOMINGO/DOCTOR

DR. LICEAGA

PASTELERÍA DEL ISTMO

BANCO SERFIN

MERCADO DE CAMPESINOS

22 DE MARZO

POST OFFICE

CASA DE DOÑA JUANA

RESTAURANT ÁNGEL

MARKET

C. ROMERO

TELECOM

Río

5 DE MAYO

PLAZA

BANAMEX

BANCOMER

BANORTE

LARGA DISTANCIA

JUANA

PALACIO MUNICIPAL

CRUZ

Tehuantepec

HOTEL OASIS

DOCTOR

GUIENGUI

ATM

RESTAURANT COLONIAL

RESTAURANT SCARU

HOTEL DONAJI

Parque Laborio

DÍAZ

LÓPEZ

METAL BRIDGE

190

200

CRISTOBAL

SALINAS

JUÁREZ

TEMPLO DE LA NATIVA EXCELSA

ZARAGOZA

0   200 yds

0   200 m

To Salina Cruz and Oaxaca

THE ISTHMUS

© BRUCE WHIPPERMAN

The Tehuantepec plaza provides a calm respite from the hubbub and bustle of the market nearby.

Markets

The most colorful downtown action goes on at the **Mercado Jesús Carranza,** just across Romero from the plaza. At midday, the market overflows with life. The center of everything is the corridor street on the market's north side, which connects the plaza with the businesses along the railroad tracks behind the market.

The buzzing *motocarros* (motorcycle mini-trucks) that you see depositing and picking passengers by the railroad track seem to be a unique Isthmus invention. They mostly follow set roundtrip routes around town for a fixed price of about half a dollar. When you get tired of walking, hop on for a breezy whirlwind tour of Tehuantepec's back streets.

Market vendors, especially women in *traje,* tend to be apprehensive of rubber-necking strangers with cameras in hand. A good strategy is to blend in. Get a *refresco* at one of the food stalls and find a low-profile spot in the shade where you can take in the passing scene.

Get some relief from the heat and bustle inside the roofed market building itself. If you're in the mood for shopping, plenty of handicrafts are available. On the bottom floor, stalls offer the **gold filigree jewelry** that the Tehuantepec women love to wear. Look farther for lots of woven goods, such as **baskets, string bags of *ixtle* fiber, hand fans,** and **hammocks.** One unusual item that you may see during the late spring are large, three-foot-long (one-meter) pods of decorative **flowers of *coyul.***

Upstairs, via the stairway on the southwest corner by the railroad track, you'll find Tehuantepec's pride—the beautiful embroidered *tehuana* **flowered blouses and skirts.** Look around, decide what you want, then bargain for it. Asking prices for the prized, embroidered flower-design blouses run as much as $30, a whole outfit about $100.

Behind the market runs the **railway track,** which has the distinct appearance of being abandoned, because dozens of vendors regularly set up where trains should come roaring through. Shopkeepers, however, report that trains actually use the track occasionally, when everyone scatters

Coyul pods spill out their seeds, popularly used for Easter decorations.

with their goods (from bananas and melons to shrimp and hammocks).

Pottery, including many big, homely items—bowls, griddles, planters, pots—is for sale at the second downtown market, the lackluster Mercado 5 de Febrero, sometimes known as the **Mercado de Campesinos,** tucked at the plaza's northwest corner. Smaller for-sale items include pots painted with bright flowers as well as woven goods, such as baskets, fans, and handmade brooms.

Besides the two aforementioned permanent daily markets near the plaza, country people flood into town for *tianguis* (street markets) on Wednesday and Sunday. Visit the Wednesday *tianguis,* set up along north-side **Calle Héroes,** most easily by riding a *motocarro* from the plaza. Alternatively, from the plaza, walk north along Hidalgo past the church. Two blocks from the plaza, turn right at Guerrero and continue several blocks to the blue-trimmed San Juan Bautista church, where you turn left at Héroes. After a few blocks, you'll see the awnings stretched along side streets.

The **Sunday *tianguis*** is much bigger, so much so that it's held on the west side across the river, beyond the big Oaxaca highway

intersection, in the open space behind the Hotel Gueixhoba.

Casa de Doña Juana Catalina Romero
The railway track so intimately close to the market is due to the speculated intimate relationship between aging President Porfirio Díaz and local beauty Doña Juana Catalina Romero. Doña Juana Catalina lived in the French-style mansion, now in faded white with fancy blue window awnings in need of serious renovation, that rises by the tracks. Doña Juana Catalina's elderly granddaughter, who occasionally enjoys receiving visitors, still lives in the mansion, along with her daughter and granddaughter.

La Cueva
If sometime you feel like an early-morning or late-afternoon walk, head for La Cueva (The Cave), as local folks call it. It's visible most of the way up the hill called Liesa, across the river about two miles (3 km) west of town. La Cueva has been hallowed ground for as long as anyone remembers. Local folks tell stories about the existence of a secret passageway somewhere at the back of the cave that leads all the way to Guiengola, the "old town," now a mysterious ruin on the mountain 10 miles (16 km) to the west. (See Excursions West of Tehuantepec.)

La Cueva still draws virtually everyone in town for a pilgrimage during both Semana Santa (Holy Week) and May 3 (Día de la Cruz). It's best not to try the climb during the heat of the day (allow at least an hour for the whole excursion). In order to get a head start, spend a dollar or two on a taxi or *motocarro* (the motorcycle-driven carts buzzing near the market) to take you to the base of the hill.

Other Sights
A number of smaller plazas dot Tehuantepec's several *barrios* (neighborhoods). If you head south along Juárez two long blocks, you'll arrive at **Plaza Laborio** and its adjacent blue-trimmed, storybook **Templo de la Natividad Excelsa.** Before you go inside to look around, notice that the right bell tower is tilted at a crazy angle, not unlike the Leaning Tower of Pisa.

JUANA CATALINA ROMERO: HEROINE OF TEHUANTEPEC

Why Tehuantepec's main downtown streets, which carry such nationally renowned labels as "Cinco de Mayo," "Juárez," and "Hidalgo," should include "Juana C. Romero" among them is a question nearly all adult townsfolk can immediately answer. "Doña Juana," they say, is Tehuantepec's heroine because she "built schools and helped the children of Tehuantepec." Some go on to say that she "got lots of help for Tehuantepec from her friend, Presidente Porfirio Díaz."

When pressed, most Tehuantepec folks acknowledge that she had a close (some even say intimate) relationship with Porfirio Díaz. Juana Catalina was an 18-year-old blue-blooded beauty when first introduced to Díaz in 1873. At that time, he was the celebrated general who beat the French at Puebla on May 5 (Cinco de Mayo), 1862, and heir apparent to the late President Benito Juárez. Although he must have been charmed by her beauty at their first meeting, most certainly nothing immediate came of it, since he was both middle-aged and married and she had her upper crust reputation to preserve.

Whatever passed between them during later years has been the subject of endless gossip. In any case, she never married, and Don Porfirio, it is speculated, had the railroad tracks laid

Juana Catalina Romero is fondly remembered by Tehuantepec people for her kindness and good works.

right past her house in downtown Tehuantepec so he could hop off the train and visit her with no fuss or muss.

Laborio (the name of the church's *barrio*) residents don't seem to worry. "It's been like that for years," they say.

Plaza Laborio is mostly sleepy, except during the August 31–September 11 **Fiesta Laborio,** when residents and visitors celebrate with a long menu of feasts, dancing, fireworks, and *calendas* (processions).

Also worth a visit, across the river, is the **Barrio de Santa María.** (Get there by bearing left at the street heading diagonally left from the highway, a block or two west of the river bridge; after about two more blocks, go left again.) The main community pride and joy is the (also bright blue and white) **Templo de la Virgen de la Asunción.** The church, by the same architect who built the famous pilgrimage church in

Juquila, is the focus of a busy round of *barrio* events. The bustle climaxes during the August 13–18 **Fiesta Patronal del Barrio de Santa María Reolotoca,** with a *calenda* (procession), a parade of flower-decorated bull-drawn carts, and earsplitting popular dances on three successive nights. Bring your earplugs.

ACCOMMODATIONS

Tehuantepec offers visitors at least three hotels, one of them, semi-deluxe, in the west suburb, and a humbler but acceptable pair downtown. Best choice downtown is the **Oasis,** a block south from the plaza hubbub, behind the *presidencia* at Melchor Ocampo 8, Tehuantepec, Oaxaca 70760, tel. 971/715-0008, fax 971/715-0835.

THE ISTHMUS

Typical colorful *tehuana* (Tehuantepec women's dress) stands out from the market hubbub.

Although at first glance the Oasis doesn't appear very exciting, a closer examination reveals the talents of the owner, friendly, English-speaking artist Julin (hoo-LEEN) Contreras, whose art decorates the hotel's restaurant wall. She also was commissioned to do the mural in the council chamber on the second floor of the *presidencia municipal.*

She offers 28 plain but clean and comfortable rooms, with colorful, thoughtfully selected bedspreads and curtains. In some rooms of the four-story tier, windows open to garden, mountain, and river views. Pottery and plants selected by the owner decorate niches and corridors. In the room-tier courtyard, a towering *chico zapote* tree stretches skyward. Other trees around the yard supply all of the seasonal grapefruits and mangos that guests can eat. A parking lot provides security for cars. All this for $13 s or d, $20 t with hot water, fans, and good, relaxed, Restaurant Almendro (Almond Tree). Credit cards are not accepted. For lovers of the way Mexico "used to be," this is the place.

Second choice downtown goes to the **Hotel Donaji** (named for Oaxaca's beloved Zapoteca heroine), two blocks south of the plaza on quiet Plaza Laborio, at Juárez 10, Tehuantepec, Oaxaca 70760, tel. 971/715-0064. The hotel, recently renovated, offers a shady, inner patio with plants and cages of chirping tropical birds. The 48 rooms, in a big two-story block, are simply but invitingly decorated. They rent for about $12 s, $17 d fan only, $21 s, $24 d with a/c; all with hot-water shower baths, TV, and parking, but credit cards not accepted. The Donaji's major pluses are air-conditioning (desirable in warm Tehuantepec) and its location on the tree-shaded, drowsy (except during the August 31–September 11 fiesta) Plaza Laborio.

The most comfortable hotel in town is the four-star **Hotel Guiexhoba** (ghee-ay-SHOW-bah), Carretera Panamericana Km 250.5, Barrio Santa María, Tehuantepec, Oaxaca 70760, tel./fax 971/715-1710 or 971/715-0416, guiex-hoba@prodigy.net.mx, which deserves extra points simply for its Zapotec label, the name of a locally abundant white flower with a fragrant scent reminiscent of jasmine. The hotel has a specimen bush, which blooms during the summer rainy season, by the front entrance. Find the hotel on Hwy. 190, inbound from Oaxaca on the right before the bridge.

The Guiexhoba's 36 spacious, clean, and comfortable rooms, in two stories, enfold a parking courtyard that fortunately shields rooms on its north side from highway noise. Staff are generally attentive, competent, and courteous. The upstairs rooms away from the highway are quiet and have fewer people walking past the windows; unfortunately, you must draw drapes for privacy. Rates run a reasonable $30 s, $39 d, $47 t, with pool, parking, good cable TV, a/c, hot-water shower baths, credit cards accepted, and the very good Restaurant Guiexhoba.

FOOD
Groceries, Breakfasts, and Treats
Tehuantepec's freshest fruit and vegetable sources by far are the luscious mounds of avocados, bananas, carrots, lettuces, mangos, pineapples, radishes, and much more in the plaza market (be sure to scrub with soap and/or peel before eating). Likewise, find the best grocery sources, such as the **Abarrotes El Centro** permanent stall, also in the market, in the covered section on the ground floor.

Breakfasts you'll probably find most conveniently at your hotel, such as the Restaurant Almendro of the Hotel Oasis and the restaurant at the Hotel Guiexhoba. Otherwise (or if you're staying at Hotel Donaji), go to the **Restaurant Colonial** two blocks south of the plaza, or Tehuantepec's best, the delightfully refined **Restaurant Scaru** (see Restaurants) three blocks south of the plaza.

Satisfy your sweet tooth with the baked offerings of the **Super Panadería y Pastelería del Istmo,** tel. 971/715-0808, open daily 7:30 A.M.–8:30 P.M. Find it on the railroad tracks, just north of the market, on the left. For evening snacks, fill up at the **taco stall** lineup behind the *presidencia municipal.*

Restaurants
Tehuantepec offers a sprinkling of good sit-down restaurants. By far the best is the showplace **Restaurant Scaru,** at south-side cul-de-sac Callejon Leona Vicario 4, tel. 971/715-0646. Here, in a graceful, airy setting, owners lovingly portray picturesque aspects of traditional Isthmus life. Walls bloom with murals of fruit, festivals, and lovely *tehuanas* in their bright, flowery costumes, while patios are sprinkled with hammocks and sheltered overhead by luxurious handcrafted *palapas.* Saturday and Sunday afternoons 2–6 P.M., a marimba band will play the *Sandunga* to your heart's content. After such a luscious introduction, the food, from a very recognizable menu of salads, soups, and eggs ($3–5), pastas ($4–6), meats (including some game), fish, and fowl ($5–10), is no less than you would expect. Open daily 8 A.M.–11 P.M.; credit cards accepted.

Get there from the plaza by walking two long blocks south along Juárez to Plaza Laborio. Turn left and walk one block to Callejon Leona Vicario on the left; the restaurant is on the uphill side of the street.

Second choice goes to the good but the more ordinarily picturesque restaurant at the **Hotel Guiexhoba** across the river, tel. 971/715-1710. The food, from a typical but tasty menu of breakfasts (eggs and pancakes), lunches (hamburgers, soups, and stews), and dinners (meat, fish, fowl, and spaghetti) sometimes comes with a flaming crepe Suzette flourish. Open daily 7:30 A.M.–10 P.M.; credit cards accepted.

Back downtown, third choice goes to the **Restaurant Colonial,** at Juana C. Romero, two blocks south of the plaza, tel. 971/715-0115. Owners have worked hard to recreate a corner of old Mexico, with sentimental country paintings, brightly hued stucco walls, all beneath a genuinely rustic tree limb–beamed ceiling.

The food is appropriately traditional, with plenty of good breakfasts (omelette with potatoes, hot cakes, corn flakes, $2–5); Mexican *antojitos* (tacos, enchiladas, tostadas, $3–5); and a long list of entrées (pasta, meat and seafood, $5–7). Find them open daily 8 A.M.–10 P.M.

Seafood lunches and dinners are the tour de force of the no-name restaurant (formerly

Restaurant Ángel) on the highway corner entrance to town, at 5 de Mayo 1, tel. 971/715-1628. You can have the best of the day's catch of *camarones, langosta, ostiones, pulpo, calamar, pescado* (shrimp, lobster, oysters, octopus, squid, fish), and much more ($5–12). The air-conditioning is a plus. Although open daily (8 A.M.–11 P.M.) for breakfast, the staff doesn't seem to wake up until about noon. Credit cards accepted.

SERVICES

Money

Tehuantepec offers several banks, all of which have ATMs. If you like a crowd, follow it to **Banamex,** on the plaza's west side, tel. 971/715-2383 (Mon.–Fri. 9 A.M.–4 P.M.); or **Bancomer,** on Cinco de Mayo, between the highway and the plaza. Find generally less crowded **Banco Santander Serfin** on the plaza's northwest side, corner of Romero, tel. 971/715-0916 or 971/715-0917 (Mon.–Fri. 9 A.M.–4 P.M., Sat. 10 A.M.–2 P.M.).

Communications

Both the *correo* (open Mon.–Fri. 8 A.M.–3 P.M., including rapid, secure **Mexpost** service), tel. 971/715-0106; and *telecomunicaciones* (money orders and public fax 971/715-0159), open Mon.–Fri. 8 A.M.–7:30 P.M. and Sat. 9 A.M.–noon), stand side by side at the north end of Juárez, at the plaza's northeast corner.

Long-distance telephone and photocopies are available at **Papelería La Esfera,** at the plaza's southeast corner next to Banamex, tel. 971/715-0042, fax 971/715-2090, open Mon.–Sat. 8:30 A.M.–8:30 P.M. and Sun. 9 A.M.–2 P.M.

Health and Emergencies

A number of town **pharmacies** provide nonprescription medicines and drugs. Perhaps the best is **Farmacia Santo Domingo,** on Romero, one block north (from Banco Serfin) of the plaza's northwest corner, tel. 971/715-0080, open Mon.–Sat. 8 A.M.–10 P.M., run by Dr. Leopoldo Vasquez, who examines, diagnoses, prescribes, and rings up the sale right on the spot.

If you need to consult a doctor, you can always find one at the *centro de salud* (health

center), three blocks from the plaza at Guerrero 19. Get there by walking from the Banco Serfin at the plaza's northwest corner. After two blocks, turn right at Guerrero and continue a long block to the *centro de salud* on the right.

Alternatively, consult with general practitioner Dr. José Manuel Vichido, on Calle Guietiqui, tel. 971/715-0862, open Mon.–Sat. 9 A.M.–1 P.M. From the plaza's southeast corner, walk south one block along Juárez; turn left at the first street, Guietiqui. The doctor's office is half a block down on the left.

Police service is available from at least two sources in Tehuantepec. Call either the *policía municipal,* tel. 971/715-0001, or the *preventiva,* tel. 971/711-2346.

GETTING THERE AND AWAY

By Bus

The main bus station is on the highway, with official address Carretera Panamericana Km 20, tel. 971/715-0108. It's at the highway intersection at the end of Calle Héroes, about a mile (2 km) northeast of downtown. Get there by taxi or *motocarro* from the plaza.

Four major bus lines, first-class **Autobuses del Oriente** (ADO) and **Cristóbal Colón** (CC) and second-class **Sur** and **Autobuses Unidos** (AU), offer many connections north across the Isthmus, northwest with Oaxaca, southwest with the Oaxaca Pacific Coast, and east with Chiapas. Direct departures connect north via Juchitán with Tuxtepec, Villahermosa, Palenque, Minatitlán, and Coatzacoalcos; northwest with Oaxaca, Puebla, and Mexico City; southwest with Salina Cruz, Bahías de Huatulco, Pochutla (Puerto Ángel), and Puerto Escondido; and east via Juchitán with Tuxtla Gutiérrez, San Cristóbal las Casas, and Tapachula at the Guatemala border.

In addition to those bus lines, a pair of reliable second-class cooperative lines, **Oaxaca Istmo** and **Fletes y Pasajes,** stop on the highway by the bus station. Oaxaca Istmo offers connections northwest with Oaxaca and southwest with Bahías de Huatulco, Pochutla (Puerto

SCOOTING AROUND BY MOTOCARRO

The city of Tehuantepec's public transportation system was long ago preempted by the city's regiment of *motocarros*—small, motorcycle-driven flat-bed trucks that buzz, putt, squeal, and skid around town continuously. The center of the action is the railroad track behind the market, where all Tehuantepec *motocarros* faithfully return for passengers and cargo.

Motocarros have thus become the end-all answer to how to get around in Tehuantepec's heat. Long ago, everyone (excepting mad dogs and Englishmen) learned that too much midday walking can produce a considerable sweat at least and sunstroke at worst. If you get overheated, do as Tehuantepec people do and take a seat in the shade and cool down with an *agua* or *refresco*. Later, continue your extended tour via *motocarro*. Fares run less than $.50 for an entire circuit of the town.

Ángel), and Puerto Escondido, while Fletes y Pasajes offers connections northwest with Oaxaca, southwest with Salina Cruz, and northeast with Juchitán.

By Car

Paved roads fan out from Tehuantepec in four directions. Highway 190 connects northeast with Juchitán (17 miles, 27 km), then splits north as Highway 185 at La Ventosa and continues north, via Matías Romero and Minatitlán all the way to the Gulf of Mexico at Coatzacoalcos, a total of 166 miles (267 km). Allow about 4.5 driving hours, either way, for this relatively easy trip.

For Tuxtepec, from Highway 185 turn onto Highway 147 at Matías Romero and continue northwest a total of 189 miles (304 km). Allow about five hours of driving time from Tehuantepec. *Warning:* Some robberies have occurred on the long, lonely Highway 147 Matías Romero–Tuxtepec leg. Authorities advise drivers to restrict their travel to *daytime only* on this stretch.

Highway 190 connects Tehuantepec northwest with Oaxaca along 155 miles (250 km) of well-maintained but winding highway. Allow about five hours Oaxaca direction (uphill), 4.5 hours in the opposite direction.

Highway 200 connects Tehuantepec west with the Oaxaca Pacific Coast, via Salina Cruz (nine miles, 15 km), Bahías de Huatulco (100 miles, 161 km, three hours), Pochutla-Puerto Ángel (124 miles, 200 km, four hours), and Puerto Escondido (170 miles, 274 km, five hours) of paved, moderately traveled, secure highway.

Highway 190 connects Tehuantepec east via Juchitán (17 miles, 27 km) and Niltepec to Tapanatepec (78 miles, 126 km) near the Chiapas border. Allow about 3.5 hours of driving time to Tapanatepec.

Drivers should fill up with **gasoline** at the Pemex *gasolinera* on the west side of the river, about a mile (2 km) west of the bridge, where the road splits southwest to Salina Cruz, northwest to Oaxaca.

EXCURSIONS WEST OF TEHUANTEPEC

The interesting destination trio of Guiengola, Jalapa del Marqués, and Tequisistlán can be combined into a full-day auto or taxi excursion (two days by bus) west of Tehuantepec. Along the way, enjoy a vigorous hike through pristine forest to the regal ruined fortress-city at Guiengola, a breezy boat ride on the Jalapa de Marqués reservoir, a soak in the community hot (actually just warm) spring, and a stop at the marble factory at Tequisistlán.

Guiengola

The mountain fortress Guiengola (ghee-ayn-GOH-lah), Big Rock in Zapotec, may have been abandoned before the Spanish arrived, but it was never forgotten. Local people refer to it as the "old town" and often hear voices when up there. If so, they rush down the mountain before dark.

Ghosts notwithstanding, an excursion to Guiengola is a chance to get some fresh air into your lungs as you enjoy the Isthmus tropical forest up close—fluttering butterflies, spiny cactus, flowery trees, and fireflies and hoot owls (if you return at dusk). At the end of the rough jeep

THE ISTHMUS

road that winds about four miles (6 km) up Guiengola Mountain, you continue on foot via a sometimes steep two-mile (three-km), one-hour hike through summer-green (but brown in spring) tropical woodland. If you start early, you might see *venado* (deer), *javelin* (wild pigs) and, if you're lucky, a *león* (mountain lion).

You know you're getting close to the ruins when the trail straightens out and you see a continuous series of vegetation-covered mounds and walls on both sides. You are following a regal street, lined with ruined houses of the nobility. Next, break out into the open, where a four-tiered unreconstructed noble pyramid, called the Pyramid of the Sun, rises at the right. On the opposite side, across a spreading, flat ceremonial plaza, another, even taller, five-tiered Pyramid of the Moon stands on your left. To the extreme left rises a big ball court, so well preserved that it appears as if a dozen persons could spend a weekend with machetes and a few shovels and put the place in order for a tournament on Monday.

What you see immediately around you is only the ceremonial center. Beneath the surrounding forest are dozens of mounds, remains of temples, ceremonial patios, and homes. The state of preservation is exceptional, partly because of the site's isolation. These structures of stone and mud mortar are delicate and mostly unexplored; please refrain from climbing on them.

Guides and Getting There: Arrive early, by 9 A.M., to avoid the midday heat and give you time to contact a guide, most likely either José Luis Toral Sánchez or Feliciano Gonzáles Mendez, whom the government has certified as official guardians of Guiengola. You will probably find one or both of them at the **Comedor Gema** or one of the other highway-front *palapas* that provide lunches (sometimes of armadillo, venison, iguana, coati, and other game), drinks, and bottled water (very necessary, since no water is available along the route). Once you've contacted your guide, you could either continue to Guiengola immediately or detour with your guide to Jalapa de Marqués and Tequisistlán and return to explore Guiengola in the late afternoon. *Warning:* Exploring the ruins without a guide could be hazardous, and could also get you into *mucho* trouble with the authorities.

By car, get there by driving your own vehicle or a rental car (agents in Oaxaca, Salina Cruz, and Juchitán) to the blue signed right turnoff that runs right past the Comedor Gema, about 10 miles (16 km) west, Oaxaca direction, along Highway 190 from Tehuantepec. Otherwise, get to the crossing by sharing a taxi, or, most cheaply and easily, via the **Autotransportes Jalapa de Marqués** buses, which leave the Tehuantepec plaza in front of the market about every half hour.

Jalapa del Marqués

During Mexico's big-dam boom in the 1950s, planners decided to conserve and control some of the trillions of gallons of water that flow via the Río Tehuantepec into the sea. A good idea, thought most, for flood control and irrigation during the long winter and spring drought.

The result is **Benito Juárez dam and reservoir,** which provides irrigation water, fish, and a

© BRUCE WHIPPERMAN

The warm mineral spring at Jalapa del Marqués provides water both for laundry and for local folks' daily baths.

tourist attraction for Jalapa del Marqués (pop. about 3,000), the biggest town on the reservoir.

The cost for all this was that the Jalapa de Marqués, originally on the bank of the Río Tehuantepec, had to be moved five miles (8 km) uphill to its present location next to Highway 190, about 18 miles (30 km) west of Tehuantepec. Now the people have everything new—wide paved streets, church, and a museum and Casa del Pueblo cultural center.

People in Jalapa del Marqués eat a lot of fish—specifically, *mojarra* (bass). A number of restaurants cook it up and serve it for visitors; try **Del Camino and El Gorda** at the east, Tehuantepec, edge of town.

The next thing to do is go fishing or take a **boat ride** on the lake. This is good anytime of year but is best in the dry winter or spring, when the silt from the summer rains has settled and the lake is invitingly clear. Arrive early enough to find one of the boatmen down at the lake before they go home for the day. A good man to ask for is Alejandro Oliveras, who charges about $12 for a two-hour ride or fishing trip. Bring your own pole, unless you want to fish by line or net as the locals do.

A popular excursion destination is **Tres Picos,** a Zapotec ruin on the far side of the lake. There, you can explore a trio of conical stone pyramids, about 30 feet (nine meters) high, and a submerged ball court. Also, if the water is low and clear enough, perhaps your boatman will take you to see the site of the submerged old Jalapa del Marqués, where you'll be able to see the old church beneath the water or even sit on its bell tower, which at low water protrudes from the lake's surface.

Before or after your boat excursion, take a look inside the **Casa del Pueblo,** on the town plaza about 600 feet (180 meters) downhill from the highway. Besides a number of giant animal bones, apparently mastodon, it has a big collection of locally gathered pre-conquest pottery, including some very phallic-looking figurines.

Get to the plaza and the lakeshore boat landing by the paved main street, marked by a huge concrete *bienvenidos* (welcome) portal on the highway. Continue downhill, past the central

plaza (.1 mile or .2 km, Casa del Pueblo on the right, uphill plaza corner). Pass a playground and traffic circle (.4 mile, .6 km); after another 1.4 mile (2.2 km) mostly on a dirt road, you arrive at the beach and boat landing. Go swimming (in your bathing suit) and enjoy a lakeside picnic.

Finally, join the folks in the community *agua caliente* (**warm spring**) about half a mile (1 km) uphill from the highway. People begin arriving around six in the morning, when it's cool. They bring their soap and clothes to be washed and stay for hours, playing in the hot-tub warm water (about 102°F, 39°C). Wear your bathing suit. If you don't have one, just go in with your clothes on like everyone else. Skinny-dipping, unless you're under three, is liable to land you in jail, besides reinforcing the local people's stereotypical view of the "loose" foreigner. Get there via the dirt street that heads uphill at the highway long-distance bus stop, a few blocks west (Oaxaca direction) of the town entrance portal. After two blocks uphill, bear left, then turn right and pass a big electrical transformer station. Continue uphill to a low ridge, where on the right side, you'll see the women washing clothes in big tanks inside an enclosure (to keep animals out). The women are friendly and also careful to keep their waste water from the lower basins, where you'll be welcome to bathe. (The basins outside the enclosure are for animals only.)

By bus, get to Jalapa del Marqués via either the Tehuantepec central bus terminal or second-class **Autotransportes Jalapa del Marqués** bus from in front of the Tehuantepec market.

Tequisistlán

This little *municipio,* officially Santa María Magdalena Tequisistlán, was on ground too high to get gobbled up by the reservoir. Consequently, the huge-in-summer (and muddy) **Río Tequisistlán** continues to run right next to town. However, during the dry, hot spring this river appears very inviting for a dip into its clear, gurgling water.

Take a look inside at the old church in the center of town. Here, folks enjoy the church's completely marble-floored atrium in front, especially handy for dancing during the July 20–24 festival in honor of Santa María Magdalena. On the church's side, you'll find the kicker: probably the world's only **marble basketball court.**

You can see the source of all this by going to the community **marble factory,** on Highway 190 about a mile (2 km) west (Oaxaca direction) of the town highway crossing. If you arrive during working hours (about 9 A.M.–2 P.M. and 4–7 P.M.), ask someone to "please show" *("favor de maestrar")* you around. You'll see dozens of men and machines working beneath a shady open-air roof, cutting, grinding, and polishing dozens of beautiful pieces of marble.

In the nearby office, feast your eyes on the beautifully polished finished products. The factory will custom-make anything you want—such as the lovely marble bathroom vanity top you've always wanted, a statuesque marble cat, or some other favorite animal.

Get there by car, via Highway 190 (30 miles, 50 km) Oaxaca direction, or an hour by bus from the Tehuantepec station. Get off at the Tequisistlán crossing and hop on the local Tequisistlán bus, which shuttles folks the two miles (3 km) to and from the highway about every 10 minutes.

Juchitán and Vicinity

Isthmus people associate the name Juchitán with both the town, Juchitán de Zaragoza, and the governmental district that it heads—a domain larger in extent than either the Distrito Federal or each of the four smallest Mexican states. The district of Juchitán (Place of Flowers) ranges from the Chimalapas, the roadless jungle refuge of dozens of Mexico's endangered species, south to the warm Pacific and the rich lagoons that border it.

But like any empire, Juchitán is the sum of its small parts—hidden slices of Mexico that few outsiders know, from the crystalline springs of Tlacotepec and Laollaga to the seemingly endless groves of the "world mango capital" at Zanatepec and the vibrant market and near-continuous community festivals—the *velas*—of busy, prosperous Juchitán de Zaragoza.

SIGHTS

Orientation

Juchitán (pop. 80,000) bustles with commerce all the daylight and early-evening hours. Main streets 16 de Septiembre and 5 de Septiembre steadily conduct a double stream of traffic to and from the north-side Highway 200 crossing. A few blocks to the west, the Río Los Perros (River of the Dogs, for the otters that hunt fish in the river) courses lazily southward, marking downtown Juchitán's western boundary.

Traffic focuses about a mile (2 km) south of the highway at the town plaza, the **Jardín Central Benito Juárez,** the town's commercial and governmental nucleus. On Calle 16 de Septiembre, on the plaza's east side, the long, white classical arcade of the *palacio municipal* fills the entire block, from Calle Efrain Gómez bordering the plaza's north edge to Calle Benito Juárez on the south. Governmental offices occupy the upper floor of the *palacio,* while businesses, crafts booths, and food stalls spread across the bottom. Behind the facade, taking up the entire city block east of the plaza, is the town market, **Mercado 5 de Septiembre.**

Around the Plaza

A fun spot to start off (or end) your day exploring Juchitán is at a table in the graceful old-Mexico patio of **Restaurant Casa Grande** on Calle Benito Juárez, on the plaza's south side. Here, a hearty breakfast or a cool lunch will invigorate you for yet another few hours of relaxed plaza sightseeing.

Stroll out and admire the fine busts of Benito Juárez on the plaza's east side and Margarita Maza, his wife, on the west side, by Calle 5 de Septiembre. On the plaza's north side, find the Monument to the Battle of September 5, 1866, where a Mexican eagle and a heroic Benito Juárez commemorate the victory of the ragtag local battalion over a superior French imperial force.

Step east, across Calle 16 de Septiembre, to the **crafts stalls** beneath the northerly (left) half of *palacio municipal* arcade. What you don't find downstairs you'll find in an upstairs market foyer. Stroll the aisles and choose from a host of excellent items customarily including, besides the famous Isthmus embroidered skirts and blouses, handwoven cotton *hamacas* (hammocks), leather huaraches and *bolsas* (purses), woven palm and reed *canastas* (baskets), *petates* (mats), and sombreros, and gold-filigree *joyería* (jewelry).

For **pottery,** walk west along Calle Juárez (which borders the plaza's south side) to the block just west of the plaza. There, along the old town church's rear wall, a lineup of stalls offers an assortment of ceramics, mostly practical traditional housewares, from huge round red *ollas* (jars) and flat *comales* (griddles) to brightly painted piggy banks and flower vases.

San Vicente Ferrer Church and Casa de la Cultura

While you're in the vicinity, visit the town's pride, the Templo de San Vicente Ferrer. Reach it by circling the block; continue west on Calle Juárez, go immediately left at 5 de Mayo, then after one block turn left again at Belisario Domínguez, to the church on the left. Although the church's early history is shrouded in mystery, the present construction appears by its style

The dignified Romanesque church of San Vicente Ferrer, often the site of festivities, nevertheless sometimes provides quiet sanctuary.

to date from the mid-19th century. Its dedication to San Vicente Ferrer, patron of survivors of the sea, appears connected to Juchitán's original founding as a refuge for survivors, perhaps of some ocean disaster, such as a terrible tsunami or hurricane, some time shortly before the conquest. Present-day Juchitecos, inheritors of their patron's zeal and ferocity, celebrate his memory with gusto to match, with no less than eight consecutive *velas*, beginning on the first Saturday of the last 15 days of May.

Across the street from the church, you might linger for a few minutes in the shady side plaza, **Parque Helidoro Charis Castro.** Here stands the bronze bust of Castro, the beloved Juchitecan *maderista* general who led the 13th Juchitecan Battalion in its bloody, but ultimately successful, revolt against dictatorial forces, from 1910 to 1914.

Afterward, look around inside the **Casa de la**

Cultura next door, west of the church, tel. 971/711-3208 (open Mon.–Fri. 10 A.M.–3 P.M. and 5–8 P.M., Sat. 10 A.M.–3 P.M.). The building, originally a Catholic school, became the Casa de la Cultura in 1972, through the efforts of celebrated Oaxaca painter Francisco Toledo. Rooms around the graceful, old-Mexico patio accommodate a café, a small archaeological museum, an art exposition gallery, and a children's library. The reception staff sell a few Spanish-language books of local history and folklore.

The Women Warriors

As an interesting downtown side-street diversion, walk across the Río Los Perros for a look at the intriguing *Women Warriors* sculptures on the west riverbank. Head west along Juárez. Two blocks west of the plaza, from the middle of the river bridge, notice the two tall sculptures of women (in Juchiteca skirts and blouses, of course), about two stories high, in what appears to be a small neighborhood park.

Local residents seem to know little about them, except that "they are guarding the people from the river." Get a better view of the sculptures (which, close-up, you'll see are of stainless sheet steel) by accessing the west riverbank from the pedestrian bridge a block upstream (north) from Juárez.

The riverbank is especially pleasant around sunset, when, standing on the Juárez bridge, you might catch a cooling breeze, enjoy the sky colors, and be entertained by the flocks of black grackles flying overhead and scrapping and cackling in riverbank trees as they settle down for the night.

ACCOMMODATIONS

Juchitán accommodates visitors with several acceptable hotels. A popular town-center choice is the once semi-deluxe, but now a bit dilapidated **Hotel Lidxi Buixa** (LEED-shee boo-EE-shah), behind the *palacio municipal* at 2 de Abril 79, Juchitán, Oaxaca 70000, tel. 971/711-1299 or 971/711-1390, fax 971/711-1623. The 26 rooms (not too clean, take a look) rent for about $16 s, $21 d, with a/c, cable TV, phones, pool, and parking. (Reservations are necessary here because it's very popular with out-of-town vendors, who rise around 5 A.M. to tend their market stalls across the street. Early morning noise may consequently be a problem.)

Rough but right at the center of everything is the **Casa de Huéspedes Echazarreta,** on Benito Juárez just west of 16 de Septiembre, Juchitán, Oaxaca 70000, no phone. It rents about 15 bare-bones, but clean, rooms with bath, around an invitingly tranquil inner courtyard, for about $10 s or d.

Moving two blocks north from the plaza along 5 de Septiembre, past Miguel Hidalgo, you'll find the welcoming **Hotel Don Alex Lena Real,** at 16 de Septiembre 48, Juchitán, Oaxaca 70000, tel. 971/711-1064, fax 971/711-0989. The 14 very clean rooms with king-size beds rent for about $17 s, $26 d, with a/c, phones, cable TV, and parking. Credit cards are not accepted.

Low water in Juchitán's Río Los Perros provides room for volleyball games.

Three more blocks north (a total of five blocks from the plaza) rises the Don Alex's sister hotel, the **Hotel López Lena Palace,** at 16 de Septiembre 70, Juchitán, Oaxaca 70000, tel. 971/711-1388, fax 971/711-1389. Designers have packed a modicum of extras, such as potted plants, airy corridors, and attractively decorated rose-colored hallways, into the four-story building. The 40 spartan-chic rooms are tiled and very clean, but with bare-bulb reading lamps. They rent for about $30 s, $40 d, and $48 t, with cable TV, phones, a/c, a bar, and a good restaurant. Credit cards are accepted.

Juchitán's best hotel is the relaxed, resort-style **Gran Hotel Santo Domingo,** on the highway across from both the bus station and the ingress road to town, at Crucero, Carretera Panamericana s/n, Juchitán, Oaxaca 70000, tel./fax 971/711-1050, 971/711-3642 or 971/711-1959. The Gran Hotel's choice attraction is a luxuriously inviting large pool and grassy patio, a welcome refuge for winding down from the heat, street noise, and bustle. The approximately 40 rooms, in a pair of double-storied tiers beyond a tropical entrance foyer, are spare but clean, spacious, high-ceilinged, and comfortable, with modern-standard bathrooms. Rentals run about $31, $42 d, $52 t, with a/c, TV, phones, good restaurant, parking, and credit cards accepted.

FOOD

Juchitán's downtown plaza food stalls do big business all day and half the night. Especially popular with local people are the market *fondas* (food stalls), bottom level at the south (right) side of the *palacio municipal.* Another, less busy *fonda* spot is on the side plaza Helidoro Charis Castro, a block south of the main plaza, in front of the church.

For baked goods, go to **Panadería Nuevo Mundo,** on 2 de Abril, between Gómez and Hidalgo, tel. 971/711-1897, open daily 8 A.M.–2 P.M. and 5–8 P.M. Find it a block east and half a block north of the plaza's northeast corner.

For pizza and snacks ($3–7) try **Pizzería**

© BRUCE WHIPPERMAN

THE ISTHMUS

VELAS: FIESTAS OF THE ISTHMUS

The Isthmus *velas* amount to a near-continuous regional party. People stay up all night, sometimes for days on end of feasting, drinking, dancing, and parading with family and friends, many of whom return from afar to renew cherished old relationships. What follows is a short list that includes only the most important Isthmus *velas.*

Date	Place	Title
January 18–21	Jalapa del Marqués	San Sebastián de las Flores
First Friday of Lent	San Pedro Huamelula	Carnaval
February 20–25	Matías Romero	Vela San Matías
First days of April	San Pedro Tehuantepec	Feria de Mango (Mango Fair)
April 15	Juchitán	Vela Ique Guia (Festival of the Chief)
April 25	Juchitán	Vela Ique Guidxi (Of the People)
April 27	Juchitán	Vela Paso Cru (Stations of the Cross)
May 3	Juchitán	Vela Guzebenda (Of the Fisherfolk)
May 3–6	Salina Cruz	Santa Cruz
May 5	Juchitán	Vela Quintu
May 8	Juchitán	Vela Guigu Dixta
May 10	Juchitán	Vela San Pedro Cantarito
May 13	Juchitán	Vela San Isidro Guete
May 15	Juchitán	Vela Guela Bene
May 16	Juchitán	Vela Iguu
Last 15 days of May	Juchitán	Fiesta de San Vicente Ferrer
	Juchitán	Vela Biadxi
	Juchitán	Vela Calvario
	Juchitán	Vela Angelica Pipi
	Juchitán	Vela San Isidro Labrador

Gato Montes (Wildcat Pizza), Colón 7, tel. 971/711-3945, open daily 7 P.M.–midnight, a block west of the church between Belisario Domínguez and Juárez.

The class-act downtown restaurant, perfect for a midday break, is the refined **Restaurant Casa Grande,** in the inner patio of an ex-mansion, at Juárez 12, tel. 971/711-3460. The mostly business and upper-class patrons choose from an international menu of soups, salads, and sandwiches ($3–5), meats and pastas ($4–9), and a number of Oaxacan regional specialties, such as

chilequiles con tasajo (chili tortillas with beef), *enchiladas de mole negro* (enchiladas with black mole sauce), and *chile relleno de picadillo* (chili stuffed with spiced meat), $4–7. Open daily 8:30 A.M.–8 P.M.

On the other hand, local fish lovers frequent seafood restaurant **Mariscos de Marlo,** at the corner of 16 de Septiembre and Hidalgo, no phone, for its long, very correctly Mexican menu of seafood and more. Have it all, including a plethora of clam, oyster, and shrimp cocktails ($3–7); soups, both clear and creamed ($2–4);

Date	Place	Title
	Juchitán	Vela San Vicente Chico
	Juchitán	Vela San Vicente Grande
	Juchitán	Vela de Cheguigo
Last week of May	Tehuantepec	Vela Sandunga
June 16	Juchitán	Vela San Antonio
June 24	Juchitán	Vela San Juan Bautista
	Juchitán	Vela Taberneros
	Juchitán	Vela Coheteros
June 24–30	San Pedro Huamelula	Fiesta del Apóstol San Pedro
June 27–30	San Pedro Tapanatepec	Fiesta Patronal de San Pedro
July 21–29	Santiago Laollaga	Fiesta de Santiago Apóstol
July	Juchitán	Vela de los Niños
August 13	Juchitán	Vela Asunción
August 15	Juchitán	Vela San Jacinto
August 13–16	Jalapa del Marqués	Fiesta de la Asunción
August 13–18	Tehuantepec	Fiesta Patronal del Barrio de Santa María Reoloteca
August 31–September 11	Tehuantepec	Fiesta del Laborio
September 3	Juchitán	Vela de la Familia Pineda
September 4	Juchitán	Vela de la Familia López
September 5	Juchitán	Vela del Triunfo del Batallón Juchiteco de 1866
	Juchitán	Vela Superior
October 1–4	San Francisco Ixhuatan	Vela del Santa Patrón
December 26	Tehuantepec	Vela Tehuantepec

fish, octopus, squid, lobster, and shrimp (cooked 10 ways, $3–8); and seven styles of *cucarachas* (cockroaches, $2–4). One block north of the plaza, open daily 8 A.M.–7 P.M.

Alternatively, escape temporarily from Mexico at the coffee shop–style **Restaurant Santa Fe,** at the highway crossing next to the bus station, tel. 971/711-1545. In the air-conditioned Denny's-like atmosphere, enjoy fresh coffee and fruit ($2), followed by tasty eggs, waffles, and pancakes for breakfast ($3–5), several hamburgers or salads ($3–5) for lunch, and finally, soups,

spaghetti, beef, chicken, and fish for dinner ($3–7). Open daily 24 hours.

ENTERTAINMENT AND EVENTS

Juchitán's substantial excess wealth goes largely to finance an impressive round of parties, locally called *velas,* in honor of a patron saint or a historically or commercially important event. The *velas* are organized and financed by entire *barrios* (neighborhoods), and led by *mayordomos,* usually a well-to-do male head

© BRUCE WHIPPERMAN

The Juchitán flower market anchors the town center's market district.

of household, but also including his spouse, children, and all relatives and friends, who usually add up to a major fraction of the population of an entire Juchitán *barrio*. The *mayordomo* family, together with male and female *capitanes* and their closest friends, make up the *mayordomía*, the core committee responsible for carrying off the celebration.

Customary activities include blossom-decorated church masses, parties in the house of the *mayordomo*, community barbecues, a parade of fruit and flower-laden floats, from which the *capitanas*, dressed like brides in their stunningly embroidered Tehuantepec outfits, throw fruit and gifts to the street-side crowds.

In all, Juchitecans celebrate 20 in-town *velas*, which fill streets with merrymakers during the last half of April, virtually the entire month of May, and several days each in June, July, August, and September, a total of about 50 days of celebrating for the entire year. This wouldn't be too excessive if it were not for the approximately 20 obligatory national holidays and the other 30 unmissable *velas* in neighboring Isthmus communities. (See the sidebar "Velas: Fiestas of the Isthmus.")

Local folks sometimes offer droll commentaries about all this celebrating: "If you go to a *mayordomo* house, I'll tell you what you'll find . . . no bed, no stove, no shoes, just happy people and lots of friends."

Lacking a local fiesta, you might want to take in a film at the genteel **Cinema Casa Grande,** on the plaza, south side; open daily, late afternoons, except Monday. Enter past the patio Restaurant Casa Grande.

INFORMATION

The local **Cámara Nacional de Comercio** (National Chamber of Commerce), second floor, above Banamex, corner of 5 de Septiembre and E. Gómez, tel. 971/711-1597, under the supervision of friendly director Cristóforo Vásquez Pineda, will try to answer your queries (in Spanish). Open Mon.–Fri. approximately 9 A.M.–1 P.M. and 4–7 P.M.

Alternatively, try travel agent **Zarymar,** at 5 de Septiembre 100B, several blocks north of the plaza, tel. 971/711-2867, for information, airline tickets, and car rentals.

SERVICES

Money

A number of downtown banks, which all have ATMs, help manage Juchitecos' money. They'll also change your money into pesos or U.S. dollars. Best choice for its long hours is **Banco Internacional** (Bital), at 16 de Septiembre 52, three blocks north of the plaza, open Mon.–Fri. 9 A.M.–5 P.M. and Sat. 9 A.M.–2 P.M. Also a good bet is **Banorte,** at Efrain Gómez 19, half a block west of the plaza's northwest corner, tel. 971/711-1160 or 971/711-3482, open Mon.–Fri. 9 A.M.–4 P.M., Sat. 10 A.M.–2 P.M. Third choice goes to **Banco Santander Serfin,** at the corner of Belasario Domínguez and the extension of 16 de Septiembre, one block south of the *palacio municipal,* tel./fax 971/711-2000; open Mon.–Fri. 9 A.M.–3 P.M., Sat. 10 A.M.–2 P.M.

Communications

The *correo* (post office), at the plaza's northeast corner, just west of the *palacio municipal,* tel. 971/711-1272, is open Mon.–Fri. 8 A.M.–7 P.M., Sat. 9 A.M.–noon. *Telecomunicaciones* (public fax and money orders), across the street, at the corner, beneath the market portal, tel. 971/711-1040, is also open Mon.–Fri. 8 A.M.–7 P.M., Sat. 9 A.M.–noon.

Photography and Cameras

A trio of downtown camera shops sell and develop film and stock some cameras and photo supplies. Try **Foto Facil,** at 16 de Septiembre 26, inside the big Mega Elektra store, west side of the street, a block and a half north of the plaza; or **Foto Color** on the same street, east side, just north of the plaza; or **Centro Fotografía Juchitán,** on 2 de Abril, east side, between Gómez and Hidalgo, open daily 8 A.M.–9 P.M. and Sun. 9 A.M.–2 P.M., a block east and half a block north of the of the plaza's northeast corner.

Health and Emergencies

A ready source of nonprescription medicines and drugs is the 24-hour **Farmacia del Istmo,** Efrain Gómez and 2 de Abril, tel. 971/711-0994 or 971/711-0316, one block behind the north side

of the *palacio municipal.* Alternatively, go to the big drugstore-style **Farmacia San Vicente,** diagonally across from the south corner of the *palacio municipal,* tel. 971/711-3259, open daily 7 A.M.–9:30 P.M.

A number of **doctors** maintain offices near the plaza. For example, general physician-surgeons Dr. Ruben Calvo López and Dr. Carlos Alonso Ruiz and gynecologist Doctora Anabel López Ruiz, have regular consulting hours at Clínica San Fernando, 16 de Septiembre between E. Gómez and Hidalgo, tel. 971/711-1569, a block and a half north of the plaza's northeast side. Alternatively, go to pharmacy and **Clínica Nuestra Señora de Exaltación,** 5 de Septiembre, tel. 971/711-1378, with about six specialists on call, on the east side of the street, half a block north of the plaza.

In an **emergency,** follow your hotel's recommendation or hire a taxi to the General Hospital Dr. Macedonio Benítez Fuentes, downtown on Efrain Gómez near the plaza, tel. 971/711-1441 or 971/711-1985.

GETTING THERE AND AWAY

By Bus

A modern long-distance *camionera central* (central bus station), at the Highway 190/200 crossing north of downtown, is the point of departure for all of the first-class and most of the second-class connections with both Oaxaca and national destinations. Both first- and second-class lines service customers from separate waiting rooms (first-class on the left, second-class in the right). The busy but clean station has snack stores and luggage-check service. Long-distance telephone and fax is available at a small office in the second-class waiting room.

Autobuses del Oriente (ADO) and affiliated lines, tel. 971/711-2565, offer direct first-class connections north with Gulf of Mexico destinations of Minatitlán, Coatzacoalcos, Villahermosa, Palenque, and Ciudad del Carmen; northwest with Oaxaca, Mexico City, Veracruz, and Tampico. Additionally, first-class carrier **Cristóbal Colón** (CC), tel. 971/711-2565, and its luxury-class subsidiary, Plus, offer connections northwest with

Oaxaca, Puebla, Mexico City, and Veracruz; southwest with Salina Cruz, Bahías de Huatulco, Pochutla (Puerto Ángel), and Puerto Escondido; and east with Chiapas destinations of Tuxtla Gutiérrez, San Cristóbal las Casas, and Tapachula, at the Guatemala border.

Second-class carriers include **Autobuses del Oriente** (ADO), which offers connections north with Coatzacoalcos; southwest with Tehuantepec and Salina Cruz; and east with Tapanatepec, including all intermediate destinations. Additionally, **Autobuses Unidos** (AU) offers second-class connections northwest with Puebla, Mexico City, Orizaba, Veracruz, and Tuxtepec; and southwest with Tehuantepec and Salina Cruz, including all intermediate destinations. Moreover, **Sur** offers second-class connections north with Coatzacoalcos, northwest with Oaxaca, southwest with Bahías de Huatulco, and east with Tapanatepec and Tapachula, including all intermediate destinations.

Semi-local bus connections with adjacent towns are available via the green-white-and-yellow **Autotransportes Istmeños** across the side street, south, less than a block toward town from the *camionera central.*

Mostly second-class **Fletes y Pasajes** buses operate out of a separate terminal, also at the Highway 190/200 crossing, but on the west side, adjacent to the Restaurant Santa Fe. Buses connect east with Chiapas destinations of Tuxtla Gutiérrez, Tapachula, and the Guatemala border; northwest, with Oaxaca, Puebla, and Mexico City; and north, with Tuxtepec and Minatitlán.

By Car

Drivers have the same highway choices and destinations as listed at the end of the Tehuantepec section. Simply subtract 30 minutes driving time (and 17 miles, 27 km distance) for northerly and easterly trips; add the same for northwesterly and southwesterly trips. In Juchitán, fill up with **gasoline** at the Pemex *gasolinera* at the Highway 190/200 town ingress crossing.

North of Juchitán

A number of uniquely interesting destinations await travelers willing to venture into the foothill hinterland northwest and north of Juchitán. Foremost among them are the storied former royal Zapotec bathing **springs** that well up, blue and crystalline, at Tlacotepec and Laollaga, an hour's travel northwest of Juchitán.

Equally ripe for exploring is the stalactite-studded **limestone cave** near the town of Santo Domingo Petapa, together with the singularly successful cooperative **company town at Lagunas,** about an hour and a half north of Juchitán.

Each of these excursions can be enjoyed from Juchitán in a leisurely day by car or a long day by bus.

THE SPRINGS AT TLACOTEPEC AND LAOLLAGA

Both of these bathing resorts were part of the territory of the Zapotec royal family of King Cosijoeza. He often used the springs as a refuge during his protracted war with Aztec emperor Ahuitzotl during the 1490s. A famous traditional story recounts how love resolved the bloody conflict. Tiring of the struggle, Ahuitzotl proposed a peace pact. In exchange for allowing Aztec traders and envoys to pass through the Isthmus lands, Cosijoeza would receive Aztec princess Coyollicatzin in marriage. One day, meditating over the proposition while bathing in the Tlacotepec spring, Cosijoeza was awestruck by a stunning apparition of Coyollicatzin. Despite his apprehension, Coyollicatzin's apparition enchanted him with her beauty. Thus persuaded, Cosijoeza soon took Coyollicatzin in marriage, sealing the pact between the two nations.

Their marriage was a happy one. Children resulted, and Cosijoeza passed the springs at Tlacotepec and Laollaga to their son Cosijopí, the king of the Isthmus lands, and their daughter,

Princess Donaji, both of whom continued to exercise authority after the conquest.

Magdalena Tlacotepec

Storied Princess Donaji (see the sidebar "The Tragic Story of Princess Donaji" in the Around the Valley of Oaxaca chapter), who after the conquest was baptized as Magdalena Donaji, donated both her Christian name and the springs and royal park at Tlacotepec to the local community, still known as Magdalena Tlacotepec.

Today, the town's springs and surrounding sanctuary are a unique asset for all Istmeño families to enjoy, which they do en masse on sunny Sundays and holidays. The source, a clear, cool underground river, wells up from a rocky basin and fills a long, meandering, aqua-blue swimming hole. Shoals of little fish that nibble and tickle your feet hide in crannies and flit along the sandy bottom. Shady mango trees overhang the bank and spread into a rustic public strolling ground on one side. On the other, entrance side, food stalls surround a parking area.

Here you can park your (self-contained) trailer or RV or set up a tent and stay a spell, walking into the surrounding hills in the morning to enjoy wildlife and wildflowers and splashing in the cool spring in the afternoons. Custodial personnel, who keep the site clean and secure, collect nominal fees for parking and camping.

Santiago Laollaga

Laollaga (lah-oh-YAH-gah) springs mark the northern boundary of the petite *municipio* of Santiago Laollaga, which you pass through on your way to the springs. A big parking lot overlooks the main series of pools (concrete basins) built into the rocky downhill channel of the Río Laollaga. Shady trees overhang the pools, and a pair of permanent open-air *comedores* on the riverbank serve drinks and food.

Visitors equipped with a self-contained trailer or RV might enjoy a stay, parking in the lot for a day or two. Fees run only a few dollars a day. Unfortunately, the water at the main pools is sometimes a bit tainted by soap from folks washing clothes upstream. You can assure pure water by following the river a quarter mile (half a km)

upstream to its source, a natural *ojo de agua* spring welling from the base of the hills. Here, great shady trees spread over a sandy riverbank, ripe for tent camping if you don't mind sharing the spot with a few townsfolk on weekdays, more on weekends.

Laollaga diversions might include strolls around the town and along dirt roads and trails, into the summer-lush native tropical woodlands. By local bus or car, you could explore farther afield, along the good gravel road (where you made your last turn left) threading the green-forested Río Los Perros valley and foothill country 15 miles (25 km) northwest to remote Santa María Guienagati.

Arrive during the last 10 days in July and join Laollaga's big **Fiesta de Santiago Apóstol** (July 20–30), which includes four separate *velas,* with fireworks, carnival rides and games, *regada* (fruit-throwing), dances, and *mojigangos* (giant dancing figures).

Small town stores can supply basic groceries.

© BRUCE WHIPPERMAN

Cool shade beneath great trees, picnic spots, and restaurants add to the enjoyment of Laollaga spring.

Pharmacies, a private doctor, a *centro de salud,* a post office, and a *caseta larga distancia* (long-distance booth) can provide basic services.

Getting There and Away

Get to Tlacotepec and Laollaga from Juchitán via Ixtepec, half an hour north of Juchitán. By bus, take one of the Ixtepec-labeled buses that frequently head northwest from the Highway 190 crossing, across the street from the *camionera central.* Half an hour later, at Ixtepec, transfer to the red-and-white Tlacotepec- or Laollaga-labeled local bus.

By car, from the Highway 190/200 crossing at Juchitán, mark your odometer and head across Highway 190/200 northwest through Ixtaltepec (five miles, 8 km) to the railroad tracks at Ixtepec (9.7 miles, 15.6 km). Immediately after crossing the tracks, turn left. After about 900 feet (270 meters) or three blocks, turn right at Ixtepec's main street, Calle 16 de Septiembre. Continue .3 mile (.5 km) and fork left at the Balneario sign (10 miles, 16.3 km). Turn left at a second sign (10.4 miles, 16.7 km), then left again at an unsigned T-intersection (10.7 miles, 17.2 km). Finally, a mile (1.6 km) farther at a Y-intersection (11.7 miles, 18.8 km), go left and continue, following the Balneario signs to Tlacotepec, a total of about 18 miles (29 km). Alternatively, bear right at the Y and continue through Chihuatán (turn left at town corner, at 16.2 miles, 26.1 km) to Santiago Laollaga town center (19.2 miles, 31 km). Turn right and continue through town. At a total of 19.7 miles (31.7 km), just before the road becomes gravel, turn left to the *balneario* (springs), whose entrance you'll see after about three blocks.

LAGUNAS: COMPANY TOWN

If success can be measured by longevity, the industrial cooperative town of Lagunas, which began producing cement in 1942, has earned its plaudits. Moreover, the unique experiment it represents seems as robust as ever. The idea began back in the 1930s, when investors were eager to exploit a mountain of local limestone that tow-

ered conveniently beside the cross-isthmus rail line. The era was, however, that of reformist President Lázaro Cárdenas, when the star of socialism was rising over Mexico from the east. The enterprise must be a cooperative, the government demanded. Investors, realizing the project's unique prospects, agreed, and Cruz Azul, a uniquely Mexican private-public cooperative, was born.

Today, the great mill beside the railroad tracks hums all day and night, producing millions of tons of cement yearly for projects from Chile to Canada. Moreover, besides supporting the livelihoods of thousands of families in the entire local hinterland, the Lagunas mill (judging from the tidy, dust-free town) appears to produce little of the debilitating cement dust that has shortened the lives of cement-mill workers the world over.

At the town center, across the tracks from the mill, a monument erected by the workers (the Cooperadores de La Cruz Azul) honors Guillermo Alvarez, Cruz Azul's guiding light, with a pair of eternally flickering electric lamps.

Along Avenida Cooperativismo facing the plant stand the town Banamex branch, the post office, the public telecommunications office, and the plant superintendent's office. Badged workers, all in pressed khakis and hard hats, walk with purpose along the sidewalks. Some turn and continue along the town's main street, Avenida Cruz Azul, and continue past the hamburger shop, *centro comercial* (company store), an immaculate bakery, and the big church, dedicated the Virgin of Guadalupe. From the commercial center, tree-lined residential streets extend past schools, a hospital, and tidy concrete houses with some of Mexico's rare, American-style unfenced yards with lawns.

SANTO DOMINGO PETAPA: LIMESTONE CAVE

Several miles past Lagunas, Santo Domingo Petapa (pop. about 2,000) marks the end of the pavement. Unless you arrive during a national holiday or the August 1–4 town festival in honor of Santo Domingo, Petapa will appear like a typical Oaxaca country town. Petapa does have, however, at least one claim to fame, and that is the grand limestone cavern on the mountainside two miles (3 km) beyond the town.

Head straight to the *presidencia municipal* and ask for a guide to show you around inside the cave. Be sure to write a letter in advance, in Spanish, addressed to the Presidente Municipal, Santo Domingo Petapa, Oaxaca, 70350, telling your date and time of arrival and that you'd be happy to pay (say $20) for an experienced guide to show you the cave. Alternatively, two or three days in advance you could ask the desk clerk at your hotel to leave a message at the Petapa *presi-dencia municipal,* tel. 972/723-4053, making the same request.

These preparations will give you a good chance of seeing the inside of the cave. Come equipped with sturdy shoes, hard hats (at least plastic), and, if possible, super-bright three- or four-celled flashlights. The cave, between one- and two-hours' walk west of town, is large, with a towering, cathedral-like entry portal and a river flowing from its mouth. Your exploration inside will take about two hours and extend past stalagmites and stalactites approximately half a mile (1 km) into the mountainside.

East of Juchitán

From south to north, the grand Isthmus landscape east of Juchitán gradually changes through three distinctive panoramas. In the south, at the Pacific Ocean, the Isthmus begins as three grand, glassy, wildlife-rich lagoons—the Laguna Superior and Inferior on the west side and the Mar Muerto (not the "Dead Sea" but the "Calm Sea") on the east. This is the home ground of the Huave people, driven to the Isthmus's salty edge an age ago by the Zapotecs, to make their living mostly from the sea. North of that lies the fertile, most prized crescent of pastures, fields, and orchards of the sizable towns of Niltepec, Zanatepec, and Tapanatepec, and the Panamerican Highway, which connects them all. Farther north rise the trans-isthmus mountains, the Sierra Atravesada, heartland of the Chimalapas, a wild kingdom of sylvan forests, rushing rivers, and deep, shadowed canyons, a final refuge of rare, endangered, and yet-to-be-discovered species of plants and animals.

First access to all this is by the Panamerican Highway east of Juchitán, then by side roads north and south from junctions such as La Venta, Zanatepec, and Tapanatepec.

LA VENTA

La Venta (The Windy Place), about 18 miles (29 km) east of Juchitán, lives up to its name, so much so that the Comisión Federal de Electricidad has installed seven towering wind generators at the very spot. The ultramodern, gleaming windmills, visible from the highway, whir obediently, doing their good work.

A side road leads to the windmills' base, where a display explains the project. So far, the seven 10-story generators have been able to average a continuous 500 kilowatts of power, enough for a modern Mexican village of 500 modern family homes. Currently, 500 kilowatts of electric power sells for about $1,000 per day, implying that each of the 500 families would have to fork out about $2 a day, $60 a month, for such power. Thus the experiment appears to be showing that although not presently affordable for most Oaxacans, Mexican wind power appears promising for industry now and for home use in a future, more prosperous Mexico.

Get to La Venta, by eastbound **ADO, Cristóbal Colón,** or **Sur** bus, from either of the central terminals at Tehuantepec or Juchitán. Drivers, simply head west half an hour along Highway 190/200 to La Venta.

The Chimalapa

A rough but mostly paved side road leads north from La Venta to the backcountry Chimalapas jumping-off point villages of **San Miguel Chimalapa** (14 miles, 23 km) and Cuauhtémoc

(17 miles, 27 km). The immense million-acre Chimalapa de facto wilderness is the communal property of two Zoque-speaking indigenous communities headquartered, respectively, at San Miguel Chimalapa and the more remote **San Martín Chimalapa,** 30 rough miles (48 km) north from the Highway 185 junction at El Mezquite.

The Chimalapa Zoque people are rightly suspicious of strangers, especially now that their lands have become one of Mexico's few remaining storehouses of valuable tropical hardwoods, endangered animals, and minerals. Legitimate visitors to the Chimalapas wilderness, if any are allowed at all, are strictly licensed by state and local authorities and must be accompanied by community guides. If you're interested in hiking and camping in the Chimalapa, first contact federal-state tourism in Oaxaca city (607 Independencia, corner of G. Vigil, tel. 951/516-0123, info@oaxaca.gob.mx), for information on how to proceed.

UNIÓN DE HIDALGO

This fair-sized *municipio* is one of the main gateways to the rich fishing grounds and tiny, Huave-speaking beach villages of the **Laguna Superior.** At the end of an approximately seven-mile (11-km) mostly-paved but bumpy road, you'll arrive at the big town plaza. In the vicinity you'll find groceries (**Abarrotes Sánchez,** Altamirano 12), a neglected hotel (the **Diush'i Nga'a Naroohba'a,** at the corner of Leona Vicario Sur and Matamoros Oriente), a pharmacy (**Farmacia San Isidro,** Nicolas Bravo 13 Oriente), police (at the *palacio municipal*), a post office, and a *telecomunicaciones* (public fax and money orders) office.

Although you'll most likely be passing through Unión de Hidalgo on the way to somewhere else, you can join the festivities (processions, mass barbecues, dancing, fruit- and gift-throwing *regadas,* carnival games and rides) if you arrive during one of the several town *velas.* The fun begins in April with the **Vela de los Pescadores** (Festival of the Fisherfolk) and continues on May 3 with the **Vela de Santa Cruz;** during the

quinceana (second 15 days) of May, *velas* honor San Vicente Chico and San Vicente Ferrer Grande. Later come the *velas* in honor of San Isidro the Farmer, Santa María Santísima, and San Pedro Apóstol, June 26–30. During the first days of August, townsfolk honor Santo Domingo de Guzmán, and September 27–30, they celebrate the town's founding. Finally, they celebrate Santa Cecilia on November 22 and the Virgin of Guadalupe on December 12.

Get to Unión Hidalgo, from Juchitán, via the Unión Hidalgo bus terminal. Best hire a taxi to take you (from the plaza, about 10 blocks along 16 de Septiembre to Calle 2 de Noviembre, thence west about seven blocks, over the railroad tracks, and bear left along the gravel road a few blocks to the terminal).

By car, from Juchitán, follow Avenida 20 de Noviembre as described in the previous paragraph, past the Unión Hidalgo bus terminal. Continue straight ahead immediately onto the paved road, that continues 12 miles (20 km) along the railroad track, to Unión Hidalgo.

PLAYA COPALITO AND SAN DIONISIO DEL MAR

From Unión de Hidalgo, turn south and continue through Chicapa de Castro a total of about 23 miles (37 km) to Playa Copalito (Little Copal Tree Beach), a tiny (but with electricity) fishing village of thatched houses and poor but friendly Huave-speaking folks. A long, sandy beach built of myriad wave-washed mussel and clam shells winds along the oft mirror-smooth Laguna Superior. Motorboats and *canoas* recline lazily on the beach. A few shoreline *copal* trees provide a bit of shade, and grassy (during the summer rainy season) spaces appear fine for RV parking or tent camping.

Here, the main work for locals and diversion for visitors is fishing. *Lanchas* routinely return with a dozen one- or two-pound *lisa* (mullet), *sierra* (mackerel), or pompano. Fishermen are willing to take visitors on a half-day fishing excursion or exploration for about $15.

Since Playa Copalito is an idyllic but isolated little place, campers should arrive well equipped with tent, food, and water. Bring insect repellent; mosquitoes may be fierce certain times of the year (although they weren't a problem one wet September). Moreover, security is good here, by virtue of the local Marine detachment, right in town.

As for food, a few village stores might supply some essentials, but best be prepared with your own fresh fruits and vegetables. The homey *palapa* **Restaurant Playa Copalita** of the friendly Pinedo Castellanos family (dad Señor Martimiano, mom Señora Reynalda, and kids Celia and Leticia), *a su servicio*, will be happy to provide fresh fish dinners.

While you're in the vicinity, the pilgrimage town of **San Dionisio del Mar** would certainly be worth a visit. The miraculous image of San Dionisio at the town church (on the east end of town) attracts thousands of pilgrims yearly, mostly around the October 6–10 festival. Things get started right away on October 6, when a carnival sets up and food stalls begin serving traditional *atole* (a nonalcoholic corn-juice drink) and tamales for the arriving pilgrims. The next day, the *mayordomía* officials crown the queen, while everyone enjoys a community dance and barbecue at the house of the *mayordomo*. Dances continue for the next two nights, punctuated by processions with fruit and gifts thrown to the celebrants, and nightly fireworks paint the sky red, blue, and green. A basic guesthouse (certainly full during the festival) is available for overnight accommodations.

Get to Copalita and San Dionisio, via Unión Hidalgo from Juchitán (see the Unión de Hidalgo section) or La Venta. Bus travelers, catch the green bus direct to San Dionisio and Copalita at the Unión Hidalgo bus terminal in Juchitán.

Drivers, from Juchitán, heading westbound, in Unión Hidalgo, turn right, south, at the Chicapa de Castro sign. Continue another two miles (3 km) to Chicapa de Castro. There, you turn left in mid-village and continue southeast another 10 miles (16 km) to Copalita (turn right at the dirt road at the edge of San Dionosio) or San Dionosio (continue to the church, at the east end of town), a total of about 24 miles (39 km) from Juchitán.

Get to Copalita and San Dionisio from La Venta (see the La Venta section) via Unión Hidalgo. At La Venta, transfer to a local bus or *colectivo* (collective taxi) south half an hour to Unión de Hidalgo, then transfer to the San Dionisio–Copalita–bound *verde* (green) bus, via Chicapa de Castro. About 45 bumpy minutes later, get off at the west edge of San Dionosio at the Playa Copalito right side road (walk about a mile, 2 km) or continue ahead to San Dionisio.

From La Venta by car or RV, set your odometer as you head south from Highway 190/200 on the side road to Unión de Hidalgo. At 7.2 miles (11.6 km), make your way through the town, asking townsfolk *"¿El camino a Chicapa?"* ("The way to Chicapa?"). Arrive at Chicapa del Castro (11 miles, 17.5 km), where you turn left, heading southeast toward San Dionisio. After a total of 21.6 miles (34.8 km), turn right at the edge of San Dionisio, at the dirt road to Playa Copalito (one mile, 2 km farther) or continue into San Dionisio del Mar, a total of about 22 miles (35 km), to the church at the east end of town.

SANTO DOMINGO ZANATEPEC

The key country town of Santo Domingo Zanatepec (pop. about 10,000), on Highway 190 about 54 miles (87 km) east of Juchitán, is the point of departure for the wild and spectacularly steep Zanatepec River Canyon. There, accompanied by a guide, you can bask in a hot spring and hike to a pair of wilderness lakes.

Zanatepec, moreover, has a restaurant and hotel. For a break, stop by the mango-shaded **Restaurant Nadxielly** (I Love You), tel. 994/721-0049, where for a few pesos you can eat all the mangos you want during April and May. The family-run establishment, well marked on the highway's north side, offers home-style *comidas* daily 6 A.M.–midnight.

Next door stands the basic **Hotel San Rafael,** Santa Domingo Zanatepec, Oaxaca 70160, same phone as the restaurant, tel. 994/721-0049. The 20 plain but clean rooms rent for about $15 s, $20 d with fan, $20 s, $30 d, or $35 t with a/c, with parking.

Zanatepec can provide a number of goods

and services through establishments located mostly along main street Hidalgo, north of the highway. Get groceries at **Abarrotes Eli,** Hidalgo s/n, tel. 994/721-0144; medicines and medical consultations with **Dr. Horacio Hernández,** at his *farmacia* on Hidalgo, tel. 994/721-0192, open Mon.–Sat. 8 A.M.–2 P.M. and 4–6 P.M.; *telecomunicaciones* (public fax and money orders), tel. 994/721-0142, open Mon.–Fri. 9 A.M.–3:30 P.M. and *correo* (post office), both at Hidalgo 200, next to the *presidencia municipal;* and *policía* (police), at Hidalgo 198, tel. 994/721-0260, the *presidencia municipal.*

Into the Río Zanatepec Canyon
The hotel also serves as contact point for guide **Hermillo Toledo,** who takes parties for excursions into the Río Zanatepec Canyon during the December–May dry season. During the rainy season, the river may be too high. Access from the highway is by a rough gravel road to the village of Agua Caliente (nine miles, 14 km); from there, visit the hot spring, then continue walking (about two hours) up the canyon to a pair of lakes, the Lago del Sol (Lake of the Sun) and Lago de la Luna (Lake of the Moon). Options include expert-level rock climbing, wildlife viewing, fishing, and wilderness camping by the river or the lakes. Expect to pay Hermillo about $30 per day for his services.

SAN PEDRO TAPANATEPEC
"Mango Capital of the World" San Pedro Tapanatepec (pop. 15,000), besides being a main access point for Rincón Juárez on the Mar Muerto (Calm Sea), also has a number of highway-side hotels, restaurants, and services.

Tapanatepec food, lodging, and services are split about evenly between the highway and the downtown, which stretches about four blocks east-west, a few blocks south of the highway.

Accommodations and Food
A trio of acceptable country hotels offer lodging in Tapanatepec. Fanciest is the **Hotel Casablanca** downtown, on the town plaza, at

A new hotel will add to the shoreline amenities—camping, fishing, boating—at Rincón Juárez.

Calle Melendez, San Pedro Tapanatepec, Oaxaca 70180, tel. 994/721-8039. The Casablanca offers about 10 comfortably furnished rooms, with private shower baths, for about $30 d with a/c. Find it in the main business district, about four blocks south of the highway.

Back on the highway, second choice goes to **Hotel Misión,** Carretera Panamericana, Km. 924, San Pedro Tapanatepec, Oaxaca 70180, tel. 994/721-8133 or 994/721-8009. The approximately 35 basic bare-bulb but clean rooms, in a motel-style layout with parking spaces in front of units, rent for about $15 s, $20 d with fan, $20 s, $30 d with a/c. All rooms have room-temperature/tepid shower baths and cable TV, but credit cards are not accepted. The hotel does offer relief from highway truck noise, if you get a room in the rear away from the highway. The Hotel Misión would be my first choice if the big shady pool in the rear were functioning. Check to see if this has changed, however.

Also acceptable, partly because of its good, longer-hours restaurant, is the **Posada Flor,** same address, across the highway, on the north side, from the Hotel Misión, tel. 994/721-8047. The approximately 15 basic but clean rooms (by the truck-noisy highway, however, so use ear plugs) go for about $15 s or d with fan, $25 with a/c. All room have tepid-water shower baths, cable TV, and parking, but credit cards are not accepted.

Any time other than the Feria del Mango (Mango Fair, first week of April) or the Fiesta Patronal de San Pedro (June 27–30), the hotels would not ordinarily require a reservation, provided you arrive before dark.

Groceries are conveniently available at markets on the highway, such as **Abarrotes La Flor,** tel. 994/721-8282.

First choice for a meal in Tapanatepec goes to the restaurant of the motel-style **Posada Flor,** on the north side of the highway, east end, open daily 8 A.M.–10 P.M. Second choice goes to the similarly good restaurant at the **Hotel Misión,** but which closes early, about 7 P.M., for supper.

Services

Most of Tapanatepec's service establishments are either on the highway or along the main business street, Calle Martín Melendez, parallel and about four blocks south of the highway. For money, find **Banamex,** with ATM, at M. Melendez 48, open Mon.–Fri. 9 A.M.–4 P.M.; for medicines, go to one of the pharmacies on the highway, or **Farmacia Espinoza,** at M. Melendez 78, tel. 994/721-8192, open daily 7 A.M.–9 P.M. A **doctor** is on duty 24 hours, at the **Seguro Social** clinic, at 16 de Septiembre 47, tel. 994/721-8119.

For a telephone, use one of the **card-operated public telephones** (Ladatel cards widely purchasable), on the highway and downtown. The *correo* (post office), tel. 994/721-8215, open Mon.–Fri. 9 A.M.–3 P.M., and **telecomunicaciones** (public fax and money orders), are both on Av. Juárez, by the *presidencia municipal,* tel. 994/721-8160, same hours. Find the

Policía Federal de Caminos (Federal Highway Patrol), tel. 994/721-8313, on the highway.

RINCÓN JUÁREZ AND THE CALM SEA

For a look at what Istmeños call the Mar Muerto (which translates, not literally as the "Dead Sea," but as the "Calm Sea," since it's tranquil by contrast with the Mar Vivo, the open ocean), head south about 14 miles (23 km) by a good paved road to Rincón Juárez village (pop. about 1000). Three or four seafood *palapas* line a sandy beach lapped by the gentle waves of a spreading, silvery sea. Life follows the drowsy rhythms of daylight and darkness, wind and tides. Mornings, early, fishermen load their nets and paddle silently out in canoes or buzz out in motorboats to try their luck. Usually, they return with about a 20-pound catch, possibly including jumbo shrimp, clams, or fish

A new *palapa* restaurant rises on the Mar Muerto shoreline at Rincón Juárez.

for sale to the wholesalers whose trucks arrive in early afternoon.

Visitors also can take pleasure from their own quiet routine, enjoying sunrises and sunsets, watching the flocks of pelicans, cormorants, and herons, and exploring the lagoon either on foot or by boat. Fishermen are willing to take parties out for wildlife-viewing or fishing excursions (expect to pay about $20 for half a day). Be prepared with your own binoculars and tackle. Alternatively, launch your own boat or inflated raft right on the beach.

Practicalities

A restaurant-store, **Los Cocos,** provides home-cooked *comidas* and basic groceries. A couple hundred yards farther east along the beach, beachfront *palapa* **Sian Kaan** also serves meals. If you're planning on staying, best come supplied with fruits and vegetables and drinking water.

Although no **hotel** had appeared at this writing, rising local prosperity due to continued high seafood prices may give rise to one or two basic lodgings by the time you read this.

Nevertheless, **tenting and RV camping** promises to be fine anywhere along the local beach for the foreseeable future. Plenty of shoreline trees provide shade and convenient branches, fine for hammocks.

Get to Rincón Juárez by bus (Tapanatepec-bound first- or second-class) from either the Juchitán or Tehuantepec central terminals. Continue by taxi ($3 roundtrip), from Tapanatepec.

By car, the Rincón Juárez trip requires about two hours, one way, from Juchitán. Set your odometer at the Juchitán Highway 190/200 crossing by the Pemex gas station. Continue east along the highway about two hours to Tapanatepec. After a total of 67 miles (108 km) (or 13 miles, 21 km from Hotel San Rafael in Zanatepec), in the middle of Tapanatepec you reach the paved highway-turnoff road for Rincón Juárez on the right. Continue through the town and over the only river-crossing bridge. Continue along another 14 miles (23 km) of paved road to Rincón Juárez, a total of about 74 miles (119 km) from Juchitán.

Salina Cruz and Vicinity

Salina Cruz was important long before the conquest. The *salinas* (salt-producing ponds) where many generations of native people had been harvesting salt for trade attracted Hernán Cortés very soon after his arrival in Mexico. He also recognized Salina Cruz's strategic position on the Isthmus, where the long-sought route to China was accessible, not by a torturous trans-Sierra journey but by a short, easy passage over the narrow, low Isthmus. Cortés lost no time in acquiring the *salinas* as part of his personal domain and building ships on nearby Playa La Ventosa with which to explore the Pacific.

His efforts have been amplified by successive generations. Beginning in the 19th century and continuing to the present day, the Isthmus regularly tempts canal builders wanting to carve a sea route between the Atlantic and Pacific. President Juárez's government settled for a rail con-

nection, begun by the American Louisiana railroad company in Salina Cruz around 1870. President Porfirio Díaz presided over the project's climax, with up-to-date Salina Cruz port facilities built by the British company Iglesias, Pearson and Son, Ltd., around 1900.

Since the 1960s, Petroleos Mexicanos (Pemex) and other government authorities have greatly extended those early efforts with a hefty trans-isthmus pipeline funneling Gulf crude oil to a grand petrochemical complex as well as elaborate new shipping docks. From these, great loads of chemicals, crude oil, gasoline, and other fuels, minerals, fruit, and much more move out via truck, train, and ship to Mexico and the Pacific. Salina Cruz has thus become the industrial engine of the southern Mexican Pacific, employing more than 10,000 workers whose wages directly and indirectly support many tens of thousands more.

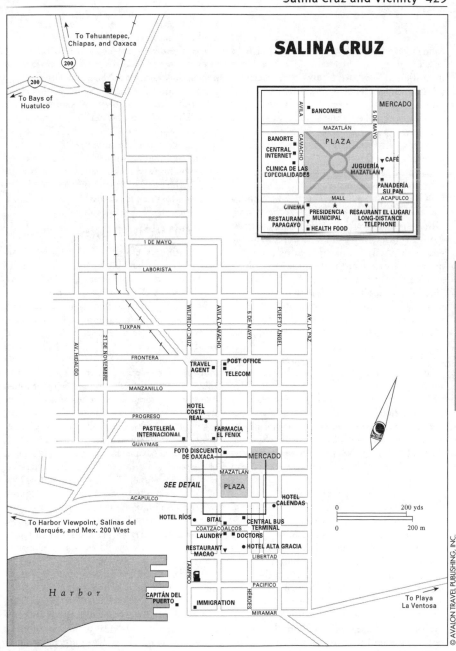

SALINA CRUZ

To Tehuantepec,
Chiapas, and Oaxaca

200

200

To Bays of
Huatulco

BANCOMER

AVILA

MERCADO

5 DE MAYO

MAZATLÁN

BANORTE

CAMACHO

PLAZA

CENTRAL
INTERNET

CLINICA DE LAS
ESPECIALIDADES

JUGUERÍA
MAZATLÁN

CAFÉ

PANADERÍA
SU PAN

MALL

ACAPULCO

CINEMA

RESTAURANT
PAPAGAYO

PRESIDENCIA
MUNICIPAL

HEALTH FOOD

RESAURANT EL LUGAR/
LONG-DISTANCE
TELEPHONE

1 DE MAYO

LABORISTA

TUXPAN

WILFREDO CRUZ

AVILA CAMACHO

5 DE MAYO

PUERTO ÁNGEL

AV. LA PAZ

21 DE NOVIEMBRE

AV. HIDALGO

FRONTERA

MANZANILLO

TRAVEL
AGENT

POST OFFICE

TELECOM

HOTEL
COSTA
REAL

PROGRESO

PASTELERÍA
INTERNACIONAL

FARMACIA
EL FENIX

GUAYMAS

FOTO DISCUENTO
DE OAXACA

MERCADO

MAZATLÁN

SEE DETAIL

PLAZA

ACAPULCO

HOTEL
CALENDAS

To Harbor Viewpoint, Salinas del
Marqués, and Mex. 200 West

HOTEL RÍOS

BITAL

COATZACOALCOS

CENTRAL BUS
TERMINAL

LAUNDRY

DOCTORS

RESTAURANT
MACAO

HOTEL ALTA GRACIA

LIBERTAD

TAMPICO

Harbor

CAPITÁN DEL
PUERTO

IMMIGRATION

PACIFICO

HEROES

MIRAMAR

To Playa
La Ventosa

0   200 yds

0   200 m

THE ISTHMUS

© AVALON TRAVEL PUBLISHING, INC.

SIGHTS

Salina Cruz (pop. 80,000), Oaxaca's third largest city, outstrips both Juchitán and Tehuantepec in hustle and bustle. In Salina Cruz, enterprise reigns and people are working. Crowds with money to spend support a host of town-center markets, stores, offices, hotels, and restaurants. If you need to buy something, Salina Cruz is the place in the Isthmus where you're most likely to get it.

Salina Cruz's big downtown stretches in a mile-long (two-km) rectangle north and south from the town plaza. Some of the north-south streets change names at the plaza, others don't. On the plaza's east side, 5 de Mayo becomes Héroes south of the plaza, while on the plaza's west side, Avila Camacho retains the same name its entire length. West another block and north of the plaza runs Wilfredo Cruz, which becomes Tampico on the south side, while a block east of 5 de Mayo, Puerto Ángel remains the same both north and south of the plaza. Thankfully, east-west streets do not change. From a block north of the plaza, moving successively south, are Guaymas, Mazatlán, Acapulco, and finally, Coatzacoalcos, a block south of the plaza.

Town activity focuses at the very pungent and busy **market,** northeast of the plaza, between Guaymas and Mazatlán. Several blocks south of the plaza are the container docks along the Calle Miramar, which leads to the drowsy beach village of **Playa Ventosa** (see the Playa Ventosa section).

Once you've gotten your fill of the sights and sounds around the plaza and market, head west to breezy harbor vista point **Faro del Marina.** Drive or ride a Salina-labeled bus or a taxi west along Acapulco, the plaza's south-side street. First you pass *dique* (DEE-kay, dry dock) no. 1 and the naval compound, then cross beneath the great rack of pipelines conducting a small river of oil and chemicals over the road. Continue, winding uphill to the summit parking lot on the right. On the harbor's near side stands the fishing fleet; on the opposite side are the smart gray naval frigates and destroyers. On the right, at the outer pier, great supertankers take on lakes of crude oil, most likely bound for Japan and the United States.

Continue west downhill to Barrio Salinas, named after Hernán Cortés's salt-producing ponds, the **Salinas del Marqués.** Although the ponds, about a mile (2 km) west of the foot of the hill, still produce salt, they are as interesting for the wildlife—flocks of waterfowl, both resident and local—that they sustain. People also live from the bounty of the *salinas*. Afternoons, next to the road that cuts north across the marshes to the highway, you can usually see men waist deep in the pond, throwing nets and hoping to haul in something for dinner.

ACCOMMODATIONS

The continuous crowd of Salina Cruz visitors supports several hotels. With the exception of the beachfront hostelries in Playa La Ventosa, they are nearly all near the town center.

Moving clockwise around the plaza, start with the **Hotel Calendas,** one long block east of plaza, just south of the corner of Acapulco and Puerto Ángel, at Puerto Ángel 408, Salina Cruz, Oaxaca 70600, tel./fax 971/714-4574. Savvy managers have created an inviting lodging of about 20 clean, spacious, thoughtfully furnished rooms in two stories around a quiet interior patio. Rentals run about $32 s, $35 d, $37 t, with hot-water shower baths, TV, a/c, and parking. Credit cards are not accepted.

The **Hotel Altagracia,** a block and a half south of the plaza at 5 de Mayo 520, Salina Cruz, Oaxaca 70600, tel./fax 971/714-0726 or 971/714-6225, offers another good choice. The 18 rooms, in a compact but invitingly decorated two-story block, are clean, with either one king-size or two double beds. They are tastefully decorated in modern style, with tile floors and some marble baths. Rooms rent for about $23 s, $27 d, $31 t, with hot-water shower baths, and a/c, but street-only parking. Credit cards are not accepted.

A good low-budget choice is the **Hotel Ríos,** at Wilfredo Cruz 405, Salina Cruz, Oaxaca 70600, tel. 971/714-0337, a block west, half a block south of the plaza. Here, the grandmotherly owner maintains three stories of about 20 plainly furnished but very clean rooms, arranged along corridors around an interior patio. Choose an upper room for more light and privacy. Rates run a very reasonable $10 s or d in one bed, $15 d, t, or q in two beds, with bath (room-temperature/tepid shower), fans, and street parking only; credit cards not accepted.

Fourth choice downtown goes to **Hotel Costa Real,** at Progreso 22, Salina Cruz, Oaxaca 70600, two blocks north, half a block west of the plaza, tel. 971/714-2870, fax 971/714-5111. A plus here is the good restaurant, especially handy for breakfast. Upstairs, although the approximately 30 rooms are clean and comfortable enough, they do not appear particularly well-maintained. Make sure everything works before you pay your money down. Rates run about $40 s and $45 d, $50 t, with hot-water shower baths, a/c, and TV. Credit cards are accepted.

Convenient for travelers with cars or RVs is the **Hotel El Parador,** at Carretera Transistmica Km 6, Colonia Aviación, Salina Cruz, Oaxaca 70670, tel./fax 971/716-2951. On the highway's east side, about four miles (6 km) north of town, the El Parador's major attraction is its big, tropical pool patio, perfect for relaxing at the end of a warm, busy day. However, the rooms, although clean, generally lack light and ventilation. Consequently, some rooms may smell of *moho* (mildew), especially during the summer-fall rainy season. Inspect various rooms until you find one satisfactory. Rentals cost $22 s or d, $25 t, with a/c, hot-water shower baths, and parking; credit cards not accepted.

FOOD

Food is plentiful in downtown Salina Cruz. If you're on a tight budget, the *fondas* (permanent food stalls) on the market's south side offer hearty country-style soups, stews, rice, tamales, and seafood, with all the tortillas you can eat. For dessert, go to one of the two close-in *panaderías* (bakeries). Try Su Pan (Your Bread) on 5 de Mayo, west side of the plaza; or Pastelería Internacional, corner of Wilfredo Cruz and Guaymas, a block north and a block west of the plaza. Find both bakeries open daily 8 A.M.–10 P.M.

Health food fanciers will appreciate the many shelves of grains, food supplements, vitamins, ginseng, herbs, and remedies at the **Centro Naturista Aquarius,** on Camacho, tel. 971/714-2180. Find it half a block south of the cinema corner, just past Restaurant Papagayo, open Mon.–Sat. 8 A.M.–8 P.M.

First restaurant choice goes to refined **Restaurant Macao Cantonesa,** which carries on Salina Cruz's Asian-food tradition, on Avila Camacho, two blocks south of the plaza-corner cinema, tel. 971/714-3834. Diners choose from a long, very recognizable menu, including lots of meat, fish, and chicken dishes, such as almond chicken ($7), pork chow mein ($6), and spareribs ($6). Lighter eaters can skip the meat and ask for rice and vegetables, such as broccoli, cabbage, tomatoes, and mushrooms only and get reduced prices ($3–5). Find them open daily 9 A.M.–9 P.M.

Also among the town center's best sit-down

Giant old trees provide welcome shade at a sidewalk food stall in downtown Salina Cruz.

© BRUCE WHIPPERMAN

THE ISTHMUS

eateries is **Restaurant Papagayo,** at Avila Camacho 407, tel. 971/714-2084, open daily 7 A.M.–11 P.M., half a block south of the plaza-corner cinema. The Chinese-Mexican owners once offered some Asian food favorites, but now they've switched exclusively to Mexican and international specialties. These include good breakfasts (hotcakes, bacon, eggs, $2–4), lunches, or dinners (hamburgers, *tortas,* soup, salad, fish, chicken, $2–6); open daily 7 A.M.–11 P.M.

Third choice near the plaza goes to **Restaurant El Lugar** (The Place), tel. 971/714-0863, where customers enjoy a perch above and away from the sidewalk hubbub, especially good for breakfast or a late snack. Beneath a squadron of cooling ceiling fans, choose from a tasty, familiar menu of soups, sandwiches, chicken, meats, eggs, and fish ($2–5). It's open long hours, daily 7–2 A.M.

For a modicum of refined tranquillity and plain good food, try the dining room of the Hotel Costa Real, at Progreso 22, open daily 7:30 A.M.–10:30 P.M., two blocks north, half a block west of the plaza.

The bounty of the Isthmus is no more apparent than at the street fruit stands of Salina Cruz.

ENTERTAINMENT AND EVENTS

True to Tehuantepec tradition, Salina Cruz folks sometimes abandon their workaday habits for fiestas. First comes the **Fiesta de la Santa Cruz,** on May 3, in a blast that includes coronation of a queen, full-costumed traditional dances, a fruit- and gift-throwing *regada* parade, carnival rides and games, and fireworks.

If you miss that fiesta, you might be lucky and get in on one later, such as the **Fiesta del Pueblo,** an all-purpose town fiesta, for several days beginning May 9; the **Fiesta de Santa Rosa de Lima** (August 26–September 2); the **Fiesta de San Francisco Asis** (October 3–5); and the **Fiesta de San Diego** (November 11–16).

If, sadly, you miss all the fiestas, at least console yourself by going to the curiously labeled **Cinema Sección 38,** right on the plazafront, southeast corner of Acapulco and Avila Camacho, where you can enjoy programs of mostly first-run American action-adventure and romantic-comedy films.

INFORMATION AND SERVICES

Money

Several banks, all with ATMs, serve downtown customers. A good first choice is **Banco Internacional** (Bital), a block south of the plaza, northeast corner of Avila Camacho and Coatzacoalcos, tel. 971/714-4476, with long hours Mon.–Sat. 8 A.M.–7 P.M. Alternatively, also on Avila Camacho, try **Bancomer,** tel. 971/714-0032, open Mon.–Fri. 8:30 A.M.–4:00 P.M., Sat. 10 A.M.–2 P.M., on the east side of the street a few steps north of the plaza; or **Banorte,** on the west side of Camacho, near the corner of Mazatlán, open Mon.–Fri. 9 A.M.–4 P.M.

Communications

The town *correo* (post office, with Mexpost secure mail service), tel. 971/714-0040, open Mon.–Sat. 8 A.M.–10 P.M., and *Telecomunicaciones* (public fax and money orders), tel./fax 971/714-0760, open Mon.–Sat. 8 A.M.–7:30 P.M., Sun. 9 A.M.–noon, stand side by side four blocks north of the plaza, east side of Avila Camacho,

© BRUCE WHIPPERMAN

Juguería Mazatlán, by the Salina Cruz market, is the perfect spot to stop for an *agua* natural fruit drink.

corner of Frontera. Moreover, a *larga distancia* (long distance) telephone office serves customers 7 A.M.–midnight, at the plaza's southeast corner, below Restaurant El Lugar.

A number of small outlets provide **Internet** services: Try **Centel,** on the plaza, west side, tel. 971/714-3375, open Mon.–Fri. 8 A.M.–11 P.M. (besides Internet, also long distance phone, fax, luggage storage, and copies), or **Internet Conección,** on Camacho, east side, a block and a half south of the plaza cinema, upstairs, open Mon.–Sat. 9 A.M.–9 P.M.

Travel Agents and Car Rentals

Travel agents, besides selling air tickets and reserving hotel rooms, are sometimes willing sources of information. Try the **Agencia de Viajes Lily Tours,** in the Hotel Costa Real, at Progreso 22, two blocks north, half a block west, of the plaza, tel. 971/714-0540 or 971/714-6694. Their services include car rentals. Find them open Mon.–Sat. 8 A.M.–8 P.M.

Altertatively, go to **Agencia de Viajes Grupo,** four blocks north of the plaza, at Avila Camacho

205 B, tel. 971/714-3266 or 971/714-3636, open Mon.–Sat. 8 A.M.–8 P.M.

Another such agency is **Lone Star,** tel./fax 971/716-2650, bubistmo@hotmail.com, on the north outskirts, along the Tehuantepec highway, about a mile (2 km) from downtown. Besides their main car rental business, they sell airline tickets, reserve hotel rooms, and provide transport.

Immigration

Being a port of entry, Salina Cruz has a **Migración** (Immigration Office). Go there, at the foot of Tampico, four blocks south of the plaza, tel. 971/714-1000 or 971/714-4531, if you lose or need an extension on your tourist permit. It's open Mon.–Fri. 9 A.M.–1 P.M.

If you arrive by **private boat** and have inspection documentation from another Mexican port, present it for check-in at the Capitán del Puerto, located just west of Migración, across Tampico. If you arrive without Mexican inspection documentation, first go to Migración for an inspection, then to the Capitán del Puerto.

Health and Emergencies

Several pharmacies sell medicines and drugs near the plaza. For discounts, go to the big **Farmacia El Fénix,** at the northwest corner of Avila Camacho and Guaymas, a block north of the plaza, tel. 971/714-0299 or 971/714-3141, open Mon.–Sat. 8 A.M.–10 P.M. If it can't supply you, try **Farmacia Pronto,** at the plaza northeast corner, across the street.

Of the several downtown doctors' offices, the **Clínica de Especialidades Médicas** (Medical Specialties Clinic), at Avila Camacho 306, west side of the plaza, tel. 971/714-4107, offers several choices: gynecologist (Mon.–Sat. 10 A.M.–1 P.M.), pediatrician (Mon.–Fri. 5–8 P.M.), orthopedist (Mon., Wed., Thurs. 6–8 P.M., Sat. 10 A.M.–1 P.M.), and general practitioner (Mon.–Fri. 5–8 P.M.).

Alternatively, at nearby offices, try **gynecologist** Doctora Gabriela Guzman Cartas, and **pediatrician** Doctor Anselmo Medero, at 1 Coatzacoalcos, a block south of the plaza, between Camacho and Héroes, tel. 971/714-1622, both open Mon.–Fri. 9 A.M.–2 P.M. and 5–8 P.M.

In a **medical emergency,** either follow your hotel recommendation or have a taxi take you to **Sanatorio del Carmen,** on Calle Francisco Villa 16, tel. 971/714-4334 or 971/714-1180. In a **police emergency,** contact the *policía municipal,* tel. 971/714-0523.

Photography and Laundry

The best town source of film (Kodak, Konica, and Fuji), developing, cameras, and supplies is **Foto Discuento de Oaxaca,** on Avila Camacho, half a block north of the plaza, tel. 971/714-4300, open Mon.–Sat. 9 A.M.–8 P.M.

Get your laundry done at **Lavandería Anabel,** Tampico 53, between Progreso and Guaymas, west side of street, a block west and a block and a half north of the plaza, tel. 971/714-0490 or 971/716-2202, open Mon.–Sat. 8 A.M.–1:30 P.M., 4–7:30 P.M. Alternatively, take your laundry to **Lavandería Carmel,** at the southeast corner of Coatzcoalcos and Camacho, a block south of the plaza.

GETTING THERE AND AWAY

Bus travelers, go to the *camionera central* (central bus terminal), on 5 de Mayo, tel. 971/714-0259, half a block south of the plaza. **Cristóbal Colón** (CC), **Plus,** and **Autobuses del Oriente** (ADO) offer luxury and first-class service (that can be booked and paid for by credit card, via the **Ticket Bus** agency's toll-free Mex. number 800/702-8000). **Autobuses Unidos** (AU) and **Sur** offer second-class service.

Cristóbal Colón departures connect northwest with Mexico City Norte via Tehuantepec and Oaxaca; southwest with Bahías de Huatulco, Pochutla (Puerto Ángel), and Puerto Escondido; east with Juchitán, Zanatepec, Tuxtla Gutiérrez, San Cristóbal las Casas, and Tapachula on the Guatemala border. Its subsidiary line, Plus, offers luxury-class connections northwest with Oaxaca, Mexico City, and Veracruz, and southwest with Bahías de Huatulco.

ADO offers first-class connections north with Tehuantepec, Juchitán, Minatitlán, Coatzacoalcos, Villahermosa, Ciudad del Carmen, Tuxpan, Veracruz, and Tampico.

AU offers second-class connections northwest with Oaxaca, Puebla, Mexico City, Orizaba, and Veracruz, and north with Tehuantepec, Juchitán, and Tuxtepec.

Sur offers second-class connections north with Tehuantepec, Juchitán, and Coatzacoalcos; east with Zanatepec and Tapanatepec, and southwest with Astata and Bahías de Huatulco.

Drivers have the same highway choices and destinations as listed at the end of the Tehuantepec section. Simply add 20 minutes to the driving time (and nine miles, 15 km distance) for northerly, northwesterly, and easterly trips; subtract the same for southwesterly trips. Fill up with **gasoline** at the Pemex *gasolinera* on the highway, Tehuantepec direction, about four miles (6 km) north of downtown.

PLAYA LA VENTOSA

Playa La Ventosa is Salina Cruz's sleepy little beach village on the historic Bahía de la Ventosa (Windy Bay) where Hernán Cortés built his first caravels to explore the Pacific. Get there by car, taxi, or white or orange Ventosa-labeled bus running west along Calle Miramar next to the container docks, four blocks south of the plaza. Drivers, bear left at the fork at the end of Miramar and continue winding over the hill toward the beach. After about two miles (3 km), you get a good view of the petrochemical plant on the left, belching a swirling, hellish plume of pollution. Fortunately for Salina Cruz (but not for other towns downwind), prevailing breezes blow the smoke away from town.

About four miles (6 km) from downtown, you arrive at Playa La Ventosa. One of the best places to land is **La Palapa de Chava**, the beachfront restaurant at the end of the main street through town. Friendly, knowledgeable owner Salvador Mendoza likes to tell visitors about Playa La Ventosa. He says that wood for Cortés's ships was cut inland and floated downstream via the **Río Tehuantepec,** which empties into the bay's east (left, facing the ocean) side. There, the summer rainy-season flood stains the entire Bahía Ventosa a muddy brown while depositing piles of driftwood on the east-side beach. In the dry winter and spring, the river dries slowly to a clear trickle and the bay becomes clear and blue.

Shift your view west and notice what appears to be a tower atop the headland, a mile or two beyond the foreground bay and beach. This tower has been known for longer than anyone remembers as **El Faro de Cortés,** The Lighthouse of Cortés. The tower's builders cut a window on the seaward side, where historians believe they placed an oil lamp to guide ships to the harbor.

If the story is true, the lighthouse would be nearly five centuries old. How could this be? Without maintenance, mortar crumbles and bricks usually fall after two or three centuries. Restaurant owner Salvador Mendoza answers that experts believe that Cortés built the tower of bricks and mortar, mixed with egg whites and yolks instead of water, which made the mortar durable enough to keep the lighthouse standing straight, without any repairs, until the present day.

Activities

Wander the beach, rocky in the rainy summer and fall, sandy in the dry winter and spring. On the east side, by the river's mouth, collect shells and driftwood, watch the antics of the pelicans, seagulls, and cormorants, and, with your binoculars, look for rarer species. On the west side, explore the tide pools beneath the rocky headland, then head inland and hike the headland's forested arroyos up to the breezy hilltop for a close-up view of Cortés's Lighthouse.

On another day, go on a fishing excursion and catch a load of silvery *mojarra* (bass), *lisa* (mullet), and *sierra* (mackerel) for a feast for everyone in the neighborhood. Go in your own boat or hire a boatman (figure on about $40) to take you out for half a day.

Accommodations

For accommodation, either park your RV, set up a tent, or stay in one of the Playa Ventosa beachfront lodgings. On the far west side of the beach, beneath the headland, is a secluded, level grassy spot that appears fine for tenting. RV-equipped travelers could simply park at one of a number of likely spots down by the beach.

Otherwise, stay at La Ventosa's best, **Posada Rústrian,** Playa Bahía la Ventosa, Salina Cruz, Oaxaca 70600, tel. 971/714-0450, so relaxing that it's worth reserving well ahead of time if you plan to arrive during high-occupancy times around Christmas, Easter, weekends, and January–April. Posada Rústrian amounts to a downscale mini-resort, perched on a breezy rise with a palm-fringed beach view. Watch for the sign on the left as you're entering town. No TV, no phones, simply about 10 basic rooms and a breezy, shaded restaurant with chairs and hammocks for resting, reading, and taking in the view. Rooms rent for about $10 s or d, $20 t, with fans and room-temperature private shower baths. (Note: Unfortunately, at this writing, the Rústrian's rooms needed a good scrubbing. I mentioned this to the owner, and hopefully he will heed the suggestion. Nevertheless, the place is still worth it, even if you have to do the scrubbing yourself.)

Three or four alternate lodgings do exist, although none so inviting as Posada Rústrian. For example, try **Casa Limones** across the main town street from Posada Rústrian, or Posada Miramar, a block farther, near the end of the street on the right just before Palapa La Chava.

EXCURSION EAST OF SALINA CRUZ: HUAVE COUNTRY

The country due east of Salina Cruz, is one of the low-lying, barrier-sand spits to which many of Oaxaca's Huave-speaking people were marginalized by the more populous Zapotecs long before the Spanish arrived. The Spanish simply continued the segregation that was already in place.

The Huave appear to have grudgingly accepted their lot. They subsist, mostly off of the cattle that graze whatever brush, grass, and cactus that grow in the sand and the fish and shrimp that they can catch in the ocean and the lagoons.

San Mateo del Mar

San Mateo del Mar (pop. around 2,000), seat of the *municipio* of the same name, has a uniquely picturesque church and a native market, making it the major destination of this eastern excursion. Get there (18 miles, 29 km) by heading

one hour east from the jumping-off spot on Highway 200, near Km marker 17.

The plaza-center of San Mateo del Mar is a block or two south (turn right) from the entrance road. The main sights are the market, which takes up much of the town plaza; the lagoon, past the plaza, a block south; and the church, just to the east of the plaza. When I was there a sullen sacristan (church keeper) didn't let me enter, claiming that the church was closed. Its colorful facade, however, is unique.

The market is where most of the town action is. Women are the actors and Huave is the language. Dress appears to be the dividing line: The women who wear *traje*—red blouse, dark skirt, striped cloth headdress trailing a bright ribbon— seem to be the ones who speak Huave only. Besides selling a few vegetables, they mostly offer the local fish and shrimp that their husbands have caught and they've dried in the sun.

Despite their historical shyness (most likely based on a communal memory of hard experience), you might get a smile when you say *"Buenos días"* or *"Buenas tardes."* The Huave reticence shows directly in the way they build their homes. Notice the walls, the older ones of sticks or brush, now increasingly of concrete, that

Huave fishing boats on the Laguna Inferior beaches at Santa María del Mar

© BRUCE WHIPPERMAN

surround each family compound. In some country lots, concrete walls appeared to have been built even before any buildings. (This, of course, is not unlike what a significant fraction of town Mexicans do, especially the well-to-do, who have historically surrounded their houses with brawny fences and encased their windows with steel bars.)

Santa María del Mar

If you have time, continue another 10 miles (16 km) to smaller Santa María del Mar (pop. 500). Here, you'll find a sleepier town plaza and a humbler church. For a bit of action, turn north (left) from the plaza to the *embarcadero* (wharf), on the Laguna Inferior beach, about a mile (2 km) from town. A detachment of marines guards the beach, apparently to keep order among the locals. The guards seemed unconcerned with me as I drove past their post.

A battalion of fishing *lanchas* (small boats) lines a broad, breezy beach. Gentle waves wash the shallow shoreline, and dogs laze in the sun. With the added security of the marines, this appears to be an especially good spot for prepared tenters or RVers (bring water and food). The most exciting time is mid- to late afternoon, when the fishermen bring in their catches. They sell whatever they can to buyers who arrive with trucks, and load the rest on wheelbarrows, which they push home for drying. The good shrimp price that the buyers were paying—about $2.50 per pound—reflects both local and world demand.

Getting There: Go by bus (ask for a "San Mateo del Mar" bus at the Salina Cruz market) or by car. The road, initially paved but potholed, finally good, all-weather gravel, takes off from near the Highway 200 Km 17 marker about three miles (5 km) north of town. Turn right (or catch a San Mateo del Mar–marked bus) at the highway traffic signal and road that heads east, by the big electrical sub-station. Drivers, set your odometer. After about five blocks, follow the traffic left; continue straight about two miles (3 km), passing through the traffic circle at the Pemex refinery gate. Cross the Río Tehuantepec at mile 4.7 (7.6 km). After the river bridge, follow the right road fork, and continue for about another 13 miles (21 km) through a couple of hamlets, just before San Mateo del Mar, 18 miles, 29 km from Highway 200.

Resources

Trailer Parks and Camping

Unlike the United States, Canada, and Europe, Oaxaca has few formal camping grounds. It does, however, have a few trailer parks and a scattering of privately, communally, or governmentally managed spots that are customarily used for camping, either by "car-RV-tent" (CRVT) or "tent only" (T). Destination chapters, listed below, locate them precisely and discuss access, arrangements, and facilities, if any.

Location	Name (if any)	Comments
OAXACA CITY		
northeast side	Oaxaca Trailer Park	(CRVT)
north side (San Felipe del Agua village)		"new" trailer park (CRVT)
AROUND THE VALLEY OF OAXACA		
Teotitlán del Valle (reservoir above town)		(CRVT)
Santa Ana del Valle (reservoir above town)		(T)
San Sebastián de las Grutas		riverside camping (CRVT)
PACIFIC RESORTS AND SOUTHERN SIERRA		
Puerto Ángel (Zipolite)	Trailer Park La Palmera	east end, above the beach (CRVT)
Puerto Ángel (Zipolite)	Fernando's Shambhala	on the beach, west end, restaurant (T)
San Agustinillo (west of Zipolite)		*palapa*-shaded parking and campsites on beach (CRVT)
Chacalapa	Balneario El Paraíso	rural pocket paradise (CRVT)
San José del Pacífico	Hotel Puesta del Sol	pine-scented air, trails, and views (T)
Bahías de Huatulco		parking in lot at Bahía Chahue marina (CRVT) and other bays (T)

Trailer Parks and Camping

Location	Name (if any)	Comments
Bahía San Agustín		sandy beach, fishing, seafood *palapas* (CRVT)
Laguna Colorada		seafood *palapas*, mangroves, beach (CRVT)
Laguna Garrapatera		wild, breezy beach (T)
Playa Cangrejo		surfing and seafood (CRVT)
Playa Brasil		(CRVT)
Puerto Escondido	Parque Trayler Palmas de Cortés	right on the beach (CRVT)
Laguna Manialtepec	Las Hamacas and La Alejandria	restaurants, lagoon, mangrove, wildlife viewing (CRVT)
Lagunas de Chacahua N.P.	Playa Cerro Hermosa	sea, sand, fishing, snorkeling (CRVT)
Charquito Atotonilco		community hot spring and sacred site (CRVT)
Playa Blanca Scenic Beach		lagoon and rustic *palapa* hotel (CRVT)
Pinotepa Nacional		Río Arena, waterfall, a few miles east of town (CRVT)
Corralero (south of Pinotepa Nacional)		uncrowded beach camping, *palapa* restaurants (CRVT)
Sola de Vega		riverside camping in grand old cypress grove (CRVT)

THE MIXTECA

Location	Name (if any)	Comments
Apoala		cave, waterfall, lodging, RV and wilderness camping (CRVT)
San Miguel Tequixtepec		small, friendly town with museum and stores (CRVT)
Tepelmeme		museum and wilderness adventure camping (T)
Yosocuta Reservoir		boating, bass fishing, and swimming (CRVT)

Trailer Parks and Camping

Location	Name (if any)	Comments
Tonalá Canyon		pristine river canyon (T)
Juxtlahuaca		Laguna Encantada natural spring, campground (CRVT)
Yosundua		waterfall and informal campground (CRVT)
Achiutla and Río Yayata		camping by creekside cypress grove; archaeological site (CRVT)

NORTHERN OAXACA

Location	Name (if any)	Comments
Benito Juárez, Cuajimoloyas	Llano de las Tarajeas and Las Vigas	pristine meadow (CRVT)
Ixtlán de Juárez vicinity	Campamento del Monte	private wooded mountainside with cabins, small campsites (CRVT)
Santa Catarina Ixtepeji		small town with eco-preserve and campground
Ixtlán de Juárez	Community Ecotours Pozuelos campsite	(CRVT)
Ixtlán de Juárez	Arco de Yagela	limestone cave (T)
Valle Nacional	Arroyo Blanco	natural spring, friendly family (CRVT)
Valle Nacional	Balneario El Zuzul	community-owned natural spring (CRVT)
Temascal Reservoir		boating, bass fishing, swimming (CRVT)
Ixcatlán		dozens of islands; choose one for your campsite (T)
Ixcatlán		Isla Soyaltepec, Chinantec-speaking island village (T)

Location	Name (if any)	Comments
THE ISTHMUS		
Tlacotepec		beautiful blue spring, picnic and camping ground (CRVT)
Laollaga		spring-fed river, picnic ground, rough trailer park (CRVT)
Unión Hidalgo		Playa Copalita; Huave fishing village (CRVT)
Zanatepec		wilderness river canyon; hot spring and lakes (T)
Rincón Juárez		Huave fishing village; seafood restaurant, quiet beach (CRVT)
Salina Cruz		Playa La Ventosa village; restaurants, beach, river (CRVT)
Santa María del Mar		Huave village east of Salina Cruz; fishing *embarcadero* and beach, secure (CRVT)

Trailer Parks and Camping

Glossary

Many of the following words have a social-historical meaning; others you will not find in the usual English-Spanish dictionary.

abarrotería—grocery store

aguardiente—Mexican "white lightning": cheap distilled liquor made from sugarcane

alcalde—mayor or municipal judge

alebrije—fanciful wooden animal, mostly made in Arrazola and Tilcajete villages

alfarería—pottery

andando—walkway, or strolling path

antojitos—native Mexican snacks, such as tamales, *chiles rellenos,* tacos, and enchiladas

artesanías—handicrafts

artesano, artesana—craftsman, craftswoman

asunción—the assumption of the Virgin Mary into heaven (as distinguished from the *ascención* of Jesus into heaven)

atole—a popular nonalcoholic drink made from corn juice

audiencia—one of the royal executive-judicial panels sent to rule Mexico during the 16th century

ayuntamiento—either the town council or the building where it meets

barrio—a town or village district or neighborhood, usually centered around its own local plaza and church

bienes raíces—literally "good roots," but popularly, real estate

boleto—ticket, boarding pass

brujo, bruja—male or female witch doctor or shaman

caballero—literally, "horseman," but popularly, gentleman

cabercera—head town of a municipal district, or headquarters in general

cabrón—literally, a cuckold, but more commonly, bastard, rat, or S.O.B.; sometimes used affectionately

cacique—local chief or boss

camionera—bus station

campesino—country person; farm worker

canasta—basket of woven reeds, with handle

cantera—local volcanic stone, widely used for colonial-era Oaxaca monuments

Carnaval—celebration preceding Lent, called Mardi Gras in the United States

casa de huéspedes—guesthouse, usually operated in a family home

caudillo—dictator or political chief

charro—gentleman cowboy

chingar—literally, to "rape," but is also the universal Spanish "f" word, the equivalent of "screw" in English

Churrigueresque—Spanish Baroque architectural style incorporated into many Mexican colonial churches, named after José Churriguera (1665–1725)

científicos—literally, scientists, but applied to President Porfirio Díaz's technocratic advisers

coa (estaca)—digging stick, used for planting corn

Cocijo—Zapotec god of rain, lightning, and thunder

cofradía—Catholic fraternal service association, either male or female, mainly in charge of financing and organizing religious festivals

colectivo—a shared public taxi or minibus that picks up and deposits passengers along a designated route

colegio—preparatory school or junior college

colonia—suburban subdivision-satellite of a larger city

comal—a flat pottery griddle, for heating tortillas

comida corrida—economical afternoon set meal, usually with four—soup, rice, entrée, and dessert—courses.

compadrazgo—the semiformal web of village and *barrio compadre* and *padrino* relationships that determine a person's lifetime obligations and loyalties

compadre—a semi-formalized "best friend" relationship that usually lasts for life

comunal—refers to the traditional indigenous

system of joint decision-making and land ownership and use

Conasupo—government store that sells basic foods at subsidized prices

correo—post office

criollo—person of all-Spanish descent born in the New World

Cuaresma—Lent

curandero, curandera—indigenous medicine man or woman

damas—ladies, as in "ladies room"

Domingo de Ramos—Palm Sunday

ejido—a constitutional, government-sponsored form of community, with shared land ownership and cooperative decision-making

encomienda—colonial award of tribute from a designated indigenous district

farmacia—pharmacy, or drugstore

finca—farm

fonda—foodstall or small restaurant, often in a traditional market complex

fraccionamiento—city sector or subdivision

fuero—the former right of clergy to be tried in separate ecclesiastical courts

gachupín—"one who wears spurs"; a derogatory term for a Spanish-born colonial

gasolinera—gasoline station

gente de razón—"people of reason"; whites and mestizos in colonial Mexico

gringo—once-derogatory but now commonly used term for North American whites

grito—impassioned cry, as in Hidalgo's Grito de Dolores

hacienda—large landed estate; also the government treasury

hamaca—hammock

hechicero—a "wizard" who leads community propitiatory ceremonies

hidalgo—nobleman; called honorifically by "Don" or "Doña"

hojalata—tinware

indígena—indigenous or aboriginal inhabitant of all-native descent who speaks his or her native tongue; commonly, but incorrectly, an *indio* (Indian)

jacal—native label for thatched, straw, and stick country house

jejenes—"no-see-um" biting gnats, especially around San Blas, Nayarit

judiciales—the federal "judicial," or investigative police, best known to motorists for their highway checkpoint inspections

jugería—stall or small restaurant providing a large array of squeezed vegetable and fruit *jugos* (juices)

juzgado—the "hoosegow," or jail

larga distancia—long-distance telephone service, or the *caseta* (booth) where it's provided

licencado—academic degree (abbrev. Lic.) approximately equivalent to a bachelor's degree in the United States

lonchería—small lunch counter, usually serving juices, sandwiches, and *antojitos*

machismo; macho—exaggerated sense of maleness; person who holds such a sense of himself

mano—the stone roller used to grind corn on the *metate*

mayordomo—community leader responsible for staging a local Catholic religious festival

mescal—alcoholic beverage distilled from the fermented hearts of maguey (century plant)

mestizo—person of mixed native-European descent

metate—a slightly concave, horizontal stone basin for grinding corn for tortillas

milagro—small religious wish medal, often pinned to an altar saint by someone requesting divine intervention

milpa—a small, family-owned field, usually planted in corn

molcajete—a stone mortar and pestle, used for hand-grinding, especially chiles and seeds

mordida—slang for bribe; "little bite"

olla—a pottery jug or pot, used for stewing—vegetables, meats, beans, coffee

padrino, padrina—godfather or godmother, often the respective *compadres* of the given child's parents

palapa—an open, thatched-roof structure, usually shading a restaurant

panela—rough brown cane sugar, sold in lumps in the market

panga—outboard launch *(lancha)*

papier-mâché—the craft of glued, multilayered paper sculpture, centered in Tonalá, Jalisco, where creations can resemble fine pottery or lacquerware

Pemex—acronym for Petróleos Mexicanos, the national oil corporation

peninsulares—the Spanish-born ruling colonial elite

peón—a poor wage-earner, usually a country native

petate—all-purpose woven mat, from palm fronds

piciete—wild tobacco

piñata—papier-mâché decoration, usually in animal or human form, filled with treats and broken open during a fiesta

plan—political manifesto, usually by a leader or group consolidating or seeking power

Porfiriata—the 34-year (1876–1910) ruling period of president-dictator Porfirio Díaz

posada—Christmas Eve procession in which participants, led by costumed Holy Mary and Joseph, knock on neighborhood doors and implore, unsuccessfully, for a room for the night

pozole—stew of hominy in broth, usually topped by shredded meat, cabbage, and diced onion

presidencia municipal—the headquarters, like a U.S. city or county hall, of a Mexican *municipio*, county-like local governmental unit

preventiva—state-funded local police

principal, anciano—a respected elder, often a member of a council of elders, whom the community consults for advice and support

pronunciamiento—declaration of rebellion by an insurgent leader

pueblo—town or people

puente—literally a "bridge," but commonly a holiday weekend, when hotel reservations are highly recommended

pulque—the fermented juice of the maguey plant, approximately equivalent to strong beer or wine in alcoholic content

puta—whore, bitch, or slut

quinta—a villa or country house

quinto—the colonial royal "fifth" tax on treasure and precious metals

regidor—a community official, often a town council member, responsible for specific government functions, such as public works

retorno—cul-de-sac

ropa típica—traditional dress, derived from the Spanish colonial tradition (in contrast to *traje*, traditional indigenous dress)

rurales—former federal country police force created to fight *bandidos* (bandits) and suppress dissent

Sabi—Mixtec god of rain

Semana Santa—Holy Week, the week before Easter

servicios—the ladder of increasingly responsible public tasks that, if successfully performed, leads to community approval, prestige, and leadership for a given individual by middle age

tapete—wool rug, made in certain east-side Valley of Oaxaca villages

taxi especial—private taxi, as distinguished from *taxi colectivo*, or collective taxi

telégrafo—telegraph office, lately converting to high-tech *telecomunicaciones*, or *telecom*, offering telegraph, telephone, and public fax services

temascal—a traditional indigenous sweat room, rock-enclosed and heated by a wood fire, usually used for healing, especially by women after childbirth

tenate—basket of woven palm leaf, with tumpline instead of a rigid handle

tepache—a wine, fermented from *panela* (sugarcane juice)

tequio—an obligatory communal task, such as local road work, street sweeping, or child care, expected of all adult villagers from time to time

tianguis—literally, "awning," but now has come to mean the awning-decorated native town market

tono—a usually benign animal guardian spirit

topil—lowest municipal job, of messenger, filled by youngest teenage boys

vaquero—cowboy

vecinidad—neighborhood

yanqui—Yankee

zócalo—town plaza or central square

Spanish Phrasebook

Your Oaxaca adventure will be more fun if you use a little Spanish. Mexican folks, although they may smile at your funny accent, will appreciate your halting efforts to break the ice and transform yourself from a foreigner to a potential friend.

Spanish commonly uses 30 letters—the familiar English 26, plus four straightforward additions: ch, ll, ñ, and rr, which are explained in "Consonants," below.

PRONUNCIATION

Once you learn them, Spanish pronunciation rules—in contrast to English—don't change. Spanish vowels generally sound softer than in English. (Note: The capitalized syllables below receive stronger accents.)

Vowels

a — like ah, as in "hah": *agua* AH-gooah (water), *pan* PAHN (bread), and *casa* CAH-sah (house)

e — like ay, as in "may:" *mesa* MAY-sah (table), *tela* TAY-lah (cloth), and *de* DAY (of, from)

i — like ee, as in "need": *diez* dee-AYZ (ten), *comida* ko-MEE-dah (meal), and *fin* FEEN (end)

o — like oh, as in "go": *peso* PAY-soh (weight), *ocho* OH-choh (eight), and *poco* POH-koh (a bit)

u — like oo, as in "cool": *uno* OO-noh (one), *cuarto* KOOAHR-toh (room), and *usted* oos-TAYD (you); when it follows a "q" the **u** is silent; when it follows an "h" or has an umlaut, it's pronounced like "w"

Consonants

b, d, f, k, l, m, n, p, q, s, t, v, w, x, y, z, and **ch** — pronounced almost as in English; **h** occurs, but is silent—not pronounced at all.

c — like k as in "keep": *cuarto* KOOAR-toh (room), Tepic tay-PEEK (capital of Nayarit state); when it precedes "e" or "i," pronounce **c** like s as in "sit": *cerveza* sayr-VAY-sah (beer), *encima* ayn-SEE-mah (atop).

g — like g as in "gift" when it precedes "a," "o,"

"u," or a consonant: *gato* GAH-toh (cat), *hago* AH-goh (I do, make); otherwise, pronounce **g** like h as in "hat": *giro* HEE-roh (money order), *gente* HAYN-tay (people)

j — like h, as in "has": *Jueves* HOOAY-vays (Thursday), *mejor* may-HOR (better)

ll — like y, as in "yes": *toalla* toh-AH-yah (towel), *ellos* AY-yohs (they, them)

ñ — like ny, as in "canyon": *año* AH-nyo (year), *señor* SAY-nyor (Mr., sir)

r — is lightly trilled, with tongue at the roof of your mouth like a very light English d, as in "ready": *pero* PAY-doh (but), *tres* TDAYS (three), *cuatro* KOOAH-tdoh (four).

rr — like a Spanish r, but with much more emphasis and trill. Let your tongue flap. Practice with *burro* (donkey), *carretera* (highway), and Carrillo (proper name), then really let go with *ferrocarril* (railroad).

Note: The single small but common exception to all of the above is the pronunciation of Spanish **y** when it's being used as the Spanish word for "and," as in "Ron y Kathy." In such case, pronounce it like the English ee, as in "keep": Ron "ee" Kathy (Ron and Kathy).

Accent

The rule for accent, the relative stress given to syllables within a given word, is straightforward. If a word ends in a vowel, an n, or an s, accent the next-to-last syllable; if not, accent the last syllable.

Pronounce *gracias* GRAH-seeahs (thank you), *orden* OHR-dayn (order), and *carretera* kah-ray-TAY-rah (highway) with stress on the next-to-last syllable.

Otherwise, accent the last syllable: *venir* vay-NEER (to come), *ferrocarril* fay-roh-cah-REEL (railroad), and *edad* ay-DAHD (age).

Exceptions to the accent rule are always marked with an accent sign: (á, é, í, ó, or ú), such as *teléfono* tay-LAY-foh-noh (telephone), *jabón* hah-BON (soap), and *rápido* RAH-pee-doh (rapid).

BASIC AND COURTEOUS EXPRESSIONS

Most Spanish-speaking people consider formalities important. Whenever approaching anyone for information or some other reason, do not forget the appropriate salutation—good morning, good evening, etc. Standing alone, the greeting *hola* (hello) can sound brusque.

Hello. — *Hola.*
Good morning. — *Buenos días.*
Good afternoon. — *Buenas tardes.*
Good evening. — *Buenas noches.*
How are you? — *¿Cómo está usted?*
Very well, thank you. — *Muy bien, gracias.*
Okay; good. — *Bien.*
Not okay; bad. — *Mal* or *feo.*
So-so. — *Más o menos.*
And you? — *¿Y usted?*
Thank you. — *Gracias.*
Thank you very much. — *Muchas gracias.*
You're very kind. — *Muy amable.*
You're welcome. — *De nada.*
Goodbye. — *Adios.*
See you later. — *Hasta luego.*
please — *por favor*
yes — *sí*
no — *no*
I don't know. — *No sé.*
Just a moment, please. — *Momentito, por favor.*
Excuse me, please (when you're trying to get attention). — *Disculpe* or *Con permiso.*
Excuse me (when you've made a boo-boo). — *Lo siento.*
Pleased to meet you. — *Mucho gusto.*
How do you say . . . in Spanish? — *¿Cómo se dice . . . en español?*
What is your name? — *¿Cómo se llama usted?*
Do you speak English? — *¿Habla usted inglés?*
Is English spoken here? (Does anyone here speak English?) — *¿Se habla inglés?*
I don't speak Spanish well. — *No hablo bien el español.*
I don't understand. — *No entiendo.*
How do you say . . . in Spanish? — *¿Cómo se dice . . . en español?*

My name is . . . — *Me llamo . . .*
Would you like . . . — *¿Quisiera usted . . .*
Let's go to . . . — *Vamos a . . .*

TERMS OF ADDRESS

When in doubt, use the formal *usted* (you) as a form of address.

I — *yo*
you (formal) — *usted*
you (familiar) — *tu*
he/him — *él*
she/her — *ella*
we/us — *nosotros*
you (plural) — *ustedes*
they/them — *ellos* (all males or mixed gender); *ellas* (all females)
Mr., sir — *señor*
Mrs., madam — *señora*
miss, young lady — *señorita*
wife — *esposa*
husband — *esposo*
friend — *amigo* (male); *amiga* (female)
sweetheart — *novio* (male); *novia* (female)
son; daughter — *hijo; hija*
brother; sister — *hermano; hermana*
father; mother — *padre; madre*
grandfather; grandmother — *abuelo; abuela*

TRANSPORTATION

Where is . . . ? — *¿Dónde está . . . ?*
How far is it to . . . ? — *¿A cuánto está . . . ?*
from . . . to . . . — *de . . . a . . .*
How many blocks? — *¿Cuántas cuadras?*
Where (Which) is the way to . . . ? — *¿Dónde está el camino a . . . ?*
the bus station — *la terminal de autobuses*
the bus stop — *la parada de autobuses*
Where is this bus going? — *¿Adónde va este autobús?*
the taxi stand — *la parada de taxis*
the train station — *la estación de ferrocarril*
the boat — *el barco*
the launch — *lancha; tiburonera*
the dock — *el muelle*

the airport — *el aeropuerto*
I'd like a ticket to . . . — *Quisiera un boleto a . . .*
first (second) class — *primera (segunda) clase*
roundtrip — *ida y vuelta*
reservation — *reservación*
baggage — *equipaje*
Stop here, please. — *Pare aquí, por favor.*
the entrance — *la entrada*
the exit — *la salida*
the ticket office — *la oficina de boletos*
(very) near; far — *(muy) cerca; lejos*
to; toward — *a*
by; through — *por*
from — *de*
the right — *la derecha*
the left — *la izquierda*
straight ahead — *derecho; directo*
in front — *en frente*
beside — *al lado*
behind — *atrás*
the corner — *la esquina*
the stoplight — *la semáforo*
a turn — *una vuelta*
right here — *aquí*
somewhere around here — *por acá*
right there — *allí*
somewhere around there — *por allá*
road — *el camino*
street; boulevard — *calle; bulevar*
block — @GI>la cuadra@P>
highway — *carretera*
kilometer — *kilómetro*
bridge; toll — *puente; cuota*
address — *dirección*
north; south — *norte; sur*
east; west — *oriente (este); poniente (oeste)*

ACCOMMODATIONS

hotel — *hotel*
Is there a room? — *¿Hay cuarto?*
May I (may we) see it? — *¿Puedo (podemos) verlo?*
What is the rate? — *¿Cuál es el precio?*
Is that your best rate? — *¿Es su mejor precio?*
Is there something cheaper? — *¿Hay algo más económico?*

a single room — *un cuarto sencillo*
a double room — *un cuarto doble*
double bed — *cama matrimonial*
twin beds — *camas gemelas*
with private bath — *con baño*
hot water — *agua caliente*
shower — *ducha*
towels — *toallas*
soap — *jabón*
toilet paper — *papel higiénico*
blanket — *frazada; manta*
sheets — *sábanas*
air-conditioned — *aire acondicionado*
fan — *abanico; ventilador*
key — *llave*
manager — *gerente*

FOOD

I'm hungry — *Tengo hambre.*
I'm thirsty. — *Tengo sed.*
menu — *carta; menú*
order — *orden*
glass — *vaso*
fork — *tenedor*
knife — *cuchillo*
spoon — *cuchara*
napkin — *servilleta*
soft drink — *refresco*
coffee — *café*
tea — *té*
drinking water — *agua pura; agua potable*
bottled carbonated water — *agua mineral*
bottled uncarbonated water — *agua sin gas*
beer — *cerveza*
wine — *vino*
milk — *leche*
juice — *jugo*
cream — *crema*
sugar — *azúcar*
cheese — *queso*
snack — *antojo; botana*
breakfast — *desayuno*
lunch — *almuerzo*
daily lunch special — *comida corrida* (or *el menú del día* depending on region)
dinner — *comida* (often eaten in late afternoon);

cena (a late-night snack)
the check — *la cuenta*
eggs — *huevos*
bread — *pan*
salad — *ensalada*
fruit — *fruta*
mango — *mango*
watermelon — *sandía*
papaya — *papaya*
banana — *plátano*
apple — *manzana*
orange — *naranja*
lime — *limón*
fish — *pescado*
shellfish — *mariscos*
shrimp — *camarones*
meat (without) — *(sin) carne*
chicken — *pollo*
pork — *puerco*
beef; steak — *res; bistec*
bacon; ham — *tocino; jamón*
fried — *frito*
roasted — *asada*
barbecue; barbecued — *barbacoa; al carbón*

SHOPPING

money — *dinero*
money-exchange bureau — *casa de cambio*
I would like to exchange traveler's checks. — *Quisiera cambiar cheques de viajero.*
What is the exchange rate? — *¿Cuál es el tipo de cambio?*
How much is the commission? — *¿Cuánto cuesta la comisión?*
Do you accept credit cards? — *¿Aceptan tarjetas de crédito?*
money order — *giro*
How much does it cost? — *¿Cuánto cuesta?*
What is your final price? — *¿Cuál es su último precio?*
expensive —*caro*
cheap — *barato; económico*
more — *más*
less — *menos*
a little — *un poco*
too much — *demasiado*

HEALTH

Help me please. — *Ayúdeme por favor.*
I am ill. — *Estoy enfermo.*
Call a doctor. — *Llame un doctor.*
Take me to . . . — *Lléveme a . . .*
hospital — *hospital; sanatorio*
drugstore — *farmacia*
pain — *dolor*
fever — *fiebre*
headache — *dolor de cabeza*
stomach ache — *dolor de estómago*
burn — *quemadura*
cramp — *calambre*
nausea — *náusea*
vomiting — *vomitar*
medicine — *medicina*
antibiotic — *antibiótico*
pill; tablet — *pastilla*
aspirin — *aspirina*
ointment; cream — *pomada; crema*
bandage — *venda*
cotton — *algodón*
sanitary napkins — use brand name, e.g., Kotex
birth control pills — *pastillas anticonceptivas*
contraceptive foam — *espuma anticonceptiva*
condoms — *preservativos; condones*
toothbrush — *cepilla dental*
dental floss — *hilo dental*
toothpaste — *crema dental*
dentist — *dentista*
toothache — *dolor de muelas*

POST OFFICE AND COMMUNICATIONS

long-distance telephone — *teléfono larga distancia*
I would like to call . . . — *Quisiera llamar a . . .*
collect — *por cobrar*
station to station — *a quien contesta*
person to person — *persona a persona*
credit card — *tarjeta de crédito*
post office — *correo*
general delivery — *lista de correo*
letter — *carta*

stamp — *estampilla, timbre*
postcard — *tarjeta*
aerogram — *aerograma*
air mail — *correo aereo*
registered — *registrado*
money order — *giro*
package; box — *paquete; caja*
string; tape — *cuerda; cinta*

AT THE BORDER

border — *frontera*
customs — *aduana*
immigration — *migración*
tourist card — *tarjeta de turista*
inspection — *inspección; revisión*
passport — *pasaporte*
profession — *profesión*
marital status — *estado civil*
single — *soltero*
married; divorced — *casado; divorciado*
widowed — *viudado*
insurance — *seguros*
title — *título*
driver's license — *licencia de manejar*

AT THE GAS STATION

gas station — *gasolinera*
gasoline — *gasolina*
unleaded — *sin plomo*
full, please — *lleno, por favor*
tire — *llanta*
tire repair shop — *vulcanizadora*
air — *aire*
water — *agua*
oil (change) — *aceite (cambio)*
grease — *grasa*
My . . . doesn't work. — *Mi . . . no sirve.*
battery — *batería*
radiator — *radiador*
alternator — *alternador*
generator — *generador*
tow truck — *grúa*
repair shop — *taller mecánico*
tune-up — *afinación*
auto parts store — *refaccionería*

VERBS

Verbs are the key to getting along in Spanish. They employ mostly predictable forms and come in three classes, which end in *ar, er,* and *ir,* respectively:

to buy — *comprar*
I buy, you (he, she, it) buys — *compro, compra*
we buy, you (they) buy — *compramos, compran*

to eat — *comer*
I eat, you (he, she, It) eats — *como, come*
we eat, you (they) eat — *comemos, comen*

to climb — *subir*
I climb, you (he, she, it) climbs — *subo, sube*
we climb, you (they) climb — *subimos, suben*

Got the idea? Here are more (with irregularities marked in **bold**).

to do or make — *hacer*
I do or make, you (he she, it) does or makes — ***hago,*** *hace*
we do or make, you (they) do or make — *hacemos, hacen*

to go — *ir*
I go, you (he, she, it) goes — ***voy, va***
we go, you (they) go — ***vamos, van***

to go (walk) — *andar*
to love — *amar*
to work — *trabajar*
to want — *desear, querer*
to need — *necesitar*
to read — *leer*
to write — *escribir*
to repair — *reparar*
to stop — *parar*
to get off (the bus) — *bajar*
to arrive — *llegar*
to stay (remain) — *quedar*
to stay (lodge) — *hospedar*
to leave — *salir* (regular except for ***salgo,*** I leave)
to look at — *mirar*

to look for — *buscar*
to give — *dar* (regular except for *doy,* I give)
to carry — *llevar*
to have — *tener* (irregular but important: ***tengo,*** ***tiene,*** *tenemos,* ***tienen***)
to come — *venir* (similarly irregular: ***vengo,*** ***viene,*** *venimos,* ***vienen***)

Spanish has two forms of "to be." Use *estar* when speaking of location or a temporary state of being: "I am at home." "***Estoy en casa.***" "I'm sick." "***Estoy enfermo.***" Use *ser* for a permanent state of being: "I am a doctor." "***Soy doctora.***"

Estar is regular except for ***estoy,*** I am. *Ser* is very irregular:

to be — *ser*
I am, you (he, she, it) is — ***soy, es***
we are, you (they) are — ***somos, son***

NUMBERS

zero — *cero*
one — *uno*
two — *dos*
three — *tres*
four — *cuatro*
five — *cinco*
six — *seis*
seven — *siete*
eight — *ocho*
nine — *nueve*
10 — *diez*
11 — *once*
12 — *doce*
13 — *trece*
14 — *catorce*
15 — *quince*
16 — *dieciseis*
17 — *diecisiete*
18 — *dieciocho*
19 — *diecinueve*
20 — *veinte*
21 — *veinte y uno* or *veintiuno*
30 — *treinta*
40 — *cuarenta*
50 — *cincuenta*
60 — *sesenta*
70 — *setenta*
80 — *ochenta*
90 — *noventa*
100 — *ciento*
101 — *ciento y uno* or *cientiuno*
200 — *doscientos*
500 — *quinientos*
1,000 — *mil*
10,000 — *diez mil*
100,000 — *cien mil*
1,000,000 — *millón*
one half — *medio*
one third — *un tercio*
one fourth — *un cuarto*

TIME

What time is it? — *¿Qué hora es?*
It's one o'clock. — *Es la una.*
It's three in the afternoon. — *Son las tres de la tarde.*
It's 4 A.M. — *Son las cuatro de la mañana.*
six-thirty — *seis y media*
a quarter till eleven — *un cuarto para las once*
a quarter past five — *las cinco y cuarto*
an hour — *una hora*

DAYS AND MONTHS

Monday — *lunes*
Tuesday — *martes*
Wednesday — *miércoles*
Thursday — *jueves*
Friday — *viernes*
Saturday — *sábado*
Sunday — *domingo*
today — *hoy*
tomorrow — *mañana*
yesterday — *ayer*
January — *enero*
February — *febrero*
March — *marzo*
April — *abril*
May — *mayo*
June — *junio*

July — *julio*
August — *agosto*
September — *septiembre*
October — *octubre*
November — *noviembre*

December — *diciembre*
a week — *una semana*
a month — *un mes*
after — *después*
before — *antes*

Suggested Reading

Some of these books are informative, others are entertaining, and all of them will increase your understanding of both Mexico and Oaxaca. Some are easier to find in Oaxaca than at home, and vice versa. Many of them are out of print, but www.amazon.com or www.barnesandnoble.com or libraries may have used copies. Take some along on your trip. If you find others that are especially noteworthy, let us know. Happy reading.

HISTORY

Blanton, E. Richard, Gary M. Feinman, Stephen A. Kowaleski, and Linda M. Nicholas. *Ancient Oaxaca*. Cambridge, New York and Melbourne: Cambridge University Press, 1999. A scholarly account of pre-Columbian Oaxaca History, for the serious reader.

Calderón de la Barca, Fanny. *Life in Mexico, with New Material from the Author's Journals*. New York: Doubleday, 1966. Edited by H.T. and M.H. Fisher. An update of the brilliant, humorous, and celebrated original 1913 book by the Scottish wife of the Spanish ambassador to Mexico.

Casasola, Gustavo. *Seis Siglos de Historia Gráfica de Mexico (Six Centuries of Mexican Graphic History)*. Mexico City: Editorial Gustavo Casasola, 1978. Six fascinating encyclopedic volumes of Mexican history in pictures, from 1325 to the present.

Chance, John K. *Conquest of the Sierra*. Norman: University of Oklahoma Press, 1990. Professor Chance uses archival sources to trace the evolution of colonial society, principally the northern Sierra Zapotec communities and how they adapted their religion, customs, and settlement patterns in response to the pressures of Spanish rule.

Collis, Maurice. *Cortés and Montezuma*. New York: New Directions Publishing Corp., 1999. A reprint of a 1954 classic piece of well-researched storytelling, Collis traces Cortés's conquest of Mexico through the defeat of his chief opponent, Aztec Emperor Montezuma. He uses contemporary eyewitnesses—notably Bernal Díaz de Castillo—to revivify one of history's greatest dramas.

Cortés, Hernán. *Letters from Mexico*. Translated by Anthony Pagden. New Haven: Yale University Press, 1986. Cortés's five long letters to his king, in which he describes contemporary Mexico in fascinating detail, including, notably, the remarkably sophisticated life of the Aztecs at the time of the conquest.

Díaz del Castillo, Bernal. *The True Story of the Conquest of Mexico*. Translated by Albert Idell. Garden City: Doubleday, 1956. A soldier's still-fresh tale of the conquest from the Spanish viewpoint.

Garfias, Luis. *The Mexican Revolution*. Mexico City: Panorama Editorial, 1985. A concise Mexican version of the 1910–1917 Mexican revolution, the crucible of present-day Mexico.

Gugliotta, Bobette. *Women of Mexico*. Encino, CA: Floricanto Press, 1989. Lively legends, tales, and biographies of remarkable Mexican women, including several from Oaxaca.

León-Portilla, Miguel. *The Broken Spears: The Aztec Account of the Conquest of Mexico*. New York: Beacon Press, 1962. Provides an interesting contrast to Díaz del Castillo's account.

Meyer, Michael, and William Sherman. *The Course of Mexican History*. New York: Oxford University Press, 1991. An insightful, 700-

plus-page college textbook in paperback. A bargain, especially if you can get it used.

Novas, Himlice. *Everything You Need to Know About Latino History.* New York: Plume Books (Penguin Group), 1994. Chicanos, Latin rhythm, La Raza, the Treaty of Guadalupe Hidalgo, and much more, interpreted from an authoritative Latino point of view.

Ridley, Jasper. *Maximilian and Juárez.* New York: Ticknor and Fields, 1999. This expert historical biography breathes new life into one of Mexico's great ironic tragedies, a drama that pitted the native Zapotec "Lincoln of Mexico" against the dreamy, idealistic Archduke Maximilian of Austria-Hungary. Despite their common liberal ideas, they were drawn into a bloody no-quarter struggle that set the Old World against the New, ended in Maximilian's execution, the insanity of his wife, and the emergence of the United States as a power to be reckoned with in world affairs. The defeat of France and Maximilian in Mexico was aided by U.S. support of the Juárez government. The Monroe Doctrine became a reality; and never again would a European power invade Mexico or any other country in the Americas.

Ruíz, Ramon Eduardo. *Triumphs and Tragedy: A History of the Mexican People.* New York: W.W. Norton, Inc., 1992. A pithy, anecdote-filled history of Mexico from an authoritative Mexican-American perspective.

Simpson, Lesley Bird. *Many Mexicos.* Berkeley: The University of California Press, 1962. A much-reprinted, fascinating broad-brush version of Mexican history.

ARCHAEOLOGY

Flannery, Kent, and Joyce Marcus. *The Cloud People.* New York: Academic Press, 1983. Eminently authoritative authors trace the divergent evolution of the Zapotec and Mixtec peoples as revealed by the archaeological record.

Marcus, Joyce, and Kent Flannery, contributor. *Zapotec Civilization.* London and New York: Thames and Hudson, 1996. The distinguished authors trace the evolution of Valley of Oaxaca civilization, from 10,000 B.C. to the Conquest, using the results from recent finds to shed light on the roots of Oaxaca's dominant linguistic group. The expertly documented text is elegantly illustrated with hundreds of maps, drawings, and photos, including many aerial views of Oaxaca archaeological sites.

Paddock, John, ed. *Ancient Oaxaca.* Palo Alto, CA: Stanford University Press, 1966. An eminent Oaxaca archaeologist edits this richly illustrated compendium of articles by major discoverers of Zapotec, Mixtec, and other antiquities.

Winter, Marcus. *Oaxaca, the Archaeological Record.* Mexico, D.F.: Minutiae Mexicana, 1992. A distinguished Oaxaca resident investigator skillfully traces a concise history of Oaxaca's pre-conquest inhabitants, based on finds at Monte Albán, Mitla, and dozens of other Oaxaca Valley and mountain sites.

UNIQUE GUIDE AND TIP BOOKS

American Automobile Association. *Mexico Travelbook.* Heathrow, FL: American Automobile Association. Short and sweet summaries of major Mexican tourist destinations and sights. Also includes information on fiestas, accommodations, restaurants, and a wealth of information relevant to car travel in Mexico. Available in bookstores, or free to AAA members at affiliate offices.

Forgey, Dr. William. *Traveler's Medical Alert Series: Mexico, A Guide to Health and Safety.* Merrillville, IN: ICS Books, 1991. Useful information on health and safety in Mexico.

Franz, Carl. *The People's Guide to Mexico.* Santa Fe, NM: Avalon Travel Publications, 12th edition, 2002. An entertaining and insightful A-to-Z general guide to the joys and pitfalls of independent economy travel in Mexico.

Freedman, Jacqueline, and Susan Gerstein. *Traveling Like Everybody Else*. Brooklyn, NY: Lambda Publishing, Inc. Your disability needn't keep you at home. This book is out of print, but www.amazon.com or www.barnesandnoble.com or libraries may have copies.

Jeffrey, Nan. *Adventuring With Children*. Avalon House Travel Series, 1995. This unusually detailed book starts where most travel-with-children books end. It contains, besides a wealth of information and practical strategies for general travel with children, specific chapters on how you can adventure—trek, kayak, river-raft, camp, bicycle, and much more—successfully with the kids in tow.

Mader, Ron. *Adventures in Nature Mexico*. Emeryville, CA: Avalon Travel Publishing, 1998. An internationally acknowledged expert on ecotravel in Latin America details dozens of environmentally sensitive adventure tours in Mexico and Oaxaca. Destinations range widely, from scuba diving off Cozumel and exploring lost Mayan cities to jeeping through the Copper Canyon to rescuing turtle eggs on Oaxaca beaches.

Martinez, Felipe, et al. *The State of Oaxaca*. Oaxaca: Government of the State of Oaxaca, 1996. Although its English translation is rough, the text of this show-and-tell book of Oaxaca provides the reader with interesting details to accompany its many beautiful color photos. Available at craft shops and the federal/state tourist information office on the plaza in downtown Oaxaca.

Simmonds, David, ed. *The Mexico File*. La Jolla, CA: Simmonds Publications (5580 La Jolla Blvd., #306, La Jolla, CA 92037). A monthly newsletter that, besides featuring pithy stories by Mexico travelers and news updates,

offers an opportunity-packed classified section of Mexico vacation rentals, publications, services, and much more. Subscribe ($39/year) by writing or dialing tel./fax 858/456-4419, tel. 800/563-9345 (voice mail), or logging on to www.mexicofile.com.

Stillman, Alan Eric. *Kwikpoint*. Alexandria, VA: GAIA Communications (P.O. Box 238, Alexandria, VA 22313-0238, www.kwikpoint.com). Kwikpoint is a super-handy, durable color foldout of pictures to point to when you need something in any foreign country. The pictures, such as a frying pan with fire under it (for "fried"), a compass (for "Which direction?"), a red lobster, and a cauliflower, are imaginative and unmistakable, anywhere, and especially in Oaxaca.

Schroeder, Dirk G., ScD, MPH. *Staying Healthy in Asia, Africa, and Latin America*. Emeryville, CA: Avalon Travel Publishing, 2000. This Volunteers in Asia book is full of tips for anyone going to the developing world, with an overview of the most common health problems and advice on how to avoid them or treat them if you do fall ill.

Weisbroth, Ericka, and Eric Ellman. *Bicycling Mexico*. New York: Hunter, 1990. These intrepid adventurers describe bike trips from Puerto Vallarta to Acapulco, coastal and highland Oaxaca, and highland Jalisco and Michoacán.

Werner, David. *Where There Is No Doctor*. Berkeley, CA: Hesperian Foundation (1919 Addison St., Berkeley, CA 94704, tel. 888/729-1796, www.hesperian.org), 1992. How to keep well in the tropical backcountry.

FICTION

Bowen, David, ed. *Pyramids of Glass*. San Antonio: Corona Publishing Co., 1994. Two dozen-odd stories that lead the reader along a month-long journey through the bedrooms, the barracks, the cafés and streets of present-day Mexico.

Doerr, Harriet. *Consider This, Señor.* New York: Harcourt Brace, 1993. Four expatriates tough it out in a Mexican small town, adapting to the excesses—blazing sun, driving rain, vast, untrammeled landscapes—meanwhile interacting with the local folks while the local folks observe them, with a mixture of fascination and tolerance.

Fuentes, Carlos. *Where the Air Is Clear.* New York: Farrar, Straus, and Giroux, 1971. The seminal work of Mexico's celebrated novelist.

Fuentes, Carlos. *The Years with Laura Díaz.* New York: Farrar, Straus, and Giroux, 2000. A panorama of Mexico from Independence to the 21st century through the eyes of one woman, Laura Díaz, and her great-grandson, the author. One reviewer said that she, "as a Mexican woman, would like to celebrate Carlos Fuentes; it is worthy of applause that a man who has seen, observed, analyzed and criticized the great occurrences of the century now has a woman, Laura Díaz, speak for him." Translated by Alfred MacAdam.

Jennings, Gary. *Aztec.* New York: Atheneum, 1980. Beautifully researched and written monumental tale of lust, compassion, love, and death in pre-conquest Mexico.

Peters, Daniel. *The Luck of Huemac.* New York: Random House, 1981. An Aztec noble family's tale of war, famine, sorcery, heroism, treachery, love, and, finally, disaster and death in the Valley of Mexico.

Porter, Katherine Ann. *The Collected Stories.* New York: Delacorte, 1970. A classic that perennially occupies many lists of the best fiction in English about Mexico.

Rulfo, Juan. *The Burning Plain.* Austin: University of Texas Press, 1967. Stories of people torn between the old and new in Mexico.

Rulfo, Juan. *Pedro Paramo.* Evanston, IL: Northwestern University Press, 1994. Rulfo's acknowledged masterpiece, first published in 1955, established his renown. The author, thinly disguised as the protagonist, Juan Preciado, fulfills his mother's dying request by returning to his shadowy Jalisco hometown, Comala, in search of this father. Although Preciado discovers that his father, Pedro Páramo (whose surname implies "wasteland"), is long dead, Preciado's search resurrects his father's restless spirit, which recounts its horrific life tale of massacre, rape, and incest.

Traven, B. *The Treasure of the Sierra Madre.* New York: Hill and Wang, 1967. Campesinos, *federales, gringos,* and *Indigenas* all figure in this modern morality tale set in Mexico's rugged outback. The most famous of the mysterious author's many novels of oppression and justice set in Mexico's jungles.

Villaseñor, Victor. *Rain of Gold.* New York: Delta Books (Bantam, Doubleday, and Dell), 1991. The moving, best-selling epic of the gritty travails of the author's family. From humble rural beginnings in the Copper Canyon, they flee revolution and certain death, struggling through parched northern deserts to sprawling border refugee camps. From there they migrate to relative safety and an eventual modicum of happiness in Southern California.

ARTS, CRAFTS, AND ARCHITECTURE

Baird, Joseph. *The Churches of Mexico, 1530–1810.* Berkeley: University of California Press, 1962. Mexican colonial architecture and art, illustrated and interpreted, with many monumental examples from Oaxaca.

Barbash, Shepard, and Vicki Ragan. *Oaxaca Wood Carving.* San Francisco: Chronicle Books, 1993. Ragan's luscious color images and Barbash's interesting, authoritative text highlight the best of Oaxacan wooden *alebrijes*, masks, dolls, toys, and much more.

Fishgrund, Andrea Stanton. *Zapotec Weavers of Teotitlán*. Santa Fe: University of New Mexico Press, 1999. Authoritative, richly color-illustrated description of the history, economics, and techniques, both traditional and contemporary, of the textile weavers of Teotitlán del Valle, in the Valley of Oaxaca.

Martínez Penaloza, Porfirio. *Popular Arts of Mexico*. Mexico City: Editorial Panorama, 1981. An excellent pocket-sized exposition of Mexican art.

Morrill, Penny C. and Berk, Carol A. *Mexican Silver*. Atglen, PA: Shiffer Publishing Co. (4880 Lower Valley Road, Atglen, PA 19310), 2001. Lovingly written and photographed exposition of the Mexican silvercraft of Taxco, Guerrero that was revitalized through the initiative of Frederick Davis and William Spratling in the 1920s and 1930s. Color photos of many beautiful, museum-quality pieces supplement the text, which describes the history and work of a score of silversmithing families who developed the Taxco craft under Spratling's leadership. Greatly adds to the traveler's appreciation of the beautiful Taxco silvercrafts widely available in Taxco, Acapulco, and Ixtapa-Zihuatanejo.

Muller, Robert J. *The Architecture and Sculpture of Oaxaca, 1530s to 1980s*. Tempe: Arizona State University, 1995. An informative stone-by-stone guide to Oaxacan monumental buildings, mostly churches. The author's solid commentary vivifies visits to every church of note in Oaxaca state and transforms what might be humdrum sightseeing for the reader-traveler to recognition, understanding, and appreciation.

Sandoval, Judith Hancock. *Shopping in Oaxaca*. Oaxaca: Government of Oaxaca, 1998. The serious shopper's and wholesaler's guide to

Oaxacan crafts, even including some food. The author illustrates a plethora of examples in black and white and authoritatively lists nearly every source of Oaxacan folk craft, from individual artisans to nearly every established crafts shop in the entire state. Has been available at crafts stores and the federal-state tourist information office on the plaza in Oaxaca city.

Sayer, Chloë. *Arts and Crafts of Mexico*. San Francisco: Chronicle Books, 1990. All you ever wanted to know about your favorite Mexican crafts, from papier-mâché to pottery and toys and Taxco silver. Beautifully illustrated by traditional etchings and David Lavender's crisp black-and-white and color photographs.

PEOPLE AND CULTURE

Augur, Helen. *Zapotec*. New York: Doubleday and Co., 1954. One woman's view of Oaxaca's history and culture: a tapestry of Oaxacan tradition from the Mixteca to the Isthmus and ancient Monte Albán to present-day Oaxaca city.

Castillo, Ana, ed. *Goddess of the Americas*. New York: Riverhead Books, 1996. Here a noted author has selected from the works of seven interpreters of Mesoamerican female deities to provide readers with visions of goddesses that range as far and wide as Sex Goddess, the Broken-Hearted, the Subversive, and the Warrior Queen.

Chinas, Beverly Newbold. *Isthmus Zapotecs: A Matrifocal Culture of Mexico*. New York: Harcourt-Brace-Jovanovich, 1997. How a female-dominant culture functions in Oaxaca.

Cohen, Jeffrey. *Cooperation and Community: Economy and Society in Oaxaca*. Austin: University of Texas Press, 1999. A pithy, authoritative account of the history, economy, politics, and folkways of the Santañeros—the people of the weaving village of Santa Ana del Valle, in the Valley of Oaxaca. Here, time-honored customs—*compadrazgo, guelaguetza, promesas*—fuse with latter-day realities to produce a culture simultaneously modern and traditional.

Cordrey, Donald, and Dorothy Cordrey. *Mexican Indian Costumes.* Austin: University of Texas Press, 1968. A lovingly photographed, written, and illustrated classic on Mexican native peoples, including many Oaxacan groups.

Covarrubias, Miguel. *Indian Art of Mexico and Central America.* New York: Knopf, 1957. A classic work by the renowned interpreter of *indígena* art and design.

Edinger, Steven T. *The Road from Mixtepec.* Fresno, CA: Asociación Cívica Benito Juárez (P.O. Box 12320, Fresno, CA 93706), 1996. A compassionately researched and photographed account of the people of San Juan Mixtepec, in the Mixtec Alta region of Oaxaca. The author, through his solid anecdotal narrative, relates the story of how a people whose means of existence have been gradually degraded for the past four hundred years maintain their lives, spirit, and traditions only by repeated emigration to work as marginal farm laborers in northern Mexico and the United States.

Greenberg, James. *Blood Ties: Life and Violence in Rural Mexico.* Tucson: University of Arizona Press, 1993. The author reveals, with a wealth of personal anecdotes, the cultural underpinnings beneath decades of deadly feuding between two leading Chatino towns in Oaxaca's southern Sierra.

Haden, Judith Cooper, and Jaffe, Matthew. *Oaxaca, the Spirit of Mexico.* New York: Artisan, division of Workman Publishing, Inc., 2002. Simply the lovliest, most sensitively photographed and crafted coffee-table book of Mexico photography yet produced. Photos by Haden, text by Jaffe.

Leslie, Charles M. *Now We Are Civilized.* Detroit: Wayne State University Press, 1960. A now-classic anecdotal study of the worldview and ways of the Zapotec people of Mitla, Oaxaca.

Martinez, Zarela. *The Food and Life of Oaxaca.* New York: Macmillan, 1997. Martinez, a New York restaurateur, leads her readers on an intriguing tour of Oaxacan folkways by way of the palate. Features chapters on Oaxaca's seven *moles,* 150 recipes, and two dozen photos of finished gastronomical creations.

Medina, Sylvia López. *Cantora.* New York: Ballantine Books, 1992. Fascinated by the stories of her grandmother, aunt, and mother, the author seeks her own center by discovering a past that she thought she wanted to forget.

Nader, Laura. *Harmony, Ideology, Justice, and Control in a Zapotec Mountain Village.* Palo Alto, CA: Stanford University Press, 1990. How some northern Sierra Zapotecs solve disputes, using religion based ideas of harmony to achieve social control.

Palmer, Colin A. *Slaves of the White God: Blacks in Mexico.* Cambridge, MA: Harvard University Press, 1976. A scholarly study of why and how Spanish authorities imported African slaves into the Americas and how they were used afterward. Replete with poignant details taken from Spanish and Mexican archives describing how the Africans struggled from bondage to eventual freedom.

Romney, Kimball, and Romaine Romney. *The Mixtecs of Juxtlahuaca.* Huntington, NY: Robert E. Krieger Publishing Co., 1966. Authors study the contemporary Mixtec culture of the western Mixteca. Pithy examples, especially of the organization of fiestas, still ring true despite the generation elapsed since the research was done.

Stephen, Lynn. *Zapotec Women.* Austin: University of Texas Press, 1992. Study of how women run much of the local economy and a significant fraction of the politics in the Oaxaca Isthmus districts of Tehuantepec and Juchitán.

Toor, Frances. *A Treasury of Mexican Folkways.* New York: Bonanza Books, 1947, reprinted 1985. An illustrated encyclopedia of vanishing Mexicana—costumes, religion, fiestas, burial practices, customs, legends—compiled during the celebrated author's 35 years' residence in Mexico in the early 20th century.

Trilling, Susana. *Seasons of My Heart.* New York: Ballantine Publishing Group, 1999. The celebrated Oaxaca author, chef, and cooking teacher leads her readers on a culinary journey of the seven regions of Oaxaca. Along the way, they stop by market towns, mountain hamlets, shoreline villages, and lush highland valleys, visiting the friends with whom she refined the dozens of recipes that introduce the best of Oaxacan cooking. *Seasons of My Heart* is the companion volume to Trilling's National Public Television series on Oaxacan cooking.

Wauchope, Robert, ed. *Handbook of Middle American Indians.* Vols. 7 and 8. Austin: University of Texas Press, 1969. Authoritative but aging surveys of important native-speaking groups in northern, central (vol. 8), and southern (vol. 7) Mexico.

GOVERNMENT, POLITICS, AND ECONOMY

Campbell, Howard. *Zapotec Renaissance: Ethnic Politics and Cultural Revival in Southern Mexico.* Albuquerque: University of New Mexico Press, 1994. A history of how the Zapotecs around Juchitán, Oaxaca, fought city hall and won.

Murphy, Arthur D., and Alex Stepick. *Social Inequality in Oaxaca.* A sociopolitical history of grassroots underclass activism in Oaxaca city during the 1960s, 1970s and 1980s.

Poleman, Thomas T. *Agricultural Development in the Mexican Tropics.* Palo Alto, CA: Stanford University Press, 1964. The successes, failures, and consequences of Mexico's great dam project in Oaxaca's Papaloapan basin.

Rubin, Jeffry W. *Decentering the Regime.* Winston-Salem, NC: Duke University Press, 1997. Ethnicity, radicalism, and democracy in Juchitán, Oaxaca.

FLORA AND FAUNA

Goodson, Gar. *Fishes of the Pacific Coast.* Stanford, CA: Stanford University Press, 1988. More than 500 beautifully detailed color drawings highlight this pocket version of all you ever wanted to know about the ocean's fishes (including common Spanish names) from Alaska to Peru.

Howell, Steve N.G., and Sophie Webb. *A Guide to the Birds of Mexico and Northern America.* Oxford: Oxford University Press, 1995. All the serious birder needs to know about Mexico's rich species treasury. Includes authoritative habitat maps and 70 excellent color plates that detail the males and females of around 1500 species. (For a more portable version of the above, check out Steve Howell's *Bird-Finding Guide to Mexico,* 1999.)

Leopold, A. Starker. *Wildlife of Mexico: The Game Birds and Mammals.* Berkeley: University of California Press, 1959. Classic, illustrated layperson's survey of common Mexican mammals and birds. Out of print.

Mason Jr., Charles T., and Patricia B. Mason. *Handbook of Mexican Roadside Flora.* Tucson: University of Arizona Press, 1987. Authoritative identification guide, with line illustrations, of all the plants you're likely to see in the Oaxaca region.

Morris, Percy A. *A Field Guide to Pacific Coast Shells.* Boston: Houghton Mifflin, 1974. The complete beachcomber's Pacific shell guide.

Pesman, M. Walter. *Meet Flora Mexicana.* Globe, AZ: D.S. King, 1962. Delightful anecdotes and illustrations of hundreds of common Mexican plants. Out of print.

Peterson, Roger Tory, and Edward L. Chalif. *Field Guide to Mexican Birds.* Boston: Houghton Mifflin, 1999. With hundreds of Peterson's crisp color drawings, this is a must for serious birders and vacationers interested in the life that teems the beaches, forests, and lagoons of Oaxaca.

Wright, N. Pelham. *A Guide to Mexican Mammals and Reptiles.* Mexico City: Minutiae Mexicana, 1989. Pocket-edition lore, history, descriptions, and pictures of commonly seen Mexican animals.

Suggested Reading

Internet Resources

A number of websites may be helpful in preparing for your Oaxaca trip:

MEXICO IN GENERAL

www.visitmexico.com
The official website of the public-private Mexico Tourism Board; a good general site for official information, such as entry requirements. It has lots of summarily informative subheadings, not unlike an abbreviated guidebook. If you can't find what you want here, call the toll-free information number tel. 800/44-MEXICO (800/446-3942), or email contact@visitmexico.com.

www.mexonline.com
Very extensive, well-organized site with many subheadings and links to Mexico's large and medium destinations, and even some small destinations. For example, Oaxaca city is typical, with about 150 connections, including about 50 hotels and bed-and-breakfast rentals. It also has the same in separate but smaller Huatulco and Puerto Escondido directories. Excellent.

www.mexconnect.com
A very good work in progress; with dozens upon dozens of subheadings and links, especially helpful for folks thinking of working, living, or retiring in Mexico.

www.go2mexico.com
An aspiring commercial site that covers the Mexican Pacific destinations of Mazatlán, Puerto Vallarta, Ixtapa-Zihuatnejo, Acapulco, Huatulco, Oaxaca, Guadalajara, and Manzanillo (including current weather reports). However, several of these destinations are incomplete at this writing. A work in progress, potentially good if completed.

www.mexicodesconocido.com.mx
The site of the excellent magazine Mexico Desconocido ("Undiscovered Mexico") that mostly features stories about unusual and off-the-beaten-track destinations, many in Oaxaca. Accesses a large library of past articles that are not unlike a Mexican version of National Geographic Traveler. Click the small "English" button at the top to translate. Excellent, hard-to-find information.

www.state.gov/travel
The U.S. State Department's information website. Lots of subheadings and links to a swarm of topics, including Mexican consular offices in the United States, U.S. consular offices in Mexico, travel advisories, and links to other government departments, such as importation of food, plants, and animals, U.S. customs information, health abroad, airline information, and exchange rates. Very good.

www.planeta.com
A grand, beautifully designed Latin-American ecotourism website and bliss of Oaxaca-based Ron Mader. Contains a huge library of information and links, mostly about Mexico, with lots of Oaxaca. Includes everything that's green—destinations, events, tour companies, conferences, organizations, book lists—and much more.

DESTINATIONS
Oaxaca in General
www.oaxaca.gob.mx/sedetur
Website of the Oaxaca Secretary of Tourism. Good Tourist Guide section with archaeological sites, recipes, churches, museums, festivals, myths and legends, recipes, murals, handicrafts, and more. Hint: To arrive at this

site, you may first have to log on to www.oax-
aca.gob.mx, then click on the "turismo" button on the left.

Oaxaca City
www.oaxaca.com
Commercial community guide to Oaxaca city
with loads of noncommercial information. It
has links to a long list of Mexico websites and
much more. The Oaxaca "Tourist Guide" link
(www.oaxaca-travel.com) would be useful to
someone planning a Oaxaca trip, if and when
it gets finished. Good.

www.oaxacainfo.com
Joint website of the Oaxaca Hotel Association and U.S.-based Zapotec Tours and Oaxaca-based Oaxaca Tours. Includes much travel
information, with (mostly up-market) hotels
and restaurants in Oaxaca city and lots of
background information on festivals, museums, maps, and much more. It has separate,
but much smaller Huatulco and Puerto Escondido sections. Good.

www.oaxacatimes.com
The website of the *Oaxaca Times* newspaper.
Its handy classified section lists restaurants,
galleries, handicrafts shops and much more,
including a very useful list of Oaxaca city
apartment, homestay, and bed-and-breakfast
rentals.

www.oaxacanstuff.com
The interesting website of master artist Douglas French, who weaves for-sale textiles, sells
art prints and mescal, and runs a trailer park,
all from the website.

The Oaxaca Coast
www.baysofhuatulco.com.mx
Restaurants, hotels, general information,
events, tour operators, water sports, land
sports. A work in progress with lots of hotels
with prices. The hotel association sub-site is
functioning well. Only in Spanish at this writing, however. Good.

www.tomzap.com
This project of Mexico lover Tom Penick is a
very informative site, especially for downscale
corners on the coasts of Jalisco, Colima, and
Oaxaca. It's especially detailed about Puerto
Escondido, Puerto Ángel, Zipolite, Mazunte,
and the Bahías de Huatulco. Information includes hotels, travel, history, surfing, scuba
and snorkeling, and more, with much helpful
advice on what to enjoy and what to avoid.
Very good.

www.puertoconnection.+com
Website for Puerto Escondido Real Estate;
besides home sales, it lists and photo-illus-
trates many moderately priced vacation
rental villas, condos, and apartments and
offers trip-planning services. Very Good.
(Note: you must attach a ".+com" as above
instead of a ".com" or you will get Puerto
Rico websites.)

www.zicatelaproperties.com
Site of Puerto Escondido's Zicatela Properties real estate company. It's especially good for
moderately priced apartment, condo, and vacation home rentals. It also lists a number of
services to help newcomers settle into Puerto
Escondido. Excellent.

Index

A

accented syllables: 447
accommodations: 90–95, 449
activism, political: 37–38
adventure tours: 252
African tulips: 10
agaves: 11
agriculture: beginnings 18; in Oaxacan economy 44; slash-and-burn 66; Suchilquitongo 215
Aguas Termales Atotonilco: 279
air travel: 102–103, 104–105, 115
alcoholic beverages: 97
alebrijes: 87
Ampaad: 67
amphibians: 16–18
Amusgo country: 297–298
Amusgos: 70–71, 297–298
Andador de Macedonio Alcalá: 145
animals, carved wooden: 87
animal sanctuaries: 280
apartments: 91
aqueduct, Oaxaca city: 147
architectural highlights: Capilla Abierta 313; church-building 200–201, 342; Templo de la Asunción 344; Yanhuitlán Dominican church 316; Zapotec 208; *see also specific place*

armadillos: 13
Arrazola: 207
arts and crafts: 84–90
ATMs: 123
Atotonilco Hot Springs: 279
ATVs: 77
Atzompa: 212–213
Aztec invasion: 21–22, 398

B

backcountry camping: 95
Bahía Cacaluta: 243
Bahía Chachacual: 244
Bahía Chahue: 241
Bahía Conejos: 241
Bahía de la Ventosa: 434–435
Bahía El Maguey: 243
Bahía El Organo: 243
Bahía San Agustín: 244
Bahías de Huatulco: accommodations 244–250; entertainment 251; food 250–251; history 238; recreation 251–253; shopping 253–254; tours 240; transportation 255–257
Bahía Tangolunda: 241
Balneario Atonalzin: 309
Balneario El Zuzul: 370

Archaeological Sites

Achiutla: 349, 350
Casa de la Cacica: 314
Cerro de la Campana: 216
Cerro de las Minas: 327–328
Cerro La Iglesia: 282
Dainzu: 185
Ejutla: 203
El Castillo de Moctezuma: 376
El Fortín: 313–314
Guiengola: 409–410
hieroglyphics: 320–321
history: 18–19
Lambityeco: 185–186
Mitla: 192–196
Monte Albán: 20, 208–212
Monte Negro: 305–306

Pueblo Viejo: 313–314
Puente Colosal: 324
San José El Mogote: 19, 213–214
San Martín Huamelulpan: 352
San Miguel Progreso: 354
Santo Domingo Tonalá: 336
Teotitlán del Valle: 188
Tilantongo: 305–306
Tres Picos: 411
Tututepec: 291
Xatachio: 310
Yagul: 191–192
Yucuita: 304–305
Yucunama: 315
Zaachila: 206

Balneario Monte Flor: 369
Balnearios Mingo: 372
banks: 123
baptism, Christian: 55–56
bargain shopping: 99
barro negro (black pottery): 197–198
basketry: 84–85, 216
bats: 13
Bay of Puerto Ángel: 278
beach buggies: 77
beachcombing: 74
bed-and-breakfasts: 91
Bee Nu'u: 315
Benito Juárez (town): 358–361
Benito Juárez dam and reservoir: 410
beverages: 97–99
billfish: 18
birds: 14–16
bird-watching: Chacalapa 237; Lagunas de Chacahua National Park 288; Playa La Ventanilla 225–226; Río Copalita wildlife sanctuary 243, 252; San Sebastián de las Grutas 205
birth rituals, traditional: 65, 70
boat tours: Bahías de Huatulco 240; Puerto Escondido 265
bodysurfing: 262
border crossing: 122–123, 451
Border Industrialization Program: 44
bread: 257
bribes: 113
bridge, colonial-era stone: 320
bromeliads: 12
bullfighting: 80
bus travel: 103, 115–117

C
cabanas: 92
Cacahuatepec: 297
cacti: 5, 11
calendar, Mesoamerican: 54–55
Calles, Plutarco Elías: 35
Calm Sea: 427
Calpulapan: 366–367
Camacho, Manuel Avila: 36
Campamento del Monte: 362
camping: accommodations 94, 440–443; gear 134
Cañada canyonland: 393–396
Capilla Abierta: 313
Cárdenas, Lázaro: 36

Beaches
general discussion: 74–75
Mazunte Beach: 224, 278
Playa Bachoco: 264
Playa Brasil: 260
Playa Carrizalillo: 264
Playa Cerro Hermosa: 288
Playa Chacahua: 289
Playa Copalito: 424
Playa Corralero: 298
Playa del Amor: 221
Playa Entrega: 243
Playa Estacahuite: 221
Playa La Ventanilla: 225–226
Playa La Ventosa: 434–436
Playa Manzanillo: 264
Playa Marinero: 262–263
Playa Mazunte: 222
Playa Panteón: 221
Playa Principal: 221, 260–261
Playa San Agustinillo: 222
Playa Santa Cruz: 243
Playa Zicatela: 263–264
Playa Zipolite: 221, 278

car insurance: 108
Carnaval: 297, 340
car permits: 121
car travel: 107–113, 117–119, 132
Casa de Cultura Rudolfa Morales: 202
Casa de la Cacica: 314
Casa de la Cultura: 414
Casa María Sabina: 389
Casas, Bartolomé de las: 25
Cascada Esmeralda: 347, 348–349
Catedral de Oaxaca: 143–144
Cavendish, Thomas: 238
Cave of Serpent: 306
caves: 75; Arco de Yagela 366; Cave of Serpent 306; Cuevas del Coyote 358; La Cueva 404; Las Campanas 328; Nindo-Da-Gé 392; San Miguel de la Cueva 339; San Sebastián de las Grutas 205; Santo Domingo Petapa 422–423; Sotano de San Agustín 392–393
Centro Cultural de Santo Domingo: 145
ceramics: 89
ceriman: 9
Cerro de Atole: 282

Cerro de la Campana: 216
Cerro de las Minas: 20, 327–328
Cerro La Iglesia: 282
Cerro Quiexobra: 3
Cerro Rabón: 11, 384
ceviche: 97
Chacalapa: 237
Chagas' disease: 129
Chalcatongo: 348
Charquito Atotonilco warm springs: 291
Chatino country: 281–287
Chatinos: 70
chicle: 10
children, traveling with: 121, 126
Chiltepec: 372
Chinantecs: 68–69
Chochos: 71, 317, 322
chocolate trees: 10
Chontal country: 259–260
Chontals: 72–73
Christian church, historical role of: 26
churches: 200–201; see also specific place
climate: 4
clothing, traditional: 85–86
cloud forests: 11–12, 366, 385–386
coatimundis: 13
COCEI (Coalición Obrero, Campesino, y Estu-
    diantil del Istmo): 38, 63
COCEO (Coalición de Obreros, Campesinos, y
    Estudiantes de Oaxaca): 38
cochineal: 27
Cochineal Farm: 198
Codex Nuttall: 315
codices, hieroglyphic: 20–21
coffee: farms 257, 281; Finca Costoche 282;
    identifying plants 9–10; La Gloria Coffee
    Farm 258–259; Mixtec industry 66
cohetes (fireworks): 332
Coixtlahuaca: 317–319
Colosio, Luis Donalo: 40
Column of Life: 195
communications: 124–126
community museums: 182
coniferous forests: 11–12
conservation projects: 280, 363
Cortés, Hernán: conquests of 22–23, 136; ex-
    plores Gulf/Pacific passage 428; Marquis of
    the Valley of Oaxaca 24
Cosijoeza, King: 212, 420
Cosijopí, King: 398

Costa Chica: 287
crafts: 84–90, 197, 198
credit cards: 124
crime: 264
criollos: 54
crocodiles: 17, 280, 288
Crucecita: 240–241, 242
Cruz, Father Domingo de la: 316
Cuajimoloyas: 358–361
Cuicatecs: 71–72
Cuicatlán: 395–396
Cuilapan de Guerrero: 207
cuisine: 95–99, 160
customs, social: 55–59, 130–133

D
Dainzu: 20, 185
dams: 36, 362, 381
dance: 87
death, customs: 56
deciduous forests, tropical: 7
dengue fever: 129
dialects: 62
diarrhea: 128
Díaz, Porfirio: 31, 32–34, 137, 373, 405
disabilities, travelers with: 126
disease, European-introduced: 26
dishes, typical Oaxacan: 160
Dominican missionaries: 309
Donaji, Princess: 212
dress: codes 58; huipiles 68, 71; packing
    133–134; traditional 85–86
drink: 97–99
driving hazards: 132
drug-growing regions: 109
duendes (spirits): 352

E
economy: 44–48; colonial 26–28; recent recov-
    ery 41; Tlaxiaco 342
ecotourism: 132
ecotours: Bahías de Huatulco 252–253; Ixtlán de
    Juárez 365; Laguna Manialtepec 279, 280;
    northern Sierra 361
eels: 16
8-Deer: 20–21, 305–306
Ejutla: 203–204
El Castillo de Moctezuma: 376
electricity: 126
El Fortín: 313–314

El Mogote: 213–214
El Tigre: 14
El Tule tree: 184
encomienda: 25
environmental issues: Bahías de Huatulco 238; desertification 319; Puerto Ángel ecological project 235
ethnicity: Costa Chica 287; criollos 28; historical mixings 28; modern groups 54–55
Etla: 214–215
evacuation, medical: 130
evergreen forests: 9–10
exchange rates: 123
Exconvento de Santa Catalina: 145
Exconvento de Santiago: 207

F
fan palms: 5
farms: coffee 257, 281; demonstration cochineal 27, 198
Faro del Marina: 430
ferns: 12
festivals: 80–83; Carnaval 297; Easter 340; Festival of San José 214; Fiesta del Apóstol de San Pablo 195; Fiesta del Dulce Nombre de Jesús 204; Guelaguetza folk dance festival 63, 164; Huaxpaltepec 293; Jamiltepec 291; Lunes del Cerro 164; Mixteca 340; Oaxaca city 164–165; Pinotepa Nacional 294; Santa María Huazolotitlán 293; Santiago Chazumba 333; Tlacolula 191; *velas* (fiestas) 416–417; Vela Tehuantepec 398; Virgin of Carmen 164; Virgin of Juquila 281; *see also specific place*
fireworks: 332
first aid: 75, 128
fish: 18, 79
fishing: 77–80; Bahías de Huatulco 243, 253; Benito Juárez reservoir 410; freshwater 80; Laguna Superior 424; licenses 80; Mar Muerto 427; Miguel Alemán Reservoir 381; Playa San Agustinillo 224; Puerto Escondido 272; Santa María del Mar 437; species descriptions 79; surf fishing 298; Yosocuta Reservoir 334–335
flora: 5–12
food: 95–99, 160, 449
forests: 5, 7–12
Fox, Vicente: 42–43
frangipanis: 7

frigate birds: 15
Frissell Museum: 195
fruit: 98

G
gardens: 323
gasoline: 109
gear: 133–134
geckos: 16
geography: 2–4, 5, 6
Gila monsters: 16
glass manufacture: 86
gods, traditional: 64
golf: 77
Gortari, Salinas de: 39
gourd trees: 7
government: 48–52; Palacio de Gobierno 139; reforms under Vicente Fox 43; regional districts, mapped 49
gratuities: 124
Green Angels: 109
greeting, phrases for: 448
Guelaguetza folk dance festival: 63, 164
Guelatao: 367
Guerrero, Vicente: 29
guesthouses: 91
guides: 119
Guiengola: 20, 409–410

H
hanging bridge: 371, 376
hazards: 75, 110
healers *(curanderos):* 68
health: 127–133, 450
heliconias: 10
herons: 15
Hidalgo, Miguel: 28
hieroglyphics: 20–21, 320–321
Hierve El Agua mineral springs: 196–197
hiking: Bahías de Huatulco 251, 252; Benito Juárez 358; Cerro de La Caja 333; Cerro de la Campana 216; Cerro Rabón 385–386; Cuajimoloyas 358; Guiengola 409–410; Ixtepeji nature reserve 363; Ixtlán de Juárez 366; La Cueva 404; Laguna Encantada 339; Las Regaderas 392; Nindo-Da-Gé cave 392; Parque Comunal de San Felipe 147; Pinotepa environs 298; Puente Colosal 324; Puerto Escondido 264; Río Santo Domingo Canyon 385; San José del Pacífico 237–238; San Sebastián

de las Grutas 205; Sotano de San Agustín 392–393
history: 18–43; Aztec invasion 21–22; civil war 34–35; colonial 25–28; contemporary 36–43; Cortés, conquests of 22–24; early civilization 18–22; independence 28–30; Monte Albán 19–20, 208; political activism 37–38; Princess Donaji 212; reforms 30–31; Spanish conquest 22–23; Tehuantepec 398; Tuxtepec 373; village era 18–19
hitchhiking: 119
Holy Cross of Huatulco: 238
homestays: 91
horseback riding: Bahías de Huatulco 252; Oaxaca city 166; Puerto Escondido 272
hotel rates: 90
hot springs: Atotonilco 279; Balneario Atonalzin 309; Charquito Atotonilco warm springs 291; Hierve El Agua mineral springs 196–197; Jalapa de Marqués 411; Santiago Astata 259
household life: 57
housing: 90–95
howler monkeys: 13
Huajuapan de León: 325–331
Huautla de Jiménez: 387
Huave country: 436–437
Huaves: 72
Huaxpaltepec: 293
Huerta de Juquila: 324
Huijazoo: 20
huipiles: 68, 71

I
iguanas: 16, 280
immigration: 119
immunizations: 127
income: average daily 3; distribution statistics 46
indígenas: 54, 62
indigenous communities: 62–73; Pinotepa Nacional 294; push for civil rights 40
industrialization: 38
industry: dams 36, 362, 381; industrialization, 20th century 38; Salina Cruz 428
inheritance customs: 57
insurance, car: 108
Internet access: 125
Isla Soyaltepec: 383–384
Isthmus, The: 397–437; geography 3; Juchitán 412–423; maps 400–401; Playa La Ventosa 434–436; Rincón Juárez 427–428; Salina

Handicrafts
general discussion: 84–90, 99
alebrijes: 87, 199, 207
Arrazola: 207
Artesanias Mitla: 376
Atzompa pottery: 212
Bahías de Huatulco: 253
basketry: 84–85
clothing: 85–86
glass manufacture: 86
Huajuapan de León: 327, 328
Huautla de Jiménez: 390
Jalapa de Díaz: 386
jewelry: 86–87, 403
leatherwork: 86
masks: 87, 293, 338
Mitla: 196
Oaxaca city: 167–169
Ocotlán area: 198
pottery: 89, 197–198, 403
Puerto Ángel: 234
Puerto Escondido: 273
Santa Ana del Valle: 190
Santa Magdalena Tiltepec: 284
stone masonry: 86
Teotitlán del Valle: 186–187
textiles: 338
woven crafts: 84–85
Yu-uku Chakuaa: 292

Cruz 428–437; Santo Domingo Zanatepec 425–426; springs 420–422; Tehuantepec 398–412; velas (fiestas) 398
Iturbide, Agustín de: 29
Ixcatecs: 71
Ixtlán de Juárez: 11, 363–368

J
Jacatepec: 371–372
jaguars: 14
jaguarundis: 14
Jalapa de Díaz: 385–387
Jalapa de Marqués: 410–411
Jamiltepec: 278, 291–293
jellyfish: 75
jewelry: 86–87, 99
jobs, creating: 44
Juárez, Benito: 364; develops shipping port 219;

and French invasion 31; in Oaxaca city history
137; as Oaxacan governor 30; reelection of
31–32; wife of 138–139
Juchitán: 412–423

KL
Kansini, King Fane: 73
kayaking: 76, 243
La Bocana: 243
La Cueva: 404
La Gloria Coffee Farm: 258–259
Laguna Colorada: 260
Laguna Encantada: 338–339
Laguna Garrapatera: 260
Laguna Inferior: 437
Laguna Manialtepec: 278–279
Lagunas: 422
Lagunas de Chacahua National Park: 278,
288–290
Laguna Superior: 424
Lambityeco: 20, 185–186
landscape: 2–4
land size: 3
language, indigenous: 61–63
Laollaga: 421
Las Campanas: 328–329
Las Regaderas: 391–392
latifundistas: 31
La Venta: 423–424
law enforcement: 132
leatherwork: 86
lipstick trees: 8
Llano Grande: 358
Los Arquitos: 147
Lunes del Cerro: 164

M
machismo: 131
Magdalena Peñasco valley: 347
Magdalena Tlacotepec: 421
maguey: 5, 11, 363
mahogany: 10
malaria: 129
mammals: 12–14
mangrove wetlands: 7; Bahías de Huatulco 260;
Laguna Manialtepec 278–279; Lagunas de
Chacahua National Park 278
marble factory: 412
Mar del Sur: 217
margays: 14

markets, native: 100, 294, 337
Mar Muerto: 427
marriage customs: 57
mask making: 87, 293, 297
masonry, stone: 86, 216
massage: 276
Maza, Margarita: 138–139
Mazateca: 385–393
Mazatecs: 67–68
Mazunte Beach: 224, 278
medical issues: *duendes*, affliction by 352; health
problems 129–130; precautions 127–128;
treatment 130
medicinal plants: 307
medicine, traditional: 351
meditation centers: 276
men, safe conduct for: 132
Mercado Juárez: 142
mescal: 190
Mesoamerican calendar: 54–55
mestizos: 28, 54
metalwork: 88–89
Miguel Alemán Dam and Reservoir: 381
Miguel de la Madrid: 382
missionaries, Christian: 24
Mitla: 20, 192–196
Mixe language: 61
Mixe people: 3, 69–70
Mixteca, The: 299–356; archaeological sites
304–306; Coixtlahuaca 317–319; Huajuapan
de León 325–331; Mixteca Baja 325–341;
Nochixtlán 300–304; Ñuiñe region 331–334;
San Miguel Tequixtepec 319–322; Tamazul-
pan 309–312; Tepelmeme de Morelos
322–324; Valle of Apoala 306–308; Yan-
huitlán 316–317; Yucunama 314–316
Mixteca Alta: 65, 342–356; Putla de Guerrero
354–356; San Miguel Progreso 353–354;
Santa María Cuqila 353; Tlaxiaco 342–347
Mixteca Baja: 65, 325–341; Huajuapan de León
325–331; Ñuiñe region 331–334; Santiago
Juxtlahuaca 337–341
Mixteca de la Costa: 65
Mixtec Coast environs: 287–298; Charquito
Atotonilco warm springs 291; Lagunas de
Chacahua National Park 288–290; Santiago
Jamiltepec 291–293; Tututepec 290–291
Mixtec expansion: 21
Mixtec people: 64, 192
Moctezuma II: 22, 23

Museums

Bee Nu'u: 315
Casa de Juárez: 146
Casa de la Cultura: 414
Centro de Fotografía Alvarez Bravo: 146
community *(museos comunitarios):* 182
El Mogote: 214
Frissell Museum: 195
Instituto de Artes Gráficos de Oaxaca: 146
Museo Arte Prehispánica de Rufino Tamayo: 144–145
Museo Comunitario Ihitalulu: 351

Museo de Arte Contemporaneo de Oaxaca: 145
Museo de la Soledad: 145
Museo Philatelica de Oaxaca: 146
San Miguel Tequixtepec: 320
Shan Dany: 189
Suchilquitongo Museo Comunitario: 215
Teotitlán del Valle: 187
Tepelmeme de Morelos: 322
Turtle Museum: 224
Yucuita: 304

money: 123–124
monkeys: 13–14
Monte Albán: 19–20, 136, 208–212
Monte Negro: 305–306
Montezuma pines: 12
Morales Foundation: 202
moray eels: 75
mordidas (bribes): 113
Morelos, José Maria: 28
motocarros: 409
mountain guides: 361
mountains: 2, 217–218
Mt. Orizaba: 358
mud baths: 243
murals, church: 241
Museo Arte Prehispánica de Rufino Tamayo: 144
Museo de Arte Contemporaneo de Oaxaca: 145
mushrooms, hallucinogenic: 387
musical instruments: 88

N

NAFTA (North American Free Trade Agreement): 39–40
naguals: 70
Nahuas: 72
names, Mexican: 346
native peoples: 62–73
Nindo-Da-Gé: 392
Nochixtlán: 300–304
Nopala: 281–284
Northern Oaxaca: 357–396; Cañada canyonland 393–396; maps 359; Mazateca 385–393, 387–393; Northern Sierra 358–368; Valle Nacional 368–371

Northern Sierra: Campamento del Monte 362; Ixtlán de Juárez 363–368
nude beaches: 222
Ñuiñe region: 331–334
numbers, Spanish: 452
nuts: 98

O

oak forests: 8–9
Oaxaca city: 135–178; accommodations 148–158; communications 173; entertainment 164–167; food 159–163; history 135–138; maps 140–141, 142; medical help 174; shopping 167–170; sights 138–148; tour guides 172–173; tourist information 170; transportation 173, 175–178
Obregón, General Alvaro: 35
ocelots: 14
Ocotlán: 199–203
oil boom: 38
Olmec people: 398
orchids: 12
Ortiz, A. Maximino Ramón: 399
Otomanguean language family: 61

P

Pacific Resorts and Southern Sierra: 217–298; Bahías de Huatulco 238–260; Chatino Country 281–287; maps 218–219; Puerto Ángel 219–238; Puerto Escondido 260–281
packing: 133–134
Palace of Columns: 194
Palacio de Gobierno: 139
palapas: 94

palms: 5–7
palm weaving: 333
Papaloapan Project: 67, 68
papier-mâché: 89
parakeets: 16
parasailing: 76
Parque Recreational: 358
parrots: 15
passports: 119
peccaries: 13
pedestrian hazards: 132
Peña Larga: 358
people: 52–73; indigenous groups 62–73; social
    customs 55–59
permits, auto: 121
pesos: 123
pets, immigrating: 121
photography: 64
phrases, common Spanish: 447–453
Piedra Colorada: 358
piñatas: 89
pine-oak forests: 8–9
Pinotepa Don Luis: 297
Pinotepa Nacional: 278, 294–297
pipeline, trans-isthmus: 428
plant life: 5–12
Playa Bachoco: 264
Playa Brasil: 260
Playa Carrizalillo: 264
Playa Cerro Hermosa: 288
Playa Chacahua: 289
Playa Copalito: 424
Playa Corralero: 298
Playa del Amor: 221
Playa Entrega: 243
Playa Estacahuite: 221
Playa La Ventanilla: 225–226
Playa La Ventosa: 434–436
Playa Manzanillo: 264
Playa Marinero: 262–263
Playa Mazunte: 222
Playa Panteón: 221
Playa Principal: 221, 260–261
Playa San Agustinillo: 222
Playa Santa Cruz: 243
Playa Zicatela: 263–264
Playa Zipolite: 221, 278
plumerias: 7
poinsettia: 8
police: 132

politics: political activism 37–38; recent reforms
    41; 20th century 39
Popolucas: 71
population: 53–55; criollos 28; historical collapse
    26
Posada La Sorpresa: 195
postal services: 125, 450
pottery: 89, 197–198, 284, 403
Presas de Huayapan: 362
PRI (Partido Revolucionario Institutional): 35,
    42
pronunciation: 447
Pueblos Mancomunados: 361
Pueblo Viejo: 313–314
Puente Colosal: 324
Puente Morelos: 335
Puente Pescadito: 382
Puerto Ángel: 219–238; accommodations
    226–231; beaches 220–226; food 231–232;
    maps 220–221, 223; recreation 232–233;
    shopping 233–234; transportation 235–236
Puerto Escondido: 260–281; accommodations
    265–269; beaches 260–265; emergency infor-
    mation 275; entertainment 271; food
    269–271; maps 262–263; recreation 272;
    transportation 276–277
Punta Arena: 241
Putla de Guerrero: 354–356

QR
Quetzalcoatl: 20
rafting: 243, 252
rainforests, tropical: 10–11
Rancho Alegre: 237
rappelling: 252, 358
religion: 59–61; Chontal 73; Mazatec 68; pil-
    grimage to Juquila 284; Chinantec 69
rental cars: 118
repairs, car: 111
reptiles: 16–18
resorts: 93
Rincón Juárez: 427–428
Río Atoyac: 215
Río Bamba valley: 260
Río Copalita wildlife sanctuary: 243, 252
Río Grande: 289, 395
Río Mixtec: 332
Río Papaloapan: 36
Río Santo Domingo Canyon: 385
Río Tequisistlán: 411

Index

Río Uluapa: 385
Río Valle Nacional: 368
Río Verde: 3, 291
Río Zanatepec Canyon: 426
road safety: 108
Roca Blanca: 290
Romero, Doña Juana Catalina: 399, 404, 405
rosa amarilla: 7
rubber trees: 10
ruins: *see* archaeological sites
RV travel: 107–113, 440–443

S
Sabina, María: 387
safety: 127–133; *bandidos* 109; financial 123; health precautions 127–128; road 108; sanitation 128; snakebite 16; social conduct 130–131; travelers 41; water sport 75–76
sailing: 76, 233
Salina Cruz: 260, 428–437; accommodations 430–431; food 431–432; industrial complex 428; map 429; transportation 434
salt, harvesting: 428
San Andres Huaxpaltepec: 293
San Andrés Huayapan: 362
San Antonio Castillo Velasco: 199
San Bartolo Coyotepec: 197–198
San Bartolomé Quialana: 192
sandbox trees: 7
San Dionisio del Mar: 425
San Felipe de Agua: 147
sanitation, water: 128
San José Chiltepec: 372
San José del Pacífico: 237–238
San José El Mogote: 19, 213–214
San Juan Colorado: 297
San Lucas Ojitlán: 384–385
San Marcos Tlapazola: 192
San Martín Chimalapa: 424
San Martín Huamelulpan: 351–353
San Martín Tilcajete: 199
San Mateo del Mar: 436–437
San Miguel Achiutla: 349–351
San Miguel Chimalpa: 423
San Miguel de la Cueva: 339
San Miguel Tequixtepec: 319–322
San Pedro Amusgos: 298
San Pedro Huamelula: 259–260
San Pedro Ixcatlán: 382–384
San Pedro Pochutla: 236–237

San Pedro Tututepec: 290–291
San Pedro Zanatepec: 426
San Sebastián de las Grutas: 204–206
Santa Ana del Valle: 188–190
Santa Anna, Antonio López: 29
Santa Catarina Ixtepeji: 362–363
Santa Catarina Juquila: 284–287
Santa Cruz de Huatulco: 241, 244, 257
Santa Magdalena Tiltepec: 284
Santa María Atzompa: 212–213
Santa María Cuqila: 353
Santa María del Mar: 437
Santa María del Tule: 184
Santa María Huatulco: 257–258
Santa María Huazolotitlán: 293–294
Santa María Jacatepec: 371–372
Santa María Xadani: 258
Santiago Astata: 259
Santiago Chazumba: 333–334
Santiago Huajolotitlán: 331–332
Santiago Jamiltepec: 291–293
Santiago Juxtlahuaca: 337–341
Santiago Laollaga: 421
Santo Domingo Petapa: 422–423
Santo Domingo Tonalá: 335–336
Santo Domingo Zanatepec: 425–426
Santos Reyes Nopala: 281–284
Santo Tomás Jalieza: 199
San Vicente Ferrer Church: 413
sarongs, Oaxacan: 295
savanna: 5–7
scorpions: 129
scuba diving: 76; Bahías de Huatulco 253; Puerto Ángel 233; Puerto Escondido 272
seabirds: 15
sea creatures: 129
seafood: 96
sea grapes: 7
sea snakes: 75
seasonal weather: 4
sea turtles: *see* turtles, sea
senior citizens: 127
sharks: 18
shell collecting: 74
shopping: 99–101, 450
shrubland, arid tropical: 11
sickness: 352
Sierra Madre del Sur: 217
slaves, African: 53–54
snakes: 16, 129

snorkeling: 76; Bahías de Huatulco 253; Playa
Cerro Hermosa 288; Puerto Ángel 233;
Puerto Escondido 272
Sola de Vega: 206
Sotano de San Agustín: 392–393
Southern Sierra: see Pacific Resorts and Southern
Sierra
spirits, nature: 352
springs: 75, 369, 420–422; >see also hot springs
statistics: comparative socioeconomic 45; economic 46; geographical 3; population changes
25
stonework: 86, 216
stranglei figs. 9
Suchilquitongo: 215–216
sulfur-lagoons: 237
sunburn: 128
surf fishing: 298
surfing: 76; Bahía San Agustín 244; Escondido
"pipeline" 263; La Bocana 243; Playa
Marinero 263; Playa Zicatela 263; Playa Zipolite 222; Puerto Escondido 272

T
Tamazulpan: 309–312
tattoos: 130
taxis: 118
Teatro Alcalá: 145
tehuana textiles: 403
Tehuantepec: 398–412; accommodations
405–407; food 407–408; history 398; maps
402; markets 403; sights 398–405; transporta-
tion 408–409; Vela Tehuantepec 398
Tejada, Lerdo de: 373
Tejupan: 310–311
telephones: 124
Temascal: 381–382
temperatures: 4
Templo de San Felipe Neri: 144
Templo de Santo Domingo: 203
Templo y Exconvento de San Agustín: 143
Templo y Exconvento de Santo Domingo: 399
tennis: 77
Tenochtitlán: 22
Teotihuacán: 20
Teotitlán del Camino: 393–395
Teotitlán del Valle: 186–188
Tepelmeme de Morelos: 322–324
Teposcolula: 313–314
Tequisistlán: 411–412

Tequixtepec: 319, 332–333
textiles: 185, 186–187, 293
thievery: 123–124; beachfront 264; gas station
109
tianguis (native markets): 100
Tilantongo: 305–306
time, telling: 452
time zone: 126
tipping: 124
Tlacochahuaya: 184–185
Tlacolula: 190–191
Tlacotepec: 421
Tlaxiaco: 342–347
Tomalá Canyon: 335
Topiltzín: 20
tourism: 47, 132
tourist cards: 119, 121
tour packages: 113–114
tours: 119
town names: 186
trailer parks: 95
train travel: 117
transportation: in-state 115–119; motocarros
409; to Oaxaca 102–114; phrases, common
Spanish 448–449
traveler's checks: 123
Tres Picos: 411
tribal dress: 85
Triques: 71
turtles, sea: 17–18; protecting 225, 226; sanctuaries for 280; Turtle Museum 224
Tututepec: 290–291
Tuxtepec: 373–380

UV
UNESCO sites: 137
Unión de Hidalgo: 424
Valle Nacional: 68, 368–371
Valle of Apoala: 306–308
Valley of Oaxaca: 179–216; accommodations
183; east side 184–197; Ejutla 203–204; geography 3, 3–4; Hierve El Agua mineral
springs 196–197; maps 180; Mitla 192–196;
Santa Ana del Valle 188–190; south side
197–207; Teotitlán del Valle 186–188; tours
181–183; transportation 180–181; west side
208–216; Yagul 191–192
vegetarian food: 96
vegetation: 5–12
velas (fiestas): 397–398, 416–417

Vela Tehuantepec: 398
verbs, common: 451
Villa, Francisco (Pancho): 34
Virgin of Guadalupe: 60
Virgin of Juquila: 284, 285
visas: 121

W
War of the Reforms: 31
water, sanitation: 128
waterfalls: 75; Cascada de San Juan Lachao 282; Cascada Esmeralda 347; Cola del Serpiente 307; Jamiltepec 292; Las Regaderas 391–392
water-skiing: 76
water sports: 75–76
weather: 4
wildflowers: 5
windsurfing: 76, 233
women, safe conduct for: 131–132
wood carving: 87–88
woven crafts: 84–85, 90

XY
Xadani: 258
Xatachio: 310

Xochicalco: 20
Yaa Tini: 358
Yagul archaeological zone: 20, 191–192
Yanhuitlán: 316–317
Yosocuta Reservoir: 334–335
Yosundua: 348–349
Yucuita: 20, 304–305
Yucunama: 314–316
Yu'u lodging: 92, 183

Z
Zaachila: 20, 206
Zapata, Emiliano: 34
Zapatista revolt: 40
Zapotalito: 288
Zapotec people: 23, 63–65; form COCEI 38; Monte Albán 208; in Oaxaca city history 136; Princess Donaji 212
Zedillo, Ernesto: 40
Zempoaltepetl: 3
Zimatlán: 204
zócalo, Oaxaca city: 139
Zoque language: 61
Zoque people: 69–70

Acknowledgments

Without the help of a host of kind Oaxacan people, this book would not have been possible. In Oaxaca city I owe many thanks to Martín Ruiz Camino, former Secretary of Tourism Development, and the present Secretary, Oscar Holm Quiroz, and his excellent staff for the abundance of support they have given me. I owe the same great debt to my friend Marí Garcia, the kind owner of Villa María, where I stayed while researching the second and third editions. Others are due the same, including Henry Wangemann, owner of the excellent Amate Books, for his kind welcome and support. For hospitality, I am in debt to both Ligia and Peter Kaiser, owners of the lovely Hacienda Los Laureles, and María Luz Díaz, owner of bed-and-breakfast Casa María. I also owe a load of thanks to Jane and Thornton Robisson, owners of Casa Colonial, for their kindness; I owe the same to excellent guide Juan Montes Lara and his wife for sharing their deep knowledge of Oaxaca with me. I'm similarly in debt to author, chef, and cooking teacher Susana Trilling for the friendly welcome that she extended to me at her Rancho Aurora cooking school.

Farther afield, in the Valley of Oaxaca, I owe a big debt to Dr. Ignacio J. del Río Dueñas for introducing me to the cultivation of cochineal at his experimental farm, Tlapanochestli. Much the same is due to Hector Joel Cruz and Victoria Jiménez Jiménez at San José El Mogote for taking the time to guide me around their town's community museum and archaeological site.

On the Pacific Coast, many thanks are due to Gloria Esperanza Johnson of Shambhala in Zipolite for her warmth and hospitality. I owe the same to Federico Roth, manager of the excellent Hotel Quinta Real in Tangolunda, and Rossana Pandolfini, owner of the very fine Restaurant Giardino del Papa in Crucecita. I also thank my gentle guides, Gregorio Cruz Cruz, at Xadani, and Frédy Zárate, at Nopala.

In the Mixteca, I owe a big debt to Juan Cruz Reyes, former Community Museum President at San Miguel Tequixtepec, for taking care of me, and to Elvia and Cari Cordoba Reyes for their kindness and excellent cooking. The same goes for sculptor Manuel Ruiz-Garcia, President of the Teposcolula Community Museum, and his simpático friend, Amancio Odriozola. I owe equal gratitude to dance master and community museum director Antonio Martínez Sánchez for his hospitality and excellent explanation of Yucunama's museum collection. Much credit is also due to Jesus Ramírez at Yucuita and Francisco Simon Reyes at San Miguel de Progreso for taking time to explain their museum collections to me.

In the north, at Huautla de Jiménez, I owe a load of thanks to Inez and Juvenal Cortez Rodríguez for taking time out to show me around their town and the same to Leonardo Altamirano and Catalina Casamiro of the Hotel Rinconcito for their kindness and hospitality.

In the Isthmus, my gratitude goes out to my guide José Luis Toral Sánchez, who went way beyond the call of duty to lead me to the Guiengola ruin at dusk, when the owls were hooting and the bats were fluttering about. The same is due to Salvador Mendoza, owner of the La Palapa de Chiva, for his patient explanation of the fascinating history of Playa La Ventosa.

Back in my hometown, I owe a mountain of thanks to the kind and sympathetic workers at my office-away-from-home, the Café Espresso Roma, whose delicious espresso lattes have become integral to my writing projects.

I give many thanks, moreover, to my friend and business partner, Halcea Valdes, who sympathetically adjusts her schedule to manage for me while I am on the road writing Moon Handbooks.

Finally, the most thanks of all go to my wife, Linda, who puts up with me being gone for long stretches, who comes to Mexico to join me for little vacations, and who skillfully manages our home front when I'm gone.

U.S.~Metric Conversion

1 inch = 2.54 centimeters (cm)
1 foot = .304 meters (m)
1 yard = 0.914 meters
1 mile = 1.6093 kilometers (km)
1 km = .6214 miles
1 fathom = 1.8288 m
1 chain = 20.1168 m
1 furlong = 201.168 m
1 acre = .4047 hectares
1 sq km = 100 hectares
1 sq mile = 2.59 square km
1 ounce = 28.35 grams
1 pound = .4536 kilograms
1 short ton = .90718 metric ton
1 short ton = 2000 pounds
1 long ton = 1.016 metric tons
1 long ton = 2240 pounds
1 metric ton = 1000 kilograms
1 quart = .94635 liters
1 US gallon = 3.7854 liters
1 Imperial gallon = 4.5459 liters
1 nautical mile = 1.852 km

To compute Celsius temperatures, subtract 32 from Fahrenheit and divide by 1.8. To go the other way, multiply Celsius by 1.8 and add 32.

Keeping Current

Although we strive to produce the most up-to-date guidebook humanly possible, change is unavoidable. Between the time this book goes to print and the moment you read it, a handful of the businesses noted in these pages will undoubtedly change prices, move, or even close their doors forever. Other worthy attractions will open for the first time. If you have a favorite gem you'd like to see included in the next edition, or see anything that needs updating, clarification, or correction, please drop us a line. Send your comments via email to atpfeedback@avalonpub.com, or use the address below.

Moon Handbooks Oaxaca
Avalon Travel Publishing
1400 65th Street, Suite 250
Emeryville, CA 94608, USA
www.moon.com

Editor: Kathryn Ettinger
Series Manager: Kevin McLain
Acquisitions Editor: Rebecca K. Browning
Copy Editor: Kim Spatz
Graphics Coordinator: Susan Snyder
Production Coordinator: Jacob Goolkasian,
 Lora Santiago
Cover Designer: Kari Gim
Interior Designers: Amber Pirker, Alvaro
 Villanueva, Kelly Pendragon
Map Editor: Olivia Solís
Cartographers: Mike Morgenfeld, Kat
 Kalamaras, Suzanne Service
Proofreader: Ana Chavier
Indexer: Rachel Kuhn

ISBN: 1-56691-502-3
ISSN: 1533-3949

Printing History
1st Edition—2000
3rd Edition—November 2004
5 4 3 2 1

Text © 2004 by Bruce Whipperman.
Maps © 2004 by Avalon Travel Publishing,
Inc.
All rights reserved.

Avalon Travel Publishing
An Imprint of Avalon Publishing
Group, Inc.

AVALON
publishing group incorporated

Some photos and illustrations are used by permission and are the property of the original copyright owners.

Front cover photo:
© Judith C. Haden Photography
Table of contents photos:
© Bruce Whipperman

Printed in USA by Malloy